CONCEPTS OF DATABASE MANAGEMENT

CONCEPTS OF DATABASE MANAGEMENT

Ninth Edition

Joy L. Starks
Indiana University—Purdue University Indianapolis

Philip J. Pratt
Grand Valley State University

Mary Z. Last

Australia • Brazil • Mexico • Singapore • United Kingdom • United States

**Concepts of Database Management,
Ninth Edition**
Joy L. Starks, Philip J. Pratt, and Mary Z. Last

SVP, GM Skills & Global Product Management:
Jonathan Lau

Product Team Manager: Kristin McNary

Associate Product Manager: Kate Mason

Senior Content Development Manager:
Leigh Hefferon

Content Developer: Maria Gargulio and
Tyler Sally

Marketing Director: Michele McTighe

Marketing Manager: Stephanie Albracht

Production Director: Patty Stephan

Content Project Manager: Michele Stulga

Art Director: Diana Graham

Cover Designer: Roycroft Design
(roycroftdesign.com)

Production Service/Composition:
Lumina Datamatics, Inc.

For product information and technology assistance, contact us at
**Cengage Customer & Sales Support, 1-800-354-9706 or
support.cengage.com.**
For permission to use material from this text or product,
submit all requests online at **www.cengage.com/permissions**.

Some of the product names and company names used in this book have been
used for identification purposes only and may be trademarks or registered
trademarks of their respective manufacturers and sellers.

Library of Congress Control Number: 2017963668

ISBN: 978-1-337-09342-2

Cengage
20 Channel Center Street
Boston, MA 02210
USA

Screenshots for this book were created using Microsoft Access®, and were used
with permission from Microsoft.

Microsoft and the Office logo are either registered trademarks or trademarks of
Microsoft Corporation in the United States and/or other countries. Cengage is an
independent entity from the Microsoft Corporation, and not affiliated with
Microsoft in any manner.

Oracle is a registered trademark, and Oracle11g is a trademark of Oracle
Corporation.

The programs in this book are for instructional purposes only. They have been
tested with care, but are not guaranteed for any particular intent beyond
educational purposes. The author and the publisher do not offer any warranties or
representations, nor do they accept any liabilities with respect to the programs.

Cengage, reserves the right to revise this publication and make changes from
time to time in its content without notice.

Cengage is a leading provider of customized learning solutions with employees
residing in nearly 40 different countries and sales in more than 125 countries
around the world. Find your local representative at **www.cengage.com**.

Cengage products are represented in Canada by Nelson Education, Ltd.

To learn more about Cengage platforms and services, visit **www.cengage.com**.
To register or access your online learning solution or purchase materials for your
course, visit **www.cengagebrain.com**.

Printed at CLDPC, USA, 08-19

TABLE OF CONTENTS

The advent of database management systems for personal computers in the 1980s moved database management beyond the realm of database professionals and into the hands of everyday users from all segments of the population. A field once limited to highly trained users of large, mainframe, database-oriented application systems became an essential productivity tool for such diverse groups as home computer users, small business owners, and end-users in large organizations.

The major PC-based database software systems have continually added features to increase their ease of use, allowing users to enjoy the benefits of database tools relatively quickly. Truly effective use of such a product, however, requires more than just knowledge of the product itself, although that knowledge is obviously important. It requires a general knowledge of the database environment, including topics such as database design, database administration, and application development using these systems. While the depth of understanding required is certainly not as great for the majority of users as it is for the information technology professional, a lack of any understanding in these areas precludes effective use of the product in all but the most limited applications.

ABOUT THIS BOOK

This book is intended for anyone who is interested in gaining some familiarity with database management. It is appropriate for students in introductory database classes in computer science or information systems programs. It is appropriate for students in database courses in related disciplines, such as business, at either the undergraduate or graduate level. Such students require a general understanding of the database environment. In addition, courses introducing students of any discipline to database management have become increasingly popular over the past few years, and this book is ideal for such courses. It also is appropriate for individuals considering purchasing a PC-based database package and who want to make effective use of such a package.

This book assumes that students have some familiarity with computers; a single introductory course is all the background that is required. While students need not have any background in programming to use this book effectively, there are certain areas where some programming experience will allow them to explore topics in more depth.

CHANGES TO THE NINTH EDITION

The Ninth Edition includes the following new features and content:

- New "Your Turn" exercises to fully engage students in critical thinking about what they have just learned.
- Full color screen shots using Access 2016.
- Hands-on steps for creating and using Microsoft Access data macros to accomplish the same functionality as SQL triggers.
- General information about creating web apps to allow data to be shared easily using the web.
- A discussion of the systems analysis approach for determining the requirements needed as the starting point for database design, including descriptions of the requirements you need to gather and how to gather these requirements.
- A new case for BITS Corporation is used to illustrate the concepts in each chapter of the book, and is also used in the end-of-chapter exercises.
- A new case for Sports Physical Therapy, along with a case for Colonial Adventure Tours, are used in the end-of-chapter cases.
- Critical-thinking questions and exercises that reinforce problem-solving and analytical skills are included in each chapter.
- Concepts of big data are presented across many chapter topics.
- A new appendix covering the use of MySQL with the database cases.

SPECIAL FEATURES

As in the Eighth Edition, the SQL material is covered using Access. Also included are generic forms of all examples that students can use on a variety of platforms, including Oracle. The Ninth Edition continues the two appendices that provide a useful reference for anyone wanting to use SQL effectively. Appendix B includes a command reference of all the SQL commands and operators that are taught in the chapters. Students can use this appendix as a quick resource when constructing commands. Each command includes a short description, a table that shows the required and optional clauses and operators, and an example and its results. Appendix C provides students with an opportunity to ask a question, such as "How do I delete rows?," and to identify the appropriate section in Appendix B to use to find the answer. Appendix C is extremely valuable when students know what they want to accomplish, but cannot remember the exact SQL command they need.

A new Appendix D introduces MySQL with instructions for downloading and installing both the server and the MySQL Workbench user interface. Students learn how to connect to the server, open and manipulate an SQL file, enter and save SQL scripts, and use the command line.

In addition to the section of Review Questions, the end of each chapter includes three sets of exercises—one featuring the BITS Corporation database and the others featuring the Colonial Adventure Tours database and the Sports Physical Therapy database—that give students "hands-on" experiences with the concepts found in the chapter.

As in the previous edition, the Ninth Edition covers entity-relationship diagrams. The database design material includes a discussion of the entity-relationship model as a database model. It also includes a discussion of a characterization of various types of primary keys.

The BITS Corporation, Colonial Adventure Tours, and Sports Physical Therapy databases will be available at *www.cengagebrain.com* and are usable with Access 2010, Access 2013, and Access 2016. For those students using database management systems that run scripts (such as Oracle), the data files also include the script files that create the tables and add the data to the tables in the databases used in the book.

For instructors who want to use an Access or SQL text as a companion to the Ninth Edition, the Instructor's Manual for this book includes detailed tips on integrating the Ninth Edition with other books from Cengage Learning that cover Access 2010, Access 2013, Access 2016, and SQL (for more information, see the "Teaching Tools" section in this preface).

Detailed Coverage of the Relational Model, Including Query-By-Example (QBE) and SQL

The book features detailed coverage of the important aspects of the relational model, including comprehensive coverage of SQL. It also covers QBE and relational algebra as well as advanced aspects of the model, such as views, the use of indexes, the catalog, and relational integrity rules.

Normalization Coverage

The Ninth Edition covers first normal form, second normal form, third normal form (Boyce-Codd normal form), and fourth normal form. The book describes in detail the update anomalies associated with lower normal forms as part of the motivation for the need for higher normal forms. Finally, the book examines correct and incorrect ways to normalize tables. This book specifically addresses this by showing students some of the mistakes people can make in the normalization process, explaining why the approach is incorrect, demonstrating the problems that would result from incorrect normalizations, and, most importantly, identifying how to avoid these mistakes.

Views Coverage

This text covers the important topic of views. It describes the process of beginning from a user perspective and then discusses the creation and use of views as well as the advantages of using views.

Database Design

The important process of database design is given detailed treatment. A highly useful method for designing databases is presented and illustrated through a variety of examples. In addition to the method, this text includes important design topics such as the use of survey forms, obtaining information by reviewing existing documents, special relationship considerations, and entity subtypes. Appendix A contains a comprehensive design example that illustrates how to apply the complete design process to a large and complex set of requirements. After mastering the design method presented in this text, students should be able to produce correct database designs for future database requirements they encounter.

Functions Provided by a Database Management System

With such a wide range of features included in current database management systems, it is important for students to know the functions that such systems should provide. These functions are presented and discussed in detail, with examples both in Access and SQL.

Database Administration

While database administration (DBA) is absolutely essential in the mainframe environment, it also is important in a personal computer environment, especially when the database is shared among several users. Thus, this text includes a detailed discussion of the database administration function.

Database Management System Selection

The process of selecting a database management system is important, considering the number of available systems from which to choose. Unfortunately, selecting the correct database management system is not an easy task. To prepare students to be able to do an effective job in this area, the text includes a detailed discussion of the selection process together with a comprehensive checklist that greatly assists in making such a selection.

Advanced Topics

The text also covers distributed database management systems, client/server systems, data warehouses, object-oriented database management systems, web access to databases, and XML. Each of these topics encompasses an enormous amount of complex information, but the goal is to introduce students to these important topics. The text also includes coverage of data macros in Access. In addition, the book presents the systems analysis approach to determining the requirements needed as the starting point for database design. After describing information systems, the book describes the requirements you need to gather and how to gather these requirements.

Numerous Realistic Examples

The book contains numerous examples illustrating each of the concepts. A running "case" example—BITS Corporation—is used throughout the book to demonstrate concepts. The examples are realistic and represent the kinds of real-world problems students will encounter in the design, manipulation, and administration of databases. Exercises that use the BITS Corporation case are included at the end of each chapter. In addition, there is another complete set of exercises at the end of each chapter that features a second and third case— Colonial Adventure Tours and Sports Physical Therapy—giving students a chance to apply what they have learned to a database that they have not seen in the chapter material.

Review Material

This text contains a wide variety of questions. At key points within the chapters, students are asked questions to reinforce their understanding of the material before proceeding. The answers to these questions follow the questions. A summary and a list of key terms appear at the end of each chapter, followed by review questions that test the students' knowledge of the important points in the chapter and that occasionally test their ability to apply what they have learned. Each chapter also contains hands-on exercises related to the BITS Corporation, Colonial Adventure Tours, and Sports Physical Therapy case examples. Critical-thinking questions that reinforce problem-solving and analytical skills are included for review questions and hands-on exercises.

Teaching Tools

When this book is used in an academic setting, instructors may obtain the following teaching tools from Cengage Learning through their sales representative or by visiting *www.cengage.com:*

- **Instructor's Manual** The Instructor's Manual has been carefully prepared and tested to ensure its accuracy and dependability. The Instructor's Manual includes suggestions and strategies for using this text, including the incorporation of companion texts on Access or SQL for those instructors who desire to do so. For instructors who want to use an Access or SQL text as a companion to the Ninth Edition, the Instructor's Manual for this book includes detailed tips on integrating the Ninth Edition with the following books, also published by Cengage Learning: *Microsoft Access 2013: Introductory Concepts and Techniques, Microsoft Access 2016: Complete Concepts and Techniques,* and *Microsoft Access 2016: Comprehensive Concepts and Techniques,* by Pratt and Last.

- **Data and Solution Files** Data and solution files are available at *www.cengage.com.* Data files consist of copies of the BITS Corporation, Colonial Adventure Tours, and Sports Physical Therapy databases that are usable in Access 2010, Access 2013, and Access 2016, and script files to create the tables and data in these databases in other systems, such as Oracle and MySQL.

Cengage Learning Testing Powered by Cognero is a flexible, online system that allows you to:

- author, edit, and manage test bank content from multiple Cengage Learning solutions
- create multiple test versions in an instant
- deliver tests from your LMS, your classroom, or wherever you want
- **PowerPoint Presentations** Microsoft PowerPoint slides are included for each chapter as a teaching aid for classroom presentations, to make available to students on a network for chapter review, or to be printed for classroom distribution. Instructors can add their own slides for additional topics they introduce to the class. The presentations are available at www.cengagebrain.com.
- **Figure Files** Figure files are included so that instructors can create their own presentations using figures appearing in the text.

ORGANIZATION OF THE TEXTBOOK

This text includes nine chapters covering general database topics that are relevant to any database management system. A brief description of the organization of topics in the chapters and an overview each chapter's contents follows.

Introduction

Chapter 1 provides a general introduction to the field of database management.

The Relational Model

The relational model is covered in detail in Chapters 2, 3, and 4. Chapter 2 covers the data definition and manipulation aspects of the model using QBE and relational algebra. The text uses Access 2016 to illustrate the QBE material. The relational algebra section includes the entire relational algebra. (*Note:* The extra material on relational algebra is optional and can be omitted if desired.)

Chapter 3 is devoted exclusively to SQL. The SQL material is illustrated using Access, but the chapter also includes generic versions of all examples that can be used with a variety of platforms, including Oracle and MySQL.

Chapter 4 covers some advanced aspects of the relational model such as views, the use of indexes, the catalog, relational integrity rules, stored procedures, triggers, and data macros.

Database Design

Chapters 5 and 6 are devoted to database design. Chapter 5 covers the normalization process, which enables students to identify and correct bad designs. This chapter discusses and illustrates the use of first, second, third, and fourth normal forms. (*Note:* The material on fourth normal form is optional and can be omitted if desired.)

Chapter 6 presents a method for database design using many examples. The material includes entity-relationship diagrams and their role in database design. It also includes discussions of several special design issues as well as the use of survey forms, obtaining information by reviewing existing documents, special relationship considerations, and entity subtypes. After completing Chapter 6, students can further challenge themselves by completing Appendix A, which includes a comprehensive design example that illustrates the application of the complete design process to a large and complex set of requirements, and Appendix E, A Systems Analysis Approach to Information-level Requirements. (*Note:* Chapters 5 and 6 can be covered immediately after Chapter 2 if desired.)

Database Management System Functions

Chapter 7 discusses the features that should be provided by a full-functioned PC-based database management system. This chapter includes coverage of journaling, forward recovery, backward recovery, authentication, and authorizations.

Database Administration

Chapter 8 is devoted to the role of database administration. Also included in this chapter is a discussion of the process of selecting a database management system.

Database Management Approaches

Chapter 9 provides an overview of several advanced topics: distributed databases, client/server systems, web access to databases, XML and related document specification standards, data warehouses, and object-oriented databases.

GENERAL NOTES TO THE STUDENT

There are many places in the text where special questions have been embedded. Sometimes the purpose of these questions is to ensure that you understand some crucial material before you proceed. In other cases, the questions are designed to give you the chance to consider some special concept in advance of its actual presentation. In all cases, the answers to these questions follow each question. You could simply read the question and its answer. You will receive maximum benefit from the text, however, if you take the time to work out the answers to the questions and then check your answer against the one provided before continuing.

You also will find *Your Turn* exercises, which allow you to stop, and try to apply the concept. These critical thinking exercises help you solidify the process and well as solve the problem. The text then follows through with a sample.

The end-of-chapter material consists of a summary, a list of key terms, review questions, and exercises for the BITS Corporation, Colonial Adventure Tours, and Sports Physical Therapy databases. The summary briefly describes the material covered in the chapter. The review questions require you to recall and apply the important material in the chapter. The BITS Corporation, Colonial Adventure Tours, and Sports Physical Therapy exercises test your knowledge of the chapter material; your instructor will assign one or more of these exercises for you to complete. Review questions and exercises include critical-thinking questions to challenge your problem-solving and analytical skills.

ACKNOWLEDGMENTS

We would like to acknowledge the following individuals who all made contributions during the preparation of this book during its multiple editions. We also appreciate the efforts of the following individuals, who have been invaluable during this book's development: Kate Mason, Associate Product Manager; Michele Stulga, Content Project Manager, Maria Garguilo and Tyler Sally, Content Developers; Diana Graham, Art Director; and Sumathy Kumaran, Associate Product Manager at Lumina Datamatics, Inc.

INTRODUCTION TO DATABASE MANAGEMENT

LEARNING OBJECTIVES

- Introduce Burk IT Solutions (BITS), the company that is used as the basis for many of the examples throughout the text
- Introduce basic database terminology
- Describe database management systems (DBMSs)
- Explain the advantages and disadvantages of database processing
- Introduce Colonial Adventure Tours, a company that is used in a case that appears at the end of each chapter
- Introduce Sports Physical Therapy, a company that is used in another case that appears at the end of each chapter

INTRODUCTION

In this chapter, you will examine the requirements of Burk IT Solutions (BITS), a company that will be used in many examples in this chapter and in the rest of the text. You will learn how BITS initially stored its data, what problems employees encountered with the storage method, and why management decided to employ a database management system (DBMS). Then you will study the basic terminology and concepts of databases, database management systems, and big data. You will learn the advantages and disadvantages of database processing. Finally, you will examine the database requirements for Colonial Adventure Tours and Sports Physical Therapy, the companies featured in the cases that appear at the end of each chapter.

BITS COMPANY BACKGROUND

Burk IT Solutions (BITS) is a local computer hardware and software consulting company whose IT consultants perform functions such as hardware repair, software installation, networking solutions, and system security—for both individuals and small businesses. As the company was getting started, they kept track of their clients in a spreadsheet; they used a homegrown job order/inventory program to keep track of work orders. Management has now determined that the company's recent growth means it is no longer feasible to use those programs to maintain its data.

What has led the managers at BITS to this decision? One of the company's spreadsheets, shown in Figure 1-1 on the next page, displays sample work order data, and illustrates the company's problems with the spreadsheet approach. For each work order, the spreadsheet displays the number and name of the client, the work order number and date, the task ID, a description, the quoted price or estimate, and the number of the consultant assigned to the client. Note that Harpersburg Bank (order number 68979) appears in two rows because this client needed two different jobs performed in its order. In the case of Prichard's Pizza & Pasta, the company placed two different orders (order numbers 67424 and 67949). In the first order, the client needed help with mobility (connectivity), which would also require an upgrade. In the second order, the client had printer issues along with a possible virus. The client also was experiencing difficulty with the network between two stores (wide area networking). The result was five lines in the spreadsheet, two work order numbers, and various job task IDs.

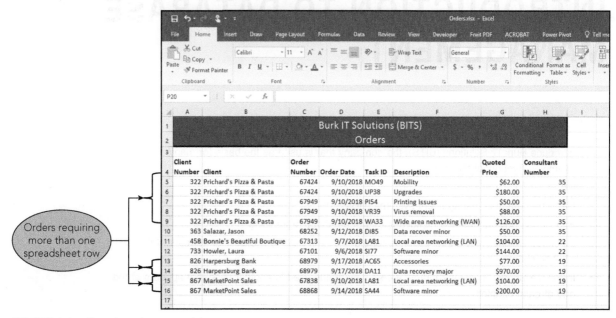

FIGURE 1-1 Sample orders spreadsheet

Redundancy is one problem that employees have with the orders spreadsheet. **Redundancy** is the duplication of data, or the storing of the same data in more than one place. In the Orders spreadsheet, redundancy occurs in the Client column because the name of a client is stored in more than one place. Both rows for client number 867, for example, store "MarketPoint Sales" as the client name. In the Orders spreadsheet, redundancy also occurs in other columns, such as the Client Number and Order Number columns.

Q & A 1-1

Question: What problems does redundancy cause?

Answer: Redundancy can cause inconsistencies in the data, leading to missing information and poor decision making from the data. The accuracy of the data is the most important factor. For example, you might enter "MarketPoint Sales" and "Market Point Sales" on separate rows in the Client column, and then be unsure about the correct version of this client's name. Further, if this client's name is spelled in two different ways and you use the search feature with one of the two values, you would find a single match instead of two matches.

When you need to change data, redundancy also makes your changes more cumbersome and time-consuming. For example, if you incorrectly enter "Harpersberg Bank" in the Client column, you would need to correct it in two places. Even if you use the global find-and-replace feature, multiple changes require more editing time than does a single change.

Finally, while storage space is relatively inexpensive, redundancy wastes space because you're storing the same data in multiple places. This extra space results in larger spreadsheets that require more space in memory and on disk. The files also take longer to save and open.

Difficulty accessing related data is another problem that employees at BITS encounter with their spreadsheets. For example, if you want to see a client's address and the scheduled date and time, you must open and search other spreadsheets that contain this data.

Spreadsheets also have limited security features to protect data from being accessed by unauthorized users. In addition, a spreadsheet's data-sharing features also prevent multiple employees from updating data in one spreadsheet at the same time. Finally, if the increase in work orders at BITS continues at its planned rate, spreadsheets have inherent size limitations that will eventually force the company to split its order data into multiple spreadsheets. Splitting the spreadsheets would create further redundancy.

Having decided to replace its spreadsheet software, management has determined that BITS must maintain the following information about its consultants, clients, categories of IT tasks, and work orders:

- The consultant number, last name, first name, address, normal weekly hours, and rate of pay for each consultant.
- The client number, name, address, current balance, and credit limit for each client, as well as the number of the consultant who typically works with the client.
- The order number, task, description, scheduled date, and quoted estimate.

BITS must store information about orders for invoicing purposes. Figure 1-2 shows a sample invoice.

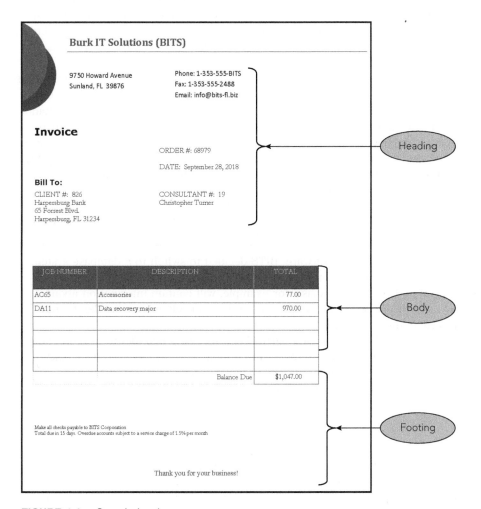

FIGURE 1-2 Sample invoice

- The heading (top) of the order contains the BITS Corporation's name, address, phone, fax, and email; the word "Invoice"; the order number and date; the client's number, name, and address; and the consultant's number and name.

- The body of the order contains one or more order lines, sometimes called line items. Each order line contains a job number, a description, and the total for the item.
- The footing (bottom) of the order contains the balance due.

BITS also must store the following items for each client's order:

- For each work order, the company must store the order number, the date the order was placed, and the number of the client that placed the order. The client's name and address as well as the number of the consultant who represents the client are stored with the client information. The name of the consultant is stored with the consultant information.
- For each order line, the company must store the order number, the task ID, the scheduled date of the repair, and the quoted estimate or price. If the job may result in taking more time or resources, the client is called and the quoted price is adjusted. Remember that the description and task category are stored with the information about the IT task.
- The overall order total is not stored. Instead, the computer calculates the total whenever an order is printed or displayed on the screen.

The problem facing BITS is common to many businesses and individuals that need to store and retrieve data in an efficient and organized way. Furthermore, most organizations are interested in more than one category of information. For example, BITS is interested in categories such as consultants, clients, orders, and tasks. A school is interested in students, faculty, and classes; a real estate agency is interested in clients, houses, and agents; a distributor is interested customers, orders, and inventory; and a car dealership is interested in clients, vehicles, and manufacturers.

Besides wanting to store data that pertains to more than one task, BITS is interested in the relationships between the clients, and consultants. For example, BITS may want to assign consultants that specialize in one area of IT. They need to be able to associate orders with the clients that ordered them, the consultants who coordinated the work, and the jobs that the client requested. Likewise, a real estate agency wants to know not only about clients, houses, and agents but also about the relationships between clients and houses (which clients have expressed interest in which houses). A real estate agency also wants to know about the relationships between agents and houses (which agent sold which house, which agent is listing which house, and which agents are receiving commissions for which houses).

DATABASE SOLUTION

After studying the alternatives to using spreadsheet software, BITS decided to switch to a database system. A database is a structure that contains data about many different categories of information and about the relationships between those categories. The BITS database, for example, will contain information about consultants, clients, orders, and tasks. It also will provide facts that relate consultants to the clients they service, and clients to the work orders they currently have placed.

With a database, employees can enter the number of a particular work order and identify which client placed the order. Alternately, employees can start with a client and find all work orders the client placed, together with descriptions of the task. Using a database, BITS not only can maintain its data better but also can use the data in the database to produce a variety of reports and to answer different types of questions.

Database Terminology

There are some terms and concepts in the database environment that are important to know. For instance, the terms *entity*, *attribute*, and *relationship* are fundamental when discussing databases. An **entity** is a person, place, object, event, or idea for which you want to store and process data. The entities of interest to BITS, for example, are consultants, clients, orders, and tasks. Entities sometimes are represented by a **table** of data in database systems.

An **attribute** is a characteristic or property of an entity. The term is used in this text exactly as it is used in everyday English. For the entity *person*, for example, the list of attributes might include such things as eye color and height. For BITS, the attributes of interest for the entity *client* are such things as client name, street, city, and so on. An attribute is also called a **field** or **column** in many database systems.

Figure 1-3 shows two entities, Consultant and Client, along with the attributes for each entity. The Consultant entity has nine attributes: ConsltNum, LastName, FirstName, Street, City, State, ZipCode, Hours, and Rate. The attributes are the same as the columns in a spreadsheet. The Client entity has nine attributes: ClientNum, ClientName, Street, City, State, ZipCode, Balance, CreditLimit, and ConsltNum. NOTE: Entity (table) names and attribute (field) names should be easy to understand, concise, indicative of their content, and contain no spaces.

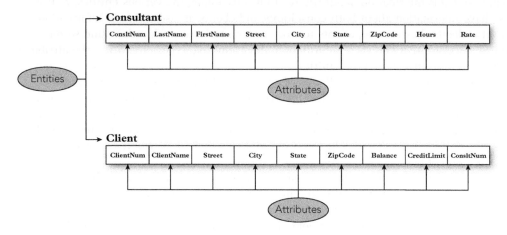

FIGURE 1-3   Entities and attributes

The final key database term is relationship. A **relationship** is an association between entities. There is an association between consultants and clients; for example, at BITS, a consultant is associated with all of his or her clients, and a client is associated with its consultant. Technically speaking, a consultant is *related to* all of his or her clients, and a client is *related to* its consultant.

This particular relationship is called a **one-to-many relationship** because each consultant is associated with *many* clients, but each client is associated with only *one* consultant. In this type of relationship, the word *many* is used differently than in everyday English; not always will it indicate a large number. In this context, for example, the term *many* means that a consultant can be associated with *any* number of clients. That is, a given consultant can be associated with zero, one, or more clients.

A one-to-many relationship often is represented visually in the manner shown in Figure 1-4. In such a diagram, entities and attributes are represented in precisely the same way as they are shown in Figure 1-3. A line connecting the entities represents the relationship. The *one* part of the relationship (in this case, Consultant) does not have an arrow on its end of the line, and the *many* part of the relationship (in this case, Client) is indicated by a single-headed arrow.

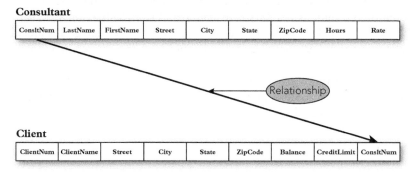

FIGURE 1-4   One-to-many relationship

Storing Data

Spreadsheets, word-processed documents, webpages, and other computer information sources are stored in files. A file that is used to store data, often called a **data file**, is the computer counterpart to an ordinary paper file you might keep in a file cabinet, an accounting ledger, or other place. A database, however, is more than a file. Unlike a typical data file, a database can store information about multiple entities.

Additionally, a database holds information about the relationships among the various entities. Not only will the BITS database have information about both consultants and clients, it also will hold information relating consultants to the clients they service, clients to work orders, tasks to work orders, and so on. Formally, a **database** is a structure that can store information about multiple types of entities, the attributes of those entities, and the relationships among the entities.

How does a database handle these entities, attributes of entities, and relationships among entities? Entities and attributes are fairly simple. Each entity has its own table. In the BITS database, for example, there will be one table for consultants, one table for clients, and so on. The attributes of an entity become the columns in the table. In the table for consultants, for example, there will be a column for the consultant number, a column for the consultant last name, and so on. Within each table, a **row** of data corresponds to one record. A **record** is a group of fields related to one item in a table.

What about relationships between entities? At BITS, there is a one-to-many relationship between consultants and clients. (Each consultant is related to the many clients that he or she represents, and each client is related to the one consultant who represents the client.) How is this relationship handled in a database system? It is handled by using common columns in the two tables. Consider Figure 1-4 on the previous page again. The ConsltNum column in the Consultant table and the ConsltNum column in the Client table are used to implement the relationship between consultants and clients. (It is not unusual to abbreviate column names in a database.) Given a consultant, you can use these columns to determine all the clients that he or she represents; given a client, you can use these columns to find the consultant who represents the client.

How will BITS store its data via tables in a database? Figure 1-5 shows sample data for BITS.

In the Consultant table, you see that there are four consultants whose numbers are 19, 22, 35, and 51. The name of consultant 19 is Christopher Turner. His street address is 554 Brown Dr. He lives in Tri City, FL, and his zip code is 32889. He typically works 40 hours a week with a pay rate of $22.50 per hour.

BITS has 12 clients at this time, which are identified with the numbers 143, 175, 299, 322, 363, 405, 449, 458, 677, 733, 826, 867. The name of client number 143 is Jarrod Hershey. (The last name is listed first for alphabetical/sorting reasons. Not all clients have a first and last name.) This client's address is 135 E. Mill Street in Easton, FL, with a zip code of 33998. The client's current balance is $1,904.55, and its credit limit is $2,500.00. The number 19 in the ConsltNum column indicates that Jarrod Hershey is represented by consultant 19 (Christopher Turner—see Consultant table).

In the table named Tasks, you see that BITS currently has 16 tasks, whose task ID numbers are AC65, DA11, DI85, HA63, HI31, LA81, MO49, OT99, PI54, SA44, SI77, SI91, UP38, VR39, WA33, and WC19. TaskID AC65 is Accessories, and BITS normal pricing is $80.00 for installing and troubleshooting accessories such as storage devices and monitors. The Accessories item is in the ACC category. Other categories include DRM (data recovery), HAM (hardware issues), and SOM (software issues), among others. The company has a $50 minimum charge on all service calls.

In the table named WorkOrders, you see that there are eight orders, which are identified with the numbers 67101, 67313, 67424, 67838, 67949, 68252, 68868, and 68979. Order number 67101 was placed on September 6, 2018, by client 733 (Laura Howler—see Client table).

Consultant

ConsltNum	LastName	FirstName	Street	City	State	ZipCode	Hours	Rate
19	Turner	Christopher	554 Brown Dr.	Tri City	FL	32889	40	$22.50
22	Jordan	Patrick	2287 Port Rd.	Easton	FL	33998	40	$22.50
35	Allen	Sarah	82 Elliott St.	Lizton	FL	34344	35	$20.00
51	Shields	Tom	373 Lincoln Ln.	Sunland	FL	39876	10	$15.00

Client

ClientNum	ClientName	Street	City	State	ZipCode	Balance	CreditLimit	ConsltNum
143	Hershey, Jarrod	135 E. Mill Street	Easton	FL	33998	$1,904.55	$2,500.00	19
175	Goduto, Sean	12 Saratoga Parkway	Tri City	FL	32889	$2,814.55	$5,000.00	19
299	Two Crafty Cousins	9787 NCR 350 West	Sunland	FL	39876	$8,354.00	$10,000.00	22
322	Prichard's Pizza & Pasta	501 Air Parkway	Lizton	FL	34344	$7,335.55	$10,000.00	35
363	Salazar, Jason	56473 Cherry Tree Dr.	Easton	FL	33998	$900.75	$2,500.00	35
405	Fisherman's Spot Shop	49 Elwood Ave.	Harpersburg	FL	31234	$4,113.40	$7,500.00	19
449	Seymour, Lindsey	4091 Brentwood Ln	Amo	FL	34466	$557.70	$5,000.00	22
458	Bonnie's Beautiful Boutique	9565 Ridge Rd.	Tri City	FL	32889	$4,053.80	$7,500.00	22
677	Yates, Nick	231 Day Rd.	Sunland	FL	39876	$2,523.80	$2,500.00	35
733	Howler, Laura	1368 E. 1000 S.	Lizton	FL	34344	$3,658.05	$5,000.00	22
826	Harpersburg Bank	65 Forrest Blvd.	Harpersburg	FL	31234	$6,824.55	$10,000.00	19
867	MarketPoint Sales	826 Host St.	Easton	FL	33998	$3,089.00	$5,000.00	19

Tasks

TaskID	Description	Category	Price
AC65	Accessories	ACC	$80.00
DA11	Data recovery major	DRM	$175.00
DI85	Data recovery minor	DRM	$50.00
HA63	Hardware major	HAM	$225.00
HI31	Hardware minor	HAM	$165.70
LA81	Local area networking (LAN)	LAN	$104 00
MO49	Mobility	MOB	$65.00
OT99	Other work	OTH	$99.99
PI54	Printing issues	PRI	$50.00
SA44	Software major	SOM	$200.00
SI77	Software minor	SOM	$144.00
SI91	Security install/repair	SIR	$126.00
UP38	Upgrades	UPG	$185.00
VR39	Virus removal	VIR	$90.00
WA33	Wide area networking (WAN)	WAN	$130.00
WC19	Web connectivity	WEC	$75.00

OrderLine

OrderNum	TaskID	ScheduledDate	QuotedPrice
67101	SI77	9/10/2018	$144.00
67313	LA81	9/12/2018	$104.00
67424	MO49	9/14/2018	$65.00
67424	UP38	9/14/2018	$185.00
67838	LA81	9/20/2018	$104.00
67949	PI54	9/21/2018	$50.00
67949	VR39	9/21/2018	$88.00
67949	WA33	9/21/2018	$126.00
68252	DI85	9/24/2018	$50.00
68868	SA44	9/24/2018	$200.00
68979	AC65	9/27/2018	$77.00
68979	DA11	9/27/2018	$970.00

WorkOrders

OrderNum	OrderDate	ClientNum
67101	9/6/2018	733
67313	9/7/2018	458
67424	9/10/2018	322
67838	9/10/2018	867
67949	9/10/2018	322
68252	9/12/2018	363
68868	9/14/2018	867
68979	9/17/2018	826

FIGURE 1-5   Sample data for BITS

The table named OrderLine on the previous page might seem strange at first glance. Why do you need a separate table for the order lines? Couldn't the order lines be included in the WorkOrders table? The answer is yes. The WorkOrders table could be structured as shown in Figure 1-6. Notice that this table contains the same orders as those shown in Figure 1-5 on the previous page, with the same dates and clients. In addition, each table row in Figure 1-6 contains all the order lines for a given order. Examining the third row, for example, you see that order 67424 has two order lines. One of the order lines is for MO49 (mobility issues), and the quoted price is $65.00. The other order line is for UP38 (upgrades), and the quoted price is $185.00.

WorkOrders

OrderNum	OrderDate	ClientNum	TaskID	QuotedPrice
67101	9/6/2018	733	SI77	$144.00
67313	9/7/2018	458	LA81	$104.00
67424	9/10/2018	322	MO49	$65.00
			UP38	$185.00
67838	9/10/2018	867	LA81	$104.00
67949	9/10/2018	322	PI54	$50.00
			VR39	$88.00
			WA33	$126.00
68252	9/12/2018	363	DI85	$50.00
68868	9/14/2018	867	SA44	$200.00
68979	9/17/2018	826	AC65	$77.00
			DA11	$970.00

FIGURE 1-6   Alternative WorkOrders table structure

Q & A 1-2

Question: How is the information in Figure 1-5 represented in Figure 1-6?
Answer: Examine the OrderLine table shown in Figure 1-5 and note the third and fourth rows. The third row indicates that there is an order line in order number 67424 for task MO49 with a quoted price of $65.00. The fourth row indicates that there is an order line in order 67424 for upgrades with a quoted price of $185.00. Thus, the information in Figure 1-6 is represented in Figure 1-5 with two separate rows rather than in one row.

Q & A 1-3

Question: Why is the quoted price in the OrderLine table different from the price listed in the Tasks table?
Answer: The estimator at BITS Corporation talks to each client or customer as he or she calls in to request services, and then enters the work order and order line. The estimator evaluates the need and may adjust the price up or down depending on the situation and how much time may be involved. In the Tasks table, the prices are listed for a typical hour related to the task at hand. The actual service or repair may take more time. For example, Task DA11 is listed at $175.00. However, in the last order line, the estimator, after talking with the client, quoted a price of $970.00 for the large amount of work involved.

It might seem inefficient to use two rows to store information that can be represented in one row. There is a problem, however, with the arrangement shown in Figure 1-6 — the table is more complicated. In Figure 1-5, there is a single entry at each position in the OrderLine table. In Figure 1-6, some of the individual positions within the table contain multiple entries, thus making it difficult to track the information between columns. In the row for order number 67424, for example, it is crucial to know that TaskID UP38 corresponds to the dollar figure $185.00 in the QuotedPrice column, not to the $65.00.

In addition, having a more complex table means that there are practical issues to worry about, such as the following:

- How much room do you allow for these multiple entries?
- What happens when an order requires more order lines than you have allowed room for?
- Given a task ID, how do you determine which orders contain order lines for that task?

Certainly, none of these problems is unsolvable. These problems do add a level of complexity, however, that is not present in the arrangement shown in Figure 1-5 on page 7. In Figure 1-5, there are no multiple entries to worry about, it does not matter how many order lines exist for any work order, and it is easy to find every order that contains an order line for a given task (just look for all order lines with the given TaskID). In general, this simpler structure is preferable, which is why the order lines appear in a separate table.

To test your understanding of the BITS data, use the data shown in Figure 1-5 on page 7 to answer the following questions.

Q & A 1-4

Question: What are the numbers of the clients represented by Christopher Turner?
Answer: 143, 175, 405, and 867. (Look up the ConsltNum value for Christopher Turner in the Consultant table and obtain the number 19. Then find all clients in the Client table that have the number 19 in the ConsltNum column.)

Q & A 1-5

Question: What is the name of the client that placed order 67424, and what is the name of the consultant who represents this client?
Answer: Prichard's Pizza & Pasta is the client, and Sarah Allen is the consultant. (Look up the ClientNum value in the Orders table for order number 67424 and obtain the number 322. Then find the client in the Client table with a ClientNum value of 322. Using this client's ConsltNum value, which is 35, find the name of the consultant in the Consultant table.)

Q & A 1-6

Question: List all the items that appear in order 67949. For each item, give the description, number ordered, and quoted price.
Answer: TaskID: PI54; description: Printing issues; category: PRI; and quoted price: $50.00. Also, TaskID: VR39; description: Virus removal; category: VIR; and quoted price $88.00. Finally, TaskID: WA33; description: Wide area networking (WAN); category: WAN; and quoted price: $126.00. The scheduled date is 9/21/2018. (Look up each OrderLine table row in which the order number is 67949. Each row contains a TaskID, the ScheduledDate, and the QuotedPrice. Use the TaskID to look up the corresponding description in the Tasks table.)

Q & A 1-7

Question: Why is the QuotedPrice column in the OrderLine table? Couldn't you just use the task ID to look up the price in the Tasks table?
Answer: If the QuotedPrice column did not appear in the OrderLine table, you would need to obtain the price for a service on an order line by looking up the price in the Tasks table. Although this might not be a bad practice, it prevents BITS from charging different prices to different clients for the same item. Because BITS wants the flexibility to quote and charge different prices to different clients, the QuotedPrice column is included in the OrderLine table. If you examine the OrderLine table, you will see cases in which the estimated price matches the actual price in the Tasks table and cases in which the estimated price differs. For example, in order number 67949, the scheduler at BITS quoted a price to Prichard's Pizza & Pasta of 126.00 (for TaskID WA33) rather than the regular price of 130.00 (shown in the Tasks table). The reduction might lead you to think the client received a slight discount for its multiple task order.

Many database administrators and IT professionals use a visual way to represent and analyze a database. It is called an **entity-relationship (E-R) diagram** (sometimes referred to as an ERD). In an E-R diagram, rectangles represent entities and their attributes; lines represent relationships between connected entities. The E-R diagram for the BITS database appears in Figure 1-7.

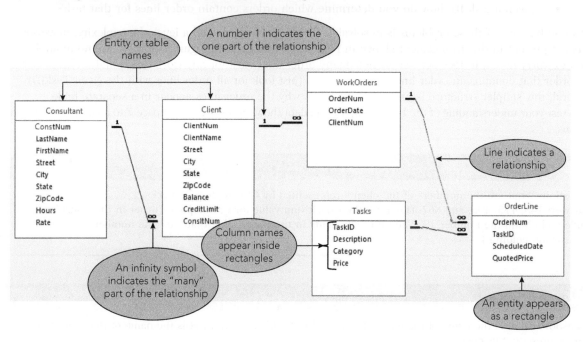

FIGURE 1-7 E-R diagram for the BITS database

Each of the five entities in the BITS database appears as a rectangle in the E-R diagram shown in Figure 1-7. The name of each entity appears above or at the top of the rectangle. The columns or attributes for each entity appear within the rectangle. Because the Consultant and Client entities have a one-to-many relationship, a line connects these two entities; similarly, a line connects the Client and WorkOrders entities, the WorkOrders and OrderLine entities, and the Tasks and OrderLine entities. The number 1, such as the one at the beginning of the Client to WorkOrders line, indicates the "one" part of the one-to-many relationship between two entities. The infinity symbol (∞) at the end of a line, such as the one at the Client end of the Consultant to Client line, indicates the "many" part of the one-to-many relationship between two entities. Older E-R diagrams may not display the number 1 at the beginning of the line and may display a solid dot at the end of the line. You will learn more about E-R diagrams in Chapter 6.

DATABASE MANAGEMENT SYSTEMS

Managing a database is inherently a complicated task. Fortunately, software packages, called database management systems, can do the job of manipulating databases for you. A **database management system (DBMS)** is a program, or a collection of programs, through which users interact with a database. The actual manipulation of the underlying database is handled by the DBMS. In some cases, users might interact with the DBMS directly, as shown in Figure 1-8.

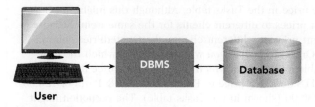

FIGURE 1-8 Using a DBMS directly

In other cases, users might interact with programs such as those created with Visual Basic, Java, Perl, PHP, or C++; these programs, in turn, interact with the DBMS, as shown in Figure 1-9. In either case, only the DBMS actually accesses the database.

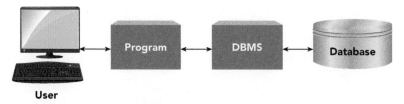

User

FIGURE 1-9   Using a DBMS through another program

With a DBMS, for example, users at BITS can ask the system to find data about task SI77; the system will either locate the item and provide the data or display a message that no such item exists in the database. All the work involved in this task is performed by the DBMS. (In a spreadsheet, you would have to search for the data manually.) If item SI77 is in the database, users then can ask for the order lines that contain the task, and the system will perform all the work involved in locating the order lines. Likewise, when users add data about a new client to the database, the DBMS performs all the tasks necessary to ensure that the client data is added and that the client is related to the appropriate consultant.

Popular DBMSs include Access, Oracle, DB2, MySQL, and SQL Server. Because BITS uses the Microsoft Office suite of programs, which includes Access, management initially elects to use Access as its DBMS. Using the tables shown in Figure 1-5 on page 7 as the starting point, a database expert at BITS determines the structure of the required database—this process is called **database design**. Then this person enters the design in the DBMS and creates several **forms**, which are screen objects used to maintain and view data from a database. Employees then use these forms to enter data.

The form that employees use to process item data is shown in Figure 1-10. Employees can use this form to enter a new task; to view, change, or delete an existing task; and to print the information for a task. No one at BITS needs to write a program to create this form; instead, the DBMS creates the form based on answers provided in response to the DBMS's questions about the form's content and appearance.

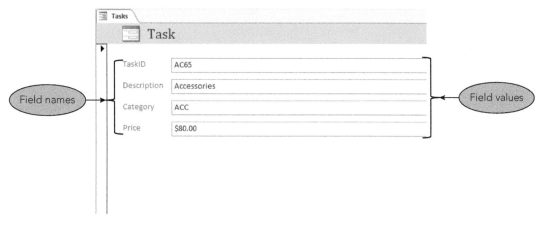

FIGURE 1-10   Task form

In this same way, you can use the DBMS to create the other forms that BITS needs. A more complicated form for processing order data is shown in Figure 1-11 on the next page. This form displays data about an order and its order lines, using data from the WorkOrders table and related data from the OrderLine table.

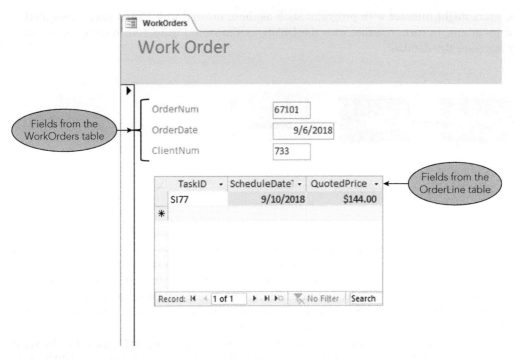

FIGURE 1-11 Work Order form

BITS can create the **reports** it needs in a similar way—the DBMS asks questions about the desired content and appearance of each report and then creates the reports automatically based on the answers. The IT Task List report, which lists the taskID, description, category, and price for each item, is shown in Figure 1-12.

IT Task List

Thursday, September 6, 2018
4:28:48 PM

TaskID	Description	Category	Price
AC65	Accessories	ACC	$80.00
DA11	Data recovery major	DRM	$175.00
DI85	Data recovery minor	DRM	$50.00
HA63	Hardware major	HAM	$225.00
HI31	Hardware minor	HAM	$165.00
LA81	Local area networking (LAN)	LAN	$104.00
MO49	Mobility	MOB	$65.00
OT99	Other work	OTH	$99.99
PI54	Printing issues	PRI	$50.00
SA44	Software major	SOM	$200.00
SI77	Software minor	SOM	$144.00
SI91	Security install/repair	SIR	$126.00
UP38	Upgrades	UPG	$185.00
VR39	Virus removal	VIR	$90.00
WA33	Wide area networking (WAN)	WAN	$130.00
WC19	Web connectivity	WEC	$75.00
			$1,963.99

Page 1 of 1

FIGURE 1-12 IT Task List report

ADVANTAGES OF DATABASE PROCESSING

The database approach to processing offers nine clear advantages over alternative data management methods. These advantages are listed in Figure 1-13 and are discussed on the following pages.

1. **Getting more information from the same amount of data**
2. **Sharing data**
3. **Balancing conflicting requirements**
4. **Controlling redundancy**
5. **Facilitating consistency**
6. **Referential integrity**
7. **Expanding security**
8. **Increasing productivity**
9. **Providing data independence**

FIGURE 1-13   Advantages of database processing

1. *Getting more information from the same amount of data.* The primary goal of a computer system is to turn data (recorded facts) into information (the knowledge gained by processing those facts). In a non-database, file-oriented environment, data often is partitioned into several disjointed systems, with each system having its own collection of files. Any request for information that necessitates accessing data from more than one of these collections can be extremely difficult to fulfill. In some cases, for all practical purposes, it is impossible. Thus, the desired information is unavailable—it has been stored in the computer, but it is scattered across multiple files. When all the data for the various systems is stored in a single database, however, the information becomes available. Given the power of a DBMS, the information is available, and the process of getting it is quick and easy.

2. *Sharing data.* The data of various users can be combined and shared among authorized users, allowing all users access to a greater pool of data. Several users can have access to the same piece of data—for example, a client's address—and still use it in a variety of ways. When one user changes a client's address, the new address immediately becomes available to all users. In addition, the existing data can be used in new ways, such as generating new types of reports, without having to create additional data files, as is the case in the nondatabase approach.

3. *Balancing conflicting requirements.* For the database approach to function adequately within an organization, a person or group should be in charge of the database, especially if the database will serve many users. This person or group is often called the **database administrator** or **database administration (DBA)**, respectively. By keeping the overall needs of the organization in mind, a DBA can structure the database in such a way that it benefits the entire organization, not just a single group. Although this approach might mean that an individual user group is served less well than it would have been if it had its own isolated system, the organization as a whole is better off. Ultimately, when the organization benefits, so do the individual groups of users.

4. *Controlling redundancy.* With database processing, data that formerly was kept separate in nondatabase, file-oriented systems is integrated into a single database, so multiple copies of the same data no longer exist. With the nondatabase approach, each user group at BITS has its own copy of each client's address. With the database approach, each client's address would occur only once, thus eliminating redundancy.

   Recall that eliminating redundancy makes the process of updating data much simpler. With the nondatebase approach, changing a client's address means making one change. With the nondatabase approach, in which data for each client might be stored in three different places, the same address change means that three changes have to be made, possibly introducing multiple errors. Although eliminating redundancy is the ideal, it is not always possible. Sometimes, for reasons having to do with performance, you might choose to introduce a limited amount of redundancy into a database. However, even in these cases, you would be able to keep the redundancy under tight control, thus obtaining the same advantages. This is why it is better to say that you *control* redundancy rather than *eliminate* it.

5. ***Facilitating consistency.*** Suppose an individual client's address appears in more than one place. Client 175, for example, might be listed at 12 Saratoga Parkway in one place and at 12 Saratoga Pky in another place. In this case, the data for the client is inconsistent. Because the potential for this sort of problem is a direct result of redundancy and because the database approach reduces redundancy, there is less potential for this sort of inconsistency occurring with the database approach.

6. ***Referential integrity.*** **Referential integrity** is a relational database concept stating that table relationships must be consistent and follow integrity constraints. An **integrity constraint** ensures that changes made to the database do not result in a loss of data consistency. For example, the consultant number given for any client must be one that is already in the database. In other words, users cannot enter an incorrect or nonexistent consultant number for a client. A database has **integrity** when the data in it satisfies all established integrity constraints. A good DBMS should provide an opportunity for users to incorporate these integrity constraints when they design the database. The DBMS then should ensure that the constraints are not violated. According to the integrity constraint about clients, the DBMS should *not allow* you to store data about a given client when the consultant number you enter is not the number of a consultant that already is in the database.

7. ***Expanding security.*** **Security** is the prevention of unauthorized access to the database. A DBMS has many features that help ensure the enforcement of security measures. For example, a DBA can assign passwords to authorized users, and then only those users who enter an acceptable password can gain access to the data in the database. Further, a DBMS lets you assign users to groups, with some groups permitted to view and update data in the database and other groups permitted only to view certain data in the database. With the nondatabase approach, you have limited security features and are more vulnerable to intentional and accidental access and changes to data.

8. ***Increasing productivity.*** A DBMS frees the programmers who are writing database access programs from having to engage in mundane data manipulation activities, such as adding new data and deleting existing data, thus making the programmers more productive. A good DBMS has many features that allow users to gain access to data in a database without having to do any programming. These features increase the productivity of programmers, who may not need to write complex programs in order to perform certain tasks, and nonprogrammers, who may be able to get the results they seek from the data in a database without waiting for a program to be written for them.

9. ***Providing data independence.*** The structure of a database often needs to be changed. For example, changing user requirements might necessitate the addition of an entity, an attribute, a record, or a relationship, or a change might be required to improve performance. A good DBMS provides **data independence**, which is a property that lets you change the structure of a database without requiring you to change the programs that access the database; examples of these programs are the forms you use to interact with the database and the reports that provide information from the database. Without data independence, programmers might need to expend a great deal of effort to update programs to match the new database structure. The presence of many programs in the system may make this effort so prohibitively difficult that management might decide to avoid changing the database, even though the change might improve the database's performance or add valuable data. With data independence, management is more likely to make the decision to change the database.

DISADVANTAGES OF DATABASE PROCESSING

As you would expect, when there are advantages to doing something in a certain way, there are also disadvantages. Database processing is no exception. In terms of numbers alone, the advantages outweigh the disadvantages; the latter are listed in Figure 1-14 and explained next.

1. **Increased complexity**
2. **Greater impact of failure**
3. **More difficult recovery**
4. **Larger file size**

FIGURE 1-14   Disadvantages of database processing

1. *Increased complexity.* The complexity and breadth of the functions provided by a DBMS make it a complex product. Users of the DBMS must master many of the features of the system in order to take full advantage of it. In the design and implementation of a new system that uses a DBMS, many decisions have to be made; it is possible to make incorrect choices, especially with an insufficient understanding of the system. Unfortunately, a few incorrect choices can spell disaster for the whole project. A sound database design is critical to the successful use of a DBMS.
2. *Greater impact of failure.* In a nondatabase, file-oriented system, each user has a completely separate system; the failure of any single user's system does not necessarily affect any other user. On the other hand, if several users are sharing the same database, a failure for any one user that damages the database in some way might affect all the other users.
3. *More difficult recovery.* Because a database inherently is more complex than a simple file, the process of recovering it in the event of a catastrophe also is more complicated. This situation is particularly true when the database is being updated by many users at the same time. The database must first be restored to the condition it was in when it was last known to be correct; any updates made by users since that time must be redone. The greater the number of users involved in updating the database, the more complicated this task becomes.
4. *Larger file size.* To support all the complex functions that it provides to users, a DBMS must be a large program that occupies a great deal of disk space as well as a substantial amount of internal memory. In addition, because all the data that the database manages for you is stored in one file, the database file requires a large amount of disk space and internal memory.

BIG DATA

Finally, companies have access to more and different kinds of data than ever before. The term **big data** describes the large volume of data produced by every digital process, system, sensor, mobile device, and even social media exchange. To extract meaningful information from big data, companies need optimal processing power, analytics capabilities, and skills.

Big data may be structured, unstructured, or a combination of both. **Structured data** is traditional in its retrieval and storage DBMS, similar to the BITS database in this chapter. **Unstructured data** is not organized or easily interpreted by traditional databases or data models. Unstructured data may involve a lot of text and **metadata**—descriptive data stored with input sources. Twitter tweets, metadata associated with photographs, and other web-based media posts are good examples of unstructured data.

Business administrators, IT personnel, and all employees need to work together to analyze big data and create useful information. Insights derived from big data enable companies to make better decisions about optimizing operations, engaging customers more fully, maintaining security, and capitalizing on

16

new revenue streams. Big data is a source for ongoing discovery and analysis, and the demand for information from big data will require new approaches to database management, architecture, tools, and practices.

INTRODUCTION TO THE COLONIAL ADVENTURE TOURS DATABASE CASE

Colonial Adventure Tours is a small business that organizes daylong, guided trips of New England. To support the company's growing business, management uses a database to ensure that the company's data is current, accurate, and easily accessible.

In running the guided tours, management gathers and organizes information about guides, trips, customers, and reservations. Figure 1-15 shows sample guide data. Each guide is identified by a unique four-character code that consists of two uppercase letters and two digits. For each guide, the table also stores the guide's last name, first name, address, city, state, zip code, telephone number, and hire date.

Guide

GuideNum	LastName	FirstName	Address	City	State	ZipCode	PhoneNum	HireDate
AM01	Abrams	Miles	54 Quest Ave.	Williamsburg	MA	01096	617-555-6032	6/3/2012
BR01	Boyers	Rita	140 Oakton Rd.	Jaffrey	NH	03452	603-555-2134	3/4/2012
DH01	Devon	Harley	25 Old Ranch Rd.	Sunderland	MA	01375	781-555-7767	1/8/2017
GZ01	Gregory	Zach	7 Moose Head Rd.	Dummer	NH	03588	603-555-8765	11/4/2013
KS01	Kiley	Susan	943 Oakton Rd.	Jaffrey	NH	03452	603-555-1230	4/8/2016
KS02	Kelly	Sam	9 Congaree Ave.	Franconia	NH	03580	603-555-0003	6/10/2016
MR01	Marston	Ray	24 Shenandoah Rd.	Springfield	MA	01101	781-555-2323	9/14/2015
RH01	Rowan	Hal	12 Heather Rd.	Mount Desert	ME	04660	207-555-9009	6/2/2014
SL01	Stevens	Lori	15 Riverton Rd.	Coventry	VT	05825	802-555-3339	9/5/2014
UG01	Unser	Glory	342 Pineview St.	Danbury	CT	06810	203-555-8534	2/2/2017

FIGURE 1-15 Sample guide data for Colonial Adventure Tours

Figure 1-16 shows sample trip data for Colonial Adventure Tours. Each trip is identified by a unique number called TripID. In addition, management tracks the trip name, the trip's starting location, the state in which the trip originates, the trip's total distance (in miles), the trip's maximum group size, the trip's type, and the trip's season.

Trip

TripID	TripName	StartLocation	State	Distance	MaxGrpSize	Type	Season
1	Arethusa Falls	Harts Location	NH	5	10	Hiking	Summer
2	Mt Ascutney - North Peak	Weathersfield	VT	5	6	Hiking	Late Spring
3	Mt Ascutney - West Peak	Weathersfield	VT	6	10	Hiking	Early Fall
4	Bradbury Mountain Ride	Lewiston-Auburn	ME	25	8	Biking	Early Fall
5	Baldpate Mountain	North Newry	ME	6	10	Hiking	Late Spring
6	Blueberry Mountain	Batchelders Grant	ME	8	8	Hiking	Early Fall
7	Bloomfield - Maidstone	Bloomfield	CT	10	6	Paddling	Late Spring
8	Black Pond	Lincoln	NH	8	12	Hiking	Summer
9	Big Rock Cave	Tamworth	NH	6	10	Hiking	Summer
10	Mt. Cardigan - Firescrew	Orange	NH	7	8	Hiking	Summer
11	Chocorua Lake Tour	Tamworth	NH	12	15	Paddling	Summer
12	Cadillac Mountain Ride	Bar Harbor	ME	8	16	Biking	Early Fall
13	Cadillac Mountain	Bar Harbor	ME	7	8	Hiking	Late Spring
14	Cannon Mtn	Franconia	NH	6	6	Hiking	Early Fall
15	Crawford Path Presidentials Hike	Crawford Notch	NH	16	4	Hiking	Summer
16	Cherry Pond	Whitefield	NH	6	16	Hiking	Spring
17	Huguenot Head Hike	Bar Harbor	ME	5	10	Hiking	Early Fall
18	Low Bald Spot Hike	Pinkam Notch	NH	8	6	Hiking	Early Fall
19	Mason's Farm	North Stratford	CT	12	7	Paddling	Late Spring
20	Lake Mephremagog Tour	Newport	VT	8	15	Paddling	Late Spring
21	Long Pond	Rutland	MA	8	12	Hiking	Summer
22	Long Pond Tour	Greenville	ME	12	10	Paddling	Summer
23	Lower Pond Tour	Poland	ME	8	15	Paddling	Late Spring
24	Mt Adams	Randolph	NH	9	6	Hiking	Summer
25	Mount Battie Ride	Camden	ME	20	8	Biking	Early Fall
26	Mount Cardigan Hike	Cardigan	NH	4	16	Hiking	Late Fall
27	Mt. Chocorua	Albany	NH	6	10	Hiking	Spring
28	Mount Garfield Hike	Woodstock	NH	5	10	Hiking	Early Fall
29	Metacomet-Monadnock Trail Hike	Pelham	MA	10	12	Hiking	Late Spring
30	McLennan Reservation Hike	Tyringham	MA	6	16	Hiking	Summer
31	Missisquoi River - VT	Lowell	VT	12	10	Paddling	Summer
32	Northern Forest Canoe Trail	Stark	NH	15	10	Paddling	Summer
33	Park Loop Ride	Mount Desert Island	ME	27	8	Biking	Late Spring
34	Pontook Reservoir Tour	Dummer	NH	15	14	Paddling	Late Spring
35	Pisgah State Park Ride	Northborough	NH	12	10	Biking	Summer
36	Pondicherry Trail Ride	White Mountains	NH	15	16	Biking	Late Spring
37	Seal Beach Harbor	Bar Harbor	ME	5	16	Hiking	Early Spring
38	Sawyer River Ride	Mount Carrigain	NH	10	18	Biking	Early Fall
39	Welch and Dickey Mountains Hike	Thorton	NH	5	10	Hiking	Summer
40	Wachusett Mountain	Princeton	MA	8	8	Hiking	Early Spring
41	Westfield River Loop	Fort Fairfield	ME	20	10	Biking	Late Spring

FIGURE 1-16   Sample trip data for Colonial Adventure Tours

Figure 1-17 on the next page shows sample customer data for Colonial Adventure Tours. Each customer is identified by a unique customer number. In addition, management stores each customer's last name, first name, address, city, state, zip code, and telephone number.

Customer

CustomerNum	LastName	FirstName	Address	City	State	ZipCode	Phone
101	Northfold	Liam	1985 Highway 17 N.	Londonderry	NH	03053	603-555-7563
102	Ocean	Arnold	2332 South St. Apt 3	Springfield	MA	01101	413-555-3212
103	Kasuma	Sujata	132 Main St. #1	East Hartford	CT	06108	860-555-0703
104	Goff	Ryan	164A South Bend Rd.	Lowell	MA	01854	781-555-8423
105	McLean	Kyle	345 Lower Ave.	Wolcott	NY	14590	585-555-5321
106	Morontoia	Joseph	156 Scholar St.	Johnston	RI	02919	401-555-4848
107	Marchand	Quinn	76 Cross Rd.	Bath	NH	03740	603-555-0456
108	Rulf	Uschi	32 Sheep Stop St.	Edinboro	PA	16412	814-555-5521
109	Caron	Jean Luc	10 Greenfield St.	Rome	ME	04963	207-555-9643
110	Bers	Martha	65 Granite St.	York	NY	14592	585-555-0111
112	Jones	Laura	373 Highland Ave.	Somerville	MA	02143	857-555-6258
115	Vaccari	Adam	1282 Ocean Walk	Ocean City	NJ	08226	609-555-5231
116	Murakami	Iris	7 Cherry Blossom St.	Weymouth	MA	02188	617-555-6665
119	Chau	Clement	18 Ark Ledge Ln.	Londonderry	VT	05148	802-555-3096
120	Gernowski	Sadie	24 Stump Rd.	Athens	ME	04912	207-555-4507
121	Bretton-Borak	Siam	10 Old Main St.	Cambridge	VT	05444	802-555-3443
122	Hefferson	Orlauh	132 South St. Apt 27	Manchester	NH	03101	603-555-3476
123	Barnett	Larry	25 Stag Rd.	Fairfield	CT	06824	860-555-9876
124	Busa	Karen	12 Foster St.	South Windsor	CT	06074	857-555-5532
125	Peterson	Becca	51 Fredrick St.	Albion	NY	14411	585-555-0900
126	Brown	Brianne	154 Central St.	Vernon	CT	06066	860-555-3234

FIGURE 1-17   Sample customer data for Colonial Adventure Tours

Figure 1-18 shows sample reservations data for Colonial Adventure Tours. Each reservation is identified by a unique reservation number that uses the last two digits of the current year followed by a five-digit number that is incremented sequentially as each reservation is received. The table also stores the trip ID, the trip date, the number of persons, the trip price per person, any additional fees for transportation and equipment rentals, and the customer number.

Reservation

ReservationID	TripID	TripDate	NumPersons	TripPrice	OtherFees	CustomerNum
1800001	40	3/26/2018	2	$55.00	$0.00	101
1800002	21	6/8/2018	2	$95.00	$0.00	101
1800003	28	9/12/2018	1	$35.00	$0.00	103
1800004	26	10/16/2018	4	$45.00	$15.00	104
1800005	39	6/25/2018	5	$55.00	$0.00	105
1800006	32	6/18/2018	1	$80.00	$20.00	106
1800007	22	7/9/2018	8	$75.00	$10.00	107
1800008	28	9/12/2018	2	$35.00	$0.00	108
1800009	38	9/11/2018	2	$90.00	$40.00	109
1800010	2	5/14/2018	3	$25.00	$0.00	102
1800011	3	9/15/2018	3	$25.00	$0.00	102
1800012	1	6/12/2018	4	$15.00	$0.00	115
1800013	8	7/9/2018	1	$20.00	$5.00	116
1800014	12	10/1/2018	2	$40.00	$5.00	119
1800015	10	7/23/2018	1	$20.00	$0.00	120
1800016	11	7/23/2018	6	$75.00	$15.00	121
1800017	39	6/18/2018	3	$20.00	$5.00	122
1800018	38	9/18/2018	4	$85.00	$15.00	126
1800019	25	8/29/2018	2	$110.00	$25.00	124
1800020	28	8/27/2018	2	$35.00	$10.00	124
1800021	32	6/11/2018	3	$90.00	$20.00	112
1800022	21	6/8/2018	1	$95.00	$25.00	119
1800024	38	9/11/2018	1	$70.00	$30.00	121
1800025	38	9/11/2018	2	$70.00	$45.00	125
1800026	12	10/1/2018	2	$40.00	$0.00	126
1800029	4	9/19/2018	4	$105.00	$25.00	120
1800030	15	7/25/2018	6	$60.00	$15.00	104

FIGURE 1-18   Sample reservations data for Colonial Adventure Tours

Q & A 1-8

Question: To check your understanding of the relationship between customers and reservations, answer the following questions: Which customer made reservation 1800010? For which trip dates does Karen Busa have reservations?

Answer: Arnold Ocean made reservation 1800010. Find the row in the Reservation table with the reservation ID 1800010 (see Figure 1-18), and then find the customer number 102. Next, review the Customer table (see Figure 1-17), and determine that the customer name with the customer number 102 is Arnold Ocean.

Karen Busa has reservations for trips on August 29, 2018, and August 27, 2018. To find the trip dates for Karen Busa, find her customer number (124) in the Customer table. Next, find all rows in the Reservation table that contain the customer number 124.

The table named TripGuides shown in Figure 1-19 is used to relate trips and guides. It includes the trip number and the guide number. The trip number in the TripGuides table matches a trip number in the Trip table, and the guide number in the TripGuides table matches a guide number in the Guide table. Note that some trips use more than one guide.

TripGuides

TripID	GuideNum
1	GZ01
1	RH01
2	AM01
2	SL01
3	SL01
4	BR01
4	GZ01
5	KS01
5	UG01
6	RH01
7	SL01
8	BR01
9	BR01
10	GZ01
11	DH01
11	KS01
11	UG01
12	BR01
13	RH01
14	KS02
15	GZ01
16	KS02
17	RH01
18	KS02

TripGuides (continued)

TripID	GuideNum
19	DH01
20	SL01
21	AM01
22	UG01
23	DH01
23	SL01
24	BR01
25	BR01
26	GZ01
27	GZ01
28	BR01
29	DH01
30	AM01
31	SL01
32	KS01
33	UG01
34	KS01
35	GZ01
36	KS02
37	RH01
38	KS02
39	BR01
40	DH01
41	BR01

FIGURE 1-19   Table used to relate trips and guides

Q & A 1-9

Question: To check your understanding of the relationship between trips and guides, answer the following questions: Which trips are led by Glory Unser? Which guides lead the Lower Pond Tour trip?

Answer: Glory Unser leads the Baldpate Mountain, Chocorua Lake Tour, Long Pond Tour, and Park Loop Ride trips. To determine those trips, first examine the Guide table (Figure 1-15) to find her guide number (UG01). Next, look for all rows in the TripGuides table (Figure 1-19) that contain her guide number (UG01), and find that these rows contain the trip numbers 5, 11, 22, and 33. Then examine the Trip table (Figure 1-16) to determine the trip names for the trips with the trip numbers 5, 11, 22, and 33 to learn the corresponding trip names: Baldpate Mountain, Chocorua Lake Tour, Long Pond Tour, and Park Look Ride.

To find the guides who lead the Lower Pond Tour trip, use the Trip table (Figure 1-16) to identify the trip number for this tour and determine that it has the trip number 23, and then look for all rows in the TripGuides table (Figure 1-19) that contain the trip number 23. There are two such rows, which contain the guide numbers DH01 and SL01. Finally, find the rows with these guide numbers in the Guide table (Figure 1-15), and then determine that Harley Devon and Lori Stevens lead the Lower Pond Tour trips.

Q & A 1-10

Question: One of Jean Luc Caron's friends called the tour office to reserve the same trip as Jean Luc, but he can't remember the trip name. Which trip did Jean Luc Caron reserve?

Answer: Jean Luc Caron has a reservation for the Sawyer River Ride trip. First, find the customer number for Jean Luc Caron in the Customer table to determine that his customer number is 109. Then review the Reservation table and find all rows with the customer number 109, and determine the trip number for that trip, which is trip number 38. Finally, review the Trip table to identify that trip number 38 is the Sawyer River Ride trip.

Q & A 1-11

Question: Which guides lead paddling trips in the summer season?

Answer: Harley Devon, Susan Kiley, Lori Stevens, and Glory Unser are leading paddling trips in the summer. To identify paddling trips that are offered in the summer, look for rows in the Trip table that have Paddling in the Type column *and* Summer in the Season column. There are four such rows with the trip numbers 11, 22, 31, and 32. Locate these trip numbers in the TripGuides table, and then determine that the guide numbers DH01, KS01, SL01, and UG01 are associated with these trip numbers. Finally, find the guide numbers DH01, KS01, SL01, and UG01 in the Guide table, and then identify the corresponding guides as Harley Devon, Susan Kiley, Lori Stevens, and Glory Unser.

The E-R diagram for the Colonial Adventure Tours database appears in Figure 1-20.

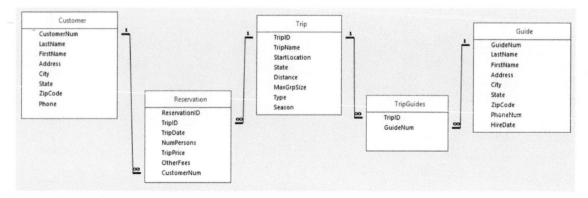

FIGURE 1-20   E-R diagram for Colonial Adventure Tours

INTRODUCTION TO THE SPORTS PHYSICAL THERAPY DATABASE CASE

Sports Physical Therapy provides evaluation, treatment, and rehabilitation of all types of acute and chronic injuries for both athletes and non-athletes. The highly skilled, certified therapists use their background of biomechanics, sport mechanics, and clinical experience to provide one-on-one comprehensive rehabilitation for all types of injuries. The company stores information about their patients, therapists, therapies, and sessions.

In the Patient table shown in Figure 1-21, Sports Physical Therapy stores information about its patients. Each patient is identified by a unique, four-digit patient number. The patient's name and address, as well as the balance due on their bill, also are stored in the table.

Patient

PatientNum	LastName	FirstName	Address	City	State	ZipCode	Balance
1010	Koehler	Robbie	119 West Bay Dr.	San Vista	TX	72510	$1,535.15
1011	King	Joseph	941 Treemont	Oak Hills	TX	74081	$212.80
1012	Houghland	Susan	7841 Lake Side Dr.	Munster	TX	72380	$1,955.40
1013	Falls	Tierra	44 Applewood Ave.	Palm Rivers	TX	72511	$1,000.35
1014	Odepaul	Ben	546 WCR 150 South	Munster	TX	74093	$525.00
1015	Venable	Isaiah	37 High School Road	Waterville	TX	74183	$432.30
1016	Waggoner	Brianna	2691 Westgrove St.	Delbert	TX	72381	$714.25
1017	Short	Tobey	1928 10th Ave.	Munster	TX	72512	$967.60
1018	Baptist	Joseph	300 Erin Dr.	Waterville	TX	76658	$1,846.75
1019	Culling	Latisha	4238 East 71st St.	San Vista	TX	74071	$1,988.50
1020	Marino	Andre	919 Horton Ave.	Georgetown	TX	72379	$688.95
1021	Wilson	Tammy	424 October Blvd.	Waterville	TX	76658	$2,015.30

FIGURE 1-21   Patient data for Sports Physical Therapy

Sports Physical Therapy records information about each of its therapy sessions. The fields of data are stored in the Session table shown in Figure 1-22. A session record will have a unique number, the session date, the patient number, and the length of the session, as well as the therapist number and therapy code.

Session

SessionNum	SessionDate	PatientNum	LengthOfSession	TherapistID	TherapyCode
27	10/10/2018	1011	45	JR085	92507
28	10/11/2018	1016	30	AS648	97010
29	10/11/2018	1014	60	SW124	97014
30	10/12/2018	1013	30	BM273	97033
31	10/15/2018	1016	90	AS648	98960
32	10/16/2018	1018	15	JR085	97035
33	10/17/2018	1017	60	SN852	97039
34	10/17/2018	1015	45	BM273	97112
35	10/18/2018	1010	30	SW124	97113
36	10/18/2018	1019	75	SN852	97116
37	10/19/2018	1020	30	BM273	97124
38	10/19/2018	1021	60	AS648	97535

FIGURE 1-22   Session data for Sports Physical Therapy

Q & A 1-12

Question: To check your understanding of the relationship between patients and sessions, answer the following questions: Which patient had therapy on October 15, 2018? What therapy code was listed for the session belonging to Isaiah Venable? What session number(s) is (are) listed for Tierra Falls?

Answer: The Session table (Figure 1-22 on the previous page) lists PatientNum 1016 as having therapy on October 15, 2018. When you look that patient up in the Patient table (Figure 1-21), you see that it is Brianna Waggoner. To find the therapy code for Isaiah Venable, you must start with the Patient table, look up his number, 1015, and then examine the Session table. Patient number 1015 had the therapy coded as 97112. Finally, Tierra Falls is patient number 1013 (Patient table). Looking up her session number in the Session table, it is 30.

Sports Physical Therapy stores information about the therapists who work in their office, as shown in the Therapist table in Figure 1-23. Each therapist is identified by a unique ID number that consists of two uppercase letters followed by a three-digit number. For each therapist, the table also includes the last name, first name, street, city, state, and zip code.

Therapist

TherapistID	LastName	FirstName	Street	City	State	ZipCode
AS648	Shields	Anthony	5222 Eagle Court	Palm Rivers	TX	72511
BM273	McClain	Bridgette	385 West Mill St.	Waterville	TX	76658
JR085	Risk	Jonathan	1010 650 North	Palm Rivers	TX	72511
SN852	Nair	Saritha	25 North Elm St.	Livewood	TX	72512
SW124	Wilder	Steven	7354 Rockville Road	San Vista	TX	72510

FIGURE 1-23 Therapist data for Sports Physical Therapy

Q & A 1-13

Question: To check your understanding of the relationship between therapists and sessions, answer the following questions: Which therapist worked with patient 1021? How many patients did Bridgette McClain work with? What were the therapy codes (TherapyCode) for those sessions?

Answer: To determine which therapist worked with patient 1021, first examine the Session table (Figure 1-22). Find patient 1021; look across the table to see the TherapistID, AS648. Then look up the TherapistID in the Therapist table (Figure 1-23) to find the name, Anthony Shields.

To determine the number of patients that Bridgette McClain worked with, look up her TherapistID number in the Therapist table (Figure 1-23). You will see that it is BM273. Then look at the Session table (Figure 1-22). In the TherapistID column, count the number of times you see BM273—it should be three. Finally, look at the TherapyCode column for each of those three sessions. You should identify therapies 97033, 97112, and 97124.

In the Therapies table, each kind of therapy is identified by a unique number, which corresponds to the medical physical therapy code sent to insurance companies for reimbursement. The TherapyCode, a description, and the billable unit of time, if any, are included in the table. Time-based therapies are billed in groups of minutes (listed in the table). Service-based therapies are billed per service (no time is listed in the table). Figure 1-24 displays data for therapies.

Therapies

TherapyCode	Description	UnitOfTime
90901	Biofeedback training by any modality	
92240	Shoulder strapping	
92507	Treatment of speech	15
92530	Knee strapping	
92540	Ankle and/or foot strapping	
95831	Extremity or trunk muscle testing	
97010	Hot or cold pack application	
97012	Mechanical traction	
97014	Electrical stimulation	
97016	Vasopneumatic devices	
97018	Paraffin bath	
97022	Whirlpool	
97026	Infrared	
97032	Electrical stimulation	15
97033	Iontophoresis	15
97035	Ultrasound	15
97039	Unlisted modality	15
97110	Therapeutic exercises to develop strength and endurance, range of motion, and flexibility	15
97112	Neuromuscular re-education of movement, balance, coordination, etc.	15
97113	Aquatic therapy with therapeutic exercises	15
97116	Gait training	15
97124	Massage	15
97139	Unlisted therapeutic procedure	
97140	Manual therapy techniques	15
97150	Group therapeutic procedure	15
97530	Dynamic activities to improve functional performance, direct (one-on-one) with the patient	15
97535	Self-care/home management training	15
97750	Physical performance test or measurement	15
97799	Unlisted physical medicine/rehabilitation service or procedure	
98941	CMT of the spine	
98960	Education and training for patient self-management	30

FIGURE 1-24   Therapies data for Sports Physical Therapy

Q & A 1-14

Question: To check your understanding of the relationship between therapies and the other tables, answer the following questions: Did any patient have a hot or cold pack application? Which therapist(s) helped a patient with gait training? How many minutes did Jonathan Risk work with his patient on speech therapy, and how many units will be billed to insurance?

Answer: To determine if any patient had an application for a hot or cold pack, look through the descriptions in the Therapies table (Figure 1-24). Note that the TherapyCode code for the procedure is 97010. Look up that number in the Sessions table (Figure 1-22). You will see that it corresponds with 28, so the answer is yes.

To look up which therapist did gait training, begin with the Therapies table (Figure 1-24). You will see that gait training is the description for therapy 97116. Move to the Sessions table (Figure 1-22) and look for 97116. You will find that session 36 lists that TherapyCode. Find the TherapistID column in the Sessions table that aligns with session 36. The TherapistID is SN852. Finally, move to the Therapist table (Figure 1-23) and look up therapist SN852. It is Saritha Nair.

The final question is a bit more difficult. How many minutes did Jonathan Risk work with his patient on speech therapy, and how many units will be billed to insurance? Looking in the Therapies table (Figure 1-24), the only description related to speech therapy is TherapyCode 92507, Treatment of Speech. Note that it is billable in 15-minute units. (You may want to write down the TherapyCode and the billable units.)

The Therapist table (Figure 1-23) will reveal that Jonathan Risk has a TherapistID number of JR085. (Again, make a note of that.)

Finally, you can use these pieces of information in the Sessions table (Figure 1-23). Look up TherapyCode 92507. Look across the row to verify that therapist JR085 performed the work. Now look at the LengthOfSession field. You will see that it was 45 minutes. With a billable unit of 15 minutes, Sports Physical Therapy will bill the insurance for three units (45 divided by 15 equals 3).

The E-R diagram for the Sports Physical Therapy database appears in Figure 1-25.

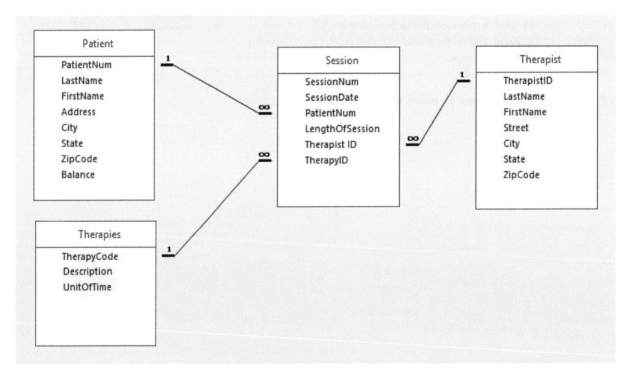

FIGURE 1-25   E-R diagram for the Sports Physical Therapy database

Summary

- Problems with nondatabase approaches to data management include redundancy, difficulties accessing related data, limited security features, limited data-sharing features, and potential size limitations.
- An entity is a person, place, object, event, or idea for which you want to store and process data—commonly that data is stored in a table. An attribute, field, or column is a characteristic or property of an entity. A relationship is an association between entities.
- A one-to-many relationship between two entities exists when each occurrence of the first entity is related to many occurrences of the second entity and each occurrence of the second entity is related to only one occurrence of the first entity.
- A database is a structure that can store information about multiple types of entities, the attributes of the entities, and the relationships among the entities.
- BITS is an organization whose requirements include information about the following entities: consultants, clients, tasks, work orders, and order lines.
- An entity-relationship (E-R) diagram represents a database visually by using a rectangle for each entity that includes the entity's name above the rectangle and the entity's columns inside the rectangle, a line to connect two entities that have a relationship, an infinity symbol at the end of a line to indicate the "many" part of a one-to-many relationship.
- A database management system (DBMS) is a program, or a collection of programs, through which users interact with a database. DBMSs let you create forms and reports quickly and easily as well as obtain answers to questions about the data stored in a database.
- Database processing offers the following advantages: getting more information from the same amount of data, sharing data, balancing conflicting requirements, controlling redundancy, facilitating consistency, improving integrity, expanding security, increasing productivity, and providing data independence.
- The disadvantages of database processing are increased complexity, greater impact of failure, more difficult recovery, and larger file sizes.
- Big data is a newer trend to use structured and unstructured data from nontraditional input sources such as electronic sensors, mobile devices, metadata, and web-based or social media entries.
- Colonial Adventure Tours is a company whose requirements include information about the following entities: guides, trips, customers, reservations, and trip guides.
- Sports Physical Therapy is a company whose requirements include information about the following entities: patients, therapists, sessions, and therapies.

Key Terms

attribute	integrity
big data	integrity constraint
column	metadata
data file	one-to-many relationship
data independence	records
database	redundancy
database administration (DBA)	referential integrity
database administrator	relationship
database design	reports
database management system (DBMS)	rows
entity	security
entity-relationship (E-R) diagram	structured data
field	table
forms	unstructured data

Review Questions

1. What is redundancy? What problems are associated with redundancy?
2. Besides redundancy, what other problems are associated with the nondatabase approach to processing data?

3. What is an entity? An attribute?

4. What is a relationship? A one-to-many relationship?

5. What is a database?

6. How do you create a one-to-many relationship in a database system?

7. What is an E-R diagram?

8. What is a DBMS?

9. What is database design?

10. What is a form?

11. How can you get more information from the same amount of data by using a database approach instead of a nondatabase approach?

12. What is meant by the sharing of data?

13. What is a DBA? What kinds of responsibilities does a DBA have in a database environment?

14. How does consistency result from controlling redundancy?

15. What is an integrity constraint? When does a database have integrity?

16. What is security? How does a DBMS provide security?

17. What is data independence? Why is it desirable?

18. How is file size a disadvantage in a database environment?

19. How can the complexity of a DBMS be a disadvantage?

20. What are some specific inputs that may result in big data?

21. Why can a failure in a database environment be more serious than an error in a nondatabase environment?

22. Why might recovery of data be more difficult in a database environment?

 23. If a database is not maintained or if incorrect data is entered into the database, serious problems can occur. What problems could occur if a student database is not maintained?

 24. An attribute is a characteristic or property of an entity. If *person* is an entity, would the same attributes be used to describe a person in different databases that store medical, student, and fitness club data? Why or why not?

BITS Corporation Exercises

Answer each of the following questions using the BITS data shown in Figure 1-5. No computer work is required.

1. List the names of all clients that have a credit limit that is less than $10,000.

2. List the descriptions of all items in the Tasks table that have the category DRM.

3. List the order numbers for orders placed by client number 322 on September 10, 2018.

4. List the order date and the scheduled date any work order involving task SA44.

5. List the name of each client that placed an order for two different tasks in the same order.

6. List the name of each client that has a credit limit of $5,000 and is represented by Patrick Jordan.

7. Find the sum of the balances for all customers represented by Christopher Turner.

8. For each order, list the order number, order date, client number, and client name.

9. For each order placed on September 10, 2018, list the order number, order date, client number, and client name.

10. For each order placed on September 17, 2018, list the order number and client name, along with the name of the client's consultant.

 11. BITS needs to be able to contact clients when problems arise concerning an order. What other attributes could BITS include in the Customer table to assist in contacting customers?

 12. BITS wants the database to include data on all its employees, not just consultants. What additional entities would the DBA need to include in the database to store this data? What attributes?

13. What kinds of unstructured data or big data might the BITS corporation want to gather in the future? What kind of devices might they use for input? How would they store the data?

Colonial Adventure Tours Case

Answer each of the following questions using the Colonial Adventure Tours data shown in Figures 1-15 through 1-19. No computer work is required.

1. List the last name of each guide who does not live in New Hampshire (NH).
2. List the trip name of each trip that has the type Paddling.
3. List the trip name of each trip that has the season Late Spring.
4. List the trip name of each trip that has the type Biking and that has a distance longer than 20 miles.
5. List the trip name of each trip that is in the state of Vermont (VT) or that has a maximum group size greater than 10.
6. List the trip name of each trip that has the season Early Fall or Late Fall.
7. How many trips are in the states of Vermont (VT) or Connecticut (CT)?
8. List the trip name of each trip that has Miles Abrams as a guide.
9. List the trip name of each trip that has the type Biking and that has Rita Boyers as a guide.
10. For each reservation that has a trip date of July 23, 2018, list the customer's last name, the trip name, and the start location.
11. How many reservations have a trip price that is greater than $50.00 but less than $100.00?
12. For each trip that has more than one guide that can lead the trip, list the trip name, the trip type, and the first and last names of each guide.
13. For each customer that has more than one reservation, list the customer's first and last names, the trip name, and the trip type.
14. For each reservation with a trip price of greater than $100.00, list the customer's last name, the trip name, and the trip type.
15. List the last name of each customer who has a reservation for a trip in Maine (ME).
 16. The trip price in the Reservation table is a per-person price. The total price for a trip includes the total of the trip price and the other fees multiplied by the number of people taking the trip. Should total price be a field in the Reservation table? Why or why not?
 17. Currently, trip cost is determined by the number of people taking the trip and the type of trip. If trip cost were based only on the type of trip, in which table would you place the trip cost field?

Sports Physical Therapy Case

Answer each of the following questions using the Sports Physical Therapy data shown in Figures 1-21 through 1-24. No computer work is required.

1. List the patient number, last name, and first name of every patient.
2. List the session number for each session that lasted 60 minutes or more.
3. List the last name, first name, and street address of every therapist who lives in Palm Rivers.
4. List the therapy description for all therapies performed by Steven Wilder.
5. List the last name, first name, and city of every patient who has a balance of more than $1,000.
6. List the therapist's name who worked with the patient named Ben Odepaul.
7. List all the therapy codes that are billed in minutes.

8. List all the therapy descriptions performed on the patient named Joseph Baptist.

9. List the full name and address of patients who visited on October 18, 2018.

 10. The Sports Physical Therapy database does not include a field for the rate of pay for each therapist. In which table would you place the information for hourly rate? Why? What other field(s) of information might you need to go along with the hourly rate, especially if the company wants to use the database for payroll?

 11. What is the relationship between the LengthOfSession field (Sessions table) and the UnitOfTime field (Therapies table)? Many therapies have no billable unit of time listed in the Therapies table. Why? Which field(s) do you think the company uses to bill insurance?

CHAPTER 2

THE RELATIONAL MODEL 1: INTRODUCTION, QBE, AND RELATIONAL ALGEBRA

LEARNING OBJECTIVES

- Describe the relational model
- Explain Query-By-Example (QBE)
- Use criteria in QBE
- Create calculated columns in QBE
- Utilize functions in QBE
- Sort data in QBE
- Join tables in QBE
- Update data using QBE
- Apply relational algebra

INTRODUCTION

The database management approach implemented by most systems is the relational model. In this chapter, you will study the relational model and examine a software method of retrieving data from relational databases, called Query-By-Example (QBE). Finally, you will learn about relational algebra, which is one of the original ways of manipulating a relational database.

RELATIONAL DATABASES

A relational database is a collection of tables like the ones you viewed for the BITS Corporation in Chapter 1. These tables also appear in Figure 2-1. You might wonder why this type of database is not called a "table" database or something similar, if a database is nothing more than a collection of tables. Formally, these tables are called relations, and this is where this type of database gets its name.

Consultant

ConsltNum	LastName	FirstName	Street	City	State	ZipCode	Hours	Rate
19	Turner	Christopher	554 Brown Dr.	Tri City	FL	32889	40	$22.50
22	Jordan	Patrick	2287 Port Rd.	Easton	FL	33998	40	$22.50
35	Allen	Sarah	82 Elliott St.	Lizton	FL	34344	35	$20.00
51	Shields	Tom	373 Lincoln Ln.	Sunland	FL	39876	10	$15.00

Client

ClientNum	ClientName	Street	City	State	ZipCode	Balance	CreditLimit	ConsltNum
143	Hershey, Jarrod	135 E. Mill Street	Easton	FL	33998	$1,904.55	$2,500.00	19
175	Goduto, Sean	12 Saratoga Parkway	Tri City	FL	32889	$2,814.55	$5,000.00	19
299	Two Crafty Cousins	9787 NCR 350 West	Sunland	FL	39876	$8,354.00	$10,000.00	22
322	Prichard's Pizza & Pasta	501 Air Parkway	Lizton	FL	34344	$7,335.55	$10,000.00	35
363	Salazar, Jason	56473 Cherry Tree Dr	Easton	FL	33998	$900.75	$2,500.00	35
405	Fisherman's Spot Shop	49 Elwood Ave.	Harpersburg	FL	31234	$4,113.40	$7,500.00	19
449	Seymour, Lindsey	4091 Brentwood Ln	Amo	FL	34466	$557.70	$5,000.00	22
458	Bonnie's Beautiful Boutique	9565 Ridge Rd.	Tri City	FL	32889	$4,053.80	$7,500.00	22
677	Yates, Nick	231 Day Rd.	Sunland	FL	39876	$2,523.80	$2,500.00	35
733	Howler, Laura	1368 E. 1000 S.	Lizton	FL	34344	$3,658.05	$5,000.00	22
826	Harpersburg Bank	65 Forrest Blvd.	Harpersburg	FL	31234	$6,824.55	$10,000.00	19
867	MarketPoint Sales	826 Host St.	Easton	FL	33998	$3,089.00	$5,000.00	19

WorkOrders

OrderNum	OrderDate	ClientNum
67101	9/6/2018	733
67313	9/7/2018	458
67424	9/10/2018	322
67838	9/10/2018	867
67949	9/10/2018	322
68252	9/12/2018	363
68868	9/14/2018	867
68979	9/17/2018	826

OrderLine

OrderNum	TaskID	ScheduledDate	QuotedPrice
67101	SI77	9/10/2018	$144.00
67313	LA81	9/12/2018	$104.00
67424	MO49	9/14/2018	$65.00
67424	UP38	9/14/2018	$185.00
67838	LA81	9/20/2018	$104.00
67949	PI54	9/21/2018	$50.00
67949	VR39	9/21/2018	$88.00
67949	WA33	9/21/2018	$126.00
68252	DI85	9/24/2018	$50.00
68868	SA44	9/24/2018	$200.00
68979	AC65	9/27/2018	$77.00
68979	DA11	9/27/2018	$970.00

Tasks

TaskID	Description	Category	Price
AC65	Accessories	ACC	$80.00
DA11	Data recovery major	DRM	$175.00
DI85	Data recovery minor	DRM	$50.00
HA63	Hardware major	HAM	$225.00
HI31	Hardware minor	HAM	$165.70
LA81	Local area networking (LAN)	LAN	$104.00
MO49	Mobility	MOB	$65.00
OT99	Other work	OTH	$99.99
PI54	Printing issues	PRI	$50.00
SA44	Software major	SOM	$200.00
SI77	Software minor	SOM	$144.00
SI91	Security install/repair	SIR	$126.00
UP38	Upgrades	UPG	$185.00
VR39	Virus removal	VIR	$90.00
WA33	Wide area networking (WAN)	WAN	$130.00
WC19	Web connectivity	WEC	$75.00

FIGURE 2-1   Sample data for BITS

How does a relational database handle entities, attributes of entities, and relationships between entities? Each entity is stored in its own table. For example, the BITS Corporation database has a table for consultants, a table for clients, and so on. The attributes of an entity become the fields or columns in the table. In the table for consultants, for example, there is a column for the consultant number, a column for the consultant's last name, and so on.

What about relationships? At BITS Corporation, there is a one-to-many relationship between consultants and clients. (Each consultant is related to the *many* clients he or she represents, and each client is related to the *one* consultant who represents it.) How is this relationship implemented in a relational database? The answer is through common columns in two or more tables. Consider Figure 2-1 again. The ConsltNum columns in the Consultant and Client tables implement the relationship between consultants and clients. For any consultant, you can use these columns to determine all the clients the consultant represents; for any client, you can use these columns to find the consultant who represents the client. If the Client table did not include the consultant number, you would not be able to identify the consultant for a given client or the clients for a given consultant.

A relation is essentially just a two-dimensional table. In Figure 2-1, you might see certain patterns or restrictions that you can place on relations. Each column in a table should have a unique name, and all entries in each column should be consistent with this column name. (For example, in the CreditLimit column, all entries should be credit limits.) And each row should be unique. After all, when two rows in a table contain identical data, the second row does not provide any information that you do not already have. In addition, for maximum flexibility, the order in which columns and rows appear in a table should be immaterial. Rows in a table (relation) are often called **records** or **tuples**. Columns in a table (relation) are often called **fields** or **attributes**.

Finally, a table's design is less complex when you restrict each location in the table to a single value; that is, you should not permit multiple entries (often called **repeating groups**) in the table. These ideas lead to the following definitions.

Definition: A **relation** is a two-dimensional table (rows and columns) in which:

1. The entries in the table are single-valued; that is, each intersection of the row and column in the table contains only one value.
2. Each column has a distinct name (technically called the attribute name).
3. All values in a column are values of the same attribute (that is, all entries must match the column name).
4. The order of the columns is not important.
5. Each row is distinct.
6. The order of rows is immaterial.

Definition: A **relational database** is a collection of relations.

Later in this text, you will encounter situations in which a structure satisfies all the properties of a relation *except for the first item*; that is, some of the entries contain repeating groups and, thus, are not single-valued. Such a structure is called an **unnormalized relation**. (This jargon is a little strange in that an unnormalized relation is not really a relation at all.) The table shown in Figure 2-2 is an example of an unnormalized relation.

WorkOrders

OrderNum	OrderDate	ClientNum	TaskID	QuotedPrice
67101	9/6/2018	733	SI77	$144.00
67313	9/7/2018	458	LA81	$104.00
67424	9/10/2018	322	MO49	$62.00
			UP38	$180.00
67838	9/10/2018	867	LA81	$104.00
67949	9/10/2018	322	PI54	$50.00
			VR39	$88.00
			WA33	$126.00
68252	9/12/2018	363	DI85	$50.00
68868	9/14/2018	867	SA44	$200.00
68979	9/17/2018	826	AC65	$77.00
			DA11	$970.00

FIGURE 2-2   Sample structure of an unnormalized relation

Relational Database Shorthand

There is a commonly accepted shorthand representation that shows the structure of a relational database. You write the name of the table and then, within parentheses, list all the columns in the table. In addition, each table should appear on its own line. Using this method, you would write the BITS Corporation database as follows:

```
Consultant (ConsltNum, LastName, FirstName, Street, City, State, ZipCode, Hours, Rate)
Client (ClientNum, ClientName, Street, City, State, ZipCode, Balance, CreditLimit, ConsltNum)
WorkOrders (OrderNum, OrderDate, ClientNum)
OrderLine (OrderNum, TaskID, ScheduledDate, QuotedPrice)
Tasks (TaskID, Description, Category, Price)
```

The BITS Corporation database contains some duplicate column names. For example, the ConsltNum column appears in *both* the Consultant table *and* the Client table. Suppose a situation exists wherein a reference to the column might be confused. For example, if you write ConsltNum, how would the computer or another user know which table you intend to use? That could be a problem. Therefore, when duplicate column names exist in a database, you need a way to indicate the column to which you are referring. One common approach to this problem is to write both the table name and the column name, separated by a period. Thus, you would write the ConsltNum column in the Client table as Client.ConsltNum. You would write ConsltNum column in the Consultant table as Consultant.ConsltNum. Technically, when you combine a column name with a table name, you say that you **qualify** the column names. It *always* is acceptable to qualify column names, even when there is no possibility of confusion. If confusion may arise, however, it is *essential* to qualify column names.

The **primary key** of a table (relation) is the column or columns that uniquely identify a given row in that table. In the Consultant table, the consultant's number uniquely identifies a given row (Figure 2-1 on page 30). For example, consultant 19 occurs in only one row of the Consultant table. Because each row contains a unique number, the ConsltNum is the primary key for the Consultant table. The primary key provides an important way of distinguishing one row in a table from another and cannot be blank or null. (*NOTE*: If more than one column is necessary to make the row unique, it is called a **composite primary key**.)

Primary keys usually are represented by underlining the column or columns that comprises the primary key for each table in the database. Thus, the complete representation for the BITS Corporation database is as follows:

```
Consultant (ConsltNum, LastName, FirstName, Street, City, State, ZipCode, Hours, Rate)
Client (ClientNum, ClientName, Street, City, State, ZipCode, Balance, CreditLimit, ConsltNum)
WorkOrders (OrderNum, OrderDate, ClientNum)
OrderLine (OrderNum, TaskID, ScheduledDate, QuotedPrice)
Tasks (TaskID, Description, Category, Price)
```

Q & A 2-1

Question: Why does the primary key of the OrderLine table consist of two columns, not just one?
Answer: No single column uniquely identifies a given row in the OrderLine table. It requires a combination of two columns: OrderNum and TaskID.

The term **foreign key** is used to refer to a primary key field used in a different column. In the above example, the field ConsltNum is a primary key in the Consultant table but a foreign key in the Client table. You will learn more about foreign keys in a future chapter.

QUERY-BY-EXAMPLE

When you ask Access or any other DBMS a question about the data in a database, the question is called a query. A **query** is simply a question represented in a way that the DBMS can recognize and process. In this section, you will investigate **Query-By-Example (QBE)**, an approach to writing queries that is extremely visual. With QBE, users ask their questions by entering column names and other criteria via an on-screen grid. Data appears on the screen in tabular form.

This chapter features a specific version of QBE, Microsoft Access 2016, to illustrate the use of QBE. The examples also match Microsoft Access as part of Office 365. Although other QBEs are not identical, the differences are relatively minor. After you have mastered one version of QBE, you can apply your skills to learn another version of QBE.

The following figures and examples will show you how to retrieve data using the Access version of QBE. *NOTE: If you plan to work through the examples in this chapter using a computer, you should use a copy of the BITS Corporation database provided with this text, because the version of the database used in subsequent chapters does not include the changes you will make.*

SIMPLE QUERIES

In Access, you create queries using the Query window, which has two panes. The upper portion of the window contains a field list for each table you want to query (see Figure 2-3). The lower pane contains the **design grid**, the area in which you specify the format of your output, the fields to be included in the query results, a sort order for the query results, and any criteria.

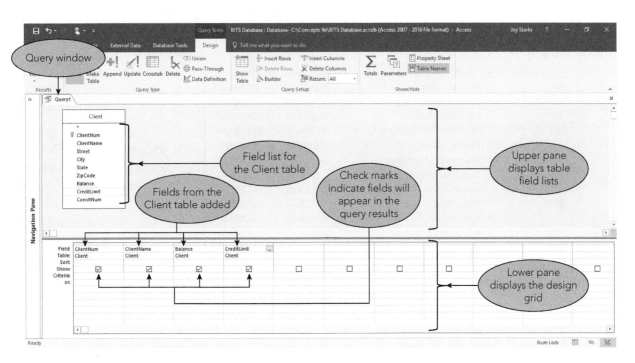

FIGURE 2-3   Fields added to the design grid

To create a new, simple query in Access, perform the following steps:

- Click Create on the ribbon to display the Create tab.
- Click the Query Design button (Create tab | Queries group) to create a query. Access will display the Show Table dialog box and a new tab on the ribbon named Query Tools Design.
- Select the table in the Show Table dialog box that you want to use in the query.
- Click the Add button (Show Table dialog box) to add the table to the query.
- Close the Show Table dialog box.

A field list for the table you selected will appear in the Query window (see Figure 2-3 on the previous page). If necessary, you can resize the field list by dragging any border of the field list to a new position. You create the query by making entries in the design grid in the lower portion of the window.

YOUR TURN 2-1

List the number, name, balance, and credit limit of all clients in the database.

Choosing Fields and Running the Query

To include a field in an Access query, double-click the field in the field list to place it in the design grid, as shown in Figure 2-3. The check marks in the Show check boxes indicate the fields that will appear in the query results. To omit a field from the query results, remove the check mark from the field's Show check box.

Clicking the Run button (Query Tools Design tab | Results group) runs or executes the query and displays the query results, as shown in Figure 2-4.

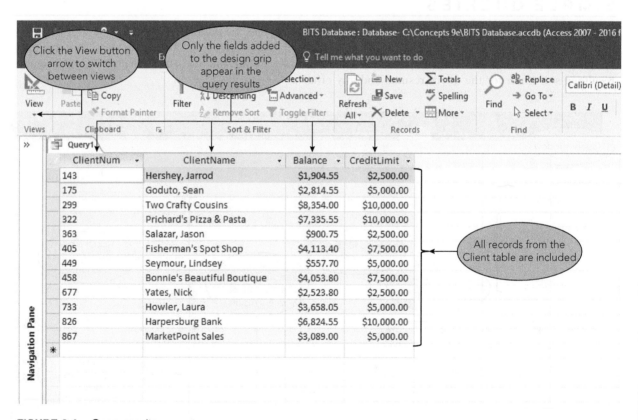

FIGURE 2-4 Query results

Q & A 2-2

Question: My first client number appears selected (white letters on a black background). Did I do something wrong?

Answer: No. The first field in the first record may appear selected. You can click elsewhere on the screen to remove the selection and thus make the data easier to read.

If you add the wrong table to a query or need to use a different table, you can remove it by right-clicking the field list and then clicking Remove Table on the shortcut menu. You can add a new table to a query by clicking the Show Table button (Query Tools Design tab | Query Setup group). Access will display the Show Table dialog box, in which you can select the desired table. *NOTE:* As an alternative to these steps, you can close the query without saving it and then start over.

You can switch between views of a query using the View button (Home tab | Views group). Clicking the arrow on the button opens the View button menu. You then click the desired view in the menu. The two query views you will use in this chapter are **Datasheet view** to see the results and **Design view** to change the design.

If you anticipate using a query more than once, you can save a query by clicking the Save button (Quick Access Toolbar), typing a name for the saved query, and then clicking the OK button (Save As dialog box). Later, if your data changes, the query will update.

After you have created and saved a query, you can use it in a variety of ways:

- To view the results of a saved query that is not currently open, open it by double-clicking the query in the Navigation Pane.
- If you want to change the design of a query that is already open, return to Design view by clicking the View button arrow (Home tab | Views group), select Design View, and then make the desired changes.
- If you want to change the design of a query that is not currently open, right-click the query in the Navigation Pane, and then click Design View on the shortcut menu to open the query in Design view.
- To print the results with the query open, click File on the ribbon, click the Print tab in the Backstage view, and then click Quick Print.
- To print the query without first opening it, select the query in the Navigation Pane, click File on the ribbon, click the Print tab in the Backstage view, and then click Quick Print.
- To save the query with a different name, open the query, click File on the ribbon to open the Backstage view, click the Save As tab to display the Save As gallery, and click Save Object As (File Types gallery). Select Save Object (Database File Types gallery) and then click the Save As button. Type the new query name and click the OK button (Save As dialog box) to save the query with the new name.

YOUR TURN 2-2

To create a list of the work orders, create a query to list all fields and all rows in the WorkOrders table.

To display all fields and all rows in the WorkOrders table, begin a new query using the WorkOrders table. As you learned previously, you could then add each field to the design grid. There is a shortcut, however. In Access, you can add all fields from a table to the design grid by double-clicking the asterisk in the table's field list. As shown in Figure 2-5 on the next page, the asterisk appears in the design grid, indicating that all fields will be included in the query results.

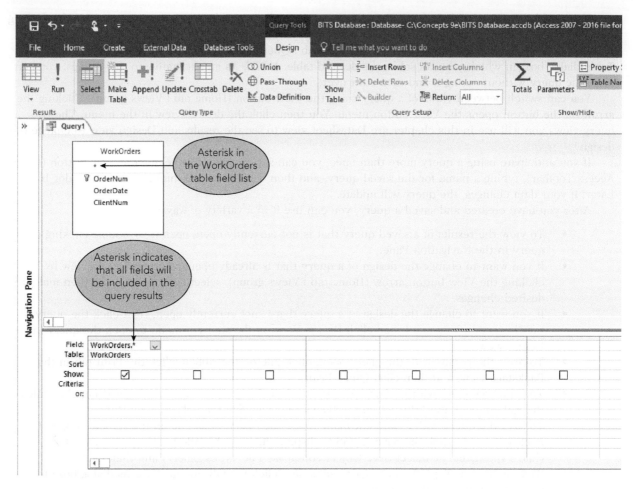

FIGURE 2-5   Query that includes all fields in the WorkOrders table

Having clicked the Run button (Query Tools Design tab | Results group), the query results appear in Figure 2-6.

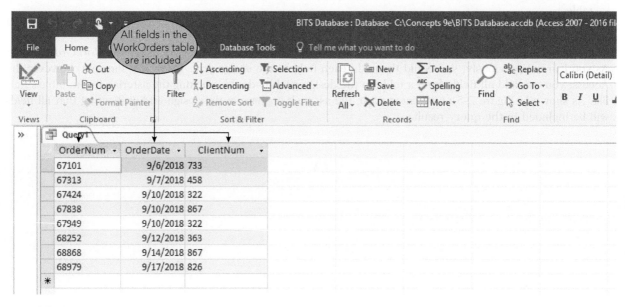

FIGURE 2-6   Query results

SIMPLE CRITERIA

When the records you want must satisfy a condition, you enter that condition in the appropriate column in the query design grid. Conditions also are called **criteria**. (A single condition is called a **criterion**.) The following example illustrates the use of a criterion to select data.

YOUR TURN 2-3

Find the name of client 458.

To enter a criterion for a field, add the table to the query, include the field or fields in the design grid, and then enter the criterion in the row labeled "Criteria" for that field, as shown in Figure 2-7.

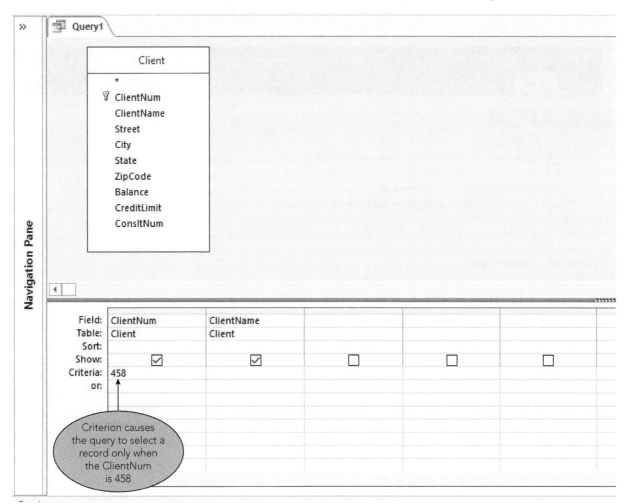

FIGURE 2-7   Query to find the name of client 458

NOTE: When you enter a criterion for some text fields, such as ClientNum, Access automatically adds double quotation marks around the value when you run the query or when you move the insertion point to another box in the design grid. Typing the quotation marks is optional. (Some database management systems use single quotation marks to enclose such values.)

Q & A 2-3

Question: Why is the ClientNum field a text field? Does it not contain numbers?
Answer: Fields such as the ClientNum field that contain numbers but are not involved in calculations are usually assigned the Short Text data type in Access. You will learn more about data types in a future chapter.

The query results shown in Figure 2-8 display an exact match; the query selects a record only when ClientNum equals 458.

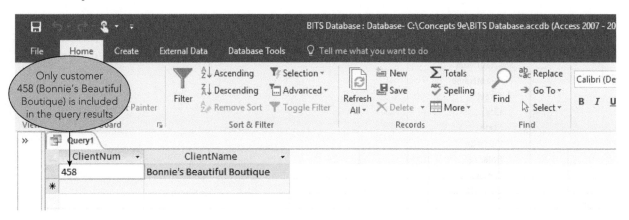

FIGURE 2-8   Query results

Parameter Queries

If you plan to use a query repeatedly, but with different criteria, you might want to save a parameter query. In Access, a **parameter query** allows you to enter criterion when you *run* the query, as opposed to placing it in the design grid. For example, if you need to search for a different client number each time you run a query, you can type a question in the Criteria row of the design grid. Then as you run it, Access will ask you the question and allow you to enter the client number. Questions must be enclosed in square brackets. Thus, if you type [What is the client number?] in the design grid, Access will display a dialog box when you run the query, allowing you to enter the client number. A parameter query is easy for novice users to supply information in saved queries.

Operators

If you want something other than an exact match, you must enter the appropriate operator. An **operator** is symbol or word that performs a mathematical operation or task related to data. Some common mathematical operators include +, −, *, and /. As you will see in the next example, a **comparison operator**, also called a **relational operator**, compares two values (binary) and returns or answers with a true or false result (boolean). The comparison operators are = (equal to), > (greater than), < (less than), >= (greater than or equal to), <= (less than or equal to), and <> (not equal to). You will learn about other types of operators as you work through the examples in this text. *NOTE:* It is common in QBE to omit the = symbol in "equal to" comparisons, although you can use it every time.

COMPOUND CRITERIA

You can use the comparison operators by themselves to create conditions. You also can combine criteria to create **compound criteria**, or **compound conditions**. In many query languages, you create compound criteria by including the word *AND* or *OR* between the separate criteria. In an **AND criterion**, both criteria must be true for the compound criterion to be true. In an **OR criterion**, the overall criterion is true if either of the individual criteria is true.

Figure 2-9 displays a table showing the different combinations of true and false criteria using AND versus using OR.

If the first criteria is:	with an operator of:	while the second criteria is:	the overall statement is:
True	AND	True	True
False	AND	True	False
True	AND	False	False
False	AND	False	False
True	OR	True	True
False	OR	True	True
True	OR	False	True
False	OR	False	False

FIGURE 2-9   AND/OR table

In QBE, to create an AND criterion, place the criteria for multiple fields on the same Criteria row in the design grid. To create an OR criterion, place the criteria for multiple fields on different Criteria rows in the design grid (see Figure 2-10 on the next page).

YOUR TURN 2-4

Using the Tasks table, list the taskID, description, category, and price for all tasks in the SOM category *and* priced more than $150.

The criteria are placed on the same Criteria row in Figure 2-10, because you want the query to select those tasks where the value in the Description field is SOM *and* where the value in the Price field is greater than 150 (which requires the use of the > comparison operator).

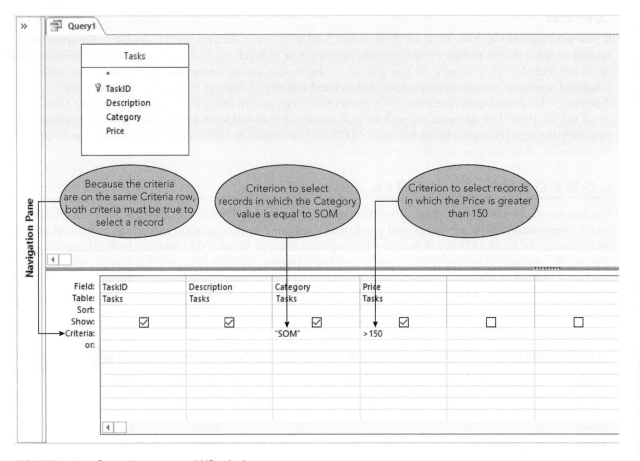

FIGURE 2-10   Query that uses an AND criterion

The query results appear in Figure 2-11.

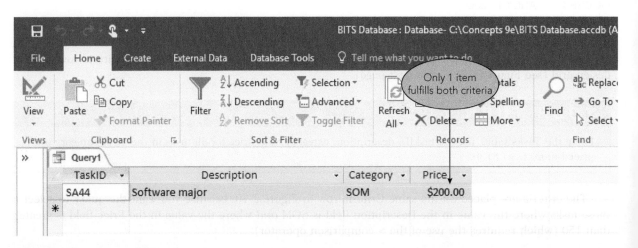

FIGURE 2-11   Query results

YOUR TURN 2-5

Using the Tasks table, list the taskID, description, category, and price for all tasks listed in the SOM (software management) category *or* all tasks priced more than $150.

The criteria are placed on two different rows in Figure 2-12, because you want to indicate that either of two conditions must be true to select a record. The first criterion is in the Criteria row for the first column, and the second criterion is in the row labeled "or."

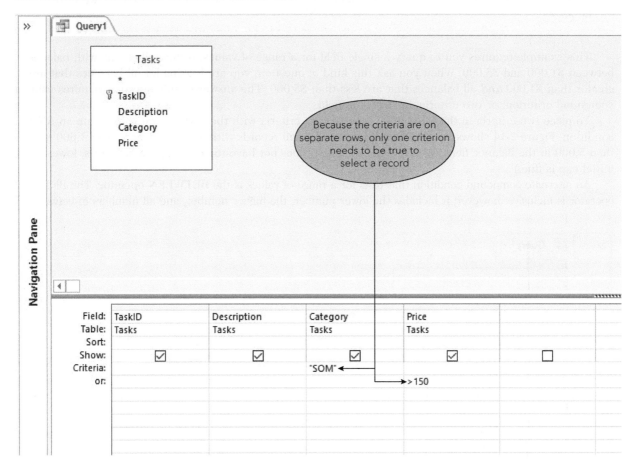

FIGURE 2-12   Query that uses an OR criterion

The query results appear in Figure 2-13.

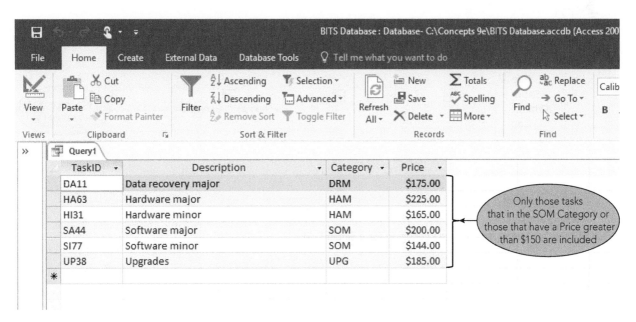

FIGURE 2-13   Query results

YOUR TURN 2-6

Using the Client table, list the number, name, and balance for each client whose balance is between $1,000 and $5,000.

This example requires you to query a single field for a range of values, to find all clients with balances between $1,000 and $5,000. When you ask this kind of question, you are looking for all balances that are greater than $1,000 *and* all balances that are less than $5,000. The answer to this question requires using a compound criterion, or two criteria, in the same field.

To place two criteria in the same field, separate the criteria with the AND operator to create an AND condition. Figure 2-14 shows the AND condition to select all records with a value of more than 1,000 and less than 5,000 in the Balance field. (*NOTE:* The word AND does not have to be in uppercase letters; lowercase or initial cap is fine.)

An alternate compound condition that tests for a range of values is the **BETWEEN operator**. The BETWEEN operator is inclusive, however; it includes the lower number, the higher number, and all numbers in-between.

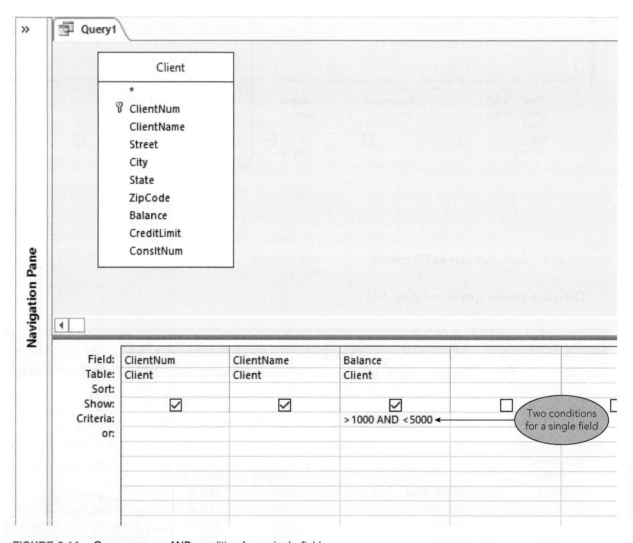

FIGURE 2-14   Query uses an AND condition for a single field

The query results appear in Figure 2-15.

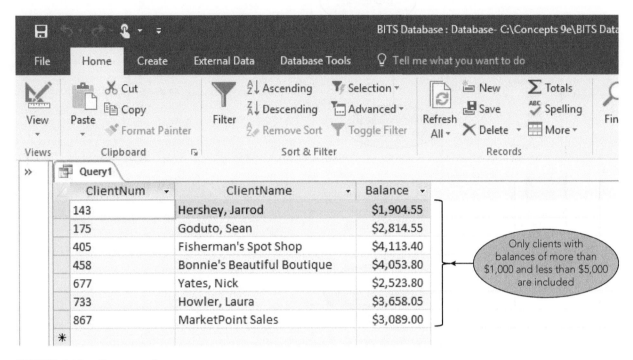

FIGURE 2-15   Query results

COMPUTED FIELDS

Sometimes you need your query to include calculated fields that are not stored in the database. A **computed field** or **calculated field** is a field that is the result of a calculation using one or more existing fields. Your Turn 2-7 illustrates the use of a calculated field.

YOUR TURN 2-7

List the number, name, and available credit for all clients.

Available credit is computed by subtracting the balance from the credit limit. Because there is no Available Credit field in the Client table, you must calculate it from the existing Balance and CreditLimit fields. To include a computed field in a query, choose a blank column in the grid. In the Field row, enter a name for the computed field, followed by a colon, and then followed by a mathematical expression.

To calculate available credit, you can enter the expression *AvailableCredit:CreditLimit - Balance* in a blank Field row in the design grid. (*AvailableCredit* is the name of the new, computed field; *CreditLimit - Balance* is the mathematical expression.) When entering an expression in the design grid, the default column size may prevent you from being able to see the complete expression. An alternative method is to right-click the column in the Field row to display the shortcut menu and then click Zoom to open the Zoom dialog box. Then you can type the expression in the Zoom dialog box, as shown in Figure 2-16.

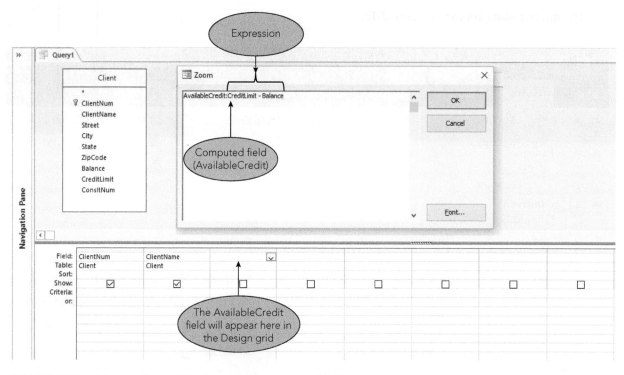

FIGURE 2-16   Using the Zoom dialog box to add a computed field to a query

Q & A 2-4

Question: When I run the calculated field query, Access asks me for a parameter value. What should I do?
Answer: You may have spelled a field name wrong or used an incorrect symbol in the new field. Double-check the syntax of the calculated field expression.

NOTE: When a field name contains spaces, you must enclose the field name in square brackets ([ ]). For example, if the field name was Credit Limit instead of CreditLimit, you would enter the expression as *[Credit Limit]-Balance.* You can enclose a field name that does not contain spaces in square brackets as well, but you do not need to do so.

After clicking the OK button (Zoom dialog box) and then clicking the Run button (Query Tools Design tab I Results group), the query results appear as shown in Figure 2-17.

ClientNum	ClientName	AvailableCredit
143	Hershey, Jarrod	$595.45
175	Goduto, Sean	$2,185.45
299	Two Crafty Cousins	$1,646.00
322	Prichard's Pizza & Pasta	$2,664.45
363	Salazar, Jason	$1,599.25
405	Fisherman's Spot Shop	$3,386.60
449	Seymour, Lindsey	$4,442.30
458	Bonnie's Beautiful Boutique	$3,446.20
677	Yates, Nick	($23.80)
733	Howler, Laura	$1,341.95
826	Harpersburg Bank	$3,175.45
867	MarketPoint Sales	$1,911.00

FIGURE 2-17   Query results

You are not restricted to subtraction in computations. You also can use addition (+), multiplication (*), or division (/). You can include parentheses in your expressions to indicate which computations Access should perform first.

FUNCTIONS

All products that support QBE, including Access, support the built-in functions shown in Figure 2-18. A **function** is a command that performs a higher-level task related to data, such as finding the highest value in a column, summing a group of numbers, or determining the length of a text field. In Access, these functions are called **aggregate functions**, because they typically work with groups of fields or numbers.

Function Name	Description
Count	returns the number of records in the field
Sum	returns the result of adding together all the records in the field
Avg	returns the result of adding together all the records in the field and then dividing by the number of records
Max	finds the largest value in a field
Min	finds the smallest value in a field
StDev	returns the standard deviation of a numeric field that tells you how tightly the data is grouped around the mean or average.
Var	returns the variance of a numeric field with a number that represents how far the data is spread out.
First	displays the first record in a field
Last	displays the last record in a field

FIGURE 2-18   Common built-in functions

To use any of these functions in an Access query, click the Totals button (Query Tools Design tab | Show/Hide group). Access will display the Total row (see Figure 2-19). You then can click the list arrow in the desired field to view and select the function or aggregate. To hide the Total row, click the Totals button a second time.

Two other statements or clauses are used with functions and queries. The Where statement is used to extract only those records that fulfill a specified condition. The Where statement is the same as using a simple criterion. The Group By statement groups records into summary rows based on the results of a different column query. For example, you might create a query for all clients who have large balances (a criterion), but you might group them together by Consultant (group by). Where and Group By sometimes are called Total row operators.

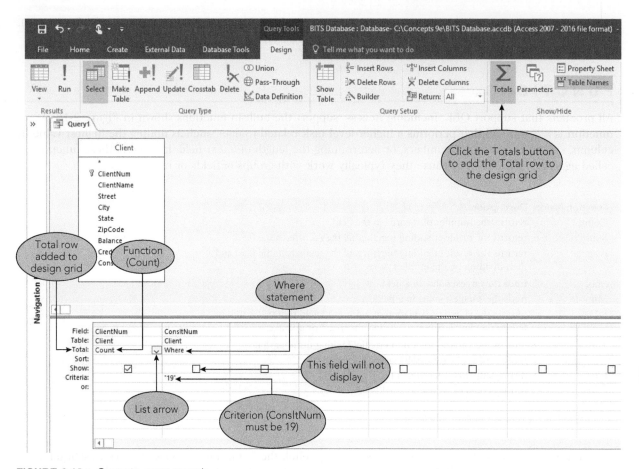

FIGURE 2-19   Query to count records

YOUR TURN 2-8

How many clients does consultant 19 represent?

To determine how many clients are represented by consultant 19, you will need to add two fields to the grid—a field to represent the clients (such as the ClientNum field) and a field to represent the consultants (such as the ConsltNum field). Then click the Total row of the ClientNum field to display its list arrow. Clicking the list arrow causes Access to display the list of aggregate operators such as Sum, Count, Max, and so on.

In this example, to count the number of clients for consultant 19, you select the Count function in the Total row for the ClientNum column. You select the Where statement in the Total row for the ConsltNum column to indicate that there will be a criterion. Then an entry of 19 in the Criteria row (ConsltNum) selects only those records for consultant number 19, as shown in Figure 2-19. Because you do not need to display the ConsltNum field, you can remove its Show check mark.

The query results appear in Figure 2-20. Notice that Access used the default name, CountOfClientNum, for the new column. *NOTE:* You could create your own column name in the query design by preceding the field name with the desired column name and a colon. For example, typing *NumberOfClients:ClientNum* changes the output name to NumberOfClients.

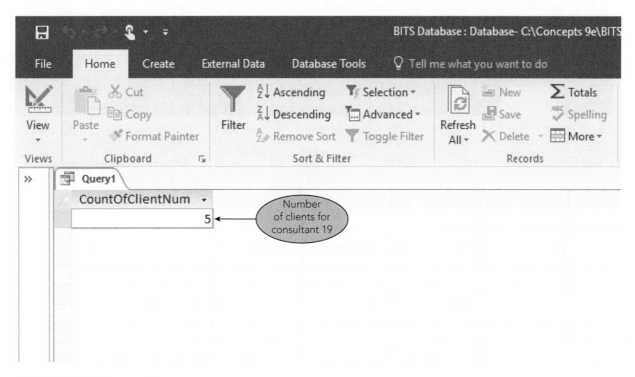

FIGURE 2-20   Query results

YOUR TURN 2-9

What is the average balance of all clients of consultant 19?

To calculate the average balance, click the Total row list arrow in the Balance field and then use the Avg function as shown in Figure 2-21.

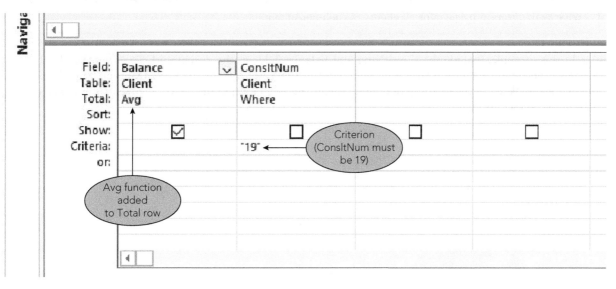

FIGURE 2-21   Query to calculate an average

The query results appear in Figure 2-22.

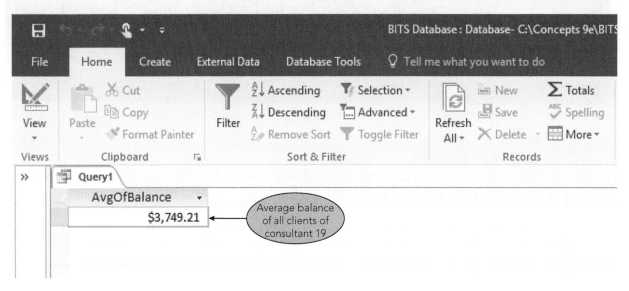

FIGURE 2-22 Query results

GROUPING

QBE programs use **grouping** as a means of creating groups of records that share some common characteristic. In grouping by ConsltNum, for example, the clients of consultant 19 would form one group, the clients of consultant 22 would form a second group, the clients of consultant 35 would form a third group, and the clients of consultant 51 would form a fourth group. You can include functions in combination with grouping. For example, you might need to calculate the average balance for all clients in each group. To group records in Access, select the Group By statement in the Total row for the field on which to group.

YOUR TURN 2-10

What is the average balance for all clients of each consultant?

In this example, include the ConsltNum and Balance fields in the design grid. To group the client records for each consultant, select the Group By statement in the Total row for the ConsltNum column. To calculate the average balance for each group of clients, select the Avg function in the Total row for the Balance column, as shown in Figure 2-23.

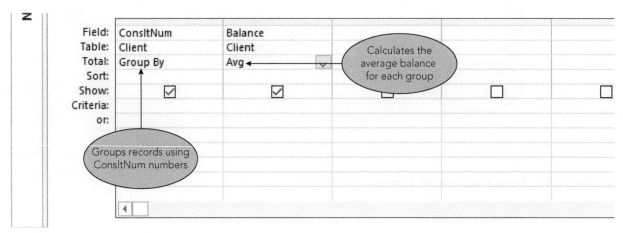

FIGURE 2-23 Query to group records

The query results appear in Figure 2-24. The record for consultant 51 does not appear in the results because this consultant has no clients yet.

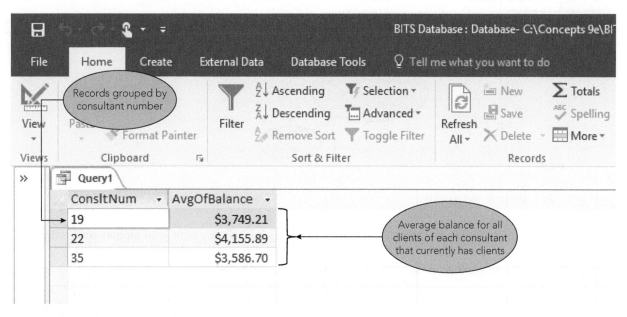

FIGURE 2-24   Query results

SORTING

In most queries, the order in which records appear does not matter. In other queries, however, the order in which records appear can be very important. You might want to see clients listed alphabetically by client name or listed by consultant number. Further, you might want to see client records listed alphabetically by client name *and* grouped by consultant number.

To list the query result records in a particular way, you need to **sort** the records. The field on which records are sorted is called the **sort key**; you can sort records using more than one field when necessary. When you are sorting records by more than one field (such as sorting by consultant number and then by client name), the first sort field (ConsltNum) is called the **major sort key** (also called the **primary sort key**) and the second sort field (ClientName) is called the **minor sort key** (also called the **secondary sort key**).

To sort in Access, specify the sort order (ascending or descending) in the Sort row of the design grid for the sort key field. You do so by clicking the Sort row arrow and then selecting the desired sort order.

YOUR TURN 2-11

List the client number, name, balance, and consultant number for each client. Sort the output alphabetically by client name.

To sort the records alphabetically using the ClientName field, select the Ascending sort order in the Sort row for the ClientName column, as shown in Figure 2-25 on the next page. (To sort the records in reverse alphabetical order, select the Descending sort order.) You can click the Totals button (Query Tools Design tab | Show/Hide group) to turn off the total in the grid.

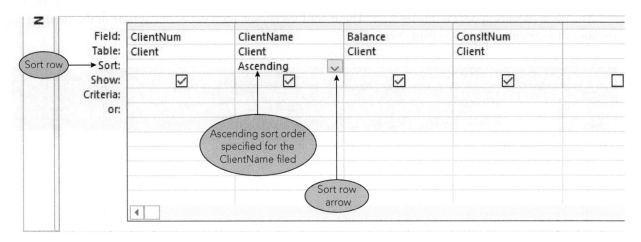

FIGURE 2-25   Query to sort records

The query results appear in Figure 2-26. Notice that the client names appear in alphabetical order.

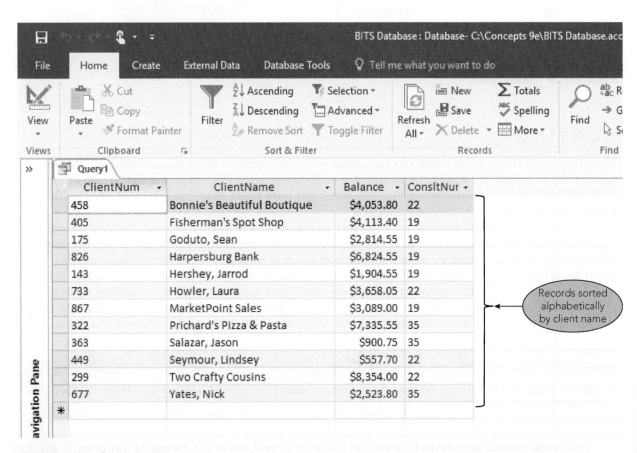

FIGURE 2-26   Query results

Sorting on Multiple Keys

You can specify more than one sort key in a query; in this case, the sort key on the left in the design grid will be the major (primary) sort key and the sort key on the right will be the minor (secondary) sort key.

YOUR TURN 2-12

List the client number, name, balance, and consultant number for each client. Sort the output by consultant number. Then, within each consultant, sort the output by client name.

To sort records by consultant number and then by client name, ConsltNum should be the major sort key and ClientName should be the minor sort key. If you simply select the sort orders for these fields in the current design grid, your results would not be sorted correctly because the fields are listed in the wrong order left to right. Figure 2-27 shows an *incorrect* query design.

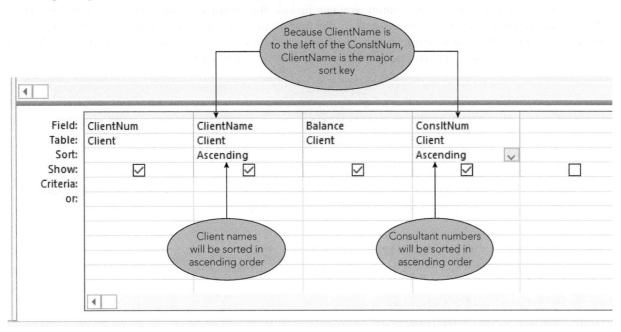

FIGURE 2-27   Incorrect query design to sort by ConsltNum and then by ClientName

In Figure 2-27, the ClientName field is to the left of the ConsltNum field in the design grid. With this order, ClientName becomes the major sort key; the data is sorted by client name first and not by consultant number, as shown in Figure 2-28.

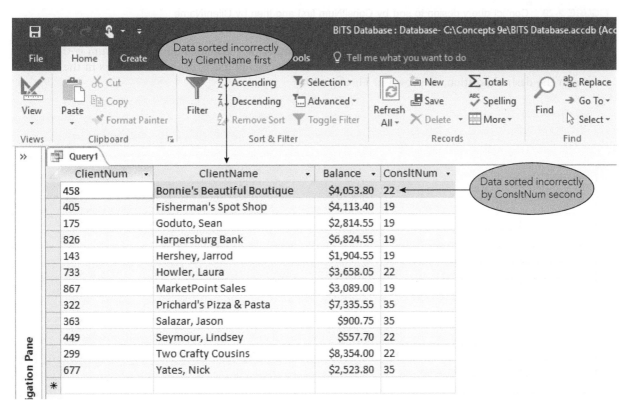

FIGURE 2-28   Query results

To correct this problem, the ConsltNum field needs to come before the Client field in the design grid. It is easy to move a field in the design grid. Point to the top of the column. When the pointer changes to a down arrow, click to select the column. Drag the column to the new location.

Moving a column changes the output order, however, which you may not want to do. If the original order is important, rather than move the column, you can include the ConsltNum field twice—once before the Client field and once after. You then can sort by the first occurrence but hide it from the output, as shown in Figure 2-29. Notice the first occurrence contains the Ascending sort order but displays no check mark in the Show check box. The second occurrence will show but has no sort order selected.

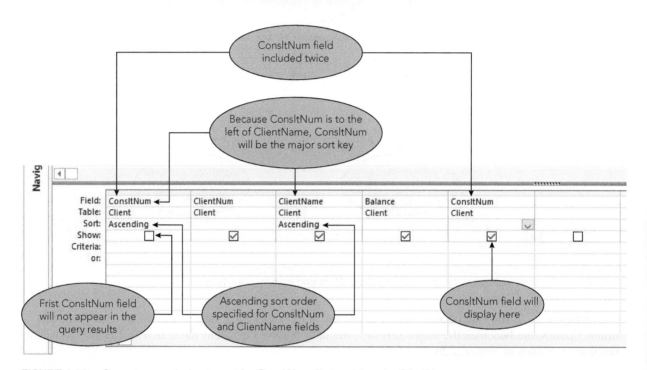

FIGURE 2-29   Correct query design to sort by ConsltNum first and then by ClientName

Because the ConsltNum field is to the left of the minor sort key (ClientName), ConsltNum is the major sort key. The second ConsltNum field in the design grid will display the consultant numbers in the query results in the desired position, as shown in Figure 2-30.

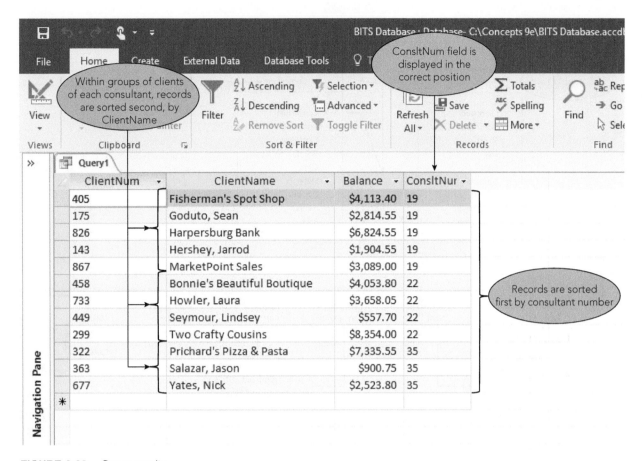

FIGURE 2-30 Query results

JOINING TABLES

So far, the queries used in the examples have displayed records from a single table. In many cases, however, you will need to create queries to select data from more than one table at the same time. To do so, it is necessary to **join** the tables based on matching fields in corresponding columns. To join tables in Access, first you add the field lists for both tables to the upper pane of the Query window. Access will draw a line, called a **join line**, between matching fields in the two tables, indicating that the tables are related. (If the corresponding fields have the same field name and at least one of the fields is the primary key of the table that contains it, Access will join the tables automatically. If a join line does not appear, you can create it by clicking and dragging one of the related fields to the other field with the same name.) Then you can select fields from either or both tables, as you will see in the next example.

You cannot create this query using a single table—the client name is in the Client table and the consultant name is in the Consultant table. The consultant number can come from either table because it is the matching field. To select the correct data, click the Show Table button (Query Tools Design tab | Query Setup group) and then use the Show Table dialog box to add the necessary tables. A join line appears, indicating how the tables are related. Finally, add the desired fields from the field lists to the design grid, as shown in Figure 2-31 on the next page.

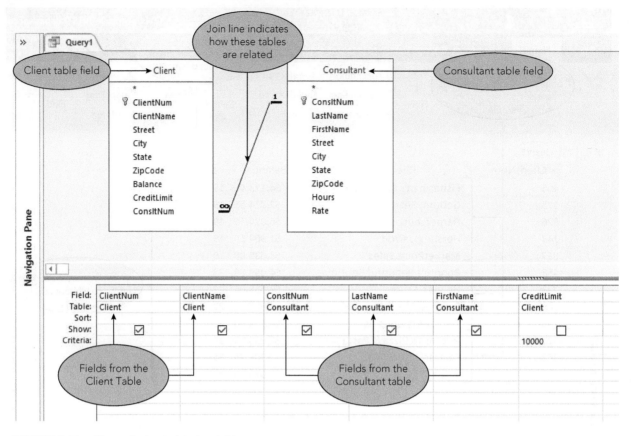

FIGURE 2-31 Query design to join two tables

Notice that the Table row in the design grid indicates the table from which each field is selected. The query results appear in Figure 2-32.

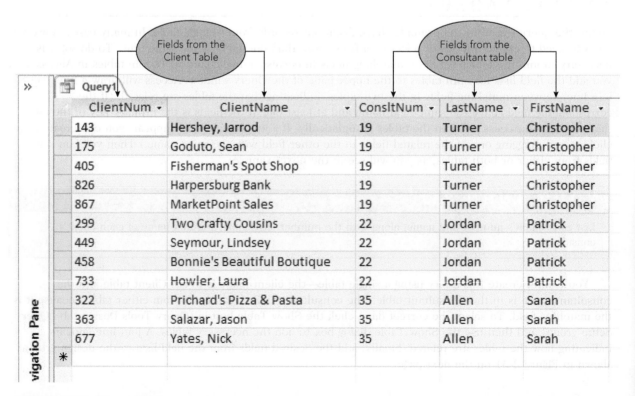

FIGURE 2-32 Query results

For each client whose credit limit is $10,000, list the client's number and name, along with the number, last name, and first name of the client's consultant. Do not display the credit limit field, as they will all be the same.

The only difference between this query and the one illustrated in Your Turn 2-13 on page 53 is that there is an extra restriction—the credit limit must be $10,000. To include this new condition, add the CreditLimit field to the design grid, enter 10000 as the criterion, and remove the check mark from the CreditLimit field's Show check box (because the CreditLimit column should not appear in the query results). The query design appears in Figure 2-33.

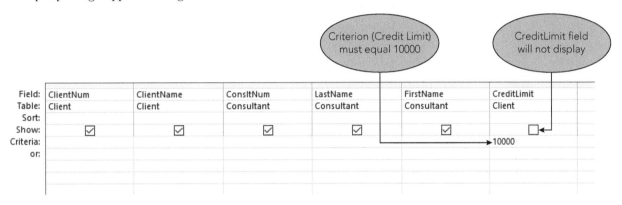

FIGURE 2-33   Query to restrict records in a join

Only clients with credit limits of $10,000 are included in the query results, as shown in Figure 2-34.

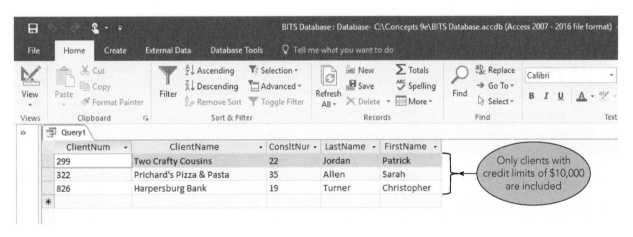

FIGURE 2-34   Query results

Joining Multiple Tables

Joining three or more tables is similar to joining two tables. First, you add the field lists for all the tables involved in the join to the upper pane; the order of the tables does not matter. Then you add the fields to appear in the query results to the design grid in the desired field order.

For each order, list the order number, order date, client number, and client name. In addition, for each order line within the order, list the taskID, description, scheduled date of service, and quoted price.

This query requires data from four tables: WorkOrders (for basic order data), Client (for the client number and name), OrderLine (for the item number, scheduled date, and quoted price), and Tasks (for the description). Figure 2-35 shows the query design.

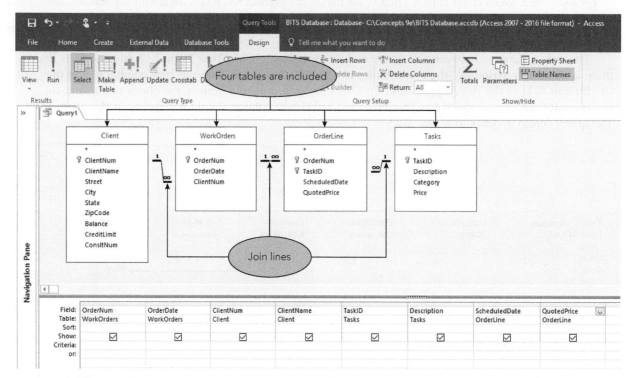

FIGURE 2-35 Query to join multiple tables

The query results appear in Figure 2-36.

OrderNum	OrderDate	ClientNum	ClientName	TaskID	Description	ScheduledDate	QuotedPrice
67101	9/6/2018	733	Howler, Laura	SI77	Software minor	9/10/2018	$144.00
67313	9/7/2018	458	Bonnie's Beautiful Boutique	LA81	Local area networking (LAN)	9/12/2018	$104.00
67424	9/10/2018	322	Prichard's Pizza & Pasta	MO49	Mobility	9/14/2018	$65.00
67424	9/10/2018	322	Prichard's Pizza & Pasta	UP38	Upgrades	9/14/2018	$185.00
67838	9/10/2018	867	MarketPoint Sales	LA81	Local area networking (LAN)	9/20/2018	$104.00
67949	9/10/2018	322	Prichard's Pizza & Pasta	PI54	Printing issues	9/21/2018	$50.00
67949	9/10/2018	322	Prichard's Pizza & Pasta	VR39	Virus removal	9/21/2018	$88.00
67949	9/10/2018	322	Prichard's Pizza & Pasta	WA33	Wide area networking (WAN)	9/21/2018	$126.00
68252	9/12/2018	363	Salazar, Jason	DI85	Data recovery minor	9/24/2018	$50.00
68868	9/14/2018	867	MarketPoint Sales	SA44	Software major	9/24/2018	$200.00
68979	9/17/2018	826	Harpersburg Bank	AC65	Accessories	9/27/2018	$77.00
68979	9/17/2018	826	Harpersburg Bank	DA11	Data recovery major	9/27/2018	$970.00

FIGURE 2-36 Query results

USING AN UPDATE QUERY

In addition to retrieving data, you can use a query to update data. A query that changes data is called an **update query**. An update query makes a specified change to all records satisfying the criteria in the query. To change a query to an update query, click the Update button (Query Tools Design tab | Query Type group). When you create an update query, a new row, called the Update To row, is added to the design grid. You use this row to indicate how to update the data selected by the query.

There is no undo feature when creating an update query. You first may want to select the data (such as those clients who live in the city of Lizton) in order to test that part of the query and make sure it selects the correct records. Doing so helps you to understand which rows will change.

YOUR TURN 2-16

The zip code for clients located in the city of Lizton is incorrect; it should be 34345. Change the zip code for those clients to the correct value.

To change the zip code for only those clients located in Lizton, include the City column in the design grid and enter a criterion of Lizton in the Criteria row. To indicate the new value for the zip code, include the ZipCode column in the design grid. Enter the new zip code value in the Update To row for the ZipCode column, as shown in Figure 2-37. When you click the Run button (Query Tools Design tab | Results group), Access indicates how many rows the query will change and gives you a chance to cancel the update, if necessary. When you click the Yes button, the query is executed and updates the data specified in the query design. Because the result of an update query is to change data in the records selected by the query, running the query does not produce a query datasheet.

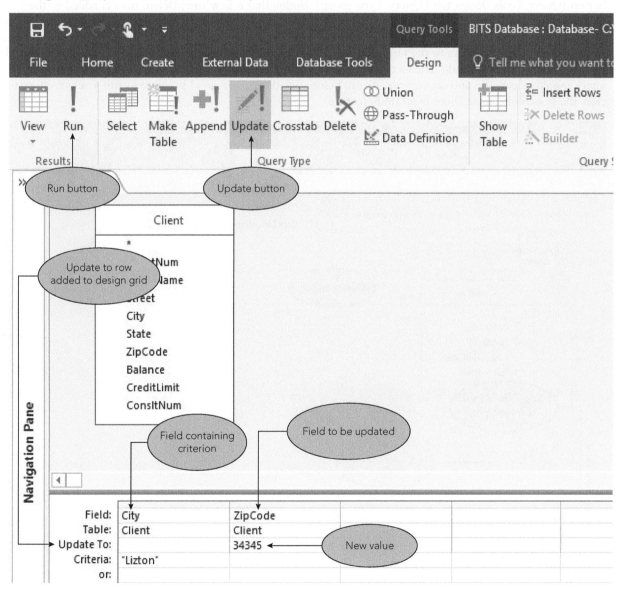

FIGURE 2-37   Query design to update data

USING A DELETE QUERY

You can use queries to delete one or more records at a time based on criteria that you specify. A **delete query** permanently deletes all the records satisfying the criteria entered in the query. For example, you can delete all the order lines associated with a certain order in the OrderLine table by using a single delete query.

YOUR TURN 2-17

Delete all order lines in which the order number is 67424.

You enter the criteria that will determine the records to be deleted just as you would enter any other criteria. In this example, include the OrderNum field in the design grid and enter the order number 67424 in the Criteria row, as shown in Figure 2-38. To change the query type to a delete query, click the Delete button (Query Tools Design tab | Query Type group). Notice that a new row, Delete row, is added to the design grid, indicating that this is a delete query. When you click the Run button, Access indicates how many rows will be deleted and gives you a chance to cancel the deletions, if necessary. If you click the Yes button, the query will delete all rows in the OrderLine table on which the order number is 67424. Because the result of a delete query permanently deletes the records it selects, you should take extra care to make sure that the query design selects the correct records. Again, before deleting, it is a good practice to run a select query to view the possible results. There is no undo feature.

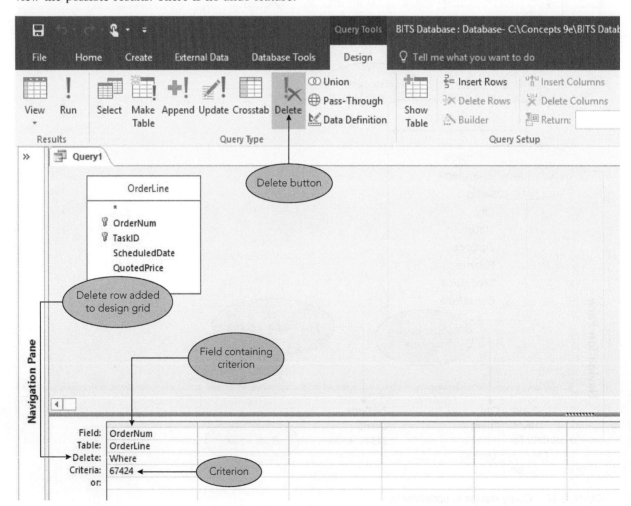

FIGURE 2-38   Query design to delete records

Q & A 2-5

Question: What happens if you run a delete query that does not include a criterion?
Answer: Because there is no criterion to select records, the query selects all records in the table and then deletes all of them from the table. Be careful!

USING A MAKE-TABLE QUERY

You can use a query to create a new table in either the current database or another database. A **make-table query** creates a new table using the results of a query. The records added to the new table are separate from the original table in which they appear. In other words, you do not move the records to a new table; you create a new table using the records selected by the query. New tables might be used for specialized reports, transferring data to other programs, or archiving the data.

YOUR TURN 2-18

Create a new table containing the client number and client name, and the number, first name, and last name of the client's consultant. Name the new table ClientRep.

First, you create a query to select the records from both the Client and Consultant tables as shown in Figure 2-39.

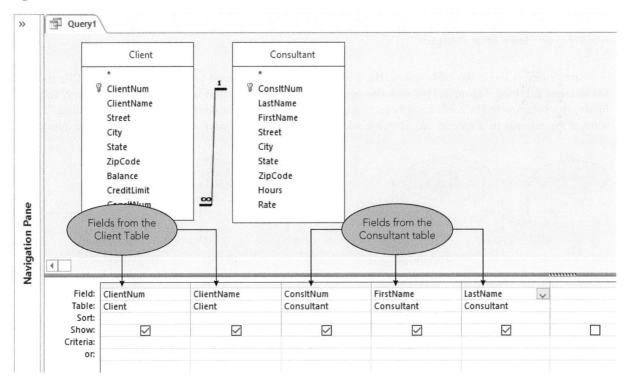

FIGURE 2-39 Preparation for a make-table query design

After you create and test the query to make sure it selects the correct records, change the query type to a make-table query by performing the following steps:

- Click the Make Table button (Query Tools Design tab | Query Type group). Access displays the Make Table dialog box (Figure 2-40).
- Enter the new table's name and choose where to create it.
- Click the OK button (Make Table dialog box).
- Run the query.
- Click the Yes button when Access indicates how many records you will paste into the new table.

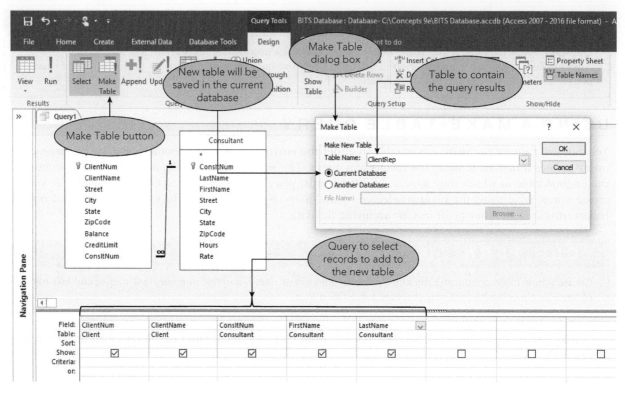

FIGURE 2-40 Make Table dialog box

After running the make-table query, the records it selects are added to a new table named ClientRep in the current database. Figure 2-41 shows the new ClientRep table created by the make-table query. In the figure, the columns in the table have been resized by dragging the boundary of the column heading. If you wanted the records in a special order, you could have specified the order within the Make Table query.

ClientNum	ClientName	ConsltNum	FirstName	LastName
143	Hershey, Jarrod	19	Christopher	Turner
175	Goduto, Sean	19	Christopher	Turner
405	Fisherman's Spot Shop	19	Christopher	Turner
826	Harpersburg Bank	19	Christopher	Turner
867	MarketPoint Sales	19	Christopher	Turner
299	Two Crafty Cousins	22	Patrick	Jordan
449	Seymour, Lindsey	22	Patrick	Jordan
458	Bonnie's Beautiful Boutique	22	Patrick	Jordan
733	Howler, Laura	22	Patrick	Jordan
322	Prichard's Pizza & Pasta	35	Sarah	Allen
363	Salazar, Jason	35	Sarah	Allen
677	Yates, Nick	35	Sarah	Allen

FIGURE 2-41 ClientRep table created by the make-table query

QUERY OPTIMIZATION

A **query optimizer** is a DBMS component that analyzes queries and attempts to determine the most efficient way to execute a given query—especially useful for large databases. Generally, the query optimizer cannot be accessed directly by users; optimization is a statistical process that occurs behind the scenes. For example, if the query asks for all clients who use consultant number 19, the optimizer "glances" through the first few records in the table and finds few clients. The internal optimizer then can determine that a search for that field's internal ID number may be more efficient than a full table scan.

The query optimizer used in Microsoft Access is very good, so you may find that simple queries are very fast. However, with larger databases and those using big data, you may want to consider the following techniques to increase the speed of the search.

- In your queries, include only the minimum number of fields necessary.
- Use list arrows where they exist—you will avoid typing errors.
- When querying multiple tables, use Join lines wherever possible. Access can search faster if the tables are joined.
- If you are searching a primary key field and another field, do not use Group By in the secondary field. Use the First aggregate operator. The results will be the same.
- Avoid using criteria in the Group By field; include the criteria in a second field (identical or different). Results are quicker when Group By stands alone.

RELATIONAL ALGEBRA

Relational algebra is a theoretical way of manipulating a relational database based on set theory. Relational algebra includes operations that act on existing tables to produce new tables, similar to the way the operations of addition and subtraction act on numbers to produce new numbers in the mathematical algebra with which you are familiar.

Retrieving data from a relational database through the use of relational algebra involves issuing relational algebra commands to operate on existing tables to form a new table containing the desired information. Sometimes you might need to execute a series of commands to obtain the desired result.

Unlike QBE, relational algebra is not used in current DBMS systems. While proprietary apps or interpreters such as RA or RelaX can be used to implement or execute relational algebra, the importance of relational algebra is the theoretical base it furnishes to the relational model and the benchmark it provides. Other approaches to querying relational databases are judged by this benchmark.

NOTE: While there is no "standard" method for representing relational algebra commands, this section illustrates one possible approach. What is important is not the particular way the commands are represented but the results they provide.

Figure 2-42 lists some of the common commands and operators used with relational algebra.

Relational Algebra Operators

Commands/Operators	Use
SELECT	chooses a subset of rows that satisfies a condition
PROJECT	reorders, selects, or deletes attributes during a query
JOIN	compounds similar rows from two tables into single longer rows, as every row of the first table is joined to every row of the second table
UNION	joins or includes all rows from two tables, eliminating duplicates
INTERSECTION	displays only rows that are common to two tables
SUBTRACT	includes rows from one table that do not exist in another table (also called SET DIFFERENT, DIFFERENCE or MINUS operation)
PRODUCT	creates a table that has all the attributes of two tables including all rows from both tables (also referred to as the CARTESIAN PRODUCT)
RENAME	assigns a name to the results of queries for future reference

FIGURE 2-42 Relational algebra operators

As you will notice in the following examples, each command ends with a GIVING clause, followed by a table name. This clause requests that the result of the command be placed in a temporary table with the specified name.

Selection

In relational algebra, the **SELECT** command takes a horizontal subset of a table; that is, it retrieves certain rows from an existing table (based on some user-specified criteria) and saves them as a new table. The SELECT command includes the word *WHERE* followed by a condition. The rows retrieved are the rows in which the condition is satisfied.

YOUR TURN 2-19

List all information about client 363 from the Client table.

```
SELECT Client WHERE ClientNum='363'
GIVING Answer
```

This command creates a new table named Answer that contains only one row on which the client number is 363, because that is the only row in which the condition is true. All the columns from the Client table are included in the new Answer table.

YOUR TURN 2-20

List all information from the Client table about all clients with credit limits of $7,500.

```
SELECT Client WHERE CreditLimit=7500
GIVING Answer
```

This command creates a new table named Answer that contains all the columns from the Client table, but only those rows on which the credit limit is $7,500.

Projection

In relational algebra, the **PROJECT** command takes a vertical subset of a table; that is, it causes only certain columns to be included in the new table. The PROJECT command includes the word *OVER* followed by a list of the columns to be included.

YOUR TURN 2-21

List the number and name of all clients.

```
PROJECT Client OVER (ClientNum, ClientName)
GIVING Answer
```

This command creates a new table named Answer that contains the ClientNum and ClientName columns for all the rows in the Client table.

YOUR TURN 2-22

List the number and name of all clients with credit limits of $7,500.

This example requires a two-step process. You first use a SELECT command to create a new table (named Temp) that contains only those clients with credit limits of $7,500. Then you project the new table to restrict the result to only the indicated columns.

```
SELECT Client WHERE CreditLimit=7500
GIVING Temp
PROJECT Temp OVER (ClientNum, ClientName)
GIVING Answer
```

The first command creates a new table named Temp that contains all the columns from the Client table, but only those rows in which the credit limit is $7,500. The second command creates a new table named Answer that contains all the rows from the Temp table (that is, only clients with credit limits of $7,500), but only the ClientNum and ClientName columns.

Joining

The **JOIN** command is a core operation of relational algebra because it allows you to extract data from more than one table. In the most common form of the join, two tables are combined based on the values in matching columns, creating a new table containing the columns in both tables. Rows in this new table are the **concatenation** (combination) of a row from the first table and a row from the second table that match on the common column (often called the **join column**). In other words, two tables are joined *on* the join column.

For example, suppose you want to join the two tables shown in Figure 2-43 on ConsltNum (the join column), creating a new table named Temp.

Client

ClientNum	ClientName	ConsltNum
143	Hershey, Jarrod	19
175	Goduto, Sean	19
299	Two Crafty Cousins	22
322	Prichard's Pizza & Pasta	35
363	Salazar, Jason	35
405	Fisherman's Spot Shop	19
449	Seymour, Lindsey	22
458	Bonnie's Beautiful Boutique	22
677	Yates, Nick	35
733	Howler, Laura	22
826	Harpersburg Bank	35
867	MarketPoint Sales	19
900	Only Cakes Bakery	75

Consultant

ConsltNum	LastName	FirstName
19	Turner	Christopher
22	Jordan	Patrick
35	Allen	Sarah
51	Shields	Tom

FIGURE 2-43   Client and Consultant tables

The result of joining the Client and Consultant tables creates the table shown in Figure 2-44. The column that joins the tables (ConsltNum) appears only once. Other than that, all columns from both tables appear in the result.

Temp

ClientNum	ClientName	ConsltNum	LastName	FirstName
143	Hershey, Jarrod	19	Turner	Christopher
175	Goduto, Sean	19	Turner	Christopher
299	Two Crafty Cousins	22	Jordan	Patrick
322	Prichard's Pizza & Pasta	35	Allen	Sarah
363	Salazar, Jason	35	Allen	Sarah
405	Fisherman's Spot Shop	19	Turner	Christopher
449	Seymour, Lindsey	22	Jordan	Patrick
458	Bonnie's Beautiful Boutique	22	Jordan	Patrick
677	Yates, Nick	35	Allen	Sarah
733	Howler, Laura	22	Jordan	Patrick
826	Harpersburg Bank	35	Allen	Sarah
867	MarketPoint Sales	19	Turner	Christopher

FIGURE 2-44   Table produced by joining the Client and Consultant tables

When a row in one table does not match any row in the other table, that row will not appear in the result of the join. Thus, the row for consultant 51 (Tom Shields) from the Consultant table does not appear in the join table because there is no client whose consultant number is 51. Likewise, the row for client 900 (Only Cakes Bakery) does not appear in the join table because there is no consultant whose number is 75.

You can restrict the output from the join to include only certain columns by using the PROJECT command, as shown in the following example.

YOUR TURN 2-23

For each client, list the client number, client name, consultant number, and consultant's last name.

```
JOIN Client Consultant
WHERE Client.ConsltNum=Consultant.ConsltNum
GIVING Temp
PROJECT Temp OVER (ClientNum, ClientName, ConsltNum, LastName)
GIVING Answer
```

In the WHERE clause of the JOIN command, the matching fields are both named ConsltNum—the field in the Consultant table named ConsltNum is supposed to match the field in the Client table named ConsltNum. Because two fields are named ConsltNum, you must qualify the field names. Just as in QBE, the ConsltNum field in the Consultant table is written as Consultant.ConsltNum and the ConsltNum field in the Client table is written as Client.ConsltNum.

In this example, the JOIN command joins the Consultant and Client tables to create a new table, named Temp. The PROJECT command creates a new table named Answer that contains all the rows from the Temp table, but only the ClientNum, ClientName, ConsltNum, and LastName columns.

The type of join used in Your Turn 2-23 is called a **natural join**. Although this type of join is the most common, there is another possibility. The other type of join, the **outer join**, is similar to the natural join, except that it also includes records from each original table that are not common in both tables. In a natural join, these unmatched records do not appear in the new table. In the outer join, unmatched records are included and the values of the fields are vacant, or **null**, for the records that do not have data common in both tables. Performing an outer join for Your Turn 2-23 produces the table shown in Figure 2-45.

Temp

ClientNum	ClientName	ConsltNum	LastName	FirstName
143	Hershey, Jarrod	19	Turner	Christopher
175	Goduto, Sean	19	Turner	Christopher
299	Two Crafty Cousins	22	Jordan	Patrick
322	Prichard's Pizza & Pasta	35	Allen	Sarah
363	Salazar, Jason	35	Allen	Sarah
405	Fisherman's Spot Shop	19	Turner	Christopher
449	Seymour, Lindsey	22	Jordan	Patrick
458	Bonnie's Beautiful Boutique	22	Jordan	Patrick
677	Yates, Nick	35	Allen	Sarah
733	Howler, Laura	22	Jordan	Patrick
826	Harpersburg Bank	35	Allen	Sarah
867	MarketPoint Sales	19	Turner	Christopher
900	Only Cakes Bakery	75		
		51	Shields	Tom

FIGURE 2-45　Table produced by an outer join of the Client and Consultant tables

Union

The **union** of tables A and B is a table containing all rows that are in either table A or table B or in both table A and table B. The union operation is performed by the **UNION** command in relational algebra; however, there is a restriction on the operation. It does not make sense, for example, to talk about the union of the Consultant table and the Client table because the tables do not contain the same columns. The two tables *must* have the same structure for a union to be appropriate; the formal term is *union compatible*. Two tables are **union compatible** when they have the same number of columns and when their corresponding columns represent the same type of data. For example, if the first column in table A contains client numbers, the first column in table B must also contain client numbers.

YOUR TURN 2-24

List the numbers and names of those clients that have orders *or* are represented by consultant 22, or both.

You can create a table containing the number and name of all clients that have orders by joining the WorkOrders table and the Client table (Temp1 in the following example) and then projecting the result over ClientNum and ClientName (Temp2). You can also create a table containing the number and name of all clients represented by consultant 22 by selecting from the Client table (Temp3) and then projecting the result (Temp4). The two tables ultimately created by this process (Temp2 and Temp4) have the same structure. They each have two fields: ClientNum and ClientName. Because these two tables are union compatible, it is appropriate to take the union of these two tables. This process is accomplished in relational algebra using the following code:

```
JOIN WorkOrders, Client
WHERE WorkOrders.ClientNum=Client.ClientNum
GIVING Temp1
PROJECT Temp1 OVER ClientNum, ClientName
GIVING Temp2
SELECT Client WHERE ConsltNum='22'
GIVING Temp3
PROJECT Temp3 OVER ClientNum, ClientName
GIVING Temp4
UNION Temp2 WITH Temp4 GIVING Answer
```

Intersection

The **intersection** of two tables is a table containing all rows that are common in both table A and table B. As you would expect, using the intersection operation is very similar to using the union operation; in fact, the two tables must be union compatible for the intersection to work. Syntactically, the only difference is that you replace the UNION command with the **INTERSECT** command, as illustrated in the following example.

YOUR TURN 2-25

List the number and name of clients that have orders *and* that are represented by consultant 22.

In this example, you need to intersect the two tables instead of taking their union. The code to accomplish this is as follows:

```
JOIN WorkOrders, Client
WHERE WorkOrders.ClientNum=Client.ClientNum
GIVING Temp1
PROJECT Temp1 OVER ClientNum, ClientName
GIVING Temp2
SELECT Client WHERE ConsltNum='22'
GIVING Temp3
PROJECT Temp3 OVER ClientNum, ClientName
GIVING Temp4
INTERSECT Temp2 WITH Temp4 GIVING Answer
```

Difference

The **difference** of two tables A and B (referred to as "A minus B") is the set of all rows that are in table A but that are not in table B. As with intersection, the two tables must be union compatible for the difference to work. The difference operation is performed by the **SUBTRACT** command in relational algebra.

YOUR TURN 2-26

List the number and name of those clients that have orders but that are *not* represented by consultant 22.

This process is virtually identical to the one you encountered in the union and intersection examples, but in this case, you subtract one of the tables from the other instead of taking their union or intersection. This process is accomplished in relational algebra using the following command:

```
JOIN WorkOrders, Client
WHERE WorkOrders.ClientNum=Client.ClientNum
GIVING Temp1
PROJECT Temp1 OVER ClientNum, ClientName
GIVING Temp2
SELECT Client WHERE ConsltNum='22'
GIVING Temp3
PROJECT Temp3 OVER ClientNum, ClientName
GIVING Temp4
SUBTRACT Temp4 FROM Temp2 GIVING Answer
```

Product

Used infrequently, the **product** of two tables (mathematically called the **Cartesian product**) is the table obtained by concatenating every row in the first table with every row in the second table. The product of the WorkOrders table and the Tasks table, which are both shown in Figure 2-46, appears in the figure as the table labeled "Product of WorkOrders and Tasks."

WorkOrders

OrderNum	OrderDate
67101	9/6/2018
67313	9/7/2018
67424	9/10/2018

Tasks

TaskID	Description
AC65	Accessories
PI54	Printing issues

Product of WorkOrders and Tasks

OrderNum	OrderDate	PartNum	Description
67101	9/6/2018	AC65	Accessories
67101	9/6/2018	PI54	Printing issues
67313	9/7/2018	AC65	Accessories
67313	9/7/2018	PI54	Printing issues
67424	9/10/2018	AC65	Accessories
67424	9/10/2018	PI54	Printing issues

FIGURE 2-46 Product of two tables

Every row in the WorkOrders table is matched with every row in the Tasks table. If the WorkOrders table has m rows and the Tasks table has n rows, there would be m *times* n rows in the product. If, as is typically the case, the tables have many rows, the number of rows in the product can be so great that it is not practical to form the product. Usually, you want only those combinations that satisfy certain restrictions;

thus, you almost always would use the join operation instead of the product operation. Also, avoid creating a product with very large databases as it has the possibility of creating millions of rows and crashing systems.

Division

The **division** process also is used infrequently. It is best illustrated by considering the division of a table with two columns by a table with a single column, which is the most common situation in which this operation is used. Consider the first two tables shown in Figure 2-47. The first table contains two columns: OrderNum and TaskID. The second table contains only a single column, PartNum.

OrderLine

OrderNum	TaskID
72608	C-3D3F
72610	B-7H5Q
72610	M-3R2X
72613	C-3D3F
72629	B-7H5Q
72630	C-3D3F
72630	M-3R2X

Item

PartNum
B-7H5Q
M-3R2X

Result of dividing OrderLine by Item

OrderNum
72610

FIGURE 2-47   Dividing one table by another

The quotient (the result of the division) is a new table with a single column named OrderNum (the column from table A that is *not* in table B). The rows in this new table contain those order numbers from the OrderLine table that "match" *all* the tasks appearing in the Item table. For an order number to appear in the quotient, a row in the OrderLine table must have that order number in the OrderNum column and, using the first PartNum in the Item table, have B-7H5Q in the TaskID column. In the second case, the OrderLine table must have a row with this same order number in the OrderNum column and M-3R2X in the TaskID column. It does not matter if other rows in the OrderLine table contain the same order number as long as the rows with *both* B-7H5Q *and* M-3R2X are present. With the sample data, only order number 72610 qualifies. Thus, the result is the final table shown in Figure 2-47.

Summary

- A relation is a two-dimensional table in which the entries are single-valued, each field has a distinct name, all the values in a field are values of the same attribute (the one identified by the field name); the order of fields does not affect queries. Each row is distinct, and the order of rows also is immaterial.
- A relational database is a collection of relations.
- An unnormalized relation is a structure in which entries need not be single-valued but that satisfies all the other properties of a relation.
- A field name is qualified by preceding it with the table name and a period (for example, Consultant. ConsltNum).
- A table's primary key is the field or fields that uniquely identify a given row within the table.
- Query-By-Example (QBE) is a visual tool for manipulating relational databases. QBE queries are created by completing on-screen forms.
- To include a field in an Access query, place the field in the design grid, and make sure a check mark appears in the field's Show check box.
- To indicate criteria in an Access query, place the criteria in the appropriate columns in the design grid of the Query window.
- To indicate AND criteria in an Access query, place both criteria in the same Criteria row of the design grid; to indicate OR criteria, place the criteria on separate Criteria rows of the design grid.
- To create a computed field in Access, enter an appropriate expression in the desired column of the design grid.
- To use functions to perform calculations in Access, include the appropriate function in the Total row for the appropriate column of the design grid.
- To sort query results in Access, select Ascending or Descending in the Sort row for the field or fields that are sort keys.
- When sorting query results using more than one field, the leftmost sort key in the design grid is the major sort key (also called the primary sort key) and the sort key to its right is the minor sort key (also called the secondary sort key).
- To join tables in Access, place field lists for both tables in the upper pane of the Query window.
- To make the same change to all records that satisfy certain criteria, use an update query.
- To delete all records that satisfy certain criteria, use a delete query.
- To save the results of a query as a table, use a make-table query.
- Relational algebra is a theoretical method of manipulating relational databases.
- The SELECT command in relational algebra selects only certain rows from a table.
- The PROJECT command in relational algebra selects only certain columns from a table.
- The JOIN command in relational algebra combines data from two or more tables based on common columns.
- The UNION command in relational algebra creates a table that with the all of the rows from two tables. For a union operation to make sense, the tables must be union compatible.
- Two tables are union compatible when they have the same number of columns and their corresponding columns represent the same type of data.
- The INTERSECT command in relational algebra creates a table with the common rows from two tables. For an intersection operation to make sense, the tables must be union compatible.
- The SUBTRACT command in relational algebra, also called the difference, creates a table with rows which are present in one table but not in the other. For a subtract operation to make sense, the tables must be union compatible.
- The PRODUCT of two tables (mathematically called the Cartesian product) is the table obtained by concatenating every row in the first table with every row in the second table.
- The DIVISION process in relational algebra divides one table by another table.

Key Terms

aggregate function	comparison operator
AND criterion	composite primary key
attribute	compound condition
BETWEEN operator	compound criteria
calculated field	computed field
Cartesian product	concatenation

criteria

criterion

Datasheet view

delete query

design grid

Design view

difference

division

field

foreign key

function

Group By statement

grouping

INTERSECT

intersection

JOIN

join column

join line

major sort key

make-table query

minor sort key

natural join

null

operator

OR criterion

outer join

parameter query

primary key

primary sort key

product

PROJECT

qualify

query

Query-By-Example (QBE)

query optimizer

record

relation

relational algebra

relational database

relational operator

RENAME

repeating group

secondary sort key

SELECT

sort

sort key

SUBTRACT

tuple

UNION

union compatible

unnormalized relation

update query

Where statement

Review Questions

1. What is a relation?

2. What is a relational database?

3. What is an unnormalized relation? Is it a relation according to the definition of the word *relation*?

4. How is the term *attribute* used in the relational model? What is a more common name for *attribute*?

5. Describe the shorthand representation of the structure of a relational database. Illustrate this technique by representing the database for Colonial Adventure Tours shown in Figures 1-15 through 1-19 in Chapter 1.

6. What does it mean to qualify a field name? How would you qualify the Street field in the Client table?

7. What is a primary key? What is the primary key for each table in the Colonial Adventure Tours database shown in Figures 1-15 through 1-19 in Chapter 1?

8. How do you include a field in an Access query?

9. How do you indicate criteria in an Access query?

10. How do you use an AND criterion to combine criteria in an Access query? How do you use an OR criterion to combine criteria?

11. How do you create a computed field in an Access query?

12. In which row of the Access design grid do you include functions? What functions can you use in Access queries?

13. How do you sort data in an Access query?

14. When sorting data on more than one field in an Access query, which field is the major sort key? Which field is the minor sort key? What effect do these keys have on the order in which the rows are displayed?

15. How do you join tables in an Access query?

16. When do you use an update query?

17. When do you use a delete query?

18. When do you use a make-table query?

19. What is relational algebra?

20. Describe the purpose of the SELECT command in relational algebra.

21. Describe the purpose of the PROJECT command in relational algebra.

22. Describe the purpose of the JOIN command in relational algebra.

23. Describe the purpose of the UNION command in relational algebra.

24. Are there any restrictions on the tables when using the UNION command? If so, what are these restrictions?

25. Describe the purpose of the INTERSECT command in relational algebra.

26. Describe the purpose of the SUBTRACT command in relational algebra.

27. Describe the purpose of the product process in relational algebra.

28. Describe the results of the division process in relational algebra.

29. In the BITS Corporation database shown in Figure 2-1, the Consultant table contains four rows and the Client table contains 12 rows. How many rows would be contained in the Cartesian product of these two tables?

30. In Your Turn 2-23 on page 64, would you get the same result if you performed the PROJECT command before the JOIN command? Why or why not?

BITS Corporation Exercises: QBE

In the following exercises, you will use the data in the BITS Corporation database shown in Figure 2-1. (If you use a computer to complete these exercises, use a copy of the BITS Corporation database so you will still have the original data when you complete Chapter 3.) In each step, use QBE to obtain the desired results. You can use the query feature in a DBMS to complete the exercises using a computer, or you can simply write a description of how you would complete the task. Check with your instructor if you are uncertain about which approach to take.

1. List the number and name of all clients.

2. List the complete Tasks table.

3. List the number and name of all clients represented by consultant 19.

4. List the number and name of all clients that are represented by consultant 19 *and* that have a credit limit of $10,000.

5. List the number and name of all clients that are represented by consultant 19 *or* that have a credit limit of $10,000.

6. For each order, list the order number, order date, number of the client that placed the order, and name of the client that placed the order.

7. List the number and name of all clients represented by Patrick Jordan.

8. How many clients have a credit limit of $5,000?

9. Find the total of the balances for all clients represented by consultant 22.

10. List the ClientNum, CreditLimit, and Balance, and list the available credit (CreditLimit - Balance) for each client represented by consultant 19.

11. List all columns and all records in the Consultant table. Sort the results by last name.

12. List all columns and all records in the Tasks table. Sort the results by price within category.

13. List the category and price for all orders. Group the results by category.

14. Create a new table named ScheduledClients to contain client's name, the scheduled date of service, task ID, description of the service, and the quoted price.

15. In the ScheduledClients table, change the description of item VR39 to "Virus detection and removal." Adjust the column widths as necessary.

16. In the ScheduledClients table, delete every row on which the price is greater than $500.

17. There are two ways to create the query in Exercise 11. What are they? Which one did you use?

18. An employee of BITS Corporation created the query shown in Figure 2-48. She wants to list the client number and the task IDs associated with each order. Will the query results be correct? If so, list other fields that would be useful. If not, how should she modify the query to achieve this result?

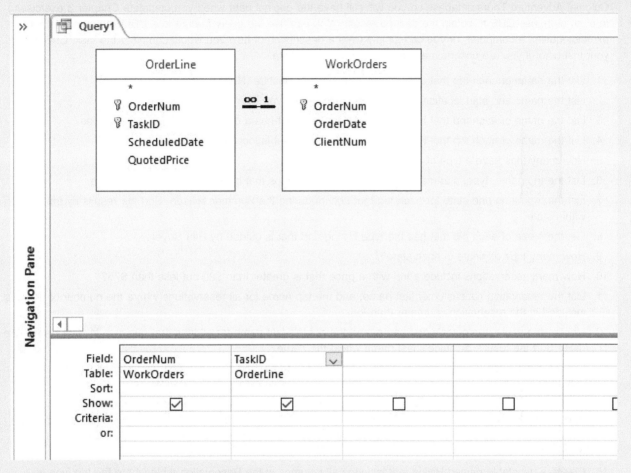

FIGURE 2-48   Query to count items in a work order

BITS Corporation Exercises: Relational Algebra

In the following exercises, you will use the data in the BITS Corporation database shown in Figure 2-1. In each step, indicate how to use relational algebra to obtain the desired results.

1. List the number and name of all consultants.

2. List all information from the Tasks table for item WC19.

3. List the order number, order date, client number, and client name for each order.

4. List the order number, order date, client number, and client name for each order placed by any client represented by the consultant whose last name is Turner.

5. List the number and date of all orders that were placed on 9/10/2018 or that were placed by a client whose consultant number is 19.

6. List the number and date of all orders that were placed on 9/10/2018 by a client whose consultant number is 35.

7. List the number and date of all orders that were placed on 9/10/2018 but *not* by a client whose consultant number is 35.

Colonial Adventure Tours Case

The owner of Colonial Adventure Tours knows that being able to run queries is one of the most important benefits of using a DBMS. In the following exercises, you will use the data in the Colonial Adventure Tours database shown in Figures 1-15 through 1-19 in Chapter 1. (If you use a computer to complete these exercises, use a copy of the Colonial Adventure Tours database so you will still have the original data when you complete Chapter 3 exercises.) In each step, use QBE to obtain the desired results. You can use the query feature in a DBMS to complete the exercises using a computer, or you can simply write a description of how you would complete the task. Check with your instructor if you are uncertain about which approach to take.

1. List the name of each trip that does not start in New Hampshire (NH).

2. List the name and start location for each trip that has the type Biking.

3. List the name of each trip that has the type Hiking and that has a distance greater than six miles.

4. List the name of each trip that has the type Paddling or that is located in Vermont (VT).

5. How many trips have a type of Hiking or Biking?

6. List the trip name, type, and maximum group size for all trips that have Susan Kiley as a guide.

7. List the trip name and state for each trip that occurs during the Summer season. Sort the results by trip name within state.

8. List the name of each trip that has the type Hiking and that is guided by Rita Boyers.

9. How many trips originate in each state?

10. How many reservations include a trip with a price that is greater than $20 but less than $75?

11. List the reservation ID, customer last name, and the trip name for all reservations where the number of persons included in the reservation is greater than four.

12. List the trip name, the guide's first name, and the guide's last name for all trips that originate in New Hampshire (NH). Sort the results by guide's last name within trip name.

13. List the reservation ID, customer number, customer last name, and customer first name for all trips that occur in July 2018.

14. Colonial Adventure Tours calculates the total price of a trip by adding the trip price plus other fees and multiplying the result by the number of persons included in the reservation. List the reservation ID, trip name, customer's last name, customer's first name, and total cost for all trips where the number of persons is greater than four.

15. Create a new table named Hiking that includes all columns in the Reservation table where the trip type is Hiking.

16. Use an update query to change the OtherFees value in the Hiking table to $5.00 for all records on which the OtherFees value is $0.00.

17. Use a delete query to delete all trips in the Hiking table where the trip date is 6/12/2018.

18. One of the reservations agents at Colonial Adventure Tours created the query shown in Figure 2-49 to list each trip name and the last name and first name of each corresponding guide. The query results included 410 records, and he knows that this result is incorrect. Why did he get so many records? What should he change in the query design to get the correct query results?

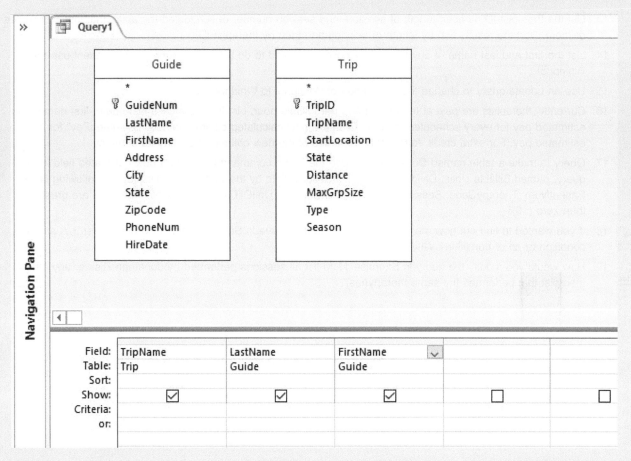

FIGURE 2-49   Query to list trip names and guide names

Sports Physical Therapy Case

In the following exercises, you will use the data in the Sports Physical Therapy database shown in Figures 1-21 through 1-24 in Chapter 1. (If you use a computer to complete these exercises, use a copy of the Sports Physical Therapy database so you will still have the original data when you complete Chapter 3 exercises.) In each step, use QBE to obtain the desired results. You can use the query feature in a DBMS to complete the exercises using a computer, or you can simply write a description of how you would complete the task. Check with your instructor if you are uncertain about which approach to take.

1. List the patient number, last name, and first name of every patient.

2. List the complete Therapist table (all rows and all columns).

3. List the last name and first name of every patient located in Waterville.

4. List the last name and first name of every patient not located in Waterville.

5. List the full name and address of every patient whose balance is greater than $1000.

6. List all the therapies that are billed in units of 15 minutes.

7. Calculate the total balance due for Sports Physical Therapy.

8. List the patient number and length of session for each patient with the TherapyCode of 97535.

9. For every session, list the patient's full name and the therapist's full name.

10. List the description for all scheduled therapies for 10/18/2018.

11. List every therapy description performed by Jonathan Risk.

12. How many patients are scheduled for more than one therapy?

74

13. List the therapist ID number, length of session, and session number of scheduled therapies that last 15 minutes or more. Sort the results first by length of session and then by therapist ID.

14. List the first and last name of any therapist who is scheduled to do a Massage *or* have the patient use the Whirlpool.

15. Use an update query to change the description of Whirlpool to Whirlpool bath.

16. Currently, therapists are paid at the rate of $35 per billable hour. List the therapist's last name, first name, and estimated pay for every scheduled therapy. Create a new calculated column named "EstimatedPay" for the estimated pay. For extra credit, format the properties of the new column to display as currency.

17. Query to make a table named CurrentBilling. Use the Zoom command to create a new calculated field in the query, named Billable Units. Divide the LengthOfSession field by the UnitOfTime. Display the following fields PatientNum, TherapyCode, SessionDate, LengthOfSession, UnitOfTime, and Billable Units that are greater than zero (>0).

 18. If you wanted to find out how many patients and therapists live in San Vista, would you consider that an *and* condition or an *or* condition? Why?

19. How would you modify the query in Exercise 11 to list all sessions performed by Jonathan Risk or any other therapist that performed the same therapy(ies)?

CHAPTER **3**

THE RELATIONAL MODEL 2: SQL

LEARNING OBJECTIVES

- Introduce Structured Query Language (SQL)
- Create simple and compound conditions in SQL
- Compute fields in SQL
- Apply built-in SQL functions
- Use subqueries in SQL
- Group records in SQL
- Join tables using SQL
- Perform union operations in SQL
- Use SQL to update data
- Create a table using an SQL query

INTRODUCTION

In this chapter, you will examine the language called **SQL (Structured Query Language)**. Like Access and Query-By-Example (QBE), SQL provides users with the capability of querying a relational database. However, in SQL, you must enter commands to obtain the desired results rather than complete an on-screen form as you do in Access and QBE. SQL uses commands to create and update tables and to retrieve data from tables. SQL is used by database managers and others to communicate with many different kinds of databases.

SQL was developed under the name SEQUEL as the data manipulation language for IBM's prototype relational DBMS, System R, in the mid-1970s. In 1980, it was renamed SQL (but still pronounced "sequel"). Most people now say "S-Q-L" ("ess-cue-ell") to avoid confusion with an unrelated hardware product called SEQUEL. SQL is the standard language for relational database manipulation. The SQL version used in the following examples is Microsoft Access 2016. Although the various versions of SQL are not identical, the differences are relatively minor. After you have mastered one version of SQL, you can apply your skills to learn another version of SQL.

Q & A 3-1

Question: Can I specify which version of Access SQL I wish to use?
Answer: Internally, Access uses a version of SQL called SQL-89 by default. If you wish to change the version, click Options on the File tab and then click Object Designers. In the Query design area, select SQL Server Compatible Syntax (ANSI 92), which is an Oracle-compatible version of SQL.

You will begin studying SQL by examining how to use it to create a table. You will examine simple retrieval methods and compound conditions. You then will use computed fields in SQL and learn how to sort data. Next, you will learn how to use built-in functions, subqueries, and grouping. You will learn how to join tables and use the UNION operator. Finally, you will use SQL to update data in a database. The end of this chapter includes generic versions of all the SQL commands presented in the chapter.

GETTING STARTED WITH SQL

In this chapter, you will be reading the material and examining the figures to understand how to use SQL to manipulate a relational database. The examples in this chapter were created in Access 2016, however, you can use Access 2007 or later to execute the SQL commands. You may use another DBMS to practice database manipulation. Some of the examples in this text change the data in the database. If you plan to work through the examples using Access, you should use a *copy* of the original BITS database because the version of the database that is used in subsequent chapters does not include these changes.

Opening an SQL Query Window in Access

To open an SQL query window in Access and execute SQL commands shown in the figures in this book, perform the following steps:

- Open the BITS database in Access.
- Click Create on the ribbon to display the Create tab.
- Click the Query Design button (Create tab | Queries group).
- When Access displays the Show Table dialog box, click the Close button without adding a table.
- Click the View button arrow (Query Tools Design tab | Results group) and then click SQL View.
- The Query1 tab displays the query window in SQL view, ready for you to type your SQL commands (Figure 3-1).

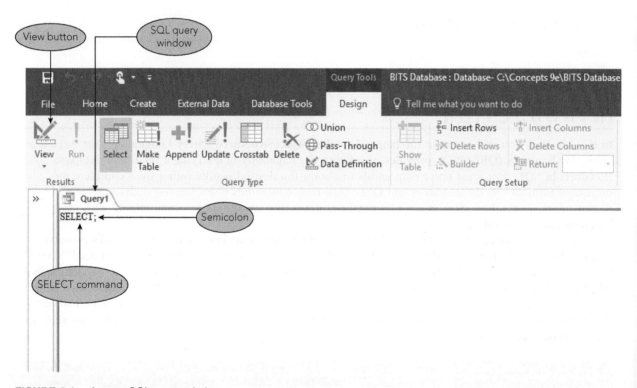

FIGURE 3-1   Access SQL query window

Q & A 3-2

Question: What text appears in the SQL query window?
Answer: Access 2016 places the SQL command, SELECT, in the query window, followed by a semicolon to indicate the end of the command. The command may be selected or highlighted.

> ## Q & A 3-3
>
> **Question:** Can I change the size of the SQL text in Access?
> **Answer:** Yes. Click the File tab. Click Options. Click Object Designers. In the Query design area, you can change the font and font size.

As you type in the query window, you can correct typing errors in a command just as you would correct errors in a document, by using the keyboard arrow keys to move the insertion point and using the Backspace or Delete keys to delete text. After completing the code and making any corrections, you can run SQL commands by clicking the Run button (Query Tools Design tab | Results group). To return to SQL view, click the View button arrow (Home tab | Views group), and then click SQL View.

TABLE CREATION

While the tables for the BITS database (and the databases at the end of the chapter) have been created already, you still should learn how to create a new table. The SQL **CREATE TABLE** command makes a new table by describing its layout. After the words *CREATE TABLE*, you type the name of the table to be created. You then enter the names, data types, and length of the columns (fields) that make up the table.

Naming Conventions

The rules for naming tables and columns vary slightly from one version of SQL to another and from one vendor to another. If you have any doubts about the validity of any of the names you have chosen, you should consult the Help application for your version of SQL.

Some common restrictions placed on table and column (field) names by DBMSs are as follows:

- The names cannot exceed 18 characters.
- The names must start with a letter.
- The names can contain only letters, numbers, and underscores (_).
- The names cannot contain spaces.

Unlike some other versions of SQL, Access SQL permits the use of spaces within table and column names. There is a restriction, however, on the way names that contain spaces are used in SQL commands. To avoid problems, it is a good practice not to include spaces in table names or column names. If the database you are using already contains a space, however, you must enclose it in square brackets in Access SQL. For example, if the name of the CreditLimit column were changed to Credit Limit (with a space between *Credit* and *Limit*), you would write the column as [Credit Limit] because the name includes a space.

In systems that permit the use of uppercase and lowercase letters in table and column names, you can avoid using spaces by capitalizing the first letter of each word in the name and using lowercase letters for the remaining letters in the words (sometimes called CamelCase). For example, the name of the credit limit column would be CreditLimit. In systems that do not permit the use of spaces or mixed case letters, some programmers use an underscore to separate words. For example, the name of the credit limit column would be CREDIT_LIMIT.

Data Types

For each column or field in a table, you must specify the type of data that the column can store and, in some cases, its length. Although the actual data types will vary slightly from one implementation of SQL to another, the following list indicates the data types you commonly will encounter:

- **INTEGER**: Stores integers, which are numbers without a decimal part. The valid data range is –2147483648 to 2147483647. You can use the contents of INTEGER fields for calculations. You do not have to specify a length for an INTEGER.
- **SMALLINT**: Stores integers but uses less storage space than the INTEGER data type. The valid data range is –32768 to 32767. SMALLINT is a better choice than INTEGER when you are certain that the field will store numbers within the indicated range. You can use the contents of SMALLINT fields for calculations. You do not have to specify a length for a SMALLINT.

- **DECIMAL(p,q):** Stores a decimal number p digits long with q of these digits being decimal places. For example, DECIMAL(5,2) represents a five-digit number with three places to the left and two places to the right of the decimal. You can use the contents of DECIMAL fields for calculations. (Unlike other SQL implementations, some versions of Access do not have a DECIMAL data type. To create numbers with decimals, you must use either the CURRENCY or the NUMBER data type. Use the CURRENCY data type for fields that will contain currency values; use the NUMBER data type for all other numeric fields.)
- **CHAR(n):** Stores a character string n characters long. The value for n must be an integer. You use the CHAR type for fields that contain letters and other special characters and for fields that contain numbers that will not be used in calculations. In the BITS database, because neither consultant numbers nor client numbers will be used in any calculations, both are assigned CHAR as the data type. (Some DBMSs use SHORT TEXT rather than CHAR, but the two data types mean the same thing.)
- **DATE:** Stores dates in the form DD-MON-YYYY or MM/DD/YYYY. For example, May 12, 2019, could be stored as 12-MAY-2019 or 5/12/2019.

The following SQL CREATE TABLE command creates a table named Consultant with nine fields:

```
CREATE TABLE Consultant (
    ConsltNum CHAR(2),
    LastName CHAR(15),
    FirstName CHAR(15),
    Street CHAR(15),
    City CHAR(15),
    State CHAR(2),
    ZipCode CHAR(5),
    Hours SMALLINT,
    Rate DECIMAL(3,2) )
;
```

As noted above, in Access, the DECIMAL data types must be changed. *Note:* This table has been created already in the Access database for BITS, so you do not have to enter this command.

```
CREATE TABLE Consultant (
    ConsltNum CHAR(2),
    LastName CHAR(15),
    FirstName CHAR(15),
    Street CHAR(15),
    City CHAR(15),
    State CHAR(2),
    ZipCode CHAR(5),
    Hours SMALLINT,
    Rate CURRENCY )
;
```

In both the generic SQL and the Access version, you are describing a table that will be named Consultant. The table contains nine fields: ConsltNum is a character field that is two positions in length. LastName is a character field with 15 characters, and so on. Hours is a numeric field that stores an integer. Similarly, Rate is a numeric field that stores three digits, including two decimal places, or in the case of Access, it is set to the CURRENCY data type.

Notice the list of field names is enclosed in parentheses. Commas separate each field. The entire multi-line command ends with a semicolon (;). Because many versions of SQL require you to end a command with a semicolon, commands in this text will end with semicolons.

Notice also that the fields are entered on separate lines. SQL does not require separate lines; SQL commands are free-format. No rule says that a specific word must begin in a particular position on the line. The previous SQL command could have been written as follows:

```
CREATE TABLE Consultant (ConsltNum CHAR(2), LastName CHAR(15), FirstName CHAR(15), Street
CHAR(15), City CHAR(15), State CHAR(2), ZipCode CHAR(5), Hours SMALLINT, Rate CURRENCY ) ;
```

Using separate lines and indentation simply makes the command more readable. In general, you should strive for such readability when you write SQL commands.

SIMPLE RETRIEVAL

When using SQL to display data, the basic form of an SQL retrieval command is SELECT-FROM-WHERE. After the word *SELECT*, you list the fields you want to display in the query results. This portion of the command is called the **SELECT clause**. The fields will appear in the query results in the order in which they are listed in the SELECT clause. After the word *FROM*, you list the table or tables that contain the data to display in the query results. This portion of the command is called the **FROM clause**. Finally, after the word *WHERE*, you list any conditions or criteria that you want to apply, such as indicating that the credit limit must equal $10,000. This portion of the command, which is optional, is called the **WHERE clause**.

Again, there are no special line-formatting rules in SQL—the examples in this text include the SELECT, FROM, and WHERE clauses on separate lines to make the commands more readable. In addition, this text uses a common style in which words that are part of the SQL language, called **reserved words**, appear in all uppercase letters. All other words in commands appear in a combination of uppercase and lowercase letters.

YOUR TURN 3-1

Using the BITS database, list the number, name, and balance of all clients.

Because you want to list all clients, you will not need to use the WHERE clause—you do not need to put any restrictions on the data to retrieve. Figure 3-2 shows the query to select the number, name, and balance of all clients using the SQL implementation in Access 2016.

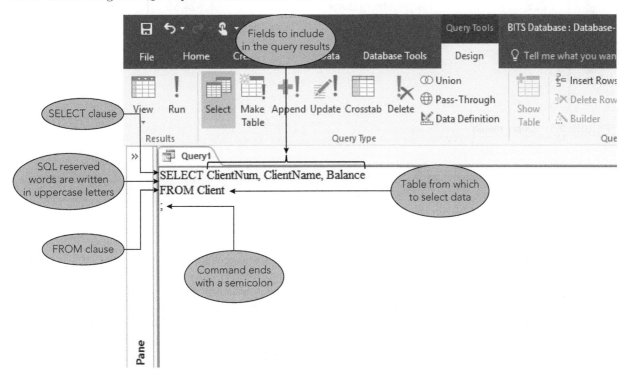

FIGURE 3-2   SQL query to select client data (Access)

The results of executing the query shown in Figure 3-2 in Access 2016 appear in Figure 3-3. To return to SQL view in Access, click the View button arrow (Home tab | Views group) and then click SQL View.

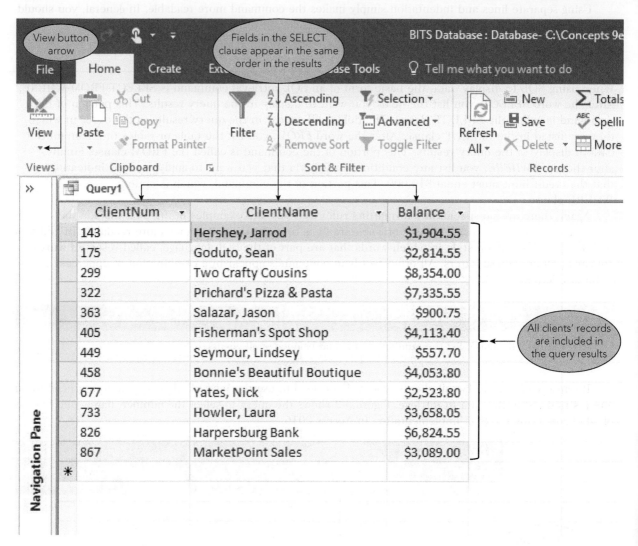

FIGURE 3-3   Query results

YOUR TURN 3-2

List the complete Tasks table.

To list all the fields in the Tasks table, you could use the same approach shown in Figure 3-2 by listing each field in the SELECT clause. However, there is a shortcut. Instead of listing all the field names in the SELECT clause, you can use the * (asterisk) symbol. When used after the word *SELECT*, the * symbol indicates that you want to include all fields in the query results in the order in which you described them to the DBMS when you created the table. To include all the fields in the query results, but in a different order, you would have to type the names of the fields in the order in which you want them to appear. In this case, assuming the default order is appropriate, the query design appears in Figure 3-4.

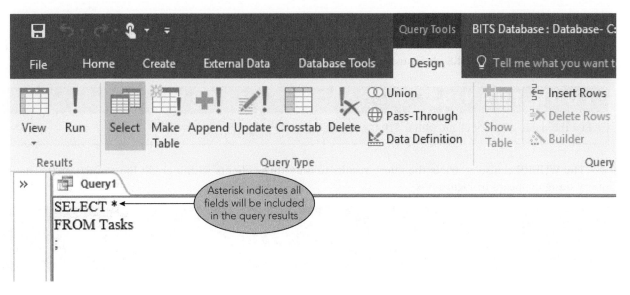

FIGURE 3-4   SQL query to list the complete Tasks table

The query results appear in Figure 3-5.

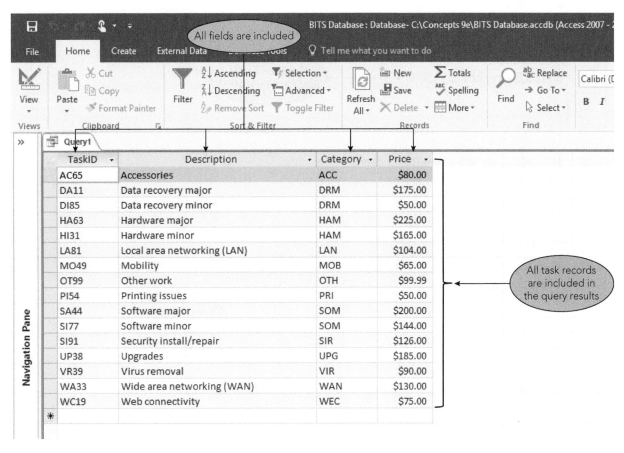

FIGURE 3-5   Query results

Numeric Criteria

Recall that queries use criteria or conditions to limit or search for specific rows or records of data. Numeric criteria can be specified in the WHERE clause using digits (no commas, dollar signs, or spaces within the numbers).

YOUR TURN 3-3

List the name of every client with a $10,000 credit limit.

The WHERE clause restricts the query results to only those clients with a credit limit of $10,000. The query design appears in Figure 3-6.

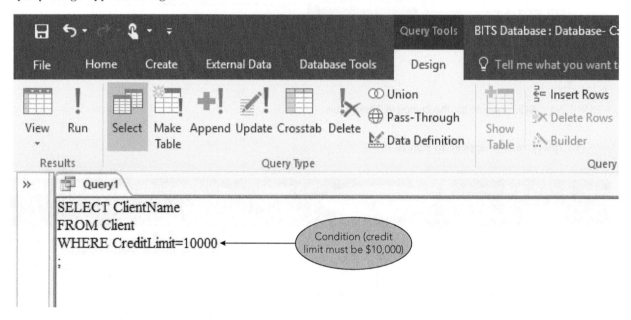

FIGURE 3-6   SQL query with a WHERE condition

The query results appear in Figure 3-7.

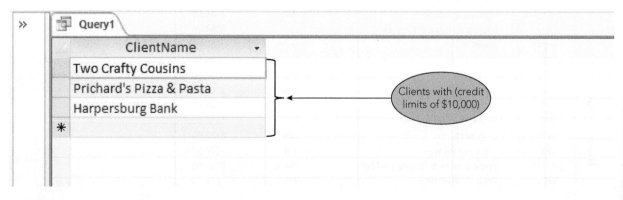

FIGURE 3-7   Query results

The WHERE clause shown in Figure 3-6 includes a simple condition. A **simple condition** includes the field name, a comparison operator, and either another field name or a value, such as CreditLimit = 10000. The spaces around the equals sign are optional.

Figure 3-8 lists the comparison operators that you can use in SQL commands. Notice that there are two versions of the "not equal to" operator: < > and !=. You must use the correct one for your version of SQL. If you use the wrong one, your system will generate an error, in which case you will know to use the other version. Access uses the < > version of the "not equal to" operator.

SQL Comparison Operators

Comparison Operator	Meaning
=	Equal to
<	Less than
>	Greater than
<=	Less than or equal to
>=	Greater than or equal to
<>	Not equal to (used by most implementations of SQL)
!=	Not equal to (used by some implementations of SQL)

FIGURE 3-8   Comparison operators used in SQL commands

Character Criteria

In Figure 3-6, the WHERE clause compared a numeric field (CreditLimit) to a number (10000). You also can search for characters or text. When a query involves a character field, such as ClientNum or ClientName, you must enclose the value to which the field is being compared in single quotation marks.

Q & A 3-4

Question: Is ClientNum a character field?
Answer: Yes. Even though the column contains only numbers, no math is performed on the field, and the data is saved as characters. Some client numbers and account numbers may contain letters or special characters, forcing the data to be stored as nonnumeric characters.

YOUR TURN 3-4

Find the name of client 458.

The query design appears in Figure 3-9 on the next page. Because ClientNum is a character field, the value 458 is enclosed in quotation marks.

84

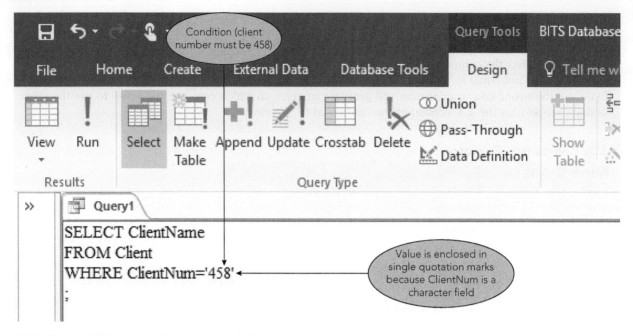

FIGURE 3-9 SQL query to find the name of client 458

The query results appear in Figure 3-10. Only a single record appears in the query results because the ClientNum field is the primary key for the Client table; there can be only one client with the number 458.

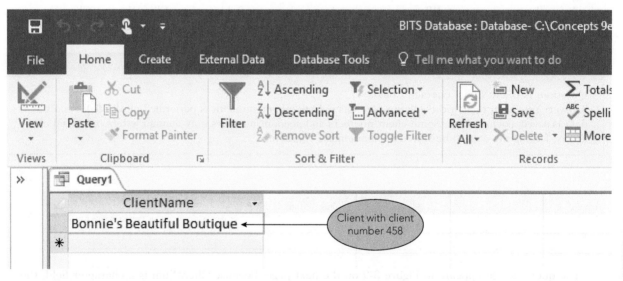

FIGURE 3-10 Query results

YOUR TURN 3-5

Find the client name for every client located in the city of Easton.

The query design appears in Figure 3-11.

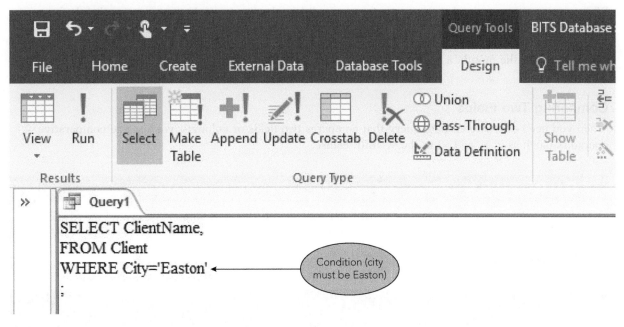

FIGURE 3-11   SQL query to find all clients located in Easton

The query results appear in Figure 3-12. Because more than one client is located in Easton, more than one record appears in the query results.

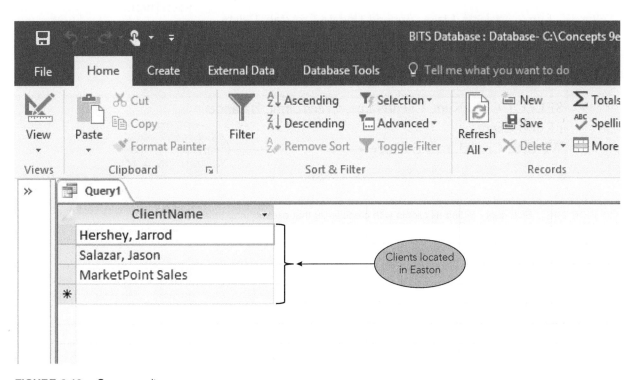

FIGURE 3-12   Query results

Date Criteria

When you want to use the date in a criterion or condition, the format of the query varies slightly from one implementation of SQL to another. In Access, you place number signs (or hash tags) around the date (for example, #11/15/2018#). In other programs, you enter the day of the month, a hyphen, the three-character abbreviation for the month, a hyphen, and the year, all enclosed in single quotation marks (for example, '15-NOV-2018').

Comparing Two Fields

When you need to create an SQL query that compares two fields or columns, you use the comparative operators (such as <, >, and =) in the WHERE clause.

YOUR TURN 3-6

List the number, name, credit limit, and balance for all clients with credit limits that exceed their balances.

The query design appears in Figure 3-13.

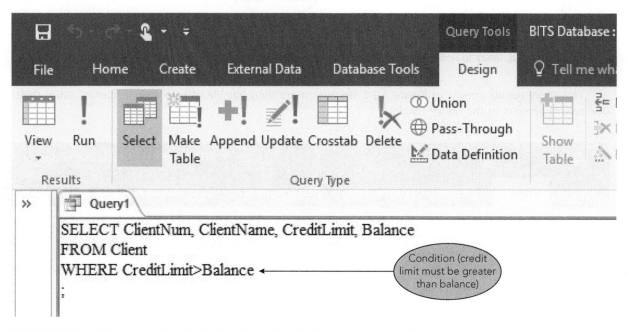

FIGURE 3-13   SQL query to find all clients with credit limits that exceed their balances

The query results appear in Figure 3-14.

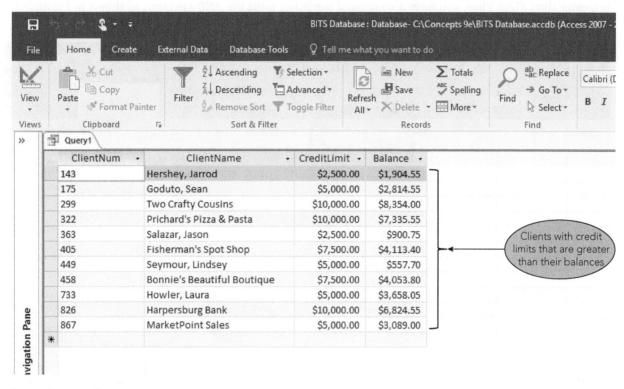

FIGURE 3-14   Query results

Saving SQL queries in Access is similar to saving the queries in Chapter 2.

- You can save SQL queries by clicking the Save button on the Quick Access Toolbar, typing a name for the saved query, and then clicking the OK button.
- To change the design of a query that is open already, return to SQL view by clicking the View button (Query Tools Design tab | Results group) and selecting SQL View.
- To change the design of a saved query that is not currently open, double-click the query in the Navigation Pane. If necessary, return to SQL view by clicking the View button arrow (Query Tools Design tab | Results group) and selecting SQL View.

COMPOUND CONDITIONS

The conditions you have seen so far are called simple conditions. The following examples require compound conditions. A **compound condition** is formed by connecting two or more simple conditions using one or both of the following operators: AND and OR. A lesser used BETWEEN operator allows you to specify a range. You also can precede a single condition with the NOT operator to negate a condition.

When you connect simple conditions using the AND operator, all the simple conditions must be true for the compound condition to be true. When you connect simple conditions using the OR operator, the compound condition will be true whenever any of the simple conditions are true. Preceding a condition with the NOT operator reverses the result of the original condition. That is, if the original condition is true, the new condition will be false; if the original condition is false, the new one will be true.

YOUR TURN 3-7

List the descriptions of all tasks in the SOM category *and* priced more than $150.

In this example, you want to list those tasks for which *both* the category is equal to SOM *and* the price is greater than $150. Thus, you form a compound condition using the AND operator, as shown in Figure 3-15. It is common practice to place the AND condition on a separate line and indent it for readability.

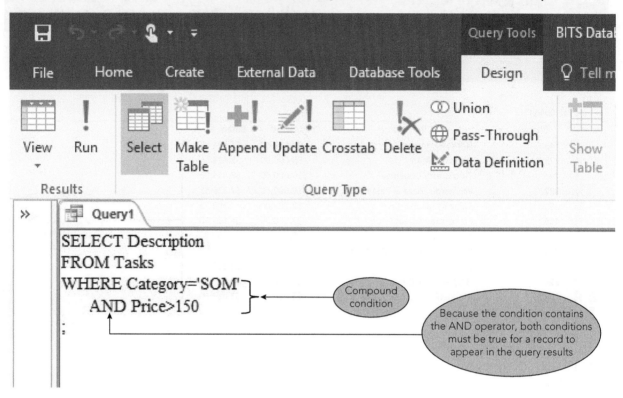

FIGURE 3-15   Compound condition that uses the AND operator

The query results appear in Figure 3-16.

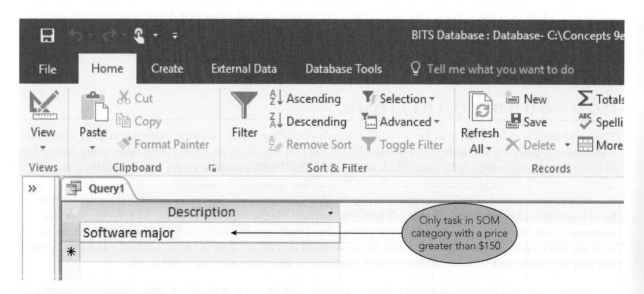

FIGURE 3-16   Query results

YOUR TURN 3-8

List the descriptions of all tasks in the SOM category *or* priced more than $150 or both.

As you would expect, you form compound conditions with the OR operator similar to the way you use the AND operator. The compound condition shown in Figure 3-17 uses the OR operator instead of the AND operator. It is common practice to place the OR condition on a separate line and indent it for readability.

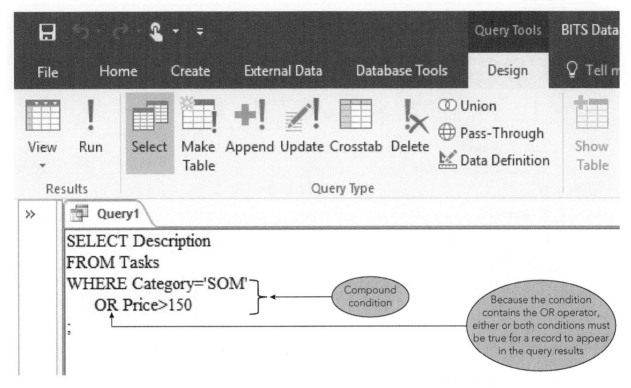

FIGURE 3-17   Compound condition that uses the OR operator

The query results appear in Figure 3-18.

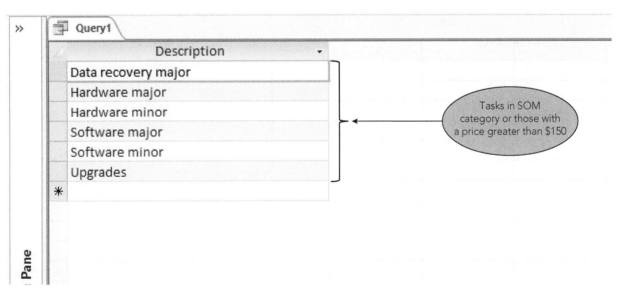

FIGURE 3-18   Query results

YOUR TURN 3-9

List the descriptions of all tasks that are not in the SOM category.

For this example, you could use a simple condition and the "not equal to" operator (< >). As an alternative, you could use the "equals" operator (=) in the condition but precede the entire condition with the NOT operator, as shown in Figure 3-19.

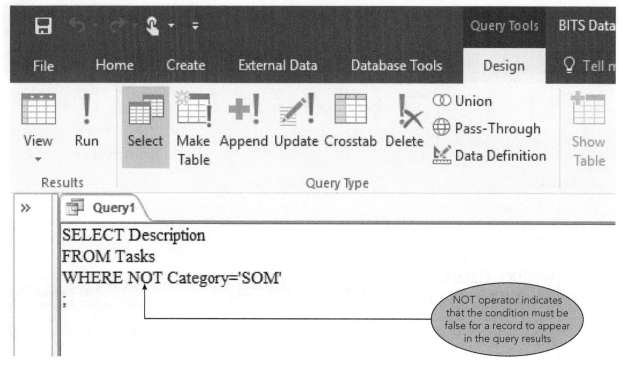

FIGURE 3-19 SQL query with the NOT operator

The query results appear in Figure 3-20.

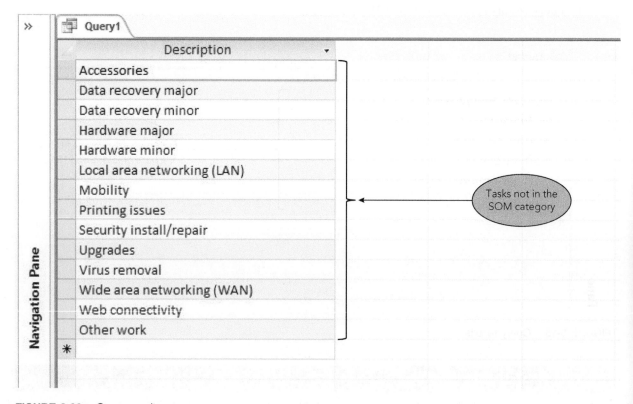

FIGURE 3-20 Query results

YOUR TURN 3-10

List the number, name, and balance of all clients with balances greater than or equal to $1,000 and less than or equal to $5,000.

You could use a WHERE clause and the AND operator (Balance>=1000 AND Balance<=5000). An alternative to this approach uses the BETWEEN operator, as shown in Figure 3-21. The BETWEEN operator is inclusive; it includes the lower number, the higher number, and all numbers in-between.

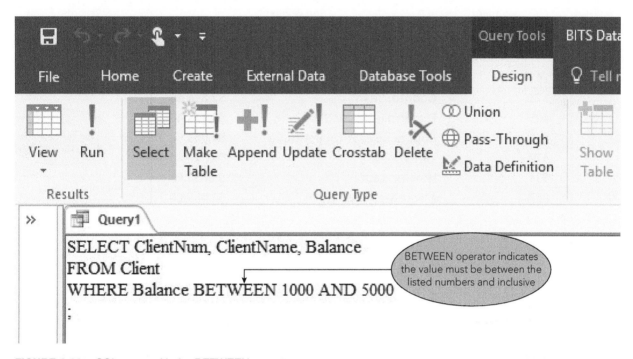

FIGURE 3-21   SQL query with the BETWEEN operator

The query results appear in Figure 3-22.

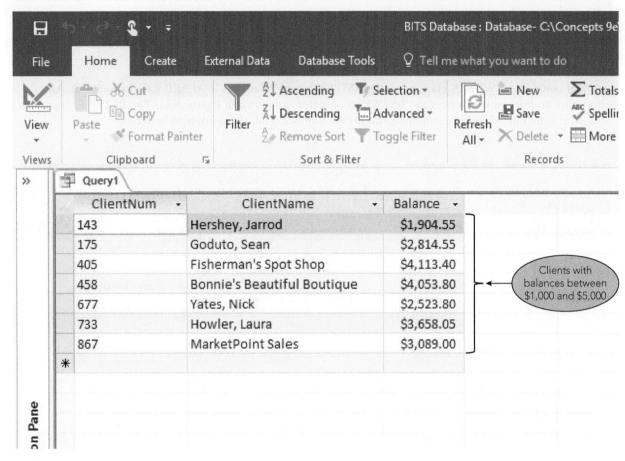

FIGURE 3-22 Query results

The BETWEEN operator is not an essential feature of SQL; you can use the AND operator to obtain the same results. Using the BETWEEN operator, however, does make some SELECT clauses easier to construct.

COMPUTED FIELDS

Similar to QBE, you can include fields in queries that are not in the database but whose values can be computed from existing database fields. A field whose values you derive from existing fields is called a computed field or calculated field. Computed fields can involve addition (+), subtraction (−), multiplication (*), or division (/). The query in Your Turn 3-11, for example, uses subtraction.

YOUR TURN 3-11

List the number, name, and available credit for all clients.

There is no field in the database that stores available credit, but you can compute it using two fields that *are* present in the database: CreditLimit and Balance. The query design shown in Figure 3-23 creates a new field named AvailableCredit, which is computed by subtracting the value in the Balance field from the value in the CreditLimit field (CreditLimit–Balance). By using the word *AS* after the computation, followed by AvailableCredit, you can assign a name to the computed field.

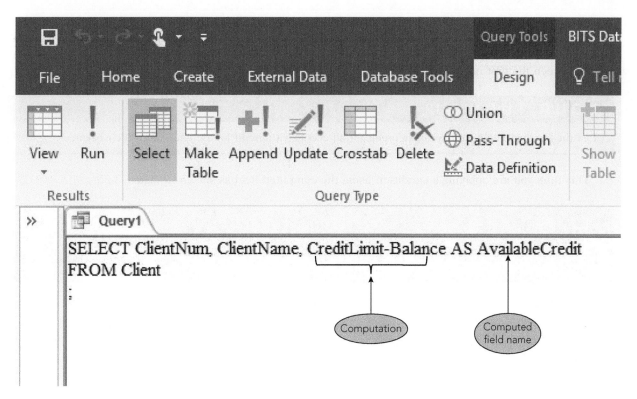

FIGURE 3-23   SQL query with a computed field

The query results appear in Figure 3-24. The column heading for the computed field is the name that you specified in the SELECT clause. (The columns have been resized, which you accomplish by dragging the right boundary of the column heading.)

ClientNum	ClientName	AvailableCredit
143	Hershey, Jarrod	$595.45
175	Goduto, Sean	$2,185.45
299	Two Crafty Cousins	$1,646.00
322	Prichard's Pizza & Pasta	$2,664.45
363	Salazar, Jason	$1,599.25
405	Fisherman's Spot Shop	$3,386.60
449	Seymour, Lindsey	$4,442.30
458	Bonnie's Beautiful Boutique	$3,446.20
677	Yates, Nick	($23.80)
733	Howler, Laura	$1,341.95
826	Harpersburg Bank	$3,175.45
867	MarketPoint Sales	$1,911.00

Computed field name

Available credit amounts

Parentheses indicate a negative amount

FIGURE 3-24   Query results

Computations are not limited to values in number fields. You can combine values in character fields as well. For example, in Access you can combine the values in the FirstName and LastName fields into a single computed field by using the **& operator**. The expression would be *FirstName&' '&LastName*, which places a space between the first name and the last name. The process is called **concatenation**.

YOUR TURN 3-12

List the number, name, and available credit for all clients with credit limits that exceed their balances.

This time you are applying a condition using the computed field as shown in Figure 3-25.

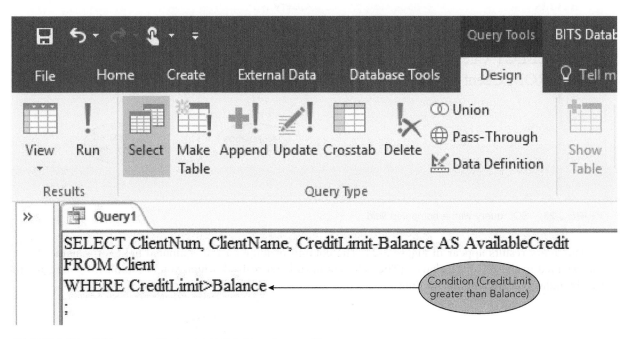

FIGURE 3-25 SQL query with a computed field and a condition

The query results appear in Figure 3-26.

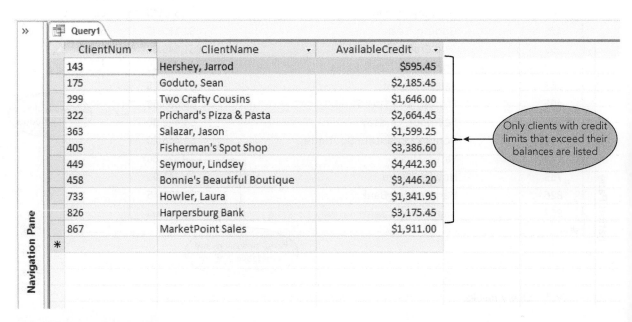

ClientNum	ClientName	AvailableCredit
143	Hershey, Jarrod	$595.45
175	Goduto, Sean	$2,185.45
299	Two Crafty Cousins	$1,646.00
322	Prichard's Pizza & Pasta	$2,664.45
363	Salazar, Jason	$1,599.25
405	Fisherman's Spot Shop	$3,386.60
449	Seymour, Lindsey	$4,442.30
458	Bonnie's Beautiful Boutique	$3,446.20
733	Howler, Laura	$1,341.95
826	Harpersburg Bank	$3,175.45
867	MarketPoint Sales	$1,911.00

Only clients with credit limits that exceed their balances are listed

FIGURE 3-26 Query results

USING SPECIAL OPERATORS (LIKE AND IN)

In most cases, your conditions will involve exact matches, such as finding all clients located in the city of Easton. In some cases, however, exact matches will not work. For example, you might know only that the desired value contains a certain collection of characters. In such cases, you use the LIKE operator with a wildcard.

YOUR TURN 3-13

List the number, name, and complete address of every client located on a street that contains the letters *wood*.

All you know is that the addresses that you want contain a certain collection of characters (*wood*) somewhere in the Street field, but you do not know where. In Access SQL, the asterisk (*) is used as a **wildcard** to represent any collection of characters. (In other versions of SQL, the percent sign (%) is used as a wildcard to represent any collection of characters.) To use a wildcard, include the LIKE operator in the WHERE clause. The query design shown in Figure 3-27 will retrieve information for every client whose street contains some collection of characters including the consecutive letters *wood*. Note that the wildcard(s) and search text are enclosed in single quotation marks.

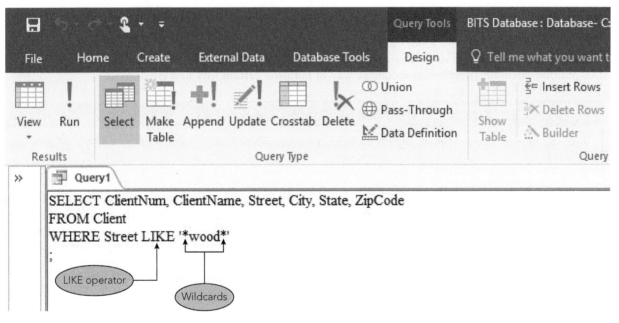

FIGURE 3-27   SQL query with a LIKE operator

The query results appear in Figure 3-28.

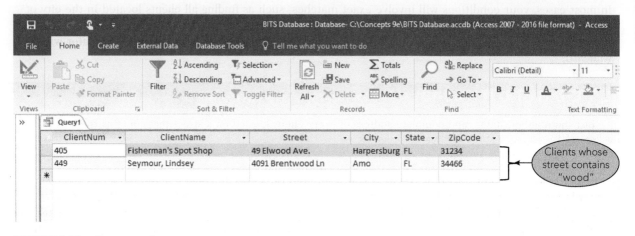

FIGURE 3-28 Query results

Another wildcard in Access SQL is the question mark (?), which represents any individual character. For example, *T?m* represents the letter *T* followed by any single character, followed by the letter *m*. When used in a WHERE clause, it retrieves records that include the words *Tim*, *Tom*, or *T3m*, for example. Other versions of SQL use an underscore (_) instead of the question mark to represent any individual character. *Note:* In a large database, you should use wildcards only when absolutely necessary. Searches involving wildcards can be extremely slow to process.

Another operator, IN, provides a concise way of phrasing certain lists in a condition.

YOUR TURN 3-14

List the number, name, street, and credit limit for every client with a credit limit of $5,000, $7,500, or $10,000.

In this query, you can use the SQL IN operator to determine whether a credit limit is $5,000, $7,500, or $10,000 as shown in Figure 3-29. You could have obtained the same result by using the condition WHERE CreditLimit = 5000 OR CreditLimit = 7500 OR CreditLimit = 10000. The IN approach is a bit simpler, however—the IN clause contains the collection of values 5000, 7500, and 10000, enclosed in parentheses and separated by commas. Recall that numeric data does not need quotation marks. The condition is true for those rows on which the value in the CreditLimit column is in this collection of values.

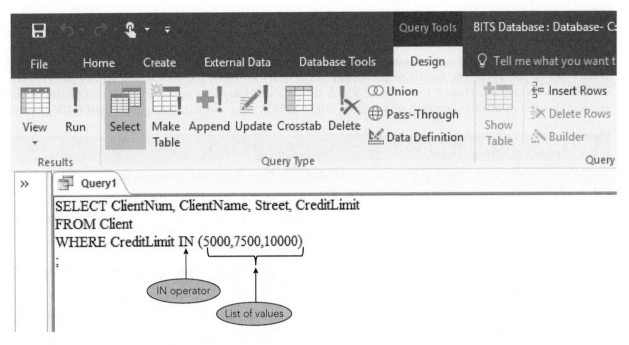

FIGURE 3-29   SQL query with an IN operator

The query results appear in Figure 3-30.

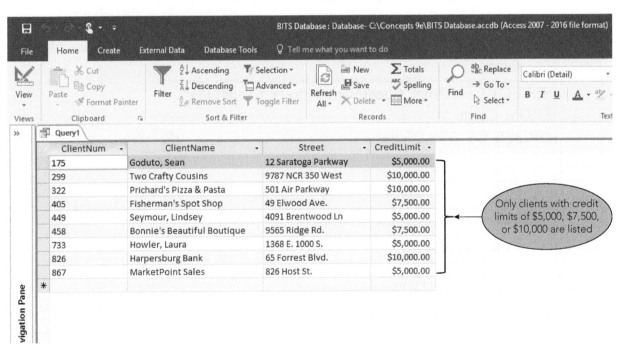

FIGURE 3-30   Query results

SORTING

Recall that the order of rows in a table is considered to be immaterial. From a practical standpoint, this means that when you query a relational database, there are no guarantees concerning the order in which the results will be displayed. The results might appear in the order in which the data was originally entered, but even this is not certain. Thus, if the order in which the data is displayed is important, you *specifically* should request that the results be displayed in a desired order. In SQL, you sort data using the **ORDER BY clause**.

YOUR TURN 3-15

List the number, name, street, and credit limit of all clients. Order (sort) the clients by name.

The field on which to sort data is called a sort key. To sort the output, you include the words *ORDER BY* in the SQL query, followed by the sort key field, as shown in Figure 3-31.

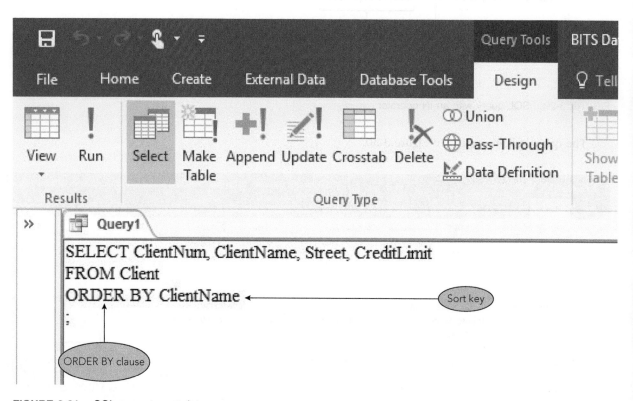

FIGURE 3-31　SQL query to sort data

The query results appear in Figure 3-32.

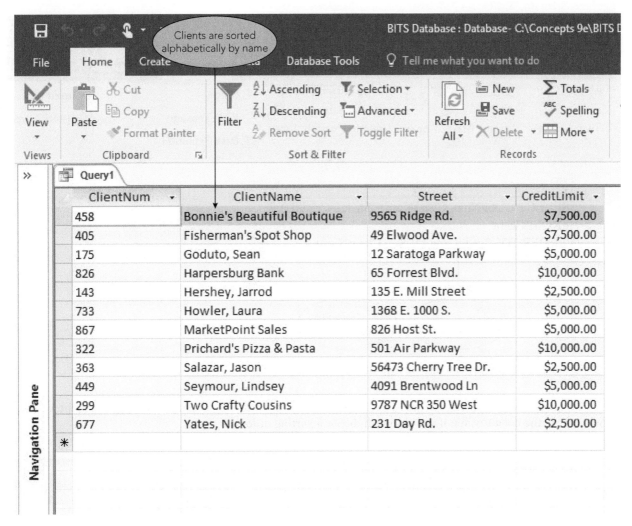

FIGURE 3-32   Query results

Sorting on Multiple Fields

When you need to sort data on two fields, the more important sort key is called the major sort key (also referred to as the primary sort key) and the less important sort key is called the minor sort key (also referred to as the secondary sort key). The major sort key should be listed first in SQL statements.

YOUR TURN 3-16

List the number, name, street, and credit limit of all clients. Order the clients by name within descending credit limit. (In other words, sort the clients by credit limit in descending order. Within each group of clients that have a common credit limit, sort the clients by name.)

In this case, because you need to sort the output by name within credit limit, the CreditLimit field is the major sort key and the ClientName field is the minor sort key. You can specify to sort the output in descending (high-to-low) order by following the sort key with the word *DESC*, as shown in Figure 3-33 on the next page.

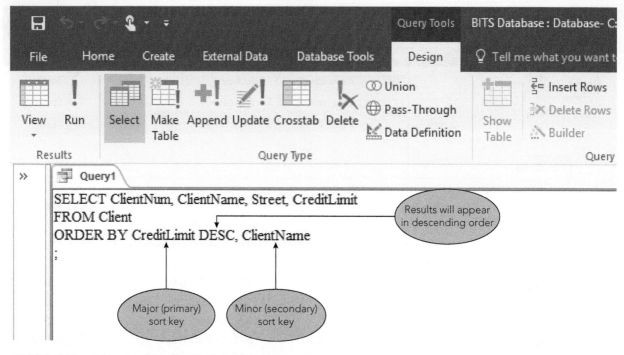

FIGURE 3-33 SQL query to sort data on multiple fields

The query results appear in Figure 3-34. If you wanted to sort in ascending order, SQL uses the word *ASC*. *ASC* is the default value if you do not indicate a sorting order.

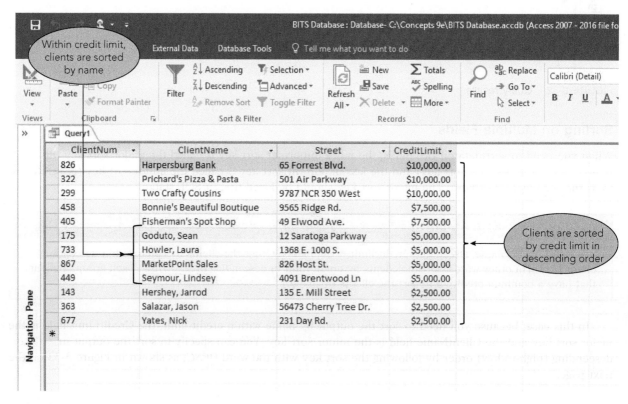

FIGURE 3-34 Query results

BUILT-IN FUNCTIONS

As in QBE applications, SQL has built-in functions (also called aggregate functions) to calculate the number of entries, the sum or average of all the entries in a given column, or the largest or smallest values in a given column. In SQL, these functions are called COUNT, SUM, AVG, MAX, and MIN, respectively.

YOUR TURN 3-17

How many items are in category SOM?

In this query, you need to count the number of rows in the query results that have the value SOM in the Category field. SQL uses an asterisk (*) wildcard with the COUNT function to return the count of all rows, as shown in Figure 3-35. Alternately, you could include a column name in the parentheses to count the number of TaskIDs for example, or the number of descriptions, or the number of entries in any other field. It does not matter which column you choose because all columns will yield the correct count if data is present in the field.

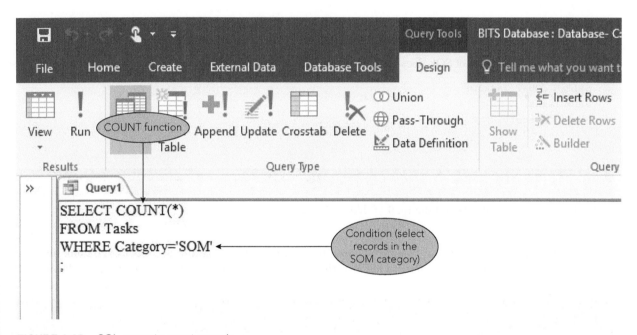

FIGURE 3-35   SQL query to count records

The query results appear in Figure 3-36 on the next page.

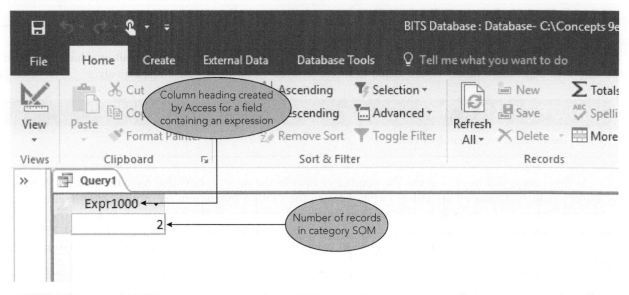

FIGURE 3-36   Query results

If your implementation of SQL does not permit the use of the * symbol, you could write the query as follows:

```
SELECT COUNT(TaskID)
FROM Tasks
WHERE Category='SOM'
;
```

YOUR TURN 3-18

Find the number of clients and the total of their balances.

This example uses COUNT and SUM. When you use the SUM function, you *must* specify the numeric field for which you want a total. (You cannot use SUM with character fields.) The query design appears in Figure 3-37.

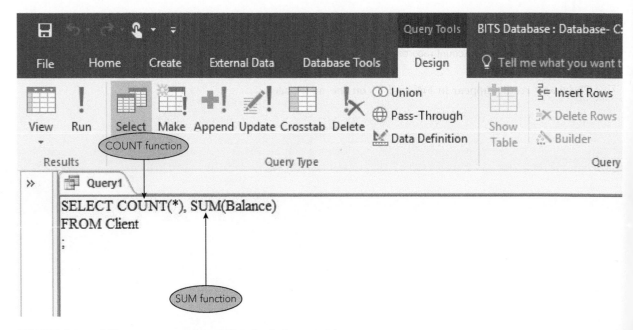

FIGURE 3-37   SQL query to count records and calculate a total

The query results appear in Figure 3-38. (The use of AVG, MAX, and MIN is similar to the use of SUM in that they require numeric fields.)

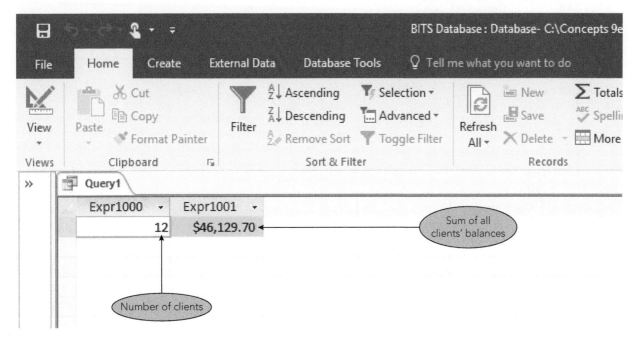

FIGURE 3-38   Query results

YOUR TURN 3-19

Find the total number of clients and the total of their balances. Change the column names for the number of clients and the total of their balances to ClientCount and BalanceTotal, respectively.

As with computed fields, you can use the word *AS* to assign names to these computations, as shown in Figure 3-39.

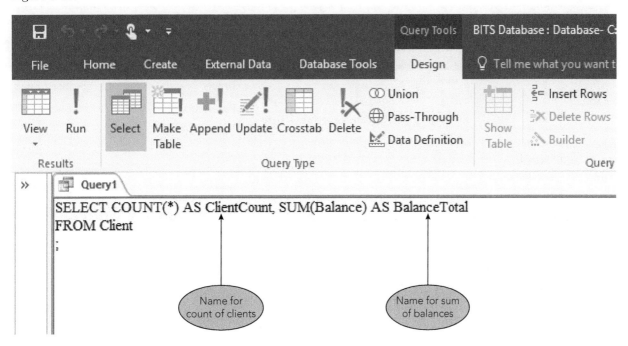

FIGURE 3-39   SQL query to perform calculations and rename columns

The query results appear in Figure 3-40. (The columns have been resized to fit the column names.)

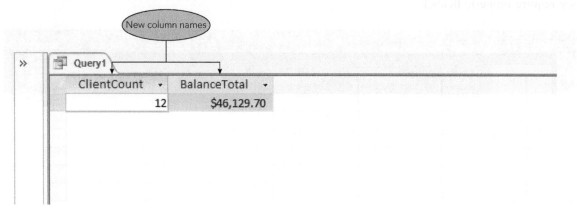

FIGURE 3-40   Query results

SUBQUERIES

In some cases, it is useful to obtain the results you want in two stages. You can do so by placing one query inside another. The inner query is called a **subquery** and is evaluated first. After the subquery has been evaluated, the outer query is evaluated. Although not required, it is common to enclose subqueries in parentheses and indent them for readability.

YOUR TURN 3-20

Using the OrderLine table, list the order number for each order that has a task in the LAN category.

Because the category is not contained in the OrderLine table, you will need to look in the Tasks table first. Use the Tasks table to create a list of TaskIDs for the LAN category (inner query or subquery). Then for the outer query, you can use the OrderLine table to find those order numbers present in any row on which the TASKID is in the results of the inner query. The corresponding query design appears in Figure 3-41. The inner query appears indented for readability purposes only.

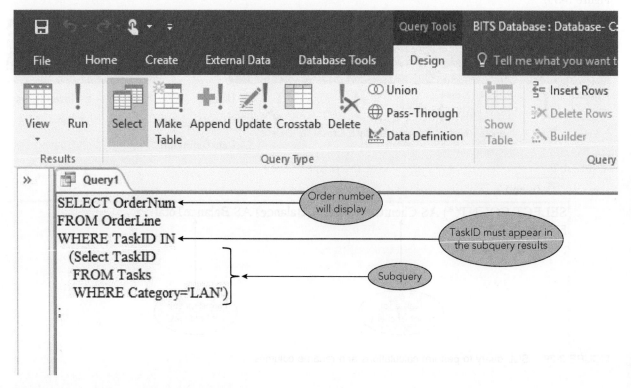

FIGURE 3-41   SQL query with a subquery

The query results appear in Figure 3-42.

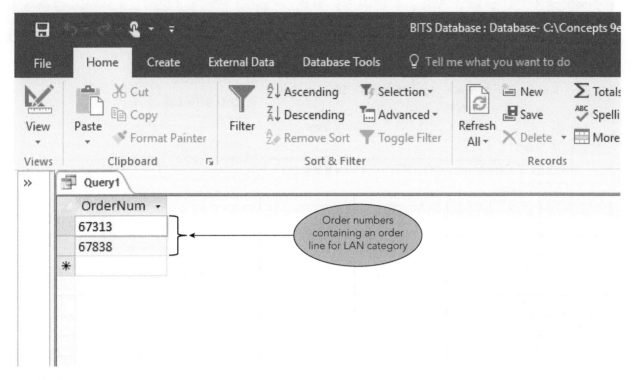

FIGURE 3-42   Query results

The subquery finds all the TaskIDs in the Tasks table with a category of LAN. The subquery is evaluated first, producing a list of TaskIDs internally. After the subquery has been evaluated, the outer query is evaluated. The order numbers display.

GROUPING

Recall from Chapter 2 that grouping means creating groups of records that share some common characteristic. When grouping clients by consultant number, for example, the clients of consultant 19 would form one group, the clients of consultant 22 would form a second group, and the clients of consultant 35 would form a third group.

YOUR TURN 3-21

For each consultant, list the consultant number, the number of clients assigned to the consultant, and the average balance of the consultant's clients. Group the records by consultant number, and order the records by consultant number.

This type of query requires grouping by consultant number to make the correct calculations for each group. To indicate grouping in SQL, you use the **GROUP BY clause**, as shown in Figure 3-43 on the next page. It is important to note that the GROUP BY clause does not mean that the query results will be sorted. To display the query results in a particular order, you must use the **ORDER BY clause**. The query design in Figure 3-43 uses the ORDER BY clause to sort the query results by consultant number.

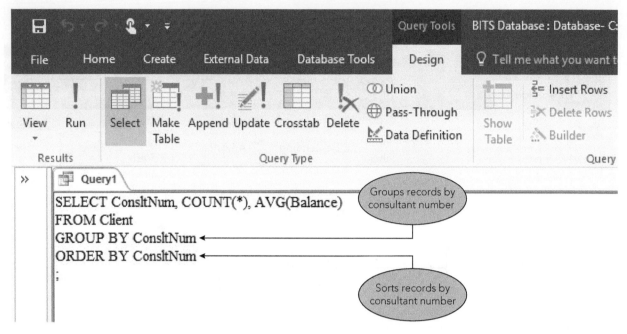

FIGURE 3-43   SQL query to group and sort records

The query results appear in Figure 3-44.

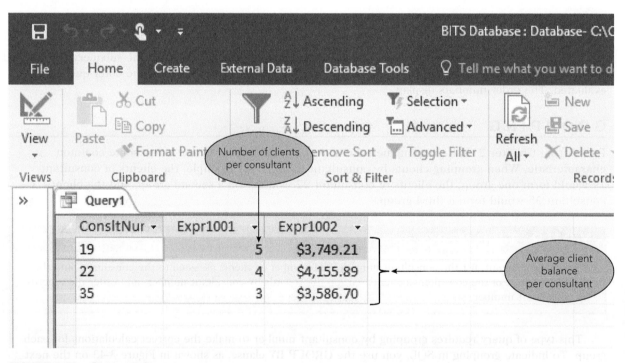

FIGURE 3-44   Query results

When rows are grouped, one line of output is produced for each group. Only statistics calculated for the group or fields whose values are the same for all rows in a group can be displayed in the grouped results.

Q & A 3-5

Question: Why is it appropriate to display the consultant number?
Answer: Because the output is grouped by consultant number, the consultant number in one row in a group must be the same as the consultant number in any other row in the group.

Q & A 3-6

Question: Would it be appropriate to display a client number?
Answer: No, because the client number will vary from one row in a group to another. (SQL could not determine which client number to display for the group.)

YOUR TURN 3-22

For each consultant whose clients' average balance is less than $4,000, list the consultant number, the number of clients assigned to the consultant, and the average balance of the consultant's clients. Rename the count of the number of clients and the average of the balances to NumClients and AverageBalance, respectively. Order the groups by consultant number.

Your Turn 3-21 and 3-22 are similar, but there are two important differences: In Your Turn 3-22, you need to rename the fields, and there is a restriction to display the calculations for only those consultants with clients having an average balance of less than $4,000. In other words, you want to display only those groups for which AVG(Balance) is less than $4,000. This restriction does not apply to individual rows but to *groups*. Because the WHERE clause applies only to rows, it is not the appropriate clause to accomplish the kind of selection you need. Fortunately, the **HAVING clause** is to groups as the WHERE clause is to rows (Figure 3-45).

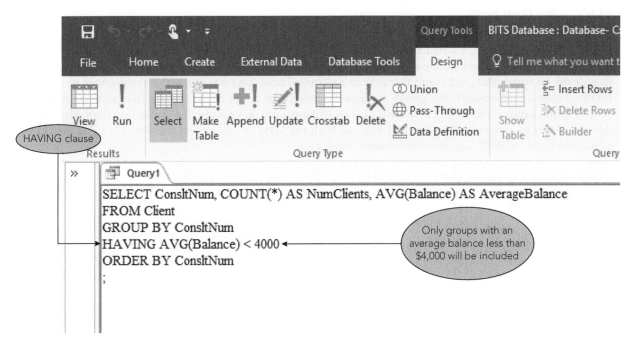

FIGURE 3-45 SQL query to restrict the groups that are included

Q & A 3-7

Question: How is the SELECT clause used when grouping in SQL?

Answer: The SELECT clause only can contain aggregate functions or fields that are then listed in the GROUP BY clause.

The query results appear in Figure 3-46. In this case, the row created for a group will be displayed only when the average client balance is less than $4,000.

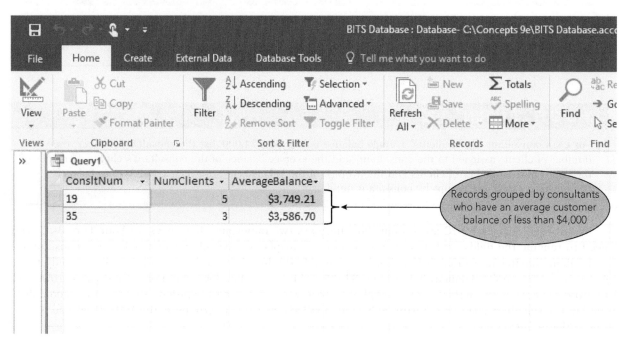

FIGURE 3-46   Query results

You can include both a WHERE clause and a HAVING clause in the same query design, as shown in Figure 3-47. In this example, the condition in the WHERE clause restricts the rows from the Client table to those rows on which the credit limit is less than $10,000. These rows are grouped by consultant number. The HAVING clause then restricts the groups to those for which the count of the rows in the group is greater than two. In other words, more than two clients of a consultant must have a credit limit of less than $10,000 for the consultant to appear in the results. If you use both the WHERE clause and the GROUP BY clause in the same query, the WHERE clause should always come first.

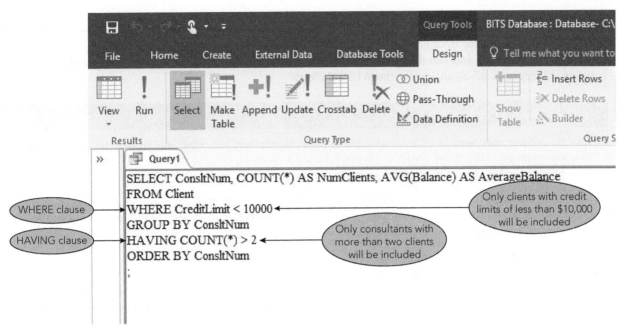

FIGURE 3-47 SQL query that includes WHERE and HAVING clauses

The query results appear in Figure 3-48.

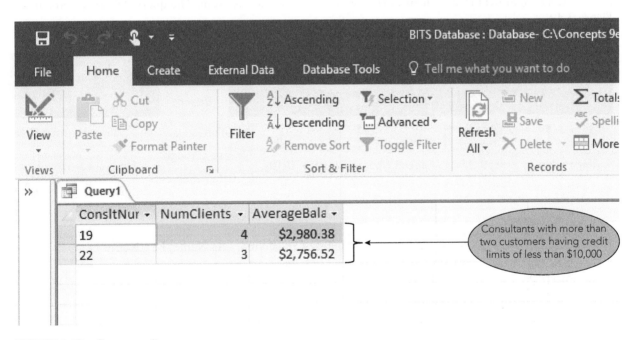

FIGURE 3-48 Query results

JOINING TABLES

Many queries require data from more than one table. As with QBE and relational algebra, it is necessary to be able to join tables so you can find rows in two or more related tables. In SQL, this is accomplished by entering the appropriate conditions in the WHERE clause.

YOUR TURN 3-23

List the number and name of each client together with the number, last name, and first name of the consultant who represents the client. Order the records by client number.

Because the numbers and names of clients are in the Client table and the numbers and names of consultants are in the Consultant table, you need to include both tables in your SQL query. To join the tables, you will construct the SQL command as follows:

1. In the SELECT clause, list all fields you want to display.
2. In the FROM clause, list all tables involved in the query.
3. In the WHERE clause, give the condition that will restrict the data to be retrieved to only those rows from the two tables that match; that is, you'll restrict it to the rows that have common values in matching fields.

As in relational algebra, it is often necessary to qualify a field name to specify the particular field you are referencing. To qualify a field name, precede the name of the field with the name of the table, followed by a period. For example, the ConsltNum field in the Consultant table is written as Consultant.ConsltNum, and the ConsltNum field in the Client table is written as Client.ConsltNum. The query design appears in Figure 3-49.

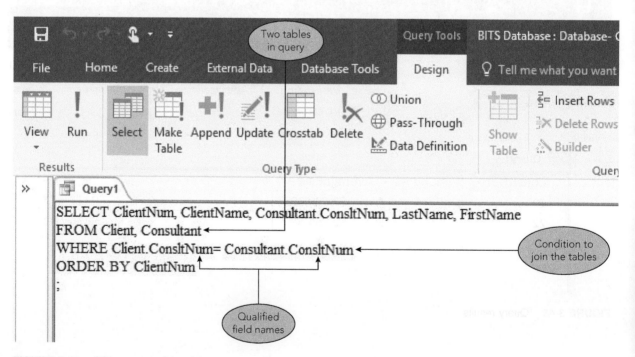

FIGURE 3-49 SQL query to join tables

The query results appear in Figure 3-50.

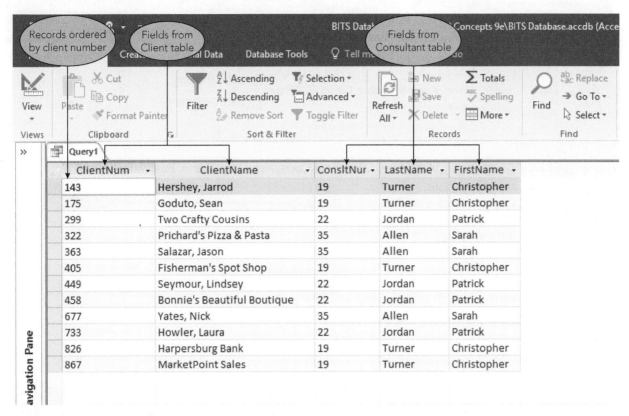

FIGURE 3-50   Query results

When there is potential ambiguity in listing field names, you *must* qualify the fields involved; that is, if two fields are named the same in two different tables, you must list the table name. It is permissible to qualify other fields as well, even if there is no possible confusion. Some people prefer to qualify all fields; however, it does make the code more difficult to read. In this text, however, you will qualify fields only when it is necessary to do so.

YOUR TURN 3-24

List the number and name of each client whose credit limit is $10,000, together with the number, last name, and first name of the consultant who represents the client. Order the records by client number.

Previously, in Figure 3-49, the condition in the WHERE clause served only to relate a client to a consultant. Although relating a client to a consultant is essential in Your Turn 3-24 as well, you also need to restrict the output to only those clients with credit limits of $10,000. You can accomplish this goal by using the AND operator to create a compound condition, as shown in Figure 3-51 on the next page. It is good practice to list the join criteria in the WHERE clause before indicating any row conditions or restrictions.

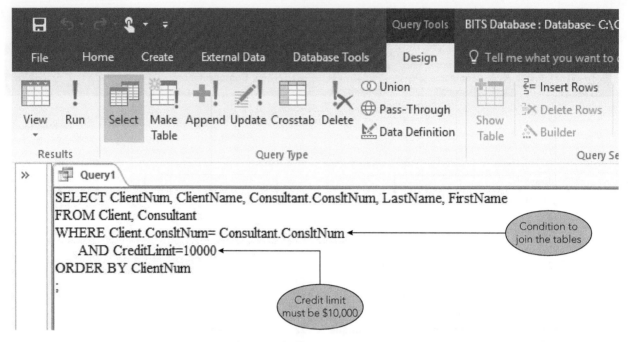

FIGURE 3-51   SQL query to restrict the records in a join

The query results appear in Figure 3-52.

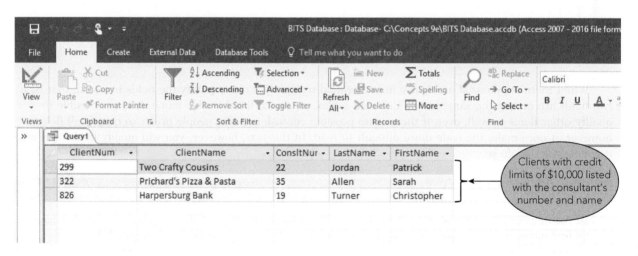

FIGURE 3-52   Query results

Complex Joins

It is possible to join more than two tables which is called a **complex join**. The procedure for joining more than two tables is essentially the same as the one for joining two tables. For each pair of tables to join, you must include a condition indicating how the tables are related. The number of join criteria conditions is always one less than the number of tables. For example. if you are joining three tables, you will need two conditions; if you are joining four tables, you will need three conditions; and so on.

The order number and date are stored in the WorkOrders table. The client number and name are stored in the Client table. The TaskID and description are stored in the Tasks table. The description and quoted price are stored in the OrderLine table. Thus, you need to join *four* tables: WorkOrders, Client, Tasks, and OrderLine, which requires that the condition in the WHERE clause be a compound condition, as shown in Figure 3-53. The first condition relates an order to a client, using the common ClientNum columns. The second condition relates the order to an order line, using the common OrderNum columns. The final condition relates the order line to an item, using the common TaskID columns.

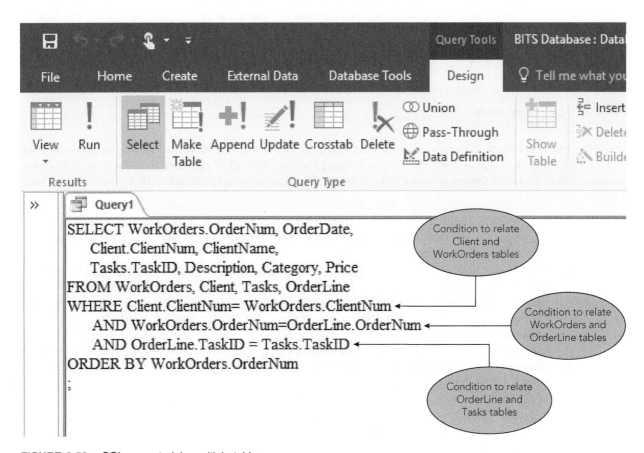

FIGURE 3-53   SQL query to join multiple tables

The query results appear in Figure 3-54.

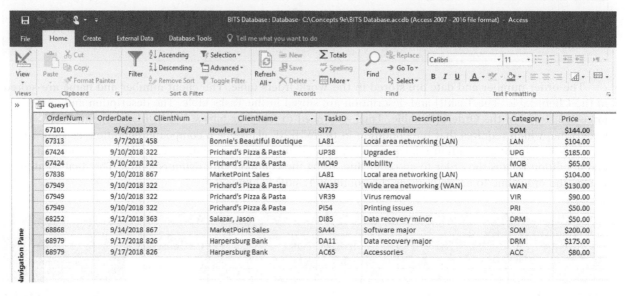

FIGURE 3-54 Query results

The query shown in Figure 3-53 on the previous page is more complex than many of the previous ones. You might think that SQL is not such an easy language to use after all. If you take it one step at a time, however, you will find that the query is not very difficult. To construct a detailed query in a systematic fashion, do the following:

1. List in the SELECT clause all the columns you want to display. If the name of a column appears in more than one table, precede the column name with the table name and a period; that is, qualify the column name.

2. List in the FROM clause all the tables involved in the query. Usually you include the tables that contain the columns listed in the SELECT clause. Occasionally, however, there might be a table that does not contain any columns used in the SELECT clause but that does contain columns used in the WHERE clause. In this case, you must also list the table in the FROM clause. For example, if you do not need to list a client number or name but you do need to list the consultant name, you would not include any columns from the Client table in the SELECT clause. The Client table is still required in the FROM clause, however, because you must include columns from it in the WHERE clause.

3. Make sure the join criteria in the WHERE clause precedes any restrictions.

4. Take one pair of related tables at a time and indicate, in the WHERE clause, the condition that relates the tables. Join these conditions with the AND operator. When there are other conditions, include them in the WHERE clause and connect them to the other conditions with the AND operator.

UNION

Recall from Chapter 2 that the union of two tables is a table containing all rows that are in the first table, the second table, or both tables. The two tables involved in a union *must* have the same structure, or be union compatible; in other words, they must have the same number of fields, and their corresponding fields must have the same data types. If, for example, the first field in one table contains client numbers, the first field in the other table also must contain client numbers.

YOUR TURN 3-26

List the number and name of all clients that are represented by consultant 19 or that currently have orders on file or both.

Because the two criteria are so different, you cannot use a simple OR criterion. Instead, you can create a table containing the number and name of all clients that are represented by consultant 19 by selecting client numbers and names from the Client table in which the consultant number is 19. You can then create another table containing the number and name of every client that currently has orders on file by joining the Client and WorkOrders tables. The two tables created by this process have the same structure—fields named ClientNum and ClientName. Because the tables are union compatible, it is possible to take the union of these two tables, which is the appropriate operation for this example, as shown in Figure 3-55.

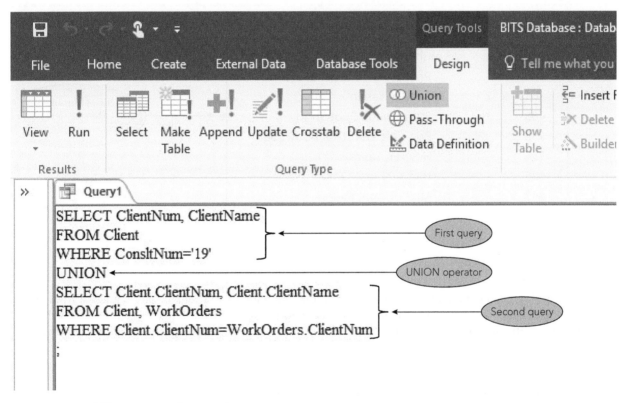

FIGURE 3-55   SQL query to perform a union

The query results appear in Figure 3-56.

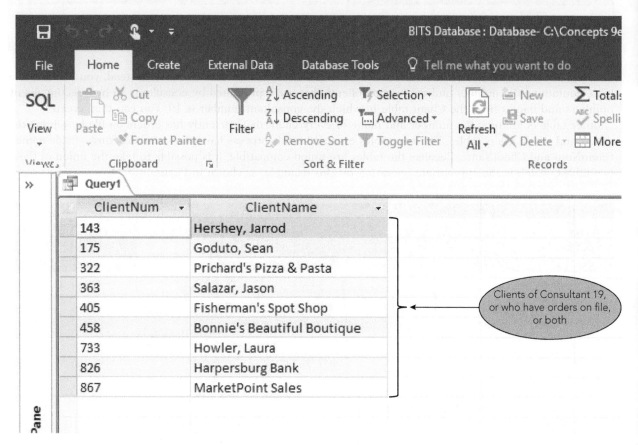

FIGURE 3-56 Query results

If the SQL implementation truly supports the union operation, it will remove any duplicate rows. For instance, any clients that are represented by consultant 19 *and* that currently have orders on file will not appear twice in the query results. Some SQL implementations have a union operation but will not remove duplicate values.

UPDATING TABLES

There are more uses for SQL than simply retrieving data from a database and creating tables. SQL has several other capabilities, including the ability to update a database, as demonstrated in the following examples.

Again, if you plan to work through the examples in this section using Access, you should use a copy of the original BITS database because the version of the database used in subsequent chapters does not include these changes. As an alternative, if you are using a DBMS (such as Oracle or SQL Server) that supports the ROLLBACK command, which reverses changes to a database, you can ensure that your changes are undone by typing the word *ROLLBACK* before exiting the DBMS. If you have any questions concerning which of these (or other) approaches is appropriate for you, check with your instructor.

YOUR TURN 3-27

Change the street address of client 677 to 1445 Rivard.

You can use the SQL **UPDATE** and **SET** commands to make changes to existing data. After the word *UPDATE*, you indicate the table to be updated. After the word *SET*, you indicate the field to be changed, followed by an equals sign and the new value. Finally, include a condition in the WHERE clause so that only the records that satisfy the condition will be changed; otherwise, you will change all records in the table. These changes are permanent; there is no undo or rollback process. The SQL command for this example appears in Figure 3-57. When you run this query in Access, a dialog box opens and indicates the number of records the UPDATE command will affect. In this case, you would update only one record because the WHERE clause selects only one record, for client 677.

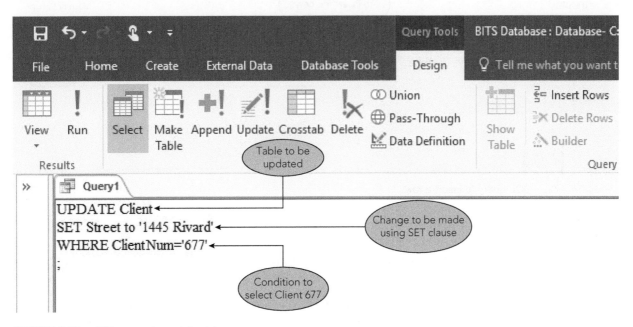

FIGURE 3-57   SQL query to update data

YOUR TURN 3-28

Add a new consultant to the Consultant table. Her number is 75; her name is Bernita Argy; and her address is 424 Bournemouth, Easton, FL 33998. She will work 40 hours a week and earn $17.50 an hour.

To add new data to a table, you use the **INSERT** command. After the words *INSERT INTO*, you list the name of the table, followed by the word *VALUES*. Then you list the values in parentheses for each of the columns, as shown in Figure 3-58 on the next page. All values must be in the same order as the fields were defined, or they must be listed explicitly. Character values must be enclosed within quotation marks, and the values for each column are separated by commas. When you run this query in Access, a dialog box opens and indicates the number of records the INSERT command will append to the table. In this case, you would add one record to the Consultant table.

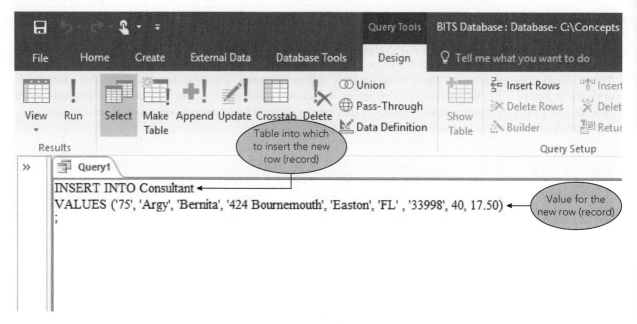

FIGURE 3-58   SQL query to insert a row

YOUR TURN 3-29

Delete any row in the OrderLine table in which the TaskID is UP38.

To delete data from the database, use the **DELETE** command, which consists of the word *DELETE* followed by a FROM clause identifying the table. Use a WHERE clause to specify a condition to select the records to delete. If you omit the condition for selecting the records to delete, when you run the query, it will delete all records from the table.

The DELETE command for this example is shown in Figure 3-59. When you run this query in Access, a dialog box opens and indicates the number of records the DELETE command will delete. In this case, you would delete only one record because the WHERE clause selects TaskID UP38 and there is only one such order line.

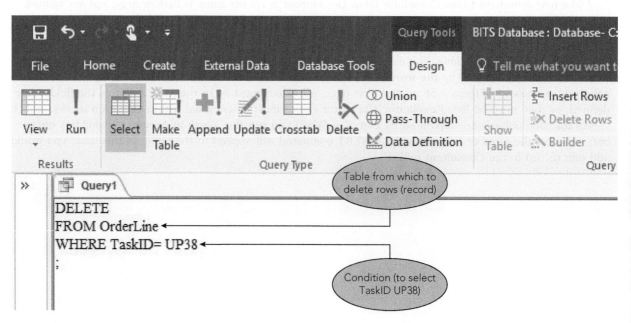

FIGURE 3-59   SQL query to delete rows

CREATING A TABLE FROM A QUERY

You can save the results of a query as a table by including the **INTO clause** in the query, as illustrated in Your Turn 3-30.

YOUR TURN 3-30

Create a new table named SmallClient consisting of all fields from the Client table in which the credit limit is less than or equal to $7,500.

To create the SmallClient table, create a query to select all fields from the Client table, include a WHERE clause to restrict the rows to those in which CreditLimit <= 7500, and include an INTO clause. The INTO clause precedes the FROM clause and consists of the word *INTO* followed by the name of the table to be created. The query appears in Figure 3-60. When you run this query in Access, a dialog box opens and indicates the number of records the INTO clause will paste into the new table. In this case, you would add nine rows to the SmallClient table.

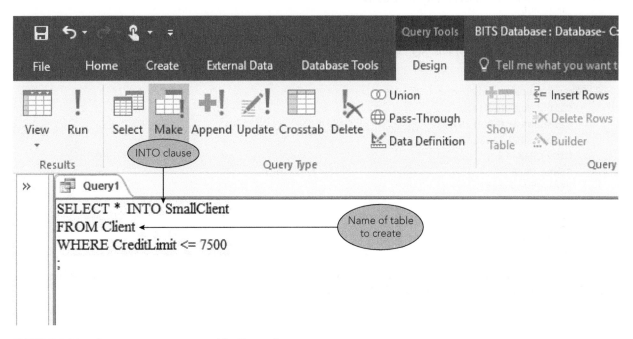

FIGURE 3-60   Query to create a new table (Access)

After you execute this query, you can use the SmallClient table shown in Figure 3-61 on the next page, just as any other table.

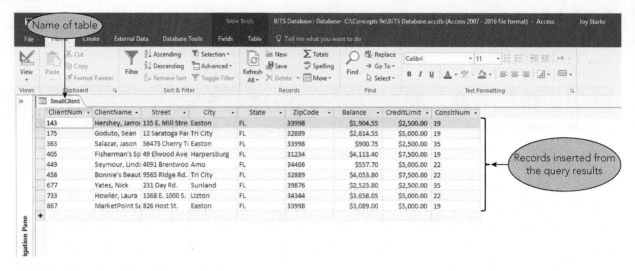

FIGURE 3-61　SmallClient table created by query

Note: The SQL implementation for Oracle does not support the query shown in Figure 3-60. To accomplish the same task using Oracle SQL, you would create the SmallClient table using the following CREATE TABLE command.

```
CREATE TABLE SmallClient (
   ClientNum CHAR(3),
   ClientName CHAR(35),
   Street CHAR(15),
   City CHAR(15),
   State CHAR(2),
   ZipCode CHAR(5),
   Balance DECIMAL(8,2),
   CreditLimit DECIMAL(8,2),
   ConsltNum CHAR(2) )
;
```

After executing the CREATE TABLE command, you would then use the following INSERT command to insert the appropriate data into the SmallClient table.

```
INSERT INTO SmallClient
SELECT *
FROM Client
WHERE CreditLimit<=7500

;
```

SUMMARY OF SQL COMMANDS

This section contains generic versions of SQL commands for every Your Turn example presented in this chapter. (The example numbers match the ones used in the chapter, making it easy to return to the page in the chapter on which the example is described.) In most cases, commands in Access are identical to the generic versions. For those commands that differ in other SQL implementations, both the generic version and the Access version are included. (If you use a computer to complete these exercises, use a copy of the BITS database so you will still have the original data when you complete Chapter 4.)

YOUR TURN 3-1

Using the BITS database, list the number, name, and balance of all clients.

```
SELECT ClientNum, ClientName, Balance
FROM Client
;
```

YOUR TURN 3-2

List the complete Tasks table.

```
SELECT *
FROM Tasks
;
```

YOUR TURN 3-3

List the name of every client with a $10,000 credit limit.

```
SELECT ClientName
FROM Client
WHERE CreditLimit=10000
;
```

YOUR TURN 3-4

Find the name of client 458.

```
SELECT ClientName
FROM Client
WHERE ClientNum='458'
;
```

YOUR TURN 3-5

Find the client name for every client located in the city of Easton.

```
SELECT ClientName
FROM Client
WHERE City='Easton'
;
```

YOUR TURN 3-6

List the number, name, credit limit, and balance for all clients with credit limits that exceed their balances.

```
SELECT ClientNum, ClientName, CreditLimit, Balance
FROM Client
WHERE CreditLimit>Balance
;
```

YOUR TURN 3-7

List the descriptions of all tasks in the SOM category *and* priced more than $150.

```
SELECT Description
FROM Tasks
WHERE Category='SOM'
  AND Price>150
;
```

YOUR TURN 3-8

List the descriptions of all tasks in the SOM category *or* priced more than $150 or both.

```
SELECT Description
FROM Tasks
WHERE Category = 'SOM'
  OR Price>150
;
```

YOUR TURN 3-9

List the descriptions of all tasks that are not in the SOM category.

```
SELECT Description
FROM Tasks
WHERE NOT Category = 'SOM'
;
```

YOUR TURN 3-10

List the number, name, and balance of all clients with balances greater than or equal to $1,000 and less than or equal to $5,000.

```
SELECT ClientNum, ClientName, Balance
FROM Client
WHERE Balance BETWEEN 1000 AND 5000
;
```

YOUR TURN 3-11

List the number, name, and available credit for all clients.

```
SELECT ClientNum, ClientName, CreditLimit-Balance AS AvailableCredit
FROM Client
;
```

YOUR TURN 3-12

List the number, name, and available credit for all clients with credit limits that exceed their balances.

```
SELECT ClientNum, ClientName, CreditLimit-Balance AS AvailableCredit
FROM Client
WHERE CreditLimit>Balance
;
```

YOUR TURN 3-13

List the number, name, and complete address of every client located on a street that contains the letters *wood*.

```
SELECT ClientNum, ClientName, Street, City, State, ZipCode
FROM Client
WHERE Street LIKE '%wood%'
;
```

Access:

```
SELECT ClientNum, ClientName, Street, City, State, ZipCode
FROM Client
WHERE Street LIKE '*wood*'
;
```

YOUR TURN 3-14

List the number, name, street, and credit limit for every client with a credit limit of $5,000, $7,500, or $10,000.

```
SELECT ClientNum, ClientName, Street, CreditLimit
FROM Client
WHERE CreditLimit IN (5000, 7500, 10000)
;
```

YOUR TURN 3-15

List the number, name, street, and credit limit of all clients. Order (sort) the clients by name.

```
SELECT ClientNum, ClientName, Street, CreditLimit
FROM Client
ORDER BY ClientName
;
```

YOUR TURN 3-16

List the number, name, street, and credit limit of all clients. Order the clients by name within descending credit limit. (In other words, sort the clients by credit limit in descending order. Within each group of clients that have a common credit limit, sort the clients by name.)

```
SELECT ClientNum, ClientName, Street, CreditLimit
FROM Client
ORDER BY CreditLimit DESC, ClientName
;
```

YOUR TURN 3-17

How many items are in category SOM?

```
SELECT COUNT(*)
FROM Tasks
WHERE Category = 'SOM'
;
```

YOUR TURN 3-18

Find the number of clients and the total of their balances.

```
SELECT COUNT(*), SUM(Balance)
FROM Client
;
```

YOUR TURN 3-19

Find the total number of clients and the total of their balances. Change the column names for the number of clients and the total of their balances to ClientCount and BalanceTotal, respectively.

```
SELECT COUNT(*) AS ClientCount, SUM(Balance) AS BalanceTotal
From Client
;
```

YOUR TURN 3-20

Using the OrderLine table, list the order number for each order that has a task in the LAN category.

```
SELECT OrderNum
FROM OrderLine
WHERE TaskID IN (
    SELECT TaskID
    FROM Tasks
    WHERE Category = 'LAN')
;
```

YOUR TURN 3-21

For each consultant, list the consultant number, the number of clients assigned to the consultant, and the average balance of the consultant's clients. Group the records by consultant number, and order the records by consultant number.

```
SELECT ConsltNum, COUNT(*), AVG(Balance)
FROM Client
GROUP BY ConsltNum
ORDER BY ConsltNum
;
```

YOUR TURN 3-22

For each consultant whose clients' average balance is less than $4,000, list the consultant number, the number of clients assigned to the consultant, and the average balance of the consultant's clients. Rename the count of the number of clients and the average of the balances to NumClients and AverageBalance, respectively. Order the groups by consultant number.

```sql
SELECT ConsltNum, COUNT(*) AS NumClients, AVG(Balance) AS AverageBalance
FROM Client
GROUP BY ConsltNum
HAVING AVG(Balance)<4000
ORDER BY ConsltNum
;
```

YOUR TURN 3-23

List the number and name of each client together with the number, last name, and first name of the consultant who represents the client. Order the records by client number.

```sql
SELECT ClientNum, ClientName, Consultant.ConsltNum, LastName, FirstName
FROM Client, Consultant
WHERE Client.ConsltNum=Consultant.ConsltNum
ORDER BY ClientNum
;
```

YOUR TURN 3-24

List the number and name of each client whose credit limit is $10,000, together with the number, last name, and first name of the consultant who represents the client. Order the records by client number.

```sql
SELECT ClientNum, ClientName, Consultant.ConsltNum, LastName, FirstName
FROM Client, Consultant
WHERE Client.ConsltNum=Consultant.ConsltNum
  AND CreditLimit=10000
ORDER BY ClientNum
;
```

YOUR TURN 3-25

For every work order, list the order number, order date, client number, and client name. In addition, for each order line within the order, list the TaskID, description, category, and price. Order the records by order number.

```sql
SELECT WorkOrders.OrderNum, OrderDate, Client.ClientNum,
   ClientName, Tasks.TaskID, Description, Category, QuotedPrice
FROM WorkOrders, Client, OrderLine, Item
WHERE Client.ClientNum=WorkOrders.ClientNum
  AND WorkOrders.OrderNum=OrderLine.OrderNum
  AND OrderLine.TaskID=Tasks.TaskID
ORDER BY WorkOrders.OrderNum
;
```

YOUR TURN 3-26

List the number and name of all clients that are represented by consultant 19 or that currently have orders on file or both.

```
SELECT ClientNum, ClientName
FROM Client
WHERE ConsltNum='19'
UNION
SELECT Client.ClientNum, ClientName
FROM Client, WorkOrders
WHERE Client.ClientNum=WorkOrders.ClientNum
;
```

YOUR TURN 3-27

Change the street address of client 677 to 1445 Rivard.

```
UPDATE Client
SET Street = '1445 Rivard'
WHERE ClientNum = '677'
;
```

YOUR TURN 3-28

Add a new consultant to the Consultant table. Her number is 75; her name is Bernita Argy; and her address is 424 Bournemouth, Easton, FL 33998. She will work 40 hours a week and earn $17.50 an hour.

```
INSERT INTO Consultant
VALUES ('75','Argy','Bernita','424 Bournemouth','Easton','FL','33998',40,17.50)
;
```

YOUR TURN 3-29

Delete any row in the OrderLine table in which the TaskID is UP38.

```
DELETE
FROM OrderLine
WHERE TaskID='UP38'
;
```

YOUR TURN 3-30

Create a new table named SmallClient consisting of all fields from the Client table in which the credit limit is less than or equal to $7,500.

```
SELECT * INTO SmallClient
FROM Client
WHERE CreditLimit<=7500
;
```

Summary

- Structured Query Language (SQL) is a language that is used to manipulate relational databases.
- The basic form of an SQL query is SELECT-FROM-WHERE.
- Use the CREATE TABLE command to describe a table's layout to the DBMS, which creates the table in the database.
- In SQL retrieval commands, fields are listed in the SELECT clause, tables are listed in the FROM clause, and conditions are listed in the WHERE clause.
- In conditions, character values must be enclosed in single quotation marks.
- Compound conditions are formed by combining simple conditions using either or both of the following operators: AND and OR.
- Sorting is accomplished using the ORDER BY clause. The field on which the records are sorted is called the sort key. When the data is sorted in more than one field, the more important field is called the major sort key or primary sort key. The less important field is called the minor sort key or secondary sort key.
- Grouping is accomplished in SQL by using the GROUP BY clause. To restrict the rows to be displayed, use the HAVING clause.
- Joining tables is accomplished in SQL by using a condition that relates matching rows in the tables to be joined.
- SQL has the built-in (also called aggregate) functions COUNT, SUM, AVG, MAX, and MIN.
- One SQL query can be placed inside another. The subquery is evaluated first.
- The union of the results of two queries is specified by placing the UNION operator between the two queries.
- Computed fields are specified in SQL queries by including the expression, followed by the word *AS*, followed by the name of the computed field.
- The INSERT command is used to add a new row to a table.
- The UPDATE command is used to change existing data.
- The DELETE command is used to delete records.
- The INTO clause is used in a SELECT clause to create a table containing the results of the query.

Key Terms

& operator	INTEGER
CHAR(*n*)	INTO clause
complex join	ORDER BY clause
compound condition	reserved word
concatenation	SELECT clause
CREATE TABLE	SET
DATE	simple condition
DECIMAL(*p*, *q*)	SMALLINT
DELETE	SQL (Structured Query Language)
FROM clause	subquery
GROUP BY clause	UPDATE
HAVING clause	WHERE clause
INSERT	wildcard

Review Questions

1. Describe the process of creating a table in SQL and the different data types you can use for fields.

2. What is the purpose of the WHERE clause in SQL? Which comparison operators can you use in a WHERE clause?

3. How do you write a compound condition in an SQL query? When is a compound condition true?

4. What is a computed field? How can you use one in an SQL query? How do you assign a name to a computed field?

5. How do you use the LIKE operator in an SQL query?

6. How do you use the IN operator in an SQL query?

7. How do you sort data in SQL? When there is more than one sort key, how do you indicate which one is the major sort key? How do you sort data in descending order?

8. What are the SQL built-in functions? How do you use them in an SQL query?

9. What is a subquery? When is a subquery executed?

10. How do you group data in SQL? When you group data in SQL, are there any restrictions on the items that you can include in the SELECT clause? Explain.

11. How do you join tables in SQL?

12. In a complex join, how is the number of tables you wish to join related to the number of WHERE conditions?

13. How do you qualify the name of a field in an SQL query? When is it necessary to do so?

14. How do you take the union of two tables in SQL? What criteria must the tables meet to make a union possible?

15. Describe the three update commands in SQL.

16. How do you save the results of an SQL query as a table?

17. Why is the data type for the ZipCode field CHAR and not SMALLINT or INTEGER? Is the length of the field long enough? Why or why not?

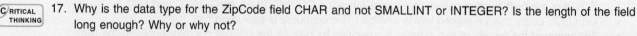
18. You need to delete the OrderLine table from the BITS database. Will the following command work? Why or why not?

```
DELETE
FROM OrderLine
;
```

BITS Corporation Exercises

In the following exercises, you will use the data in the BITS database shown in Figure 1-5 in Chapter 1. (If you use a computer to complete these exercises, use a copy of the original BITS database so you will still have the original data when you complete Chapter 4.) In each step, use SQL to obtain the desired results. You can use a DBMS to complete the exercises using a computer, or you can simply write the SQL command to complete each step. Check with your instructor if you are uncertain about which approach to take.

1. List the number and name of all clients.

2. List the complete Tasks table.

3. List the number and name of every client represented by consultant 22.

4. List the number and name of all clients that are represented by consultant 22 *and* that have credit limits of $10,000.

5. List the number and name of all clients that are represented by consultant 22 *or* that have credit limits of $10,000.

6. For each work order, list the order number, order date, number of the client that placed the order, and name of the client that placed the order.

7. List the number and name of all clients represented by Sarah Allen.

8. How many clients have a credit limit of $10,000?

9. Find the total of the balances for all clients represented by consultant 35.

10. List the name and remaining credit (CreditLimit−Balance) for each client.

11. List all columns and all rows in the Client table. Sort the results by name.

12. List all columns and all rows in the Tasks table. Sort the results by price within category.

13. For each consultant, list the consultant last name, the average balance of the consultant's clients, and the number of clients assigned to the consultant. Group the records by consultant name, and order the records by consultant name.

14. Create a new table named Sept21 to contain the columns OrderNum, TaskID, Description, ScheduledDate, QuotedPrice for all rows on which the ScheduledDate is 9/21/2018.

15. In the Sept21 table, change the description of TaskID PI54 to "Misc. Printing."

16. In the Sept21 table, add a new order. The order number is 69123. The TaskID is OT99. The scheduled date is 9/21/2018. The quoted price is $99.99. The description is Other work.

17. There are two ways to create the query in Exercise 12. Write the SQL command that you used and then write the alternate command that also would obtain the correct result.

18. How would you modify the query in Exercise 6 to limit retrieval only to work orders that were placed on 9/10/2018?

Colonial Adventure Tours Case

The owner of Colonial Adventure Tours knows the importance of the SQL language in database management. He realizes that he can use SQL to perform the same functions that you performed with queries in Chapter 2. In each of the following steps, use SQL to obtain the desired results using the data shown in Figures 1-15 through 1-19 in Chapter 1. (If you use a computer to complete these exercises, use a copy of the Colonial Adventure Tours database, so you will still have the original data when you complete Chapter 4.) You can use a DBMS to complete the exercises using a computer, or you can simply write the SQL command to complete each step. Check with your instructor if you are uncertain about which approach to take.

1. List the name of each trip that does not start in New Hampshire (NH).

2. List the name and start location for each trip that has the type Biking.

3. List the name of each trip that has the type Hiking and that has a distance of greater than six miles.

4. List the name of each trip that has the type Paddling or that is located in Vermont (VT).

5. How many trips have a type of Hiking or Biking?

6. List the trip name, type, and maximum group size for all trips that have Susan Kiley as a guide.

7. List the trip name and state for each trip that occurs during the Summer season. Sort the results by trip name within state.

8. List the name of each trip that has the type Hiking and that is guided by Rita Boyers.

9. How many trips originate in each state?

10. How many reservations include a trip with a price that is greater than $20 but less than $75?

11. List the reservation ID, customer last name, and the trip name for all reservations where the number of persons included in the reservation is greater than four.

12. List the trip name, the guide's first name, and the guide's last name for all trips that originate in New Hampshire (NH). Sort the results by guide's last name within trip name.

13. List the reservation ID, customer number, customer last name, and customer first name for all trips that occur in July 2018.

14. Colonial Adventure Tours calculates the total price of a trip by adding the trip price plus other fees and multiplying the result by the number of persons included in the reservation. List the reservation ID, trip name, customer's last name, customer's first name, and total cost for all reservations where the number of persons is greater than four. Use the column name TotalCost for the calculated field.

15. Create a new table named Solo that includes the reservation ID, trip ID, trip date, trip price, other fees, and customer number for all reservations that are for only one person.

16. Use an update query to change the OtherFees value in the Solo table to $5.00 for all records on which the OtherFees value is $0.00.

17. Use a delete query to delete all trips in the Solo table where the trip date is 9/12/2018.

18. There are multiple ways to create the query in Step 13. Write the SQL command that you used and then write an alternate command that also would obtain the correct result.

19. The following SQL code produces an error message. What is wrong with the code and how would you correct it?

```
SELECT ReservationID, TripID, TripName
FROM Reservation, Trip
WHERE Reservation.TripID=Trip.TripID
;
```

Sports Physical Therapy Case

In the following exercises, you will use the data in the Sports Physical Therapy database shown in Figures 1-21 through 1-24 in Chapter 1. (If you use a computer to complete these exercises, use a copy of the Sports Physical Therapy database so you will still have the original data when you complete Chapter 4.) In each step, use SQL to obtain the desired results. You can use the query feature in a DBMS to complete the exercises using a computer, or you can simply write the SQL command to complete each step. Check with your instructor if you are uncertain about which approach to take.

1. List the patient number, last name, and first name of every patient.
2. List the complete Session table (all rows and all columns).
3. List the last name and first name of every therapist located in Palm Rivers.
4. List the last name and first name of every therapist *not* located in Palm Rivers.
5. List the patient number, first name, and last name or every patient whose balance is greater than or equal to $3,000.
6. List the session number and patient number for every therapy that lasted 60 minutes.
7. List the TherapyCode for every therapy performed on 10/17/2018.
8. List the TherapyCode and description for all therapies that are billed in 15-minute units. Sort them in order by description.
9. How many patients are scheduled for more than one therapy?
10. Currently, therapists are paid at the rate of $35 per billable hour. List the therapist's last name, first name, and estimated pay for every scheduled therapy. Create a new calculated column named "EstimatedPay" for the estimated pay.
11. List the patient number and last name for all patients who live in Palm Rivers, Waterville, or Munster.
12. List every therapy description performed by Bridgette McClain. Sort the results by description.
13. How many sessions happened on 10/19/2018?
14. Calculate the average session time of all sessions performed in October.
15. Concatenate the first and last name of any therapist who is scheduled to do a Massage *or* have the patient use the Whirlpool. Display the name(s).
16. List the patient number and length of session for each patient with the TherapyCode of 97535.
17. Change the description of Whirlpool to Whirlpool bath.
18. Make a table named CurrentBilling. Create a new calculated field named BillableUnits (LengthOfSession / UnitOfTime). Add the following fields: PatientNum, TherapyCode, SessionDate, LengthOfSession, UnitOfTime, and BillableUnits. (Note: the BillableUnits field will be blank for those records with no UnitOfTime.)
19. List all rows in the new table, CurrentBilling, that have billable units greater than zero.

20. Use a delete query to delete all rows in the CurrentBilling table in which the billable units are blank or null. (Hint: you can use the IS NULL function in your comparison.)

21. There are two ways to create the query in Step 11. Write the SQL command that you used and then write the alternate command that also would obtain the correct result.

22. What WHERE clause would you use if you wanted to find all therapies where the description included the word "training" anywhere in the Description field?

CHAPTER **4**

THE RELATIONAL MODEL 3: ADVANCED TOPICS

LEARNING OBJECTIVES

- Define, describe, and use views
- Use indexes to improve database performance
- Examine the security features of a DBMS
- Discuss entity, referential, and legal-values integrity
- Make changes to the structure of a relational database
- Define and use the system catalog
- Explain the use of stored procedures, triggers, and data macros

INTRODUCTION

In Chapter 3, you used SQL to define and manipulate table data. In this chapter, you will investigate some other aspects of the relational model. You will learn about views, which represent a way of giving each user his or her own view of the data in a database. You will examine indexes and use them to improve database performance. You also will investigate the features of a DBMS that provide security. You then will learn about important integrity rules and examine ways to change the structure of a database. You will use the system catalog found in many relational DBMSs to provide users with information about the structure of a database. You will examine the use of stored procedures and triggers. Finally, you will see how Access 2016 provides the functionality of triggers using data macros. *NOTE:* If you plan to work through the examples in this chapter using a computer, you should use a copy of the original BITS database because the version of the database used in this chapter does not include the changes made in Chapters 2 and 3.

VIEWS

Most DBMSs support the creation of views. A **view** is an application program's or an individual user's picture of the database. An individual can use a view to create reports, charts, and other objects using database data. In many cases, an individual can use a view to examine table data as well. Because a view is usually less involved than the full database, its use can represent a great simplification. Views also provide a measure of security because omitting sensitive tables or fields from a view will render them unavailable to anyone who is accessing the database via that view.

To illustrate the idea of a view, suppose Antonio is interested in the TaskID, description, and price for BITS tasks that have to do specifically with hardware—those with categories of ACC, HAM, PRI, and UPG. He is not interested in any of the rows that correspond to items in other categories such as networking or software. Viewing this data would be simpler for Antonio if the other rows and fields were not even present.

Although you cannot change the structure of the Tasks table and omit some of its rows just for Antonio, you can do the next best thing. You can provide him with a view that consists of precisely the rows and fields he needs to access. Using SQL, the following CREATE VIEW command creates the view that Antonio can use to see the data he needs.

```
CREATE VIEW Hardware AS
    SELECT TaskID, Description, Price
    FROM TASKS
    WHERE Category IN ('ACC', 'HAM', 'PRI', 'UPG')
;
```

Q & A 4-1

Question: Does Access support views?
Answer: In most cases, Access requires you to use a query to create a view. The CREATE VIEW command does not work directly in Access because of the internal database engine.

Q & A 4-2

Question: Can you update a view?
Answer: In some DBMSs such as Oracle, if you want to update a view, you can use the syntax of REPLACE. For example, to include the Other work category (OTH) in the view you would use the following command.

```
CREATE or REPLACE VIEW Hardware AS
    SELECT TaskID, Description, Price
    FROM TASKS
    WHERE Category IN ('ACC', 'HAM', 'PRI', 'UPG', 'OTH')
;
```

The SELECT command that creates the view, which is called the **defining query**, indicates what to include in the view. Conceptually, given the current data in the BITS database, this view will contain the data shown in Figure 4-1. The data does not really exist in this form, however; nor will it *ever* exist in this form. It is tempting to think that when this view is used, the query is executed and will produce some sort of temporary table named Hardware, which Antonio then could access, but that is *not* what happens.

Hardware

TaskID	Description	Price
AC65	Accessories	$80.00
HA63	Hardware major	$225.00
HI31	Hardware minor	$165.00
PI54	Printing issues	$50.00
UP38	Upgrades	$185.00

FIGURE 4-1   Hardware view

Instead, the query acts as a sort of window into the database, as shown in Figure 4-2. As far as Antonio is concerned, the entire database is just the darker-shaded portion of the Tasks table. Antonio can see any change that affects the darker portion of the Tasks table, but he is totally unaware of any other changes that are made in the database.

Tasks

TaskID	Description	Category	Price
AC65	Accessories	ACC	$80.00
DA11	Data recovery major	DRM	$175.00
DI85	Data recovery minor	DRM	$50.00
HA63	Hardware major	HAM	$225.00
HI31	Hardware minor	HAM	$165.00
LA81	Local area networking (LAN)	LAN	$104.00
MO49	Mobility	MOB	$65.00
OT99	Other work	OTH	$99.99
PI54	Printing issues	PRI	$50.00
SA44	Software major	SOM	$200.00
SI77	Software minor	SOM	$144.00
SI91	Security install/repair	SIR	$126.00
UP38	Upgrades	UPG	$185.00
VR39	Virus removal	VIR	$90.00
WA33	Wide area networking (WAN)	WAN	$130.00
WC19	Web connectivity	WEC	$75.00

FIGURE 4-2 Hardware view of the BITS database (shaded portion)

When you create a query that involves a view, the DBMS changes the query to one that selects data from the table(s) in the database that created the view. Suppose, for example, Antonio creates the following query:

```
SELECT *
FROM Hardware
WHERE Price<150
;
```

The DBMS does *not* execute the query in this form. Instead, it merges the query Antonio entered with the query that defines the view, to form the query that is actually executed. When the DBMS merges the query that creates the view with the query to select rows where the Price value is less than 150, the query that the DBMS actually executes is as follows:

```
SELECT TaskID, Description, Price
FROM Tasks
WHERE Category IN ('ACC', 'HAM', 'PRI', 'UPG')
   AND Price<150
;
```

In the query that the DBMS executes, the FROM clause lists the Tasks table rather than the Hardware view. The SELECT clause lists fields from the Tasks table instead of * to select all fields from the Hardware view. The WHERE clause contains a compound condition to select only those items in the given categories (as Antonio sees in the Hardware view) and only those items with Price values of less than 150.

Antonio, however, is unaware that this kind of activity is taking place. To Antonio, it seems as though he is using a table named Hardware. One advantage of this approach is that, because the Hardware view never exists in its own right, any update to the Tasks table is *immediately* available in Antonio's Hardware view. If the Hardware view were really a table, then that would not be the case.

To create a view in Access, you simply create and save a query. For example, to create the Hardware view, you would include the TaskID, Description, Category, and Price fields from the Tasks table. You would also include the Category field in the design grid and enter the categories ACC, HAM, PRI, and UPG as the criterion. Because the Category field is not included in the view, you would remove the check mark from the

Category field's Show check box. Finally, you would save the query using the name Hardware, as shown in Figure 4-3 on the next page. *NOTE:* To save a query, click the Save button on the Quick Access Toolbar and then name the query.

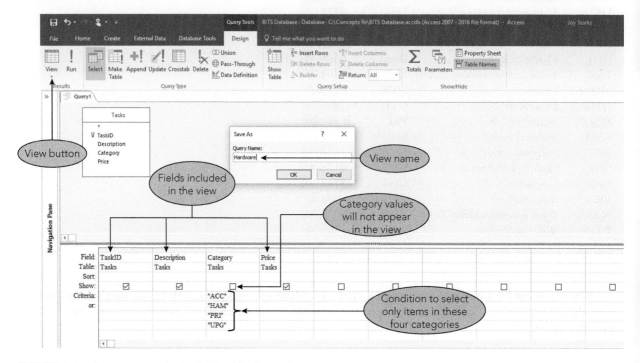

FIGURE 4-3 Access query design for the Hardware view

Q & A 4-3

Question: Do other DBMS programs support views?
Answer: Yes. In some DBMSs, views are a permanent addition to database schema. They do not disappear when the user logs out.

After creating the view, you can use it right away. Figure 4-4 shows the data in the Hardware view created by running the query in Figure 4-3. You can create a form for the view, base a report on the view, and treat the view as though it were a table, permanently stored in the database.

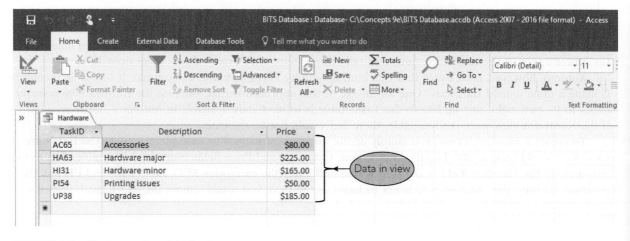

FIGURE 4-4 Hardware view datasheet

What if Antonio wanted different names for the fields? You can use SQL to change the field names in a view by including the new field names in the CREATE VIEW command. For example, if Antonio wanted the names of the TaskID, Description, and Price fields to be TNum, TDesc, and Price, respectively, the CREATE VIEW command would be as follows:

```
CREATE VIEW Hardware (TNum, TDesc, Price) AS
   SELECT TaskID, Description, Price
   FROM Tasks
   WHERE Category IN ('ACC', 'HAM', 'PRI', 'UPG')
;
```

Now when Antonio accesses the Hardware view, he uses the field names TNum, TDesc, and Price rather than TaskID, Description, and Price, respectively.

In Access, you can change the field names by preceding the name of the field with the desired name, followed by a colon, as shown in Figure 4-5.

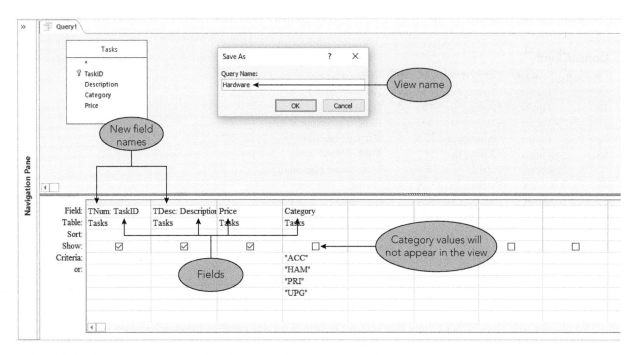

FIGURE 4-5 Access query design of the Hardware view with changed field names

In the query results shown in Figure 4-6, the column headings are TNum, TDesc, and Price.

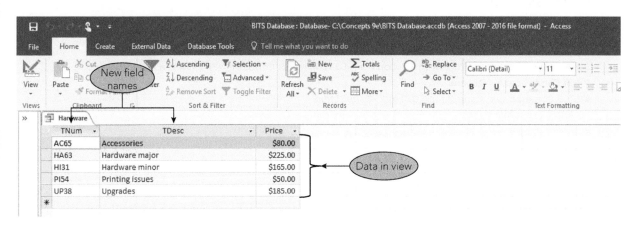

FIGURE 4-6 Datasheet for the Hardware view with changed field names

The Hardware view is an example of a **row-and-column subset view** because it consists of a subset of the rows and columns in some individual table, which, in this case, is the Tasks table. Because the query can be any SQL query, a view also can join two or more tables.

Suppose, for example, Cecilia needs to know the number and name of each consultant, along with the number and name of the clients represented by each consultant. It would be much simpler for her if this information were stored in a single table instead of in two tables that she has to join together. She would like a single table that contains the consultant number, consultant name, client number, and client name. Suppose she also would like these fields to be named ConNum, ConLast, ConFirst, CliNum, and CliName, respectively. She could use a join in the CREATE VIEW command as follows:

```
CREATE VIEW ConsltClient (ConNum, ConLast, ConFirst, CliNum, CliName) AS
    SELECT Consultant.ConsltNum, LastName, FirstName, ClientNum, ClientName
    FROM Consultant, Client
    WHERE Consultant.ConsltNum=Client.ConsltNum
;
```

Given the current data in the BITS database, conceptually this view is the table shown in Figure 4-7.

ConsltClient

ConNum	ConLast	ConFirst	CliNum	CliName
19	Turner	Christopher	143	Hershey, Jarrod
19	Turner	Christopher	175	Goduto, Sean
19	Turner	Christopher	405	Fisherman's Spot Shop
19	Turner	Christopher	826	Harpersburg Bank
19	Turner	Christopher	867	MarketPoint Sales
22	Jordan	Patrick	299	Two Crafty Cousins
22	Jordan	Patrick	449	Seymour, Lindsey
22	Jordan	Patrick	458	Bonnie's Beautiful Boutique
22	Jordan	Patrick	733	Howler, Laura
35	Allen	Sarah	322	Prichard's Pizza & Pasta
35	Allen	Sarah	363	Salazar, Jason
35	Allen	Sarah	677	Yates, Nick

FIGURE 4-7 ConsltClient view

To Cecilia, the ConsltClient view is a real table; she does not need to know what goes on behind the scenes in order to use it. She could find the number and name of the consultant who represents client 175, for example, by using the following query:

```
SELECT ConNum, ConLast, ConFirst
FROM ConsltClient
WHERE CliNum='175'
;
```

Cecilia is completely unaware that, behind the scenes, the DBMS converts her query as follows:

```
SELECT Consultant.ConsltNum AS ConNum, LastName AS ConLast, FirstName AS ConFirst
FROM Consultant, Client
WHERE Consultant.ConsltNum=Client.ConsltNum
    AND ClientNum='175'
;
```

In Access, the query for the `ConsltClient` view appears in Figure 4-8.

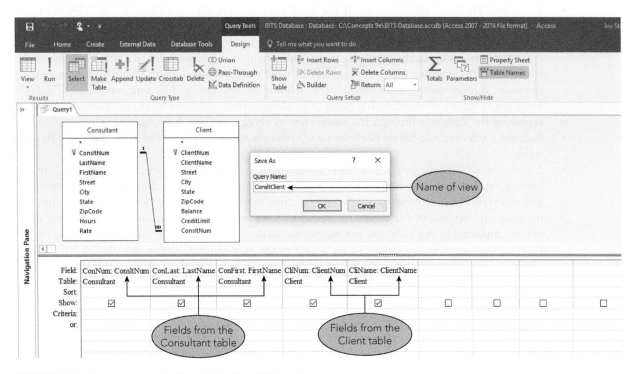

FIGURE 4-8 Access query design of the ConsltClient view

The Datasheet view for the `ConsltClient` view appears in Figure 4-9.

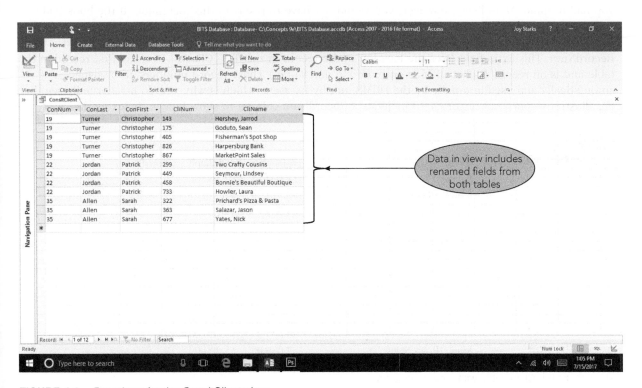

FIGURE 4-9 Datasheet for the ConsltClient view

The use of views provides several advantages:

- Views provide data independence. If the database structure changes (because of fields being added or relationships changing between tables, for example) in such a way that the view can still be derived from existing data, the user still can access and use the same view. If adding extra fields to tables in the database is the only change and these fields are not required by the view's user, the defining query may not even need to be changed for the user to continue using the view. If relationships are changed, the defining query may be different, but because users need not be aware of the defining query, this difference is unknown to them. They continue accessing the database through the same view as though nothing has changed.
- Because each user has his or her own view, different users can view the same data in different ways.
- A view should contain only those fields required by a given user. This practice has two advantages. First, because the view, in all probability, contains fewer fields than the overall database and the view is conceptually a single table, rather than a collection of tables, it greatly simplifies the user's perception of the database. Second, views provide a measure of security. Fields that are not included in the view are not accessible to the view's user. For example, omitting the Balance field from a view ensures that a user of the view cannot access any client's balance. Likewise, rows that are not included in the view are not accessible. A user of the Hardware view, for example, cannot obtain any information about items in the SOM or DRM categories.

INDEXES

Within relational model systems, the main mechanism for increasing the efficiency with which data is retrieved from the database is the **index**. An index is a database-generated copy of a selected column organized so that it directly refers to the storage location of the data. As a data structure, an index is used to improve the execution time of queries and searches in large databases.

Conceptually, these indexes are very much like the index in a book. If you want to find a discussion of a given topic in a book, you could scan the entire book from start to finish, looking for references to the topic you had in mind. More likely, however, you would not have to resort to this technique. If the book had a good index, you could use it to quickly identify the pages on which your topic is discussed.

Consider Figure 4-10, for example, which shows the Client table for BITS together with one extra field, RecordNum. This extra field gives the location of the record in the file. (Client 143 is the first record in the table and is on record 1, client 175 is on record 2, and so on.) These record numbers are assigned automatically and used internally by the DBMS, not by its users, which is why you do not normally see them. For illustrative purposes, Figure 4-10 includes a RecordNum column to show how an index works.

Client

RecordNum	ClientNum	ClientName	...	Balance	CreditLimit	ConsltNum
1	143	Hershey, Jarrod	...	$1,904.55	$2,500.00	19
2	175	Goduto, Sean	...	$2,814.55	$5,000.00	19
3	299	Two Crafty Cousins	...	$8,354.00	$10,000.00	22
4	322	Prichard's Pizza & Pasta	...	$7,335.55	$10,000.00	35
5	363	Salazar, Jason	...	$900.75	$2,500.00	35
6	405	Fisherman's Spot Shop	...	$4,113.40	$7,500.00	19
7	449	Seymour, Lindsey	...	$557.70	$5,000.00	22
8	458	Bonnie's Beautiful Boutique	...	$4,053.80	$7,500.00	22
9	677	Yates, Nick	...	$2,523.80	$2,500.00	35
10	733	Howler, Laura	...	$3,658.05	$5,000.00	22
11	826	Harpersburg Bank	...	$6,824.55	$10,000.00	19
12	867	MarketPoint Sales	...	$3,089.00	$5,000.00	19

FIGURE 4-10 Client table with record numbers

To rapidly access a client's record on the basis of his or her record number, you might choose to create and use an index, as shown in Figure 4-11.

Client Index

ClientNum	RecordNum
143	1
175	2
299	3
322	4
363	5
405	6
449	7
458	8
677	9
733	10
826	11
867	12

FIGURE 4-11   Index for the Client table on the ClientNum field

The index has two fields. The first field contains a client number, and the second field contains the number of the record on which the client number is found. Because client numbers are unique, there is only a single corresponding record number in this index. That is not always the case, however. Suppose, for example, you wanted to quickly access all clients with a specific credit limit or all clients that are represented by a specific consultant. You might choose to create and use an index on credit limit as well as an index on consultant number. These two indexes are shown in Figure 4-12.

CreditLimit Index

CreditLimit	RecordNum
$2,500	1, 5, 9
$5,000.00	2, 7, 10, 12
$7,500.00	6, 8
$10,000.00	3, 4, 11

ConsltNum Index

ConsltNum	RecordNum
19	1, 2, 6, 11, 12
22	3, 7, 8, 10
35	4, 5, 9

FIGURE 4-12   Indexes for the Client table on the CreditLimit and ConsltNum fields

By examining the CreditLimit index in Figure 4-12, you can see that each credit limit occurs in the index along with the numbers of the records on which that credit limit occurs. Credit limit $7,500, for example, occurs on records 6, and 8. Further, the credit limits appear in the index in numerical order. If the DBMS uses this index to find those records on which the credit limit is $10,000, for example, it could scan the credit limits in the index to find $10,000. After doing that, it would determine the corresponding record numbers (3, 4, and 11) and then immediately go to those records in the Client table, finding these clients more quickly than if it had to scan the entire Client table one record at a time. Thus, indexes can make the process of retrieving records fast and efficient.

With relatively small tables, the increased efficiency associated with indexes is not readily apparent. In practice, it is common to encounter tables with thousands, tens of thousands, or even hundreds of thousands of records. In such cases, the increase in efficiency is dramatic. In fact, without indexes, many operations in such databases would simply not be practical—they would take too long to complete.

The field or combination of fields on which the index is built is called the **index key**. In the index shown in Figure 4-11, the index key is ClientNum; in the indexes shown in Figure 4-12, the index keys are CreditLimit and ConsltNum. The index key for an index can be any field or combination of fields in any table.

After creating an index, you can use it to facilitate data retrieval. In powerful mainframe relational systems, the decision concerning which index(es) to use (if any) during a particular type of retrieval is a function of the DBMS.

As you would expect, the use of any index is not purely advantageous or disadvantageous. An advantage already was mentioned: An index makes certain types of retrieval more efficient. A disadvantage is the fact that the DBMS must update the index whenever corresponding data in the database is updated. This kind of maintenance overhead slows down the process in large databases. Without the index, the DBMS would not need to make these updates.

The main question you must ask when considering whether to create a given index is this: Do the benefits derived during retrieval outweigh the extra processing involved in update operations and, in large databases, the additional storage required? The following guidelines should help you make this determination. You should create an index on a field (or combination of fields) when one or more of the following conditions exist:

- The field is the primary key of the table. (In some systems, the DBMS might create this index automatically.)
- The field is the foreign key in a relationship you have created.
- You will use the field frequently as a sort field.
- You will need to locate a record frequently based on a value in this field.

You can add and delete indexes as necessary. You can create an index after the database is built—the index does not need to be created at the same time as the database. Likewise, when it appears that an existing index is unnecessary, you can delete it.

The exact process for creating an index varies from one DBMS to another. A common SQL command to create an index is as follows:

```
CREATE INDEX ClientName
   ON Client (ClientName)
;
```

This **CREATE INDEX** command creates an index named ClientName. The index is for the Client table, and the index key is the ClientName field. In this example, the index name is the same as the index key. This format is not a requirement, but it is a good general practice.

Figure 4-13 shows the creation of an index on the ClientName field in the Client table Design View using Access. As illustrated in the figure, there are three choices for index options when you click the row named, Indexed: No, Yes (Duplicates OK), and Yes (No Duplicates).

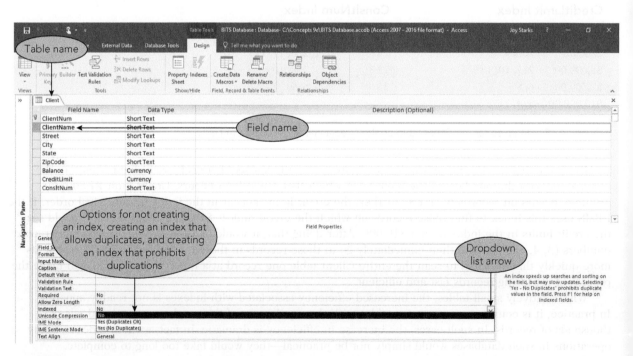

FIGURE 4-13   Creating an index on a single field in Access

The first Indexed option, No, is the default. You select No when you need to remove a previously created index. You select Yes (Duplicates OK) to create an index that allows duplicate values. In this case, Access allows more than one client with the same name. When you select Yes (No Duplicates), Access creates the index, but you cannot add a client with the same name as an existing client in the database. The third option is used to enforce uniqueness when it is appropriate. For example, the third option would be a good choice for a Social Security number field.

When you create an index whose key is a single field, you have created a **single-field index** (also called a **single-column index**). A **multiple-field index** (also called a **multiple-column index** or **composite key**) is an index with more than one key field. When creating a multiple-field index, you list the more important key first. In addition, if data for either key appears in descending order, you must follow the field name with the word *DESC*.

To create an index named ConsltBal with the keys ConsltNum and Balance and with the balances listed in descending order, you could use the following SQL command:

```
CREATE INDEX ConsltBal
   ON Client (ConsltNum, Balance DESC)
;
```

Creating multiple-field indexes in Access involves a slightly different process than creating single-field indexes. To create multiple-field indexes, click the Indexes button (Table Tools Design tab | Show/Hide group), enter a name for the index, and then select the fields that make up the index key. If data for any of the fields is to appear in descending order, change the corresponding entry in the Sort Order column to Descending, as shown in Figure 4-14.

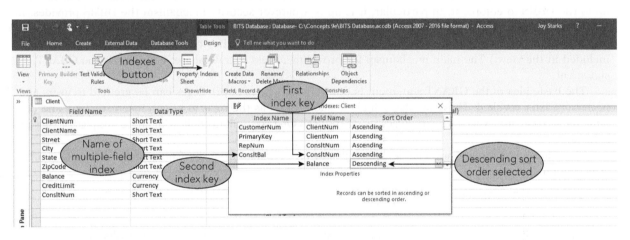

FIGURE 4-14   Creating a multiple-field index in Access

The SQL command used to drop (delete) an index that is no longer necessary is **DROP INDEX**, which consists of the words *DROP INDEX* followed by the name of the index to drop. To drop the ConsltBal index, for example, the command is as follows:

```
DROP INDEX ConsltBal
;
```

To delete an index in Access, right-click the index in the Indexes dialog box (shown in Figure 4-14) and then click Delete Rows on the shortcut menu.

> **Q & A 4-4**
>
> **Question:** When do you need to delete an index?
> **Answer:** You may find that your current index is inefficient, not selective enough, or slow. In addition, database administrators can run programs to see if indexes are being used or read consistently. In large databases, unused indexes may slow down your inserts, deletes, and updates.

Finally, if you are retrieving data based on a field in a large database, an index can help performance; however, indexes should not be overused due to the maintenance overhead.

SECURITY

Security is the prevention of unauthorized access to the database. Within an organization, the database administrator determines the types of access various users can have to the database. Some users may be able to retrieve and update anything in the database. Other users may be able to retrieve any data from the database but not make any changes to it. Still other users may be able to access only a portion of the database. For example, Bill Kaiser may be able to retrieve and update consultant and client data, but not be permitted to retrieve data about items and orders. Mary Smith may be able to retrieve item data and nothing else. Kyung Park may be able to retrieve and update data on items in the GME category but not in other categories.

After the database administrator has determined the access different users of the database will have, it is up to the DBMS to enforce it. In particular, it is up to whatever security mechanism the DBMS provides. In SQL systems, there are two security mechanisms. You already have seen that views furnish a certain amount of security. (When users are accessing the database through a view, they cannot access any data that is not included in the view.) The main mechanism for providing access to a database, however, is the GRANT statement.

The basic idea of the **GRANT** statement is that different types of privileges can be granted to users and, if necessary, later revoked. These privileges include such things as the right to select, insert, update, and delete table data. You can revoke user privileges using the **REVOKE** statement. Following are examples of these two statements.

The following command will enable user Jones to retrieve data from the Client table but not take any other action.

```
GRANT SELECT ON Client TO Jones
;
```

The following command enables users Smith and Park to add new records to the Tasks table.

```
GRANT INSERT ON Tasks TO Smith, Park
;
```

The following command revokes the ability to retrieve Client records from user Jones; that is, Jones no longer has the privilege granted earlier.

```
REVOKE SELECT ON Client FROM Jones
;
```

NOTE: While other DBMSs allow you to grant and revoke user privileges, user-level security features have been removed from Access 2016.

INTEGRITY RULES

Recall than an integrity rule is a constraint established to keep users from making errors when editing a database. A relational DBMS must enforce two important integrity rules that were defined by Dr. E. F. Codd of IBM in 1979. Both rules are related to two special types of keys: primary keys and foreign keys. The two integrity rules are called entity integrity and referential integrity.

Entity Integrity

In some DBMSs, when you describe a database, you can indicate that certain fields can accept a special value, called null. Essentially, setting the value in a given field to null is similar to not entering a value in the field at all. Nulls are used when a value is missing, unknown, or inapplicable. It is *not* the same as a blank or zero value, both of which are actual values. For example, a value of zero in the Balance field for a particular client indicates that the client has a zero balance. A value of null in a client's Balance field, on the other hand, indicates that, for whatever reason, the client's balance is unknown.

When you indicate that the Balance field can be null, you are saying that this situation (a client with an unknown balance) is something you want to allow. If you do not want to allow unknown values, you indicate this by specifying that Balance field values cannot be null.

The decision about allowing nulls is generally made on a field-by-field basis. There is one type of field for which you should *never* allow nulls, however, and that is the primary key. After all, the primary key is supposed to uniquely identify a given row, which would not happen if nulls were allowed. How, for example, could you tell two clients apart if both had null client numbers? The restriction that the primary key cannot allow null values is called entity integrity.

Entity integrity is the rule that no field that is part of the primary key may accept null values. Entity integrity guarantees that each record indeed has its own identity. In other words, preventing the primary key from accepting null values ensures that you can distinguish one record from another. Typically, the DBMS handles this distinction automatically. All you need to do is specify which field or fields make up the primary key.

In SQL, you can specify the primary key by entering a **PRIMARY KEY clause** in either an ALTER TABLE (covered later in this chapter) or a CREATE TABLE command. For example, to use the PRIMARY KEY clause to indicate that ClientNum is the primary key for the Client table, the clause would be as follows:

```
PRIMARY KEY (ClientNum)
```

In general, the PRIMARY KEY clause has the form PRIMARY KEY followed, in parentheses, by the field or fields that make up the primary key. When more than one field is included, the fields are separated by commas. Thus, the PRIMARY KEY clause for the OrderLine table is as follows:

```
PRIMARY KEY (OrderNum, TaskID)
```

In Access, you designate the primary key by selecting the primary key field in Table Design view and clicking the Primary Key button (Table Tools Design tab | Tools group). A key symbol appears in the field's row selector to indicate that it is the primary key, as shown in Figure 4-15.

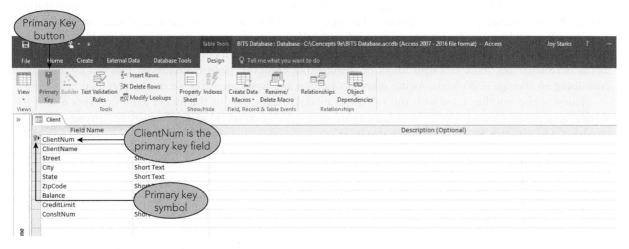

FIGURE 4-15   Specifying a primary key in Access

If the primary key consists of more than one field, select the first field, press and hold down the Ctrl key, and then click the other field or fields that make up the primary key. Clicking the Primary Key button adds the key symbol to the row selectors of the primary key fields, as shown in Figure 4-16.

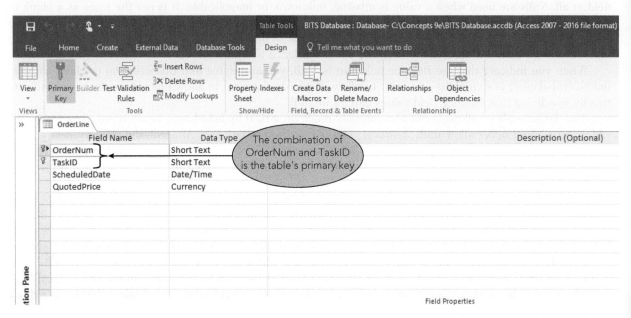

FIGURE 4-16   Specifying a primary key consisting of more than one field in Access

Referential Integrity

In the relational model you have examined thus far, you have created the relationships between tables by having common fields in two or more tables. The relationship between consultants and clients, for example, is accomplished by including the primary key of the Consultant table (ConsltNum) as a field in the Client table.

This approach has several drawbacks. First, relationships are not very obvious. If you were not already familiar with the relationships in the BITS database, you would have to find the matching fields in separate tables in order to locate the relationship. Even then, you could not be sure that the matching field names indicated a relationship. Two fields having the same name could be just a coincidence—the fields might have nothing to do with each other. Second, what if the primary key in the Consultant table is named ConsltNum, but the corresponding field in the Client table is named RepNo? Unless you are aware that these two fields are identical, the relationship between clients and consultants would not be clear. In a database having as few tables and fields as the BITS database, these problems might be manageable. However, picture a database that has 20 tables, each containing an average of 30 fields. As the number of tables and fields increases, so do the potential problems.

There is also another issue with the relational model. Nothing about the model itself prevents a user from storing data about a client whose consultant number did not correspond to any consultant already in the database. Clearly, this is not a desirable situation.

Fortunately, a solution exists for both issues. It involves using foreign keys. Recall that a foreign key is a field (or collection of fields) in a table whose value is required to match the value of the primary key for a second table.

The ConsltNum field in the Client table is a foreign key that must match the primary key of the Consultant table. In practice, this means that the consultant number for any client must be the same as the number of a consultant that is already in the database.

There is one possible exception to this rule. Perhaps BITS does not require a client to have a consultant—it is strictly optional. This situation could be indicated in the Client table by setting such a client's consultant number to null. Technically, however, a null consultant number would violate the restrictions that you have indicated for a foreign key. Thus, if you were to use a null consultant number, you would have to modify the definition of a foreign key to include the possibility of nulls. You would insist, however, that if the foreign key contained a value *other than null*, it would have to match the value of the primary key in some row in the other table. (In the example, for instance, a client's consultant number could be null. If it were not null, it would have to be the number of an actual consultant.) This general property is called referential integrity.

Therefore, **referential integrity** is the rule that if table A contains a foreign key that matches the primary key of table B, the values of this foreign key must match the value of the primary key for some row in table B or be null.

Usually a foreign key is in a table that is different from the table whose primary key it is required to match. In the BITS database, for example, to be able to determine the consultant for any client, you include the consultant number as a foreign key in the Client table that must match the primary key in the Consultant table. It is possible for the foreign key and the matching primary key to be in the same table, however, which is sometimes called a self-referencing or **recursive** foreign key. As an example of this situation, suppose one of the requirements in a particular database is that, given an employee, you must be able to determine the manager of that employee. You might have an Employee table with a primary key of EmployeeNum (the employee number). To determine the employee's manager, you would include the manager's employee number as a foreign key in the Employee table. Because the manager is also an employee, however, the manager will be in the same Employee table. Thus, this foreign key in the Employee table would need to match the primary key in the same Employee table. The only restriction is that the foreign key must have a name that is different from the primary key because the fields are in the same table. For example, you could name the foreign key ManagerEmployeeNum.

Using foreign keys solves the previously mentioned problems. Indicating that the ConsltNum field in the Client table is a foreign key that must match the ConsltNum field in the Consultant table explicitly specifies the relationship between clients and consultants—you do not need to look for common fields in several tables. Further, with foreign keys, matching fields that have different names no longer pose a problem. For example, it would not matter if the name of the foreign key in the Client table were RepNo and the primary key in the Consultant table were ConsltNum; the only thing that *would* matter is that this field is a foreign key that matches the Consultant table. Finally, through referential integrity, it is possible for a client not to have a consultant number, but it is not possible for a client to have an *invalid* consultant number; that is, a client's consultant number *must* be null or *must* be the number of a consultant who is already in the database.

In SQL, you specify referential integrity using a **FOREIGN KEY clause** in either the CREATE TABLE or ALTER TABLE commands. To specify a foreign key, you need to specify both the field that is a foreign key and the table whose primary key it is to match. In the Client table, for example, the ConsltNum field is a foreign key that must match the primary key in the Consultant table as follows:

```
FOREIGN KEY (ConsltNum) REFERENCES Consultant
```

The general form of this clause is FOREIGN KEY, followed by the field or combination of fields that make up the foreign key, which is followed by the word *REFERENCES* and the name of the table containing the primary key that the foreign key is supposed to match.

In Access, referential integrity is specified as defining relationships. After clicking the Relationships button (Database Tools tab I Relationships group), both tables must be added to the window, as shown in Figure 4-17.

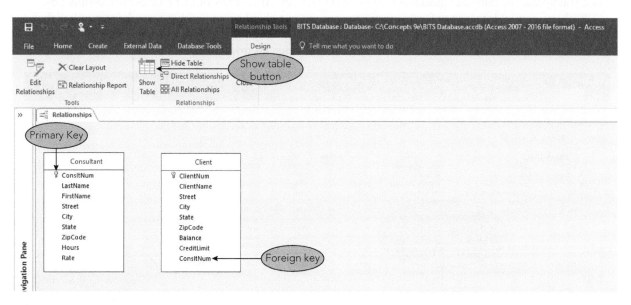

FIGURE 4-17 Using the Relationships window to relate tables in Access

You use the pointer (or mouse) to drag the primary key (ConsltNum) of the Consultant table to the foreign key (ConsltNum) of the Client table. After releasing the mouse button, you can request Access to enforce referential integrity by selecting the Enforce Referential Integrity check box (Edit Relationships dialog box), as shown in Figure 4-18. You also can specify whether update or delete operations cascade. Selecting the Cascade Delete Related Records check box ensures that the deletion of a consultant record also deletes all client records related to that consultant (also known as **cascade delete**). Selecting the Cascade Update Related Fields check box ensures that changes made to the primary key of a consultant record are also made in the related client record (also known as **cascade update**). In Figure 4-18, the cascade delete and cascade update options are not selected.

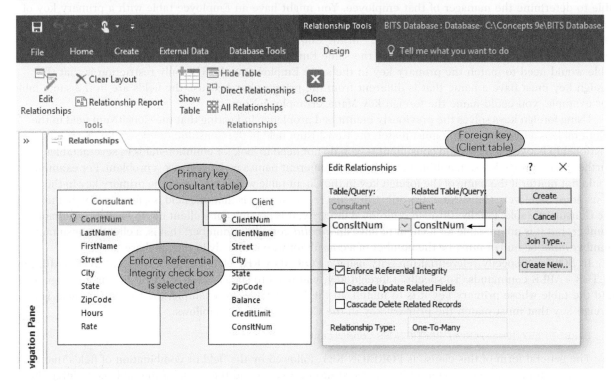

FIGURE 4-18   Specifying referential integrity in Access

NOTE: In some other DBMS programs, such as Oracle, a cascade update is accomplished by adding a constraint when you update the table and including the ON UPDATE CASCADE or ON DELETE CASCADE commands.

With referential integrity enforced, users cannot enter a client record with a consultant number that does not match any consultant number currently in the Consultant table. An error message, such as the one shown in Figure 4-19, appears when a user attempts to enter an invalid consultant number.

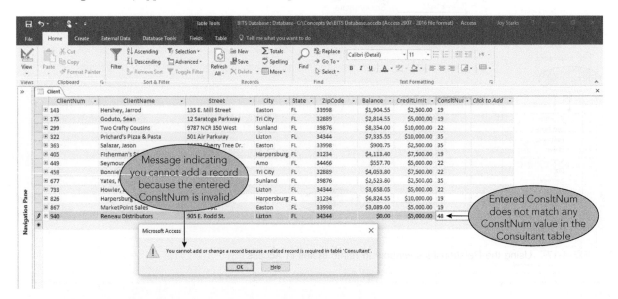

FIGURE 4-19   Referential integrity violation when attempting to add a record

Deleting a consultant who currently has clients on file would also violate referential integrity because the consultant's clients would no longer match any consultant in the Consultant table. The DBMS must prevent this type of deletion and then produce an error message, such as the one shown in Figure 4-20. If consultant 19 leaves BITS, all of his clients would need to be assigned to other consultants before his record could be deleted from the Consultant table.

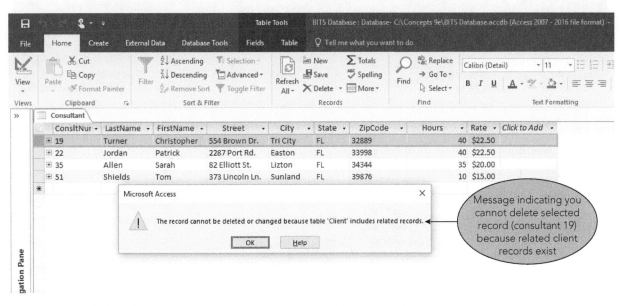

FIGURE 4-20   Referential integrity violation when attempting to delete a record

Legal-Values Integrity

In addition to the two integrity rules defined by Codd, there is a third type of integrity, called **legal-values integrity**. Often there is a particular set of values called legal values that are allowable in a field (sometimes called check constraints). Legal-values integrity is the property that states that no record can exist in the database with a value in the field other than one of the legal values. For example, at BITS, the legal values for the CreditLimit field are $2,500, $5,000, $7,500, and $10,000. The DBMS must reject an attempt to enter a record with a credit limit of $12,500.

In SQL, you use the **CHECK** clause to enforce legal-values integrity. For example, to ensure that the only legal values for credit limits are $2,500. $5,000, $7,500, or $10,000, include the following CHECK clause in a CREATE TABLE or ALTER TABLE command:

```
CHECK (CreditLimit IN (2500, 5000, 7500, 10000))
```

The general form of the CHECK clause is the word *CHECK* followed by a condition. In the previous CHECK clause, the credit limit must be in the set consisting of 2500, 5000, 7500, or 10000. The DBMS automatically rejects any update to the database that violates the condition in the CHECK clause.

In Access, you can restrict the legal values accepted by a field by entering an appropriate **validation rule** that data entered in the field must follow. Figure 4-21 shows the validation rule that restricts entries in the CreditLimit field to 2500, 5000, 7500, and 10000. Along with the validation rule, you usually enter **validation text** to inform the user of the reason for the rejection when the user attempts to enter data that violates the rule.

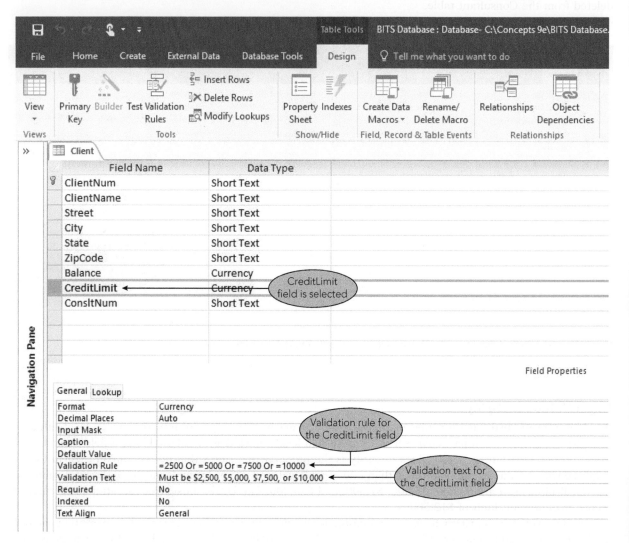

FIGURE 4-21   Specifying a validation rule in Access

STRUCTURE CHANGES

An important feature of relational DBMSs is the ease with which you can change the database structure by adding and removing tables and fields, by changing the characteristics of existing fields, or by creating and dropping indexes. Although the exact manner in which you accomplish these changes varies from one system to another, most systems allow you to make all of these changes quickly and easily.

Changes to a table's structure are made using the SQL **ALTER TABLE** command. Virtually every implementation of SQL allows the creation of new fields in existing tables. For example, suppose you need to maintain a client type for each client in the BITS database. You can decide to assign individual clients type I, companies type C, and special clients type S. To implement this change, you would add a new field named ClientType to the Client table as follows:

```
ALTER TABLE Client
    ADD ClientType CHAR(1)
;
```

In Access, you can add a field in Table Design view at any time. Figure 4-22 shows the Client table after adding the ClientType field.

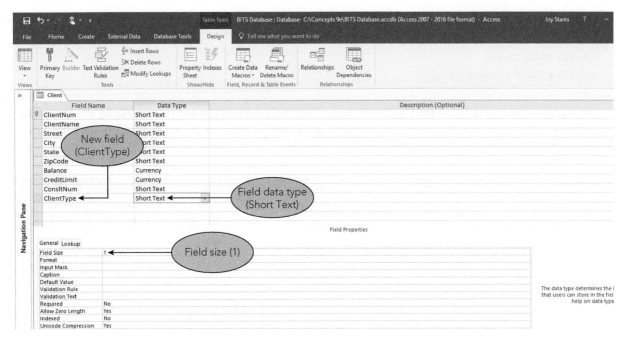

FIGURE 4-22 Adding a field in Access

At this point, the Client table contains an extra field, ClientType. For rows (clients) added from this point on, the value of ClientType is entered just like any other field. For existing rows, ClientType typically is assigned a null value by the DBMS automatically. The user can then change these values if desired.

Some systems allow changes to the properties of existing fields, such as increasing the length of a character field. For example, to increase the field size of the ClientName field in the Client table from 35 to 40 characters, use the following SQL ALTER TABLE command:

```
ALTER TABLE Client
    MODIFY ClientName CHAR(40)
;
```

In Access, you can change field properties in Table Design view. Figure 4-23 shows the ClientName field after increasing its field size from 35 to 40 characters.

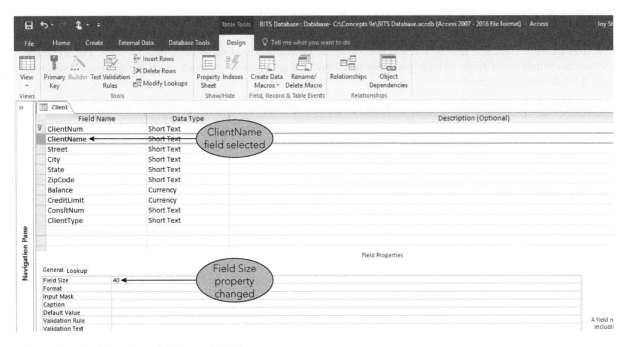

FIGURE 4-23 Changing a field property in Access

Some systems allow existing fields to be deleted. (Oracle is one system that does not allow existing fields to be deleted.) For example, the following SQL command deletes the Category field from the Tasks table:

```
ALTER TABLE Tasks
    DROP COLUMN Category
;
```

In Access, you can delete a field in Table Design view by selecting the field and pressing the Delete key. Access asks you to confirm the deletion of the field, as shown in Figure 4-24. Be careful; clicking the Yes button permanently deletes the field and the data it stores.

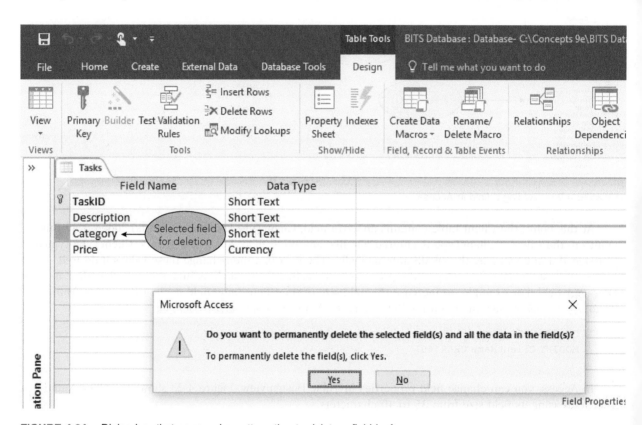

FIGURE 4-24   Dialog box that opens when attempting to delete a field in Access

You can use the SQL **DROP TABLE** command to delete a table that is no longer needed. For example, to delete the SmallClient table (which you may have created in Chapter 3) from the BITS database, you would use the following command:

```
DROP TABLE SmallClient
;
```

The table and all indexes and views defined on the table would be deleted. The DROP TABLE command deletes the table structure as well as its data.

In Access, you can drop (delete) a table by right-clicking the table on the Navigation Pane and then clicking Delete on the shortcut menu, as shown in Figure 4-25.

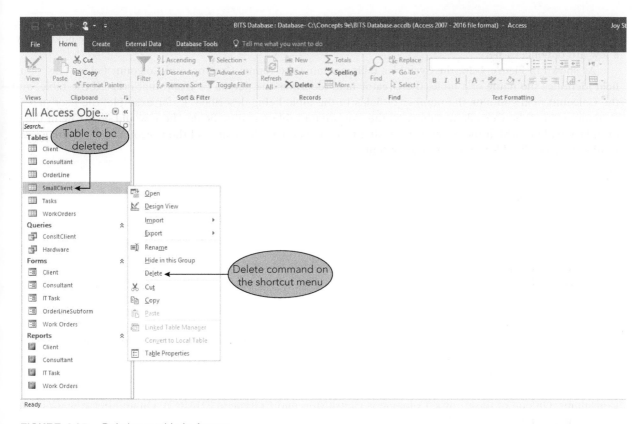

FIGURE 4-25   Deleting a table in Access

MAKING COMPLEX CHANGES

In some cases, you might need to change a table's structure in ways that are beyond the capabilities of your DBMS. Perhaps you need to eliminate a field, change the field order, or combine data from two tables into one, but your system does not allow these types of changes. For example, some systems, including Oracle, do not allow you to reduce the size of a field or change its data type. In these situations, you can use the CREATE TABLE command to describe the new table, and then insert values into it using the INSERT command combined with an appropriate SELECT clause, as you learned in Chapter 3. If you are using a version of SQL that supports the SELECT INTO command, as Access does, you can use it to create the new table in a single operation, such as when you want to create a backup of your table

```
SELECT *
INTO WorkOrdersBackupMarch2019
FROM WorkOrders
;
```

SYSTEM CATALOG

Information about tables in the database is kept in the **system catalog** (or the **catalog**). The catalog is maintained automatically by the DBMS. When a user adds a new table, changes the structure of an existing table, or deletes a table, the DBMS updates the catalog to reflect these changes.

This section describes the types of items kept in the catalog and the way in which you can query it to determine information about the database structure. (This description represents the way catalogs are used in a typical SQL implementation.) Although catalogs in individual relational DBMSs vary from the examples shown here, the general ideas apply to most relational systems.

The catalog you will consider contains two tables: **Systables** (information about the tables known to SQL) and **Syscolumns** (information about the columns or fields within these tables). An actual catalog contains other tables as well, such as **Sysindexes** (information about the indexes that are defined on these tables) and **Sysviews** (information about the views that have been created). Although these tables have many fields, only a few are of concern here.

As shown in Figure 4-26, the Systables table contains the Name, Creator, and Colcount fields. The Name field identifies the name of a table, the Creator field identifies the person or group that created the table, and the Colcount field contains the number of fields in the table being described. If, for example, the user named Graham created the Consultant table and the Consultant table has nine fields, there would be a row in the Systables table in which the Name is Consultant, the Creator is Graham, and the Colcount is 9. Similar rows would exist for all tables known to the system.

Systables

Name	Creator	Colcount
Client	Graham	9
Tasks	Graham	4
WorkOrders	Graham	3
OrderLine	Graham	4
Consultant	Graham	9

FIGURE 4-26   Systables table

The Syscolumns table contains the Colname, Tbname, and Coltype fields, as shown in Figure 4-27. The Colname field identifies the name of a field in one of the tables. The table in which the field is found is stored in the Tbname field, and the data type for the field is found in the Coltype field. There is a row in the Syscolumns table for each field in the Consultant table, for example. On each of these rows, Tbname is Consultant. On one of these rows, Colname is ConsltNum and Coltype is CHAR(2). On another row, Colname is LastName and Coltype is CHAR(15).

Syscolumns

Colname	Tbname	Coltype
Balance	Client	DECIMAL(8,2)
Category	Tasks	CHAR(3)
City	Client	CHAR(15)
City	Consultant	CHAR(15)
ClientName	Client	CHAR(35)
ClientNum	Client	CHAR(3)
ClientNum	WorkOrders	CHAR(3)
ConsltNum	Client	CHAR(2)
ConsltNum	Consultant	CHAR(2)
CreditLimit	Client	DECIMAL(8,2)
Description	Tasks	CHAR(30)
FirstName	Consultant	CHAR(15)
Hours	Consultant	DECIMAL(2,0)
LastName	Consultant	CHAR(15)
OrderDate	WorkOrders	DATE
OrderNum	OrderLine	CHAR(5)
OrderNum	WorkOrders	CHAR(5)
Price	Tasks	DECIMAL(6,2)
QuotedPrice	OrderLine	DECIMAL(6,2)
Rate	Consultant	DECIMAL(3,2)
ScheduledDate	OrderLine	DATE
State	Client	CHAR(2)
State	Consultant	CHAR(2)
Street	Client	CHAR(20)
Street	Consultant	CHAR(15)
TaskID	OrderLine	CHAR(4)
TaskID	Tasks	CHAR(4)
ZipCode	Client	CHAR(5)
ZipCode	Consultant	CHAR(5)

FIGURE 4-27   Syscolumns table

A DBMS furnishes ways of using the catalog to determine information about the structure of the database. In some cases, this simply involves using SQL to query the tables in the catalog. For example, to list the name and type of all fields (columns) in the Tasks table, you could use the following SQL command:

```
SELECT Colname, Coltype
FROM Syscolumns
WHERE Tbname='Tasks'
;
```

NOTE: In Oracle, the equivalent tables for SYSTABLES, SYSCOLUMNS, and SYSVIEWS are named DBA_TABLES, DBA_TAB_COLUMNS, and DBA_VIEWS, respectively.

In other cases, special tools provide the desired documentation. For example, Access has a tool called the Database **Documenter**, which allows you to print detailed documentation about any table, query, report, form, or other object in the database. To document the objects in an Access database, click the Database Documenter button (Database Tools tab | Analyze group).

STORED PROCEDURES

In a **client/server system**, the database resides on a computer called the **server**, and users access the database through clients. A **client** is a computer that is connected to a network and has access through the server to the database. Every time a user executes a query, the DBMS must determine the best way to process the query and provide the results. For example, the DBMS must determine which indexes are available and whether it can use those indexes to make the processing of the query more efficient.

If you anticipate running a particular query often for example, you can improve overall performance by saving the query in a special file called a **stored procedure**. The stored procedure is placed on the server. The DBMS compiles the stored procedure (translating it into machine code) and creates an execution plan, which is the most efficient way of obtaining the results. From that point on, users execute the compiled, optimized code in the stored procedure.

Another reason for saving a query as a stored procedure, even when you are not working in a client/server system, is convenience. Rather than retyping the entire query each time you need it, you can use the stored procedure. For example, suppose you frequently execute a query to change a client's credit limit. You can use the same query to select the record using the client's number and to change the credit limit. Instead of running the query each time and changing the client number and the credit limit, it would be simpler to store the query in a stored procedure. When you run the stored procedure, you need to enter only the appropriate client number and the new credit limit.

Stored procedures are more complex than views. Views do not accept parameters, and must be queried in a manner similar to tables. Stored procedures can have both input and output parameters and can contain statements to control the flow of the code, such as IF and WHILE. It is good practice to use stored procedures for all repetitive actions in the database.

Although Access does not support stored procedures, you can achieve some of the same convenience by creating and saving a parameter query that you learned about in Chapter 3. Recall that a parameter query prompts the user for the arguments you would otherwise use in a stored procedure.

TRIGGERS

A **trigger** is an action that occurs automatically in response to an associated database operation such as INSERT, UPDATE, or DELETE. Like a stored procedure, a trigger is stored and compiled on the server. Unlike a stored procedure, which is executed manually in response to a user request, a trigger is executed in response to a command that causes the associated database operation to occur.

Triggers in Access 2016

Access does not use the term "trigger" but offers the functionality of triggers through data macros. A **data macro** enables you to add logic to table events such as adding, changing, or deleting data. You can create data macros associated with specific events such as before you change or delete a record, or after you insert, update, or delete a record, by using the options on the Table Tools Table tab, as shown in Figure 4-28.

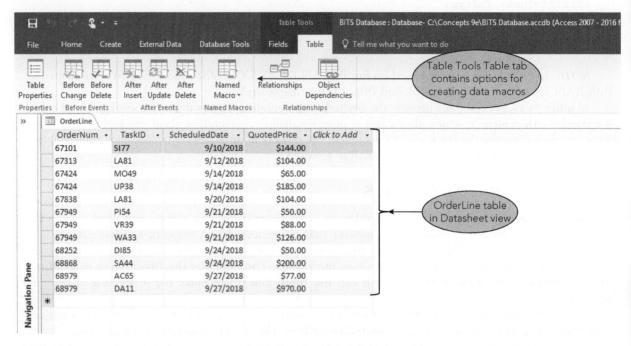

FIGURE 4-28   Data macro options to create triggers for the OrderLine table

Each of the events on the Table Tools Table tab opens a window with a dropdown button to begin preparing your data macro. From the dropdown list, you can choose one of various program flow, data block, or data action commands. Alternately, you can choose a command from the Action Catalog.

Once you choose a command, you can set parameters, such as updating a field or specifying a condition. Many commands require additional information, called **arguments**, to complete the action. If you select a command or action that requires arguments, the arguments appear along with the action allowing you to make any necessary changes to them.

Before Macros

Before macros are triggered when a change is made to the table, but before the table is saved to storage. For example, if you change any value in a field, this event is triggered when you leave the field, but before the table is saved.

Figure 4-29 displays the data macro for a Before Change event associated with the Client table. This example assumes there is a new column named Payment in the OrderLine table. This column represents the payment amount of the last payment the client made. (There might be other columns, such as PaymentDate, PaymentType, etc.) The employee who handles payments enters the amount in the Payment column. The macro should subtract that payment from the Balance column amount and update the Balance field.

The steps that must be taken are as follows:

- Check to see if it is the Payment field that has been changed.
- If so, subtract the payment from the old balance.
- Store the result of the subtraction in the Balance field.
- Save the macro.

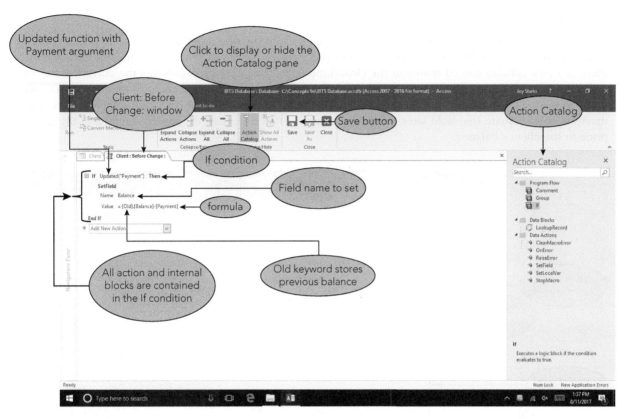

FIGURE 4-29 Macro Designer window for the Before Change event associated with the Client table

Specifically, this macro uses blocks, program flow commands, functions, and keywords. A block is a set of code, with a beginning and end, that is only executed based on the first line of the block. Examples of blocks include LookUpRecord, If, SetField, and others. Access allows you to select the block header or first line from a drop-down list. Access also insert the ending line.

The *If* condition is a program flow command that specifies to look in a certain table and column for a desired value. If the condition is true, the block is entered.

A function performs a task in the macro. Functions may need to use (or take) arguments to perform tasks. The arguments may be field names or actual values. Many times, arguments are enclosed in parentheses. Functions also may produce answers (called return values).

Figure 4-29 uses the function called *Updated*. The function takes a field name as its argument, evaluates if the field has been updated, and then returns a true or false. Notice in the first line of the data macro, the If condition looks to see if that update has been performed. If it has—meaning the Update function has returned a true value—the macro continues to the *Then* portion of the block. Notice the field name is enclosed in quotation marks.

```
If Updated["Payment"] then
```

Within the If condition is a *SetField* action. SetField allows you to choose one of the fields that you would like to change or edit. In this case, you are wanting to set the Balance field to a new value.

The final entry is to do some subtraction. You need to take the balance before the change, and subtract the payment. The OLD keyword holds the previous value of a field. After you type the word, OLD, you must type a period followed by the field name. As you enter steps in the Macro Designer window, Access will offer you choices to auto-complete your code, along with appropriate punctuation such as brackets. When the macro is excuted, the Balance field will be overwritten with the new value.

```
Value = [OLD].[Balance] - [Payment]
```

After Macros

Figure 4-30 displays the data macro for an After Update event for the OrderLine table. After macros are triggered after a change has been made, and after the changes are saved to storage. This example assumes there is a new column named Status in the OrderLine table. This column represents the current status of the orders: pending (P), complete (C), or deleted (D). For example, once the consultant notifies the BITS office that the service has been completed, the DBMS user updates the column with a C for complete. The data macro should evaluate that field after an update occurs. If it is a C, then the macro should add the quoted price to the client's balance.

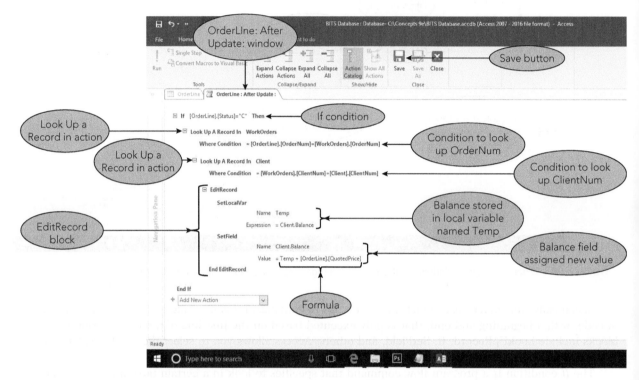

FIGURE 4-30 Macro Designer window for the After Update event associated with the OrderLine table

The steps that must be taken are as follows:

- Check to see if the table update changed the status to C.
- Look up the order number in the WorkOrders table and get the client number.
- Look up the client number in the Client table and get the balance.
- Store the old balance temporarily.
- Create a new balance by adding the old balance and the quoted price.
- Save the macro.

The first command chosen is an If. In this case, it looks in the OrderLine table, in the field or column named, Status, for the value "C" as shown in Figure 4-30. The C must be in quotation marks.

```
If [OrderLine].[Status] = "C" then
```

Notice that Access adds square brackets around the table and field names used in the If condition. When this condition is true, then the data macro proceeds. If it is false, the block finishes.

Next comes a *Look Up A Record In* block. This block looks for a record in a different table. Because you want to update the client's balance, you need to find the client number. The client number is not in the OrderLine table, so the data macro must reference the WorkOrder table to find that number. The *Where* condition specifies that you are looking for a match of the order number from the record that was updated:

```
Where [OrderLine].[OrderNum] = [WorkOrders].[OrderNum]
```

The Where condition is true only if a match occurs. If it is false, the macro finishes with no changes to the data.

Next, you need to find the exact client record. Again, a Look Up A Record In block searches for a match in the client number from both the WorkOrders table and the Client table.

```
Where [WorkOrders].[ClientNum] = [Client].[ ClientNum]
```

When a match occurs, the data macro continues.

With the correct record located, it is time to edit or update the record. From the dropdown, you choose the *Edit Record* block, and then the *SetLocalVar* action. In this example, you are storing the client's balance temporarily. Access calls this setting a local variable, because you are just using the value as storage for the duration of the current data macro. (You cannot use the Old keyword, because Balance is not in the OrderLine table.) The SetLocalVar action uses two arguments to change the contents of a field. The Name value is chosen by the user in this case. The Value argument can be a reference to a column, or you can enter a piece of data. In Figure 4-30, the Name of the local variable is *Temp* and the Value is [Client].[Balance].

Finally, the SetField action updates the field. Like the previous action, it takes two arguments. The Name argument is the field you wish to set; the Value argument is the new data for the field. In this case, it indicates that the new value is the result of adding the current value of Balance (stored in *Temp*) with the [OrderLine].[QuotedPrice] value. A period separates the table and the field. Access adds brackets.

```
Value = Temp + [OrderLine].[QuotePrice]
```

This data macro is triggered when the OrderLine table is updated and saved.

Access has many other blocks, flow controls, functions, and actions—many of which are listed in the Action Catalog. See your instructor for ways to use these data macro commands.

Summary

- Views are used to give each user his or her own view of the data in a database. In SQL, a defining query creates a view. When you enter a query that references a view, it is merged with the defining query to produce the query that is actually executed. In Access, views are created by saving queries that select the data to use in the view.
- Indexes are often used to facilitate data retrieval from the database. You can create an index on any field or combination of fields.
- Security is provided in SQL systems by using the GRANT and REVOKE commands.
- Entity integrity is the property that states that no field that is part of the primary key can accept null values.
- Referential integrity is the property that states that the value in any foreign key field must be null or must match an actual value in the primary key field of the table it references. Referential integrity is specified in SQL using the FOREIGN KEY clause. In Access, foreign keys are specified by creating relationships.
- Legal-values integrity is the property that states that the value entered in a field must be one of the legal values that satisfies some particular condition. Legal-values integrity is specified in SQL using the CHECK clause. In Access, legal-values integrity is specified using validation rules.
- The ALTER TABLE command allows you to add fields to a table, delete fields, or change the characteristics of fields. In Access, you can change the structure of a table by making the desired changes in the table design.
- The DROP TABLE command lets you delete a table from a database. In Access, you can delete a table by selecting the Delete command on the table's shortcut menu in the Navigation Pane.
- The system catalog is a feature of many relational DBMSs that stores information about the structure of a database. The system updates the catalog automatically. Each DBMS includes features to produce documentation of the database structure using the information in the catalog.
- A stored procedure is a query saved in a file that users can execute later.
- A trigger is an action that occurs automatically in response to an associated database operation such as INSERT, UPDATE, or DELETE. Like a stored procedure, a trigger is stored and compiled on the server. Unlike a stored procedure, which is executed in response to a user request, a trigger is executed in response to a command that causes the associated database operation to occur. Access provides the functionality of triggers through the use of data macros.

Key Terms

argument	multiple-column index
ALTER TABLE	multiple-field index
cascade delete	PRIMARY KEY clause
cascade update	recursive
catalog	referential integrity
CHECK	REVOKE
client	row-and-column subset view
client/server system	security
composite key	server
CREATE INDEX	single-column index
data macro	single-field index
defining query	stored procedure
Documenter	Syscolumns
DROP INDEX	Sysindexes
DROP TABLE	Systables
entity integrity	system catalog
FOREIGN KEY clause	Sysviews
GRANT	trigger
index	validation rule
index key	validation text
legal-values integrity	view

Review Questions

1. What is a view? How do you define a view? Does the data described in a view definition ever exist in that form? What happens when a user accesses a database through a view?

2. Using data from the BITS database, define a view named TopLevelClient. It consists of the number, name, address, balance, and credit limit of all clients with credit limits that are greater than or equal to $10,000.
   a. Using SQL, write the view definition for TopLevelClient.
   b. Write an SQL query to retrieve the number and name of all clients as well as the difference between their credit limit and balance in the TopLevelClient view.
   c. Convert the query you wrote in Question 2b to the query that the DBMS will actually execute.

3. Define a view named ItemOrder. It consists of the TaskID, description, price, order number, order date, and quoted price for all order lines currently on file.
   a. Using SQL, write the view definition for ItemOrder.
   b. Write an SQL query to retrieve the TaskID, description, order number, and quoted price for all orders in the ItemOrder view for items with quoted prices that exceed $100.
   c. Convert the query you wrote in Question 3b to the query that the DBMS will actually execute.

4. What is an index? What are the advantages and disadvantages of using indexes? How do you use SQL to create an index?

5. Describe the GRANT statement and explain how it relates to security. What types of privileges may be granted? How are they revoked?

6. Write the SQL commands to grant the following privileges:
   a. User Stetson must be able to retrieve data from the Client table.
   b. Users Webster and Bremer must be able to add new orders and order lines.

7. Write the SQL command to revoke user Stetson's privilege.

8. What is the system catalog? Name three items about which the catalog maintains information.

9. Write the SQL commands to obtain the following information from the system catalog:
   a. List every table that you created.
   b. List every field in the Client table and its associated data type.
   c. List every table that contains a field named TaskID.

10. Why is it a good idea for the DBMS to update the catalog automatically when a change is made in the database structure? Could users cause problems by updating the catalog themselves? Explain.

11. What are nulls? Which field cannot accept null values? Why?

12. State the three integrity rules. Indicate the reasons for enforcing each rule.

13. The WorkOrders table contains a foreign key, ClientNum, which must match the primary key of the Client table.
    a. What type of update to the WorkOrders table would violate referential integrity?
    b. If deletes do not cascade, what type of update to the Client table would violate referential integrity?
    c. If deletes do cascade, what would happen when a client was deleted?

14. How would you use SQL to change a table's structure? What general types of changes are possible? Which commands are used to implement these changes?

15. What are stored procedures? What purpose do they serve?

16. What are triggers? What purpose do they serve? How do you gain the functionality of a trigger using Access 2016?

17. You have a table that contains the following fields: MemberLastName, MemberFirstName, Street, City, State, ZipCode, and MembershipFee. There are 75,000 records in the table. What indexes would you create for the table, and why would you create these indexes?

18. MarketPoint Sales currently has a credit limit of $5,000. Because MarketPoint Sales has an excellent credit rating, BITS is increasing the company's credit limit to $10,000. If you run the SQL query in Question 2b after the credit limit has been increased, would MarketPoint Sales be included in the query results? Why or why not?

BITS Corporation Exercises

In the following exercises, you will use the data in the BITS database shown in Figure 2-1 in Chapter 2. (If you use a computer to complete these exercises, use a copy of the original BITS database so your data will not reflect the changes you made in Chapter 3.) If you have access to a DBMS, use the DBMS to perform the tasks and explain the steps you used in the process. If not, explain how you would use SQL to obtain the desired results. Check with your instructor if you are uncertain about which approach to take.

1. Create a view named TopLevelCust view. It consists of the number, name, address, balance, and credit limit of all clients with credit limits that are greater than or equal to $10,000. Display the data in the view.

2. Create a view named ItemOrder view. It consists of the TaskID, description, price, order number, order date, and quoted price for all order lines currently on file. Display the data in the view.

3. Create the following indexes. If it is necessary to name the index in your DBMS, use the indicated name.
   a. Create an index named ItemIndex1 on the TaskID field in the OrderLine table.
   b. Create an index named ItemIndex2 on the Description field in the Tasks table.
   c. Create an index named ItemIndex3 on the Description and Category fields in the Tasks table.
   d. Create an index named ItemIndex4 on the Description and Category fields in the Tasks table and list Category in descending order.

4. Drop the ItemIndex3 index from the Tasks table.

5. Assume the Client table has been created, but there are no integrity constraints. Create the necessary integrity constraint to ensure that the only allowable values for the CreditLimit field are 2500, 5000, 7500 or 10000. Ensure that the ClientNum field is the primary key in the Client table, and foreign key in the WorkOrders table.

6. Because BITS is about to obtain client number 1000, increase the length of the ClientNum field in the Client table to four characters. Insert yourself as client number 1001 with sample data. Display all the data in the Client table.

7. Add a field named TimeAllocation to the Tasks table. The allocation is a number representing the number of minutes that have been initially allocated for the task. Set all Allocation values to 60, as the company has a one hour minimum charge. Display all the data in the Tasks table.

8. Delete the Time Allocation field from the Tasks table. Display all the data in the Tasks table.

9. What command would you use to delete the Tasks table from the BITS database? (Do not delete the Tasks table.)

10. If you are using Access 2016, do the following.
    a. Add a field to the Client table named AvailableCredit. Set the field to currency.
    b. Create a data macro associated with the After Update event for the Client table. When a user updates the Balance field, the macro should subtract the new balance from the credit limit and place that value in the AvailableCredit field.
    c. Create a data macro associated with the After Delete event for the OrderLine table. When a user deletes a record because it is complete or cancelled, the macro should look up the order number in the WorkOrders table and delete it there as well. Use the For Each Record in the WorkOrders table. *Hint:* You can use the OLD keyword in the Where Condition: *[Old].[OrderNum] = [WorkOrders].[OrderNum]*. Test the data macro by deleting a record from the OrderLine table and ensuring that the record also is deleted from the WorkOrders table.

 11. Using Access 2016, an employee at BITS tried to delete TaskID PI54 from the Tasks table and received the following error message: "The record cannot be deleted or changed because table 'OrderLine' includes related records." Why did the employee receive this error message? What change is needed in the database to allow the deletion of records from the Tasks table?

 12. BITS has decided to include I.T. training in its service line and has assigned the item to the category OTH. What change is needed in the database to add items in category OTH to the Tasks table? Would you add any integrity constraints to the fields in the Tasks table? Why or why not?

Colonial Adventure Tours Case

The owner of Colonial Adventure Tours would like you to complete the following tasks to help him maintain his database. In the following exercises, you will use the data in the Colonial Adventure Tours database shown in Figures 1-15 through 1-19 in Chapter 1. (If you use a computer to complete these exercises, use a copy of the original Colonial Adventure Tours database so your data will not reflect the changes you made in Chapter 3.) If you have access to a DBMS, use the DBMS to perform the tasks and explain the steps you used in the process. If not, explain how you would use SQL to obtain the desired results. Check with your instructor if you are uncertain about which approach to take.

1. Create a view named NHTrips. It consists of the trip ID, trip name, start location, distance, maximum group size, type, and season for every trip located in New Hampshire (NH). Display the data in the view.

2. Create a view named Hiking. It consists of the trip ID, trip name, start location, state, distance, maximum group size, and season for every hiking trip. Display the data in the view.

3. Create a view named ReservationCustomer. It consists of the reservation ID, trip ID, trip date, customer number, customer last name, customer first name, and phone number. Display the data in the view.

4. Create the following indexes. If it is necessary to name the index in your DBMS, use the indicated name.
   a. Create an index named TripIndex1 on the TripName field in the Trip table.
   b. Create an index named TripIndex2 on the Type field in the Trip table.
   c. Create an index named TripIndex3 on the Type and Season fields in the Trip table and list the seasons in descending order.

5. Drop the TripIndex3 index from the Trip table.

6. Specify the integrity constraint that the distance of any trip must be equal to or greater than 4.

7. Ensure that the following are foreign keys (that is, specify referential integrity within the Colonial Adventure Tours database).
   a. CustomerNum is a foreign key in the Reservation table.
   b. TripID is a foreign key in the Reservation table.

8. Add to the Customer table a new character field named Waiver that is one character in length.

9. Change the value in the Waiver field in the Customer table to Y for the customer with the last name of Ocean.

10. Change the length of the StartLocation field in the Trip table to 60.

11. What command would you use to delete the Trip table from the Colonial Adventure Tours database? (Do not delete the Trip table.)

12. If you are using Access 2016, complete the following steps.
   a. Add a PreviousTrip field to the Customer table. Create and run a totals query on the Reservation table to count the number of reservations by customer. Manually update the Customer table with these values. Assign the value 0 to customers 110 and 123.
   b. Create a data macro associated with the After Insert event for the Reservation table to increment the PreviousTrip field for the appropriate customer when inserting a row in the Reservation table. Test the data macro by adding a record to the Reservation table and ensuring that the corresponding customer's previous trip total is updated correctly.
   c. Create a data macro associated with the After Delete event for the Reservation table to subtract one on the record being deleted from the customer's previous trip total. Test the data macro by deleting a record from the Reservation table and ensuring that the corresponding customer's previous trip total is updated correctly.

13. In Question 7, you specified referential integrity for the Reservation table. What other table(s) in the Colonial Adventure Tours database require that you specify referential integrity? Identify the foreign keys in the table(s).

14. Review the trip data for Colonial Adventure Tours shown in Figure 1-16 on page 17. In addition to the integrity constraint specified in Question 6, what other integrity constraints could you add to at least two other fields in the Trip table?

Sports Physical Therapy Case

In the following exercises, you will use the data in the Sports Physical Therapy database shown in Figures 1-21 through 1-24 in Chapter 1. (If you use a computer to complete these exercises, use a copy of the Sports Physical Therapy database so your data will not reflect the changes you made in Chapter 3.) If you have access to a DBMS, use the DBMS to perform the tasks and explain the steps you used in the process. If not, explain how you would use SQL to obtain the desired results. Check with your instructor if you are uncertain about which approach to take.

1. Create a view named HighBalance using the patient number, last name, first name, street, city, and zip code for those patients with a balance greater than $1,000. Display the data in the view.

2. Create a view named SingleBillingTherapies using the therapy code and description fields, for every therapy in which the unit of time is blank. Display the data in the view.

3. Create a view named McClainPatients using all fields from the Session table, where the TherapistID is BM273. Display the data in the view.

4. Create the following indexes. If it is necessary to name the index in your DBMS, use the indicated name.
   a. Create an index named PatientIndex1 on the City field in the Patient table.
   b. Create an index named PatientIndex2 on the LastName field in the Patient table.
   c. Create an index named PatientIndex3 on the City field in the Patient table and list the cities in descending order.

5. Drop the PatientIndex3 index from the Patient table.

6. Assume the Session table has been created, but there are no integrity constraints. Create the necessary integrity constraints so that the length of session must be greater than 0.

7. Ensure that the following are foreign keys (that is, specify referential integrity) in the Sports Physical Therapy database.
   a. TherapyCode is a foreign key in the Session table.
   b. PatientNum is a foreign key in the Session table.
   c. TherapistID is a foreign key in the Session table.

8. Add to the Patient table a new character field named Overdue that is one character in length. On all records, change the value for the Overdue field to N.

9. Change the value in the Overdue field in the Patient table to Y for the patient named Tobey Short.

10. Change the length of the LastName field in the Patient table to 25.

11. If you are using Access 2016, complete the following steps.
    a. Add a new field to the Patient table named, PaidInFull. Set the Length to 1. Set an integrity rule to accept only the following characters: Y or N. Set all fields to N. Save the table with the new field.
    b. Create a data macro associated with the After Update event for the saved Patient table. The macro should look at the PaidInFull field. If it is a Y, then the macro should change the Balance to zero. Test the data macro by changing the PaidInFull value on two patients, ensuring that the PaidInFull field for the corresponding patient is updated correctly.

12. The management of Sports Physical Therapy wants to assign certain therapists to certain therapies in which they specialize. What tables would have to be updated? Would it be appropriate to add a new field to the Therapies table? Would management encounter any problems in restricting a field in the Session table? What additional updates would management need to make to ensure that the data in the database is correct?

CHAPTER 5

DATABASE DESIGN 1: NORMALIZATION

LEARNING OBJECTIVES

- Discuss functional dependence and primary keys
- Define first normal form, second normal form, third normal form, and fourth normal form
- Describe the problems associated with tables (relations) that are not in first normal form, second normal form, or third normal form, along with the mechanism for converting to all three
- Discuss the problems associated with incorrect conversions to third normal form
- Describe the problems associated with tables (relations) that are not in fourth normal form and describe the mechanism for converting to fourth normal form
- Understand how normalization is used in the database design process

INTRODUCTION

You have examined the basic relational model, its structure, and the various ways of manipulating data within a relational database. In this chapter, you will learn about the normalization process and its underlying concepts and features. The **normalization process** is a series of steps that enable you to identify the existence of potential problems or anomalies in the database along with methods for correcting these problems. An **update anomaly** is a data inconsistency that results from data redundancy, the use of inappropriate nulls, or from a partial update. A **deletion anomaly** is the unintended loss of data due to deletion of other data. An **insertion anomaly** results when you cannot add data to the database due to absence of other data.

To correct anomalies in a database, you must convert tables to various types of **normal forms**. A table in a particular normal form possesses a certain desirable collection of properties. The most common normal forms are first normal form (1NF), second normal form (2NF), third normal form (3NF), and the lesser-used fourth normal form (4NF). Normalization is a progression in which a table that is in first normal form is better (freer from problems) than a table that is not in first normal form, a table that is in second normal form is better than one that is in first normal form, and so on. The goal of normalization is to take a table or collection of tables and produce a new collection of tables that represents the same information but that is free of all anomalies.

In this chapter, you will learn about two crucial concepts that are fundamental to understanding the normalization process: functional dependence and keys. You also will learn about first, second, third, and fourth normal forms.

Many of the examples in this chapter use data from the BITS database, which is shown in Figure 5-1.

Consultant

ConsltNum	LastName	FirstName	Street	City	State	ZipCode	Hours	Rate
19	Turner	Christopher	554 Brown Dr.	Tri City	FL	32889	40	$22.50
22	Jordan	Patrick	2287 Port Rd.	Easton	FL	33998	40	$22.50
35	Allen	Sarah	82 Elliott St.	Lizton	FL	34344	35	$20.00
51	Shields	Tom	373 Lincoln Ln.	Sunland	FL	39876	10	$15.00

Client

ClientNum	ClientName	Street	City	State	ZipCode	Balance	CreditLimit	ConsltNum
143	Hershey, Jarrod	135 E. Mill Street	Easton	FL	33998	$1,904.55	$2,500.00	19
175	Goduto, Sean	12 Saratoga Parkway	Tri City	FL	32889	$2,814.55	$5,000.00	19
299	Two Crafty Cousins	9787 NCR 350 West	Sunland	FL	39876	$8,354.00	$10,000.00	22
322	Prichard's Pizza & Pasta	501 Air Parkway	Lizton	FL	34344	$7,335.55	$10,000.00	35
363	Salazar, Jason	56473 Cherry Tree Dr.	Easton	FL	33998	$900.75	$2,500.00	35
405	Fisherman's Spot Shop	49 Elwood Ave.	Harpersburg	FL	31234	$4,113.40	$7,500.00	19
449	Seymour, Lindsey	4091 Brentwood Ln.	Amo	FL	34466	$557.70	$5,000.00	22
458	Bonnie's Beautiful Boutique	9565 Ridge Rd.	Tri City	FL	32889	$4,053.80	$7,500.00	22
677	Yates, Nick	231 Day Rd.	Sunland	FL	39876	$2,523.80	$2,500.00	35
733	Howler, Laura	1368 E. 1000 S.	Lizton	FL	34344	$3,658.05	$5,000.00	22
826	Harpersburg Bank	65 Forrest Blvd.	Harpersburg	FL	31234	$6,824.55	$10,000.00	19
867	MarketPoint Sales	826 Host St.	Easton	FL	33998	$3,089.00	$5,000.00	19

Tasks

TaskID	Description	Category	Price
AC65	Accessories	ACC	$80.00
DA11	Data recovery major	DRM	$175.00
DI85	Data recovery minor	DRM	$50.00
HA63	Hardware major	HAM	$225.00
HI31	Hardware minor	HAM	$165.70
LA81	Local area networking (LAN)	LAN	$104 00
MO49	Mobility	MOB	$65.00
OT99	Other work	OTH	$99.99
PI54	Printing issues	PRI	$50.00
SA44	Software major	SOM	$200.00
SI77	Software minor	SOM	$144.00
SI91	Security install/repair	SIR	$126.00
UP38	Upgrades	UPG	$185.00
VR39	Virus removal	VIR	$90.00
WA33	Wide area networking (WAN)	WAN	$130.00
WC19	Web connectivity	WEC	$75.00

OrderLine

OrderNum	TaskID	ScheduledDate	QuotedPrice
67101	SI77	9/10/2018	$144.00
67313	LA81	9/12/2018	$104.00
67424	MO49	9/14/2018	$65.00
67424	UP38	9/14/2018	$185.00
67838	LA81	9/20/2018	$104.00
67949	PI54	9/21/2018	$50.00
67949	VR39	9/21/2018	$88.00
67949	WA33	9/21/2018	$126.00
68252	DI85	9/24/2018	$50.00
68868	SA44	9/24/2018	$200.00
68979	AC65	9/27/2018	$77.00
68979	DA11	9/27/2018	$970.00

WorkOrders

OrderNum	OrderDate	ClientNum
67101	9/6/2018	733
67313	9/7/2018	458
67424	9/10/2018	322
67838	9/10/2018	867
67949	9/10/2018	322
68252	9/12/2018	363
68868	9/14/2018	867
68979	9/17/2018	826

FIGURE 5-1 Sample data for BITS

FUNCTIONAL DEPENDENCE

Understanding functional dependence is crucial to learning the material in the rest of this chapter. Functional dependence is a formal name for what is basically a simple idea — columns depending on other columns. To understand functional dependence, suppose the Consultant table for BITS contains an additional column named PayClass, as shown in Figure 5-2.

Consultant

ConsltNum	LastName	FirstName	Street	City	State	ZipCode	Hours	PayClass	Rate
19	Turner	Christopher	554 Brown Dr.	Tri City	FL	32889	40	1	$22.50
22	Jordan	Patrick	2287 Port Rd.	Easton	FL	33998	40	2	$22.50
35	Allen	Sarah	82 Elliott St.	Lizton	FL	34344	35	1	$20.00
51	Shields	Tom	373 Lincoln Ln.	Sunland	FL	39876	10	1	$15.00

FIGURE 5-2   Consultant table with additional column, PayClass

Assume one of the policies at BITS is that all consultants in any given pay class earn the same pay rate. How might you convey this fact to someone else? You might say that a consultant's pay class *determines* his or her pay rate. Another way to convey this fact is to say that a consultant's pay rate *depends on* his or her pay class. This phrasing uses the words *determines* and *depends on* exactly the way you will use them in connection with database design. If you wanted to be more formal, you would precede either expression with the word *functionally*. Thus, you might say, "A consultant's pay class *functionally determines* his or her pay rate" or "A consultant's pay rate *functionally depends on* his or her pay class."

The formal definition of functional dependence is as follows:

Definition: Column (attribute) B is **functionally dependent** on another column A (or possibly a collection of columns) when each value for A in the database is associated with exactly one value of B.

You can think of functional dependence as follows: If you are given a value for A in the database, do you know whether it will be associated with exactly one value of B? If so, B is functionally dependent on A (written as A → B). If B is functionally dependent on A, you can also say that A **functionally determines** B.

In the Consultant table, LastName is functionally dependent on ConsltNum. If you are given a value of 19 for ConsltNum, for example, you know that you will find a *single* LastName (in this case, Turner) associated with it. (*NOTE:* You need to be concerned only with actual values of ConsltNum in the database. If you are given a value of 31 for ConsltNum, for example, you will not find any names associated with it because there is no row in the Consultant table in which the consultant number is 31.)

Q & A 5-1

Question: In the Client table, is ClientName functionally dependent on ConsltNum?
Answer: No. Consultant number 35, for example, occurs on a row in which the client name is Prichard's Pizza and Pasta, on a row in which the client name is Salazar, Jason, and on a row in which the client name is Yates, Nick. Thus, a consultant number can be associated with more than one client name.

Q & A 5-2

Question: In the OrderLine table, is QuotedPrice functionally dependent on OrderNum?
Answer: No. Order number 67424, for example, occurs on a row in which the quoted price is $65.00 and on another row in which the quoted price is $185.00. Thus, an order number can be associated with more than one quoted price.

> ## Q & A 5-3
>
> **Question:** On which columns is QuotedPrice functionally dependent?
> **Answer:** For any combination of OrderNum and TaskID, there can be only one row in the OrderLine table. Thus, any combination of OrderNum and TaskID in the OrderLine table is associated with exactly one quoted price. Consequently, QuotedPrice is functionally dependent on the combination (formally called the concatenation) of OrderNum and TaskID.

At this point, a question naturally arises: How do you determine functional dependencies? Can you determine them by looking at sample data, for example? The answer is no, not always.

Consider the Consultant table shown in Figure 5-3, in which all last names are unique. It is very tempting to say that LastName functionally determines Street, City, State, and ZipCode (or equivalently that Street, City, State, and ZipCode are all functionally dependent on LastName). After all, given the last name of a consultant, you can find his or her address.

Consultant

ConsltNum	LastName	FirstName	Street	City	State	ZipCode	Hours	Rate
19	Turner	Christopher	554 Brown Dr.	Tri City	FL	32889	40	$22.50
22	Jordan	Patrick	2287 Port Rd.	Easton	FL	33998	40	$22.50
35	Allen	Sarah	82 Elliott St.	Lizton	FL	34344	35	$20.00
51	Shields	Tom	373 Lincoln Ln.	Sunland	FL	39876	10	$15.00

FIGURE 5-3 Consultant table

What happens if the last name of consultant 51 also happens to be Turner? Now you have the situation illustrated in Figure 5-4. If the last name you are given is Turner, you no longer can find a single address. Thus, you were misled by the original sample data. The only way to determine the functional dependencies that exist is to examine user policies through discussions with users, an examination of user documentation, and so on.

Consultant

ConsltNum	LastName	FirstName	Street	City	State	ZipCode	Hours	Rate
19	Turner	Christopher	554 Brown Dr.	Tri City	FL	32889	40	$22.50
22	Jordan	Patrick	2287 Port Rd.	Easton	FL	33998	40	$22.50
35	Allen	Sarah	82 Elliott St.	Lizton	FL	34344	35	$20.00
51	Turner	Tom	373 Lincoln Ln.	Sunland	FL	39876	10	$15.00

FIGURE 5-4 Consultant table with a second consultant named Turner

> ## Q & A 5-4
>
> **Question:** Assume the following columns exist in a relation named Student:
>
> - StudentNum (student number)
> - StudentLast (student last name)
> - StudentFirst (student first name)
> - HighSchoolNum (number of the high school from which the student graduated)
> - HighSchoolName (name of the high school from which the student graduated)
> - AdvisorNum (number of the student's advisor)
> - AdvisorLast (last name of the student's advisor)
> - AdvisorFirst (first name of the student's advisor)

Q & A 5-4 (continued)

Student numbers, high school numbers, and advisor numbers are unique; no two students have the same number, no two high schools have the same number, and no two advisors have the same number. Use this information to determine the functional dependencies in the Student relation.

Answer: Because student numbers are unique, any given student number in the database is associated with a single last name, first name, high school number, high school name, advisor number, advisor last name, and advisor first name. Thus, all the other columns in the Student relation are functionally dependent on StudentNum, which is represented as follows:

StudentNum → StudentLast, StudentFirst, HighSchoolNum, HighSchoolName, AdvisorNum,
    AdvisorLast, AdvisorFirst

Because two students can have the same first and last names, StudentFirst and StudentLast do not determine anything else. Because high school numbers are unique, any given high school number is associated with exactly one high school name. If high school 128 is Robbins High, for example, any student whose high school number is 128 *must* have the high school name Robbins High. Thus, HighSchoolName is functionally dependent on HighSchoolNum, which is represented as follows:

HighSchoolNum → HighSchoolName

Because advisor numbers are unique, any given advisor number is associated with exactly one advisor first name and exactly one advisor last name. If advisor 20 is Mary Webb, for example, any student whose advisor number is 20 *must* have the advisor's first name Mary and the advisor's last name Webb. Thus, AdvisorFirst and AdvisorLast are functionally dependent on AdvisorNum, which is represented as follows:

AdvisorNum → AdvisorLast, AdvisorFirst

As with students, an advisor's first and last names are not necessarily unique, so AdvisorFirst and AdvisorLast do not determine anything.

KEYS

A second underlying concept of the normalization process is that of the primary key. You already encountered the basic concept of the primary key in earlier chapters. In this chapter, however, you need a more precise definition.

Definition: Column A (or a collection of columns) is the **primary key** for a relation (table) R, if:

Property 1. *All* columns in R are functionally dependent on A.

Property 2. No subcollection of the columns in A (assuming A is a collection of columns and not just a single column) also has Property 1, above.

Q & A 5-5

Question: Is the Category column the primary key for the Tasks table?
Answer: No, because the other columns are not functionally dependent on the category. The category DRM, for example, appears on a row in the Tasks table in which the TaskID is DA11 and a row in which the TaskID is DI85. The category DRM is associated with two TaskIDs, so the TaskID column is not functionally dependent on the category.

Q & A 5-6

Question: Is ClientNum the primary key for the Client table?
Answer: Yes, because client numbers are unique. A given client number cannot appear on more than one row. Thus, each client number is associated with a single name, a single street, a single city, a single state, a single zip code, a single balance, a single credit limit, and a single consultant number. In other words, all columns in the Client table are functionally dependent on ClientNum.

ClientNum → CientName, Street, City, State, ZipCode, Balance, CreditLimit, ConsltNum

Q & A 5-7

Question: Is OrderNum the primary key for the OrderLine table?
Answer: No, because it does not uniquely determine ScheduledDate or QuotedPrice. The order number 68979, for example, appears on a row in the OrderLine table in which the TaskID is AC65 and the quoted price is $77.00 and also on a row in which the TaskID is DA11 and the quoted price is $970.00 (see Figure 5-1 on page 168).

Q & A 5-8

Question: Is the combination of OrderNum and TaskID the primary key for the OrderLine table?
Answer: Yes, because all columns are functionally dependent on this combination. Any combination of OrderNum and TaskID occurs on only one row in the OrderLine table and is associated with only one value for ScheduledDate and only one value for QuotedPrice. Further, neither OrderNum nor TaskID alone has this property. For example, order number 67424 appears on more than one row, as does TaskID LA81.

Q & A 5-9

Question: Is the combination of TaskID and Description the primary key for the Tasks table?
Answer: No. It is true that this combination functionally determines all columns in the Tasks table. TaskID alone, however, also has this property, so it violates Property 2.

Q & A 5-10

Question: You already determined the functional dependencies in a Student relation containing the following columns: StudentNum, StudentLast, StudentFirst, HighSchoolNum, HighSchoolName, AdvisorNum, AdvisorLast, and AdvisorFirst. The functional dependencies you determined were as follows:

```
StudentNum → StudentLast, StudentFirst, HighSchoolNum, HighSchoolName, AdvisorNum,
    AdvisorLast, AdvisorFirst
HighSchoolNum → HighSchoolName
AdvisorNum → AdvisorLast, AdvisorFirst
```

What is the primary key for the Student relation?
Answer: The only column that determines all the other columns is StudentNum, so it is the primary key for the Student relation.

Occasionally (but not often), there might be more than one possibility for the primary key. For example, if the BITS database included an Employee table to store employee numbers and Social Security numbers, either the employee number or the Social Security number could serve as the table's primary key. In this case, both columns are referred to as candidate keys. Similar to a primary key, a **candidate key** is a column or a collection of columns on which all columns in the table are functionally dependent. From all the candidate keys, one is chosen to be the primary key. The candidate keys that are not chosen as the primary key are often referred to as **alternate keys**.

The primary key is often called simply the *key* in other studies on database management and the relational model. This text will continue to use the term *primary key* to distinguish between the different definitions of a key that you will encounter throughout this text.

FIRST NORMAL FORM

A relation (table) that contains a **repeating group** (or multiple entries for a single record) is called an **unnormalized relation**. Sometimes a repeating group is one that contains more than one piece of data in a single cell (field and record intersection). Removing repeating groups is the starting point in the quest to create tables that are as free of problems as possible. Tables without repeating groups are said to be in first normal form.

Definition: A table (relation) is in **first normal form (1NF)** when it does not contain repeating groups.

As an example, consider the sample WorkOrders table shown in Figure 5-5, in which there is a repeating group (multiple entries for a single record) consisting of TaskID and QuotedPrice.

WorkOrders

OrderNum	OrderDate	TaskID	QuotedPrice
67101	9/6/2018	SI77	$144.00
67313	9/7/2018	LA81	$104.00
67424	9/10/2018	MO49	$65.00
		UP38	$185.00
67838	9/10/2018	LA81	$104.00
67949	9/10/2018	PI54	$50.00
		VR39	$88.00
		WA33	$126.00
68252	9/12/2018	DI85	$50.00
68868	9/14/2018	SA44	$200.00
68979	9/17/2018	AC65	$77.00
		DA11	$970.00

FIGURE 5-5 Sample unnormalized table

The notation for describing the WorkOrders table is as follows:

```
WorkOrders (OrderNum, OrderDate, (TaskID, QuotedPrice))
```

This notation indicates a table named WorkOrders consisting of a primary key (OrderNum) and a column named OrderDate. The inner parentheses indicate that there is a repeating group. The repeating group contains two columns, TaskID and QuotedPrice. This means that for a single order, there can be multiple combinations of a TaskID and a corresponding QuotedPrice, as illustrated in Figure 5-5. The row for order 67424, for example, contains two such combinations. In the first combination, the TaskID is MO49 and the QuotedPrice is $65.00. In the second combination, the TaskID is UP38 and the QuotedPrice is $185.00.

To convert the WorkOrders table to first normal form, you remove the repeating group as follows:

```
WorkOrders (OrderNum, OrderDate, TaskID, QuotedPrice)
```

Figure 5-6 shows the new table, which is now in first normal form.

WorkOrders

OrderNum	OrderDate	TaskID	NumOrdered
67101	9/6/2018	SI77	$144.00
67313	9/7/2018	LA81	$104.00
67424	9/10/2018	MO49	$65.00
67424	9/10/2018	UP38	$185.00
67838	9/10/2018	LA81	$104.00
67949	9/10/2018	PI54	$50.00
67949	9/10/2018	VR39	$88.00
67949	9/10/2018	WA33	$126.00
68252	9/12/2018	DI85	$50.00
68868	9/14/2018	SA44	$200.00
68979	9/17/2018	AC65	$77.00
68979	9/17/2018	DA11	$970.00

FIGURE 5-6 Result of normalization (conversion to first normal form)

Note that the third row of the unnormalized table (see Figure 5-5) indicates that TaskID MO49 and TaskID UP38 are both present for order 67424. In the normalized table (see Figure 5-6), this information is represented by *two* rows, the third and fourth. The primary key to the unnormalized WorkOrders table was OrderNum alone. The primary key to the normalized table is now the combination of OrderNum and TaskID.

In general, when converting a table to first normal form, the primary key usually will include the original primary key concatenated with the key to the repeating group (the column that distinguishes one occurrence of the repeating group from another). In this case, TaskID is the key to the repeating group; thus, TaskID becomes part of the primary key in the first normal form table.

SECOND NORMAL FORM

A table that is in first normal form still might contain problems that will require you to restructure it. Consider the following table:

WorkOrders (<u>OrderNum</u>, OrderDate, <u>TaskID</u>, Description, ScheduledDate, QuotedPrice)

This table has the following functional dependencies:

OrderNum → OrderDate
TaskID → Description
OrderNum, TaskID → ScheduledDate, QuotedPrice, OrderDate, Description

This notation indicates that OrderNum alone determines OrderDate and that TaskID alone determines Description; however, *both* an OrderNum *and* a TaskID are required to determine either ScheduledDate or QuotedPrice. (The combination of OrderNum and TaskID also determines both OrderDate and Description because OrderNum determines OrderDate and TaskID determines Description.) Consider the sample of this table shown in Figure 5-7.

WorkOrders

OrderNum	OrderDate	TaskID	Description	ScheduledDate	QuotedPrice
67101	9/6/2018	SI77	Software minor	9/10/2018	$144.00
67313	9/7/2018	LA81	Local area networking (LAN)	9/12/2018	$104.00
67424	9/10/2018	MO49	Mobility	9/14/2018	$65.00
67424	9/10/2018	UP38	Upgrades	9/14/2018	$185.00
67838	9/10/2018	LA81	Local area networking (LAN)	9/20/2018	$104.00
67949	9/10/2018	PI54	Printing issues	9/21/2018	$50.00
67949	9/10/2018	VR39	Virus removal	9/21/2018	$88.00
67949	9/10/2018	WA33	Wide area networking (WAN)	9/21/2018	$126.00
68252	9/12/2018	DI85	Data recovery minor	9/24/2018	$50.00
68868	9/14/2018	SA44	Software major	9/24/2018	$200.00
68979	9/17/2018	AC65	Accessories	9/27/2018	$77.00
68979	9/17/2018	DA11	Data recovery major	9/27/2018	$970.00

FIGURE 5-7   Sample WorkOrders table

The description of a specific task, LA81, occurs twice in the table. This redundancy causes several problems. It is wasteful of space, but that is not nearly as serious as some of the other problems. These other problems are anomalies, and they fall into the following categories:

1. *Update.* A change to the description of task LA81 requires not one change to the table, but two changes—you have to change each row on which TaskID LA81 appears. Changing multiple rows makes the update process more cumbersome; it also is more complicated logically, takes more time to update, and may introduce new errors.

2. *Inconsistent data.* There is nothing about the design that would prohibit task LA81 from having two different descriptions in this table. In fact, if TaskID LA81 were to occur on 20 rows, it could potentially have 20 *different* descriptions in the database!

3. **Additions.** You have a real problem when you try to add a new task and its description to the database. Because the primary key for the table consists of both OrderNum and TaskID, you need values for both columns when you want to add a new row. If you have a task to add, but there are no orders for it yet, what order number do you use? The only solution is to use a fictitious order number and then replace it with a real order number after BITS receives an order for the new task. Certainly, this is not an acceptable solution.

4. **Deletions.** If you deleted order 67101 from the database, you would *lose* all information about task SI77. For example, you would no longer know that TaskID SI77 is Software minor.

These problems occur because you have a nonkey column, Description, that is dependent on only a portion of the primary key (TaskID) and *not* on the complete primary key (OrderNum and TaskID). Second normal form represents an improvement over first normal form because it eliminates update anomalies in these situations.This problem leads to the definition of second normal form.

Definition: A table (relation) is in **second normal form (2NF)** when it is in first normal form and no nonkey column is dependent on only a portion of the primary key. A column is a **nonkey column** (also called a **nonkey attribute**) when it is not a part of the primary key.

When a table's primary key contains only one column, the table is automatically in second normal form because there would be no way for a column to be dependent on only a portion of the primary key.

For another perspective on second normal form, consider Figure 5-8. This type of diagram, sometimes called a **dependency diagram**, uses arrows to indicate all the functional dependencies present in the WorkOrders table (Figure 5-7). The arrows above the boxes indicate the normal dependencies that should be present; in other words, the primary key functionally determines all other columns. (In the WorkOrders table, the concatenation of OrderNum and TaskID determines all other columns.) The arrows below the boxes prevent the table from being in second normal form. These arrows represent types of dependencies that are often called **partial dependencies**, which are dependencies on only a portion of the primary key. In fact, another definition for second normal form is a table that is in first normal form but that contains no partial dependencies.

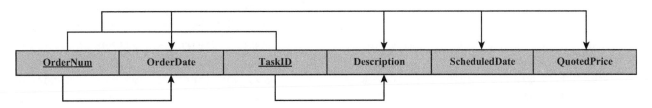

FIGURE 5-8 Dependencies in the WorkOrders table

Regardless of which definition of second normal form you use, you now can identify the fundamental problem with the WorkOrders table: It is *not* in second normal form. Although it may be pleasing to have a name for the problem, what you really need is a method to *correct* it; you need a way to convert tables to second normal form. To do so, first take each subset of the set of columns that makes up the primary key; then begin a new table with this subset as the primary key. For the WorkOrders table, this would give the following:

```
(OrderNum,
(TaskID,
(OrderNum, TaskID,
```

Next, place each of the other columns with its appropriate primary key; that is, place each primary key with the minimal collection of columns on which it depends. For the WorkOrders table, this would yield the following:

```
(OrderNum, OrderDate)
(TaskID, Description)
(OrderNum, TaskID, ScheduledDate, QuotedPrice)
```

Now you can give each new table a name that is descriptive of the table's contents, such as WorkOrders, Tasks, or OrderLine. Figure 5-9 shows the original WorkOrders table on top; the resulting WorkOrders, Tasks, and OrderLine tables created after the WorkOrders table was converted to second normal form appear below it.

WorkOrders

OrderNum	OrderDate	TaskID	Description	ScheduledDate	QuotedPrice
67101	9/6/2018	SI77	Software minor	9/10/2018	$144.00
67313	9/7/2018	LA81	Local area networking (LAN)	9/12/2018	$104.00
67424	9/10/2018	MO49	Mobility	9/14/2018	$65.00
67424	9/10/2018	UP38	Upgrades	9/14/2018	$185.00
67838	9/10/2018	LA81	Local area networking (LAN)	9/20/2018	$104.00
67949	9/10/2018	PI54	Printing issues	9/21/2018	$50.00
67949	9/10/2018	VR39	Virus removal	9/21/2018	$88.00
67949	9/10/2018	WA33	Wide area networking (WAN)	9/21/2018	$126.00
68252	9/12/2018	DI85	Data recovery minor	9/24/2018	$50.00
68868	9/14/2018	SA44	Software major	9/24/2018	$200.00
68979	9/17/2018	AC65	Accessories	9/27/2018	$77.00
68979	9/17/2018	DA11	Data recovery major	9/27/2018	$970.00

WorkOrders

OrderNum	OrderDate
67101	9/6/2018
67313	9/7/2018
67424	9/10/2018
67838	9/10/2018
67949	9/10/2018
68252	9/12/2018
68868	9/14/2018
68979	9/17/2018

Tasks

TaskID	Description
AC65	Accessories
DA11	Data recovery major
DI85	Data recovery minor
HA63	Hardware major
HI31	Hardware minor
LA81	Local area networking (LAN)
MO49	Mobility
OT99	Other work
PI54	Printing issues
SA44	Software major
SI77	Software minor
SI91	Security install/repair
UP38	Upgrades
VR39	Virus removal
WA33	Wide area networking (WAN)
WC19	Web connectivity

OrderLine

OrderNum	TaskID	ScheduledDate	QuotedPrice
67101	SI77	9/10/2018	$144.00
67313	LA81	9/12/2018	$104.00
67424	MO49	9/14/2018	$65.00
67424	UP38	9/14/2018	$185.00
67838	LA81	9/20/2018	$104.00
67949	PI54	9/21/2018	$50.00
67949	VR39	9/21/2018	$88.00
67949	WA33	9/21/2018	$126.00
68252	DI85	9/24/2018	$50.00
68868	SA44	9/24/2018	$200.00
68979	AC65	9/27/2018	$77.00
68979	DA11	9/27/2018	$970.00

FIGURE 5-9 Conversion to second normal

With this conversion, you have eliminated the update anomalies. A description appears only once for each task, so you do not have the redundancy that you did in the previous design. Changing the description for TaskID LA81, for example, now is a simple process involving a single change. Because the description for a task occurs in a single place, it is not possible to have multiple descriptions for a single task in the database at the same time.

To add a new task and its description, you simply create a new row in the Tasks table; there is no need to have an existing order for that task. Also, deleting order 67101 does not delete task SI77 from the Tasks table; you still have its description, Software minor, in the database. Finally, you have not lost any information in the process—you can reconstruct the data in the original design from the data in the new design.

THIRD NORMAL FORM

Problems can still exist with tables that are in second normal form. Consider the following Client table:

Client (<u>ClientNum</u>, ClientName, Balance, CreditLimit, <u>ConsltNum</u>, LastName, FirstName)

The functional dependencies in this table are as follows:

ClientNum → ClientName, Balance, CreditLimit, ConsltNum, LastName, FirstName
ConsltNum → LastName, FirstName

ClientNum determines all the other columns, and this is the primary key. In addition, ConsltNum determines LastName and FirstName.

When the primary key of a table is a single column, the table is automatically in second normal form. (If the table were not in second normal form, some columns would be dependent on only a *portion* of the primary key, which is impossible when the primary key is just one column.) Thus, the Client table is in second normal form.

The sample Client table shown in Figure 5-10 illustrates that this table possesses redundancy problems similar to those encountered earlier, even though it is in second normal form. In this case, the name of a consultant can occur many times in the table; see consultant 19 (Christopher Turner), for example.

Client

Client Num	ClientName	Street	City	State	ZipCode	Balance	CreditLimit	ConsltNum	LastName	FirstName
143	Hershey, Jarrod	135 E. Mill Street	Easton	FL	33998	$1,904.55	$2,500.00	19	Turner	Christopher
175	Goduto, Sean	12 Saratoga Parkway	Tri City	FL	32889	$2,814.55	$5,000.00	19	Turner	Christopher
299	Two Crafty Cousins	9787 NCR 350 West	Sunland	FL	39876	$8,354.00	$10,000.00	22	Jordan	Patrick
322	Prichard's Pizza & Pasta	501 Air Parkway	Lizton	FL	34344	$7,335.55	$10,000.00	35	Allen	Sarah
363	Salazar, Jason	56473 Cherry Tree Dr.	Easton	FL	33998	$900.75	$2,500.00	35	Allen	Sarah
405	Fisherman's Spot Shop	49 Elwood Ave.	Harpersburg	FL	31234	$4,113.40	$7,500.00	19	Turner	Christopher
449	Seymour, Lindsey	4091 Brentwood Ln.	Amo	FL	34466	$557.70	$5,000.00	22	Jordan	Patrick
458	Bonnie's Beautiful Boutique	9565 Ridge Rd.	Tri City	FL	32889	$4,053.80	$7,500.00	22	Jordan	Patrick
677	Yates, Nick	231 Day Rd.	Sunland	FL	39876	$2,523.80	$2,500.00	35	Allen	Sarah
733	Howler, Laura	1368 E. 1000 S.	Lizton	FL	34344	$3,658.05	$5,000.00	22	Jordan	Patrick
826	Harpersburg Bank	65 Forrest Blvd.	Harpersburg	FL	31234	$6,824.55	$10,000.00	19	Turner	Christopher
867	MarketPoint Sales	826 Host St.	Easton	FL	33998	$3,089.00	$5,000.00	19	Turner	Christopher

FIGURE 5-10 Sample Client table

In addition to the problem of wasted space, you have anomalies as follows:

1. **Updates.** A change to the name of a consultant requires not one change to the table but several, making the update process cumbersome.
2. **Inconsistent data.** There is nothing about the design that would prohibit a consultant from having two different names in the database. In fact, if the same consultant represents 20 clients (and thus would be found on 20 different rows), he or she could have 20 *different* names in the database.
3. **Additions.** In order to add consultant 87 (Mary Webb) to the database, she must already represent at least one client. If she has not yet been assigned any clients, you must add her record and create a fictitious client for her to represent. Again, this is not a desirable solution to the problem.
4. **Deletions.** If you deleted all the clients of consultant 35 from the database, you would lose all information concerning consultant 35.

These anomalies are due to the fact that ConsltNum determines LastName and FirstName, even though ConsltNum is not the primary key. As a result, the same ConsltNum and consequently the same LastName and FirstName can appear on many different rows.

You have seen that second normal form is an improvement over first normal form, but to eliminate second normal form problems, you need an even better strategy for creating tables in the database. Third normal form provides that strategy.

First, any column (or collection of columns) that determines another column is called a **determinant**. Certainly, the primary key in a table is a determinant. In fact, by definition, any candidate key is a determinant. (Remember that a candidate key is a column or a collection of columns that could function as the primary key.) In this case, ConsltNum is a determinant, but it is not a candidate key, and that is the problem.

Therefore, a table (relation) is in **third normal form (3NF)** when it is in second normal form and the only determinants it contains are candidate keys. *NOTE:* Third normal form is sometimes referred to as **Boyce–Codd normal form (BCNF)**, which is a stricter version of 3NF than previous definitions. This text will not differentiate between 3NF and BCNF.

Again, for an additional perspective, you can use a dependency diagram, as shown in Figure 5-11. The arrows above the boxes represent the normal dependencies of all columns on the primary key. The arrows below the boxes represent the problem—these arrows make ConsltNum a determinant. If there were arrows from ConsltNum to all the columns, ConsltNum would be a candidate key and you would not have a problem. The absence of these arrows indicates that this table contains a determinant that is not a candidate key. Thus, the table is not in third normal form.

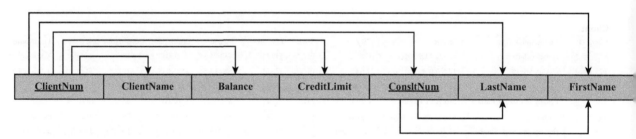

FIGURE 5-11   Dependencies in the Client table

You now have identified the problem with the Client table: It is not in third normal form. The following method corrects the deficiency in the Client table and in all tables having similar deficiencies.

First, for each determinant that is not a candidate key, remove from the table the columns that depend on this determinant (but do not remove the determinant). Next, create a new table containing all the columns from the original table that depend on this determinant. Finally, make the determinant the primary key of this new table. In the Client table, for example, you would remove LastName and FirstName because they depend on the determinant ConsltNum, which is not a candidate key. A new table is formed, consisting of ConsltNum (as the primary key), LastName, and FirstName.

```
Client (ClientNum, ClientName, Balance, CreditLimit, ConsltNum)
Consultant (ConsltNum, LastName, FirstName)
```

Figure 5-12 shows samples of the revised Client table and the new Consultant table.

Client

ClientNum	ClientName	Balance	CreditLimit	ConsltNum	LastName	FirstName
143	Hershey, Jarrod	$1,904.55	$2,500.00	19	Turner	Christopher
175	Goduto, Sean	$2,814.55	$5,000.00	19	Turner	Christopher
299	Two Crafty Cousins	$8,354.00	$10,000.00	22	Jordan	Patrick
322	Prichard's Pizza & Pasta	$7,335.55	$10,000.00	35	Allen	Sarah
363	Salazar, Jason	$900.75	$2,500.00	35	Allen	Sarah
405	Fisherman's Spot Shop	$4,113.40	$7,500.00	19	Turner	Christopher
449	Seymour, Lindsey	$557.70	$5,000.00	22	Jordan	Patrick
458	Bonnie's Beautiful Boutique	$4,053.80	$7,500.00	22	Jordan	Patrick
677	Yates, Nick	$2,523.80	$2,500.00	35	Allen	Sarah
733	Howler, Laura	$3,658.05	$5,000.00	22	Jordan	Patrick
826	Harpersburg Bank	$6,824.55	$10,000.00	19	Turner	Christopher
867	MarketPoint Sales	$3,089.00	$5,000.00	19	Turner	Christopher

Client

ClientNum	ClientName	Balance	CreditLimit	ConsltNum
143	Hershey, Jarrod	$1,904.55	$2,500.00	19
175	Goduto, Sean	$2,814.55	$5,000.00	19
299	Two Crafty Cousins	$8,354.00	$10,000.00	22
322	Prichard's Pizza & Pasta	$7,335.55	$10,000.00	35
363	Salazar, Jason	$900.75	$2,500.00	35
405	Fisherman's Spot Shop	$4,113.40	$7,500.00	19
449	Seymour, Lindsey	$557.70	$5,000.00	22
458	Bonnie's Beautiful Boutique	$4,053.80	$7,500.00	22
677	Yates, Nick	$2,523.80	$2,500.00	35
733	Howler, Laura	$3,658.05	$5,000.00	22
826	Harpersburg Bank	$6,824.55	$10,000.00	19
867	MarketPoint Sales	$3,089.00	$5,000.00	19

Consultant

ConsltNum	LastName	FirstName
19	Turner	Christopher
22	Jordan	Patrick
35	Allen	Sarah
51	Shields	Tom

FIGURE 5-12 Conversion to third normal form

Have you now corrected all previously identified problems? A consultant's name appears only once, thus avoiding redundancy and simplifying the process of changing a consultant's name. With this design, it is not possible for the same consultant to have different names in the database. To add a new consultant to the database, you can add a row in the Consultant table without requiring the consultant to have at least one assigned Client. Finally, deleting all the clients of a given consultant will not remove the consultant's record from the Consultant table, retaining the consultant's name. In addition, you can reconstruct all the data in the original table from the data in the new collection of tables. All previously mentioned problems have indeed been solved.

INCORRECT DECOMPOSITIONS

When you normalize a table by breaking down the relations into progressively finer levels of detail, it is called **decomposition**. It is important to note that the decomposition of a table into two or more third normal form tables *must* be accomplished by the method indicated in the previous section, even though there are other possibilities that at first glance might seem to be legitimate. For example, you can examine two other decompositions of the Client table into third normal form tables to understand the difficulties they pose. Assume in the decomposition process that

Client (<u>ClientNum</u>, ClientName, Balance, CreditLimit, ConsltNum, LastName, FirstName)

is incorrectly replaced by the following, with ClientNum being the primary key for both tables.

Client (<u>ClientNum</u>, ClientName, Balance, CreditLimit, ConsltNum)
Consultant (<u>ClientNum</u>, LastName, FirstName)

Samples of these incorrect tables appear in Figure 5-13. Both new tables are in third normal form, but still suffer from some of the same kinds of problems as the original Client table.

Client

ClientNum	ClientName	Balance	CreditLimit	ConsltNum	LastName	FirstName
143	Hershey, Jarrod	$1,904.55	$2,500.00	19	Turner	Christopher
175	Goduto, Sean	$2,814.55	$5,000.00	19	Turner	Christopher
299	Two Crafty Cousins	$8,354.00	$10,000.00	22	Jordan	Patrick
322	Prichard's Pizza & Pasta	$7,335.55	$10,000.00	35	Allen	Sarah
363	Salazar, Jason	$900.75	$2,500.00	35	Allen	Sarah
405	Fisherman's Spot Shop	$4,113.40	$7,500.00	19	Turner	Christopher
449	Seymour, Lindsey	$557.70	$5,000.00	22	Jordan	Patrick
458	Bonnie's Beautiful	$4,053.80	$7,500.00	22	Jordan	Patrick
677	Yates, Nick	$2,523.80	$2,500.00	35	Allen	Sarah
733	Howler, Laura	$3,658.05	$5,000.00	22	Jordan	Patrick
826	Harpersburg Bank	$6,824.55	$10,000.00	19	Turner	Christopher
867	MarketPoint Sales	$3,089.00	$5,000.00	19	Turner	Christopher

Client

ClientNum	ClientName	Balance	CreditLimit	ConsltNum
143	Hershey, Jarrod	$1,904.55	$2,500.00	19
175	Goduto, Sean	$2,814.55	$5,000.00	19
299	Two Crafty Cousins	$8,354.00	$10,000.00	22
322	Prichard's Pizza & Pasta	$7,335.55	$10,000.00	35
363	Salazar, Jason	$900.75	$2,500.00	35
405	Fisherman's Spot Shop	$4,113.40	$7,500.00	19
449	Seymour, Lindsey	$557.70	$5,000.00	22
458	Bonnie's Beautiful	$4,053.80	$7,500.00	22
677	Yates, Nick	$2,523.80	$2,500.00	35
733	Howler, Laura	$3,658.05	$5,000.00	22
826	Harpersburg Bank	$6,824.55	$10,000.00	19
867	MarketPoint Sales	$3,089.00	$5,000.00	19

Consultant

ClientNum	LastName	FirstName
143	Turner	Christopher
175	Turner	Christopher
299	Jordan	Patrick
322	Allen	Sarah
363	Allen	Sarah
405	Turner	Christopher
449	Jordan	Patrick
458	Jordan	Patrick
677	Allen	Sarah
733	Jordan	Patrick
826	Turner	Christopher
867	Turner	Christopher

FIGURE 5-13 Incorrect decomposition of the Client table

Consider, for example, the redundancy in the storage of consultants' names, the problem encountered in changing the name of a consultant, and the difficulty of adding a new consultant who represents no clients. In addition, because the consultant number and consultant names are in different tables, you have actually *split a functional dependence across two different tables.* Thus, this seemingly valid decomposition is definitely not a desirable way to create third normal form tables.

There is another incorrect decomposition that you might choose, and that is to replace

Client (<u>ClientNum</u>, ClientName, Balance, CreditLimit, ConsltNum, LastName, FirstName)

with

Client (<u>ClientNum</u>, ClientName, Balance, CreditLimit, LastName, FirstName)
Consultant (<u>ConsltNum</u>, LastName, FirstName)

Samples of these tables appear in Figure 5-14.

Client

ClientNum	ClientName	Balance	CreditLimit	ConsltNum	LastName	FirstName
299	Two Crafty Cousins	$8,354.00	$10,000.00	22	Jordan	Patrick
322	Prichard's Pizza & Pasta	$7,335.55	$10,000.00	35	Allen	Sarah
363	Salazar, Jason	$900.75	$2,500.00	35	Allen	Sarah
449	Seymour, Lindsey	$557.70	$5,000.00	22	Jordan	Patrick
458	Bonnie's Beautiful Boutique	$4,053.80	$7,500.00	22	Jordan	Patrick
677	Yates, Nick	$2,523.80	$2,500.00	35	Allen	Sarah
733	Howler, Laura	$3,658.05	$5,000.00	22	Jordan	Patrick

Client

ClientNum	ClientName	Balance	CreditLimit	LastName	FirstName
175	Goduto, Sean	$2,814.55	$5,000.00	Turner	Christopher
299	Two Crafty Cousins	$8,354.00	$10,000.00	Jordan	Patrick
322	Prichard's Pizza & Pasta	$7,335.55	$10,000.00	Allen	Sarah
363	Salazar, Jason	$900.75	$2,500.00	Allen	Sarah
449	Seymour, Lindsey	$557.70	$5,000.00	Jordan	Patrick
458	Bonnie's Beautiful	$4,053.80	$7,500.00	Jordan	Patrick
733	Howler, Laura	$3,658.05	$5,000.00	Jordan	Patrick
826	Harpersburg Bank	$6,824.55	$10,000.00	Turner	Christopher

Consultant

ConsltNum	LastName	FirstName
22	Jordan	Patrick
35	Allen	Sarah
51	Shields	Tom

FIGURE 5-14 Incorrect decomposition of the Client table

This new design seems to be a possibility. Not only are both tables in third normal form, but joining them together based on LastName and FirstName seems to reconstruct the data in the original table. Or does it? Suppose two different consultants, with consultant numbers 19 and 51, happen to have the same name, Christopher Turner. In this case, when you join the two new tables, there would be no way to identify correctly which Christopher Turner represents which clients. Thus, you would get a row on which client 143 (Hershey, Jarrod) is associated with consultant 19 (Christopher Turner) and *another* row on which client 143 is associated with consultant 51 (the other Christopher Turner). Because you obviously want decompositions that preserve the original information, this design is not appropriate.

Q & A 5-11

Question: Using the types of entities found in a college environment (faculty, students, departments, courses, and so on), create an example of a table that is in first normal form but not in second normal form and an example of a table that is in second normal form but not in third normal form. In each case, justify your solutions and show how to convert to the higher forms.

Answer: There are many possible solutions. Your answer may differ from the following solution, but that does not mean it is an unsatisfactory solution.

To create a first normal form table that is not in second normal form, you need a table that has no repeating groups and that has at least one column that is dependent on only a portion of the primary key. For a column to be dependent on a portion of the primary key, the primary key must contain at least two columns. Following is a picture of what you need:

(1, 2, 3, 4)

This table contains four columns, numbered 1, 2, 3, and 4, in which the combination of columns 1 and 2 functionally determines both columns 3 and 4. In addition, neither column 1 nor column 2 can determine *all* other columns; if either one could, the primary key would contain only this one column. Finally, you want part of the primary key (say, column 2) to determine another column (say, column 4).

Now that you know the pattern you need, you would like to find columns from within the college environment to fit it. One example is as follows:

(StudentNum, CourseNum, Grade, CourseDescription)

In this example, the concatenation of StudentNum and CourseNum determines both Grade and CourseDescription. Both columns are required to determine Grade; thus, the primary key consists of their concatenation. CourseDescription, however, is dependent only on CourseNum, which violates second normal form. To convert this table to second normal form, you would replace it with two tables. Recall that for each non-candidate determinant, you should remove the columns that depend on this determinant (but do not remove the determinant itself). The result is as follows:

(StudentNum, CourseNum, Grade)
(CourseNum, CourseDescription)

You now would give these tables appropriate names.

To create a table that is in second normal form but not in third normal form, you need a second normal form table in which there is a determinant that is *not* a candidate key. If you choose a table that has a single column as the primary key, it is automatically in second normal form, so the real problem is the determinant. You need a table like the following:

(1, 2, 3)

This table contains three columns, numbered 1, 2, and 3, in which column 1 determines each of the others and thus is the primary key. When column 2 also determines column 3, column 2 is a determinant. When column 2 does not also determine column 1, column 2 is not a candidate key. One example that fits this pattern is as follows:

(StudentNum, AdvisorNum, AdvisorName)

In this case, the StudentNum determines both the student's AdvisorNum and AdvisorName. AdvisorNum determines AdvisorName, but AdvisorNum does not determine StudentNum because one advisor can have many advisees. This table is in second normal form but not in third normal form. To convert it to third normal form, you would replace it with the following:

(StudentNum, AdvisorNum)
(AdvisorNum, AdvisorName)

Q & A 5-12

Question: Convert the following table to third normal form. In this table, StudentNum determines StudentName, NumCredits, AdvisorNum, and AdvisorName. AdvisorNum determines AdvisorName. CourseNum determines Description. The combination of StudentNum and CourseNum determines Grade.

```
Student (StudentNum, StudentName, NumCredits, AdvisorNum, AdvisorName, (CourseNum,
    Description, Grade))
```

Answer: Step 1. Remove the repeating group to convert it to first normal form, yielding the following:

```
Student (StudentNum, StudentName, NumCredits, AdvisorNum, AdvisorName, CourseNum,
    Description, Grade)
```

This table is now in first normal form because it has no repeating groups. It is not, however, in second normal form because StudentName, for example, is dependent only on StudentNum, which is only a portion of the primary key.

Step 2. Convert the first normal form table to second normal form. First, for each subset of the primary key, start a table with that subset as its key, yielding the following:

```
(StudentNum,
(CourseNum,
(StudentNum, CourseNum,
```

Next, place the rest of the columns with the smallest collection of columns on which they depend, giving the following:

```
(StudentNum, StudentName, NumCredits, AdvisorNum, AdvisorName)
(CourseNum, Description)
(StudentNum, CourseNum, Grade)
```

Finally, assign names to each of the newly created tables as follows:

```
Student (StudentNum, StudentName, NumCredits, AdvisorNum, AdvisorName)
Course (CourseNum, Description)
StudentCourse (StudentNum, CourseNum, Grade)
```

Although these tables are all in second normal form, Course and StudentCourse are also in third normal form. The Student table is not in third normal form, however, because it contains a determinant (AdvisorNum) that is not a candidate key.

Step 3. Convert the second normal form of the Student table to third normal form by removing the column that depends on the determinant AdvisorNum and placing it in a separate table.

```
(StudentNum, StudentName, NumCredits, AdvisorNum)
(AdvisorNum, AdvisorName)
```

Step 4. Name these tables and put the entire collection together, giving the following:

```
Student (StudentNum, StudentName, NumCredits, AdvisorNum)
Advisor (AdvisorNum, AdvisorName)
Course (CourseNum, Description)
StudentCourse (StudentNum, CourseNum, Grade)
```

MULTIVALUED DEPENDENCIES AND FOURTH NORMAL FORM

By converting a given collection of tables to an equivalent third normal form collection of tables, you remove problems arising from functional dependencies. Usually this means that you eliminate the types of previously discussed anomalies. Converting to third normal form does not avoid all problems related to dependencies, however. A different kind of dependency also can lead to the same types of problems.

To illustrate the problem, suppose you are interested in faculty members at Marvel College. In addition to faculty members, you are interested in the students they advise and the committees on which the faculty members serve. A faculty member can advise many students. Because students can have more than one major, a student can have more than one faculty member as an advisor. A faculty member can serve on zero, one, or more committees. As an initial relational design for this situation, suppose you chose the following unnormalized table:

Faculty (<u>FacultyNum</u>, (StudentNum), (CommitteeCode))

The single Faculty table has a primary key of FacultyNum (the number that identifies the faculty member) and two separate repeating groups, StudentNum (the number that identifies the student) and CommitteeCode (the code that identifies the committee, such as ADV for Advisory committee, PER for Personnel committee, and CUR for Curriculum committee). To convert this table to first normal form, you might be tempted to remove the two repeating groups and expand the primary key to include both StudentNum and CommitteeCode. That solution would give the following table:

Faculty (<u>FacultyNum</u>, <u>StudentNum</u>, <u>CommitteeCode</u>)

Samples of the table with repeating groups and with the repeating groups removed appear in Figure 5-15.

Faculty

FacultyNum	StudentNum	CommitteeCode
123	12805 24139	ADV PER HSG
444	57384	HSG
456	24139 36273 37573	CUR

Faculty

FacultyNum	StudentNum	CommitteeCode
123	12805	ADV
123	12805	PER
123	12805	HSG
123	24139	ADV
123	24139	PER
123	24139	HSG
444	57384	HSG
456	24139	CUR
456	36273	CUR
456	37573	CUR

FIGURE 5-15   Incorrect way to remove repeating groups-relation is not in fourth normal form

You already may have suspected that this approach has some problems. If so, you are correct. It is a strange way to normalize the original table. Yet it is precisely this approach for removing repeating groups that leads to the problems concerning multivalued dependencies. You will see how this table should have been normalized to avoid the problems altogether. For now, however, you will examine this table to see what kinds of problems are present.

The first thing you should observe about this table is that it is in third normal form because no groups repeat, no column is dependent on only a portion of the primary key, and no determinants exist that are not candidate keys. There are several problems, however, with this third normal form table.

1. *Update.* Changing the CommitteeCode for faculty member 123 requires more than one change. If this faculty member changes from an Advisory committee member to a Curriculum committee member, you would need to change the CommitteeCode from ADV to CUR in rows 1 and 4 of the table. After all, it does not make sense to say that the committee is ADV when associated with student 12805 and CUR when associated with student 24139. The same committee is served on by the same faculty member. The faculty member does not serve on one committee when advising one student and a different committee when advising another student.

2. *Additions.* Suppose faculty member 555 joins the faculty at Marvel College. Also suppose that this faculty member does not yet serve on a committee. When this faculty member begins advising student 44332, you have a problem because CommitteeCode is part of the primary key. You need to enter a fictitious CommitteeCode in this situation.

3. *Deletions.* If faculty member 444 no longer advises student 57384 and you delete the appropriate row from the table, you lose the information that faculty member 444 serves on the Housing committee (HSG).

These problems are similar to those encountered in the discussions of both second normal form and third normal form, but there are no functional dependencies among the columns in this table. A given faculty member is not associated with one student, as he or she would be if this were a functional dependence. Each faculty member, however, is associated with a specific collection of students. More importantly, this association is *independent* of any association with committees. This independence is what causes the problem. This type of dependency is called a multivalued dependency.

Definition: In a table with columns A, B, and C, there is a **multivalued dependence** of column B on column A (also read as "B is **multidependent** on A" or "A **multidetermines** B") when each value for A is associated with a specific collection of values for B, and further, this collection is independent of any values for C. This is usually written as follows:

A → → B

Definition: A table (relation) is in **fourth normal form (4NF)** when it is in third normal form and there are no multivalued dependencies.

As you might expect, converting a table to fourth normal form is similar to the normalization process used in the treatments of second normal form and third normal form. You split the third normal form table into separate tables, each containing the column that multidetermines the others, which, in this case, is FacultyNum. This means you replace

    Faculty (FacultyNum, StudentNum, CommitteeCode)

with

    FacStudent (FacultyNum, StudentNum)
    FacCommittee (FacultyNum, CommitteeCode)

Figure 5-16 shows samples of these tables. As before, the problems have disappeared. There is no problem with changing the CommitteeCode ADV to CUR for faculty member 123 because the committee code occurs in only one place. To add the information that faculty member 555 advises student 44332, you need to add a row to the Fac-Student table—it does not matter whether this faculty member serves on a committee. Finally, to delete the information that faculty member 444 advises student 57384, you need to remove a row from the FacStudent table. In this case, you do not lose the information that this faculty member serves on the Housing committee.

Faculty

FacultyNum	StudentNum	CommitteeCode
123	12805	ADV
123	12805	PER
123	12805	HSG
123	24139	ADV
123	24139	PER
123	24139	HSG
444	57384	HSG
456	24139	CUR
456	36273	CUR
456	37573	CUR

FacStudent

FacultyNum	StudentNum
123	12805
123	24139
456	37573
456	24139
456	36273
444	57384

FacCommittee

FacultyNum	CommitteeCode
123	ADV
123	PER
123	HSG
456	CUR
444	HSG

FIGURE 5-16   Conversion to fourth normal form

AVOIDING THE PROBLEM WITH MULTIVALUED DEPENDENCIES

Any table that is not in fourth normal form suffers some serious problems, but there is a way to avoid dealing with the issue. You should have a design methodology for normalizing tables that prevents this situation from occurring in the first place. You already have most of such a methodology in place from the discussion of the first normal form, second normal form, and third normal form normalization processes. All you need is a slightly more sophisticated method for converting an unnormalized table to first normal form.

The conversion of an unnormalized table to first normal form requires the removal of repeating groups. When this was first demonstrated, you merely removed the repeating group symbol and expanded the primary key. You will recall, for example, that

```
WorkOrders (OrderNum, OrderDate, (TaskID, ScheduledDate))
```

became

```
WorkOrders (OrderNum, OrderDate, TaskID, ScheduledDate)
```

The primary key was expanded to include the primary key of the original table together with the key to the repeating group.

What happens when there are two or more repeating groups? The method you used earlier is inadequate for such situations. Instead, you must place each repeating group in a separate table. Each table will contain all the columns that make up the given repeating group, as well as the primary key of the original unnormalized table. The primary key to each new table will be the concatenation of the primary key of the original table and the primary key of the repeating group. For example, consider the following unnormalized table that contains two repeating groups:

```
Faculty (FacultyNum, FacultyName, (StudentNum, StudentName), (CommitteeCode, CommitteeName))
```

In this example, FacultyName is the name of the faculty member and StudentName is the name of the student. The columns CommitteeCode and CommitteeName refer to the committee's code and name. (For example, one row in this table would have PER in the CommitteeCode column and Personnel Committee in the CommitteeName column.) Applying this new method to create first normal form tables would produce the following:

```
Faculty (FacultyNum, FacultyName)
FacStudent (FacultyNum, StudentNum, StudentName)
FacCommittee (FacultyNum, CommitteeCode, CommitteeName)
```

As you can see, this collection of tables avoids the problems with multivalued dependencies. At this point, you have a collection of first normal form tables that you still need to convert to third normal form. By using this process, however, you can guarantee that the result will also be in fourth normal form.

Summary of Normal Forms

Figure 5-17 summarizes the four normal forms.

Normal Form	Meaning/Required Conditions	Notes
1NF	No repeating groups.	
2NF	1NF and no nonkey column is dependent on only a portion of the primary key.	Automatically 2NF if the primary key contains only a single column.
3NF	2NF and the only determinants are candidate keys.	Actually Boyce-Codd normal form (BCNF).
4NF	3NF and no multivalued dependencies.	

FIGURE 5-17   Normal forms

APPLICATION TO DATABASE DESIGN

The normalization process used to convert a relation or collection of relations to an equivalent collection of third normal form tables is a crucial part of the database design process. By following a careful and appropriate normalization methodology, you need not worry about normal forms higher than third normal form. There are three aspects concerning normalization that you need to keep in mind, however.

First, you should carefully convert tables to third normal form. Suppose the following columns exist in a table about Coaches (the Coach relation). *NOTE:* The ellipsis (…) represents additional columns that exist but are not included in this example.

```
Coach (CoachNum, LastName, FirstName, Street, City, State, ZipCode,...)
```

In addition to the functional dependencies that all the columns have on CoachNum, there are two other functional dependencies. As originally designed by the United States Postal Service, a zip code determines both the state and city.

Does this mean that you should replace the Coach relation with the following?

```
Coach (CoachNum, LastName, FirstName, Street, ZipCode,...)
ZipCodeInfo (ZipCode, City, State)
```

If you are determined to ensure that every relation is in third normal form, you could replace the Coach relation with the revised Coach relation and the new ZipCodeInfo relation, but this approach is probably unnecessary. If you review the list of problems normally associated with relations that are not in third normal form, you will see that they do not apply here. Are you likely to need to change the state in which a given zip code is located? Do you need to add the fact that a zip code corresponds to a particular city, if you have no clients who live in Allendale, for example? In this case, the design of the original Coach relation is sufficient.

Second, there are currently situations where the same zip code corresponds to more than one city or even to more than one state in rare circumstances. This situation illustrates the wisdom in not making the change and the fact that the requirements and, consequently, the functional dependencies, can change over time. It is critical to review assumptions and dependencies periodically to see if any changes to the design are warranted.

Third, by splitting relations to achieve third normal form tables, you create the need to express an **interrelation constraint**, a condition that involves two or more relations. In the example given earlier for converting to third normal form, you split the Client relation in the BITS database from

```
Client (ClientNum, ClientName, Balance, CreditLimit, ConsltNum, LastName, FirstName)
```

to

```
Client (ClientNum, ClientName, Balance, CreditLimit, ConsltNum)
Consultant (ConsltNum, LastName, FirstName)
```

Nothing about these two relations by themselves would force the ConsltNum on a row in the Client relation to match a value of ConsltNum in the Consultant relation. Requiring this to take place is an example of an interrelation constraint. Foreign keys handle this type of interrelation constraint. You will learn more about foreign keys and how to specify them during the database design process in Chapter 6.

Summary

- Column (attribute) B is functionally dependent on another column A (or possibly a collection of columns) when each value for A in the database is associated with exactly one value of B.
- The primary key is a column (or a collection of columns) A such that all other columns are functionally dependent on A and no subcollection of the columns in A also has this property.
- When there is more than one choice for the primary key, one of the possibilities is chosen to be *the* primary key. The others are referred to as candidate keys.
- A table (relation) is in first normal form (1NF) when it does not contain repeating groups.
- A column is a nonkey column (also called a nonkey attribute) when it is not a part of the primary key.
- A table (relation) is in second normal form (2NF) when it is in first normal form and no nonkey column is dependent on only a portion of the primary key.
- A determinant is any column that functionally determines another column.
- A table (relation) is in third normal form (3NF) when it is in second normal form and the only determinants it contains are candidate keys.
- A collection of tables (relations) that is not in third normal form has inherent problems called anomalies. Replacing this collection with an equivalent collection of tables (relations) that is in third normal form removes these anomalies. This replacement must be done carefully, following a method like the one proposed in this text. If not, other problems, such as those discussed in this chapter, may be introduced.
- A table (relation) is in fourth normal form (4NF) when it is in third normal form and there are no multivalued dependencies.

Key Terms

alternate key	multidetermine
Boyce–Codd normal form (BCNF)	multivalued dependence
candidate key	nonkey attribute
decomposition	nonkey column
deletion anomaly	normal form
dependency diagram	normalization process
determinant	partial dependency
first normal form (1NF)	primary key
fourth normal form (4NF)	repeating group
functionally dependent	second normal form (2NF)
functionally determines	third normal form (3NF)
insertion anomaly	unnormalized relation
interrelation constraint	update anomaly
multidependent	

Review Questions

1. Define functional dependence.
2. Give an example of a column A and a column B such that B is functionally dependent on A. Give an example of a column C and a column D such that D is *not* functionally dependent on C.
3. Define primary key.
4. Define candidate key.
5. Define first normal form.
6. Define second normal form. What types of problems would you find in tables that are not in second normal form?
7. Define third normal form. What types of problems would you find in tables that are not in third normal form?
8. Define fourth normal form. What types of problems would you find in tables that are not in fourth normal form?
9. Define interrelation constraint and give one example of such a constraint. How are interrelation constraints addressed?

10. Consider a Student table containing StudentNum, StudentName, StudentMajor, AdvisorNum, AdvisorName, AdvisorOfficeNum, AdvisorPhone, NumCredits, and Category (freshman, sophomore, and so on). List the functional dependencies that exist, along with the assumptions that would support those dependencies.

11. Convert the following table to an equivalent collection of tables that are in third normal form. This table contains information about patients of a dentist. Each patient belongs to a household.

```
Patient (HouseholdNum, HouseholdName, Street, City, State, ZipCode,
    Balance, PatientNum, PatientName, (ServiceCode, Description,
    Fee, Date))
```

The following dependencies exist in the Patient table:

```
PatientNum → HouseholdNum, HouseholdName, Street, City, State,
    ZipCode, Balance, PatientName

HouseholdNum → HouseholdName, Street, City, State, ZipCode, Balance

ServiceCode → Description, Fee

PatientNum, ServiceCode → Date
```

12. Using your knowledge of the college environment, determine the functional dependencies that exist in the following table. After determining the functional dependencies, convert this table to an equivalent collection of tables that are in third normal form:

```
Student (StudentNum, StudentName, NumCredits, AdvisorNum,
    AdvisorName, DeptNum, DeptName, (CourseNum, Description,
    Term, Grade))
```

13. Again, using your knowledge of the college environment, determine the functional or multivalued dependencies that exist in the following table. After determining the functional dependencies, convert this table to an equivalent collection of tables that are in fourth normal form. ActivityNum and ActivityName refer to activities in which a student can choose to participate. For example, activity number 1 might be soccer, activity 2 might be band, and activity 3 might be the debate team. A student can choose to participate in multiple activities. CourseNum and Description refer to courses the student is taking.

```
Student (StudentNum, StudentName, ActivityNum, ActivityName,
    CourseNum, Description)
```

14. Assume the same scenario as that given in Question 13 but replace CourseNum and Description with AdvisorNum, LastName, and FirstName as shown. Advisor refers to the advisor responsible for the activity. One advisor can be responsible for many activities, but each activity has only one advisor.

```
Student (StudentNum, StudentName, ActivityNum, ActivityName,
    AdvisorNum, LastName, FirstName)
```

15. The requirements shown in Question 11 have changed. The dentist's office would like to add the date of the patient's last payment. In which relation (table) would you place this attribute? Why?

BITS Corporation Exercises

The following exercises are based on the BITS database shown in Figure 5-1.

1. Using your knowledge of BITS, determine the functional dependencies that exist in the following table. After determining the functional dependencies, convert this table to an equivalent collection of tables that are in third normal form:

```
Tasks (TaskID, Description, Category, Price, (OrderNum,
    OrderDate, ClientNum, ClientName, ConsltNum, LastName,
    FirstName, ScheduledDate, QuotedPrice))
```

2. List the functional dependencies in the following table that concern invoicing (an application BITS is considering adding to its database), subject to the specified conditions. For a given invoice (identified by the InvoiceNum), there will be a single client. The client's number, name, and complete address appear on the invoice, as does the date. Also, there may be several different tasks appearing on the invoice. For each task that appears,

display the TaskID, description, category, and price. Assume that each client that requests a particular service task pays the same price. Convert this table to an equivalent collection of tables that are in third normal form:

```
Invoice (InvoiceNum, ClientNum, LastName, FirstName, Street, City,
    State, ZipCode, Date, (TaskID, Description, Category, Price))
```

3. BITS wants to store information about the supervisors, including their supervisor number and the relationship to consultants. Supervisors can work with multiple consultants, but consultants only have one supervisor. In addition, supervisors specialize in working with clients in specific task categories. Using this information, convert the following unnormalized relation to fourth normal form:

```
Consultant (ConsltNum, LastName, FirstName, Street, City, ZipCode,
    Hours, Rate, (SupervisorNum, SupervisorName), (Tasks, Description,
    Category, Price, SupervisorNum))
```

4. BITS is considering changing its business model so that many consultants can service one client and one consultant can represent many clients. Using this information, convert the following unnormalized relation to fourth normal form:

```
Client (ClientNum, ClientName, Street, City, State, ZipCode,
    Balance, CreditLimit, (ConsltNum, LastName, FirstName, Street,
    City, State, ZipCode, Hours, Rate))
```

5. Convert the following unnormalized relation to fourth normal form using the same requirements as in Question 4 (many consultants can represent one client, and one consultant can represent many clients):

```
Consultant (ConsltNum, LastName, FirstName, Street, City, State, ZipCode,
    Rate, (ClientNum, ClientName, Street, City, State, ZipCode, Balance,
    CreditLimit))
```

6. Is there any difference between the tables you created in Questions 4 and 5? Why or why not?

Colonial Adventure Tours Case

The following exercises are based on the Colonial Adventure Tours database shown in Figures 1-15 through 1-19 in Chapter 1. No computer work is required.

1. Using the types of entities found in the Colonial Adventure Tours database (trips, guides, clients, and reservations), create an example of a table that is in first normal form but not in second normal form and an example of a table that is in second normal form but not in third normal form. In each case, justify your answers and show how to convert to the higher forms.

2. Colonial Adventure Tours is considering changing the way it handles reservations. Instead of storing the number of persons associated with one reservation, the company would like to store the name and address of each person associated with each reservation. If Colonial Adventure Tours decides to implement this change, the trip price and other fee amounts for each trip would be dependent on only the trip ID. Determine the multivalued dependencies in the following table, and then convert this table to an equivalent collection of tables that are in fourth normal form:

```
Reservation (ReservationID, TripID, TripDate, TripPrice, OtherFees,
    (ClientNum, ClientLastName, ClientFirstName, Address, City, State,
    ZipCode, Phone))
```

3. Identify the functional dependencies in the following unnormalized table. Convert the table to third normal form. Is the result also in fourth normal form? Why or why not?

```
Trip (TripID, TripName, StateAbbreviation, StateName,
    (GuideNum, GuideLast, GuideFirst))
```

4. Currently, each trip is identified with only season. For example, the Arethusa Falls trip is offered only in the Summer season. Colonial Adventure Tours is considering offering the same trip in more than one season; that is, the Arethusa Falls trip could be offered in both the Summer and Late Spring seasons. Using this new information, identify all dependencies and convert the current Trip table to third normal form. You may need to make some assumptions. Identify these assumptions in your solution.

Sports Physical Therapy Case

The following exercises are based on the Sports Physical Therapy database shown in Figures 1-21 through 1-24. No computer work is required.

1. Using the types of entities found in the Sports Physical Therapy database (clients, session, therapies, and therapists), create an example of a table that is in first normal form but not in second normal form and an example of a table that is in second normal form but not in third normal form. In each case, justify your answer and show how to convert to the higher forms.

2. Determine the functional dependencies that exist in the following table, and then convert this table to an equivalent collection of tables that are in third normal form:

    Patient (<u>PatientNum</u>, LastName, (SessionDate, LengthOfSession, TherapistID, TherapyCode))

3. Determine the functional dependencies that exist in the following table, and then convert this table to an equivalent collection of tables that are in third normal form:

    Session (<u>SessionNum</u>, SessionDate, PatientNum, LengthOfSession, TherapistID, TherapyCode, Description, UnitOfTime)

4. Sports Physical Therapy is considering adding doctor information to the database. Determine the functional dependencies that exist in the following table, and then convert this table to an equivalent collection of tables that are in third normal form:

    Session (<u>SessionNum</u>, SessionDate, PatientNum, LengthOfSession, TherapistID, TherapyCode, Description, UnitOfTime, DoctorNum, DrLastName, DrFirstName)

5. What type of relationship exists between doctors and sessions? Why? What type of relationship exists between doctors and patients? Why?

CHAPTER **6**

DATABASE DESIGN 2: DESIGN METHOD

LEARNING OBJECTIVES

- Discuss the general process and goals of database design
- Define user views and explain their function
- Use Database Design Language (DBDL) to document database designs
- Create an entity-relationship (E-R) diagram to represent a database design visually
- Present a method for database design at the information level and view examples illustrating this method
- Explain the physical-level design process
- Discuss top-down and bottom-up approaches to database design and examine the advantages and disadvantages of both methods
- Use a survey form to obtain information from users prior to beginning the database design process
- Review existing documents to obtain information prior to beginning the database design
- Discuss special issues related to implementing one-to-one relationships and many-to-many relationships involving more than two entities
- Identify entity subtypes and their relationships to nulls
- Learn how to avoid potential problems when merging third normal form relations
- Examine the entity-relationship model for representing and designing databases

INTRODUCTION

Now that you have learned how to identify and correct poor table designs, you will turn your attention to the design process by determining the tables (relations) and columns (attributes) that make up the database. In addition, you will determine the relationships between the various tables.

Most designers tackle database design using a two-step process. In the first step, the database designers design a database that satisfies the organization's requirements as cleanly as possible. This step, which is called **information-level design**, or conceptual design, is completed *independently* of any particular DBMS that the organization will ultimately use. In the second step, which is called the **physical-level design**, designers adapt the information-level design for the specific DBMS that the organization will use. During the physical-level design, designers must consider the characteristics of that particular DBMS.

After examining the information-level design process, you will explore the general database design method and view examples illustrating this method. You will construct entity-relationship (E-R) diagrams to represent the database design visually. You then will learn about the physical-level design process and compare top-down and bottom-up approaches to database design.

You will explore special issues related to database design, including survey forms and their use in database design and the way to obtain important information from existing documents. You will examine issues related to the implementation of some special types of relationships. You will learn about entity subtypes and their relationship to nulls. You will look at issues related to merging third normal form relations. Finally, you will learn about the E-R model.

USER VIEWS

Regardless of which approach an organization adopts to implement its database design, a complete database design that satisfies all the organization's requirements is rarely a one-step process. Unless the requirements are simple, an organization usually divides the overall job of database design into many smaller tasks by identifying the individual pieces of the design problem, called user views. A **user view** is the set of requirements that is necessary to support the operations of a particular database user; it is a logical way of looking at the database setup to support the activities of a user or a group of users. User views may come in a variety of formats such as a requirements list, a set of reports, output products, a previous manual system, or a personal discussion with database users. For example, a growing company may be producing manual invoices. That "view" includes many fields the company must store as they proceed to an electronic system.

In another example, an interview with several users and managers indicates the need to store customer data for easy access—some users need names and email addresses; others need physical addresses, still others need balances and payment history. Each of those needs becomes a user view. The interviews also may uncover synonyms from different users such as customers, clients, and regulars.

At the BITS Corporation, a requirement is that the database must be capable of storing each task ID, description, category, and price. It is critical to analyze and determine these user views carefully before beginning the design process.

For each user view, designers must develop the database structure to support the view and then merge it into a **cumulative design** that supports all the user views encountered during the design process. Each user view is generally much simpler than the total collection of requirements, so working on individual user views is usually more manageable than attempting to turn the design of the entire database into one large task.

INFORMATION-LEVEL DESIGN METHOD

The information-level design method in this text involves representing individual user views, refining them to eliminate any problems, and then merging them into a cumulative design. After you have represented and merged all user views, you can complete the cumulative design for the entire database.

When creating user views, a "user" can be a person or a group that will use the system, a report that the system must produce, or a type of transaction that the system must support. In the last two instances, you might think of the user as the person who will use the report or enter the transaction. In fact, if the same user requires three separate reports, for example, it is more efficient to consider each report as a separate user view, even though only one user is involved, because smaller user views are easier to construct.

For each user view, the information-level design method requires you to complete the following steps:

1. Represent the user view as a collection of tables.
2. Normalize these tables.
3. Identify all keys in these tables.
4. Merge the result of Steps 1 through 3 into the cumulative design.

In the following sections, you will examine each of these steps in detail.

Step 1: Represent the User View as a Collection of Tables

When provided with samples or some sort of stated requirements, you must develop a collection of tables. In some cases, the collection of tables may be obvious to you. For example, suppose you are dealing with departments and employees. Each department can hire many employees, and each employee can work in only one department (a typical restriction). A table or relation design similar to the following may have naturally occurred to you. It is an appropriate design.

```
Department (DepartmentNum, Name, Location)
Employee (EmployeeNum, LastName, FirstName, Street, City,
     State, ZipCode, WageRate, SocSecNum, DepartmentNum)
```

Undoubtedly you will find that the more designs you complete, the easier it will be for you to develop such a collection without resorting to any special procedure. The real question is this: What procedure should you follow when the correct design is not so obvious? In that case, you should work through the following four substeps.

Step 1a. Determine the entities involved and create a separate table for each type of entity. At this point, you do not need to do anything more than name the tables. For example, if a user view involves departments and employees, you can create a Department table and an Employee table. Therefore, you will write something like this:

```
Department (
Employee (
```

That is, you will write the name of a table and an opening parenthesis, *and that is all*. You will assign columns to these tables in later steps.

Step 1b. Determine the primary key for each table. In this step, you can add one or more columns depending on how many columns are required for the primary key. You will add additional columns later. Even though you have yet to determine the columns in the table, you can usually determine the primary key. For example, the primary key in an Employee table will probably be EmployeeNum, and the primary key in a Department table will probably be DepartmentNum.

The primary key is the unique identifier, so the essential question is this: What does it take to identify an employee or a department uniquely? Even if you are trying to automate a previously designed manual system, you usually can find a unique identifier in that system. If no unique identifier is available, you will need to assign one. For example, in a manual system, customers may not have been assigned numbers because the customer base was small and the organization did not require or use customer numbers. Because the organization is computerizing its records, however, now is a good time to assign customer numbers to become the unique identifiers you are seeking.

After creating unique identifiers, you add these primary keys to what you have written already. At this point, you will have something like the following:

```
Department (DepartmentNum,
Employee (EmployeeNum,
```

Now you have the name of the table and the primary key, but that is all. In later steps, you will add the other columns.

Step 1c. Determine the properties for each entity. You can look at the user requirements and then determine the other required properties of each entity. These properties, along with the primary key identified in Step 1b, will become columns in the appropriate tables. For example, an Employee entity may require columns for LastName, FirstName, Street, City, State, ZipCode, WageRate, and SocSecNum (Social Security number). The Department entity may require columns for Name (department name) and Location (department location). Adding these columns to what is already in place produces the following:

```
Department (DepartmentNum, Name, Location
Employee (EmployeeNum, LastName, FirstName, Street, City,
     State, ZipCode, WageRate, SocSecNum
```

Step 1d. Determine relationships between the entities. The basic relationships are one-to-many, many-to-many, and one-to-one. You will see how to handle each type of relationship next.

To create a one-to-many relationship, include the primary key of the "one" table as a foreign key in the "many" table. For example, assume each employee works in a single department but a department can have many employees. Thus, *one* department is related to *many* employees. In this case, you would include the primary key of the Department table (the "one" part) as a foreign key in the Employee table (the "many" part). The tables would now look like this:

```
Department (DepartmentNum, Name, Location)
Employee (EmployeeNum, LastName, FirstName, Street, City,
     State, ZipCode, WageRate, SocSecNum, DepartmentNum)
```

You create a **many-to-many relationship** by creating a new table whose primary key is the combination of the primary keys of the original tables. Assume each employee can work in multiple departments and each department can have many employees. In this case, you would create a new table whose primary key is the combination of EmployeeNum and DepartmentNum. Because the new table represents the fact that an employee *works in* a department, you might choose to call it WorksIn. (Another method is to use a name that combines the names of the two tables being related. Using the second approach, the new table's name could be DepartmentEmployee or EmployeeDepartment.) After creating the new table, the collection of tables is as follows:

```
Department (DepartmentNum, Name, Location)
Employee (EmployeeNum, LastName, FirstName, Street,
    City, State, ZipCode, WageRate, SocSecNum)
WorksIn (EmployeeNum, DepartmentNum)
```

In this design, there is a one-to-many relationship between the Department and WorksIn tables and a one-to-many relationship between the Employee and WorksIn tables. By creating the WorksIn table, which includes foreign keys from the Department and Employee tables, you have created a new table to implement a many-to-many relationship. The one-to-many relationship between each of the original tables with the new table creates the many-to-many relationship between the two original tables.

In some situations, no other columns (attributes) are required in the new table. The other columns in the WorksIn table would be those columns that depend on both the employee and the department, if such columns existed. One possibility, for example, would be the date the department hired the employee because it depends on *both* the employee *and* the department.

If each employee works in a single department, and each department has only one employee, the relationship between employees and departments is a **one-to-one relationship**. (In practice, such relationships are rare.) The simplest way to implement a one-to-one relationship is to treat it as a one-to-many relationship. Which table is the "one" part of the relationship, and which table is the "many" part? Sometimes looking ahead helps. For example, you might ask this question: If the relationship changes in the future, is it more likely that one employee will work in many departments or that one department will hire several employees rather than just one? If your research determines that it is more likely that a department will hire more than one employee, you would make the Employee table the "many" part of the relationship. If both situations might happen, you could treat the relationship as many-to-many. If neither situation is likely to occur, you could arbitrarily choose the "many" part of the relationship.

Step 2: Normalize the Tables

After establishing the relationships between the entities, Step 2 is to normalize each table. Recall that 1NF requires that the data not contain repeating groups. 2NF builds on 1NF, narrowing the tables to a single purpose so that all nonkey columns are dependent on the table's primary key. Finally, 3NF builds on 2NF and ensures referential integrity—all the attributes in a table are determined only by candidate keys. Your target is this third normal form. (The target is actually fourth normal form, but careful planning in the early phases of the normalization process usually rules out the need to consider fourth normal form.)

Step 3: Identify All Keys

Step 3 of the information-level design method requires you to identify all keys. For each table, you must identify the primary key and any alternate keys, secondary keys, and foreign keys. In the database containing information about employees and departments, you already determined the primary keys for each table in an earlier step.

Recall that an alternate key is a column or collection of columns that could have been chosen as a primary key but was not. It is not common to have alternate keys; if they do exist and the system must enforce their uniqueness, you should note them. You usually implement this restriction by creating a unique index on the field. If there are any **secondary keys** (columns that are of interest strictly for the purpose of retrieval), you should represent them at this point. If a user were to indicate, for example, that rapidly retrieving an employee record based on his or her last name and first name was important, you would designate the LastName and FirstName columns as a secondary key. You usually create a nonunique index for each secondary key. A **nonunique index** is used to improve query performance in frequently used columns by maintaining a sorted order; it does not enforce constraints.

In many ways, the foreign key is the most important key because it is through foreign keys that you create relationships between tables and enforce certain types of integrity constraints in a database. Remember that a foreign key is a column (or collection of columns) in one table that is required to match the value of the primary key for some row in another table or is required to be null. (This property is called referential integrity.) Consider, for example, the following tables:

```
Department (DepartmentNum, Name, Location)
Employee (EmployeeNum, LastName, FirstName, Street,
    City, State, ZipCode, WageRate, SocSecNum, DepartmentNum)
```

As before, the DepartmentNum column in the Employee table indicates the department in which the employee works. In this case, you say that the DepartmentNum column in the Employee table is a foreign key that *identifies* Department. Thus, the number in this column on any row in the Employee table must be a department number that is already in the database, or the value must be set to null. (Null indicates that, for whatever reason, the employee is not assigned to a department.)

Types of Primary Keys

There are three types of primary keys that you can use in your database design. A **natural key** (also called a **logical key** or an **intelligent key**) is a primary key that consists of a column that uniquely identifies an entity, such as a person's Social Security number, a book's ISBN (International Standard Book Number), a product's UPC (Universal Product Code), or a vehicle's VIN (Vehicle Identification Number). These characteristics are inherent to the entity and visible to users. If a natural key exists for an entity, you usually can select it as the primary key.

If a natural key does not exist for an entity, it is common to create a primary key column that will be unique and accessible to users. The primary keys in the BITS database (ConsltNum, ClientNum, OrderNum, and TaskID) were created to serve as the primary keys. A column that you create for an entity to serve solely as the primary key and that is visible to users is called an **artificial key**. Even if there is a natural key, you may want or need to create an artificial key. For instance, if database users are not supposed to see each other's Social Security numbers, an EmployeeNum may be a better choice as an artificial key.

The final type of primary key, which is called a **surrogate key** (or a **synthetic key**), is a system-generated primary key that is usually hidden from users. When a DBMS creates a surrogate key, it is usually an automatic numbering data type, such as the Access AutoNumber data type. For example, suppose you have the following relation (table) for Customer payments:

```
Payment (CustomerNum, PaymentDate, PaymentAmount)
```

Because a customer can make multiple payments, CustomerNum cannot be the primary key. Assuming it is possible for a customer to make more than one payment on a particular day, the combination of CustomerNum and PaymentDate cannot be the primary key either. Adding an artificial key, such as PaymentNum, means you would have to assign a PaymentNum every time the customer makes a payment. Adding a surrogate key, such as PaymentID, would make more sense because the DBMS will automatically assign a unique value to each payment. Users do not need to be aware of the PaymentID value, however.

DATABASE DESIGN LANGUAGE (DBDL)

To carry out the design process, you must have a mechanism for representing tables and keys. The standard notation you have used thus far for representing tables is fine, but it does not go far enough—there is no way to represent alternate, secondary, or foreign keys. Because the information-level design method is based on the relational model, it is desirable to represent tables with the standard notation. To do so, you will add additional features capable of representing additional information. One approach to doing this is called **Database Design Language (DBDL)**. Figure 6-1 shows sample DBDL documentation for the Employee table.

```
Employee(EmployeeNum, LastName, FirstName, Street, City, State, ZipCode,
      WageRate, SocSecNum, DepartmentNum)
      AK    SocSecNum
      SK    LastName, FirstName
      FK    DepartmentNum → Department
```

FIGURE 6-1   DBDL for the Employee table

In DBDL, you represent a table by listing all columns and then underlining the primary key. Below the table definition, you list any alternate keys, secondary keys, and foreign keys, using the abbreviations AK, SK, and FK, respectively. For alternate and secondary keys, you can list the column or collection of columns by name. In the case of foreign keys, however, you must also represent the table whose primary key the foreign key must match. In DBDL, you write the foreign key followed by an arrow pointing to the table that the foreign key identifies.

The rules for defining tables and their keys using DBDL are as follows:

- Tables (relations), columns (attributes), and primary keys are written by first listing the table name and then, in parentheses, listing the columns that make up the table. The column(s) that make up the primary key are underlined.

- Alternate keys are identified by the abbreviation AK, followed by the column(s) that make up the alternate key.
- Secondary keys are identified by the abbreviation SK, followed by the column(s) that make up the secondary key.
- Foreign keys are identified by the abbreviation FK, followed by the column(s) that make up the foreign key. Foreign keys are followed by an arrow pointing to the table identified by the foreign key. When several tables are listed, a common practice places the table containing the foreign key below the table that the foreign key identifies, if possible.

Figure 6-1 on the previous page shows that there is a table named Employee containing the columns EmployeeNum, LastName, FirstName, Street, City, State, ZipCode, WageRate, SocSecNum, and DepartmentNum. The primary key is EmployeeNum. Another possible primary key is SocSecNum, which is listed as an alternate key. The combination of LastName and FirstName columns is a secondary key, which allows you to retrieve data more efficiently based on an employee's name. (You can add additional secondary key designations later as necessary.) The DepartmentNum column is a foreign key that identifies the department number in the Department table in which the employee works.

Entity-Relationship (E-R) Diagrams

A popular type of diagram that visually represents the structure of a database is the entity-relationship (E-R) diagram. Recall from Chapter 1 that in an E-R diagram, rectangles represent the entities (tables). Foreign key restrictions determine relationships between the tables, and these relationships are represented as lines joining the corresponding rectangles.

There are several different styles of E-R diagrams currently in use. In this chapter, you will begin with a style called **IDEF1X** (Integration Definition for Information Modeling). IDEF1X is part of the Integrated Definition family of modeling languages (IDEF) created by the U.S. Air Force in 1983. The style produces E-R diagrams that are compatible with object-oriented programming constructs and the relationship diagrams created in Microsoft Access.

Consider the following database design written in DBDL:

```
Department (DepartmentNum, Name, Location)
Employee (EmployeeNum, LastName, FirstName, Street, City, State, ZipCode, WageRate,
    SocSecNum, DepartmentNum)
    AK → SocSecNum
    SK → LastName, FirstName
    FK → DepartmentNum → Department
```

The E-R diagram for the preceding database design appears in Figure 6-2.

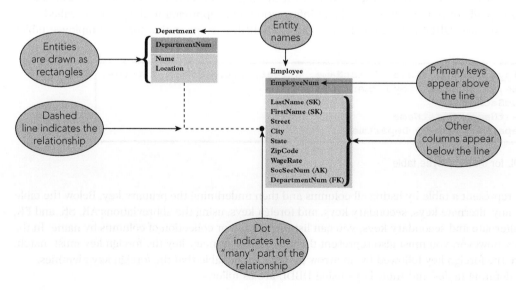

FIGURE 6-2 E-R diagram

The E-R diagram shown in Figure 6-2 has the following characteristics:

- A rectangle represents each entity in the E-R diagram—there is one rectangle for the Department entity and a second rectangle for the Employee entity. The name of each entity appears above the rectangle.
- The primary key for each entity appears above the line in the rectangle for each entity. DepartmentNum is the primary key of the Department entity, and EmployeeNum is the primary key of the Employee entity.
- The other columns in each entity appear below the line within each rectangle.
- The letters AK, SK, and FK appear in parentheses following the alternate key, secondary key, and foreign key, respectively, in the Employee entity. (The Department entity does not have an alternate, secondary, or foreign key.)
- For each foreign key, there is a dotted line leading from the rectangle that corresponds to the table being identified to the rectangle that corresponds to the table containing the foreign key. The dot at the end of the line indicates the "many" part of the one-to-many relationship between the Department and Employee entities. Recall that Access uses an infinity symbol (∞) rather than the dot; the concept is the same. (In Figure 6-2, *one* department is related to *many* employees, so the dot is at the end of the line connected to the Employee entity.)

When you use an E-R diagram to represent a database, it visually illustrates all the information listed in the DBDL. Thus, you would not need to include the DBDL version of the design. There are other styles, however, that do not include such information within the diagram. In that case, you should represent the design with *both* the diagram *and* the DBDL.

Step 4: Merge the Result into the Design

As soon as you have completed Steps 1 through 3 for a given user view, you can merge the results into the cumulative design. If the view on which you have been working is the first user view, the cumulative design will be identical to the design for the first user view. Otherwise, you merge all the tables for other user views with those tables that are currently in the cumulative design.

As you create subsequent views, sometimes you find that more than one table in your cumulative design has the same primary key. You need to combine those tables to form a new table. The new table contains all the columns from both tables, with the common primary key. In the case of duplicate columns, you remove all but one copy of the column. For example, if the cumulative design already contains the following table:

```
Employee (EmployeeNum, LastName, FirstName, WageRate, SocSecNum, DepartmentNum)
```

and the user view you just completed contains the following table:

```
Employee (EmployeeNum, LastName, FirstName, Street, City, State, ZipCode)
```

you would combine the two tables because they have the same primary key. All the columns from both tables are in the new table, but without any duplicate columns. Thus, LastName and FirstName appear only once, even though they are in each table. The end result is as follows:

```
Employee (EmployeeNum, LastName, FirstName, WageRate, SocSecNum, DepartmentNum, Street,
    City, State, ZipCode)
```

If necessary, you could reorder the columns at this point. For example, you might move the Street, City, State, and ZipCode columns to follow the FirstName column, which is the more traditional arrangement of this type of data. This change would give the following:

```
Employee (EmployeeNum, LastName, FirstName, Street, City, State, ZipCode, WageRate,
    SocSecNum, DepartmentNum)
```

At this point, you need to check the new design to ensure that it is still in third normal form. If it is not, you should convert it to third normal form before proceeding.

Figure 6-3 on the next page summarizes the process that is repeated for each user view until all user views have been examined. At that point, the design is reviewed to resolve any problems that may remain and to ensure that it can meet the needs of all individual users. After all user view requirements have been satisfied, the information-level design is considered complete.

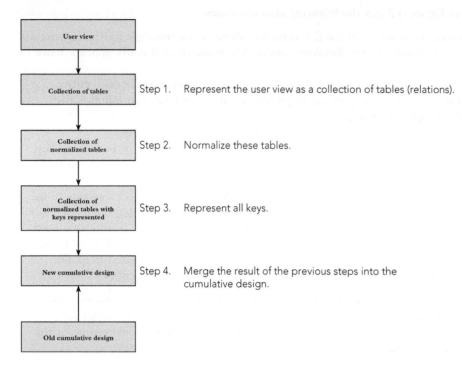

Step 1. Represent the user view as a collection of tables (relations).

Step 2. Normalize these tables.

Step 3. Represent all keys.

Step 4. Merge the result of the previous steps into the cumulative design.

FIGURE 6-3 Information-level design method

DATABASE DESIGN EXAMPLES

Now that you understand how to represent a database in DBDL and in an E-R diagram, you can examine the requirements of another database, the BITS database. In this process, you will see how the initial set of requirements provided by BITS led to the database with which you have been working throughout this text.

YOUR TURN 6-1

Complete an information-level design for a database that satisfies the following constraints and user view requirements for a company that stores information about consultants, clients, tasks, and work orders.

User View 1 Requirements: For a consultant, store the consultant's number, name, address, hours, and rate.

User View 2 Requirements: For a client, store the client's number, name, address, balance, and credit limit. In addition, store the number and name of the consultant who represents this client. A consultant can represent many clients, but a client must have exactly one consultant. (A client *must have* a consultant and cannot have more than *one* consultant.)

User View 3 Requirements: For each service task, store the task's ID number, description, category, and price.

User View 4 Requirements: For an order, store the order number; order date; number, name, and address of the client who placed the order; and number of the consultant who services that client. In addition, for each line item within the order, store the task ID number, description, scheduled date, and quoted price. The user also has supplied the following constraints:

a. Each order must be placed by a client who is already in the Client table.

b. There is only one client per order.

c. On a given order, there is, at most, one line item for a given task. For example, task LA81 cannot appear in several lines within the same order.

d. The quoted price might not match the current price in the Tasks table, allowing the company to provide services to different clients at different prices. The user wants to be able to change the price for a task without affecting orders that are currently on file.

What are the user views in Your Turn 6-1? In particular, how should the design proceed if you are given requirements that are not stated specifically in the form of user views? Sometimes you might encounter a series of well-developed user views in a form that you can easily merge into the design. Other times you might be given only a set of requirements, such as those described in Your Turn 6-1. In another situation, you might be given a list of reports and updates that a system must support. In addition to the requirements, when you are able to interview users and document their needs before beginning the design process, you can make sure that you understand the specifics of their user views *prior* to starting the design process. On the other hand, you may have to take information as you get it and in whatever format it is provided.

When the user views are not clearly defined, you should consider each stated requirement as a separate user view. Thus, you can think of each report or update transaction that the system must support, as well as any other stated requirement, as an individual user view. In fact, even when the requirements are presented as user views already, you may want to split a complex user view into smaller pieces and consider each piece as a separate user view for the design process.

To transform each user view into DBDL, examine the requirements individually, and create the necessary entities, keys, and relationships.

User View 1: For a consultant, store the consultant's number, name, address, hours, and rate. You will need to create only one table to support this view:

```
Consultant (ConsltNum, LastName, FirstName, Street, City, State, ZipCode, Hours, Rate)
```

This table is in third normal form. Because there are no foreign, alternate, or secondary keys, the DBDL representation of the table is the same as the relational model representation.

Notice that you have assumed the consultant's number (ConsltNum) is the Consultant table's primary key—this is a reasonable assumption. Because the user did not provide this information, however, you would need to verify its accuracy with the user. In each of the following requirements, you can assume the obvious column (ClientNum, TaskID, and OrderNum) is the primary key. Because you are working on the first user view, the "merge" step of the design method produces a cumulative design consisting of only the Consultant table, which is shown in Figure 6-4. This design is simple, so you do not need to represent it with an E-R diagram.

```
Consultant (ConsltNum, LastName, FirstName, Street, City, State, ZipCode,
            Hours, Rate)
```

FIGURE 6-4   Cumulative design after first user view

User View 2: Because the first user view was simple, you were able to create the necessary table without having to complete each step mentioned in the information-level design method section. The second user view is more complicated, however, so you will use all the steps to determine the tables. (If you already have determined what the tables should be, you have a natural feel for the process. If so, please be patient and work through the process.)

For a client, store the client's number, name, address, balance, and credit limit. In addition, store the number and name of the consultant who represents this client. You will take two different approaches to this requirement, allowing you to see how they both can lead to the same result. The only difference between the two approaches is the entities that you initially identify. In the first approach, suppose you identify two required entities for consultants and clients. You would begin by listing the following two tables:

```
Consultant (
Client (
```

After determining the unique identifiers, you add the primary keys, which creates the following:

```
Consultant (ConsltNum,
Client (ClientNum,
```

Adding columns for the properties of each of these entities yields this:

```
Consultant (ConsltNum, LastName, FirstName
Client (ClientNum, ClientName, Street, City, State, ZipCode, Balance, CreditLimit
```

Finally, you deal with the relationship: *One* consultant is related to *many* clients. To implement this one-to-many relationship, include the key of the "one" table as a foreign key in the "many" table. In this case, you would include the ConsltNum column in the Client table. Thus, you would have the following:

```
Consultant (ConsltNum, LastName, FirstName)
Client (ClientNum, ClientName, Street, City, State, ZipCode, Balance, CreditLimit, ConsltNum)
```

Both tables are in third normal form, so you can move on to representing the keys. Before doing that, however, consider another approach that you could have used to determine the tables.

Suppose you did not realize that there were really two entities, and you created only a single table for clients. You would begin by listing the table as follows:

```
Client (
```

Adding the unique identifier as the primary key gives this table:

```
Client (ClientNum,
```

Finally, adding the other properties as additional columns yields the following:

```
Client (ClientNum, ClientName, Street, City, State,
    ZipCode, Balance, CreditLimit, ConsltNum, LastName, FirstName)
```

A problem occurs, however, when you examine the functional dependencies that exist in the Client entity. The ClientNum column determines all the other columns, as it should. However, the ConsltNum column determines the LastName and FirstName columns, but ConsltNum is not an alternate key. This table is in second normal form because no column depends on a portion of the primary key, but it is not in third normal form. Converting the table to third normal form produces the following two tables:

```
Client (ClientNum, ClientName, Street, City, State,
    ZipCode, Balance, CreditLimit, ConsltNum)
Consultant (ConsltNum, LastName, FirstName)
```

Notice that these are the same tables you determined with the first approach—it just took a little longer to get there.

Besides the obvious primary keys, ClientNum for Client and ConsltNum for Consultant, the Client table now contains a foreign key, ConsltNum. There are no alternate keys, nor did the requirements state anything that would require a secondary key. If there were a requirement to retrieve the client based on the client's name, for example, you would probably choose to make ClientName a secondary key.

The next step is to merge User View 1 and User View 2. You now could represent the Consultant table in DBDL in preparation for merging these two tables into the existing cumulative design. Looking ahead, however, you see that because the User View 2 table has the same primary key as the Consultant table from the first user view, you can merge the two tables to form a single table that has the common column ConsltNum as its primary key and that contains all the other columns from both tables without duplication. In the second user view, the only columns in the Consultant table other than the primary key are LastName and FirstName. These columns were already in the Consultant table from the first user view that you added to the cumulative design. The cumulative design now contains the Consultant and Client tables shown in Figure 6-5.

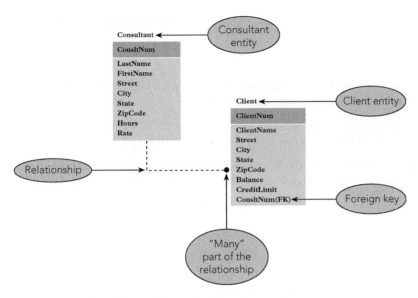

FIGURE 6-5 Cumulative design after second user view

User View 3: Like the first user view, this one poses no special problems. For a task, store the task ID number, description, category, and price. Only one table is required to support this user view:

```
Tasks (TaskID, Description, Category, Price)
```

This table is in third normal form. The DBDL representation is identical to the relational model representation.

Because TaskID has not been used as the primary key of any previous table, merging this table into the cumulative design produces the design shown in Figure 6-6, which contains the Consultant, Client, and Tasks tables.

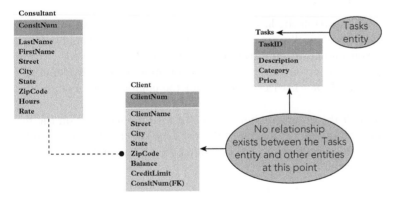

FIGURE 6-6 Cumulative design after third user view

User View 4: This user view is more complicated, and you can approach it in several ways. For an order, store the order number; order date; number, name, and address of the client who placed the order; and number of the consultant who represents that client. In addition, for each line item within the order, store the task ID number, description, scheduled date, and quoted price.

Suppose that you decide you need to create only a single entity for orders. You might create the following table:

```
Orders (
```

Because order numbers uniquely identify orders, you would add the OrderNum column as the primary key, giving this table:

```
Orders (OrderNum,
```

Examining the various properties of an order, such as the date, client number, and so on, as listed in the requirements, you would add the appropriate columns, giving the following:

```
Orders (OrderNum, OrderDate, ClientNum, ClientName,
    Street, City, State, ZipCode, ConsltNum,
```

What about the fact that you are supposed to store the item number, description, scheduled date, and quoted price for each order line in this order? One way of doing this would be to include all these columns within the Orders table as a repeating group (because an order can contain many order lines). This would yield the following:

```
Orders (OrderNum, OrderDate, ClientNum, ClientName,
    Street, City, State, ZipCode, ConsltNum, (TaskID, Description,
    ScheduledDate, QuotedPrice) )
```

At this point, you have a table that contains all the necessary columns. Now you must convert this table to an equivalent collection of tables that are in third normal form. Because this table is not even in first normal form, you would remove the repeating group and expand the primary key to produce the following:

```
Orders (OrderNum, OrderDate, ClientNum, ClientName,
    Street, City, State, ZipCode, ConsltNum, TaskID, Description, ScheduledDate,
    QuotedPrice)
```

In the new Orders table, you have the following functional dependencies:

```
OrderNum → OrderDate, ClientNum, ClientName, Street,
    City, State, ZipCode, ConsltNum
ClientNum → ClientName, Street, City, State, ZipCode, ConsltNum
TaskID → Description
OrderNum, TaskID → ScheduledDate, QuotedPrice
```

Notice the combination of OrderNum and TaskID in the last line. In reality, those two keys functionally determine all attributes from both tables. While technically correct, adding all of those fields would only clutter the list of dependencies. In general, you should list an attribute after the smallest possible combination that determines it. For example, because you can determine Description by TaskID alone, you *should* list Description after TaskID, but you *should not* list Description after the combination of OrderNum and TaskID.

The quoted price, however, depends on *both* the order number and the task ID number, not on the task ID number alone. Because some columns depend on only a portion of the primary key, the Orders table is not in second normal form. Converting to second normal form (and renaming the Orders table to WorkOrders to further differentiate) would yield the following:

```
WorkOrders (OrderNum, OrderDate, ClientNum, ClientName,
    Street, City, State, ZipCode, ConsltNum)
Tasks (TaskID, Description)
OrderLine (OrderNum, TaskID, ScheduledDate, QuotedPrice)
```

The Tasks and OrderLine tables are in third normal form. The WorkOrders table is not in third normal form because ClientNum determines ClientName, Street, City, State, ZipCode, and ConsltNum. ClientNum is not an alternate key, however, because one client may have multiple orders. Converting the WorkOrders table to third normal form and leaving the other tables as written would produce the following design for this user view requirement:

```
WorkOrders (OrderNum, OrderDate, ClientNum)
Client (ClientNum, ClientName,
    Street, City, State, ZipCode, ConsltNum)
```

```
Tasks (TaskID, Description)

OrderLine (OrderNum, TaskID, ScheduledDate, QuotedPrice)
```

You can represent this collection of tables in DBDL and then merge them into the cumulative design. Again, however, you can look ahead and see that you can merge this Client table with the existing Client table and this Tasks table with the existing Tasks table. In both cases, you will not need to add anything to the Client and Tasks tables already in the cumulative design, so the Client and Tasks tables for this user view do not affect the overall design. The DBDL representation for the WorkOrders and OrderLine tables appears in Figure 6-7.

```
WorkOrders (OrderNum, OrderDate, ClientNum)
       FK      ClientNum → Client

OrderLine (OrderNum, TaskID, ScheduledDate, QuotedPrice)
       FK      OrderNum → WorkOrders
       FK      TaskID   → Tasks
```

FIGURE 6-7   DBDL for WorkOrders and OrderLine tables

At this point, you have completed the process for each user view. Now it is time to review the design to make sure it will fulfill all the stated requirements. If the design contains problems or new information arises, you must modify the design to meet the new user views. Based on the assumption that you do not have to modify the design further, the final information-level design appears in Figure 6-8.

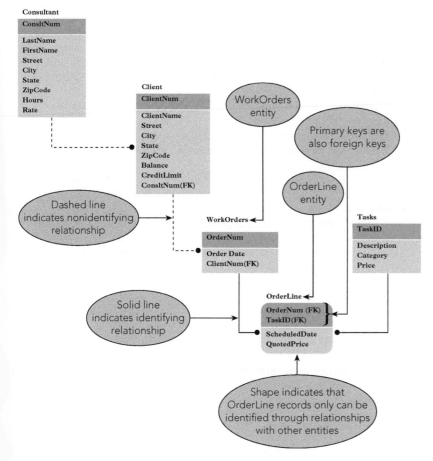

FIGURE 6-8   Final information-level design

There are some differences between the E-R diagram shown in Figure 6-8 on the previous page and earlier ones. The OrderLine entity appears as a rectangle with rounded corners. Further, the relationships from Work-Orders to OrderLine and from Tasks to OrderLine are represented with solid lines instead of dashed lines.

Both of these differences occur because the primary key of the OrderLine entity contains foreign keys. In the OrderLine entity, both columns that compose the primary key (OrderNum and TaskID) are foreign keys. Thus, to identify an order line, you need to know the order number and the task ID number to which the order corresponds.

This situation is different from one in which the primary key does not contain one or more foreign keys. Consider the Client table, for example, in which the primary key is ClientNum, which is not a foreign key. (The Client table does contain a foreign key, ConsltNum, which identifies the Consultant table.) To identify a client, all you need is the client number; you do not need to know the consultant number. In other words, you do not need to know the consultant to which the client corresponds.

An entity that does not require a relationship to another entity for identification is called an **independent entity**, and one that does require such a relationship is called a **dependent entity**. Thus, the Client entity is independent, whereas the OrderLine entity is dependent. Independent entities have square corners in the diagram, and dependent entities have rounded corners.

A relationship that is necessary for identification is called an **identifying relationship**, whereas one that is not necessary is called a **nonidentifying relationship**. Thus, the relationship between the Consultant and Client entities is nonidentifying, and the relationship between the WorkOrders and OrderLine entities is identifying. In an E-R diagram, a solid line represents an identifying relationship and a dashed line represents a nonidentifying relationship.

YOUR TURN 6-2

Ray Henry, the owner of a bookstore chain named Henry Books, gathers and organizes information about branches, publishers, authors, and books. Each local branch of the bookstore has a number that uniquely identifies the branch. In addition, Ray tracks the branch's name, location, and number of employees. Each publisher has a code that uniquely identifies the publisher. In addition, Ray tracks the publisher's name and city. The only user of the Book database is Ray, but you do not want to treat the entire project as a single user view. Ray has provided you with all the reports the system must produce, and you will treat each report as a user view. Ray has given you the following requirements:

User View 1 Requirements: For each publisher, list the publisher code, publisher name, and city in which the publisher is located.

User View 2 Requirements: For each branch, list the number, name, and location.

User View 3 Requirements: For each book, list its code, title, publisher code, publisher name, and whether it is a paperback.

User View 4 Requirements: For each book, list its code, title, and type. In addition, list the name(s) of the author(s). If a book has more than one author, all names must appear in the order in which they are listed on the book's cover. The author order is not always alphabetical.

User View 5 Requirements: For each branch, list its number and name. In addition, for each copy of a book in the branch, list the code and title of the book, the condition of the book, and the price. A branch may have multiple copies of the same book, each with a different quality (condition) and price. The copies of the same book in a branch are assigned numbers to distinguish one copy from another.

User View 6 Requirements: For each book, list its code and title. In addition, for each branch that currently has a copy of the book in stock, list the copy number, quality, and price of the book.

To transform each user view into DBDL, examine the requirements and create the necessary entities, keys, and relationships.

User View 1: For each publisher, list the publisher code, publisher name, and city in which the publisher is located.

The only entity in this user view is Publisher.

```
Publisher (PublisherCode, PublisherName, City)
```

This table is in third normal form; the primary key is PublisherCode. There are no alternate or foreign keys. Assume Ray wants to access a publisher rapidly based on its name. You will need to specify the PublisherName column as a secondary key.

Because this is the first user view, there is no previous cumulative design. Thus, at this point, the new cumulative design consists only of the design for this user view, as shown in Figure 6-9. There is no need for an E-R diagram at this point.

```
Publisher (PublisherCode, PublisherName, City)
     SK    PublisherName
```

FIGURE 6-9   DBDL for Book database after first user view

User View 2: For each branch, list the number, name, and location.
The only entity in this user view is Branch.

```
Branch (BranchNum, BranchName, BranchLocation)
```

This table is in third normal form. The primary key is BranchNum, and there are no alternate or foreign keys. Ray wants to be able to access a branch rapidly based on its name, so you will make the BranchName column a secondary key.

Because there is no table in the cumulative design with the BranchNum column as its primary key, you can add the Branch table to the cumulative design during the merge step, as shown in Figure 6-10. Again, there is no need for an E-R diagram with this simple design.

```
Publisher (PublisherCode, PublisherName, City)
     SK    PublisherName

Branch (BranchNum, BranchName, BranchLocation)
     SK    BranchName
```

FIGURE 6-10   DBDL for Book database after second user view

User View 3: For each book, list its code, title, publisher code and name, and whether it is paperback. To satisfy this user requirement, you will need to create entities for publishers and books and establish a one-to-many relationship between them. This leads to the following:

```
Publisher (PublisherCode, PublisherName)
Book (BookCode, Title, Paperback, PublisherCode)
```

The PublisherCode column in the Book table is a foreign key identifying the publisher. Merging these tables with the ones you already created does not add any new columns to the Publisher table, but it does add columns to the Book table. The result of merging the Book table with the cumulative design is shown in Figure 6-11. Assuming Ray will need to access books based on their titles, you will designate the Title column as a secondary key.

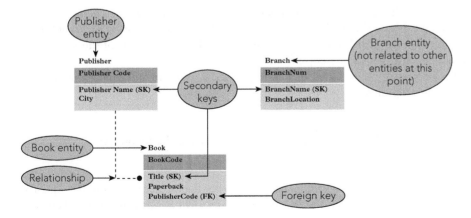

FIGURE 6-11   Cumulative design after third user view

User View 4: For each book, list its code, title, and type. In addition, list the name(s) of the author(s). If a book has more than one author, all names must appear in the order in which they are listed on the book's cover. The author order is not always alphabetical.

There are two entities in the user view for books and authors. The relationship between them is many-to-many (one author can write many books, and one book can have many authors). Creating tables for each entity and the relationship between them gives the following:

```
Author (AuthorNum, AuthorLast, AuthorFirst)
Book (BookCode, Title, Type)
Wrote (BookCode, AuthorNum)
```

The third table is named Wrote because it represents the fact that an author *wrote* a particular book. In this user view, you need to be able to list the authors for a book in the appropriate order. To accomplish this goal, add a sequence number column to the Wrote table. This completes the tables for this user view, which are as follows:

```
Author (AuthorNum, AuthorLast, AuthorFirst)
Book (BookCode, Title, Type)
Wrote (BookCode, AuthorNum, Sequence)
```

The Author and Wrote tables are new; merging the Book table adds nothing new. Because it may be important to find an author based on the author's last name, the AuthorLast column is a secondary key. The result of the merge step is shown in Figure 6-12.

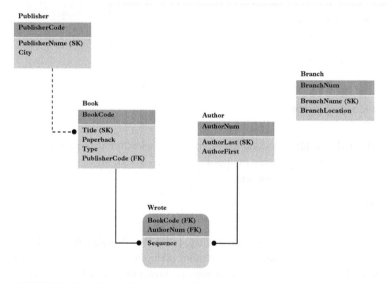

FIGURE 6-12 Cumulative design after fourth user view

User View 5 Requirements: For each branch, list its number and name. In addition, for each copy of a book in the branch, list the code and title of the book, the quality of the book, and the price. A branch might have multiple copies of the same book, each with a different quality and price. The copies of the same book in a branch are assigned numbers to distinguish one copy from another.

Suppose you decide that the only entity mentioned in this requirement contains information about branches. You would create the following table:

```
Branch (
```

You would then add the BranchNum column as the primary key, producing the following:

```
Branch (BranchNum,
```

The other columns include the branch name as well as the book code, book title, copy number, quality, and price. Because a branch will have several books, the last five columns form a repeating group. Thus, you have the following:

```
Branch (BranchNum, BranchName, (BookCode, Title, CopyNum, Quality, Price) )
```

You convert this table to first normal form by removing the repeating group and expanding the primary key. This gives the following:

Branch (<u>BranchNum</u>, BranchName, <u>BookCode</u>, Title, <u>CopyNum</u>, Quality, Price)

Q & A 6-1

Question: Why is CopyNum part of the primary key?
Answer: A branch can have more than one copy of the same book in stock. The Branch entity, as currently designed, could include multiple rows with the same branch number and the same book code. To uniquely identify a specific book, you also need the copy number. Thus, CopyNum must be part of the primary key.

In this table, you have the following functional dependencies:

BranchNum → BranchName
BookCode → Title
BranchNum, BookCode, CopyNum → Quality, Price

The table is not in second normal form because some columns depend on just a portion of the primary key. Converting to second normal form gives the following:

Branch (<u>BranchNum</u>, BranchName)
Book (<u>BookCode</u>, Title)
Copy (<u>BranchNum</u>, <u>BookCode</u>, <u>CopyNum</u>, Quality, Price)

You can name the new table Copy because it represents information about individual copies of books. In the Copy table, the BranchNum column is a foreign key that identifies the Branch table, and the BookCode column is a foreign key that identifies the Book table. In other words, for a row to exist in the Copy table, *both* the branch number *and* the book code must already be in the database.

You can merge this Branch table with the existing Branch table without adding any new columns or relationships to the database, and you can merge this Book table with the existing Book table without adding any new columns or relationships to the database. After adding the Copy table to the existing cumulative design, you have the design shown in Figure 6-13.

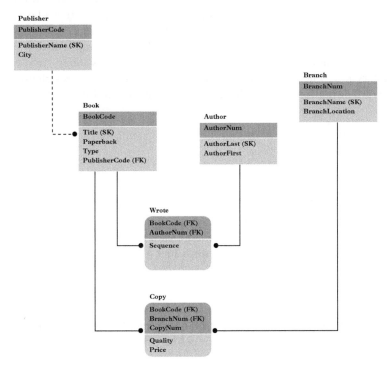

FIGURE 6-13   Cumulative design after fifth user view

NOTE: When you are using a software tool to produce these diagrams, the software may change the order of the columns that make up the primary key from the order you intended. For example, the diagram in Figure 6-13 indicates that the primary key for the Copy table is BookCode, BranchNum, and CopyNum, even though you intended it to be BranchNum, BookCode, and CopyNum. This change in order is not a problem. What is significant is the collection of fields that make up the primary key, not the order in which they appear.

User View 6 Requirements: For each book, list its code and title. In addition, for each branch that currently has a copy of the book in stock, list the copy number, quality, and price of the book.

This user view leads to precisely the same set of tables that were created for User View 5.

You have satisfied all the requirements, and the design shown in Figure 6-13 represents the complete information-level design.

Q & A 6-2

Question: In the Wrote table, Sequence is not part of the primary key. In the Copy table, CopyNum is part of the primary key. These fields seem to play similar roles in tables. Why is there a difference?

Answer: In the Wrote table, there will only be one row with a given book code and author number. The sequence number simply helps ensure that the authors for a given book appear in the correct order when listed in queries and reports. It is not necessary in distinguishing one row from another. On the other hand, in the Copy table, there can be multiple rows with the same branch number and book code combination, and with the same or a different condition and price. The copy number is essential to distinguish one copy of a given book at a given branch from another.

PHYSICAL-LEVEL DESIGN

After the information-level design is complete, you are ready to begin the physical-level design process by implementing the design for the specific DBMS selected by the organization.

Because most DBMSs are relational and the final information-level design already exists in a relational format, producing the design for the chosen DBMS is usually an easy task—you simply use the same tables and columns. At this point, you also need to supply format details, such as specifying that the ClientNum field will store characters and that its length is three.

Most DBMSs support primary, alternate, secondary, and foreign keys. If you are using a system that supports these keys, you can use these features to implement the various types of keys that are listed in the final DBDL version of the information-level design. When working in DBMSs that do not support these keys, you need to devise a scheme for handling them to ensure the uniqueness of primary and alternate keys. In addition, you must ensure that values in foreign keys are legitimate; they must match the value of the primary key in some row in another table. For secondary keys, you must ensure that it is possible to retrieve data rapidly based on a value of the secondary key. These kinds of decisions are called **enforcing restrictions**.

For instance, suppose you are implementing the Employee table shown in Figure 6-1 and it has the following DBDL:

```
Employee (EmployeeNum, LastName, FirstName, Street, City,
    State, ZipCode, WageRate, SocSecNum, DepartmentNum)
AK → SocSecNum
SK → LastName
FK → DepartmentNum → Department
```

The Employee table uses the EmployeeNum column as its primary key, the SocSecNum column as its alternate key, the LastName column as its secondary key, and the DepartmentNum column as a foreign key that matches the DepartmentNum column in the Department table. You must find a way for the DBMS to ensure that the following conditions hold true:

- Employee numbers are unique.
- Social Security numbers are unique.
- Access to an employee's record on the basis of his or her last name is rapid. (This restriction differs in that it merely states that a certain type of activity must be efficient, but it is an important restriction nonetheless.)
- Department numbers must match the number of a department currently in the database.

When the DBMS cannot enforce these restrictions, who should enforce them? Two choices are possible: the users of the system or the programmers. If users must enforce these restrictions, they must be careful not to enter two employees with the same EmployeeNum, an employee with an invalid DepartmentNum, and so on. Clearly, this type of enforcement puts a tremendous burden on users.

When the DBMS cannot enforce these restrictions, the appropriate place for the enforcement to take place is in the peripheral programs written to access the data in the database. Thus, the responsibility for this enforcement should fall on the programmers who write these programs. Users therefore *must* update the data through these programs and *not* through the built-in features of the DBMS in such circumstances; otherwise, the users would be able to bypass all the controls you are attempting to program into the system.

To enforce restrictions, programmers must include logic in their programs. With respect to the DBDL for the Employee table, this means the following:

1. Before an employee is added, the program should determine and process three restrictions:
   a. Determine whether an employee with the same EmployeeNum is already in the database. If so, the program should reject the update.
   b. Determine whether an employee with the same Social Security number is already in the database. If so, the program should reject the update.
   c. Determine whether the inputted department number matches a department number that is already in the database; if it does not, the program should reject the update.
2. When a user changes the department number of an existing employee, the program should check to make sure the new number matches a department number that is already in the database. If it does not, the program should reject the update.
3. When a user deletes a department number, the program should verify that no employees work in the department. If the employees do work in the department and the program allows the deletion of the department, these employees will have invalid department numbers. In this case, the program should reject the update.

Programs must perform these verifications efficiently; in most systems, this means the database administrator will create indexes for each column (or combination of columns) that is a primary key, an alternate key, a secondary key, or a foreign key.

TOP-DOWN VERSUS BOTTOM-UP DESIGN

Another way to design a database is to use a **bottom-up design method** in which specific user requirements are synthesized into a design. The opposite of a bottom-up design method is a **top-down design method**, which begins with a general database design that models the overall enterprise and repeatedly refines the model to achieve a design that supports all necessary applications. The original design and refinements are often represented with E-R diagrams.

Both strategies have their advantages. The top-down approach lends a more global feel to the project; you at least have some idea where you are headed, which is not so with a strictly bottom-up approach. On the other hand, a bottom-up approach provides a rigorous way of tackling each separate requirement and ensuring that it is met. In particular, tables are created to satisfy each user view or requirement precisely. When these tables are correctly merged into the cumulative design, you can be sure that you have satisfied the requirements for each user view.

The ideal strategy combines the best of both approaches. Assuming the design problem is sufficiently complicated to warrant the benefits of the top-down approach, you could begin the design process for BITS using a top-down approach by completing the following steps:

1. After gathering data on all user views, review them without attempting to create any tables. In other words, try to get a general feel for the task at hand.
2. From this information, determine the basic entities of interest to the organization (consultants, clients, orders, and tasks). Do not be overly concerned that you might miss an entity. If you do miss one, it will show up in later steps of the design method.
3. For each entity, start a table. For example, if the entities are consultants, clients, orders, and tasks, you will have the following:

```
Consultant (
Client (
WorkOrders (
Tasks (
```

4. Determine and list a primary key for each table. In this example, you might have the following:

```
Consultant (ConsltNum,
Client (ClientNum,
WorkOrders (OrderNum,
Tasks (TaskID,
```

5. For each one-to-many relationship that you can identify among these entities, optionally create and document an appropriate foreign key. For example, if there is a one-to-many relationship between the Consultant and Client tables, add the foreign key ConsltNum to the Client table. If you omit this step or fail to list any foreign keys, you will usually find the foreign keys when you examine the individual user views later.

After completing the steps for a top-down approach, you can then apply the bottom-up method for examining individual user views. As you design each user view, keep in mind the tables you have created in the initial top-down approach and their keys. When you need to determine the primary key for a table, look for a primary key in your cumulative design. When it is time to determine a foreign key, check the entity's primary key to see if a match exists in the cumulative design. In either case, if the primary key already exists, use the existing name as a foreign key to ensure that you can merge the tables properly. At the end of the design process, you can consider removing any tables that do not contain columns and that have no foreign keys matching them.

Adding these steps to the process brings the benefits of the top-down approach to the approach you have been using. As you proceed through the design process for the individual user views, you will have a general idea of the overall picture.

SURVEY FORM

When designing a database, you might find it helpful to design a survey form to obtain the required information from users. You can ask users to complete the form, or you may want to complete the form yourself during an interview with the user. Before beginning the interview, you can identify all existing data by viewing various reports, documents, and so on. In any case, it is imperative that the completed survey form contain all the information necessary for the design process.

To be truly valuable to the design process, the survey form must contain the following information:

- *Entity information.* For each entity (consultants, clients, tasks, and so on), record a name and description, and identify any synonyms for the entity. For example, at BITS, your survey might reveal that what one user calls "tasks" another user calls "services." In addition, record any general information about the entity, such as its use within the organization.
- *Attribute (column) information.* For each attribute of an entity, list its name, description, synonyms, and physical characteristics (such as being 20 characters long and alphanumeric, or a number with five digits), along with general information concerning its use. In addition, list any restrictions on values and the place from which the values for the item originate. (For example, the values might originate from time cards or from orders placed by customers, or be computed from values from other attributes, such as when subtracting the balance from the credit limit to obtain available credit). Finally, list any security restrictions that apply to the attribute.
- *Relationships.* For any relationship, the survey form should include the entities involved, the type of relationship (one-to-one, one-to-many, or many-to-many), the significance of the relationship (that is, what determines when two objects are related), and any restrictions on the relationship.
- *Functional dependencies.* The survey form should include information concerning the functional dependencies that exist among the columns. To obtain this information, you might ask the user a question such as this: If you know a particular employee number, can you establish other information, such as the name? If so, you can determine that the name is functionally dependent on the employee number. Another question you might ask is this: Do you know the number of the department to which the employee is assigned? If so, you can determine that the department number is functionally dependent on the employee number. If a given employee can be assigned to more than one department, you would not know the department number, and the department number would not be dependent on the employee number. Users probably will not understand the term *functional dependency*; therefore, it is important to ask the right questions so that you can identify any functional dependencies. An accurate list of functional dependencies is absolutely essential to the design process.

- **Processing information.** The survey form should include a description of the manner in which the various types of processing (updates to the database, reports that must be produced, and so on) are to take place. To obtain this information, pose questions such as these:

  - How exactly is the report to be produced?
  - Where do the entries on the report come from?
  - How are the report entries calculated?
  - When a user enters a new order, from where does the data come?
  - Which entities and columns must be updated and how?

In addition, you need to obtain estimates on processing volumes by asking questions such as these:

- How often is the report produced?
- On average, how many pages or screens is the report?
- What is the maximum length of the report?
- What is the maximum number of orders the system receives per day?
- What is the average number of orders the system receives per day?
- What is the maximum number of invoices the system prints per day?
- What is the average number of invoices the system prints per day?

OBTAINING INFORMATION FROM EXISTING DOCUMENTS

Existing documents can often furnish helpful information concerning the database design. You need to take an existing document, like the invoice for the company named Holt Distributors shown in Figure 6-14, and determine the tables and columns that would be required to produce the document.

10/15/2018						Invoice 11025

HOLT DISTRIBUTORS
146 NELSON PLACE
BRONSTON, MI 49802

SOLD TO:	Smith Rentals 153 Main St. Suite 102 Grandville, MI 49494		SHIP TO:	A & B Supplies 2180 Halton Pl. Arendville, MI 49232		

Customer	P.O. No.	Our Order No.	Order Date	Ship Date	Sales Rep
1354	PO3351	12424	10/02/2015	10/15/2015	10-Brown, Sam

Quantity						
Order	Ship	B/O	Item Number	Description	Price	Amount
6	5	1	AT414	Lounge Chair	$42.00	$210.00
4	4	0	BT222	Chair Arm	$51.00	$204.00
				Freight		$42.50

	Pay This Amount
	$456.50

FIGURE 6-14 Invoice for Holt Distributors

The first step in obtaining information from an existing document is to identify and list all columns and give them appropriate names. Figure 6-15 lists the columns you can determine from the invoice shown in Figure 6-14 on the previous page.

```
InvoiceNumber
InvoiceDate
CustomerNumber
CustomerSoldToName
CustomerSoldToAddressLine1
CustomerSoldToAddressLine2
CustomerSoldToCity
CustomerSoldToState
CustomerSoldToZipCode
CustomerShipToName
CustomerShipToAddress
CustomerShipToCity
CustomerShipToState
CustomerShipToZipCode
CustomerPONumber
OrderNumber
OrderDate
ShipDate
CustomerRepNumber
CustomerRepLastName
CustomerRepFirstName
ItemNumber
ItemDescription
ItemQuantityOrdered
ItemQuantityShipped
ItemQuantityBackordered
ItemPrice
ItemAmount
Freight
InvoiceTotal
```

FIGURE 6-15　List of possible attributes for Holt Distributors invoice

The names the user chose for many of these columns might differ from the names you select, but this difference is not important at this stage. After interviewing the user, you might learn that a required column was not apparent on the document you reviewed. For example, the shipping address for the client shown in Figure 6-14 did not require a second line, so you simply listed CustomerShipToAddress rather than CustomerShipToAddressLine1 and CustomerShipToAddressLine2 in your preliminary list of columns (see Figure 6-15). If you later determine that you might need two lines for a client's address, you could replace CustomerShipToAddress with CustomerShipToAddressLine1 and CustomerShipToAddressLine 2 at the next step. Some columns that you identify may not be required. For example, when the ship date is the same as the invoice date, a separate ShipDate column is unnecessary. Clearly, the user's help is needed to clarify these types of issues.

Next, you need to identify functional dependencies. If you are unfamiliar with the document you are examining, you might not be able to determine its functional dependencies. In this case, you will need to interview the user to determine the functional dependencies that exist. Sometimes you can make intelligent guesses based on your general knowledge of the type of document you are studying. You may make mistakes, of course, but you can correct them when you interview the user. After initially determining the functional dependencies shown in Figure 6-16, you may find additional information.

```
CustomerNumber →

        CustomerSoldToName
        CustomerSoldToAddressLine1
        CustomerSoldToAddressLine2
        CustomerSoldToCity
        CustomerSoldToState
        CustomerSoldToZipCode
        CustomerShipToName
        CustomerShipToAddressLine1
        CustomerShipToAddressLine2
        CustomerShipToCity
        CustomerShipToState
        CustomerShipToZipCode
        CustomerRepNumber
        CustomerRepLastName
        CustomerRepFirstName

ItemNumber →
        ItemDescription
        ItemPrice

InvoiceNumber →
        InvoiceDate
        CustomerNumber
        OrderNumber
        OrderDate
        ShipDate
        Freight
        InvoiceTotal

InvoiceNumber, ItemNumber →
        ItemQuantityOrdered
        ItemQuantityShipped
        ItemQuantityBackordered
        ItemAmount
```

FIGURE 6-16   Tentative list of functional dependencies for the Holt Distributors invoice

Based on your list of functional dependencies, you may learn that the shipping address for a given client varies from one invoice to another. In other words, the shipping address depends on the invoice number, not the client number. A default shipping address may be defined for a given client in case no shipping address is entered with an order. However, the address that actually appears on the invoice depends on the invoice number. You may also determine that several columns actually depend on the order that was initially entered. The order date, client, shipping address, and quantities ordered on each line of the invoice may have been entered as part of the initial order. At the time the invoice was printed, additional information, such as the quantities shipped, the quantities back-ordered, and the freight charges, may have been added. You may also find that the price is not necessarily the one stored with the item and that the price can vary from one order to another. Given all these corrections, a revised list of functional dependencies might look like Figure 6-17 on the next page.

```
CustomerNumber →
         CustomerSoldToName
         CustomerSoldToAddressLine1
         CustomerSoldToAddressLine2
         CustomerSoldToCity
         CustomerSoldToState
         CustomerSoldToZipCode
         CustomerRepNumber
         CustomerRepLastName
         CustomerRepFirstName

ItemNumber →
         ItemDescription
         ItemPrice

InvoiceNumber →
         InvoiceDate
         OrderNumber
         ShipDate
         Freight
         InvoiceTotal

OrderNumber →
         OrderDate
         CustomerPONumber
         CustomerShipToName
         CustomerShipToAddressLine1
         CustomerShipToAddressLine2
         CustomerShipToCity
         CustomerShipToState
         CustomerShipToZipCode

OrderNumber, ItemNumber →
         ItemQuantityOrdered (added when order is entered)
         ItemQuantityShipped (added during invoicing)
         ItemQuantityBackordered (added during invoicing)
         ItemPrice (added when order is entered)
```

FIGURE 6-17 Revised list of functional dependencies for the Holt Distributors invoice

After you have determined the preliminary functional dependencies, you can begin determining the tables and assigning columns. You could create tables with the determinant (the column or columns to the left of the arrow) as the primary key and with the columns to the right of the arrow as the remaining columns. This would lead to the following initial collection of tables:

```
Customer (CustomerNumber, CustomerSoldToName,
    CustomerSoldToAddressLine1, CustomerSoldToAddressLine2,
    CustomerSoldToCity, CustomerSoldToState, CustomerSoldToZipCode,
    CustomerRepNumber, CustomerRepLastName, CustomerRepFirstName)
Item (ItemNum, ItemDescription, ItemPrice)
Invoice (InvoiceNumber, InvoiceDate, OrderNumber, ShipDate,
    Freight, InvoiceTotal)
Order (OrderNumber, OrderDate, CustomerPONumber,
    CustomerShipToName, CustomerShipToAddressLine1,
    CustomerShipToAddressLine2, CustomerShipToCity,
    CustomerShipToState, CustomerShipToZipCode)
OrderLine (OrderNumber, ItemNum, ItemQuantityOrdered,
    ItemQuantityShipped, ItemQuantityBackordered, ItemPrice)
```

These tables would then need to be converted to third normal form and the result merged into the cumulative design.

Some people prefer not to get so specific at this point. Rather, they examine the various columns and determine a preliminary list of entities, as shown in Figure 6-18.

```
Orders
Customer
Rep
Item
```

FIGURE 6-18   Tentative list of entities

After examining the functional dependencies, they refine this list, producing a list similar to the one shown in Figure 6-19. At this point, they create tables for these entities and position each column in the table in which it seems to fit best.

```
Invoice
Customer
Rep
Item
Orders
OrderLine
```

FIGURE 6-19   Expanded list of entities

Whichever approach you take, this kind of effort is certainly worthwhile; it gives you a better feel for the problem when you interact with the user. You can change your work based on your interview with the user. Even if your work proves to be accurate, you still need to ask additional questions of the user. These questions might include the following:

- What names do you think are appropriate for the various entities and attributes?
- What synonyms are in use?
- What restrictions exist?
- What are the meanings of the various entities, attributes, and relationships?

If the organization has a computerized system, current file layouts can provide you with additional information about entities and attributes. Current file sizes can provide information on volume. Examining the logic in current programs and their operational instructions can yield processing information. Again, however, this is just a starting point. You still need further information from the user, which you can obtain by asking questions such as these:

- How many invoices do you expect to print?
- Exactly how are the values on the invoice calculated, and where do they come from?
- What updates must be made during the invoicing cycle of processing?
- What fields in the Customer table will be updated?

ONE-TO-ONE RELATIONSHIP CONSIDERATIONS

What, if anything, is wrong with implementing a one-to-one relationship by simply including the primary key of each table as a foreign key in the other table? For example, suppose each BITS client has a single consultant and each consultant represents a single client. Applying the suggested technique to this one-to-one relationship produces two tables:

```
Consultant (ConsltNum, LastName, FirstName, ClientNum)
Client (ClientNum, ClientName, ConsltNum)
```

In practice, these tables would contain any additional consultant or client columns of interest in the design problem. For the purposes of illustration, however, assume these are the only columns in these tables.

Samples of these tables are shown in Figure 6-20. This design clearly forces a consultant to be related to a single client. Because the client number is a column in the Consultant table, there can be only one client for each consultant. Likewise, this design forces a consultant to be related to a single client.

Consultant

ConsltNum	LastName	FirstName	ClientNum
19	Turner	Christopher	143
22	Jorden	Patrick	299
35	Allen	Sarah	322

Client

ClientNum	ClientName	ConsltNum
143	Hershey, Jarrod	19
299	Two Crafty Cousins	22
322	Prichard's Pizza & Pasta	35

FIGURE 6-20 One-to-one relationship implemented by including the primary key of each table as a foreign key in the other

Q & A 6-3

Question: What is the potential problem with this solution?
Answer: There is no guarantee that the information will match. Consider Figure 6-21, for example. The data in the first table indicates that consultant 19 represents client 143. The data in the second table, on the other hand, indicates that client 143 is represented by consultant 22! This solution may be the simplest way of implementing a one-to-one relationship from a conceptual standpoint, but it clearly introduces the risk of update anomalies and inconsistency in the database. The programs themselves would have to ensure that the data in the two tables match, a task that the design should be able to accomplish on its own.

Consultant

ConsltNum	LastName	FirstName	ClientNum
19	Turner	Christopher	143
22	Jorden	Patrick	299
35	Allen	Sarah	322

Client

ClientNum	ClientName	ConsltNum
143	Hershey, Jarrod	22
299	Two Crafty Cousins	19
322	Prichard's Pizza & Pasta	35

FIGURE 6-21 Implementation of a one-to-one relationship in which information does not match

To avoid these types of problems when creating one-to-one relationships, the first solution is to create a single table such as this:

```
Client (ClientNum, ClientName, ConsltNum, LastName, FirstName)
```

A sample of this table is shown in Figure 6-22. Which column should be the primary key? If it is the client number, there is nothing to prevent all three rows from containing the same consultant number. On the other hand, if it were the consultant number, the same would hold true for the client number.

Client

ClientNum	ClientName	ConsltNum	LastName	FirstName
143	Hershey, Jarrod	19	Turner	Christopher
299	Two Crafty Cousins	11	Jordan	Patrick
322	Prichard's Pizza & Pasta	35	Allen	Sarah

FIGURE 6-22   One-to-one relationship implemented in a single table

The solution is to choose either the client number or the consultant number as the primary key and make the other column the alternate key. In other words, the DBMS should enforce the uniqueness of both client numbers and consultant numbers. Because each client and each consultant will appear in exactly one row, there is a one-to-one relationship between them.

Although this solution is workable, it has two features that are not particularly attractive. First, it combines columns of two different entities into a single table. It certainly would seem more natural to have one table with client columns and a second table with consultant columns. Second, if it is possible for one entity to exist without the other (for example, when a client has no consultant), this structure is going to cause problems.

A better solution is to create separate tables for clients and consultants and to include the primary key of one of them as a foreign key in the other. This foreign key would also be designated as an alternate key. Thus, you could choose either

```
Consultant (ConsltNum, LastName, FirstName, ClientNum)
Client (ClientNum, ClientName)
```

or

```
Consultant (ConsltNum, LastName, FirstName)
Client (ClientNum, ClientName, ConsltNum)
```

Samples of these two possibilities are shown in Figure 6-23. In either case, you must enforce the uniqueness of the foreign key that you added. In the first solution, for example, if client numbers need not be unique, all three rows might contain client 143, violating the one-to-one relationship. You can enforce the uniqueness by designating these foreign keys as alternate keys. They also will be foreign keys because they must match an actual row in the other table.

Solution 1:
Consultant

ConsltNum	LastName	FirstName	ClientNum
19	Turner	Christopher	143
22	Jordan	Patrick	299
35	Allen	Sarah	322

Client

ClientNum	ClientName
143	Hershey, Jarrod
299	Two Crafty Cousins
322	Prichard's Pizza & Pasta

Solution 2:
Consultant

ConsltNum	LastName	FirstName
19	Turner	Christopher
22	Jordan	Patrick
35	Allen	Sarah

Client

ClientNum	ClientName	ConsltNum
143	Hershey, Jarrod	15
299	Two Crafty Cousins	30
322	Prichard's Pizza & Pasta	45

FIGURE 6-23   One-to-one relationship implemented by including the primary key of one table as a foreign key (and alternate key) in the other table

How do you make a choice between the possibilities? In some cases, it really makes no difference which arrangement you choose. Suppose, however, you anticipate the possibility that this relationship may not always be one-to-one. Suppose there is likelihood in the future that a consultant might represent more than one client but that each client still will be assigned to exactly one consultant.

The relationship would then be one-to-many, and it would be implemented with a structure similar to Solution 2. In fact, the structure would differ only in that the consultant number in the Client table would not be an alternate key. Thus, to convert from the second alternative to the appropriate structure would be a simple matter—you would remove the restriction that the consultant number in the Client table is an alternate key. This situation would lead you to favor the second alternative.

MANY-TO-MANY RELATIONSHIP CONSIDERATIONS

Complex issues arise when more than two entities are related in a many-to-many relationship. For example, suppose BITS needs to know which consultants provided which tasks to which clients. A table is produced named Services. In this example, there are no restrictions on which clients a given consultant may service, or on the tasks that a consultant may perform. Sample data for this relationship is shown in Figure 6-24.

Services

ConsltNum	ClientNum	TaskID
19	143	LA81
19	143	MO49
22	143	WA33
22	677	LA81
35	143	WA33
35	299	VR39
35	363	WA33

FIGURE 6-24   Sample services data

The first row in the table indicates that consultant 19 performed task LA81 for client 143. The second row indicates that consultant 19 performed task MO49 for client 143.

Q & A 6-4

Question: What is the primary key of the Services table?
Answer: Clearly, in Figure 6-24, none of the three columns (ConsltNum, ClientNum, and TaskID) alone will uniquely identify a record. The combination of ConsltNum and ClientNum does not work because there are two rows on which the consultant number is 19 and the client number is 143. The combination of ConsltNum and TaskID does not work because there are two rows on which the consultant number is 35 and the task ID number is WA33. Finally, the combination of ClientNum and TaskID does not work because there are two rows on which the client number is 143 and the task ID number is WA33. Thus, the primary key for the Services table must be the combination of all three columns, as follows:

```
Services (ConsltNum, ClientNum, TaskID)
```

Attempting to model this particular situation as two (or three) many-to-many relationships is not legitimate. Consider the following code and the data shown in Figure 6-25, for example, in which the same data is split into three tables:

```
ConsultantClient (ConsltNum, ClientNum)
ClientTasks (ClientNum, TaskID)
TasksConsultant (TaskID, ConsltNum)
```

ConsultantClient

ConsltNum	ClientNum
19	143
22	143
22	677
35	143
35	299
35	363

ClientTasks

ClientNum	TaskID
143	LA81
143	MO49
143	WA33
299	VR39
363	WA33
677	LA81

TasksConsultant

TaskID	ConsltNum
LA81	19
LA81	22
MO49	19
VR39	35
WA33	22
WA33	35

FIGURE 6-25   Results obtained by splitting the services table into three tables

Figure 6-26 shows the result of joining these three tables. Note that it contains inaccurate information. The third row, for example, indicates that consultant 22 performed task LA81 for client 143. If you look back to Figure 6-24, you will see that is not the case.

Services

ConsltNum	ClientNum	TaskID
19	143	LA81
19	143	MO49
22	143	LA81 !!!!
22	143	TR40
22	677	LA81
35	143	LA81 !!!!
35	143	TR40
35	299	VR39
35	363	TR40

FIGURE 6-26   Result obtained by joining three tables—the third and sixth rows are in error

The row appears in the join because consultant 22 is related to client 143 in the ConsultantClient table (consultant 22 performed a task for client 143). Client 143 is related to task LA81 in the ClientTasks table (client 143 received service task LA81 from some consultant). Finally, task LA81 is related to consultant 22 in the TasksConsultant table (consultant 22 performed task LA81 for some client).

In other words, consultant 22 performed services for client 143, client 143 requested task LA81 from some consultant, and consultant 22 provided service task LA81 to someone. Of course, these three facts do not imply that consultant 22 performed service LA81 for client 143. Very confusing!

The problem with the preceding relationship is that it involves all three entities—consultants, clients, and tasks. Splitting the Services table shown in Figure 6-26 any further is inappropriate. Such a relationship is called a **many-to-many-to-many relationship**.

Remember from the discussion of fourth normal form that there are examples of three-way relationships in which you must split the tables. In particular, if the relationship between consultants and clients has nothing to do with the relationship between consultants and tasks, this table would violate fourth normal form and would need to be split.

The crucial issue in making the determination between a single many-to-many-to-many relationship and two (or three) many-to-many relationships is the independence. When all three entities are critical in the relationship, the three-way relationship (like Services) is appropriate. When there is independence among the individual relationships, separate many-to-many relationships are appropriate. Incidentally, if a many-to-many-to-many relationship is created when it is not appropriate to do so, the conversion to fourth normal form will correct the problem.

NULLS AND ENTITY SUBTYPES

Recall that a null is a special value that represents the *absence* of a value in a field. In other words, setting a particular field to null is equivalent to not entering a value in the field. Nulls are used when a value is either unknown or inapplicable. This section focuses on the second possibility—when the value is inapplicable.

Consider, for example, a Student table in which one of the columns, DormNum, is a foreign key that identifies a Dorm (dormitory) table. The DormNum column indicates the number of the dormitory in which a student currently resides. This foreign key is allowed to be null because some students do not live in a dormitory; for these students, DormNum is inapplicable. Thus, for some rows in the Student table, the DormNum column would be null.

When there are many students who do not live in dorms, you can avoid using null values in the DormNum column by removing the DormNum column from the Student table and creating a separate table named StudentDorm that contains the columns StudentNum (the primary key) and DormNum. Students living in a dorm would have a row in this new table. Students not living in a dorm would have a row in the Student table but not in the StudentDorm table.

This change is illustrated in Figure 6-27. Note that StudentNum, the primary key of the StudentDorm table, is also a foreign key that must match a student number in the Student table.

Student

StudentNum	LastName	FirstName	DormNum
1253	Johnson	Ann	3
1662	Anderson	Tom	1
2108	Lewis	Bill	
2546	Davis	Mary	2
2867	Albers	Cathy	2
2992	Matthew	Mark	
3011	Candela	Tim	3
3574	Talen	Sue	

Student

StudentNum	LastName	FirstName
1253	Johnson	Ann
1662	Anderson	Tom
2108	Lewis	Bill
2546	Davis	Mary
2867	Albers	Cathy
2992	Matthew	Mark
3011	Candela	Tim
3574	Talen	Sue

StudentDorm

StudentNum	DormNum
1253	3
1662	1
2546	2
2867	2
3011	3

FIGURE 6-27   Student table split to avoid use of null values

In the process, you have created what formally is called an entity **subtype**. You can say that the StudentDorm table is a subtype of the Student table. (Conversely, you can say that the Student table is the **supertype**.) In other words, "students living in dorms" is a subtype (or subset) of "students." A subtype **discriminator** is the specific attribute that determines the subtype-supertype relationship.

Some design methods have specific ways of denoting entity subtypes, but it is not necessary to denote entity subtypes in DBDL. You can recognize entity subtypes by the fact that the primary key is also a foreign key, as shown in Figure 6-28.

```
Student(StudentNum, LastName, FirstName)

StudentDorm (StudentNum, DormNum)
    FK    StudentNum → Student
    FK    DormNum → Dorm
```

FIGURE 6-28   Sample DBDL with entity subtypes

Most approaches to diagramming database designs have ways of representing subtypes. In IDEF1X, for example, a subtype, which is called a **category** in IDEF1X terminology, is represented in the manner shown in Figure 6-29. The circle is the symbol used for a category. The single horizontal line below the category symbol indicates that the category is an **incomplete category**; that is, there are students who do not fall into the StudentDorm category.

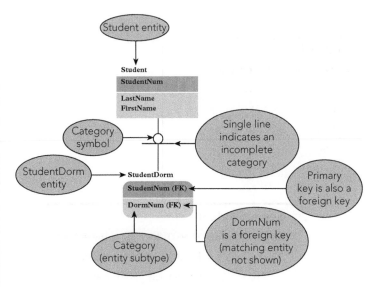

FIGURE 6-29   Entity subtype in an E-R diagram

The issue is more complicated when more than one column can accept null values. Suppose the DormNum, ThesisTitle, and ThesisArea columns in the following Student table can be null.

```
Student (StudentNum, LastName, FirstName, DormNum, ThesisTitle, ThesisArea)
```

In this table, the dorm number is the number of the dorm in which the student resides or is null if the student does not live in a dorm. In addition, students at this college must write a senior thesis. After students attain senior standing, they must select a thesis title in the area in which they will write their thesis. Thus, seniors will have a thesis title and a thesis area, whereas other students will not. You can handle this situation by allowing the fields ThesisTitle and ThesisArea to be null.

The Student table now has three different columns—DormNum, ThesisTitle, and ThesisArea—that can be null. The DormNum column will be null for students who do not live in a dorm. The ThesisTitle and ThesisArea columns will be null for students who have not yet attained senior standing. It would not make much sense to combine all three of these columns into a single table. A better choice would be to create the following table for students living in dorms:

```
StudentDorm (StudentNum, DormNum)
```

For seniors, you could create a second table as follows:

```
SeniorStudent (StudentNum, ThesisTitle, ThesisArea)
```

Samples of these tables are shown in Figure 6-30. The StudentDorm and SeniorStudent tables represent entity subtypes. In both tables, the primary key (StudentNum) will also be a foreign key matching the student number in the new Student table.

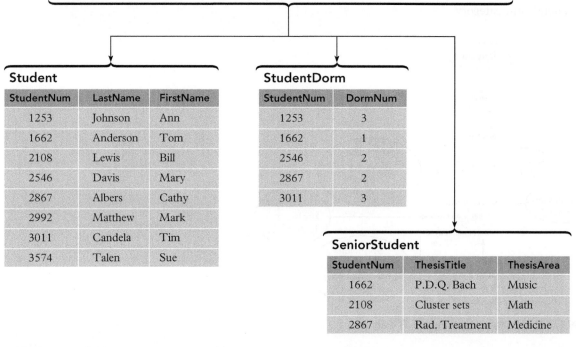

Student

StudentNum	LastName	FirstName	DormNum	ThesisTitle	ThesisArea
1253	Johnson	Ann	3		
1662	Anderson	Tom	1	P.D.Q. Bach	Music
2108	Lewis	Bill		Cluster sets	Math
2546	Davis	Mary	2		
2867	Albers	Cathy	2	Rad. Treatment	Medicine
2992	Matthew	Mark			
3011	Candela	Tim	3		
3574	Talen	Sue			

Student

StudentNum	LastName	FirstName
1253	Johnson	Ann
1662	Anderson	Tom
2108	Lewis	Bill
2546	Davis	Mary
2867	Albers	Cathy
2992	Matthew	Mark
3011	Candela	Tim
3574	Talen	Sue

StudentDorm

StudentNum	DormNum
1253	3
1662	1
2546	2
2867	2
3011	3

SeniorStudent

StudentNum	ThesisTitle	ThesisArea
1662	P.D.Q. Bach	Music
2108	Cluster sets	Math
2867	Rad. Treatment	Medicine

FIGURE 6-30   Student table split to avoid use of null values

The DBDL for these tables appears in Figure 6-31. The primary key of the StudentDorm and SeniorStudent tables (StudentNum) is also a foreign key matching the student number in the revised Student table.

```
Student (StudentNum, LastName, FirstName)

StudentDorm (StudentNum, DormNum)
    FK    StudentNum → Student
    FK    DormNum → Dorm

SeniorStudent (StudentNum, ThesisTitle, ThesisArea)
    FK    StudentNum → Student
```

FIGURE 6-31   Sample DBDL with entity subtypes

To represent two subtypes (categories) in IDEF1X, you use the same category symbol shown in Figure 6-29. The difference is that there will be two lines coming out of the category symbol—one to each category, as shown in Figure 6-32. Because there are students who do not live in dorms and who are not seniors, these categories are also incomplete; so there is only one horizontal line below the category symbol.

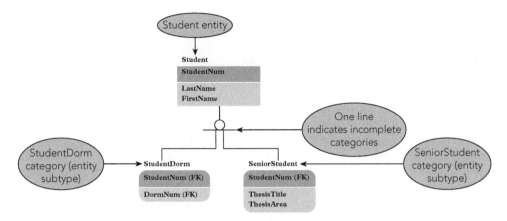

FIGURE 6-32 Two entity subtypes—incomplete categories

By contrast, Figure 6-33 represents a slightly different situation. There are two categories: students who live in dorms (StudentDorm) and students who do not (StudentNonDorm) live in dorms. For students who live in dorms, the attribute of interest is DormNum. For students who do not live in dorms, the attributes of interest are the ones that give the students' local addresses (LocalStreet, LocalCity, LocalState, and LocalZipCode). The difference between this example and the one shown in Figure 6-32 is that every student *must* be in one of these two categories. These are called **complete categories** and are represented by two horizontal lines below the category symbol.

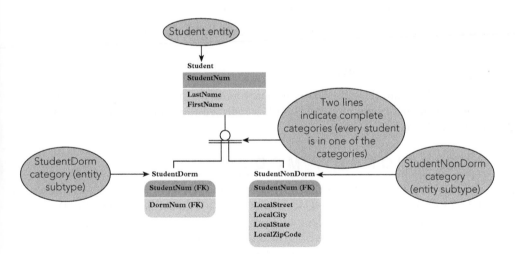

FIGURE 6-33 Two entity subtypes—complete categories

You should group columns that can be null by function. If a given subset of the entity in question can have nulls in a certain collection of columns, you should note this fact. When available, you should strongly consider splitting columns that can have nulls into a separate table (an entity subtype), as explained previously. If you create an entity subtype, you should give the entity subtype a name that suggests the related entity type, such as SeniorStudent for students who are seniors. In addition, you should carefully document the meaning of the entity subtype, especially the conditions that will cause an occurrence of the entity type also to be an occurrence of the entity subtype. If you do not create such an entity subtype, you must at least document precisely when the columns might take on null as a value.

AVOIDING PROBLEMS WITH THIRD NORMAL FORM WHEN MERGING TABLES

When you combine third normal form tables, the result might not be in third normal form. For example, both of the following tables are in third normal form:

```
Client (ClientNum, ClientName, ConsltNum)
Client (ClientNum, ClientName, LastName, FirstName)
```

When you combine them, however, you get the following table:

```
Client (ClientNum, ClientName, ConsltNum, LastName, FirstName)
```

This table is not in third normal form. You would have to convert it to third normal form before proceeding to the next user view.

You can attempt to avoid the problem of creating a table that is not in third normal form by being cautious when representing user views. This problem occurs when a column A in one user view functionally determines a column B in a second user view. Thus, column A is a *determinant* for column B, yet column A is not a column in the second user view.

In the preceding example, the ConsltNum column in the first table determines the columns LastName and FirstName in the second table. (The columns refer to the last name and first name of the consultant, not the client). However, the ConsltNum column is not one of the columns in the second table. If you always attempt to determine whether determinants exist and include them in the tables, you often will avoid this problem. For example, a user may be used to referring to the consultant by name only (using the name in all data interactions); thus, the table for that user view was created with a name. You should ask the user whether any special way has been provided for consultants to be uniquely identified within the organization in the case that two consultants might have the same name. Even though this user evidently does not need the consultant number, he or she might very well be aware of the existence of such a number. If so, you would include this number in the table. Having done this, you would have the following table in this user view:

```
Client (ClientNum, ClientName, ConsltNum, LastName, FirstName)
```

Now the normalization process for this user view would produce the following two tables:

```
Client (ClientNum, ClientName, ConsltNum)
Consultant (ConsltNum, LastName, FirstName)
```

When you merge these two tables into the cumulative design, you do not produce any tables that are not in third normal form. Notice that the determinant ConsltNum has replaced the columns that it determines, LastName and FirstName, in the Client table.

THE ENTITY-RELATIONSHIP MODEL

You have examined the use of E-R diagrams (IDEF1X) to illustrate visually the relations and keys represented in DBDL. Another approach is the **entity-relationship (E-R) model**. The E-R model (also called ERM) uses diagrams to represent the high-level abstract and conceptual representation of data, along with entities, attributes, and relationships. (*Note*: sometimes the diagrams in the E-R models also are called E-R diagrams, which leads to confusion with the IDEF1X E-R diagrams.) In 1976, Peter Chen of the MIT Sloan School of Management proposed the E-R model, which has been widely accepted as a graphical approach to database representation and database design.

In the E-R model, entities are drawn as rectangles and relationships are drawn as diamonds, with lines connecting the entities involved in relationships. Both entities and relationships are named in the E-R model. The lines are labeled to indicate the type of relationship. For example, in Figure 6-34, the one-to-many relationship between consultants and clients at BITS is represented as "1" to "n." (The letter *n* denotes *any* number.)

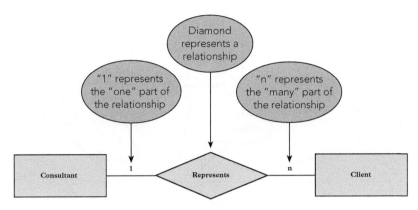

FIGURE 6-34 One-to-many relationship

In Figure 6-35, the many-to-many relationship between orders and tasks is represented as "m" to "n."

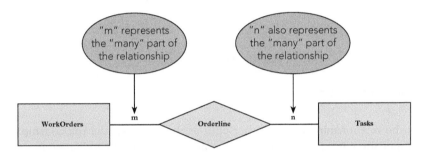

FIGURE 6-35 Many-to-many relationship

Finally, the many-to-many-to-many relationship between consultants, clients, and tasks is represented as "m" to "n" to "p," as shown in Figure 6-36.

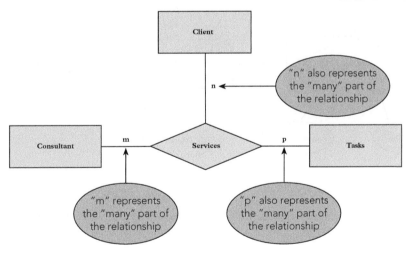

FIGURE 6-36 Many-to-many-to-many relationship

If desired, you also can indicate attributes in the E-R model by placing them in ovals and attaching them to the corresponding rectangles (entities), as shown in Figure 6-37 on the next page. As in the relational model representation, primary keys are underlined.

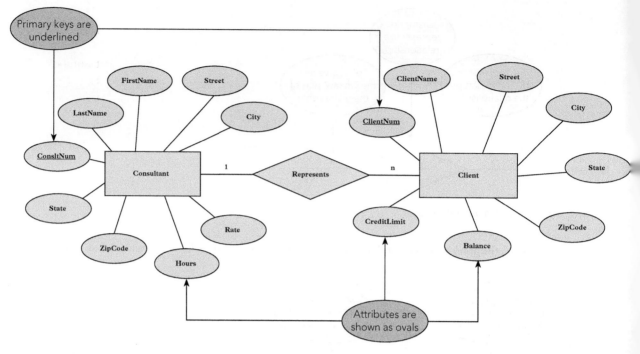

FIGURE 6-37 One-to-many relationship with attributes added

Sometimes an entity can serve as the relationship between other entities. In that case, the relationship may possess attributes. Known as a **composite entity**, it is represented in an E-R diagram by a diamond within a rectangle. Figure 6-38 shows this approach.

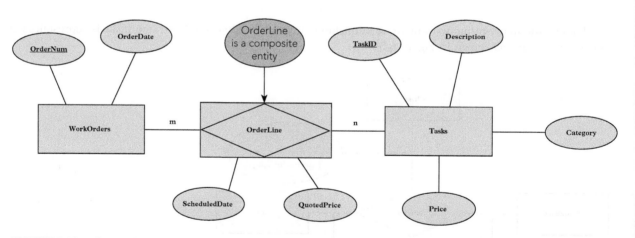

FIGURE 6-38 Composite entity

A complete E-R diagram for the BITS database appears in Figure 6-39. Notice that OrderLine is represented as a composite entity.

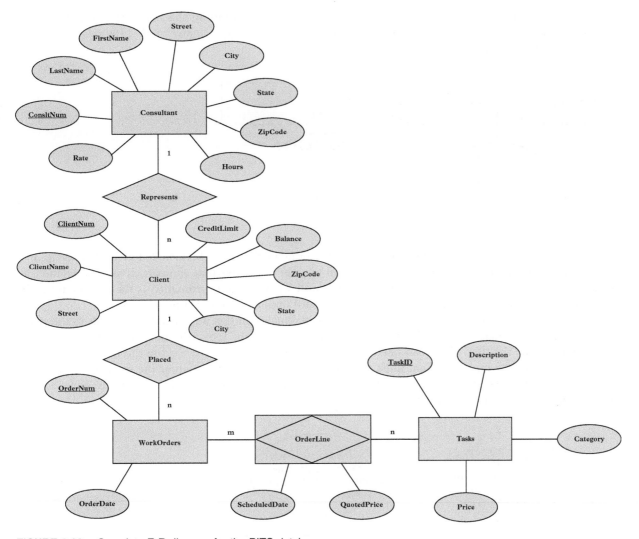

FIGURE 6-39   Complete E-R diagram for the BITS database

When the existence of one entity depends on the existence of another related entity, there is an **existence dependency**. For example, because an order cannot exist without a client, the relationship between clients and orders is an existence dependency. You indicate an existence dependency by placing an *E* in the relationship diamond, as shown in Figure 6-40. An entity that depends on another entity for its own existence is called a **weak entity**. A double rectangle encloses a weak entity. A weak entity corresponds to the term *dependent entity*, which was previously defined in this chapter.

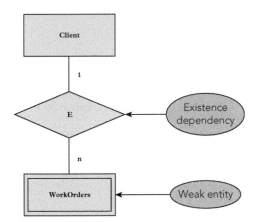

FIGURE 6-40   E-R diagram with an existence dependency and a weak entity

There is another popular way to indicate a one-to-many relationship. In this alternative, you do not label the "one" end of the relationship; instead, you place a crow's foot at the "many" end of the relationship. Figure 6-41 illustrates this style.

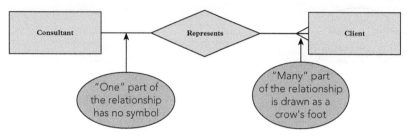

FIGURE 6-41 E-R diagram with a crow's foot

Some people represent **cardinality**, or the number of items that must be included in a relationship, in an E-R diagram. **Maximum cardinality** is the maximum number of entities that can participate in a relationship: one-to-one [1:1], one-to-many [1:N], or many-to-many [N:M]. **Minimum cardinality**: is the minimum number of entities that must participate in a relationship: zero [0] optional or one [1] mandatory.

Figure 6-42 shows an E-R diagram that represents cardinality in this way. The two symbols to the right of the Consultant rectangle are both the number 1. The 1 closest to the rectangle indicates that the maximum cardinality is one; that is, a client can have at most one consultant. The 1 closest to the relationship is the minimum cardinality; that is, a client must have at least one consultant. Together the two symbols indicate that a client must have exactly one consultant. (If the minimum cardinality were zero, for example, a client would not be required to have a consultant.)

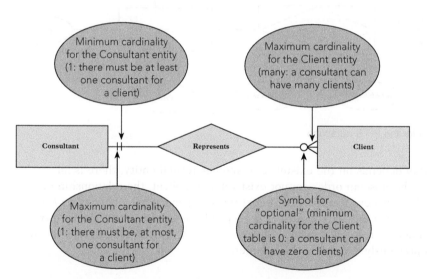

FIGURE 6-42 E-R diagram that represents cardinality

The crow's foot to left of the Client rectangle indicates that the maximum cardinality is "many." The circle to the left of the crow's foot indicates that the minimum cardinality is zero; that is, a consultant could be associated with zero clients. An entity in a relationship with minimum cardinality of zero plays an **optional role** in the relationship. An entity with a minimum cardinality of one plays a **mandatory role** in the relationship.

Both the E-R model and the E-R diagram (IDEF1X) are used in modern database design and in DBDLs, so it is important that you understand how to use them.

Summary

- Database design is a two-part process of determining an appropriate database structure to satisfy a given set of requirements. In the information-level design, a clean DBMS design that is not dependent on a particular DBMS is created to satisfy the requirements. In the physical-level design, the final information-level design is converted into an appropriate design for the particular DBMS that will be used.
- A user view is the set of necessary requirements to support a particular user's operations. To simplify the design process, the overall set of requirements is split into user views.
- The information-level design method involves applying the following steps to each user view: Represent the user view as a collection of tables, normalize these tables (convert the collection into an equivalent collection that is in third normal form), represent all keys (primary, alternate, secondary, and foreign), and merge the results into the cumulative design.
- A database design is represented in a language called Database Design Language (DBDL).
- Designs can be represented visually using entity-relationship (E-R) diagrams, which have the following characteristics. There is a rectangle for each entity; the name of the entity appears above the rectangle; the primary key appears above the line in the rectangle; the remaining columns appear below the line. Alternate keys, secondary keys, and foreign keys are identified with the letters AK, SK, and FK, respectively. For each foreign key, there is a dashed line from the table (rectangle) being identified, to the table (rectangle) containing the foreign key. A dot at the end of the line indicates the "many" part of a one-to-many relationship.
- When a relational DBMS is going to be used, the physical-level design process consists of creating a table for each entity in the DBDL design. Any constraints (primary key, alternate key, or foreign key) that the DBMS cannot enforce must be enforced by the programs in the system; this fact must be documented for the programmers.
- The design method presented in this chapter is a bottom-up method. By listing potential relations before beginning the method, you have the advantages of both the top-down and bottom-up approaches.
- A survey form is useful for documenting the information gathered for the database design process.
- To obtain information from existing documents, list all attributes present in the documents, identify potential functional dependencies, make a tentative list of tables, and use the functional dependencies to refine the list.
- To implement a one-to-one relationship, include the primary key of one of the two tables in the other table as a foreign key and then indicate the foreign key as an alternate key.
- If a table's primary key consists of three (or more) columns, you must determine whether there are independent relationships between pairs of these columns. If there are independent relationships, the table is not in fourth normal form, and you must split it. If there are no independent relationships, you cannot split the table because doing so produces incorrect information.
- If a table contains columns that can be null and the nulls represent the fact that the column is inapplicable for some rows, you can split the table, placing the null column(s) in separate tables. These new tables represent entity subtypes.
- It is possible that the result of merging third normal form tables may not be in third normal form. To avoid this problem, include determinants for columns in the individual tables before merging them.
- The entity-relationship (E-R) model is another method of representing the structure of a database using a conceptual diagram. In the E-R model, a rectangle represents an entity, a diamond represents a relationship, and an oval represents an attribute.

Key Terms

artificial key	entity-relationship model
bottom-up design method	existence dependency
cardinality	IDEF1X
category	identifying relationship
composite entity	incomplete category
cumulative design	independent entity
Database Design Language (DBDL)	information-level design
dependent entity	intelligent key
enforcing restrictions	logical key

mandatory role	physical-level design
many-to-many relationship	secondary key
many-to-many-to-many relationship	subtype
maximum cardinality	supertype
minimum cardinality	surrogate key
natural key	synthetic key
nonidentifying relationship	top-down design method
nonunique index	user view
one-to-one relationship	weak entity
optional role	

Review Questions

1. Define the term *user view* as it applies to database design.

2. What is the purpose of breaking down the overall design problem into a consideration of individual user views?

3. Under what circumstances would you not need to break down an overall design into a consideration of individual user views?

4. The information-level design method presented in this chapter contains steps that must be repeated for each user view. List the steps and briefly describe the kinds of activities that must take place at each step.

5. Describe the function of each of the following types of keys: primary, alternate, secondary, and foreign.

6. A database at a college is required to support the following requirements. Complete the information-level design for this set of requirements. Use your own experience to determine any constraints you need that are not stated in the problem. Represent the answer in DBDL.

   a. For a department, store its number and name.

   b. For an advisor, store his or her number and name and the number of the department to which he or she is assigned.

   c. For a course, store its code and description (for example, MTH110 or Algebra).

   d. For a student, store his or her number and name. For each course the student has taken, store the course code, course description, and grade received. In addition, store the number and name of the student's advisor. Assume that an advisor may advise any number of students but that each student has just one advisor.

7. List the changes you would need to make in your answer to Question 7 if a student could have more than one advisor.

8. Suppose in addition to the requirements specified in Question 7, you must store the number of the department in which the student is majoring. Indicate the changes this would cause in the design in the following two situations:

   a. The student must be assigned an advisor who is in the department in which the student is majoring.

   b. The student's advisor does not necessarily have to be in the department in which the student is majoring.

9. Describe the different ways of implementing one-to-one relationships. Assume you are maintaining information on offices (office numbers, buildings, and phone numbers) and faculty (numbers and names). No office houses more than one faculty member; no faculty member is assigned more than one office. Illustrate the ways of implementing one-to-one relationships using offices and faculty. Which option would be best in each of the following situations?

   a. A faculty member must have an office, and each office must be occupied by a faculty member.

   b. A faculty member must have an office, but some offices are not currently occupied. You must maintain information about the unoccupied offices in an Office relation.

   c. Some faculty members do not have an office, but all offices are occupied.

   d. Some faculty members do not have an office, but some offices are not occupied.

10. For each of the following collections of relations, give the assumptions concerning the relationship between students, courses, and faculty members that are implied by the collection. In each relation, only the primary keys are shown.

a. `Student (`<u>`StudentNum`</u>`, `<u>`CourseNum`</u>`, `<u>`FacultyNum`</u>`)`

b. `Student (`<u>`StudentNum`</u>`, `<u>`CourseNum`</u>`)`
   `Faculty (`<u>`CourseNum`</u>`, FacultyNum)`

c. `Student (`<u>`StudentNum`</u>`, `<u>`CourseNum`</u>`)`
   `Faculty (`<u>`CourseNum`</u>`, FacultyNum)`
   `StudentFaculty (`<u>`StudentNum`</u>`, `<u>`CourseNum`</u>`, `<u>`FacultyNum`</u>`)`

d. `Student (`<u>`StudentNum`</u>`, `<u>`CourseNum`</u>`, `<u>`FacultyNum`</u>`)`

e. `Student (`<u>`StudentNum`</u>`, `<u>`CourseNum`</u>`)`
   `Faculty (`<u>`CourseNum`</u>`, FacultyNum)`
   `StudentFaculty (`<u>`StudentNum`</u>`, `<u>`FacultyNum`</u>`)`

11. Describe the relationship between columns that can be null and entity subtypes. Under what circumstances would these columns lead to more than one entity subtype?

12. Describe the entity-relationship model. How are entities, relationships, and attributes represented in this model? What is a composite entity? Describe the approach to diagrams that use a crow's foot. Describe how you would represent cardinality in an E-R diagram.

13. Design a survey form of your own. Fill it out as it might have been completed during the database design for Henry Books. For any questions you have too little information to answer, make a reasonable guess.

14. Using a document at your own school (for example, a class schedule), determine the attributes present in the document. Using your knowledge of the policies at your school, determine the functional dependencies present in the document. Use these dependencies to create a set of tables and columns that you could use to produce the document.

BITS Corporation Exercises

The following exercises are based on the BITS database user views as designed in Your Turn 6-1 in this chapter. In each exercise, represent your answer in DBDL and with a diagram. You may use any of the styles presented in this chapter for the diagram.

1. Indicate the changes you need to make to the design of the BITS database to support the following situation. A client is not necessarily represented by a single consultant but can be represented by several consultants.

2. Indicate the changes you need to make to the design of the BITS database to support the following situation. There is no relationship between clients and consultants. When a client places an order (service request), it may be performed by any consultant. On the order, identify both the client placing the order and the consultant responsible for the order.

3. Indicate the changes you need to make to the BITS database design to support the following situation. The region where clients are located is divided into territories. For each territory, store the territory number (a unique identifier) and territory name. Each consultant is assigned to a single territory. Each client also is assigned to a single territory, but the territory *must be* the same as the territory to which the client's consultant is assigned.

4. Indicate the changes you need to make to the BITS database design to support the following situation. The region where clients are located is divided into territories. For each territory, store the territory number (a unique identifier) and territory name. Each consultant is assigned to a single territory. Each client also is assigned to a single territory, which *may not be* the same as the territory to which the client's consultant is assigned.

5. Indicate the changes you need to make to the BITS database design to support the following situation. The client address may or may not be the same as the Bill To address on the client's invoice.

Colonial Adventure Tours Case

Complete the following tasks. In each exercise, represent your answer in both DBDL and with a diagram. You may use any of the styles presented in this chapter for the diagram.

1. Design a database to produce the following reports. Do not use any surrogate keys in your design.
   a. For each guide, list the guide number, guide last name, guide first name, address, city, state, postal code, telephone number, and date hired.
   b. For each trip, list the trip ID number, the trip name, the location from which the trip starts, the state in which the trip originates, the trip distance, the maximum group size, the type of trip (hiking, biking, or paddling), the season in which the trip occurs, and the guide number, first name, and last name of each guide. A guide may lead many trips and a trip may be led by many different guides.
   c. For each client, list the client number, client last name, client first name, address, city, state, postal code, and telephone number.

2. Colonial Adventure Tours is considering offering outdoor adventure classes. These classes would better prepare people to participate in hiking, biking, and paddling adventures. Only one class is taught on any given day. Participants can enroll in one class or several classes. Classes are taught by the guides that Colonial Adventure employs. Colonial Adventure Tours needs your help with the database design for this new venture. In each step, represent your answer in DBDL with a diagram. You may use any of the styles presented in this chapter for the diagram. Colonial Adventure Tours needs to produce the following reports:
   a. For each participant, list his or her number, last name, first name, address, city, state, postal code, telephone number, and date of birth.
   b. For each adventure class, list the class number, class description, maximum number of persons in the class, and class fee.
   c. For each participant, list his or her number, last name, first name, and the class number, class description, and date of the class for all classes in which the participant is enrolled.

3. Expand the database design you created in Exercise 3 so it will support the following report: Colonial Adventure Tours needs to send an invoice to each participant, listing the classes in which the participant is enrolled as well as the total fees for the classes. The invoice should include the participant's full name and address.

Sports Physical Therapy Case

Complete the following tasks. In each exercise, represent your answer in both DBDL and with a diagram. You may use any of the styles presented in this chapter for the diagram.

1. Design a database to produce the following reports. Do not use any surrogate keys in your design.
   a. For each therapist, list the therapist ID, last name, first name, street, city, state, and zip code.
   b. For each patient, list the patient number, last name, first name, address, city, state, zip code, and balance.
   c. For each therapist, list the sessions, the date, the length of session, therapist ID, and therapy code.

2. Expand the database design you created in Exercise 1 so that it will also support the following situation: A specific therapist handles each therapy (a therapist can handle more than one). Along with all the details concerning sessions listed in Exercise 1, list the ID, last name, and first name of the therapist assigned to handle the request.

3. Sports Physical Therapy has a list of approved vendors who supply things such as office supplies, therapy tools, towels, and wraps. Design a database to meet the following requirements:
   a. For each vendor, list the vendor ID number, vendor name, address, city, state, zip code, telephone number, and type of supply provided.
   b. For each supply, list the product number (UPC or SKU), product name, description, vendor ID number, quantity, and price.
   c. For each order, list the product number, product name, vendor ID number, quantity, total price, date ordered, and expected date of arrival.

DBMS FUNCTIONS

LEARNING OBJECTIVES

- Introduce the functions, or services, provided by a DBMS
- Describe how a DBMS handles updating and retrieving data
- Examine the catalog feature of a DBMS
- Illustrate the concurrent update problem and describe how a DBMS handles this problem
- Explain the data recovery process in a database environment
- Describe the security services provided by a DBMS
- Examine the data integrity features provided by a DBMS
- Discuss the extent to which a DBMS achieves data independence
- Define and describe data replication
- Present the utility services provided by a DBMS

INTRODUCTION

In this chapter, you will learn about nine critical functions performed by a DBMS. Some of the functions have been introduced in previous chapters; however, they are emphasized again here because they are key processing components of a DBMS. The nine functions of a DBMS are as follows:

- *Update and retrieve data.* A DBMS must provide users with the ability to update and retrieve data in a database.
- *Provide catalog services.* A DBMS must store data about the data in a database and make this data accessible to users.
- *Support concurrent update.* A DBMS must ensure that the database is updated correctly when multiple users update the database at the same time.
- *Recover data.* A DBMS must provide methods to recover a database in the event that the database is damaged in any way.
- *Provide security services.* A DBMS must provide ways to ensure that only authorized users can access the database.
- *Provide data integrity features.* A DBMS must follow rules so that it updates data accurately and consistently.
- *Support data independence.* A DBMS must provide facilities to support the independence of programs from the structure of a database.
- *Support data replication.* A DBMS must manage multiple copies of the same data at multiple locations.
- *Provide utility services.* A DBMS must provide services that assist in the general maintenance of a database.

UPDATE AND RETRIEVE DATA

A DBMS must provide users with the ability to update and retrieve data in a database; this is the fundamental job of a DBMS. Unless a DBMS provides this capability, further discussion of what a DBMS does is irrelevant. In updating and retrieving data, users do not need to know how data is physically structured on a storage medium or which processes the DBMS uses to manipulate the data. These structures and manipulations are solely the responsibility of the DBMS.

Updating data in a database includes adding new records, and changing and deleting existing records. For example, suppose that Karen must update the BITS database by adding data for task TR27, which is a new task. As shown in Figure 7-1, Karen enters the data for task AE27 and then requests that the DBMS add the data to the database. To add this data, the DBMS handles all the work to verify that task TR27 does not already exist in the database, stores the task TR27 data in the database, and then informs Karen that the task was completed successfully. How the DBMS performs these steps, where the DBMS stores the data in the database, how the DBMS stores the data, and all other processing details are invisible to Karen.

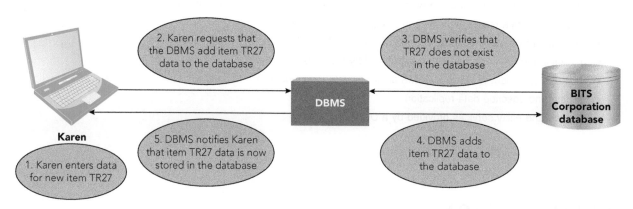

FIGURE 7-1 Adding a new item to the BITS database

Suppose that Karen must also update the BITS database by changing the price for task DI85. As shown in Figure 7-2, Karen requests the data for the item and enters the change, but the DBMS performs the tasks of locating and reading the item data, displaying the data for Karen, and changing the price in the database. Once again, Karen does not need to be aware of the tasks that the DBMS completes or how the DBMS completes them.

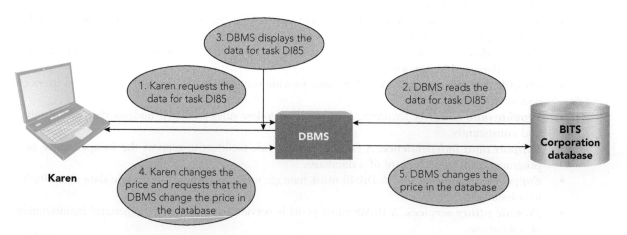

FIGURE 7-2 Changing the price of an item in the BITS database

Deleting data in a database requires both user and DBMS processing steps similar to those used to change data. The only differences occur in Steps 4 and 5 in Figure 7-2. In Step 4, the user requests that the DBMS delete the designated record. In Step 5, the DBMS deletes the record.

Figure 7-3 shows Karen retrieving the balance amount for MarketPoint Sales, a client in the BITS database. The DBMS finds the MarketPoint Sales record using the same strategy it used when it added the client to the database; Karen does not need to know the strategy the DBMS uses to find and read the data. After finding and reading the MarketPoint Sales record in the database, the DBMS displays the client's balance amount for Karen.

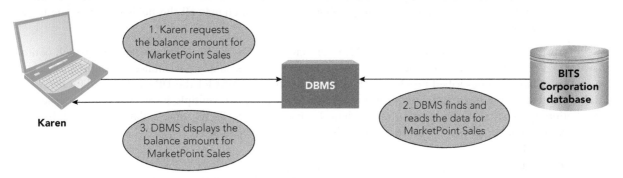

FIGURE 7-3   Retrieving a balance amount from the BITS database

PROVIDE CATALOG SERVICES

A DBMS must store information about the data in a database and make this information accessible to users. Information about the data in a database, or **metadata**, includes table descriptions and field definitions. As described in Chapter 4, the catalog, which is maintained automatically by the DBMS, contains table and field metadata. In addition, the catalog contains metadata about table relationships, views, indexes, users, privileges, and replicated data; the last three items are discussed later in this chapter.

The catalogs for many DBMSs consist of a set of special tables that are included in the database. The DBMS hides these special tables from everyday users of the database. However, the DBMS lets the DBA (database administrator) access and update the tables because the DBA must know the contents of the database and must create and define tables, fields, views, indexes, and other metadata. The DBA can authorize access for some catalog tables to other users as necessary.

In some database systems, such as Microsoft Access, users can access and update the metadata about the fields, tables, relationships, and indexes in a database. However, individuals and companies that create databases for other people usually hide this metadata so that users cannot access or update the metadata.

When the DBA uses the DBMS to access the catalog in the database, the DBA asks questions such as the following:

- What tables and fields are included in the database? What are their names?
- What are the properties of these fields? For example, is the Street field in the Client table 15 or 30 characters long? Is the ClientNum field a numeric field, or is it a character field? How many decimal places are in the Rate field in the Consultant table?
- What are the possible values for the various fields? For example, are there any restrictions on the possible values for the CreditLimit field in the Client table or for the Category field in the Tasks table?
- What are the meanings of the various fields? For example, what exactly is the Category field in the Tasks table, and what does a Category field value of SOM mean?
- What relationships between the tables exist in the database? Which relationships are one-to-many, many-to-many, and one-to-one? Must the relationship always exist? For example, must a client always have a sales consultant?

- In which fields and combinations of fields can you rapidly search for specific values because they are indexed? Which fields that are not indexed are candidates for indexes because they often are used in searches?
- Which users have access to the database? For example, which fields can Karen access for retrieval purposes but not update? Which fields can Karen update?
- Which programs or objects (queries, forms, and reports) access which data within the database? How do they access it? Do these programs merely retrieve the data, or do they update it too? What kinds of updates do the programs perform? Can a certain program add a new client, for example, or can it merely make changes to information about clients that are already in the database? When a program changes client data, can it change all the fields or only some fields? Which fields?

Enterprise DBMSs, such as Oracle and DB2, often have a catalog called a **data dictionary**, which contains answers to all these questions and more. The data dictionary serves as a super catalog containing metadata beyond what has been described previously. For example, these DBMSs let the DBA split the data in a database and store the fragmented data on multiple storage devices at multiple locations. In these cases, the data dictionary must track the location of the data. PC-based DBMSs do not offer a data dictionary, but they have a catalog that provides answers to most of the preceding questions.

SUPPORT CONCURRENT UPDATE

A DBMS must ensure that the database is updated correctly when multiple users update the database at the same time.

Sometimes a person uses a database stored on a single computer. At other times, several people might update a database, but only one person at a time does so. For example, several people might take turns with one computer to update a database. A DBMS handles these situations easily. However, the use of network DBMSs, capable of allowing several users to update the same database, raises a problem that the DBMS must address: concurrent update.

Concurrent update occurs when multiple users make updates to the same database at the same time. On the surface, you might think that a concurrent update does not present any problem. Why would 2, 3, or 50 users, updating the database simultaneously, cause a problem?

The Concurrent Update Problem

To illustrate the problem with concurrent update, suppose that Micah and Karen are two users who work at BITS. Micah is currently updating the BITS database to process orders and, among other actions, to increase clients' balances by the amount of their orders. For example, Micah needs to increase the balance of client 405 (Fisherman's Spot Shop) by $100.00. Karen, on the other hand, is updating the BITS database to post client payments and, among other things, to decrease clients' balances by the amounts of their payments. Coincidentally, Karen has a $100.00 payment from Fisherman's Spot Shop, so she will decrease that client's balance by $100.00. The balance for Fisherman's Spot Shop is $575.00 before the start of these updates. Because the amount of the increase exactly matches the amount of the decrease, the balance should still be $575.00 after their updates. But will it? That depends on how the database handles the updates.

How does the DBMS make the required update for Micah? First, as shown in Figure 7-4, the DBMS reads the data for Fisherman's Spot Shop from the database on disk into Micah's work area in memory (RAM). Second, Micah enters the order data for Fisherman's Spot Shop. At this point, Micah's order entry takes place in his work area in memory, including the addition of the order total of $100.00 to the balance of $575.00, bringing the balance to $675.00. This change has not yet taken place in the database; it has taken place *only* in Micah's work area in memory. Finally, after Micah finishes entering the order data for Fisherman's Spot Shop, the DBMS updates the database with Micah's changes.

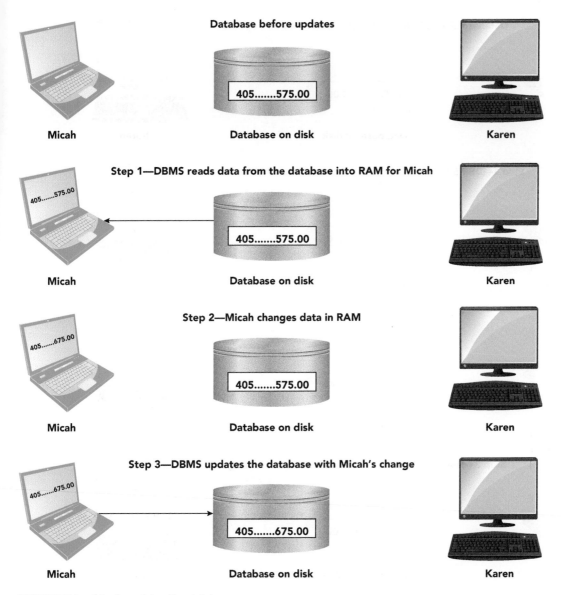

FIGURE 7-4 Micah updates the database

Suppose that Karen begins her update at this point. As shown in Figure 7-5, the DBMS reads the data for Fisherman's Spot Shop from the database, including the new balance of $675.00. Karen then enters the payment of $100.00, which decreases the client balance to $575.00 in her work area in memory. Finally, the DBMS updates the database with Karen's change. The balance for Fisherman's Spot Shop in the database is now $575.00, which is correct.

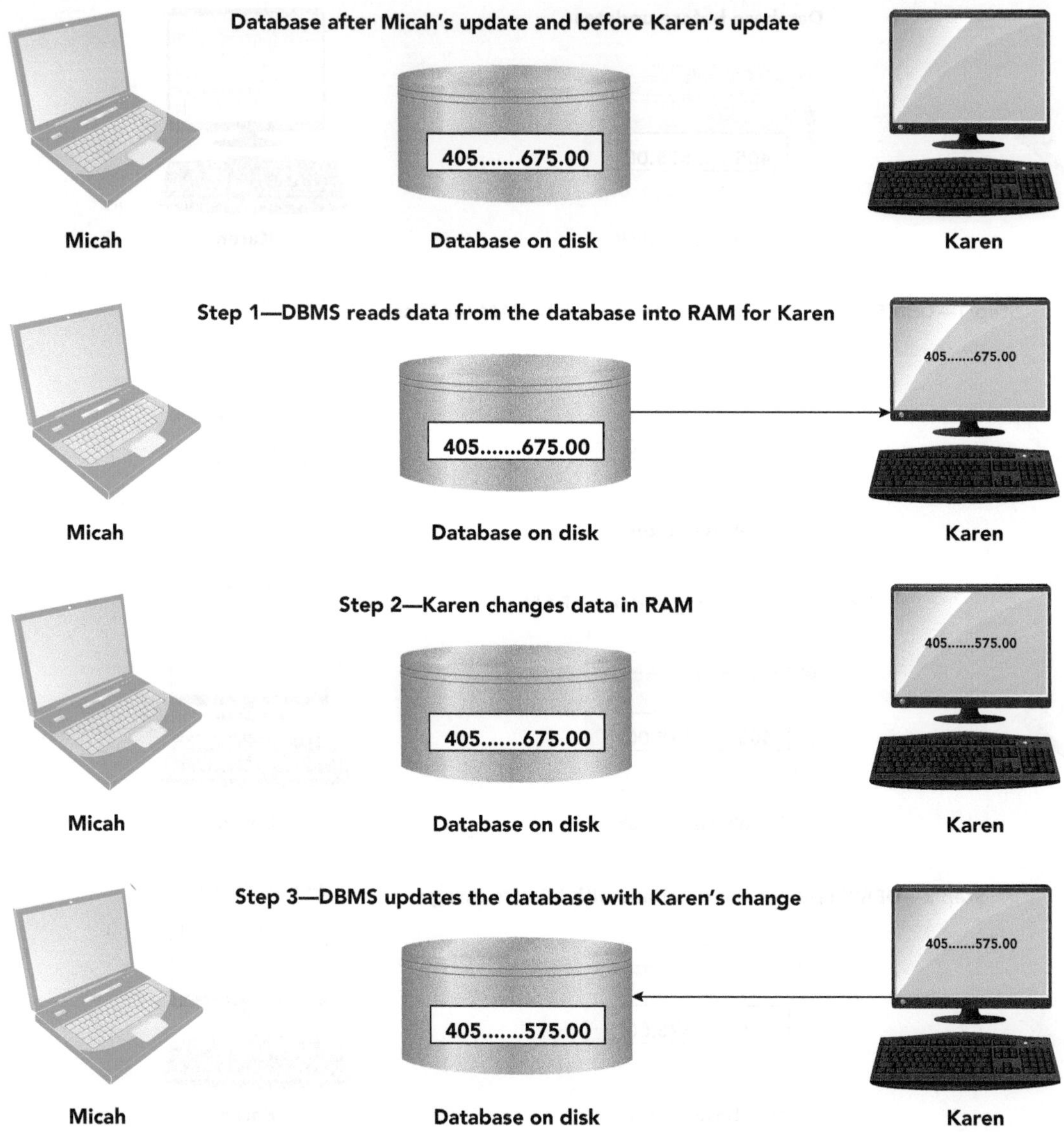

Database after Micah's update and before Karen's update

405.......675.00

Micah   Database on disk   Karen

Step 1—DBMS reads data from the database into RAM for Karen

405.......675.00

405.......675.00

Micah   Database on disk   Karen

Step 2—Karen changes data in RAM

405.......675.00

405.......575.00

Micah   Database on disk   Karen

Step 3—DBMS updates the database with Karen's change

405.......575.00

405.......575.00

Micah   Database on disk   Karen

FIGURE 7-5   Karen updates the database

In the preceding sequence of updates, everything worked out correctly, but this is not always the case. Do you see how the updates to the database could occur in a way that would lead to an incorrect result?

What if the updates occur in the sequence shown in Figure 7-6 instead? First, the DBMS reads the data from the database into Micah's work area in memory. At about the same time, the DBMS reads the data from the database into Karen's separate work area in memory. At this point, both Micah and Karen have the correct data for Fisherman's Spot Shop, including a balance of $575.00. Micah adds $100.00 to the balance in his work area, and Karen subtracts $100.00 from the balance in her work area. At this point, in Micah's work area in memory the balance is $675.00, while in Karen's work area in memory the balance is $475.00. The DBMS now updates the database with Micah's change. At this moment, Fisherman's Spot Shop has a balance of $675.00 in the database. Finally, the DBMS updates the database with Karen's change. Her update replaces Micah's change. Now the balance for Fisherman's Spot Shop in the database is $475.00! Had the DBMS updated the database in the reverse order, the final balance would have been $675.00. In either case, you would now have incorrect data in the database—one of the updates has been lost. The DBMS must prevent these lost updates from affecting the database.

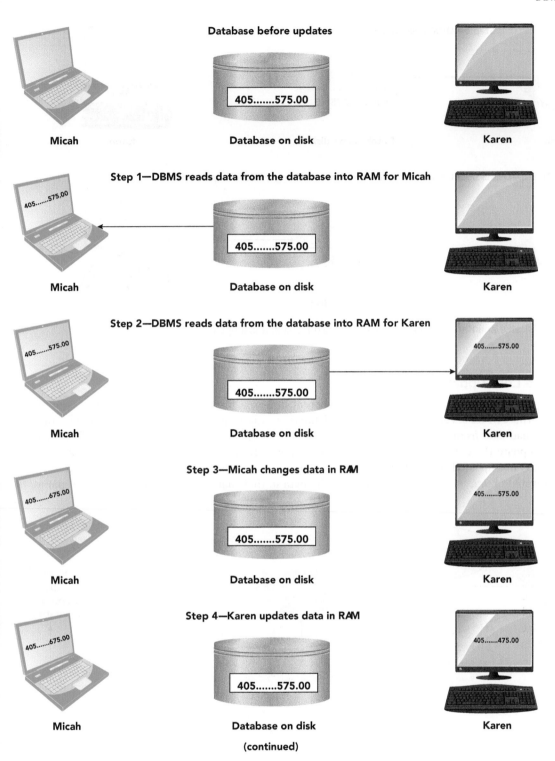

FIGURE 7-6 Micah's and Karen's updates to the database result in a lost update *(continued)*

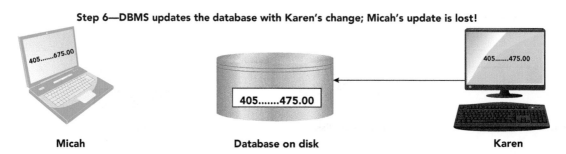

Step 5—DBMS updates the database with Micah's change

Micah   Database on disk   Karen

405.......675.00

405.......675.00

405.......475.00

Step 6—DBMS updates the database with Karen's change; Micah's update is lost!

405.......675.00

405.......475.00

405.......475.00

Micah   Database on disk   Karen

FIGURE 7-6   Micah's and Karen's updates to the database result in a lost update

Avoiding the Lost Update Problem

One way to prevent lost updates is to prohibit concurrent update. This may seem drastic, but it is not really so farfetched. You can let several users access the database at the same time, but for retrieval only; that is, the users can read data from the database, but they cannot update any data in the database. When these users need to update the database, such as increasing a client's balance or changing the price of an item, the database itself is not updated. Instead, as shown in Figure 7-7, a special program, which a computer programmer would create for the users to use with the data in their database, adds a record to a separate file.

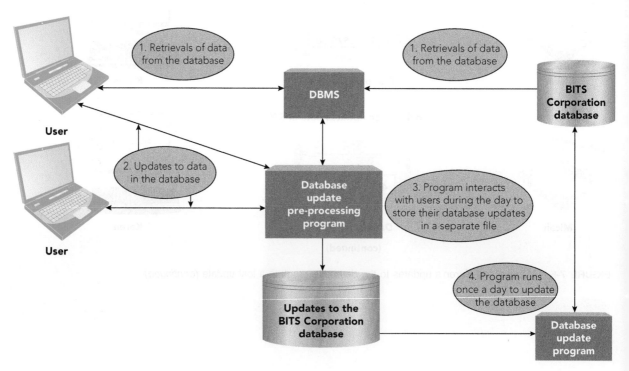

1. Retrievals of data from the database

1. Retrievals of data from the database

DBMS

BITS Corporation database

User

2. Updates to data in the database

Database update pre-processing program

3. Program interacts with users during the day to store their database updates in a separate file

User

4. Program runs once a day to update the database

Updates to the BITS Corporation database

Database update program

FIGURE 7-7   Delaying updates to the BITS database to avoid the lost update problem

A record in this separate file might indicate, for example, that BITS received a $100 payment from client 405 on a certain date. Periodically, usually once a day, a single update program reads the *batch* of records in this file one at a time and performs the appropriate updates to the database; this processing technique is called **batch processing**. Because this program is the only way to update the database, you eliminate the problems associated with concurrent update.

Although this approach avoids the lost update problem, it creates another problem. From the time that users start updating (adding records to the special batch file) until the time the batch-processing program actually updates the database, the data in the database is out of date. If a client's balance in the database is $4,500, the true balance is $5,500 (because a user had entered an order for this client increasing its balance by $1,000). If the client has a $5,000 credit limit, the client is now over that credit limit by $500. And, if a query is made to provide a client with his or her balance, the amount easily could be wrong.

The batch-processing approach does not work in any situation that requires the data in the database to be current such as with credit card processing, banking, inventory control, and airline reservations. Other simple alternative solutions to the concurrent update problem, such as permitting only one user to update the database (perhaps making the database read-only for other users), also will not work in these situations because many users need to update the database in a timely way.

Two-Phase Locking

In most situations, you cannot solve the concurrent update problem by avoiding it; you need the DBMS to have a strategy for dealing with it. One such strategy is for the DBMS to process an update completely before it begins processing the next update. For example, the DBMS can prevent Karen from beginning her update to the Fisherman's Spot Shop data until the DBMS completes Micah's update to that data, or vice versa.

To accomplish such a serial processing of updates, many DBMSs use locking. **Locking** denies other users access to data while the DBMS processes one user's updates to the database. An example of locking using Micah's and Karen's updates appears in Figure 7-8. After the DBMS reads the data in the database for Micah's update, the DBMS locks the data, denying access to the data by Karen and any other user. The DBMS retains the locks until Micah completes his change; then the DBMS updates the database. For the duration of the locks, the DBMS rejects all attempts by Karen to access the data, and it notifies Karen that the data is locked. If she chooses to do so, she can keep attempting to access the data until the DBMS releases the locks, at which time the DBMS can process her update. In this simple case at least, the locking technique appears to solve the lost update problem.

Database before updates

Micah   Database on disk   Karen

405.......575.00

Step 1—DBMS reads data from the database into RAM for Micah and locks the record

405.......575.00

Micah   Database on disk   Karen

405.......575.00

Step 2—Karen requests the same record from the database and her request fails

405.......575.00

Record locked; read fails

Micah   Database on disk   Karen

405.......575.00

Step 3—Micah changes data in RAM; Karen's request for the same record again fails

405.......675.00

Record locked; read fails

Micah   Database on disk   Karen

405.......575.00

Step 4—DBMS updates the database with Micah's change; Karen's request for the same record again fails

405.......675.00

Record locked; read fails

Micah   Database on disk   Karen

405.......675.00

(continued)

FIGURE 7-8   The DBMS uses a locking scheme to apply the updates for Micah and Karen to the database *(continued)*

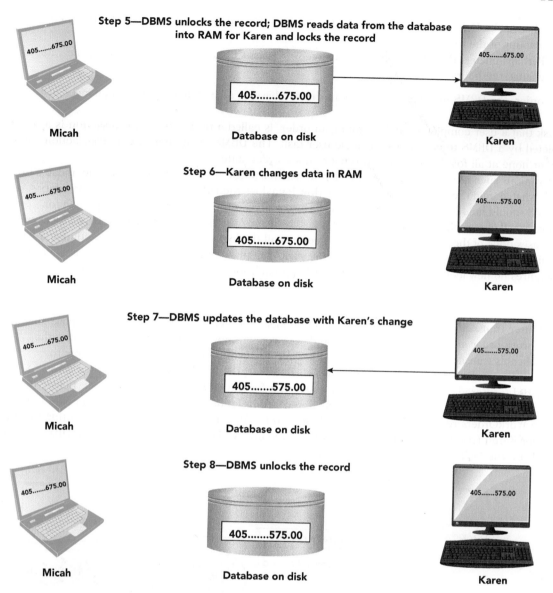

Step 5—DBMS unlocks the record; DBMS reads data from the database into RAM for Karen and locks the record

Micah — 405.......675.00
Database on disk — 405.......675.00
Karen — 405.......675.00

Step 6—Karen changes data in RAM

Micah — 405.......675.00
Database on disk — 405.......675.00
Karen — 405.......575.00

Step 7—DBMS updates the database with Karen's change

Micah — 405.......675.00
Database on disk — 405.......575.00
Karen — 405.......575.00

Step 8—DBMS unlocks the record

Micah — 405.......675.00
Database on disk — 405.......575.00
Karen — 405.......575.00

FIGURE 7-8 The DBMS uses a locking scheme to apply the updates for Micah and Karen to the database

How long should the DBMS hold a lock? If the update involves changing field values in a single row in a single table, such as changing a client's name and address, the lock no longer is necessary after this row is updated. However, sometimes an update is more involved.

Consider the task of scheduling a service order for a new BITS client. Micah might think that adding a new client is a single process and then scheduling an order involves a second action. He simply creates a new client and then adds a record to the OrderLine table. Behind the scenes, though, creating an order for a new client requires that the DBMS update several records in the database. For example, suppose Micah adds a new client, Hobby Express, and schedules a new service request that includes a virus removal and an upgrade. He must also schedule a consultant. Therefore, to schedule this order, the DBMS must update the records in the database as follows:

- Add a new record (Hobby Express) to the Client table including a consultant (Christopher Turner) and a credit limit ($5,000).
- Add one record to the WorkOrders table for the new order.
- Add one record to the OrderLine table for virus removal.
- Add one record to the OrderLine table for the upgrade.

- Change the Hobby Express record in the Client table to increase the balance by the total amount of the order.
- Perhaps change the Christopher Turner record in the Consultant table to increase the rate or change the hours.

For this order, the DBMS updates six records in the database; it adds four records and changes two records.

Each task that a user completes, such as filling an order, is called a transaction. A **transaction** is a set of steps completed by a DBMS to accomplish a single user task. The DBMS must complete all transaction steps successfully or none at all for the database to remain in a correct state.

For transactions such as scheduling a work order, in which a single user task requires several updates in the database, what should the DBMS do about locks? How long does the DBMS hold each lock? For safety's sake, the DBMS should hold locks until it completes all the updates in the transaction. This approach for handling locks is called **two-phase locking**. The first phase is the **growing phase**, in which the DBMS locks more rows and releases none of the locks. After the DBMS acquires all the locks needed for the transaction and has completed all database updates, the second phase is the **shrinking phase**, in which the DBMS releases all the locks and acquires no new locks. This two-phase locking approach solves the lost update problem.

Deadlock

Because each user transaction can require more than one lock, another problem can occur. Suppose Micah has entered a work order and is attempting to schedule the virus removal while Karen is scheduling the upgrade. For Micah's transaction, the DBMS places a lock on the WorkOrders record and attempts to schedule a record in OrderLine, as shown in Figure 7-9. However, the DBMS has already locked the OrderLine record for Karen's transaction, so Micah must wait for the DBMS to release the lock. Before the DBMS releases the lock on the OrderLine record for Karen's transaction, however, it needs to update (and thus lock) the WorkOrders record, which is currently locked for Micah's transaction. Micah is waiting for the DBMS to act for Karen (release the lock on the OrderLine record), while Karen is waiting for the DBMS to act for Micah (release the lock on the WorkOrders record).

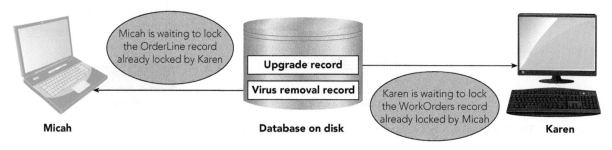

FIGURE 7-9 Two users experiencing deadlock

Without the aid of some intervention, this dilemma could continue indefinitely. Terms used to describe such situations are **deadlock** and the **deadly embrace**. Obviously, some strategy is necessary to prevent, minimize, or manage deadlocks. You can minimize the occurrence of deadlocks by making sure all programs lock records in the same order whenever possible. For example, all programs for the BITS database should lock records in the WorkOrders table and then lock records in the OrderLine table consistently. A consistent locking strategy prevents situations in which a user locks a record in the WorkOrders table, a second user locks a record in the OrderLine table, and both users are deadlocked while they wait for the release of records they need to lock next.

One strategy to manage deadlocks is to let them occur and then have the DBMS detect and break any deadlock. To detect a deadlock, the DBMS must keep track of the collection of records it has locked for each transaction, as well as the records it is waiting to lock. If two transactions are waiting for records held by the other, a deadlock has occurred. Actually, more than two users could be involved. Micah could be waiting for a record held by Karen, while Karen is waiting for a record held by Pat, who in turn is waiting for a record held by Micah.

After the DBMS detects deadlock, the DBMS must break the deadlock. To break the deadlock, the DBMS chooses one deadlocked user to be the **victim** (the person who has to wait for their update). For the victim's transaction, the DBMS rolls back all completed updates, releases all locks, and reschedules the transaction. Using this method of handling deadlocks, the user notices only a delay in the time needed to complete the transaction.

Locking on PC-Based DBMSs

Enterprise DBMSs—systems that are support large databases and concurrent users—typically offer sophisticated schemes for locking as well as for detecting and handling deadlocks. PC-based DBMSs provide facilities for the same purposes, but they usually are much more limited than the facilities provided by enterprise DBMSs. These limitations, in turn, put an additional burden on the programmers who write the programs that allow concurrent update.

Although the exact features for handling the problems associated with concurrent update vary from one PC-based DBMS to another, the following list is fairly typical of the types of facilities provided:

- Programs can lock an entire table or an individual row within a table, but only one or the other. As long as one program has a row or table locked, no other program may access that row or table.
- Programs can release any or all of the locks that they currently hold.
- Programs can inquire whether a given row or table is locked.

This list, although short, makes up the complete set of facilities provided by many PC-based DBMSs. Consequently, the following guidelines have been devised for writing programs for concurrent update:

- If an update transaction must lock more than one row in the same table, you must lock the entire table.
- When a program attempts to read a row that is locked, the program may wait a short period of time and then try to read the row again. This process can continue until the row becomes unlocked. However, it usually is preferable to impose a limit on the number of times a program may attempt to read the row. In this case, reading is done in a loop, which proceeds until the read is successful or the maximum number of times that the program can repeat the operation is reached. Programs vary in terms of what action is taken should the loop be terminated without the read being successful. One possibility is to notify the user of the problem and let the user decide whether to try the same update again or move on to something else.
- Because there is no facility to *detect and handle* deadlocks, you must try to *prevent* them. A common approach to this problem is for every program in the system to attempt to lock all the rows and/or tables it needs before beginning an update. Assuming each program is successful in this attempt, it can then perform the required updates. If any row or table that the program needs is already locked, the program should immediately release all the locks that it currently holds, wait some specified period of time, and then try the entire process again. In some cases, it might be better to notify the user of the problem and see whether the user wants to try again. In effect, this means that any program that encounters a problem will immediately get out of the way of all the other programs rather than be involved in a deadlock situation.
- Because locks prevent other users from accessing a portion of the database, it is important that no user keep rows or tables locked any longer than necessary. This is especially significant for update programs. Suppose, for example, that a user is employing an update program to update information about clients. Suppose further that after the user enters the number of the client to be updated, the client row is locked and remains locked until the user has entered all the new data and the update has taken place. What if the user is interrupted by a phone call before he or she has finished entering the new data? What if the user goes to lunch? The row might remain locked for an extended period of time. If the update involves several rows, all of which must be locked, the problem becomes that much worse. In fact, in many DBMSs, if more than one row from the same table must be locked, the entire table must be locked, which means that entire tables might be locked for extended periods of time. Clearly, this situation must not be permitted to occur. A variation on the timestamping technique used by some enterprise DBMSs is a programming strategy you can use to overcome this problem.

Timestamping

An alternative to two-phase locking is timestamping. With **timestamping**, the DBMS assigns to each database update the unique time when the update started; this time is called a **timestamp**. In addition, every database row includes the timestamp associated with the last update to the row. The DBMS processes updates to the database in timestamp order. If two users try to change the same row at approximately the same time, the DBMS processes the change that has the slightly earlier timestamp. The other transaction will be restarted and assigned a new timestamp value.

Timestamping avoids the need to lock rows in the database and eliminates the processing time needed to apply and release locks and to detect and resolve deadlocks. On the other hand, additional storage and memory space are required to store the timestamp values; in addition, the DBMS uses extra processing time to update the timestamp values.

One might naturally ask at this point whether the ability to have concurrent update is worth the complexity that it adds to the DBMS. In some cases, the answer is no. Concurrent update may be far from a necessity. In most cases, however, concurrent update is necessary to the productivity of the users of the system. In these cases, implementation of locking, timestamping, or some other strategy is essential to the proper performance of the system.

RECOVER DATA

A DBMS must provide methods to recover a database in the event the database is damaged in any way. A database can be damaged or destroyed in many ways. Users can enter data that is incorrect, transactions that are updating the database can end abnormally during an update, a hardware problem can occur, and so on. After any such event has occurred, the database might contain invalid or inconsistent data. It may even be totally destroyed.

Obviously, a situation in which data has been damaged or destroyed must not be allowed to go uncorrected. The database must be returned to a correct state. **Recovery** is the process of returning the database to a state that is known to be correct from a state known to be incorrect; in performing such a process, you say that you *recover* the database. In situations where indexes or other physical structures in the database have been damaged but the data has not, many DBMSs provide a feature that you can use to repair the database automatically.

To address cases in which the data in a database has been damaged, the simplest approach to recovery involves periodically making a copy of the database (called a **backup** or a **save**). If a problem occurs, the database is recovered by copying this backup copy over it. In effect, the damage is undone by returning the database to the state it was in when the last backup was made.

Unfortunately, other activity besides that which caused the destruction also is undone. Suppose the database is backed up at 10:00 p.m. and users begin updating it at 8:00 a.m. the next day. Further, suppose that at 11:30 a.m., something happens that destroys the database. If the previous night's backup is used to recover the database, the entire database is returned to the state it was in at 10:00 p.m. All updates made in the morning are lost, not just the update or updates that were in progress at the time the problem occurred. Thus, during the final part of the recovery process, users would have to redo all the work they had done since 8:00 a.m.

Journaling

As you might expect, enterprise DBMSs provide sophisticated features to avoid the costly and time-consuming process of having users redo their work. These features include **journaling**, which involves maintaining a **journal** or **log** of all updates to the database. The log is a separate file from the database; thus, the log is still available if a catastrophe destroys the database.

Several types of information are typically kept in the log for each transaction. This information includes the transaction ID and the date and time of each individual update. The log also includes a record of what the data in the row looked like before the update (called a **before image**) and a record of what the data in the row looked like after the update (called an **after image**). In addition, the log contains an entry to indicate the start of a transaction and the successful completion (**commit**) of a transaction.

To illustrate the use of a log by a DBMS, consider the four sample transactions shown in Figure 7-10. Three transactions—1, 3, and 4—require a single update to the database. The second transaction, which is Micah's order transaction for Hobby Express, requires six updates to the database.

Transaction ID	Transaction Description
1	1. In the Tasks table, change the Price value for TaskID WC19 to $125.00
2	1. Add a new record to the Client table: ClientNum of 521, ClientName of Hobby Express, address of 250 N. Green Street, Sunland, FL 39876, Balance of zero, CreditLimit of $2,500.00, Consultant of 19 2. Add a new record to the WorkOrders table: OrderNum of 69163, OrderDate of 9/24/2018, ClientNum of 521 3. Add a record to the OrderLine table: OrderNum of 69163, TaskID of VR39, ScheduledDate of 9/30/2018, QuotedPrice of $90.00 4. Add a record to the OrderLine table: OrderNum of 69163, TaskID of UP38, ScheduledDate of 9/30/2018, QuotedPrice of $185.00 5. Change the Balance value in the Client table for ClientNum 521 to $275.00 6. Change the Rate value in the Consultant table for ConsltNum 19 to $25.00
3	1. In the Consultant table, increase ConsltNum 51 to full time (change Hours to 40)
4	1. Delete task AC65

FIGURE 7-10   Four sample transactions

245

Suppose these four transactions are the first transactions in a day, immediately following a backup of the database, and they all complete successfully. In this case, the log might look like the sample log shown in Figure 7-11. The four transactions are shaded for reference to the previous figure.

Transaction ID	Time	Action	Record Updated	Before Image	After Image
1	8:00	Start			
2	8:01	Start			
2	8:02	Insert	Client (521)		(new values)
1	8:03	Update	Tasks (WC19, $125.00)	(old values)	(new values)
2	8:04	Insert	WorkOrders (69163)		(new values)
1	8:05	Commit			
3	8:06	Start			
2	8:07	Insert	OrderLine (69163, VR39)		(new values)
2	8:08	Insert	OrderLine (69163, UP38)		(new values)
4	8:09	Start			
2	8:10	Update	Client (521, $275.00)	(old values)	(new values)
2	8:11	Update	Consultant (19, $25.00)	(old values)	(new values)
2	8:12	Commit			
3	8:13	Update	Consultant (51, 40)	(old values)	(new values)
3	8:14	Commit			
4	8:15	Delete	Tasks (AC65)	(old values)	
4	8:16	Commit			

FIGURE 7-11   Sample log in which all four transactions commit normally

Before studying how the log is used in the recovery process, examine the log itself. Each record in the log includes the ID of the transaction, as well as the time the particular action occurred. The actual time would be more precise than in the example, the DBMS would process the actions much faster, and the date also would be included in the log. For simplicity in this example, each action occurs one minute after the preceding action.

The actions are *Start* to indicate the start of a transaction, *Commit* to indicate that the transaction completed successfully, *Insert* to identify the addition of a record to the database, *Update* to identify the change of a record, and *Delete* to identify the deletion of a record. For an Insert action, no before image appears in the log because the data did not exist prior to the action. Similarly, for a Delete action, no after image appears in the log.

The sample log shows, for example, shows the following for transaction 2. It began at 8:01. A database change occurred at 8:02 (Client 521 inserted). At 8:04 (the WorkOrders record inserted), 8:07 (the first order line record inserted), 8:08 (the second order line record inserted), 8:10 (client 521 record updated), and 8:11 (consultant 19 record updated). At 8:12, transaction 2 was committed. During this same time span, from 8:00 to 8:16, the other three transactions were executed and committed.

Forward Recovery

How is the log used in the recovery process? Suppose a catastrophe destroys the database just after 8:11. In this case, the recovery of the database begins with the most recent database backup from the previous evening at 10:00. As shown in Figure 7-12, the DBA copies the backup over the live database. Because the database is no longer current, the DBA executes a DBMS recovery program that applies the after images of committed transactions from the log to bring the database up to date. This method of recovery is called **forward recovery**.

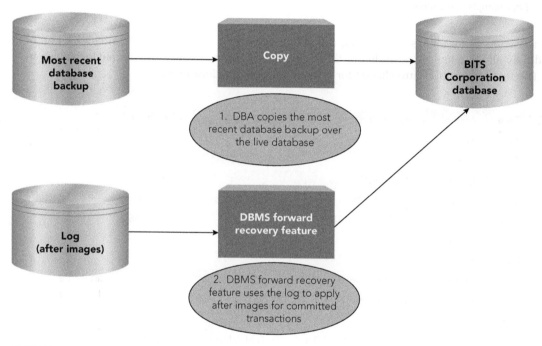

FIGURE 7-12   Forward recovery

In its simplest form, the recovery program in chronological order copies the after image of each record in the log over the actual record in the database. You can improve the recovery process by realizing that if a specific record was updated 10 times since the last backup, the recovery program copies the after image records 10 times over the database record. Thus, in reality, the first nine copies are unnecessary. The 10th after image includes all the updates accomplished in the first nine. Thus, you can improve the performance of the recovery program by having it first scan the log and then apply the last after image.

Q & A 7-1

Question: In the preceding scenario, which transactions in the sample log shown in Figure 7-11 does the recovery program use to update the restored database?
Answer: The catastrophe occurred just after 8:11. Because the recovery program applies transactions committed before the catastrophe, the program applies only transactions 1 and 3. These two transactions committed before 8:11, at which point the DBMS was still processing transactions 2 and 4.

Backward Recovery

If the database has not actually been destroyed, the problem must involve transactions that were either incorrect or, more likely, stopped in midstream. In either case, the database is currently not in a valid state. You can use **backward recovery**, or **rollback**, to recover the database to a valid state by undoing the problem transactions. The DBMS accomplishes the backward recovery by reading the log for the problem transactions and applying the before images to undo their updates, as shown in Figure 7-13.

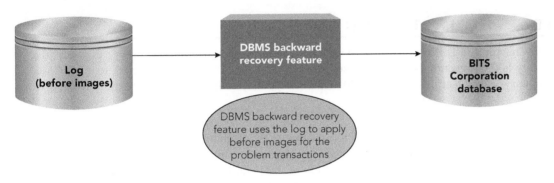

FIGURE 7-13   Backward recovery

Q & A 7-2

Question: For the sample log shown in Figure 7-11, what does the DBMS do to roll back transaction 1?
Answer: The DBMS started transaction 1 at 8:00, changed a Tasks table record at 8:04 for transaction 1, and committed transaction 1 at 8:06. To roll back transaction 1, the DBMS applies the before image of the Tasks table record.

Q & A 7-3

Question: For the sample log shown in Figure 7-11, what does the DBMS do to roll back transaction 3?
Answer: The DBMS started transaction 3 at 8:03, added a Client table record at 8:08 for transaction 3, and committed transaction 3 at 8:10. Because no before image exists for adding a record, to roll back transaction 3, the DBMS deletes the Client table record.

Recovery on PC-Based DBMSs

PC-based DBMSs generally do not offer sophisticated recovery features such as journaling. Most of them provide users with a simple way to make backup copies and to recover the database later by copying the backup over the database.

How should you handle recovery in any application system you develop with a PC-based DBMS? You could simply use the features of the DBMS to periodically make backup copies and use the most recent backup if a recovery is necessary. The more important it is to avoid redoing work, the more often you would make backups. For example, if a backup is made every eight hours, you might have to redo up to eight hours of work. If, on the other hand, a backup is made every two hours, you might have to redo up to two hours of work.

In many situations, this approach, although not particularly desirable, is acceptable. However, for systems with a large number of updates made to the database between backups, this approach is not acceptable. In such cases, the necessary recovery features that are not supplied by the DBMS must be included in application programs. Each of the programs that update the database, for example, also could write a record to a separate log file indicating the update that had taken place. Programmers could write a separate program to read the log file and re-create all the updates indicated by the records in the file. The recovery process would then consist of copying the backup over the actual database and running this special program.

Although this approach does simplify the recovery process for the users of the system, it also causes some problems. First, each of the programs in the system becomes more complicated because of the extra logic involved in adding records to the special log file. Second, someone must write a separate program to update the database with the information in this log file. Finally, every time a user completes an update, the system has extra work to do, and this additional processing may slow down the system to an unacceptable level. Thus, in any application, you must determine whether the ease of recovery provided by this approach is worth the price that you might have to pay for it. The answer will vary from one system to another.

PROVIDE SECURITY SERVICES

As discussed in Chapter 4, a DBMS must provide ways to ensure that only authorized users can access the database. **Security** is the prevention of unauthorized access, either intentional or accidental, to a database. The most common security features used by DBMSs are encryption, authentication, authorizations, and views.

Encryption

Encryption converts the data in a database to a format that is indecipherable by a word processor or another program and stores it in an encrypted format. When unauthorized users attempt to bypass the DBMS and get to the data directly, they see only the encrypted version of the data. However, authorized users accessing the data using the DBMS have no problem viewing and working with the data.

When a user updates data in the database, the DBMS encrypts the data before updating the database. Before a legitimate user retrieves the data via the DBMS, the data is decrypted, or decoded, and presented to the user in the normal format. The entire encryption process is transparent to a legitimate user; that is, he or she is not even aware it is happening.

Access lets you encrypt a database with a password and, after you have encrypted the database, you can use Access to decrypt it. **Decrypting** a database reverses the encryption. If your encrypted database takes longer to respond to user requests as it gets larger, you might consider decrypting it to improve its responsiveness.

Using Access to encrypt or decrypt a database is a four-step process:

1. Start Access, click the FILE tab on the ribbon (if necessary) to display Backstage view, and then click Open in the navigation bar.
2. Navigate to the drive and folder that contains the database in the Open dialog box, click the database name, click the Open arrow, and then click Open Exclusive.
3. Click the FILE tab, click Info if necessary, and then click the Encrypt with Password button (File tab | Info gallery). (To decrypt a database, click the Decrypt Database button.)
4. Type the password in the Password box, type the same password in the Verify box, press the enter key, and then click the OK button in the message box. (If you are decrypting the database, type the password for the database in the Password box, and then press the enter key.)

Authentication

Authentication refers to techniques for identifying the person who is attempting to access the DBMS. The use of passwords is the most common authentication technique. A **password** is a string of characters assigned by the DBA to a user that the user must enter to access the database. Users also employ passwords to access many operating systems, networks, other computer and Internet resources, and mobile devices. Biometric identification techniques and the use of smart cards are increasing in use as an alternative to password authentication. **Biometrics** identify users by physical or behavioral characteristics such as fingerprints, voiceprints, handwritten signatures, and facial characteristics. **Smart cards** are small plastic cards about the size of a driver's license that have built-in circuits containing processing logic to identify the cardholder.

Unlike individual passwords, a **database password** is a string of characters that the DBA assigns to a database and that users must enter before they can access the database. As long as the database password is known only to authorized database users, unauthorized access to the database is prevented. The DBA should use a database password that is easy for the authorized users to remember but that is not so obvious that others can easily guess the password. If a DBA encrypts an Access database, the DBA must assign a database password, as shown in Figure 7-14. To create the database password, the DBA enters the same password twice to verify that the initial entry is the one that the DBA wants.

FIGURE 7-14 Assigning a database password to the BITS database

After the DBA creates the database password for a database, as shown in Figure 7-15, users must enter it correctly before they can open the database.

FIGURE 7-15 User enters database password to open the BITS database

Authorizations

Using passwords is a security measure that applies to all users of a database; after users enter their passwords successfully, they can retrieve and update all the data in the database. Frequently, the security needs for a database are more individualized. For example, the DBA might need to let some users view and update all data and let other users view only certain data. In this situation, the DBA uses **authorization rules** that specify which users have what type of access to which data in the database.

The DBA grants users specific permissions to tables, queries, and other objects in a database. A user's **permissions** specify what kind of access the user has to objects in the database. The DBA can assign permissions to individual users or to groups of users. The DBA usually creates groups of users, sometimes called **workgroups**, assigns the appropriate permissions to each group, and then assigns each user to the appropriate group based on the permissions the user requires.

Views

Recall from Chapter 4 that a view is a snapshot of certain data in the database at a given moment in time. If a DBMS provides a facility that allows users to have their own views of a database, this facility can be used for security purposes. Tables or fields to which the user does not have access in his or her view effectively do not exist for that user.

Privacy

No discussion of security is complete without at least a brief mention of privacy. Although the terms *security* and *privacy* often are used synonymously, they are different, but related, concepts. **Privacy** refers to the right of individuals to have certain information about them kept confidential. Privacy and security are related because it is only through appropriate *security* measures that *privacy* can be ensured.

249

Laws and regulations dictate some privacy rules, and companies institute additional privacy rules. For example, HIPAA, the Health Insurance Portability and Accountability Act, passed in 1996 is a federal law that sets a national standard to protect medical records and other personal health information that identifies an individual and is maintained or exchanged electronically or in hard copy.

Confidential information varies widely among organizations. For example, salaries at governmental and many service organizations are public information, but salaries at many private enterprises are kept confidential.

PROVIDE DATA INTEGRITY FEATURES

A DBMS must follow rules so that it updates data accurately and consistently. These rules, called integrity constraints, are categorized as either key integrity constraints or data integrity constraints.

Key integrity constraints consist of primary key constraints and foreign key constraints. **Primary key constraints**, which are governed by entity integrity (as discussed in Chapter 4), enforce the uniqueness of the primary key. For example, forbidding the addition of a consultant whose number matches the number of a consultant already in the database is an example of a primary key constraint. Foreign key constraints, which are governed by referential integrity (as discussed in Chapter 4), enforce the fact that a value for a foreign key must match the value of the primary key for some row in a table in the database. Forbidding the addition of a client whose consultant is not already in the database is an example of a foreign key constraint.

Data integrity constraints help to ensure the accuracy and consistency of individual field values. Types of data integrity constraints include the following:

- *Data type.* The value entered for any field should be consistent with the data type for that field. For a numeric field, only numbers should be allowed. If the field is a date, only a legitimate date should be permitted. For instance, February 30, 2018, is an invalid date and should be rejected.
- *Legal values.* For some fields, not every possible value that is of the assigned data type is legitimate. For example, even though CreditLimit is a numeric field, only the values $2,500.00, $5,000.00, $7,500.00, and $10,000.00 are valid. For the OrderDate field in the WorkOrders table, BITS might insist that only the current date or a future date is an acceptable value when an order is updated. In addition, you should be able to specify which fields can accept null values and which fields cannot.
- *Format.* Some fields require a special entry or display format. Although the TaskID field is a character field, for example, only specially formatted strings of characters might be acceptable. Legitimate task ID numbers might have to consist of two letters followed by two digits; this is an example of an entry format constraint. Users might want the OrderDate field displayed with a four-digit year value instead of a two-digit year value; this is an example of a display format constraint.

Integrity constraints can be handled in one of four ways:

1. The constraint is ignored, in which case no attempt is made to enforce the constraint.
2. The responsibility for constraint enforcement is placed on the users. This means that users must be careful that any updates they make in the database do not violate the constraint.
3. The responsibility for constraint enforcement is placed on programmers. Programmers place into programs the logic to enforce the constraint. Users must update the database only by means of these programs and not through any of the built-in entry facilities provided by the DBMS because these would allow violation of the constraint. Programmers design the programs to reject any attempt by the users to update the database in a way that violates the constraint.
4. The responsibility for constraint enforcement is placed on the DBMS. The DBA specifies the constraint to the DBMS, which then rejects any attempt to update the database in a way that violates the constraint.

Q & A 7-4

Question: Which of these four approaches for constraint enforcement is best?
Answer: The first approach, ignoring the constraint, is undesirable because it can lead to invalid data in the database, such as two clients with the same number, item numbers with an invalid format, and invalid credit limits.

continued

The second approach, user constraint enforcement, is a little better because at least an attempt is made to enforce the constraints. However, this approach places the burden of enforcement on users. Besides meaning extra work for users, any mistake on the part of a single user, no matter how innocent, can lead to invalid data in the database.

The third approach removes the burden of enforcement from users and places it on programmers. This solution is better still because it means that users cannot violate the constraints. The disadvantage is that all update programs in the system become more complex. This complexity makes programmers less productive and makes programs more difficult to create and modify. This approach also makes changing an integrity constraint more difficult because this may mean changing all the programs that update the database. Furthermore, if the logic in any program used to enforce the constraints is faulty, the program could permit some constraint to be violated, and you might not realize that this had happened until a problem occurred at a later date. Finally, you would have to guard against a user bypassing the programs in the system in order to enter data directly into the database—for example, by using some built-in facility of the DBMS. If a user is able to bypass the programs and enters incorrect data, all the controls that were so diligently placed into the programs are helpless to prevent a violation of the constraints.

The best approach is the one the DBMS enforces. You specify the constraints to the DBMS, and the DBMS ensures that they are never violated.

Nearly all DBMSs include most of the necessary capabilities to enforce the various types of integrity constraints. Consequently, you let the DBMS enforce all the constraints that it is capable of enforcing, then let application programs enforce any other constraints. You also might create a special program whose sole purpose is to examine the data in the database to determine whether any constraints have been violated. You would run this program periodically and take corrective action to remedy any violations that the program discovers.

Microsoft Access supports key constraints. Access lets you specify a primary key, and then it builds a unique index automatically for the primary key. Access also lets you specify foreign keys, and then it enforces referential integrity automatically. You can use Access to specify data integrity constraints. As shown in Figure 7-16, you can specify the data type for each field, and you can specify data format and legal-values integrity constraints.

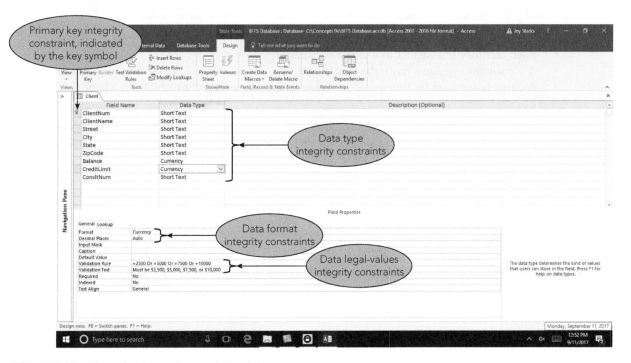

FIGURE 7-16   Example of integrity constraints in Access

SUPPORT DATA INDEPENDENCE

A DBMS must provide facilities to support the independence of programs from the structure of a database. One of the advantages of working with a DBMS is **data independence**, which is a property that lets you change the database structure without requiring you to change the programs that access the database. What types of changes could you or a DBA make to the database structure? A few of these changes include adding a field, changing a field property (such as length), creating an index, and adding or changing a relationship. The following sections describe the data independence considerations for each type of change.

Adding a Field

If you add a new field to a database, you do not need to change any program except, of course, those programs using the new field. However, when a program uses an SQL SELECT * FROM command to select all the fields from a given table, you are presented with an extra field. To prevent this from happening, you need to change the program to restrict the output to only the desired fields. To avoid the imposition of this extra work, you should list all the required fields in an SQL SELECT command instead of using the *.

Changing the Length of a Field

In general, you do not need to change associated programs because you have changed the length of a field; the DBMS handles all the details concerning this change in length. However, if a program sets aside a certain portion of the screen or a report for the field, and the length of the field has increased to the point where the previously allocated space is inadequate, you will need to change the program.

Creating an Index

To create an index, you enter a simple SQL command or select a few options. Most DBMSs use the new index automatically for all updates and queries. For some DBMSs, you might need to make minor changes in already existing programs to use the new index.

Adding or Changing a Relationship

In terms of data independence considerations, adding or changing a relationship is the trickiest of all and is best illustrated with an example. Suppose BITS now has the following requirements:

- Clients are assigned to territories.
- Each territory is assigned to a single consultant.
- A consultant can have more than one territory.
- A client is serviced by the consultant who covers the territory to which the client is assigned.

To implement these changes, you need to restructure the database. The previous one-to-many relationship between the Consultant and Client tables is no longer valid. Instead, there is now a one-to-many relationship between the Consultant table and the new Territory table, and a one-to-many relationship between the Territory table and the Client table, as follows:

```
Consultant (ConsltNum, LastName, FirstName, Street, City,
    State, ZipCode, Hours, Rate)
Territory (TerritoryNum, TerritoryDesc, ConsltNum)
Client (ClientNum, ClientName, Street, City, State, ZipCode,
    Balance, CreditLimit, TerritoryNum)
```

Further, suppose that a user accesses the database via the following view, which is named ConsultantClient:

```
CREATE VIEW ConsultantClient (CNum, CLast, CFirst, CliNum,
    CliName) AS
    SELECT Consultant.ConsltNum, LastName, FirstName, Client.ClientNum, ClientName
    FROM Consultant, Client
    WHERE Consultant.ConsltNum = Client.ConsltNum
;
```

The defining query is now invalid because there is no CNum field in the Client table. A relationship still exists between consultants and clients, however. The difference is that you now must go through the Territory table to relate the two tables. If users have been accessing the tables directly to form the relationship, their programs will have to change. If they are using the ConsultantClient view, you will need to change only the definition of the view. The new definition is as follows:

```
CREATE VIEW ConsultantClient (CNum, CLast, CFirst, CliNum,
    CliName) AS
    SELECT Consultant.ConsltNum, LastName, FirstName, Client.ClientNum, ClientName
    FROM Consultant, Territory, Client
    WHERE Consultant.ConsltNum = Territory.ConsltNum
    AND Territory.TerritoryNum = Client.TerritoryNum
;
```

The defining query is now more complicated than it was before, but this does not affect users of the view. The users continue to access the database in exactly the same way they did before, and the DBA does not need to change their programs.

SUPPORT DATA REPLICATION

A DBMS must manage multiple copies of the same data at multiple locations. For performance or other reasons, sometimes data should be duplicated—technically called **replicated**—at more than one physical location. For example, accessing data at a local site is much more efficient than accessing data remotely—especially if a large number of users are trying to access the main database. It is more efficient because using replicated data does not involve data communication and network time delays, users compete for data with fewer other users, and replicated data keeps data available to local users at times when the data might not be available at other sites.

If certain information needs to be accessed frequently from all sites, a company might choose to store the information at all its locations. At other times, users on the road—for example, consultants meeting at their clients' sites—might need access to data but would not have this access unless the data was stored on their laptop computers, mobile devices, or the Internet.

Replication allows users at different sites to use and modify copies of a database and then share their changes with the other users. Replication is a two-step process. First, the DBMS creates copies, called **replicas**, of the database at one or more sites. For example, you could create two replicas, as shown in Figure 7-17, and give the "Replica 1 database" to one user to access at a remote location and give the "Replica 2 database" to a second user to use at a different remote location.

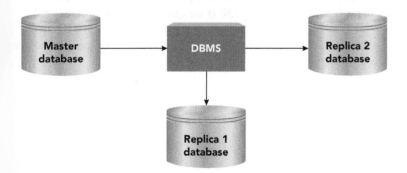

FIGURE 7-17   The DBMS creates replicas from the master database

The master database and all replicas form a replica set. Users then update their individual replicas, just as if they were updating the master database. Periodically, the DBMS exchanges all updated data between the master database and a replica in a process called **synchronization**. For example, after the second user returns from the remote site, the DBA synchronizes the master database and the "Replica 2 database," as shown in Figure 7-18. Later, after the first user returns, the DBA synchronizes the master database and the "Replica 1 database."

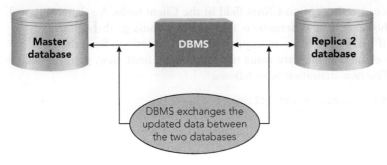

FIGURE 7-18   DBMS synchronizes two databases in a replica set

Ideally, the DBMS should handle all the issues associated with replication for you. The DBMS should do all the work to keep the various copies of data consistent behind the scenes; users should be unaware of the work involved. You will learn more about replication in Chapter 9.

PROVIDE UTILITY SERVICES

A DBMS must provide services that assist in the general maintenance of a database. In addition to the services already discussed, a DBMS provides a number of **utility services** that assist in the general maintenance of the database. The following is a list of services that might be provided by a PC-based DBMS:

- The DBMS lets you change the database structure—adding new tables and fields, deleting existing tables and fields, changing the name or properties of fields, and so on.
- The DBMS lets you add new indexes and delete indexes that are no longer needed.
- While you are using the database, the DBMS lets you use the services available from your operating system, such as Windows or Linux.
- The DBMS lets you export data to and import data from other software products. For example, you can transfer data easily between the DBMS and a spreadsheet file, a word-processing file, a graphics program file, or even another DBMS.
- The DBMS provides support for easy-to-use edit and query capabilities, screen generators, report generators, and so on.
- The DBMS provides support for both procedural and nonprocedural languages. With a **procedural language**, you must tell the computer precisely how a given task is to be accomplished; Basic, C++, and Java are examples of procedural languages. With a **nonprocedural language**, you merely describe the task you want the computer to accomplish. The nonprocedural language then determines how the computer will accomplish the task. SQL is an example of a nonprocedural language.
- The DBMS provides an easy-to-use, menu-driven interface that allows users to tap into the power of the DBMS without having to learn a complicated set of commands.

Summary

- The fundamental capability of a DBMS is to provide users with the ability to update and retrieve data in a database without users needing to know how data is structured on a storage medium or which processes the DBMS uses to manipulate the data.
- A DBMS must store metadata (data about the data) in a database and make this data accessible to users. The metadata is stored in a catalog or data dictionary.
- A DBMS must support concurrent update, allowing multiple users to update the same database at the same time. If concurrent update is not handled correctly, updates might be lost, causing the database to contain invalid data.
- Locking, which denies access by other users to data while the DBMS processes one user's updates, is one approach to concurrent update. Two-phase locking includes a growing phase, in which the DBMS locks more rows and releases none of the locks, followed by a shrinking phase, in which the DBMS releases all locks and acquires no new locks.
- Deadlock and deadly embrace are terms used to describe the situation in which two or more users are each waiting for the other(s) to release a lock before they can proceed. Enterprise DBMSs have sophisticated facilities for detecting and handling deadlock. Most PC-based DBMSs do not have such facilities, which means that programs that access the database must be written in such a way that deadlocks are avoided.
- An alternative to two-phase locking is timestamping, in which the DBMS processes updates to a database in timestamp order.
- A DBMS must provide methods to recover a database in the event that the database is damaged in any way. DBMSs provide facilities for periodically making a backup copy of the database. To recover the database when it is damaged or destroyed, your first step is to copy the backup over the damaged database.
- Enterprise DBMSs maintain a log or journal of all database updates since the last backup. If a database is destroyed, you make the database current from the last backup by using forward recovery to apply the after images of committed transactions. If you need to remove the updates of incorrect or terminated transactions, you use backward recovery or rollback to apply the before images to undo the updates.
- A DBMS must provide security features to prevent unauthorized access, either intentional or accidental, to a database. These security features include encryption (the storing of data in an encoded form), authentication (passwords, biometrics, or smart cards to identify users, and database passwords assigned to the database), authorizations (assigning authorized users to groups that have permissions for accessing the database), and views (snapshots of certain data in the database that limit a user's access to only the tables and fields included in the view).
- A DBMS must follow rules or integrity constraints so that it updates data accurately and consistently. Key integrity constraints consist of primary key and foreign key constraints. Data integrity constraints help to ensure the accuracy and consistency of individual fields and include data type, legal values, and format integrity constraints.
- A DBMS must provide facilities to support the independence of programs from the structure of a database; *data independence* is the term for this capability.
- A DBMS must provide a facility to handle replication by managing multiple copies of a database at multiple locations.
- A DBMS must provide a set of utility services that assist in the general maintenance of a database.

Key Terms

after image	database password
authentication	data dictionary
authorization rule	data independence
backup	data integrity constraints
backward recovery	deadlock
batch processing	deadly embrace
before image	decrypting
biometrics	encryption
commit	forward recovery
concurrent update	growing phase

journal   replicate
journaling   rollback
key integrity constraints   save
locking   shrinking phase
log   smart card
metadata   synchronization
nonprocedural language   timestamp
password   timestamping
permission   transaction
primary key constraints   two-phase locking
privacy   utility services
procedural language   victim
recovery   workgroup
replica

Review Questions

1. When users update and retrieve data, what tasks does a DBMS perform that are hidden from the users?

2. What is metadata? Which component of a DBMS maintains metadata?

3. How does a catalog differ from a data dictionary?

4. What is meant by concurrent update?

5. Describe a situation that could cause a lost update.

6. What is locking, and what does it accomplish?

7. What is a transaction?

8. Describe two-phase locking.

9. What is deadlock? How does it occur?

10. How do some DBMSs use timestamping to handle concurrent update?

11. What is recovery?

12. What is journaling? What two types of images does a DBMS output to its journal?

13. When does a DBA use forward recovery? What are the forward recovery steps?

14. When does a DBA use backward recovery? What does the DBMS do to perform backward recovery?

15. What is security?

16. What is encryption? How does encryption relate to security?

17. What is authentication? Describe three types of authentication.

18. What are authorization rules?

19. What are permissions? Explain the relationship between permissions and workgroups.

20. How do views relate to security?

21. What is privacy? How is privacy related to security?

22. What are integrity constraints? Describe four different ways to handle integrity constraints. Which approach is the most desirable?

23. What is data independence?

24. What is replication? What is synchronization?

25. Describe three utility services that a DBMS should provide.

26. What is a procedural language? What is a nonprocedural language?

27. Assume that you need to withdraw $100 from your checking account using your bank's ATM machine. What set of steps does the DBMS need to perform to complete your transaction?

28. How well does your school's DBMS fulfill the functions of a DBMS as described in this chapter? Which functions are fully supported? Which are partially supported? Which are not supported at all?

29. Research your DBMS help files, such as Microsoft Access Help, to identify ways to add data validation, set formats, add passwords, and make a backup. Write a brief summary with the steps and examples.

BITS Corporation Exercises

For the following exercises, you will address problems and answer questions from management at BITS. You do not use the BITS database for any of these exercises.

1. While users were updating the BITS database, one of the transactions was interrupted. You need to explain to management what steps the DBMS will take to correct the database. Using the sample log shown in Figure 7-11, list and describe the updates that the DBMS will roll back if transaction 2 is interrupted at 8:10.

2. Occasionally, users at BITS obtain incorrect results when they run queries that include built-in (aggregate, summary, or statistical) functions. The DBA told management that unrepeatable reads caused the problems. Use books, articles, and/or the Web to research the unrepeatable-read problem. Write a short report that explains the unrepeatable-read problem to management and use an example with your explanation. (*Note:* Unrepeatable reads also are called inconsistent retrievals, dirty reads, and inconsistent reads.) If you use information from the Web, use reputable sites. Do not plagiarize or copy from the Web.

3. You have explained replication to management, and some managers ask you for examples of when replication could be useful to them. Describe two situations, other than the ones given in the text, when replication would be useful to an organization.

4. The staff of the marketing department at BITS is scheduled to receive some statistical databases, and they need you to explain these databases to them. (A statistical database is a database that is intended to supply only statistical information to users; a census database is an example of a statistical database.) Using a statistical database, users should not be able to infer information about any individual record in the database. Use books, articles, and/or the Web to research statistical databases; then write a report that explains them, discusses the problem with using them, and gives the solution to the problem.

5. The DBA at BITS wants you to investigate biometric identification techniques for potential use at the company for computer authentication purposes. Use books, articles, and/or the Web to research these techniques, then write a report that describes the advantages and disadvantages of each of these techniques. In addition, recommend one technique and provide a justification for your recommendation.

6. Because most consultants access the BITS database from their mobile devices, such as smart phones and tablets, the DBA is considering the potential use of cloud computing. Use books, articles, and/or the Web to research cloud computing, then write a report that describes the advantages and disadvantages of making data available in the cloud. If you use information from the Web, use reputable sites. Do not plagiarize or copy from the Web.

Colonial Adventure Tours Case

The management of Colonial Adventure Tours wants to upgrade its database and wants you to help select a different DBMS. To help management, they would like you to complete the following exercises. You do not use the Colonial Adventure Tours database for any of these exercises.

1. Many computer magazines and Web sites present comparisons of several DBMSs. Find one such DBMS comparison article and compare the functions in this chapter to the listed features and functions in the article. Which functions from this chapter are included in the article? Which functions are missing from the article? What additional functions are included in the article? Which DBMS would you recommend for Colonial Adventure Tours? Justify your recommendation. If you use information from the Web, use reputable sites. Do not plagiarize or copy from the Web.

2. Use computer magazines and/or the Web to investigate one of these DBMSs: DB2, SQL Server, MySQL, Oracle, or SAP. Prepare a report that explains how that DBMS handles the following DBMS functions: concurrent update, data recovery, and security. (*Note:* For concurrent update, you might need to review the

concurrency control features of the DBMS.) Could Colonial Adventure Tours upgrade to the DBMS that you researched? Why or why not? If you use information from the Web, use reputable sites. Do not plagiarize or copy from the Web.

3. Use the Web to search for different ways to share an Access database, such as the one for Colonial Adventure Tours, with others using the Internet. Be sure to note any specific hardware and software resources needed. Prepare a report with your recommendations for sharing the database. If you use information from the Web, use reputable sites. Do not plagiarize or copy from the Web.

Sports Physical Therapy Case

For the following exercises, you will address problems and answer questions from the Sports Physical Therapy staff. You do not use the Sports Physical Therapy database for any of these exercises.

1. The log shown in Figure 7-19 includes four transactions that completed successfully. For each of the four transactions, list the transaction ID and the table(s) modified. In addition, list whether the modification to the table added, changed, or deleted a record.

Transaction ID	Time	Action	Record Updated	Before Image	After Image
1	10:00	Start			
2	10:01	Start			
1	10:02	Insert	Session (39)		(new values)
3	10:03	Start			
2	10:04	Update	Therapist (JR085)	(old values)	(new values)
3	10:05	Update	Patient (1012)	(old values)	(new values)
1	10:06	Commit			
4	10:07	Start			
3	10:08	Update	Therapies (92540)	(old values)	(new values)
3	10:09	Commit			
2	10:10	Update	Therapies (92540)	(old values)	(new values)
2	10:11	Commit			
4	10:12	Update	Therapies (92540)	(old values)	(new values)
4	10:13	Update	Patient (1012)	(old values)	(new values)
4	10:14	Commit			

FIGURE 7-19 Sample log in which four transactions commit normally

2. Suppose a catastrophe destroys the database just after 10:10. Which transactions in the sample log shown in Figure 7-19 would the recovery program use to update the restored database? Which transactions would have to be entered again by users?

3. If two of the four transactions shown in Figure 7-19 started at different times, deadlock could have occurred. Adjust the log to create deadlock between these two transactions.

4. Two of the five tables in the Sports Physical Therapy database are defined as follows:

```
Patient (PatientNum, LastName, FirstName, Street, City,
    State, ZipCode, Balance)
Session (SessionNum, SessionDate, PatientNum,
    LengthOfSession, TherapistID, TherapyCode)
```

Suppose that a user accesses the database via the following view:

```
CREATE VIEW PatientSession AS
    SELECT Patient.PatientNum, LastName, FirstName,
        SessionNum, TherapyCode
    FROM Patient, Session
    WHERE Patient.PatientNum= Session.PatientNum
;
```

Suppose further that the database requirements have changed so that users need to see the name of the therapist who completed the session. What other table(s) need to be added to the view in order to satisfy the new requirements? What if a patient has multiple therapies and sees multiple therapists? Write the new defining query for the view.

5. Sports Physical Therapy currently uses a PC-based DBMS. What factors should they consider in determining how often to back up their database? The factors you include should be specific to Sports Physical Therapy.

DATABASE ADMINISTRATION

INTRODUCTION

As you have learned in previous chapters, the database approach (versus other ways of storing data) has many benefits. At the same time, the use of a DBMS involves potential hazards, especially when a database serves more than one user. For example, concurrent update and security present potential problems. Whom do you allow to access various parts of the database, and in what way? How do you prevent unauthorized accesses?

Note that just managing a database involves fundamental difficulties. Users must be made aware of the database structure or at least the portion of the database they are allowed to access so that they can use the database effectively. Any changes made in the database structure must be communicated to all users, along with information about how the changes will affect them. Backup and recovery must be carefully coordinated, much more so than in a single-user environment, and this coordination presents another complication.

To manage these problems, companies appoint a DBA to manage both the database and the use of the DBMS, that is, to perform database administration tasks. In this chapter, you will learn about the responsibilities of the DBA. You will be focusing on the role of the DBA in a personal computer (PC) environment that is similar to the environment of BITS. You will learn about the DBA's role in formulating and enforcing important policies with respect to the database and its use. Then you will examine the DBA's other administrative responsibilities for DBMS evaluation and selection, DBMS maintenance, data dictionary management, and training. Finally, you will learn about the DBA's technical responsibilities for database design, testing, and performance tuning.

THE ROLE OF THE DATABASE ADMINISTRATOR

Database administrators (DBAs) use operating systems, specialized software, and computer programs to design, store, and organize data. The following sections describe the education, qualifications, skills, and potential duties of a DBA.

Education and Qualifications

If you want to be a DBA, you should obtain a bachelor's degree in business, computer technology, information technology, or computer science and have two to four years of experience in databases.

Degrees that include internships or some type of work experience are extremely valuable. Many DBAs also have experience in programming, SQL, website design, or object-oriented technology. In addition, a wide variety of skills can help you obtain employment and succeed as a DBA, including

- knowledge of the principles of database design
- problem-solving and organizational skills
- knowledge of data manipulation languages
- communication, teamwork, and flexibility skills
- understanding business requirements
- ability to meet deadlines under pressure
- staying up to date with developments in new technology
- a commitment to continuing professional development (CPD)
- an understanding of information legislation, such as the Data Protection Act

Duties and Responsibilities

The role of a DBA varies greatly depending on the business or industry. In larger corporations, the role is more administrative; in smaller companies, the DBA may do everything from database design to data entry to training.

You already have seen many of the functions of a DBA. The following general list represents some (not all) of the jobs of the DBA. As you peruse it, you may want to review those skills in previous chapters.

- Design the database schema and create any necessary database objects
- Define and model data requirements, business rules, and operational requirements
- Plan for storage
- Create new databases
- Formulate and enforce database policies
- Write application SQL
- Install and configure software
- Test all aspects of the database
- Resolve data conflicts
- Work closely with application developers and system administrators to ensure all database needs are being met
- Ensure database security is implemented to safeguard the data
- Troubleshoot all aspects of database implementation and maintenance
- Plan and implement data migration
- Archive and recover the database
- Apply patches or upgrades to the database as needed
- Maintain corporate data dictionary
- Manage the data repository

The role of the DBA is multifaceted. In large companies, that role may be divided among many different roles, including a data administrator, a data architect, and a data operations manager. These roles often overlap.

Data Administrator

The administration duties in larger corporations may result in the hiring of a specialized data administrator (as opposed to a database administrator). A **data administrator** must be able to handle most of the jobs involving data. He or she must set data-handling policies, assign data entry, organize metadata, and act as a liaison between the database administrator and the rest of the database staff. The data administrator also may take the role of data analyst and be responsible for defining data elements, establishing relationships, and assuring data integrity and security.

Data Architect

A **data architect** is a person who designs, builds, and deploys databases. In many cases, he or she manages or supervises the construction of large and comprehensive databases. The data architect works closely with software designers, design analysts, users, and others on the database team. The data architect may be involved with programming new database applications, data modeling, and data warehousing.

Database Operations Manager

A **database operations manager** (sometimes called a data manager or DM) is concerned with the ongoing maintenance of established databases. Typically, the database operations manager manages data operations or DataOps, making sure the data gets from one place to another with integrity and security. He or she is responsible for ensuring the performance and availability of critical services and applications related to the database. These managers work with quality testing, analysis and design, and data replication.

The next sections go into greater detail on specific responsibilities of the DBA, which are summarized in Figure 8-1. In application, these functions may be performed by administrators, architects, managers, or others within an organization.

```
Database Policy Formulation and Enforcement
    Access privileges
    Security
    Disaster planning
    Archiving
Other Database Administrative Functions
    DBMS evaluation and selection
    DBMS maintenance
    Data dictionary management
    Training
Database Technical Functions
    Database design
```

FIGURE 8-1   DBA responsibilities

DATABASE POLICY FORMULATION AND ENFORCEMENT

The database administrator formulates database policies, communicates those policies to users, and enforces them. Among the policies are those covering access privileges, security, disaster planning, and archiving.

Access Privileges

Access to every table and field in a database is not a necessity for every user. Henry, for example, is an employee at BITS; his main responsibility is inventory control. Although he needs access to the entire Tasks table, does he also need access to the Consultant table? It is unlikely. Figure 8-2 on the next page illustrates the permitted and denied access privileges for Henry.

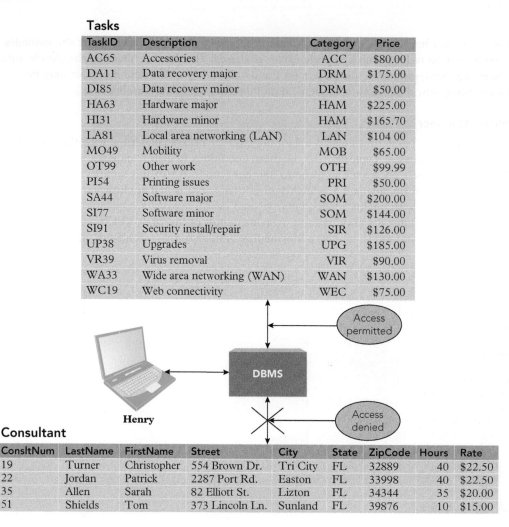

Tasks

TaskID	Description	Category	Price
AC65	Accessories	ACC	$80.00
DA11	Data recovery major	DRM	$175.00
DI85	Data recovery minor	DRM	$50.00
HA63	Hardware major	HAM	$225.00
HI31	Hardware minor	HAM	$165.70
LA81	Local area networking (LAN)	LAN	$104 00
MO49	Mobility	MOB	$65.00
OT99	Other work	OTH	$99.99
PI54	Printing issues	PRI	$50.00
SA44	Software major	SOM	$200.00
SI77	Software minor	SOM	$144.00
SI91	Security install/repair	SIR	$126.00
UP38	Upgrades	UPG	$185.00
VR39	Virus removal	VIR	$90.00
WA33	Wide area networking (WAN)	WAN	$130.00
WC19	Web connectivity	WEC	$75.00

Henry

DBMS

Access permitted

Access denied

Consultant

ConsltNum	LastName	FirstName	Street	City	State	ZipCode	Hours	Rate
19	Turner	Christopher	554 Brown Dr.	Tri City	FL	32889	40	$22.50
22	Jordan	Patrick	2287 Port Rd.	Easton	FL	33998	40	$22.50
35	Allen	Sarah	82 Elliott St.	Lizton	FL	34344	35	$20.00
51	Shields	Tom	373 Lincoln Ln.	Sunland	FL	39876	10	$15.00

FIGURE 8-2 Permitted and denied access privileges for Henry

Vicki, whose responsibility is client mailings at BITS, clearly requires access to clients' names and addresses. But what about their balances or credit limits? Should she be able to change an address? Should she be able to retrieve clients' balances or credit limits? Figure 8-3 illustrates the permitted and denied access privileges for Vicki. The denied access is shaded.

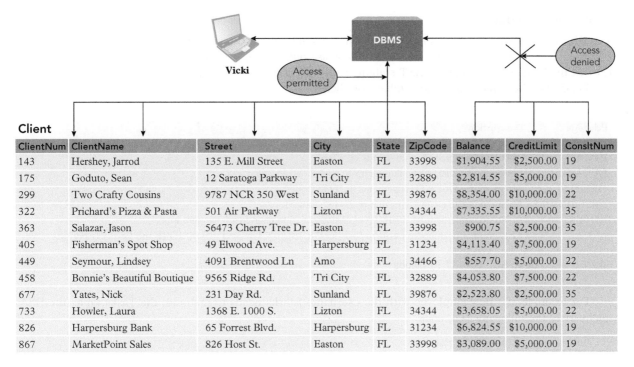

FIGURE 8-3 Permitted and denied access privileges for Vicki

Although consultant 22 (Patrick Jordan) should be able to obtain some of the information about his own clients, should he be able to obtain the same information about other clients? Figure 8-4 illustrates the permitted and denied access privileges for Patrick. The denied access is shaded.

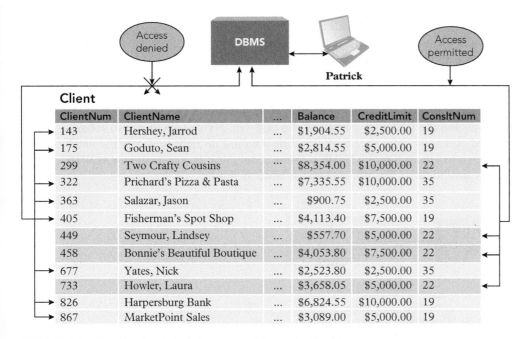

FIGURE 8-4 Permitted and denied access privileges for Patrick

Grant and Revoke

The DBA determines the access privileges for all users and enters the appropriate authorization rules in the DBMS catalog to ensure that users access the database only in ways to which they are entitled. As you learned in Chapter 4, the SQL GRANT statement defines access privileges.

Figure 8- 5 describes the basic database privileges.

Privilege	Description
SELECT	Ability to use SELECT statements on a table
INSERT	Ability to use INSERT statements on a table
UPDATE	Ability to use UPDATE statements on a table
DELETE	Ability to use DELETE statements on a table
REFERENCES	Ability to create a constraint that refers to a table
ALTER	Ability to implement ALTER TABLE statements to change a table definition
ALL	ALL grants the ability to perform SELECT, INSERT, UPDATE, DELETE, and REFERENCES

FIGURE 8-5　Basic SQL GRANT Privileges

For example, if a new employee with the username jstarks needs to maintain the Tasks table, the DBA might write the following SQL code:

```
GRANT ALL ON Tasks TO jstarks

;
```

The REVOKE statement rescinds privileges in a similar manner. For example, if the same employee should not be able to change the constraints or the table definition, the DBA might issue the following SQL command:

```
REVOKE REFERENCES, ALTER ON Tasks TO jstarks

;
```

Note that multiple privileges are delineated with commas.

The DBA also documents the access privilege policy; top-level management approves the policy, and the DBA communicates the policy to management and to all users.

Security

As discussed in previous chapters, security is the prevention of unauthorized access, either intentional or accidental, to a database, and the DBA uses views and the SQL GRANT statement as two security mechanisms. Unauthorized access includes access by someone who has no right to access the database at all. For example, as shown in Figure 8-6, the DBMS prevents Isaac, who is a programmer at BITS, from accessing the database because the DBA has not authorized Isaac as a user.

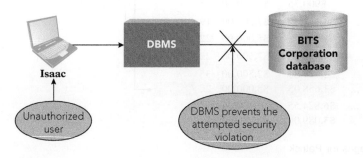

FIGURE 8-6　Attempted security violation by Isaac, who is not an authorized user

Unauthorized access also includes users who have legitimate access to some but not all data in a database and who attempt to access data for which they are not authorized. For example, the DBMS prevents Vicki from accessing client balances, as shown in Figure 8-7, because the DBA did not grant her access privileges to that data.

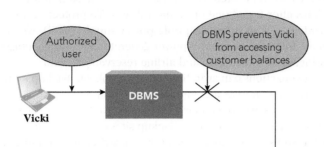

ClientNum	ClientName	...	Balance	CreditLimit	ConsltNum
143	Hershey, Jarrod	...	$1,904.55	$2,500.00	19
175	Goduto, Sean	...	$2,814.55	$5,000.00	19
299	Two Crafty Cousins	...	$8,354.00	$10,000.00	22
322	Prichard's Pizza & Pasta	...	$7,335.55	$10,000.00	35
363	Salazar, Jason	...	$900.75	$2,500.00	35
405	Fisherman's Spot Shop	...	$4,113.40	$7,500.00	19
449	Seymour, Lindsey	...	$557.70	$5,000.00	22
458	Bonnie's Beautiful Boutique	...	$4,053.80	$7,500.00	22
677	Yates, Nick	...	$2,523.80	$2,500.00	35
733	Howler, Laura	...	$3,658.05	$5,000.00	22
826	Harpersburg Bank	...	$6,824.55	$10,000.00	19
867	MarketPoint Sales	...	$3,089.00	$5,000.00	19

FIGURE 8-7   Attempted security violation by Vicki, who is authorized to access some client data but is not authorized to access client balances

The DBA takes the necessary steps to ensure that the database is secure. After the DBA determines the access privileges for each user, the DBA creates security policies and procedures, obtains management approval of the policies and procedures, and then distributes them to authorized users.

To implement and enforce security, the DBA uses the DBMS's security features, such as encryption, authentication, authorizations, and views. If a DBMS lacks essential security features, the DBA might create or purchase special security programs that provide the missing features.

In addition to relying on the security features provided by the DBMS and, if necessary, the special security programs, the DBA monitors database usage to detect potential security violations. If a security violation occurs, the DBA determines who breached security, how the violation occurred, and how to prevent a similar violation in the future.

Disaster Planning

The type of security discussed in the previous section concerns damage to the data in a database caused by authorized and unauthorized users. Damage to a database also can occur through a physical incident such as an abnormally terminated program, a software virus or worm, a disk problem, a power outage, a computer malfunction, a hurricane, a flood, a tornado, or another natural disaster.

To protect an organization's data from physical damage, the DBA creates and implements backup and recovery procedures as part of a disaster recovery plan. A **disaster recovery plan** specifies the ongoing and emergency actions and procedures required to ensure data availability if a disaster occurs. For example, a disaster recovery plan must include plans for protecting an organization's data against hard drive failures and electrical power loss.

Many businesses use cloud backup to keep copies of all their data. **Cloud backup** is an easy, secure, and scalable strategy for backing up data that sends data to an off-site server. Fees are based on capacity, bandwidth, or the number of users.

To protect against hard drive failures, organizations often use a **redundant array of inexpensive/ independent drives (RAID)**, in which database updates are replicated to multiple hard drives so that an organization can continue to process database updates after losing one of its hard drives. To protect against electrical power interruptions and outages, organizations use an **uninterruptible power supply (UPS)**, which is a power source such as a battery or fuel cell for short interruptions and a power generator for longer outages.

For some functions, such as credit card processing, stock exchanges, and airline reservations, data availability must be continuous. In these situations, organizations can switch quickly to duplicate backup systems (usually at a separate backup site) in the event of a malfunction in or a complete destruction of the main system. Other organizations contract with firms using hardware and software similar to their own so that in the event of a catastrophe, they can temporarily use these other facilities as backup sites. Backup sites can be established with different levels of preparedness. A **hot site** is a backup site that an organization can switch to in minutes or hours because the site is completely equipped with duplicate hardware, software, and data. Although hot sites are expensive, businesses such as banks and other financial institutions cannot permit any lengthy service interruptions and must have hot sites. A less expensive **warm site** is a backup site that is equipped with duplicate hardware and software but not data, so it takes longer to start processing at a warm site compared to a hot site.

Archiving

Often users need to retain certain data in a database for only a limited time. An order that has been filled, reported on a client's statement, and paid by the client is, in one sense, no longer important. Should you keep the order in the database? If you always keep data in the database as a matter of policy, the database will continually grow. The storage space that is occupied by the database will expand, and programs that access the database might take more time to perform their functions. The increased usage of storage space and the longer processing times might be good reasons to remove completed orders and all their associated order lines from the database.

On the other hand, you might need to retain orders and their associated order lines for future reference by users to answer client inquiries or to check a client's past history with the company. More critically, you need to retain data legally required to satisfy governmental laws and regulations and to meet auditing and financial requirements. Examples of legal reasons for data retention that apply to many organizations are as follows:

- The **Sarbanes–Oxley (SOX) Act** of 2002, a federal law that specifies data retention and verification requirements for public companies, requires CEOs and CFOs to certify financial statements and makes it a crime to destroy or tamper with financial records. Congress passed this law in response to major accounting scandals involving Enron, WorldCom, and Tyco.
- The **Patriot Act** of 2001 is a federal law that specifies data retention requirements for the identification of clients opening accounts at financial institutions, allows law enforcement agencies to search companies' and individuals' records and communications, and expands the government's authority to regulate financial transactions. President George W. Bush signed the Patriot Act into law 45 days after the September 11, 2001, terrorist attacks against the United States.
- The Security and Exchange Commission's Rule 17a-4 (**SEC Rule 17a-4**) specifies the retention requirements of all electronic communications and records for financial and investment entities.
- The **Department of Defense (DOD) 5015.2 Standard** of 1997 provides data management requirements for the DOD and for companies supplying or dealing with the DOD.
- The **Health Insurance Portability and Accountability Act (HIPAA)** of 1996 is a federal law that specifies the rules for storing, handling, and protecting health-care transaction data.
- The **Presidential Records Act** of 1978 is a federal law that regulates the data retention requirements for all communications, including electronic communications, of U.S. presidents and vice presidents. Congress passed this law after the scandals during the Nixon administration.

If a company does business internationally, there are even more laws governing the use of data. For example, in 2015 Australia passed a law requiring all companies doing business in Australia to keep customer data, including telephony, Internet, and email metadata, for a period of two years.

Legal compliance with the many data retention laws and regulations is a complicated and expensive process. For example, the length of time organizations must retain data ranges from two to seven years; for some laws, the time period is indefinite. The DBA is responsible for ensuring that data processed by DBMSs is retained in conformance to all laws.

One solution to data retention is to use what is known as a **data archive**, or **archive**. In ordinary usage, an archive (technically *archives*) is a place where public records and documents are kept. A data archive is similar. It is a place where a record of certain corporate data is kept. In the case of the previously mentioned completed orders and associated order lines, Figure 8-8 shows how you would remove them from the database and place them in the archive, thus storing them for future reference.

DATABASE

ARCHIVE

WorkOrders

OrderNum	OrderDate	ClientNum
67101	9/6/2018	733
67313	9/7/2018	458
67424	9/10/2018	322
67838	9/10/2018	867
67949	9/10/2018	322
68252	9/12/2018	363
68868	9/14/2018	867
68979	9/17/2018	826

WorkOrders

OrderNum	OrderDate	ClientNum
67949	9/10/2018	322

OrderLine

OrderNum	TaskID	ScheduledDate	QuotedPrice
67101	SI77	9/10/2018	$144.00
67313	LA81	9/12/2018	$104.00
67424	MO49	9/14/2018	$65.00
67424	UP38	9/14/2018	$185.00
67838	LA81	9/20/2018	$104.00
67949	PI54	9/21/2018	$50.00
67949	VR39	9/21/2018	$88.00
67949	WA33	9/21/2018	$126.00
68252	DI85	9/24/2018	$50.00
68868	SA44	9/24/2018	$200.00
68979	AC65	9/27/2018	$77.00
68979	DA11	9/27/2018	$970.00

OrderLine

OrderNum	TaskID	ScheduledDate	QuotedPrice
67949	PI54	9/21/2018	$50.00
67949	VR39	9/21/2018	$88.00
67949	WA33	9/21/2018	$126.00

FIGURE 8-8 Movement of order 67949 from the database to the archive

Typically, the DBA stores the archive on some mass storage device—for example, a disk, tape, CD, or DVD. Whichever medium the DBA uses, the DBA must store copies of both archives and database backups off-site so that recovery can take place even if a company's buildings and contents are destroyed. The off-site location must be a sufficient distance from the main site so that there is no likelihood of a disaster damaging both sites. Once again, it is up to the DBA to establish and implement procedures for the use, maintenance, and storage of the archive.

OTHER DATABASE ADMINISTRATIVE FUNCTIONS

The DBA is also responsible for DBMS evaluation and selection, DBMS maintenance, data dictionary management, and training.

DBMS Evaluation and Selection

When a company decides to purchase a new DBMS, the DBA leads the DBMS evaluation and selection effort. To evaluate the DBMS candidates objectively, the DBA usually prepares a checklist similar to the one shown in Figure 8-9. (This checklist applies specifically to a relational system because most DBMSs are, at least in part, relational. If the DBA had not already selected a data model, such as the relational model, the DBA would have added a "Choice of Data Model" category to the list.) The DBA evaluates each prospective purchase of a DBMS against the categories shown in the figure. An explanation of each category follows the figure.

1. Data Definition
   a. Data types
      (1) Numeric
      (2) Character
      (3) Date
      (4) Logical (T/F)
      (5) Memo
      (6) Currency
      (7) Binary object (pictures, drawings, sounds, and so on)
      (8) Link to an Internet, Web, or other address
      (9) User-defined data types
      (10) Other
   b. Support for nulls
   c. Support for primary keys
   d. Support for foreign keys
   e. Unique indexes
   f. Views
2. Data Restructuring
   a. Possible restructuring
      (1) Add new tables
      (2) Delete existing tables
      (3) Add new columns
      (4) Change the layout of existing columns
      (5) Delete columns
      (6) Add new indexes
      (7) Delete existing indexes
   b. Ease of restructuring
3. Nonprocedural Languages
   a. Nonprocedural languages supported
      (1) SQL
      (2) QBE
      (3) Natural language
      (4) Language unique to the DBMS. Award points based on ease of use as well as the types of operations (joining, sorting, grouping, calculating various statistics, and so on) that are available in the language. You can use SQL as a standard against which you can judge the language.
   b. Optimization done by one of the following:
      (1) User (in formulating the query)
      (2) DBMS (through built-in optimizer)
      (3) No optimization possible; system does only sequential searches.
4. Procedural Languages
   a. Procedural languages supported
      (1) Language unique to the DBMS. Award points based on the quality of this language in terms of both the types of statements and control structures available, and the database manipulation statements included in the language.
      (2) Java
      (3) C or C++
      (4) GUI language such as Visual Basic
      (5) COBOL
      (6) Other
   b. Can a nonprocedural language be used in conjunction with the procedural language (for example, could SQL be embedded in a COBOL program)?
5. Data Dictionary
   a. Type of entries
      (1) Tables
      (2) Columns
      (3) Indexes
      (4) Relationships
      (5) Users
      (6) Programs
      (7) Other
   b. Integration of data dictionary with other components of the system

FIGURE 8-9   DBMS evaluation checklist *(continued)*

6. Concurrent Update
   a. Level of locking
      (1) Field value
      (2) Row
      (3) Page
      (4) Table
      (5) Database
   b. Type of locking
      (1) Shared
      (2) Exclusive
      (3) Both
   c. Responsibility for handling deadlock
      (1) Programs
      (2) DBMS (automatic rollback of transaction causing deadlock)
7. Backup and Recovery
   a. Backup services
   b. Journaling services
   c. Recovery services
      (1) Recover from backup copy only
      (2) Recover using backup copy and journal
   d. Rollback of individual transactions
   e. Incremental backup
8. Security
   a. Encryption
   b. Passwords
   c. Authorization rules
      (1) Access to database only
      (2) Access/update access to any column or combination of columns
   d. Views
   e. Difficulty in bypassing security controls
9. Integrity
   a. Support for entity integrity
   b. Support for referential integrity
   c. Support for data integrity
   d. Support for other types of integrity constraints
10. Replication and Distributed Databases
   a. Partial replicas
   b. Handling of duplicate updates in replicas
   c. Data distribution
   d. Procedure support
      (1) Language used
      (2) Procedures stored in database
      (3) Support for remote stored procedures
      (4) Trigger support
11. Limitations
   a. Number of tables
   b. Number of columns
   c. Length of individual columns
   d. Total length of all columns in a table
   e. Number of rows per table
   f. Number of files that can be open at the same time
   g. Sizes of database, tables, and other objects
   h. Types of hardware supported
   i. Types of LANs supported
   j. Other
12. Documentation and Training
   a. Clearly written manuals
   b. Tutorial
      (1) Online
      (2) Printed
   c. Online help available
      (1) General help
      (2) Context-sensitive help
   d. Training
      (1) Vendor or other company
      (2) Location
      (3) Types (DBA, programmers, users, others)
      (4) Cost
13. Vendor Support
   a. Type of support available
   b. Quality of support available
   c. Cost of support
   d. Reputation of support
14. Performance
   a. External benchmarking done by various organizations
   b. Internal benchmarking
   c. Includes a performance monitor

FIGURE 8-9 DBMS evaluation checklist *(continued)*

```
15. Portability
    a.  Operating systems
        (1) Unix
        (2) Microsoft Windows
        (3) Linux
        (4) Other
    b.  Import/export/linking file support
        (1) Other databases
        (2) Other applications (for example, spreadsheets and
            graphics)
    c.  Internet and intranet support
16. Cost
    a.  Cost of DBMS
    b.  Cost of any additional components
    c.  Cost of any additional hardware that is required
    d.  Cost of network version (if required)
    e.  Cost and types of support
17. Future Plans
    a.  What does the vendor plan for the future of the system?
    b.  What is the history of the vendor in terms of keeping the
        system up to date?
    c.  When changes are made in the system, what is involved in
        converting to the new version?
        (1) How easy is the conversion?
        (2) What will it cost?
18. Other Considerations (Fill in your own special requirements.)
    a.  ?
    b.  ?
    c.  ?
    d.  ?
```

FIGURE 8-9   DBMS evaluation checklist *(continued)*

1. ***Data definition.*** What types of data does the DBMS support? Does it support nulls? What about primary and foreign keys? The DBMS undoubtedly provides support for indexes. But can you specify that an index is unique and then have the system enforce the uniqueness? Does the DBMS support views?

2. ***Data restructuring.*** What type of database restructuring does the DBMS allow? How easily can the DBA perform the restructuring? Will the system do most of the work, or will the DBA have to create special programs for this purpose?

3. ***Nonprocedural languages.*** What types of nonprocedural language does the DBMS support? The possibilities are SQL, QBE, natural language, and a DBMS built-in language. If the DBMS supports one of the standard languages, what is the quality of its version? If the DBMS provides its own language, how good is it? How does its functionality compare to that of SQL? How does the DBMS achieve optimization of queries? The DBMS optimizes each query, or the user must do so through the manner in which he or she states the query. If neither happens, no optimization occurs. Most desirable, of course, is the first alternative.

4. ***Procedural languages.*** What types of procedural languages does the DBMS support? Are they common languages, such as Java, C or C++, and COBOL? Is it a graphical user interface (GUI) language? Does the DBMS provide its own language? In the latter case, how complete is the language? Does it contain all the required types of statements and control structures? What facilities does the language provide for accessing the database? Does the DBMS let you use a nonprocedural language while you are using the procedural language?

5. ***Data dictionary.*** What kind of data dictionary does the DBMS provide? Is it a simple catalog? Or can it contain more content, such as information about programs and the various data items these programs access? How well is the data dictionary integrated with other components of the system—for example, the nonprocedural language?

6. ***Concurrent update.*** Does the DBMS support concurrent update? What unit may be locked (field value, row, page, table, or database)? Are exclusive locks the only ones permitted, or are shared locks also allowed? (A **shared lock** permits other users to read the data; with an **exclusive lock**, no other user may access the data in any way.) Does the DBMS resolve deadlock, or must programs resolve it?

7. ***Backup and recovery.*** What type of backup and recovery services does the DBMS provide? Does the DBMS maintain a journal of changes in the database and use the journal during the

recovery process? If a transaction terminates abnormally, does the DBMS roll back its updates? Can the DBMS perform an incremental backup of just the data that has changed?

8. *Security.* What types of security features does the DBMS provide? Does the DBMS support encryption, password support, and authorization rules? Does the DBMS provide a view mechanism that can be used for security? How difficult is it to bypass the security controls?

9. *Integrity.* What type of integrity constraints does the DBMS support? Does the DBMS support entity integrity (the fact that the primary key cannot be null) and referential integrity (the property that values in foreign keys must match values already in the database)? Does the DBMS support any other type of integrity constraints?

10. *Replication and distributed databases.* Does the DBMS support replication? If so, does the DBMS allow partial replicas (copies of selected rows and fields from tables in a database)? And how does the DBMS handle updates to the same data from two or more replicas? Can the DBMS distribute a database, that is, divide the database into segments, and store the segments on different computers? If so, what types of distribution does the DBMS allow and what types of procedure support for distribution does the DBMS provide?

11. *Limitations.* What limitations exist with respect to the number of tables and the number of fields and rows per table? How many files can you open at the same time? (For some databases, each table and each index is in a separate file. Thus, a single table with three indexes, all in use at the same time, would account for *four* files. Problems might arise if the number of files you can open is relatively small and many indexes are in use.) On what types of operating systems and hardware is the DBMS supported? What types of local area networks (LANs) can you use with the DBMS? (A **local area network [LAN]** is a configuration of several computers connected together that allows users to share a variety of hardware and software resources. One of these resources is the database. In a LAN, support for concurrent update is very important because many users might be updating the database at the same time. The relevant question here, however, is not how well the DBMS supports concurrent update but which of the LANs you can use with the DBMS.)

12. *Documentation and training.* Does the vendor of the DBMS supply printed or online training manuals? If so, how good are the manuals? Are they easy to use? Is there a good index? Is a tutorial, in either printed or online form, available to assist users in getting started with the system? Is online help available? If so, does the DBMS provide general help and context-sensitive help? (**Context-sensitive help** means that if a user is having trouble and asks for help, the DBMS will provide assistance for the particular feature being used at the time the user asks for the help.) Does the vendor provide training classes? Do other companies offer training? Are the classes on-site or off-site? Are there classes for the DBA and separate classes for programmers and others? What is the cost for each type of training?

13. *Vendor support.* What type of support does the vendor provide for the DBMS, and how good is it? What is the cost? What is the vendor's reputation for support among current users?

14. *Performance.* How well does the DBMS perform, where performance is a measure of how rapidly the DBMS completes its tasks? This is a difficult question to answer because each organization has a different number of users and a different mix of transactions and both factors affect how a DBMS performs. One way to determine relative performance among DBMSs is to look into benchmark tests that various organizations have performed on several DBMSs. Benchmarking typically is done in areas such as sorting, indexing, and reading all rows and then changing data values in all rows. For example, the Transaction Processing Performance Council (www.tpc.org) provides the results of database benchmark tests to its members. Beyond using benchmarks, if an organization has some specialized needs, it may have to set up its own benchmark tests. Does the DBMS provide a performance monitor that measures different types of performance while the DBMS is operating?

15. *Portability.* Which operating systems can you use with the DBMS? What types of files can you import or export? Can the DBMS link to other data sources, such as files and other types of DBMSs? Does the DBMS provide Internet and intranet support? (An **intranet** is an internal company network that uses software tools typically used on the Internet and the World Wide Web.) Is there a version of the DBMS for mobile devices, such as smart phones and tablets?

273

16. *Cost.* What is the cost of the DBMS and of any additional components the organization is planning to purchase? Is additional hardware required? If so, what is the associated cost? If the organization requires a special version of the DBMS for a network, what is the additional cost? What is the cost of vendor support, and what types of support plans are available?

17. *Future plans.* What plans has the vendor made for the future of the system? This information is often difficult to obtain, but you can get an idea by looking at the performance of the vendor with respect to how it has kept the existing system up to date. How easy has it been for users to convert to new versions of the system?

18. *Other considerations.* This is a final catchall category that contains any special requirements not covered in the other categories. For many organizations, existing financial and other application software and existing hardware limit the DBMS choice.

After the DBA examines each DBMS with respect to all the preceding categories, the DBA and management can compare the results. Unfortunately, this process can be difficult because of the number of categories and their generally subjective nature. To make the process more objective, the DBA can assign a numerical ranking to each DBMS in each category (for example, a number between 0 and 10, where 0 is poor and 10 is excellent). Furthermore, the DBA can assign weights to the categories. Weighting allows an organization to signify which categories are more critical than others. Then, you multiply each number used in the numerical ranking by the appropriate weight and add the results, producing a weighted total. Finally, you compare the weighted totals for each DBMS, producing the final evaluation.

How does the DBA arrive at the numbers to assign each DBMS in the various categories? Several methods are used. The DBA can request feedback from other organizations that are currently using the DBMS being considered. The DBA can read journal reviews of the various DBMSs. Sometimes the DBA can obtain a trial version of the DBMS, and members of the staff can give it a hands-on test. In practice, the DBA usually combines all three methods. Whichever method is used, however, the DBA must carefully create the checklist and determine weights before starting the evaluation; otherwise, the findings may be inadvertently slanted in a particular direction.

DBMS Maintenance

After the organization selects and purchases the DBMS, the DBA has primary responsibility for it. The DBA installs the DBMS in a way that is suitable for the organization. If the DBMS configuration needs to be changed, it is the DBA who makes the changes. When the vendor releases a new version of the DBMS, the DBA reviews it and determines whether the organization should upgrade to it. If the decision is made to convert to the new version or perhaps to a new DBMS, the DBA coordinates the conversion. The DBA also handles any fixes to problems in the DBMS that the vendor releases.

When a problem occurs that affects the database, the DBA coordinates the people required to resolve the problem. Some people, such as programmers and users, are from inside the organization, and others, such as hardware and software vendors, are from outside the organization. When users have special one-time processing needs or extensive query requirements of the database, the DBA coordinates the users so that their needs are satisfied without unduly affecting other users.

A **run-book** is a log of all database maintenance, with dates, license keys, issues or updates, involved personnel, and resolutions. It also may contain a record of where backups and archives are located.

Data Dictionary Management

The DBA also manages the data dictionary. Essentially, the data dictionary is the catalog mentioned in Chapter 7, but it often contains a wider range of information, including information about tables, fields, indexes, programs, and users.

The DBA establishes naming conventions for tables, fields, indexes, and so on. The DBA creates the data definitions for all tables, as well as for any data integrity rules and user views. The DBA also updates the contents of the data dictionary. Finally, the DBA creates and distributes appropriate reports from the data dictionary to users, programmers, and other people in the organization.

Training

The DBA provides training in the use of the DBMS and in how to access the database. The DBA also coordinates the training of users and the technical staff responsible for developing and maintaining database applications. In those cases where the vendor of the DBMS provides training, the DBA handles the scheduling to make sure users receive the training they require. Training is a big expense, but successful organizations make the investment to ensure that their employees are knowledgeable and productive in handling the critical data resource.

TECHNICAL FUNCTIONS

The DBA is also responsible for database design, testing, and performance tuning.

Database Design

The DBA establishes a sound methodology for database design, such as the one discussed in Chapter 6, and ensures that all database designers follow the methodology. The DBA also verifies that the designers obtain all pertinent information from the appropriate users. After the database designers complete the information-level design, the DBA does the physical-level design.

The DBA establishes documentation standards for all the steps in the database design process. The DBA also makes sure that these standards are followed, that the documentation is kept up to date, and that the appropriate personnel have access to the documentation they need.

Requirements do not remain stable over time; they change constantly. The DBA reviews all changes to requirements and determines whether the changes will require modifications to be made to the database. For example, suppose your school's information technology service decides to move from a single passphrase system to a 2-step verification (sometimes called a two-factor authentication). Users of the service will now have to enter a passphrase and then enter a phone number or special code. A 2-step login provides an additional layer of security when you log into technology services. When this request is presented to the DBA, he or she will have to determine what kinds of changes will be made to the database. Will there need to be new fields for every user? Will there need to be letter or number constraints? Will there need to be new code written? The answer to all of these questions is yes.

The DBA oversees all of the changes in the design and in the data in the database. The DBA also verifies that programmers modify all programs and documentation affected by the change.

Testing

The combination of hardware, software, and database for the users is called the **production system**, or **live system**. The DBA strictly controls the production system. With just two exceptions, the DBA grants access and update privileges to the production system only to authorized users. The first exception is when problems occur, for example, with software. The DBA and others must troubleshoot the problem by accessing the production system. The second exception is when programmers complete new programs or modify existing programs for the production system. For both exceptions, the DBA performs any necessary database modifications or closely controls the activities of others.

Other than for these two exceptions, the DBA does not grant programmers access to the production system. Instead, the DBA and the programmers create a separate system, called the **test system**, or **sandbox**, that programmers use to develop new programs and modify existing programs. After programmers complete the testing of their programs in the test system, a separate quality assurance group performs further tests. The DBA and the users review and approve the test results, and the DBA reviews and approves the programs and documentation. The DBA then notifies all affected users when the new or corrected features will be available. The DBA then transfers the programs to the production system and makes any required database changes, as shown in Figure 8-10.

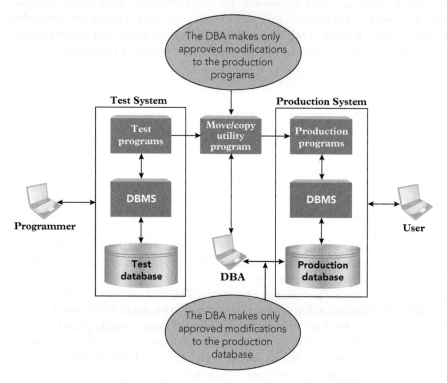

FIGURE 8-10 DBA controls the interaction between the test and production systems

A production system with a DBMS is a complex system. Having a separate test system reduces the complexity of the production system and provides an extra measure of control.

Performance Tuning

Database performance deals with the ability of the production system to serve users in a timely and responsive manner. Because funding is usually a constraint, the DBA's challenge is to get the best possible performance from the available funds.

Faster computers with faster storage media, faster network connections, faster software, and other production system expenditures help improve performance. What can the DBA do if the organization has no additional money for its production system but needs further performance improvements? The DBA can change the database design to improve performance; this process is called **tuning** the design. Some of the performance-tuning changes the DBA can make to a database design include creating and deleting indexes, splitting tables, and changing the table design.

By default, Access and some other DBMSs automatically create indexes for primary key and foreign key fields. These indexes make accessing the fields faster than accessing would be without the indexes. Further, indexing common fields improves the speed of joining related tables. If a DBMS does not automatically index primary key and foreign key fields, the DBA should create indexes for them. In addition, queries that search indexed fields run faster than comparable queries without indexes for those fields. For example, if users frequently query the Tasks table to find records based on values for the Category or Description fields, the DBA can improve performance by adding indexes on those fields. On the other hand, a table with many indexes takes longer to update. If users experience delays when they update a table, the DBA can delete some of the table's indexes to improve updating performance.

If users access only certain fields in a table, you can improve performance by splitting the table into two or more tables that each has the same primary key as the original and that collectively contain all the fields from the original table. Each resulting table is smaller than the original; the smaller amount of data moves faster between disk and memory. For example, suppose dozens of users at BITS access the Client table shown in Figure 8-11.

Client

ClientNum	ClientName	Street	City	State	ZipCode	Balance	CreditLimit	ConsltNum
143	Hershey, Jarrod	135 E. Mill Street	Easton	FL	33998	$1,904.55	$2,500.00	19
175	Goduto, Sean	12 Saratoga Parkway	Tri City	FL	32889	$2,814.55	$5,000.00	19
299	Two Crafty Cousins	9787 NCR 350 West	Sunland	FL	39876	$8,354.00	$10,000.00	22
322	Prichard's Pizza & Pasta	501 Air Parkway	Lizton	FL	34344	$7,335.55	$10,000.00	35
363	Salazar, Jason	56473 Cherry Tree Dr.	Easton	FL	33998	$900.75	$2,500.00	35
405	Fisherman's Spot Shop	49 Elwood Ave.	Harpersburg	FL	31234	$4,113.40	$7,500.00	19
449	Seymour, Lindsey	4091 Brentwood Ln	Amo	FL	34466	$557.70	$5,000.00	22
458	Bonnie's Beautiful Boutique	9565 Ridge Rd.	Tri City	FL	32889	$4,053.80	$7,500.00	22
677	Yates, Nick	231 Day Rd.	Sunland	FL	39876	$2,523.80	$2,500.00	35
733	Howler, Laura	1368 E. 1000 S.	Lizton	FL	34344	$3,658.05	$5,000.00	22
826	Harpersburg Bank	65 Forrest Blvd.	Harpersburg	FL	31234	$6,824.55	$10,000.00	19
867	MarketPoint Sales	826 Host St.	Easton	FL	33998	$3,089.00	$5,000.00	19

FIGURE 8-11   Client table for BITS

If some users access the address data from the Client table, and other users access balances and credit limits, the DBA can split the Client table into two tables, as shown in Figure 8-12, to improve performance. Users needing data from both tables can obtain that data by joining the two split tables on the ClientNum field.

ClientAddress

ClientNum	ClientName	Street	City	State	ZipCode
143	Hershey, Jarrod	135 E. Mill Street	Easton	FL	33998
175	Goduto, Sean	12 Saratoga Parkway	Tri City	FL	32889
299	Two Crafty Cousins	9787 NCR 350 West	Sunland	FL	39876
322	Prichard's Pizza & Pasta	501 Air Parkway	Lizton	FL	34344
363	Salazar, Jason	56473 Cherry Tree Dr.	Easton	FL	33998
405	Fisherman's Spot Shop	49 Elwood Ave.	Harpersburg	FL	31234
449	Seymour, Lindsey	4091 Brentwood Ln	Amo	FL	34466
458	Bonnie's Beautiful Boutique	9565 Ridge Rd.	Tri City	FL	32889
677	Yates, Nick	231 Day Rd.	Sunland	FL	39876
733	Howler, Laura	1368 E. 1000 S.	Lizton	FL	34344
826	Harpersburg Bank	65 Forrest Blvd.	Harpersburg	FL	31234
867	MarketPoint Sales	826 Host St.	Easton	FL	33998

ClientFinancial

ClientNum	Balance	CreditLimit	ConsltNum
143	$1,904.55	$2,500.00	19
175	$2,814.55	$5,000.00	19
299	$8,354.00	$10,000.00	22
322	$7,335.55	$10,000.00	35
363	$900.75	$2,500.00	35
405	$4,113.40	$7,500.00	19
449	$557.70	$5,000.00	22
458	$4,053.80	$7,500.00	22
677	$2,523.80	$2,500.00	35
733	$3,658.05	$5,000.00	22
826	$6,824.55	$10,000.00	19
867	$3,089.00	$5,000.00	19

FIGURE 8-12   Result of splitting the Client table into two tables

The DBA can also split tables for security purposes. In Figure 8-12, the ClientAddress table contains client address data, and the ClientFinancial table contains client financial data. Those users granted access only to the ClientAddress table have no access to client financial data, thus providing an added measure of security.

Although you design database tables in third normal form to prevent the anomaly problems discussed in Chapter 5, the DBA occasionally denormalizes tables to improve performance. **Denormalizing** converts a table that is in third normal form to a table that is no longer in third normal form. Usually, the conversion produces tables that are in first normal form or second normal form. Denormalizing introduces anomaly problems but can decrease the number of disk accesses that certain types of transactions require, thus improving performance. For example, suppose users who are processing order lines need task descriptions. The DBA might include task descriptions in the OrderLine table, as shown in Figure 8-13.

OrderLine

OrderNum	TaskID	Description	ScheduledDate	QuotedPrice
67101	SI77	Software minor	9/10/2018	$144.00
67313	LA81	Local area networking (LAN)	9/12/2018	$104.00
67424	MO49	Mobility	9/14/2018	$65.00
67424	UP38	Upgrades	9/14/2018	$185.00
67838	LA81	Local area networking (LAN)	9/20/2018	$104.00
67949	PI54	Printing issues	9/21/2018	$50.00
67949	VR39	Virus removal	9/21/2018	$88.00
67949	WA33	Wide area networking (WAN)	9/21/2018	$126.00
68252	DI85	Data recovery minor	9/24/2018	$50.00
68868	SA44	Software major	9/24/2018	$200.00
68979	AC65	Accessories	9/27/2018	$77.00
68979	DA11	Data recovery major	9/27/2018	$970.00

FIGURE 8-13   Including task descriptions in the OrderLine table, which creates a first normal form table

The OrderLine table in Figure 8-13 is in first normal form because there are no repeating groups. Because a task description depends only on the TaskID, which is just a portion of the primary key for the table, the OrderLine table is not in second normal form and, consequently, is not in third normal form either. As a result, the table has redundancy and anomaly problems that are inherent in tables that are not in third normal form. However, users processing order lines no longer need to join the OrderLine and Tasks tables to obtain task descriptions, thus improving performance.

A system may allow multiple computers to share access to data, software, or peripheral devices by running multiple instances of a single, shared database. A **parallel database system** takes advantage of this architecture to improve performance through parallelization of operations, such as storing data, indexing, and querying. In addition to balancing the workload among CPUs, the parallel database provides for concurrent access to data while protecting data integrity.

Finally, large databases with thousands of users often suffer periodic performance problems as users change their transaction mix. In these cases, the DBA must tune the databases to provide improved performance to all users.

Summary

- The DBA is the person who is responsible for supervising the database and the use of the DBMS.
- The DBA formulates and enforces policies about those users who can access the database, the portions of the database they may access, and in what manner they can access the database.
- The DBA formulates and enforces policies about security, which is the prevention of unauthorized access, either intentional or accidental, to a database. The DBA uses the DBMS's security features and special security programs, if necessary, and monitors database usage to detect potential security violations.
- The DBA creates and implements backup and recovery procedures as part of a disaster recovery plan to protect an organization's data from physical damage.
- The DBA formulates and enforces policies that govern the management of an archive for data that is no longer needed in the database but that must be retained for reference purposes or for compliance with federal laws.
- The DBA leads the effort to evaluate and select a new DBMS. The DBA develops a checklist of desirable features for a DBMS and evaluates each prospective purchase of a DBMS against this checklist.
- The DBA installs and maintains the DBMS after it has been selected and procured.
- The DBA maintains the data dictionary, establishes naming conventions for its contents, and provides information from it to others in the organization.
- The DBA provides database and DBMS training and schedules training by outside vendors.
- The DBA verifies all information-level database designs, completes all physical-level database designs, and creates documentation standards. The DBA also evaluates changes in requirements to determine whether he or she needs to change the database design and the data in the database.
- The DBA controls the production system, which is accessible only to authorized users. Other than when authorized by the DBA to access the production system in exceptional situations, programmers access a separate test system. The DBA migrates tested programs to the production system and makes any required database changes.
- The DBA tunes the database design to improve performance. Included among the performance tuning changes the DBA makes are creating and deleting indexes, splitting tables, and denormalizing tables.

Key Terms

archive	local area network (LAN)
cloud backup	parallel database system
context-sensitive help	Presidential Records Act
data administrator	production system
data architect	RAID (redundant array of inexpensive/independent drives)
data archive	run-book
database operations manager	sandbox
denormalizing	Sarbanes–Oxley (SOX) Act
Department of Defense (DOD) 5015.2 Standard	SEC Rule 17a-4
disaster recovery plan	shared lock
exclusive lock	test system
Health Insurance Portability and Accountability Act (HIPAA)	tuning
hot site	uninterruptible power supply (UPS)
intranet	warm site
live system	

Review Questions

1. What is a DBA? Why is this position necessary?
2. What are the DBA's responsibilities regarding access privileges?
3. List and describe the five SQL privileges available with the GRANT or REVOKE statements.
4. What are the DBA's responsibilities regarding security?

5. What is a disaster recovery plan?

6. What are data archives? What purpose do they serve? What is the relationship between a database and its data archives?

7. Name five categories that you usually find on a DBMS evaluation and selection checklist.

8. What is a shared lock? What is an exclusive lock?

9. What is a LAN?

10. What is context-sensitive help?

11. What is an intranet?

12. After a DBMS has been selected, what is the DBA's role in DBMS maintenance?

13. What are the DBA's responsibilities with regard to the data dictionary?

14. Who trains computer users in an organization? What is the DBA's role in this training?

15. What are the DBA's database design responsibilities?

16. What is the difference between production and test systems?

17. What is meant by "tuning a design?"

18. How can splitting a table improve performance?

19. What is denormalization?

20. You are employed as a DBA for a medical practice. You have implemented multiple safeguards to protect patient privacy and conform to HIPAA regulations. What other practical, common-sense measures should you take to ensure that the database system is secure? Identify at least three measures and explain the purpose of each one. If you use information from the Web, use reputable sites. Do not plagiarize or copy from the Web.

21. For credit card processing, stock exchanges, and airline reservations, data availability must be continuous. There are many other examples of mission-critical applications. Research the Internet to find four additional mission-critical applications and explain why data availability must be continuous for these applications. If you use information from the Web, use reputable sites. Do not plagiarize or copy from the Web. Be sure to cite your references.

BITS Corporation Exercises

For the following exercises, you do not use the BITS database.

1. Write the SQL for the following privileges as they related to the Client table:
   a. Give all rights to sburton.
   b. Give insert, delete, and update rights to creneau.
   c. Give select rights to lneilson.
   d. Revoke delete privileges to sburton.
   e. Revoke the ability to add constraints or change the table definition to tknudsen.

2. The DBA asks for your help in planning the data archive (not backup) for the following BITS database:

```
Consultant (ConsltNum, LastName, FirstName, Street,
    City, State, ZipCode, Hours, Rate)

Client (ClientNum, ClientName, Street, City,
    State, ZipCode, Balance, CreditLimit, ConsltNum)

WorkOrders (OrderNum, OrderDate, ClientNum)

OrderLine (OrderNum, TaskID, ScheduledDate,
    QuotedPrice)

Tasks (TaskID, Description, Category, Price)
```

Determine which data from the database to archive; that is, for each table, specify whether data needs to be archived. If it does, specify which data, when it should be archived, and whether it should be archived with data from another table.

3. The DBA denormalized some of the data in the BITS database to improve performance, and one of the resulting tables is the following:

```
Client (ClientNum, ClientName, Street, City,
        State, ZipCode, Balance, CreditLimit, ConsltNum, ConsltName)
```

Which field or fields cause the table no longer to be in third normal form? In which normal form is the denormalized table?

4. Does your school have a formal disaster recovery plan? If it does, describe the general steps in the plan. If it does not, describe the informal steps that would be taken if a disaster occurred.

5. Use computer magazines, books, or the Internet to investigate the role cloud computing plays in disaster recovery planning. Then prepare a report that defines cloud computing and explains how it can be used in disaster recovery planning. If you use information from the Web, use reputable sites. Do not plagiarize or copy from the Web. Cite your references.

Colonial Adventure Tours Case

The management of Colonial Adventure Tours wants you to complete the following exercises. You do not use the Colonial Adventure Tours database for any of these exercises.

1. The DBA asks for your help in planning the data archive (not backup) for the following Colonial Adventure Tours database:

```
Guide (GuideNum, LastName, FirstName, Address, City,
       State, ZipCode, PhoneNum, HireDate)

Trip (TripID, TripName, StartLocation, State,
      Distance, MaxGrpSize, Type, Season)

Client (ClientNum, LastName, FirstName, Address,
        City, State, ZipCode, Phone)

Reservation (ReservationID, TripID, TripDate,
             NumPersons, TripPrice, OtherFees, ClientNum)

TripGuides (TripID, GuideNum)
```

Determine which data from the database to archive; that is, for each table, specify whether data needs to be archived. If it does, specify which data, when it should be archived, and whether it should be archived with data from another table.

2. The DBA denormalized some of the data in the Colonial Adventure Tours database to improve performance, and one of the resulting tables is the following:

```
Reservation (ReservationID, TripID, TripDate,
    NumPersons, TripPrice, OtherFees, ClientNum,
    LastName, FirstName)
```

Which field or fields cause the table no longer to be in third normal form? In which normal form is the denormalized table?

3. Interview the DBA at your school or at a local business to determine the safeguards used to segregate the production system from the test system.

4. You are the DBA for Colonial Adventure Tours. The company is considering accepting reservations from sports clubs, such as hiking clubs. The reservation would be for the entire group. What changes to the database structure would you need to make to accommodate accepting reservations from groups or organizations as well as individuals?

Sports Physical Therapy Case

For the following exercises, you do not use the Sports Physical Therapy database.

1. The DBA asks for your help in planning the data archive (not backup) for the following Sports Physical Therapy database:

   ```
   Patient (PatientNum, LastName, FirstName, Address,
            City, State, ZipCode, Balance)
   Session (SessionNum, SessionDate, PatientNum,
            LengthOfSession, Therapist ID, TherapyCode)
   Therapies (TherapyCode, Description, UnitOfTime)
   Therapist (TherapistID, LastName, FirstName, Street,
              City, State, ZipCode)
   ```

   Determine which data from the database to archive; that is, for each table, specify whether data needs to be archived. If it does, specify which data to archive, when it should be archived, and whether it should be archived with data from another table.

2. The DBA denormalized some of the data in the Sports Physical Therapy database to improve performance, and one of the resulting tables is the following:

   ```
   Patient (PatientNum, LastName, FirstName, Address,
            City, State, ZipCode, Balance, TherapistID,
            LastName, FirstName)
   ```

   Which field or fields cause the table no longer to be in third normal form? In which normal form is the denormalized table? What other problems do you see in the table?

3. Write the SQL to give appropriate permissions to the data entry operator at BITS. Explain why the DBA might limit some privileges.

 4. Interview the DBA at your school or at a local business to determine the security and access privilege procedures used to safeguard data, and then document your findings in a report.

 5. Regression testing is one technique that quality assurance individuals use to test a database system. Use computer magazines, books, or the Internet to research regression testing. Then prepare a report that defines regression testing and explain its importance in the database system testing process. If you use information from the Web, use reputable sites. Do not plagiarize or copy from the Web. Cite your references.

CHAPTER 9

DATABASE MANAGEMENT APPROACHES

INTRODUCTION

In previous chapters, you learned about relational DBMSs (RDBMSs), which dominate the database market today. In this chapter, you will examine several database management topics, most of which are applicable to relational systems.

The centralized approach to processing data, in which users access a central computer through personal computers (PCs) and workstations, dominated organizations from the late 1960s through the mid-1980s because there was no alternative approach to compete with it. The introduction of reasonably priced PCs during the 1980s, however, facilitated the placement of computers at various locations within an organization; users could access a database directly at those locations. Networks connected these computers, so users could access not only data located on their local computers but also data located anywhere along the entire network. In the next section, you will study the issues involved in distributed databases where a database is stored on more than one computer.

Organizations often off-load, or shift, data communications functions from central computers to smaller computers to improve processing speed. Similarly, organizations often use client/server systems to off-load database access functions from central computers to other computers; you will study these client/server systems. In addition, you will learn about accessing databases on the web and the importance of XML and related document standard specifications. You will examine special database systems, called data warehouses, which allow you to retrieve data rapidly. Finally, you will study object-oriented systems, which treat data as objects, and the actions that operate on the objects.

DISTRIBUTED DATABASES

BITS Corporation has multiple locations nationwide. Each location has its own consultants and client base, and each location maintains its own list of services or tasks. Instead of using a single centralized computer accessed by all the separate locations, BITS Corporation is considering installing a computer at each site. If it does so, each site would maintain its own data about its consultants, clients, tasks, and orders. Occasionally, an order at one site might involve specialized consultants from another site. In addition, a client serviced at one site might require service for its subsidiaries that are located closer to other sites. Consequently, the computer at a particular site would need to communicate with the computers at all the other sites. The computers would have to be connected in a **communications network**, or **network**, as illustrated in Figure 9-1.

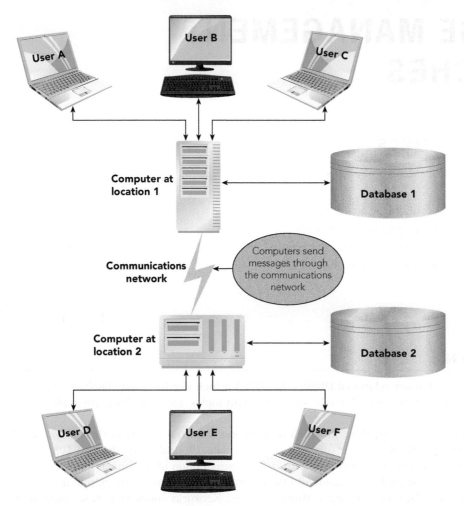

FIGURE 9-1   Communications network

BITS Corporation also would divide its existing database, and distribute to each site the data needed at that site. In doing so, BITS Corporation would be creating a distributed database. A **distributed database** is a single logical database that is physically divided among computers at several sites on a network. To make such a distributed database work properly, BITS Corporation needs to purchase a **distributed database management system (DDBMS)**, which is a DBMS capable of supporting and manipulating distributed databases.

Computers in a network communicate through **messages**; that is, one computer sends a message to another. The word *message* is used in a fairly broad way here. A computer might send a message to request data from another computer, or a computer might send a message to indicate a problem. For example, one computer might send a message to another computer to indicate that the requested data is not available. Additionally, a computer might send the requested data as a message to another computer.

Accessing data using messages over a network is substantially slower than accessing data on a disk. For example, to access data rapidly in a centralized database, you make design decisions to minimize the number of disk accesses. In a distributed database system, you must attempt to minimize the number of messages. The length of time required to send one message—an indicator of database efficiency—depends on the length of the message and the characteristics of the network. A fixed amount of time, sometimes called the **access delay**, is required for every message. The time to send a message includes the time it takes to transmit all the characters in the message. The formula for message transmission time is as follows:

```
Communication time = access delay + (data volume / transmission rate)
```

To illustrate the importance of minimizing the number of messages, suppose you have a network with an access delay of 2 seconds and a transmission rate of 750,000 bits per second. Also, suppose you send a message that consists of 10,000 records, each of which is 800 bits long, or 8 million bits. (The 10,000 records are equivalent to approximately 250 pages of single-spaced text.) In this example, you calculate the communication time as follows:

```
Communication time = 2 + ((10,000 * 800) / 750,000)
                   = 2 + (8,000,000 / 750,000)
                   = 2 + 10.67
                   = 12.67 seconds
```

If you send a message that is 100 bits long, your communication time calculation is as follows:

```
Communication time = 2 + (100 / 750,000)
                   = 2 + .0001
                   = 2.0001 seconds or, for practical purposes,
                   = 2 seconds
```

As you can see, in short messages, the access delay becomes the dominant factor. Thus, in general, it is preferable to send a small number of lengthy messages rather than a large number of short messages.

CHARACTERISTICS OF DISTRIBUTED SYSTEMS

Because a DDBMS effectively contains a local DBMS at each site, an important property of DDBMSs is that they are either homogeneous or heterogeneous. A **homogeneous DDBMS** is one that has the same local DBMS at each site. A **heterogeneous DDBMS** is one that does not; there are at least two sites at which the local DBMSs are different. Heterogeneous DDBMSs are more complex than homogeneous DDBMSs and, consequently, have more problems and are more difficult to manage.

All DDBMSs share several important characteristics. Among these characteristics are location transparency, replication transparency, and fragmentation transparency.

Location Transparency

The definition of a distributed database says nothing about the *ease* with which users access data that is stored at other sites. Systems that support distributed databases should let a user access data at a **remote site**—a site other than the one at which the user is located—just as easily as the user accesses data from the **local site**—the site at which the user is located. Response times for accessing data stored at a remote site might be much slower, but except for this difference, a user should *feel* as though the entire database is stored at the local site. **Location transparency** is the characteristic of a DDBMS that users do not need to be aware of the location of data in a distributed database.

Replication Transparency

As described in Chapter 7, replication allows users at different sites to use and update copies of a database, and then share their updates with other users. However, data replication creates update problems that can lead to data inconsistencies. If you update the record of a single item at BITS Corporation, the DDBMS must make the update at every location at which data concerning this item is stored. Not only do multiple updates make the process more time-consuming and complicated, but also, should one of the copies of data for this item be overlooked, the database would contain inconsistent data. Ideally, the DDBMS should correctly handle the updating of replicated data. The steps taken by the DDBMS to update the various copies of data should be done behind the scenes; users should be unaware of the steps. This DDBMS characteristic is called **replication transparency**.

Fragmentation Transparency

A DDBMS supports **data fragmentation** if the DDBMS can divide and manage a logical object, such as the records in a table, among the various locations under its control. The main purpose of data fragmentation is to place data at the location where the data is most often accessed.

Suppose BITS Corporation has a local DBMS at each of the three states in a tri-state area. BITS wants to fragment its Consultants table data, which is shown in Figure 9-2, by placing the consultants who live in that state in the local database.

Consultant

ConsltNum	LastName	FirstName	Street	City	State	ZipCode	Hours	Rate
65	Beard	Peter	8162 Mayor Blvd.	Littleton	IN	46327	40	$25.00
62	Benedict	Nathan	5109 North Oak Avenue	Durham	IL	60052	40	$22.50
71	Carver	Jason	Route 2 Box 71	Littleton	IN	46327	10	$20.00
61	Chorbajian	Laura	488 Flaggor Road	Key City	IL	60023	40	$25.00
63	Ciupak	Katie	6121 Rodd St.	Grant	IN	46325	15	$17.50
67	Daily	John	9183 County Road 800	Montgomery	WI	53106	35	$17.50
68	Hefner	Tim	2004 Grainville Road	Beauville	WI	53107	40	$22.50
79	Louks	Donna	246 W. 3rd Street	Green Glee	IL	60030	40	$22.50
60	Neilson	Amanda	367 Broadway	Hallis	IL	60003	30	$20.00
57	Reneau	Anita	125 Ironton Street	Key City	IL	60023	40	$22.50
69	Swentor	Brett	1215 NE 81st Terrace	Montgomery	WI	53106	40	$20.00

FIGURE 9-2 BITS Corporation Consultant table for tri-state area

Using SQL-type statements, you can define the following fragments:

```
DEFINE FRAGMENT Consultant1 AS
SELECT ConsltNum, LastName, FirstName, Street, City, State, ZipCode, Hours, Rate
FROM Consultant
WHERE State ='WI'

DEFINE FRAGMENT Consultant2 AS
SELECT ConsltNum, LastName, FirstName, Street, City, State, ZipCode, Hours, Rate
FROM Consultant
WHERE State ='IL'

DEFINE FRAGMENT Consultant3 AS
SELECT ConsltNum, LastName, FirstName, Street, City, State, ZipCode, Hours, Rate
FROM Consultant
WHERE State ='IN'
```

Each fragment definition indicates which Consultant table data to select for the fragment. Note that the entire Consultant table does not actually exist in any one place. Rather, the Consultant table exists in three pieces. You assign these pieces, or fragments, to the databases defined by the city location, as shown in Figure 9-3.

Fragment Consultant1

ConsltNum	LastName	FirstName	Street	City	State	ZipCode	Hours	Rate
67	Daily	John	9183 County Road 800	Montgomery	WI	53106	35	$17.50
68	Hefner	Tim	2004 Grainville Road	Beauville	WI	53107	40	$22.50
69	Swentor	Brett	1215 NE 81st Terrace	Montgomery	WI	53106	40	$20.00

Fragment Consultant2

ConsltNum	LastName	FirstName	Street	City	State	ZipCode	Hours	Rate
62	Benedict	Nathan	5109 North Oak Avenue	Durham	IL	60052	40	$22.50
61	Chorbajian	Laura	488 Flaggor Road	Key City	IL	60023	40	$25.00
79	Louks	Donna	246 W. 3rd Street	Green Glee	IL	60030	40	$22.50
60	Neilson	Amanda	367 Broadway	Hallis	IL	60003	30	$20.00
57	Reneau	Anita	125 Ironton Street	Key City	IL	60023	40	$22.50

Fragment Consultant3

ConsltNum	LastName	FirstName	Street	City	State	ZipCode	Hours	Rate
65	Beard	Peter	8162 Mayor Blvd.	Littleton	IN	46327	40	$25.00
71	Carver	Jason	Route 2 Box 71	Littleton	IN	46327	10	$20.00
63	Ciupak	Katie	6121 Rodd St.	Grant	IN	46325	15	$17.50

FIGURE 9-3 Fragmentation of tri-state Consultant table data by state

You assign Fragment Consultant1 to the database in Wisconsin, Fragment Consultant2 to the database in Illinois, and Fragment Consultant3 to the database in Indiana. The effect of these assignments is that data about each consultant is stored in the database at the location where the consultant lives. You can access the complete Consultant table by taking the union of the three fragments.

In the larger scheme of things, users should not be aware of the fragmentation—they should feel as if they are using a single central database. When users are unaware of fragmentation, the DDBMS has **fragmentation transparency**.

ADVANTAGES OF DISTRIBUTED DATABASES

When compared with a single centralized database, distributed databases offer the following advantages:

- *Local control of data.* Because each location retains its own data, a location can exercise greater control over that data. With a single centralized database, on the other hand, the central site that maintains the database is usually unaware of all the local issues at the various sites served by the database.
- *Increasing database capacity.* In a properly designed and installed distributed database, the process of increasing system capacity is often simpler than in a centralized database. If the size of the storage medium at a single site becomes inadequate for its database, you need to increase the capacity of the storage medium only at that site. Furthermore, you can increase the capacity of the entire database simply by adding a new site.
- *System availability.* When a centralized database becomes unavailable for any reason, *no* users can continue processing. In contrast, if one of the local databases in a distributed database becomes unavailable, only users who need data in that particular database are affected; other users can continue processing in a normal fashion. In addition, if the data has been replicated (another copy of it exists in other local databases), potentially all users can continue processing. However, processing for users at the site of the unavailable database will be much less efficient because data that was formerly obtained locally must now be obtained through communication with a remote site.
- *Improved performance.* When data is available locally, you eliminate network communication delays and can retrieve data faster than with a remote centralized database.

287

DISADVANTAGES OF DISTRIBUTED DATABASES

Distributed databases have the following disadvantages:

- *Update of replicated data.* Replicating data can improve processing speed and ensure that the overall system remains available even when the database at one site is unavailable. However, replication can cause update problems, most obviously in terms of the extra time needed to update all the copies. Instead of updating a single copy of the data, the DBMS must update several copies. Because most of these copies are at sites other than the site initiating the update, each update transaction requires extra time to update each copy and extra time to communicate all the update messages over the network.

    Replicated data causes another, slightly more serious problem. Assume an update transaction must update data that is replicated at five sites and that the fifth site is currently unavailable. If all updates must be made or none at all, the update transaction fails. Because the data at a single site is unavailable for update, that data is unavailable for update at *all* sites. This situation certainly contradicts the earlier advantage of increased system availability. On the other hand, if you do not require that all updates be made, the data will be inconsistent.

    Often a DDBMS uses a compromise strategy. The DDBMS designates one copy of the data to be the **primary copy**. As long as the primary copy is updated, the DDBMS considers the update to be complete. The primary site and the DDBMS must ensure that all the other copies are in sync. The primary site sends update transactions to the other sites and notes whether any sites are currently unavailable. If a site is unavailable, the primary site must try to send the update again at some later time and continue trying until it succeeds. This strategy overcomes the basic problem, but it obviously uses more time. Further, if the primary site is unavailable, the problem remains unresolved.

- *More complex query processing.* Processing queries is more complex in a distributed database. The complexity occurs because of the difference in the time it takes to send messages between sites and the time it takes to access a disk. As discussed earlier, minimizing message traffic is extremely important in a distributed database environment. To illustrate the complexity involved with query processing, consider the following query for BITS Corporation: List all tasks in the HAM category with a price that is more than $100.00. For this query, assume (1) the Tasks table contains 1,000 rows and is stored at a remote site; (2) each record in the Tasks table is 500 bits long; (3) there is no special structure, such as an index, that would be helpful in processing this query faster; and (4) only 10 of the 1,000 rows in the Tasks table satisfy the conditions. How would you process this query?

    One query strategy involves retrieving each row from the remote site and examining the category and price to determine whether the row should be included in the result. For each row, this solution requires two messages. The first is a message from the local site to the remote site requesting a row. It is followed by the second message, which is from the remote site to the local site, containing the data or, ultimately, an indication that there is no more data because you have retrieved every row in the table. Thus, in addition to the database accesses, this strategy requires 2,000 messages. Once again, suppose you have a network with an access delay of 2 seconds and a transmission rate of 750,000 bits per second. Based on the calculations for communication time earlier in this chapter, each message requires approximately 2 seconds. You calculate the communication time for this query strategy as follows:

$$\text{Communication time} = 2 * 2,000$$
$$= 4,000 \text{ seconds, or } 66.7 \text{ minutes}$$

A second query strategy involves sending a single message from the local site to the remote site, requesting the complete answer to the query. The remote site examines each row in the table and finds the 10 rows that satisfy the query. The remote site then sends a single message back to the local site, containing all 10 rows in the answer. You calculate the communication time for this query strategy as follows:

$$\text{Communication time} = 2 + (2 + ((10 * 500) / 750,000))$$
$$= 2 + (2 + (5000 / 750,000))$$
$$= 2 + (2 + 0.006)$$
$$= 4.006 \text{ seconds}$$

Even if the second message is lengthy, especially where many rows satisfied the conditions, this second query strategy is a vast improvement over the first strategy. A small number of lengthy messages is preferable to a large number of short messages.

Systems that are record-at-a-time-oriented can create severe performance problems in distributed systems. If the only choice is to transmit every record from one site to another site as a message and then examine it at the other site, the communication time required can become unacceptably high. DDBMSs that permit a request for a set of records, as opposed to an individual record, outperform record-at-a-time systems.

- *More complex treatment of concurrent update.* Concurrent update in a distributed database is treated basically the same way it is treated in nondistributed databases. A user transaction acquires locks, and the locking is two-phase. (Locks are acquired in a growing phase, during which time no locks are released and the DDBMS applies the updates. All locks are released during the shrinking phase.) The DDBMS detects and breaks deadlocks, and then the DDBMS rolls back interrupted transactions. The primary distinction lies not in the kinds of activities that take place but in the additional level of complexity created by the very nature of a distributed database.

If all the records to be updated by a particular transaction occur at one site, the problem is essentially the same as in a nondistributed database. However, the records in a distributed database might be stored at many different sites. Furthermore, if the data is replicated, each occurrence might be stored at several sites, each requiring the same update to be performed. Assuming each record occurrence has replicas at three different sites, an update that would affect 5 record occurrences in a nondistributed system might affect 20 different record occurrences in a distributed system (each record occurrence together with its three replica occurrences).

Having more record occurrences to update is only part of the problem. Assuming each site keeps its own locks, the DDBMS must send many messages for each record to be updated: a request for a lock, a message indicating that the record is already locked by another user or that the lock has been granted, a message directing that the update be performed, an acknowledgment of the update, and, finally, a message indicating that the record is to be unlocked. Because all those messages must be sent for each record and its occurrences, the total time for an update can be substantially longer in a distributed database.

A partial solution to minimize the number of messages involves the use of the primary copy mentioned earlier. Recall that one of the replicas of a given record occurrence is designated as the primary copy. Locking the primary copy, rather than all copies, is sufficient and reduces the number of messages required to lock and unlock records. The number of messages might still be large, however, and the unavailability of the primary copy can cause an entire transaction to fail. Thus, even this partial solution presents problems.

Just as in a nondistributed database, deadlock is a possibility in a distributed database. In a distributed database, however, deadlock is more complicated because two types of deadlock— local deadlock and global deadlock—are possible. **Local deadlock** is deadlock that occurs at a single site in a distributed database. If each of two transactions is waiting for a record held by the other at the same site, the local DBMS can detect and resolve the deadlock with a minimum number of messages needed to communicate the situation to the other DBMSs in the distributed system.

On the other hand, **global deadlock** involves one transaction that requires a record held by a second transaction at one site, while the second transaction requires a record held by the first transaction at a different site. In this case, neither site has information individually to allow this deadlock to be detected resulting in a global deadlock. It can be detected and resolved only by sending a large number of messages between the DBMSs at the two sites.

The various factors involved in supporting concurrent update greatly add to the complexity and the communications time in a distributed database.

- *More complex recovery measures.* Although the basic recovery process for a distributed database is the same as the one described in Chapter 7, there is an additional potential problem. To make sure that the database remains consistent, each database update should be made permanent or aborted and undone, in which case *none* of its changes will be made. In a distributed database, with an individual transaction updating several local databases, it is possible—because of problems affecting individual sites—for local DBMSs to commit the updates at some sites and undo the updates at other sites, thereby creating an inconsistent state in the distributed database. The DDBMS *must not* allow this inconsistency to occur.

  A DDBMS usually prevents this potential inconsistency through the use of **two-phase commit**. The basic idea of two-phase commit is that one site, often the site initiating the update, acts as **coordinator**. In the first phase, the coordinator sends messages to all other sites requesting that they prepare to update the database; in other words, each site acquires all necessary locks. The sites do not update at this point, however, but they do send messages to the coordinator stating that they are ready to update. If for any reason any site cannot secure the necessary locks or if any site must abort its updates, the site sends a message to the coordinator that all sites must abort the transaction. The coordinator waits for replies from all sites involved before determining whether to commit the update. If all replies are positive, the coordinator sends a message to each site to commit the update. At this point, each site *must* proceed with the commit process. If any reply is negative, the coordinator sends a message to each site to abort the update, and each site *must* follow this instruction. In this way, the DDBMS guarantees consistency.

  While a process similar to two-phase commit is essential to the consistency of the database, two problems are associated with it. For one thing, many messages are sent during the process. For another, during the second phase, each site must follow the instructions from the coordinator; otherwise, the process will not accomplish its intended result. This process means that the sites are not as independent as you would like them to be.

- *More difficult management of the data dictionary.* A distributed database introduces further complexity to the management of the data dictionary or catalog. Where should the data dictionary entries be stored? The three possibilities are as follows: choose one site and store the complete data dictionary at that site and that site alone; store a complete copy of the data dictionary at each site; and distribute the data dictionary entries, possibly with replication, among the various sites.

  Although storing the complete data dictionary at a single site is a relatively simple approach to administer, retrieving information in the data dictionary from any other site is more time-consuming because of the communication involved. Storing a complete copy of the data dictionary at every site solves the retrieval problem because a local DBMS can handle any retrieval locally. Because this second approach involves total replication (every data dictionary occurrence is replicated at every site), updates to the data dictionary are more time-consuming. If the data dictionary is updated with any frequency, the extra time needed to update all copies of the data dictionary might be unacceptable. Thus, you usually implement an intermediate strategy.

  One intermediate strategy is to partition the data by storing data dictionary entries at the site at which the data they describe are located. Interestingly, this approach also suffers from a problem. If a user queries the data dictionary to access an entry not stored at the user's site, the system has no way of knowing the entry's location. Satisfying this user's query might involve sending a message to every other site, which involves a considerable amount of network and DDBMS overhead.

- *More complex database design.* A distributed database adds another level of complexity to database design. Distributing data does not affect the information-level design. During the physical-level design in a nondistributed database, disk activity—both the number of disk accesses and the volumes of data to be transported—is one of the principal concerns. Although disk activity is also a factor in a distributed database, communication activity becomes another concern during the physical-level design. Because transmitting data from one site to another is much slower than transferring data to and from disk, in many situations, communication activity is the most important physical-level design factor. In addition, you must consider possible fragmentation and replication during the physical-level design.

- *More complicated security and backup requirements.* With a single central database, you need to secure the central physical site, the central database, and the network connecting users to the database at the central site. The security requirements for a distributed database are more demanding, requiring you to secure every physical site and every database, in addition to securing the network. Backing up a distributed database is also more complicated and is best initiated and controlled from a single site.

RULES FOR DISTRIBUTED DATABASES

C. J. Date (Date, C. J. "Twelve Rules for a Distributed Database." *ComputerWorld* 21.23, June 8, 1987) formulated 12 rules that distributed databases should follow. The basic goal is that a distributed database should feel like a nondistributed database to users; that is, users should not be aware that the database is distributed. The 12 rules serve as a benchmark against which you can measure DDBMSs. The 12 rules are as follows:

1. *Local autonomy.* No site should depend on another site to perform its database functions.
2. *No reliance on a central site.* The DDBMS should not rely on a single central site to control specific types of operations. These operations include data dictionary management, query processing, update management, database recovery, and concurrent update.
3. *Continuous operation.* Performing functions such as adding sites, changing versions of DBMSs, creating backups, and modifying hardware should not require planned shutdowns of the entire distributed database.
4. *Location transparency.* Users should not be concerned with the location of any specific data in the database. Users should feel as if the entire database is stored at their location.
5. *Fragmentation transparency.* Users should not be aware of any data fragmentation that has occurred in the database. Users should feel as if they are using a single central database.
6. *Replication transparency.* Users should not be aware of any data replication. The DDBMS should perform all the work required to keep the replicas consistent; users should be unaware of the data synchronization work carried out by the DDBMS.
7. *Distributed query processing.* You already learned about the complexities of query processing in a distributed database. The DDBMS must process queries as rapidly as possible.
8. *Distributed transaction management.* You already learned about the complexities of update management in a distributed database and the need for the two-phase commit strategy. The DDBMS must effectively manage transaction updates at multiple sites.
9. *Hardware independence.* Organizations usually have many different types of hardware, and a DDBMS must be able to run on this hardware. Without this capability, users are restricted to accessing data stored only on similar computers, disks, and so on.
10. *Operating system independence.* Even if an organization uses similar hardware, different operating systems might be used within the organization. For the same reason that it is desirable for a DDBMS to support different types of hardware, a DDBMS must be able to run on different operating systems.
11. *Network independence.* Because different sites within an organization might use different communications networks, a DDBMS must run on different types of networks and not be restricted to a single type of network.
12. *DBMS independence.* Another way of stating this requirement is that a DDBMS should be heterogeneous; that is, a DDBMS must support different local DBMSs. Supporting heterogeneous DBMSs is a difficult task. In practice, each local DBMS must "speak" a common language; this common language most likely is SQL.

CLIENT/SERVER SYSTEMS

Networks often include a file server, as shown in Figure 9-4. The **file server** stores the files required by the users on the network. When users need data from a file or a group of files, they send requests to the file server. The file server then sends the requested file or files to the user's computer; that is, the file server sends entire files, not just the data needed by users. Although this approach works to supply data to users, sending entire files generates a high level of communication activity on the network. Adding users to the network and larger files to the file server adds higher levels of communication activity and eventually causes longer delays in supplying data to users.

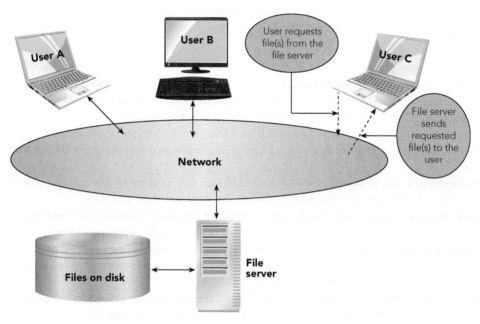

FIGURE 9-4 File server architecture

An alternative architecture, which is called **client/server**, is illustrated in Figure 9-5. In client/server terminology, the **server** is a computer providing data to the **clients**, which are the computers, such as PC-based computers, tablets, or other mobile devices, that are connected to a network and that people use to access data stored on the server. A server is also called a **back-end processor** or a **back-end machine**, and a client is also called a **front-end processor** or a **front-end machine**.

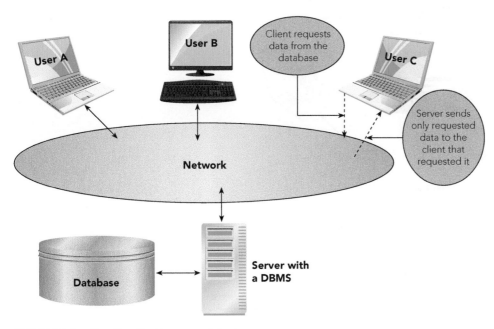

Client computers connected to a network

FIGURE 9-5 Two-tier client/server architecture

With this alternative architecture, a DBMS runs on the server. A client sends a request to the server not for entire *files*, but for specific *data*. The DBMS on the server processes the request, extracts the requested data, and then sends only the requested data back to the client. Compared to a file server architecture, a client/server architecture reduces communication activity on a network, which reduces delays in supplying data to users. Because the clients and the server perform different functions and can run different operating systems, this arrangement of client/server architecture is called a **two-tier architecture**.

In a two-tier architecture, the server performs database functions and the clients perform the presentation functions (or user interface functions), such as determining which form to display on the screen and how to format the form's data. Which of the two tiers, server or clients, performs the business functions, such as the calculations BITS Corporation uses to determine taxes and order totals? When the clients perform the business functions—each client is called a **fat client**. In this arrangement, you have a client maintenance problem. Whenever programmers make changes to the business functions, they must make sure that they place the updated business functions on every client. For organizations with thousands of clients, updating the business functions for all clients is an almost impossible task.

To eliminate the fat client maintenance problem, you can place the business functions on the server. Because clients perform only the presentation functions in this arrangement, each client is called a **thin client**. Although you have now eliminated the fat client maintenance problem by moving the business functions to the server, you have created a scalability problem. **Scalability** is the ability of a computer system to continue to function well as utilization of the system increases. Because the server performs both database and business functions, increasing the number of clients eventually causes a bottleneck on the server and degrades the system's responsiveness to clients. To improve a system's scalability, some organizations use a three-tier client/server architecture, as shown in Figure 9-6 on the next page. In a **three-tier architecture**, the clients perform the presentation functions, a **database server** performs the database functions, and separate computers (called **application servers**) perform the business functions and serve as an interface between clients and the database server. A three-tier architecture distributes the processing functions so that you eliminate the fat client maintenance problem and maximize the scalability of the system. As the number of users increases, you can upgrade the application and database servers by adding faster processors, disks, and other hardware without changing any client computers. A three-tier architecture is sometimes referred to as an **n-tier architecture** because additional application servers can be added for scalability without affecting the design for the client or the database server.

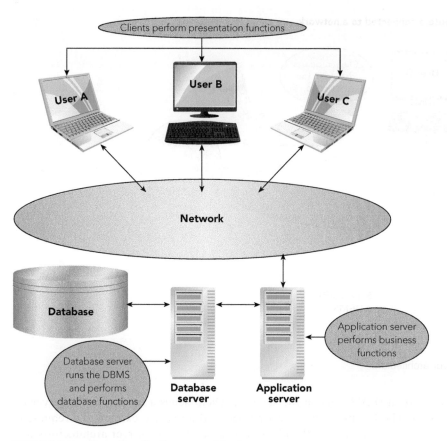

FIGURE 9-6 Three-tier client/server architecture

NOTE: A client/server system stores the database on a single server, and the DBMS resides and processes on that server. Only with a DDBMS is the database itself distributed to multiple computers. However, you can combine a DDBMS with a client/server system to distribute both data and processing functions across multiple computers.

Advantages of Client/Server Systems

Compared to file server systems, a client/server system has the following advantages:

- *Lower network traffic.* A client/server system transmits only the necessary data, rather than entire files, across the network.
- *Improved processing distribution.* A client/server system lets you distribute processing functions among multiple computers.
- *Thinner clients.* Because the application and database servers handle most of the processing in a client/server system, clients do not need to be as powerful or as expensive as they would in a file/server environment.
- *Greater processing transparency.* As far as a user is concerned, all processing occurs on the client just as it does on a stand-alone system. Users do not need to learn any special commands or techniques to work in a client/server environment.
- *Increased network, hardware, and software transparency.* Because client/server systems use SQL as a common language, it is easier for users to access data from a variety of sources. A single operation could access data from different networks, different computers, and different operating systems.
- *Improved security.* Client/server systems can provide a greater level of security than file server systems. In addition to the DBMS security features located on the database server, you can place additional security features on the application servers and on the network.
- *Decreased costs.* Client/server systems have proven to be powerful enough that organizations have replaced enterprise applications and mainframe databases with PC applications and databases managed by client/server systems. The replacement has resulted in a considerable cost savings.

- *Increased scalability.* A three-tier client/server system is more scalable than file-server and two-tier architectures. If an application server or database server becomes a bottleneck, you can upgrade the appropriate server or add additional processors to share the processing load.

WEB ACCESS TO DATABASES

The **Internet**, which is a worldwide collection of millions of interconnected computers and computer networks that share resources, is used daily by most people and is an essential portal for all organizations. In particular, people and organizations use the **World Wide Web** (or the **web**), which is a vast collection of digital documents available on the Internet. Each digital document on the web is called a **webpage**, each computer on which an individual or organization stores webpages for access on the Internet is called a **web server**, and each computer requesting a webpage from a web server is called a **web client**.

Each webpage is assigned an Internet address called a **Uniform Resource Locator (URL)**; the URL identifies where the webpage is stored—both the location of the web server and the name and location of the webpage on that server. For example, http://www.irs.gov/individuals/index.html is a URL that identifies the web server (www.irs.gov), the location path (*individuals*) on the web server, and the webpage name (*index.html*). The beginning of the URL (*http*) specifies **Hypertext Transfer Protocol (HTTP)**, which is the data communication method used by web clients and web servers to exchange data on the Internet.

You use a computer program called a **web browser** to retrieve a webpage from a web client; popular web browsers include Google Chrome, Microsoft Edge, Mozilla Firefox, Safari, and Opera. As shown in Figure 9-7, a user enters the webpage's URL in a web browser on a web client and then sends the request for the webpage over the Internet using HTTP and **Transmission Control Protocol/Internet Protocol (TCP/IP)**, which is the standard protocol for all communication on the Internet. The request for the webpage arrives at the web server designated in the transmitted URL, and the web server locates the requested webpage on a disk connected to the web server and retrieves the webpage. The web server then responds to the web client by transmitting the webpage over the Internet using HTTP and TCP/IP, and the web browser displays the webpage on the user's screen. Note that web clients on an intranet bypass the Internet and directly access internal company webpages through the organization's web server.

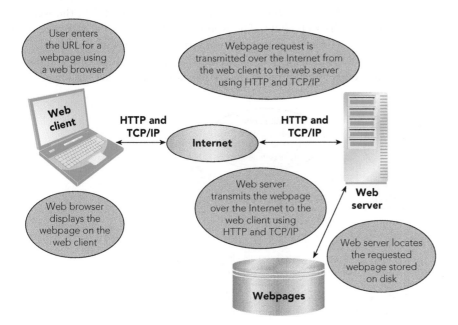

FIGURE 9-7   Retrieving a webpage on the Internet

Each webpage usually is created using a language called **Hypertext Markup Language (HTML)**. You can use a program such as ColdFusion or Adobe Dreamweaver to create the HTML code for webpages without needing to learn HTML. Many programs, including Microsoft Access, have built-in tools that convert and export objects such as tables and queries to HTML documents.

Webpages that display the same content for all web clients are called **static webpages**. At the heart of most web processing today are activities—such as paying bills, ordering merchandise, buying and selling stocks, and bidding in online auctions—for which the webpages need to change depending on the web client's input and responses; these business activities are called **electronic commerce (e-commerce)**. For e-commerce activities, web servers cannot use static webpages. Instead, web servers use **dynamic webpages**, which are pages whose content changes in response to the different inputs and choices made using web clients. A dynamic webpage includes, or triggers, instructions to tell the web server how to process the page (**server-side extensions** or **server-side scripts**) and possibly other instructions for the web browser to process (**client-side extensions** or **client-side scripts**). Client-side extensions can be embedded in HTML documents or contained in separate files that are referenced within the HTML documents, while server-side extensions are usually separately executed programs. Client-side extensions can change the user interface in response to user input actions; JavaScript and VBScript are examples of client-side extension languages. Because of the processing complexities of server-side extensions and the difficulty of creating them, most server-side extensions are created using programming development frameworks, such as PHP, ASP.NET, or ColdFusion.

Web servers must have a mechanism for communicating with server-side extensions; Common Gateway Interface (CGI) and Application Program Interface (API) are standard interfaces that provide this capability. In addition, server-side extensions usually include interaction with databases to send web clients requested data from databases and to update databases with data supplied by web clients. Several standard software interfaces have been developed to interact with DBMSs; Open Database Connectivity (ODBC), Java Database Connectivity (JDBC), and ADO.NET are examples of these standard interfaces. These standard software interfaces include many DBMS-specific drivers so that a given web server can work with many different DBMSs.

One common web-based architecture for dealing with dynamic webpages, shown in Figure 9-8, uses a three-tier architecture, with the web clients, a web server, and a database server as the three tiers. A user on a web client sends a request for a webpage to the web server over the Internet using TCP/IP and HTTP. The web server receives the request, retrieves the webpage, and then runs server-side extensions associated with the webpage using API. These extensions, among other actions, include instructions for interacting with the database, usually in the form of SQL commands, using API and ODBC in this example. The database server, which contains the DBMS, deals directly with the database and returns the required data back through the ODBC/API interfaces to the web server. The web server customizes the HTML document based on the server-side extensions and the data from the database and the web client; then, using TCP/IP and HTTP, the web server transmits the webpage over the Internet to the web client. The web browser displays the webpage on the user's screen, executing any client-side extensions as appropriate. Interaction between the web client, the web server, and the database server continues in a similar fashion as the user at the web client fills in data or chooses options in the delivered webpage and sends follow-up webpage requests to the web server.

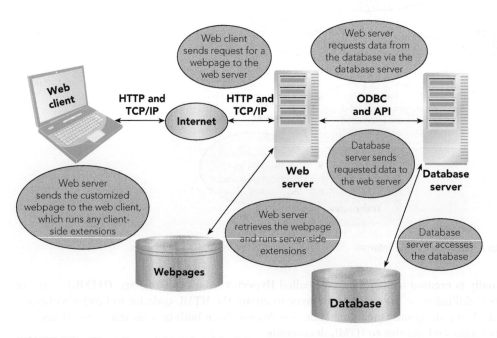

FIGURE 9-8 Three-tier web-based architecture

A further complication for database processing over the web is that HTTP is inherently a **stateless** protocol, which means that, once the web server responds to a web client request for a webpage by delivering the page, the connection between the two is closed and the web server retains no information about the request or the web client. The stateless nature of HTTP allows for maximum throughput of webpages through the Internet. However, the stateless nature of webpages is at odds with most e-commerce processing. Consider placing an order over the Internet. If you have ever done so, you know that you might view and interact with dozens of webpages to select the products you want to buy and to place them in a shopping cart. You then view the shopping cart webpage, making adjustments to the products you are ordering; view another webpage to confirm the order; enter your name and address information in another webpage; enter your credit card information in a different webpage; and finally go through additional webpages to confirm and place the final order. In this scenario, the vendor's web server somehow must remember the key data from many different webpages, even though each delivered webpage is stateless. Organizations use several techniques to remember key data supplied by a web client. Among the client-side techniques are **cookies** (small files written on a web client's hard drive by a web server) and hidden form fields, while server-side solutions usually include storing session information in a database or using other forms of session management, where a **session** is the duration of a web client's connection to a web server.

Organizations benefit in many ways from using the web for database processing. They can transfer data to and from their databases to suppliers, clients, and others outside the company; this provides current information in a timely way to those needing the information. As another example, a company can allow clients to place orders that directly update the organization's database and trigger the processing required to fulfill the orders. Additionally, web clients can access an organization's webpages at their convenience 24/7. The tradeoffs for an organization using the web for database processing include the increased complexities and cost of maintaining an always-available web presence and reliance on the Internet with potential data communication contention difficulties and increased security exposure.

X M L

Many different software languages, software products, computer hardware devices, and standards exist to make e-commerce possible. As e-commerce evolves, these web components are constantly changing and improving, with new components appearing frequently. Since 1994, the international **World Wide Web Consortium (W3C)** has developed web standards, specifications, guidelines, and recommendations, including HTML standards. HTML is a text-based **markup language**, which means that it contains pieces of code or **tags** that describe the content and appearance of the webpage; however, HTML does not describe the structure and meaning of the data it contains. That is, within the HTML, you cannot identify which data elements are in the webpage, what each data element means, and how those data elements are related. This limitation is not a problem for webpages used in the traditional way, in which a user requests and works with webpages using a web browser. However, e-commerce between organizations, called **business to business (B2B)**, is an important part of communication across the Internet. Organizations send data from their databases to the databases of other organizations, and those organizations that send data need to receive data in return. In these situations, the structure and meaning of the transmitted data are of utmost importance because organizations structure common data, such as product data and cost data, in their databases in different ways. Somehow the document containing the data being transmitted between organizations must convey the structure and meaning of the data it contains. To address the inability of HTML to specify the structure and meaning of data and to address the need for the exchange of data between organizations, XML was developed and became a W3C recommendation in 1998.

Extensible Markup Language (XML) is a **metalanguage** or a language used to define another language. XML is designed for the exchange of data on the web. Using XML, you can create text documents that follow simple, specific rules for their content, and you can define new tags that define the data in the document and the structure of the data so that programs running on any platform can interpret and process the document.

Figure 9-9 on the next page shows the key portions of a file that was created by using Access to export the original Consultant table in the BITS database as an XML document.

298

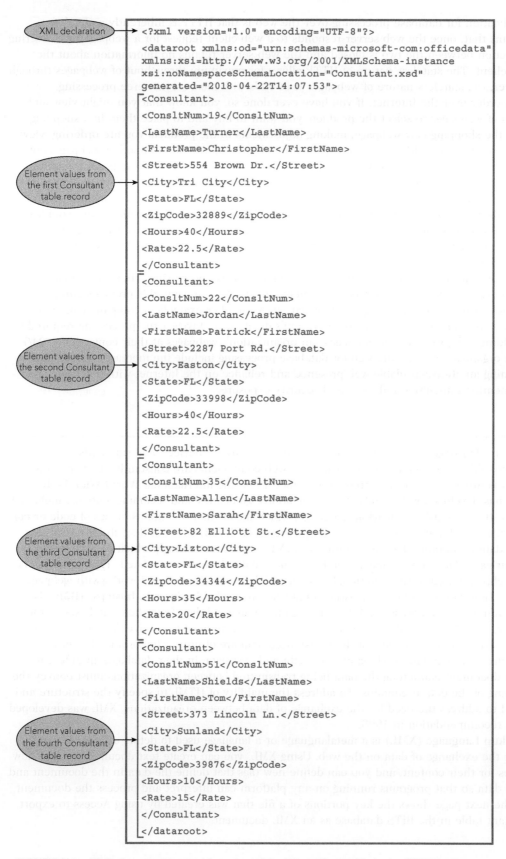

```xml
<?xml version="1.0" encoding="UTF-8"?>
<dataroot xmlns:od="urn:schemas-microsoft-com:officedata"
xmlns:xsi=http://www.w3.org/2001/XMLSchema-instance
xsi:noNamespaceSchemaLocation="Consultant.xsd"
generated="2018-04-22T14:07:53">
<Consultant>
<ConsltNum>19</ConsltNum>
<LastName>Turner</LastName>
<FirstName>Christopher</FirstName>
<Street>554 Brown Dr.</Street>
<City>Tri City</City>
<State>FL</State>
<ZipCode>32889</ZipCode>
<Hours>40</Hours>
<Rate>22.5</Rate>
</Consultant>
<Consultant>
<ConsltNum>22</ConsltNum>
<LastName>Jordan</LastName>
<FirstName>Patrick</FirstName>
<Street>2287 Port Rd.</Street>
<City>Easton</City>
<State>FL</State>
<ZipCode>33998</ZipCode>
<Hours>40</Hours>
<Rate>22.5</Rate>
</Consultant>
<Consultant>
<ConsltNum>35</ConsltNum>
<LastName>Allen</LastName>
<FirstName>Sarah</FirstName>
<Street>82 Elliott St.</Street>
<City>Lizton</City>
<State>FL</State>
<ZipCode>34344</ZipCode>
<Hours>35</Hours>
<Rate>20</Rate>
</Consultant>
<Consultant>
<ConsltNum>51</ConsltNum>
<LastName>Shields</LastName>
<FirstName>Tom</FirstName>
<Street>373 Lincoln Ln.</Street>
<City>Sunland</City>
<State>FL</State>
<ZipCode>39876</ZipCode>
<Hours>10</Hours>
<Rate>15</Rate>
</Consultant>
</dataroot>
```

Labels pointing to the XML document:
- XML declaration
- Element values from the first Consultant table record
- Element values from the second Consultant table record
- Element values from the third Consultant table record
- Element values from the fourth Consultant table record

FIGURE 9-9 XML document created from the original Consultant table in the BITS database

An XML document should begin with an **XML declaration** that specifies to an XML processor which version of XML to use, as shown in the first line of Figure 9-9. Following the XML declaration, the <dataroot> tag identifies a standard element in Office 2016 exported XML documents. The dataroot element serves as a container for all the other elements defined in the XML document. Its matching </dataroot> tag at the end of the document identifies the end of the scope of the dataroot element. The dataroot element also can specify the location of a schema file that describes the XML elements and the date that the file was generated.

In between the <dataroot> and </dataroot> tags in Figure 9-9, there are four groups of statements, one group for each record from the Consultant table. Each statement group starts with a <Consultant> tag and ends with a matching closing </Consultant> tag; those tags identify the beginning and end of one Consultant record. User-defined tag pairs (such as <Rate> and </Rate>) enclose field values, which are called element values (such as 22.5, 22.5, 20, and 15) from the Consultant records. Each tag must have a matching closing tag in an XML document.

Webpages continue to be written in HTML, but the last W3C recommendation was for HTML 5.1 in 2016. Since then, W3C has focused on recommendations for **Extensible Hypertext Markup Language (XHTML)**, which is a markup language based on XML and, thus, is a stricter version of HTML. Web browsers continue to support HTML and all major browsers support the XHTML specification.

An XML document contains element tags and element values. How does an XML processor understand the meaning of the tags and the characteristics and structure of the data in an XML document? You use either a document type definition or an XML schema to provide those important facts about the data. A **document type definition (DTD)** specifies the elements (tags), the attributes (characteristics associated with each tag), and the element relationships for an XML document. The DTD can be a separate file with a .dtd extension, or you can include it at the beginning of an XML document. An **XML schema** is a newer form of DTD that more closely matches database features and terminology; you can embed it at the beginning of an XML document or place it in a separate file with an .xsd extension. Figure 9-10 shows the portion of an XML schema specifying the characteristics of the Rate field from the Consultant table. Notice how closely the attributes for the Rate element in the XML schema match the properties for the Rate field in the Consultant table.

```
<xsd:element name="Rate" minOccurs="0" jetType="double"
        sqlSType="float" type="xsd:double">
<xsd:annotation>
<xsd:appinfo>
<fieldProperty name="ColumnWidth" type="3" value="840"/>
<fieldProperty name="ColumnOrder" type="3" value="0"/>
<fieldProperty name="ColumnHidden" type="1" value="0"/>
<fieldProperty name="DecimalPlaces" type="2" value="255"/>
<fieldProperty name="Required" type="1" value="0"/>
<fieldProperty name="DisplayControl" type="3" value="109"/>
<fieldProperty name="TextAlign" type="2" value="0"/>
<fieldProperty name="AggregateType" type="4" value="-1"/>
</xsd:appinfo>
</xsd:annotation>
</xsd:element>
```

FIGURE 9-10   XML schema for the Rate element from the Consultant table

XML documents contain data; DTDs and XML schemas define the structure, characteristics, and relationships of the data. In addition, XHTML documents focus on data, not on presentation details. The presentation aspects of an XML or XHTML document can be described by a stylesheet. The **Extensible**

Stylesheet Language (XSL) is a standard W3C language for creating stylesheets for XML documents; a **stylesheet** is a document that specifies how to process the data contained in another document and present the data in a web browser, in a printed report, on a mobile device, in a sound device, or in other presentation media. A related W3C standard language is **XSL Transformations (XSLT)**, which defines the rules to process an XML document and change it into another document, such as an HTML or XHTML document.

As more and more data is being stored, exchanged, and presented using XML, the W3C has developed **XQuery**, which is a language for querying web-based documents and similarly structured data repositories.

One example of the inroads made by XML is Microsoft's Office suite. Starting with the Office 2007 suite, Microsoft switched from its native file formats to a new file format that it calls Office Open XML for the Excel, PowerPoint, and Word programs. The **Office Open XML** file format is a compressed version of XML, but you can save Office files in a more traditional XML-based format.

Figure 9-11 illustrates the interaction between XML and the languages that are closely related to XML.

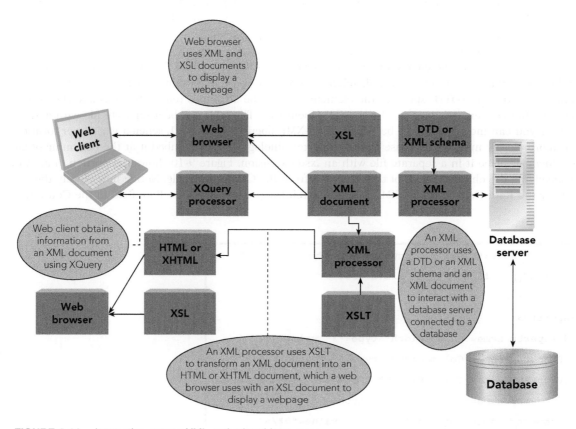

FIGURE 9-11   Interaction among XML and related languages

DATA WAREHOUSES

Among the objectives that organizations have when they use RDBMSs are data integrity, high performance, and ample availability. The leading RDBMSs are able to satisfy these requirements. Typically, when users interact with an RDBMS, they use transactions, such as adding a new order and changing a client's consultant. Thus, these types of systems are called **online transaction processing (OLTP)** systems.

For each transaction, OLTP typically deals with a few rows from the tables in a database in a highly structured, repetitive, and predetermined way. If you need to know the status of specific clients, items, and orders or if you need to update data for specific clients, items, and orders, an RDBMS and OLTP are the ideal tools to use.

When you need to analyze data from a database, however, an RDBMS and OLTP often suffer from severe performance problems. For example, finding total sales by site and by month requires the joining of all the rows in many tables; such processing takes a considerable number of database accesses and considerable time to accomplish. Consequently, many organizations continue to use RDBMSs and OLTP for their normal day-to-day processing or for *operational purposes*, but the organizations have turned to data warehouses for the *analysis* of their data. The following definition for a data warehouse is credited to W. H. Inmon (Inmon, W. H. *Building the Data Warehouse*. QED, 1990), who originally coined the phrase.

DEFINITION: A **data warehouse** is a subject-oriented, integrated, time-variant, nonvolatile collection of data in support of management's decision-making process.

Subject-oriented means that data is organized by entity rather than by the application that uses the data. For example, Figure 9-12 shows the databases for typical operational applications such as inventory, order entry, production, and accounts payable. When the data from these operational databases is loaded into a data warehouse, it is transformed into subjects such as product, customer, vendor, and financial. Data about products appears once in the warehouse even though it might appear in many files and databases in the operational environment.

Operational applications

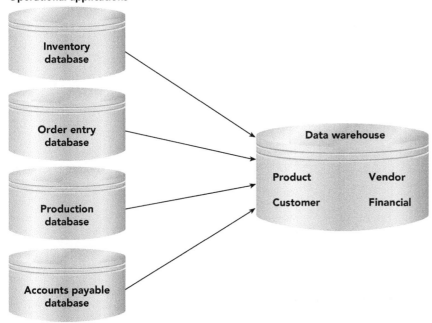

FIGURE 9-12   Data warehouse architecture

NOTE: For the operational applications shown in Figure 9-12, large organizations use a variety of DBMSs and file-processing systems that have been developed over a period of many years.

Integrated means that data is stored in one place in the data warehouse even though the data originates from everywhere in the organization and from a variety of external sources. The data can come from recently developed applications or from legacy systems developed many years ago.

Time-variant means that data in a data warehouse represents snapshots of data at various points in time in the past, such as at the end of each month. This is unlike an operational application, which has data that is accurate as of the moment. Data warehouses also retain historical data for long periods of time; that data is summarized to specific time periods, such as daily, weekly, monthly, and annually.

Nonvolatile means that data is read-only. Data is loaded into a data warehouse periodically, but users cannot update a data warehouse directly.

In summary, a data warehouse contains read-only snapshots of highly consolidated and summarized data from multiple internal and external sources that are refreshed periodically, usually on a daily or weekly basis. Companies use data warehouses in support of their decision-making processing, which typically consists of unstructured and nonrepetitive requests for exactly the type of information contained in a data warehouse.

Data Warehouse Structure and Access

A typical data warehouse structure is shown in Figure 9-13. The central ServiceCalls table is called a **fact table**. A **fact table** consists of rows that contain consolidated and summarized data. The fact table contains a multipart primary key, each part of which is a foreign key to the surrounding dimension tables. Each **dimension table** contains a single-part primary key that serves as an index for the fact table and that contains other fields associated with the primary key value. The overall structure shown in Figure 9-13 is called a **star schema** because of its conceptual shape.

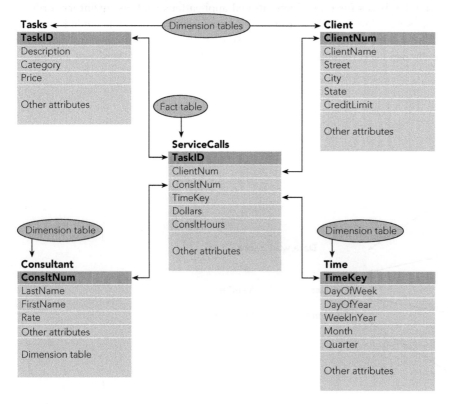

FIGURE 9-13 A star schema with four dimension tables and a central fact table

Access to a data warehouse is accomplished through the use of **online analytical processing (OLAP)** software. OLAP software, whether it is part of the DBMS or a separate product, is optimized to work efficiently with data warehouses.

Users access a data warehouse using OLAP software to answer questions such as the following: How has the average client balance changed each year over the past five years? What is the total income by month for this year, and how does it compare to last year?

In posing those types of questions, users perceive the data in a data warehouse as a **multidimensional database**. For example, if users' questions pertain to the Tasks, Client, and Time dimensions, which appear in Figure 9-13, users might visualize the data warehouse as a multidimensional database in the shape of a **data cube**, as shown in Figure 9-14. Each axis in the data cube (Tasks, Client, and Time) represents data from a dimension table in Figure 9-13, and the cells in the data cube represent task and dollar data from the ServiceCalls fact table in Figure 9-13.

When users access a data warehouse, their queries usually involve aggregate data, such as total income by month and average hours by client. As users view the aggregate results from their queries, they often need to perform further analyses of the data they are viewing. OLAP software should let users perform these analyses as easily and quickly as possible.

Users' analyses typically involve actions that include the following:

- **Slice and dice.** Instead of viewing all data in a data cube, users typically view only portions of the data. You **slice and dice** data to select portions of the available data or to reduce the data cube. For example, suppose the Time dimension in the conceptual data cube that appears in Figure 9-14 contains detailed service data on a weekly basis for BITS Corporation. Further, suppose the manager queries the data warehouse to view this week's total business, both in dollars and by task as shown in Figure 9-15.

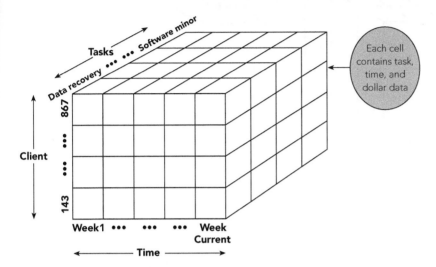

FIGURE 9-14   A data cube representation of the Tasks, Client, and Time dimensions

TotalDollars	ConsultantHours
$5,385.72	82

FIGURE 9-15   Total dollars query results

Conceptually, the manager's query slices the data cube to reduce it to the shaded "Week Current" portion, which is shown in Figure 9-16.

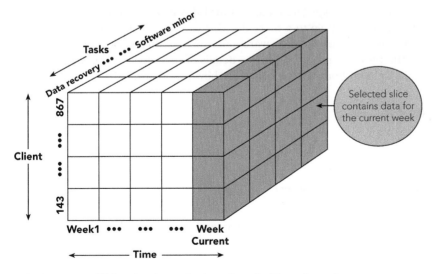

FIGURE 9-16   Slicing the data cube based on the Time dimension

If the manager's next query displays this week's total dollars and hours for the Software minor task, the query dices the sliced data cube, reducing it to the shaded portion shown in Figure 9-17.

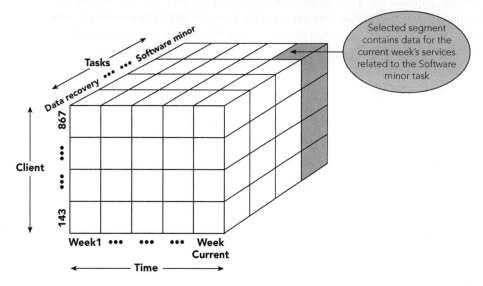

FIGURE 9-17 Dicing the sliced data cube based on the Tasks dimension

The results for the manager's queries for this diced portion of the data cube appear in Figure 9-18.

TotalDollars	ConsultantHours
$350.85	10

FIGURE 9-18 Query results for total dollars and hours for the Software minor task

The manager's first query sliced the data cube to focus on the current week's income, and the second query reduced the slice by dicing only the cells in the data cube that are for the Software minor task.

- **Drill down.** When you view specific aggregate data, you **drill down** the data to view and analyze lower levels of aggregation; that is, you go to a more detailed view of the data. For example, suppose again that the manager queries the data warehouse to view this week's total income, as shown in Figure 9-15 on the previous page. To analyze details of this income, the manager might drill down to view total dollars and hours by category, as shown in Figure 9-19.

Category	TotalDollars	ConsultantHours
DRM	$413.65	15
HAM	$4,090.47	42
SOM	$857.60	25

FIGURE 9-19 Query results for total dollars and hours by category

Finally, the manager might drill down to view total dollars and hours by task within category, as shown in Figure 9-20.

Category	Description	TotalDollars	ConsultantHours
DRM	Data recovery major	$273.75	10
DRM	Data recovery minor	$139.90	5
HAM	Hardware major	$3,048.47	15
HAM	Hardware minor	$1,048.00	20
SOM	Software major	$524.75	15
SOM	Software minor	$350.85	5

FIGURE 9-20   Query results for total dollars and hours by category and task

- *Roll up.* When you view specific aggregate data, you **roll up** the data to view and analyze higher levels of aggregation. Rolling up the data is the exact opposite of drilling down the data. For example, the manager might start with the query results for total dollars by category and task (see Figure 9-20), click the appropriate button to roll up the data for the query results for the total dollars by category (see Figure 9-19), and then click another button to roll up the data for the query results for total dollars (see Figure 9-15 on page 303).

Data mining consists of uncovering new knowledge, patterns, trends, and rules from the data stored in a data warehouse. You use data mining software to answer questions such as the following:

- Which services best attract new clients?
- What factors best predict which clients default in making payments?
- What are the optimal number of consultants to hire based on predicted economic factors?
- What is the optimal number of clients to assign to each consultant?

Because data warehouses often contain enormous amounts of data, users cannot sift through the data in them to find answers to those questions. Instead, with minimal user interaction, data mining software attempts to answer the questions by using sophisticated analytical, mathematical, and statistical techniques.

Rules for OLAP Systems

E. F. Codd and colleagues [Codd, E. F., S. B. Codd, and C. T. Salley. "Providing OLAP (On-line Analytical Processing) to UserAnalysts: An IT Mandate." Arbor Software, August, 1993] formulated 12 rules that OLAP systems should follow. The 12 rules serve as a benchmark against which you can measure OLAP systems. The 12 rules are as follows:

1. *Multidimensional conceptual view.* Users must be able to view data in a multidimensional way, matching the way data appears naturally in an organization. For example, users can view data about the relationships between data using the dimensions of tasks, client locations, consultants, and time.
2. *Transparency.* Users should not have to know they are using a multidimensional database nor need to use special software tools to access data. For example, if users usually access data using a spreadsheet, they should still be able to use a spreadsheet to access a multidimensional database.
3. *Accessibility.* Users should perceive data as a single user view even though the data may be physically located in several heterogeneous locations and in different forms, such as relational databases and standard files.
4. *Consistent reporting performance.* Retrieval performance should not degrade as the number of dimensions and the size of the warehouse grow.
5. *Client/server architecture.* The server component of OLAP software must be intelligent enough that a variety of clients can be connected with minimal effort.
6. *Generic dimensionality.* Every dimension table must be equivalent in both its structural and operational capabilities. For example, you should be able to obtain information about tasks as easily as you obtain information about consultants.
7. *Dynamic sparse matrix handling.* Missing data should be handled correctly and efficiently and not affect the accuracy or speed of data retrieval.

8. *Multiuser support.* OLAP software must provide secure, concurrent retrieval of data. Because you do not update a data warehouse when you are using it, concurrent update is not an issue, so problems of security and access are less difficult than in an OLTP environment.

9. *Unrestricted, cross-dimensional operations.* Users must be able to perform the same operations across any number of dimensions. For example, you should be able to ask for statistics based on the dimensions of time, location, and task just as easily as you would ask for statistics based on the single dimension of location.

10. *Intuitive data manipulation.* Users should be able to act directly on individual data values without needing to use menus or other interfaces. Of course, these other interfaces can be used, but they should not be the required method of processing.

11. *Flexible reporting.* Users should be able to retrieve data results and view them any way they want for analysis.

12. *Unlimited dimensions and aggregation levels.* OLAP software should allow at least 15 data dimensions and an unlimited number of aggregation (summary) levels.

OBJECT-ORIENTED SYSTEMS

Organizations use relational databases to store and access data consisting of text and numbers. Additionally, some organizations store and access graphics, drawings, photographs, video, sound, voice mail, spreadsheets, and other complex objects in their databases. RDBMSs store these complex objects using special data types, generically called **binary large objects (BLOBs)**. Some applications, such as computer-aided design and manufacturing (CAD/CAM) and geographic information systems (GIS), have as their primary focus the storage and management of complex objects. For these systems, many companies use object-oriented DBMSs.

What Is an Object-Oriented DBMS?

The relational model, which has a strong theoretical foundation, is the foundation for RDBMSs. Although object-oriented DBMSs do not have a corresponding theoretical foundation, they all exhibit several common characteristics. Central to all object-oriented systems is the concept of an object. An **object** is a set of related attributes along with the actions that are associated with the set of attributes. A client object, for example, consists of the attributes associated with clients (number, name, balance, and so on) together with the actions that are associated with client data (add client, change credit limit, delete client, and so on).

In relational systems, you create the actions as part of data manipulation (in the programs that update the database) rather than as part of the data definition. In contrast, in object-oriented systems, you define the actions as part of the data definition and then use the actions whenever they are required. In an object-oriented system, the data and actions are **encapsulated**, which means that you define an object to contain both the data and its associated actions. Thus, an **object-oriented database management system (OODBMS)** is a database management system in which data and the actions that operate on the data are encapsulated into objects.

To become familiar with OODBMSs, you should have a general understanding of the following object-oriented concepts: objects, classes, methods, messages, and inheritance.

Objects and Classes

To understand the distinction between objects and classes, you will examine an object-oriented representation of the following relational model representation of the BITS Corporation database.

```
Consultant (ConsltNum, LastName, FirstName, Street, City, State, ZipCode, Hours, Rate)
Client (ClientNum, ClientName, Street, City, State, ZipCode, Balance, CreditLimit, ConsltNum)
WorkOrders (OrderNum, OrderDate, ClientNum)
OrderLine (OrderNum, TaskID, ScheduledDate, QuotedPrice)
Tasks (TaskID, Description, Category, Price, Allocated)
```

This version of the BITS database contains an extra field, Allocated, in the Tasks table. The Allocated field stores the amount of time scheduled for the service. Figure 9-21 shows a representation of this database as a collection of objects.

```
Consultant OBJECT
ConsltNum:              Consultant Numbers
LastName:               Last Names
FirstName:              First Names
Street:                 Addresses
City:                   Cities
State:                  States
ZipCode:                Zip Codes
Hours                   Number of Hours per Week
Rate:                   Hourly Rates
Client:                 Client OBJECT; MV

Client OBJECT
ClientNum:              Client Numbers
ClientName:             Client Names
Street:                 Addresses
City:                   Cities
State:                  States
ZipCode:                ZipCodes
Balance:                Balances
CreditLimit:            Credit Limits
Consultant:             Consultant OBJECT; SUBSET[ConsltNum, LastName, FirstName]

Tasks OBJECT
TaskID:                 Task ID Numbers
Description:            Task Descriptions
Category:               Task Categories
Price:                  Prices
Allocated:              Hours
OrderLine:              OrderLine OBJECT; MV

WorkOrders OBJECT
OrderNum:               Order Numbers
OrderDate:              Dates
Client:                 Client OBJECT; SUBSET[ClientNum, ClientName, ConsltNum]
OrderLine:              OrderLine OBJECT; MV

OrderLine OBJECT
OrderNum:               Order Numbers
TaskID:                 Task Numbers
ScheduledDate:          Dates
QuotedPrice:            Prices
```

FIGURE 9-21   Object-oriented representation of the BITS Corporation database

Notice the following differences between the collection of objects in Figure 9-21 and the relational model representation:

- Each entity (Consultant, Client, and so on) is represented as an *object* rather than a relation.
- The attributes are listed vertically below the object names. In addition, each attribute is followed by the name of the domain associated with the attribute. A **domain** is the set of values permitted for an attribute.
- Objects can contain other objects. For example, the Consultant object contains the Client object as one of its attributes. In the Consultant object, the letters *MV* following the Client object indicate that the Client object is multivalued. In other words, a single occurrence of the Consultant object can contain multiple occurrences of the Client object. Roughly speaking, this is analogous to a relation containing a repeating group.
- An object can contain a portion of another object. The Client object, for example, contains the Consultant object. The word *SUBSET* indicates, however, that the Client object contains only a subset of the Consultant object. In this case, the Client object contains three of the Consultant object attributes: ConsltNum, LastName, and FirstName.

Notice that each of two objects can appear to contain the other. The Consultant object contains the Client object, and the Client object contains the Consultant object (or at least a subset of it). The important thing to keep in mind is that users deal with *objects*. If the users of the Client object require access to the Consultant's number and name, the Consultant's number and name are part of the Client object. If the users of the Consultant object require data about all the clients of a consultant, the Client object is part of the Consultant object. This arrangement is not to imply, of course, that the data is physically stored this way, but this is the way its users perceive the data.

Objects can contain more than one other object. Notice that the WorkOrders object contains the Client object and the OrderLine object, with the OrderLine object being multivalued. Nevertheless, users of the WorkOrders object perceive it as a single unit.

Technically, the objects in Figure 9-21 are classes. The term **class** refers to the general structure. The term *object* refers to a specific occurrence of a class. Thus, Consultant is a class, whereas the data for Consultant 19 is an object.

Methods and Messages

Methods are the actions defined for a class. Figure 9-22 shows two methods associated with the WorkOrders object. The first method, Add WorkOrder, adds an order to the database. In this example, users enter data, and then the program places the data temporarily in computer memory in a work area named WOrders. (In this example, the *W* prefix indicates a temporary work order, record, or field.) The WOrders record consists of a user-entered value for the order number stored in WOrderNum, a user-entered value for the order date stored in WOrderDate, and so on.

```
Add WorkOrder (WOrders)
        Add row to WorkOrders table
                OrderNum      = WOrderNum
                OrderDate     = WOrderDate
                ClientNum     = WClientNum
        For each OrderLine record in WOrders DO
                Add row to OrderLine table
                        OrderNum      = WOrderNum
                        TaskID        = WTaskIDNum
                        ScheduledDate = WScheduledDate
                        QuotedPrice   = WQuotedPrice
                        Allocated     = WAllocated
                Update Tasks table (WHERE TaskID = WTaskIDNum)
                        TotalAllocated = TotalAllocated + WAllocated
Delete WorkOrder (WOrderNum)
        Delete row from WorkOrders table (WHERE OrderNum = WOrderNum)
        For each OrderLine record (WHERE OrderNum = WOrderNum) DO
                Delete row from OrderLine table
                Update Tasks table (WHERE Tasks.TaskID = OrderLine.TaskID)
                        TotalAllocated = TotalAllocated – WAllocated
```

FIGURE 9-22   Two methods for the BITS Corporation object-oriented database

Q & A 9-1

Question: Describe the steps in the Add Order method.
Answer: The steps accomplish the following:

- Add a row to the WorkOrders table for the new order.
- For each order line record associated with the order, add a row to the OrderLine table.
- For each matched order line record, update the Allocated value in the Tasks table for the corresponding item.

In Figure 9-22, the second method, Delete Order, deletes an order. The only data a user inputs to this method is the order number to be deleted, which is placed temporarily in WOrderNum.

Question: Describe the steps in the Delete Order method.
Answer: The steps accomplish the following:

- Delete the order with the user-entered order number (WOrderNum) from the WorkOrders table.
- For each order line record in which the order number matches the value of WOrderNum, delete the record.
- For each matched order line record, subtract the NumOrdered value from the Allocated value for the corresponding part in the Tasks table. (Because the method deletes the order line record, the items are no longer allocated.)

You define methods during the data definition process. To execute the steps in a method, a user sends a message to the object. A message is a request to execute a method. As part of sending the message to an object, the user sends the required data (for example, full order data for the Add Order method, but only the order number for the Delete Order method). The process is similar to the process of calling a subroutine or invoking a procedure in a standard programming language.

Inheritance

A key feature of object-oriented systems is **inheritance**. For any class, you can define a **subclass**. Every occurrence of the subclass is also considered an occurrence of the class. The subclass *inherits* the structure of the class as well as its methods. In addition, you can define additional attributes and methods for the subclass.

As an example, suppose BITS Corporation has a special type of order that has all the characteristics of other orders. In addition, it contains a discount that is calculated in a special way. Rather than create a new class for this type of order, you can define it as a subclass of the WorkOrders class. In that way, the special order type automatically has all the attributes of the WorkOrders class. The new subclass also has all the same methods of the WorkOrders class, including the update of the Allocated field in the Tasks table whenever orders are added or deleted. The only thing you would have to add would be those attributes and methods that are specific to this new type of order, thus greatly simplifying the entire process.

Unified Modeling Language (UML)

The **Unified Modeling Language (UML)** is an approach you can use to model all the various aspects of software development for object-oriented systems. UML includes a way to represent database designs.

UML includes several types of diagrams, each with its own special purpose. Figure 9-23 describes the purpose of some of the most commonly used UML diagrams.

Diagram Type	Description
Class	For each class, shows the name, attributes, and methods of the class, as well as the relationships between the classes in the database.
Use Case	Describes how the system is to behave from the standpoint of the system's users.
State	Shows the possible states of an object. (For example, an order could be in the placed, open, filled, or invoiced states.) Also shows the possible transitions between states (for example, placed→open→filled→invoiced).
Sequence	Shows the sequence of possible interactions between objects over time.
Activity	Shows the business and operational step-by-step workflows of components in a system.
Component	Complex software systems are usually subdivided into smaller components. This type of diagram shows these components and their relationships with each other.

FIGURE 9-23   UML diagrams

The type of diagram most relevant to database design is the **class diagram**. Figure 9-24 shows a sample class diagram for the BITS Corporation database. A rectangle represents a class. The top portion of a rectangle contains the name of the class, the middle portion contains the attributes, and the bottom portion contains the methods. The lines joining the classes represent the relationships and are called **associations** in UML.

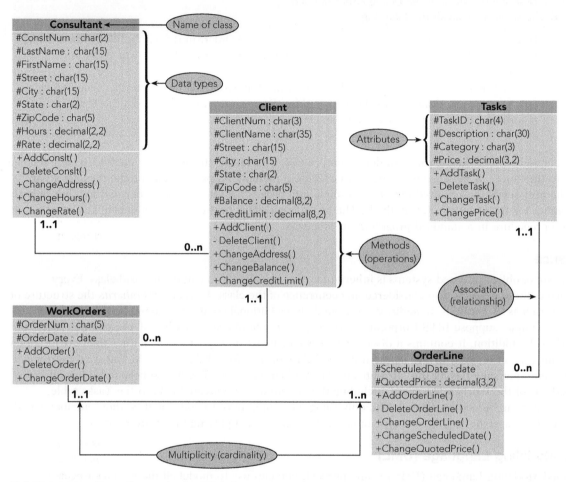

FIGURE 9-24 Class diagram for the BITS Corporation database

In a class diagram, a visibility symbol precedes each attribute. The **visibility symbol** indicates whether other classes can view or update the value in the attribute. The possible visibility symbols are public visibility (+), protected visibility (#), and private visibility (−). With **public visibility**, any other class can view or update the value. With **protected visibility**, only the class itself or public or protected subclasses of the class can view or update the value. With **private visibility**, only the class itself can view or update the value. The name of the attribute, a colon, and then the data type for the attribute follow the visibility symbol.

At each end of each association is an expression that represents the multiplicity, or cardinality, of the relationship. **Multiplicity** indicates the number of objects that can be related to an individual object at the other end of the relationship. UML provides various alternatives for representing multiplicity. In the alternative shown in Figure 9-24, two periods separate two symbols. The first symbol represents the minimum number of objects, and the second symbol represents the maximum number of objects. A second number of n indicates that there is no maximum number of objects.

In the association between Client and WorkOrders, for example, the multiplicity for Client is 1..1. This multiplicity indicates that an order must correspond to at least one client and can correspond to, at most, one client. In other words, an order must correspond to *exactly* one client. The multiplicity for WorkOrders is 0..n, indicating that a client can have as few as zero orders (that is, a client does not have to have any orders currently in the database) and that there is no limit on the number of orders a client can have. In the association between WorkOrders and OrderLine, the multiplicity for OrderLine is 1..n rather than 0..n. This multiplicity indicates that each order must have *at least one* order line but that the number of order lines is unlimited. If, on the other hand, the multiplicity for OrderLine were 1..5, an order would be required to have anywhere from one to five order lines.

You can also specify constraints, which are restrictions on the data that can be stored in the database. You enter the constraint in the shape shown in Figure 9-25 and then connect the shape to the class to which it applies.

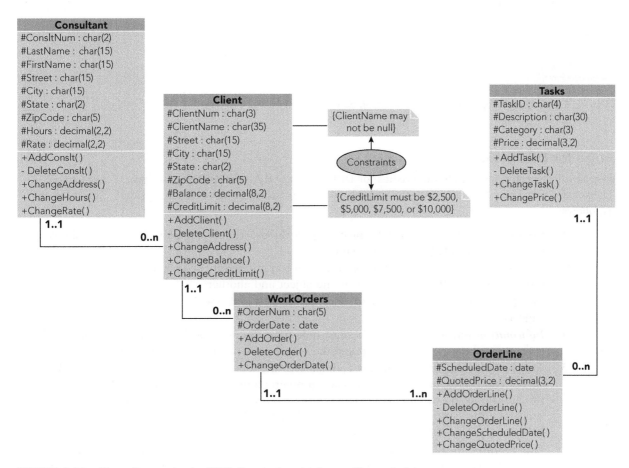

FIGURE 9-25   Class diagram for the BITS Corporation database with constraints

You learned about entity subtypes and how to represent them in E-R diagrams. In UML, these entity subtypes are called subclasses. In addition, when one class is a subclass of a second class, you call the second class a **superclass** of the first class. The relationship between a superclass and a subclass is called a **generalization**, which is shown in Figure 9-26. This class diagram represents the relationship between the class of students and the subclass of students who live in dorms.

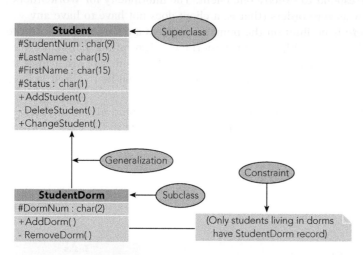

FIGURE 9-26   Class diagram with a generalization and a constraint

Rules for OODBMSs

Just as rules specify desired characteristics for DDBMSs and OLAP, OODBMSs also have a set of rules. These rules serve as a benchmark against which you can measure object-oriented systems. The rules are as follows:

1. ***Complex objects.*** An OODBMS must support the creation of complex objects from simple objects such as integers and characters.
2. ***Object identity.*** An OODBMS must provide a way to identify objects; that is, the OODBMS must provide a way to distinguish between one object and another.
3. ***Encapsulation.*** An OODBMS must encapsulate data and associated methods together in the database.
4. ***Information hiding.*** An OODBMS must hide from the users of the database the details concerning the way data is stored and the actual implementation of the methods.
5. ***Types or classes.*** You are already familiar with the idea of a class. Types are very similar to classes and correspond to abstract types in programming languages. The differences between the two are subtle and will not be explored here. It is important to know, however, that an OODBMS supports either abstract types or classes (it does not matter which).
6. ***Inheritance.*** An OODBMS must support inheritance.
7. ***Late binding.*** In this case, **binding** refers to the association of operations to actual program code. With late binding, this association does not happen until runtime, that is, until some user actually invokes the operation. Late binding lets you use the same name for different operations, which is called **polymorphism** in object-oriented systems. For example, an operation to display an object on the screen requires different program code when the object is a picture than when it is text. With late binding, you can use the same name for both operations. At the time a user invokes this "display" operation, the system determines the object being displayed and then binds the operation to the appropriate program code.

8. *Computational completeness.* You can use functions in the language of the OODBMS to perform various computations.

9. *Extensibility.* Any DBMS, object-oriented or not, comes with a set of predefined data types, such as numeric and character. An OODBMS should be **extensible**, meaning that it is possible to define new data types. Furthermore, the OODBMS should make no distinction between the data types provided by the system and the new data types.

10. *Persistence.* In object-oriented programming, **persistence** refers to the ability to have a program *remember* its data from one execution to the next. Although this is unusual in programming languages, it is common in all database systems. After all, one of the fundamental capabilities of any DBMS is its ability to store data for later use.

11. *Performance.* An OODBMS should have sufficient performance capabilities to manage very large databases effectively.

12. *Concurrent update support.* An OODBMS must support concurrent update. (You learned about concurrent update in Chapter 7.)

13. *Recovery support.* An OODBMS must provide recovery services. (You learned about recovery services in Chapter 7.)

14. *Query facility.* An OODBMS must provide query facilities. (You learned about query facilities such as QBE and SQL in Chapters 2 and 3, respectively.)

Summary

- A distributed database is a single logical database that is physically divided among computers at several sites on a network. A user at any site can access data at any other site. A DDBMS is a DBMS capable of supporting and manipulating distributed databases.
- Computers in a network communicate through messages. Minimizing the number of messages is important for rapid access to distributed databases.
- A homogenous DDBMS is one that has the same local DBMS at each site, whereas a heterogeneous DDBMS is one that does not.
- Location transparency, replication transparency, and fragmentation transparency are important characteristics of DDBMSs.
- DDBMSs permit local control of data, increased database capacity, improved system availability, and added efficiency.
- The two-phase commit usually uses a coordinator to manage concurrent update.
- C. J. Date presented 12 rules that serve as a benchmark against which you can measure DDBMSs. These rules include local autonomy, no reliance on a central site, continuous operation, location transparency, fragmentation transparency, replication transparency, distributed query processing, distributed transaction management, hardware independence, operating system independence, network independence, and DBMS independence.
- A file server stores the files required by users and sends entire files to the users.
- In a two-tier client/server architecture, a DBMS runs on a file server and the server sends only the requested data to the clients. The server performs database functions, and the clients perform presentation functions. A fat client can perform the business functions, or the server can perform the business functions in a thin client arrangement.
- In a three-tier client/server architecture, the clients perform the presentation functions, database servers perform the database functions, and application servers perform business functions. A three-tier architecture is more scalable than a two-tier architecture.
- The advantages of client/server systems are lower network traffic; improved processing distribution; thinner clients; greater processing transparency; increased network, hardware, and software transparency; improved security; decreased costs; and increased scalability.
- Web servers interact with web clients using HTTP and TCP/IP to display HTML webpages on web clients' screens.
- Dynamic webpages, not static webpages, are used in e-commerce; server-side and client-side extensions provide the dynamic capabilities, including the capability to interact with databases.
- Cookies and session management techniques are used to counteract the stateless nature of HTTP.
- XML was developed in response to the need for data exchange between organizations and due to the inability of HTML to specify the structure and meaning of its data.
- The W3C has developed recommendations for other languages related to XML. These languages include XHTML, a markup language based on XML and a stricter version of HTML; DTD and XML schema, both used to specify the structure and meaning of data in an XML document; XSL, a language for creating stylesheets; XSLT, which transforms an XML document into another document; and XQuery, which is an XML query language.
- OLTP is used with relational database management systems, and OLAP is used with data warehouses.
- A data warehouse is a subject-oriented, integrated, time-variant, nonvolatile collection of data in support of management's decision-making process.
- A typical data warehouse data structure is a star schema consisting of a central fact table surrounded by dimension tables.
- Users perceive the data in a data warehouse as a multidimensional database in the shape of a data cube. OLAP software lets users slice and dice data, drill down data, and roll up data.
- Data mining consists of uncovering new knowledge, patterns, trends, and rules from the data stored in a data warehouse.
- E. F. Codd presented 12 rules that serve as a benchmark against which you can measure OLAP systems. These rules are multidimensional conceptual view; transparency; accessibility; consistent reporting performance; client/server architecture; generic dimensionality; dynamic sparse matrix handling; multiuser support; unrestricted, cross-dimensional operations; intuitive data manipulation; flexible reporting; and unlimited dimensions and aggregation levels.
- Object-oriented DBMSs deal with data as objects. An object is a set of related attributes along with the actions that are associated with the set of attributes. An OODBMS is a database management system in which data and the actions that operate on the data are encapsulated into objects. A domain is the set of

values that are permitted for an attribute. The term *class* refers to the general structure, and the term *object* refers to a specific occurrence of a class. Methods are the actions defined for a class, and a message is a request to execute a method. A subclass inherits the structure and methods of its superclass.

- UML is an approach to model all the various aspects of software development for object-oriented systems. The class diagram represents the design of an object-oriented database. Relationships are called associations, and visibility symbols indicate whether other classes can view or change the value in an attribute. Multiplicity indicates the number of objects that can be related to an individual object at the other end of the relationship. Generalization is the relationship between a superclass and a subclass.
- Properties that serve as a benchmark against which you can measure object-oriented systems are complex objects, object identity, encapsulation, information hiding, types or classes, inheritance, late binding, computational completeness, extensibility, persistence, performance, concurrent update support, recovery support, and query facility.

Key Terms

access delay	Extensible Stylesheet Language (XSL)
application server	fact table
association	fat client
back-end machine	file server
back-end processor	fragmentation transparency
binary large object (BLOB)	front-end machine
binding	front-end processor
business to business (B2B)	generalization
class	global deadlock
class diagram	heterogeneous DDBMS
client	homogeneous DDBMS
client/server	Hypertext Markup Language (HTML)
client-side extension	Hypertext Transfer Protocol (HTTP)
client-side script	inheritance
communications network	Internet
cookie	local deadlock
coordinator	local site
database server	location transparency
data cube	markup language
data fragmentation	message
data mining	metalanguage
data warehouse	method
dimension table	multidimensional database
distributed database	multiplicity
distributed database management system (DDBMS)	network
document type definition (DTD)	n-tier architecture
domain	object
drill down	object-oriented database management system (OODBMS)
dynamic webpage	
electronic commerce (e-commerce)	Office Open XML
encapsulated	online analytical processing (OLAP)
extensible	online transaction processing (OLTP)
Extensible Hypertext Markup Language (XHTML)	persistence
Extensible Markup Language (XML)	polymorphism

primary copy	tag
private visibility	thin client
protected visibility	three-tier architecture
public visibility	Transmission Control Protocol/Internet Protocol (TCP/IP)
remote site	two-phase commit
replication transparency	two-tier architecture
roll up	Unified Modeling Language (UML)
scalability	Uniform Resource Locator (URL)
server	visibility symbol
server-side extension	web browser
server-side script	web client
session	web server
slice and dice	webpage
star schema	World Wide Web (web)
stateless	World Wide Web Consortium (W3C)
static webpage	XML declaration
stylesheet	XML schema
subclass	XQuery
superclass	XSL Transformations (XSLT)

Review Questions

1. What is a distributed database? What is a DDBMS?
2. What different design decisions do you make to access data rapidly in a centralized database compared to a distributed database?
3. How does a homogeneous DDBMS differ from a heterogeneous DDBMS? Which is more complex?
4. What is meant by a local site? By a remote site?
5. What is location transparency?
6. What is replication? Why is it used? What benefit is derived from using it? What are the biggest potential problems?
7. What is replication transparency?
8. What is data fragmentation? What purpose does data fragmentation serve?
9. What is fragmentation transparency?
10. Why is local control of data an advantage in a distributed database?
11. Why is the ability to increase system capacity an advantage in a distributed database?
12. Why is system availability an advantage in a distributed database?
13. What are two disadvantages of updating replicated data in a distributed database?
14. What causes query processing to be more complex in a distributed database?
15. What is meant by local deadlock? By global deadlock?
16. Describe the two-phase commit process. How does it work? Why is it necessary?
17. Describe three possible approaches to storing data dictionary entries in a distributed system.
18. What additional factors must you consider during the information-level design of a distributed database?
19. What additional factors must you consider during the physical-level design of a distributed database?
20. What is the difference between a file server and a client/server system?
21. In a two-tier client/server architecture, what problems occur when you place the business functions on the clients? On the server?

22. What is a fat client? What is a thin client?

23. What is scalability?

24. What is a three-tier architecture?

25. List the advantages of a client/server architecture as compared to a file server.

26. What are dynamic webpages? How can you augment HTML to provide the dynamic capability?

27. Explain why HTTP is a stateless protocol and what types of techniques are used in e-commerce to deal with this complication.

28. What is XML? Why was it developed?

29. What are the characteristics of OLTP systems?

30. What is a data warehouse?

31. What does it mean when a data warehouse is nonvolatile?

32. What is a fact table in a data warehouse?

33. When do you use OLAP?

34. What three types of actions do users typically perform when they use OLAP software?

35. What is data mining?

36. What is an OODBMS?

37. How do classes relate to objects?

38. What is a method? What is a message? How do messages relate to methods?

39. What is inheritance? What are the benefits of inheritance?

40. What is UML?

41. What are relationships called in UML?

42. What is a visibility symbol in UML?

43. What is multiplicity?

44. What is generalization?

45. Use a web browser to find three examples of static webpages and three examples of dynamic webpages, and note the URLs for each page you find. Explain the purpose of each page and why you believe it was created as a static page or a dynamic page. For dynamic pages, what kinds of processing happen on each page?

46. Using your knowledge of the college environment, identify three transactions that might be handled by online transaction processing (OLTP) systems.

47. Using your knowledge of the college environment, identify three questions to answer using online analytical processing (OLAP) software.

BITS Corporation Exercises

For the following exercises, you will answer problems and questions from management at BITS Corporation. You do not use the BITS Corporation database for any of these exercises.

1. Fragment the Client table so that clients of Consultant 19 form a fragment named ClientConslt19, clients of Consultant 22 form a fragment named ClientConslt22, clients of Consultant 35 form a fragment named ClientConslt35, and clients of Consultant 51 form a fragment named ClientConslt51. (Include all fields from the Client table in each fragment.) In addition, you need to fragment the WorkOrders table so that orders are distributed and stored with the clients that placed the orders. For example, fragment OrdersConslt19 consists of those orders placed by clients of Consultant 19. Write the SQL-type statements to create these fragments.

2. Create a class diagram for the BITS Corporation database, as shown in Figure 1-5 in Chapter 1. If you need to make any assumptions when preparing the class diagram, document those assumptions.

3. A user queries the Tasks table in the BITS Corporation database over the company intranet. Assume the Tasks table contains 5,000 rows, each row is 1,000 bits long, the access delay is 2.5 seconds, the transmission rate is 50,000 bits per second, and only 20 of the 5,000 rows in the Tasks table satisfy the query conditions. Calculate

the total communication time required for this query based on retrieving all table rows one row at a time, and then calculate the total communication time required based on retrieving the 20 rows that satisfy the query conditions in a single message.

4. BITS Corporation is interested in open source distributed database management systems (DDBMSs). Use the Internet to research open source DDBMS software. Use Date's 12 rules for distributed databases to evaluate the software. Are there any open source DDBMS software programs that follow all 12 rules? Which open source DDBMS would you recommend BITS Corporation use? Justify your recommendation and be sure to cite your references. If you use information from the web, use reputable sites. Do not plagiarize or copy from the web.

Colonial Adventure Tours Case

The management of Colonial Adventure Tours asks you to research improvements it might make to its database processing. To help management, they would like you to complete the following exercises.

1. Create a class diagram for the Colonial Adventure Tours database, as shown in Figures 1-15 through 1-19 in Chapter 1. If you need to make any assumptions when preparing the class diagram, document those assumptions.

2. Colonial Adventure Tours is interested in learning more about data mining and how it can help the company target more clients. Use the Internet to research how data mining is being used in the tourism industry. Then prepare a report that details the use of data mining in tourism and explain how Colonial Adventure Tours could use data mining. Be sure to cite your references. If you use information from the web, use reputable sites. Do not plagiarize or copy from the web.

3. Colonial Adventure Tours would like to use XML to share the Trip table with a local hiking club. If you have access to a DBMS such as Access 2016, export the Trip table as an XML document. If you do not have access to a DBMS, use Figure 9-9 as a guide and create an XML document for the first two records (with TripID 1 and 2) in the Trip table.

Sports Physical Therapy Case

For the following exercises, you will answer questions from the Sports Physical Therapy staff. You do not use the Sports Physical Therapy database for any of these exercises.

1. Create a class diagram for the Sports Physical Therapy database, as shown in Figures 1-21 through 1-24 in Chapter 1. If you need to make any assumptions when preparing the diagram, document those assumptions.

2. Sports Physical Therapy is considering upgrading to a client/server system. Use computer magazines, books, or the Internet to investigate one of the following web services: Application Programming Interface (API); Common Gateway Interface (CGI); Simple Object Access Protocol (SOAP); Universal Description, Discovery, and Integration (UDDI); or Web Services Description Language (WSDL). Then prepare a report that defines the web service, explains its purpose, and includes the potential advantages and disadvantages of its use by Sports Physical Therapy. If you use information from the web, use reputable sites. Do not plagiarize or copy from the web.

COMPREHENSIVE DESIGN EXAMPLE: DOUGLAS COLLEGE

Douglas College has decided to computerize its operations. In this appendix, you will design a database that satisfies many user requirements by applying the design techniques you learned in Chapter 6 to a significant set of requirements.

DOUGLAS COLLEGE REQUIREMENTS

Douglas College has provided you with the following requirements that its new system must satisfy. You will use these requirements to design a new database.

General Description

Douglas College is organized by department (Mathematics, Physics, English, and so on). Most departments offer more than one major; for example, the Mathematics department might offer majors in calculus, applied mathematics, and statistics. Each major, however, is offered by only one department. Each faculty member is assigned to a single department. Students can have more than one major, but most students have only one. Each student is assigned a faculty member as an advisor for his or her major; students who have more than one major are assigned a faculty advisor for each major. The faculty member may or may not be assigned to the department offering the major.

A code that has up to three characters (CS for Computer Science, MTH for Mathematics, PHY for Physics, ENG for English, and so on) identifies each department. The combination of the department code and a three-digit number (CS 162 for Programming I, MTH 201 for Calculus I, ENG 102 for Creative Writing, and so on) identifies each course. The number of credits offered by a particular course does not vary; that is, all students who pass the same course receive the same amount of credit.

A two-character code identifies the semester in which a course is taught (FA for fall, SP for spring, and SU for summer). The code is combined with two digits that designate the year (for example, FA18 represents the fall semester of 2018). For a given semester, a department assigns each section of each course a four-digit schedule code (schedule code 1295 for section A of MTH 201, code 1297 for section B of MTH 201, code 1302 for section C of MTH 201, and so on). The schedule codes might vary from semester to semester. The schedule codes are listed in the school's time schedule, and students use them to indicate the sections in which they want to enroll. (You will learn more about the enrollment process later in this section.)

After all students have completed the enrollment process for a given semester, each faculty member receives a class list for each section he or she will be teaching. In addition to listing the students in each section, the class list provides space to record the grade each student earns in the course. At the end of the semester, the faculty member enters the students' grades in this list and sends a copy of the list to the records office, where the grades are entered into the database. (In the future, the college plans to automate this part of the process.)

After an employee of the records office posts the grades (by entering them into the database), the DBMS generates a report card for each student; then the report cards are mailed to the addresses printed on the report card. The grades earned by a student become part of his or her permanent record and will appear on the student's transcript.

Report Requirements

Employees at Douglas College require several reports to manage students, classes, schedules, and faculty members; these reports have the following requirements.

Report card: At the end of each semester, the system must produce a report card for each student. A sample report card is shown in Figure A-1.

DOUGLAS COLLEGE

Department	Course Number	Course Description	Grade	Credits Taken	Credits Earned	Grade Points
Computer Science	CS 162	Programming I	A	4	4	16.0
Mathematics	MTH 201	Calculus I	B+	3	3	9.9

Current Semester Totals

7	7	3.70	25.9
Credits Taken	Credits Earned	GPA	Total Points

Semester: FA18

Cumulative Totals

44	44	3.39	149.2
Credits Taken	Credits Earned	GPA	Total Points

Student Number: 381124188

Student Name & Address	Local Address (IF DIFFERENT)
Fredrick Starks 8006 Howard Ave. Baring, ID 83224	1605b College Park Douglas, ID 83260

FIGURE A-1   Sample report card for Douglas College

Class list: The system must produce a class list for each section of each course (for the faculty member); a sample class list is shown in Figure A-2. Note that space is provided for the grades. At the end of the semester, the instructor enters each student's grade and sends a copy of the class list to the records office.

CLASS LIST

Department: CS   Computer Science   Term: FA18
Course: 162   Programming I   (4 CREDITS)
Section: B
Schedule Code: 2366

Time: 1:00 - 1:50 M, T, W, F
PLACE: 118 SCR

Instructor: 462   Diane Johnson

Student Number	Student Name	Class Standing	Grade
381124188	Fredrick Starks	2	
.	.	.	
.	.	.	
.	.	.	

FIGURE A-2   Sample class list for Douglas College

Grade verification report: After the records office processes the class list, it returns the class list to the instructor with the grades entered in the report. The instructor uses the report to verify that the records office entered the students' grades correctly.

Time schedule: The time schedule shown in Figure A-3 lists all sections of all courses offered during a given semester. Each section has a unique four-digit schedule code. The time schedule lists the schedule code; the department offering the course; the course's number, section letter, and title; the instructor teaching the course; the time the course meets; the room in which the course meets; the number of credits generated by the course; and the prerequisites for the course. In addition to the information shown in Figure A-3, the time schedule includes the date the semester begins and ends, the date final exams begin and end, and the last withdrawal date (the last date on which students may withdraw from a course for a refund and without academic penalty).

```
┌─────────────────────────────────────────────────────────────────────┐
│                  TIME SCHEDULE      Term: FA18                       │
│                                                                       │
│  Course #    Code #   Sect   Time              Room      Faculty     │
│  ...............................................................     │
│         .         .         .              .         .               │
│         .         .         .              .         .               │
│         .         .         .              .         .               │
│                                                                       │
│  CHEMISTRY (CHM) Office: 341 NSB                                      │
│                                                                       │
│   111  Chemistry I                             4 CREDITS             │
│          1740     A      10:00-10:50 M, T, W, F   102 WRN   Johnson  │
│          1745     B      12:00-12:50 M, T, W, F   102 WRN   Lawrence │
│            .         .         .               .         .           │
│            .         .         .               .         .           │
│            .         .         .               .         .           │
│            .         .         .               .         .           │
│          Prerequisite:  MTH 110                                      │
│   112  Chemistry II                            4 CREDITS             │
│          1790     A      10:00-11:50 M, W        109 WRN   Adams     │
│          1795     B      12:00-1:50 T, R         102 WRN   Nelson    │
│            .         .         .               .         .           │
│            .         .         .               .         .           │
│            .         .         .               .         .           │
│          Prerequisite:  CHM 111                                      │
│   114  ....                                                          │
└─────────────────────────────────────────────────────────────────────┘
```

FIGURE A-3   Sample time schedule for Douglas College

Registration request form: A sample registration request form is shown in Figure A-4 on the next page. A student uses this form to request classes for the upcoming semester. Students indicate the sections for which they want to register by entering each section's schedule code; for each of these sections, students may also enter a code for an alternative section in case the first requested section is full.

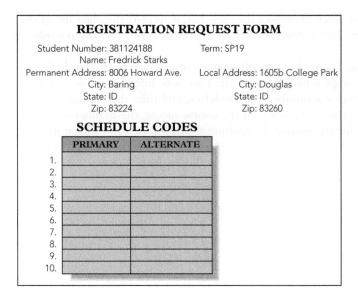

FIGURE A-4   Sample registration request form for Douglas College

Student schedule: After all students have been assigned to sections, the system produces a student schedule form, which is mailed to students so that they know the classes in which they have been enrolled. A sample student schedule form is shown in Figure A-5. This form shows the schedule for an individual student for the indicated semester.

STUDENT SCHEDULE

Student Number: 381124188   Term: SP19
Name: Fredrick Starks
Permanent Address: 8006 Howard Ave.   Local Address: 1605b College Park
City: Baring   City: Douglas
State: ID   State: ID
Zip: 83224   Zip: 83260

Schedule Code	Course Number	Course Description	Section	Credits	Time	Room
2366	CS 253	Programming II	B	4	1:00–1:50 M, T, W, F	118 SCR
.	.	.	.	.		
.	.	.	.	.		
.	.	.	.	.		
		Total Credits:		16		

FIGURE A-5   Sample student schedule for Douglas College

Full student information report: This report lists complete information about a student, including his or her major(s) and all grades received to date. A sample of a full student information report is shown in Figure A-6.

FULL STUDENT INFORMATION

Student Number: 381124188   Term: FA18
           Name: Fredrick Starks
Current Address: 8006 Howard Ave.   Local Address: 1605b College Park
          City: Baring   City: Douglas
         State: ID   State: ID
          Zip: 83224   Zip: 83260

Major 1: Information Sys.   Department: Computer Science   Advisor: Mark Lawerence
Major 2: Accounting   Department: Business   Advisor: Jill Thomas
Major 3:   Department: Advisor:

Term	Course Number		Credits	Grade Earned	
SP13	MTH 123	Trigonometry	4	A	16.0
	HST 201	Western Civilization	3	A-	11.1
	ENG 101	American Literature	3	A	12.0
FA13	CS 162	Programming I	4	A	16.0
	MTH 201	Calculus I	4	B+	9.9

Credits Attempted: 44
  Credits Earned: 44
    Grade Points: 149.2
 Grade Point Avg: 3.39
  Class Standing: 2

FIGURE A-6   Sample full student information report for Douglas College

Faculty information report: This report lists all faculty by department and contains each faculty member's ID number, name, address, office location, phone number, current rank (Instructor, Assistant Professor, Associate Professor, or Professor), and starting date of employment. It also lists the number, name, and local and permanent addresses of each faculty member's advisees; the code number and description of the major in which the faculty member is advising each advisee; and the code number and description of the department to which this major is assigned. (Remember that this department need not be the one to which the faculty member is assigned.)

Work version of the time schedule: Although this report is similar to the original time schedule (see Figure A-3), it is designed for the college's internal use. It shows the current enrollments in each section of each course, as well as the maximum enrollment permitted per section. It is more current than the time schedule. (When students register for courses, enrollment figures are updated on the work version of the time schedule. When room or faculty assignments are changed, this information also is updated. A new version of this report that reflects the revised figures is printed after being updated.)

Course report: For each course, this report lists the code and name of the department that is offering the course, the course number, the description of the course, and the number of credits awarded. This report also includes the department and course number for each prerequisite course.

Update (Transaction) Requirements

In addition to being able to add, change, and delete any information in the report requirements, the system must be able to accomplish the following update requirements:

Enrollment: When a student attempts to register for a section of a course, the system must determine whether the student has received credit for all prerequisites to the course. If the student is eligible to enroll in the course and the number of students currently enrolled in the section is less than the maximum enrollment, enroll the student.

Post grades: For each section of each course, the system must post the grades that are indicated on the class list submitted by the instructor and produce a grade verification report. (*Posting the grades* is the formal term for the process of entering the grades permanently in the students' computerized records.)

Purge: Douglas College retains section information, including grades earned by the students in each section, for two semesters following the end of the semester, then the system removes this information. (Grades assigned to students are retained by course but not by section.)

DOUGLAS COLLEGE INFORMATION-LEVEL DESIGN

You should consider the overall requirements before you apply the method to the individual user requirements. For example, by examining the documents shown in Figures A-1 through A-6, you may have identified the following entities: department, major, faculty member, student, course, and semester.

NOTE: Your list might include the section and grade entities. On the other hand, you might not have included the semester entity. In the end, as long as the list is reasonable, what you include will not make much difference. In fact, you may remember that this step is not even necessary. The better you do your job now, however, the simpler the process will be later on.

After identifying the entities, you assign a primary key to each one. In general, this step will require some type of consultation with users. You may need to ask users directly for the required information, or you may be able to obtain it from some type of survey form. Assume that having had such a consultation, you created a relation for each of these entities and assigned them the following primary keys:

```
Department (DepartmentCode,
Major (MajorNum,
Faculty (FacultyNum,
Student (StudentNum,
Course (DepartmentCode, CourseNum,
Semester (SemesterCode,
```

Note that the primary key for the Course table consists of two attributes, DepartmentCode (such as CS) and CourseNum (such as 153), both of which are required. The database could contain, for example, CS 153 and CS 353. Thus, the department code alone cannot be the primary key. Similarly, the database could contain ART 101 and MUS 101, two courses with the same course number but with different department codes. Thus, the course number alone cannot be the primary key either.

Now you can begin examining the individual user views as stated in the requirements. You can create relations for these user views, represent any keys, and merge the new user views into the cumulative design. Your first task is to determine the individual user views. The term *user view* never appeared in the list of requirements. Instead, Douglas College provided a general description of the system, together with a collection of report requirements and another collection of update requirements. How do these requirements relate to user views?

Certainly, you can think of each report requirement and each update requirement as a user view, but what do you do with the general description? Do you think of each paragraph (or perhaps each sentence) in the report as representing a user view, or do you use each paragraph or sentence to furnish additional information about the report and update requirements? Both approaches are acceptable. Because the second approach is often easier, you will follow the approach in this text. Think of the report and update requirements as user views and when needed, use the statements in the general description as additional information about these user views. You will also consider the general description during the review process to ensure that your final design satisfies all the functionality it describes.

First, consider one of the simpler user views, the course report. (Technically, you can examine user views in any order. Sometimes you take them in the order in which they are listed. In other cases, you may be able to come up with a better order. Often, examining some of the simpler user views first is a reasonable approach.)

Before you proceed with the design, consider the following method. First, with some of the user views, you will attempt to determine the relations involved by carefully determining the entities and relationships between them and using this information when creating the relations. This process means that from the outset, the collection of tables created will be in or close to third normal form. With other user views, you will create a single relation that may contain some number of repeating groups. In these cases, as you will see, the normalization process still produces a correct design, but it also involves more work. In practice, the more experience a designer has, the more likely he or she is to create third normal form relations immediately.

Second, the name of an entity or attribute may vary from one user view to another, and this difference requires resolution. You will attempt to use names that are the same.

User View 1—Course report: For each course, list the code and name of the department that is offering the course, the course number, the course title, and the number of credits awarded. This report also includes the department and course number for each prerequisite course. Forgetting for the moment the requirement to list prerequisite courses, the basic relation necessary to support this report is as follows:

```
Course (DepartmentCode, DepartmentName, CourseNum, CourseTitle, NumCredits)
```

The combination of DepartmentCode and CourseNum uniquely determines all the other attributes. In this relation, DepartmentCode determines DepartmentName; thus, the table is not in second normal form. (An attribute depends on only a portion of the key.) To correct this situation, the table is split into the following two tables:

```
Course (DepartmentCode, CourseNum, CourseTitle, NumCredits)
Department (DepartmentCode, DepartmentName)
```

The DepartmentCode attribute in the first relation is a foreign key identifying the second relation. To maintain prerequisite information, you need to create the relation Prereq:

```
Prereq (DepartmentCode, CourseNum, DepartmentCode/1, CourseNum/1)
```

In this table, the attributes DepartmentCode and CourseNum refer to the course and the attributes DepartmentCode/1 and CourseNum/1 refer to the prerequisite course. If CS 362 has a prerequisite of MTH 345, for example, there will be a row in the Prereq table in which the DepartmentCode is CS, the CourseNum is 362, the DepartmentCode/1 is MTH, and the CourseNum/1 is 345.

NOTE: Because the Prereq relation contains two attributes named DepartmentCode and two attributes named CourseNum, you must be able to distinguish between them. The software used to produce these diagrams makes the distinction by appending the characters /1 to one of the names, which is why these names appear in the Prereq table. In this example, the DepartmentCode/ 1 and CourseNum/1 attributes represent the department code and course number of the prerequisite course, respectively. When it is time to implement the design, you typically assign them names that are more descriptive. For instance, you might name them PrereqDepartmentCode and PrereqCourseNum, respectively.

The DBDL version of these tables is shown in Figure A-7.

```
Department (DepartmentCode, DepartmentName)

Course (DepartmentCode, CourseNum, CourseTitle, NumCredits)
    FK DepartmentCode → Department

Prereq (DepartmentCode, CourseNum, DepartmentCode/1,
    CourseNum/1)
    FK DepartmentCode, CourseNum → Course
    FK DepartmentCode/1, CourseNum/1 → Course
```

FIGURE A-7   DBDL for User View 1

The result of merging these relations into the cumulative design appears in the E-R diagram shown in Figure A-8. Notice that the Department and Course tables have been merged with the existing Department and Course tables in the cumulative design. In the process, the attribute DepartmentName was added to the Department table and the attributes CourseTitle and NumCredits were added to the Course table. In addition, the attribute DepartmentCode in the Course table is a foreign key. Because the Prereq table is new, it was added to the cumulative design in its entirety. Notice also that you do not yet have any relationships among the entities Student, Major, Faculty, and Semester.

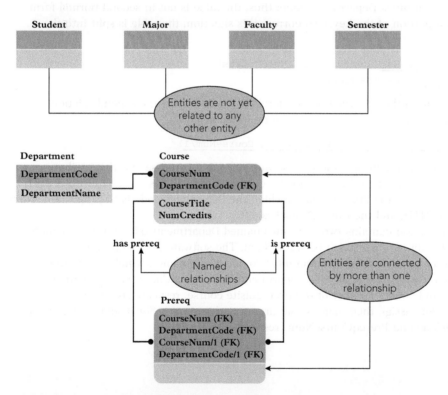

FIGURE A-8   Cumulative design after User View 1

In Figure A-8, there are two relationships between Course and Prereq. To distinguish between them, it is necessary to name the relationships. In the figure, the name for the first relationship is "has prereq" and the name for the second relationship is "is prereq."

NOTE: When using a software tool to produce E-R diagrams, the software might reverse the order of the fields that make up the primary key. For example, the E-R diagram in Figure A-8 indicates that the primary key for the Course table is CourseNum and then DepartmentCode, even though you intended it to be DepartmentCode and then CourseNum. This difference is not a problem. Indicating the fields that make up the primary key is significant, not the order in which they appear.

User View 2—Faculty information report: List all faculty by department and each faculty member's ID number, name, address, office location, phone number, current rank (Instructor, Assistant Professor, Associate Professor, or Full Professor), and starting date of employment. In addition, list the number, name, and local and permanent addresses of each faculty member's advisees; the code number and description of the major in which the faculty member is advising each advisee; and the code number and description of the department to which this major is assigned. This user view involves three entities (departments, faculty, and advisees), so you can create the following three tables:

```
Department (
Faculty (
Advisee (
```

The next step is to assign a primary key to each table. Before doing so, however, you should briefly examine the tables in the cumulative design and use the same names for any existing tables or attributes. In this case, you would use DepartmentCode as the primary key for the Department table and FacultyNum as the primary key for the Faculty table. There is no Advisee table in the cumulative collection, but there is a Student table. Because advisees and students are the same, rename the Advisee entity to Student and use the StudentNum attribute as the primary key rather than AdvisorNum. Your efforts yield the following tables and primary keys:

```
Department (DepartmentCode,
Faculty (FacultyNum,
Student (StudentNum,
```

Next, add the remaining attributes to the tables:

```
Department (DepartmentCode, DepartmentName)
Faculty (FacultyNum, LastName, FirstName, Street, City, State,
    PostalCode, OfficeNum, Phone, CurrentRank, StartDate, DepartmentCode)
Student (StudentNum, LastName, FirstName, LocalStreet,
    LocalCity, LocalState, LocalPostalCode, PermStreet, PermCity,
    PermState, PermPostalCode, (MajorNum, Description,
    DepartmentCode, FacultyNum, LastName, FirstName) )
```

The DepartmentCode attribute is included in the Faculty table because there is a one-to-many relationship between departments and faculty members. Because a student can have more than one major, the information about majors (number, description, department, and the number and name of the faculty member who advises this student in this major) is a repeating group.

Because the key to the repeating group in the Student table is MajorNum, removing this repeating group yields the following:

```
Student (StudentNum, LastName, FirstName, LocalStreet,
    LocalCity, LocalState, LocalPostalCode, PermStreet,
    PermCity, PermState, PermPostalCode, MajorNum, Description,
    DepartmentCode, FacultyNum, LastName, FirstName)
```

Converting this relation to second normal form produces the following tables:

```
Student (StudentNum, LastName, FirstName, LocalStreet,
    LocalCity, LocalState, LocalPostalCode, PermStreet,
    PermCity, PermState, PermPostalCode)
Major (MajorNum, Description, DepartmentCode, DepartmentName)
Advises (StudentNum, MajorNum, FacultyNum)
```

In this case, you must remove the following dependencies to create third normal form tables: OfficeNum determines Phone in the Faculty table, and DepartmentCode determines DepartmentName in the Major table. Removing these dependencies produces the following collection of tables:

```
Department (DepartmentCode, DepartmentName)
Faculty (FacultyNum, LastName, FirstName, Street, City, State,
    PostalCode, OfficeNum, CurrentRank, StartDate, DepartmentCode)
Student (StudentNum, LastName, FirstName, LocalStreet, LocalCity,
    LocalState, LocalPostalCode, PermStreet, PermCity, PermState, PermPostalCode)
Advises (StudentNum, MajorNum, FacultyNum)
Office (OfficeNum, Phone)
Major (MajorNum, Description, DepartmentCode)
```

The DBDL representation is shown in Figure A-9.

```
Department (DepartmentCode, DepartmentName)

Student (StudentNum, LastName, FirstName, LocalStreet, LocalCity,
    LocalState, LocalPostalCode, PermStreet, PermCity, PermState, PermPostalCode)

Office (OfficeNum, Phone)

Faculty (FacultyNum, LastName, FirstName, Street, City, State, PostalCode,
        OfficeNum, CurrentRank, StartDate, DepartmentCode)
    FK OfficeNum → Office
    FK DepartmentCode → Department

Major (MajorNum, Description, DepartmentCode)
    FK DepartmentCode → Department

Advises (StudentNum, MajorNum, FacultyNum)
    FK StudentNum → Student
    FK FacultyNum → Faculty
    FK MajorNum → Major
```

FIGURE A-9   DBDL for User View 2

The result of merging these tables into the cumulative design is shown in Figure A-10. The tables Student, Faculty, Major, and Department are merged with the existing tables with the same primary keys and with the same names. Nothing new is added to the Department table in the process, but the other tables receive additional attributes. In addition, the Faculty table also receives two foreign keys, OfficeNum and DepartmentCode. The Major table receives one foreign key, DepartmentCode. The Advises and Office tables are new and thus are added directly to the cumulative design.

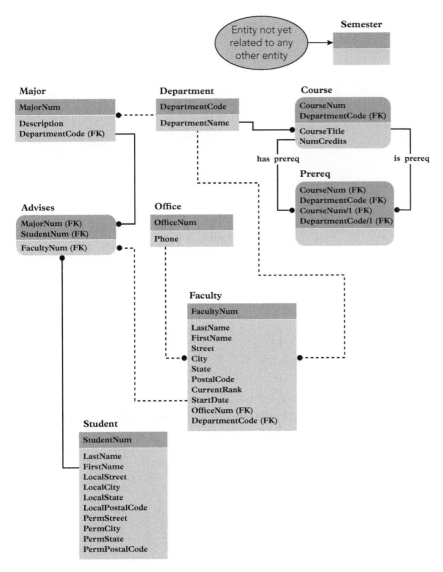

FIGURE A-10 Cumulative design after User View 2

User View 3—Report card: At the end of each semester, the system must produce a report card for each student. Report cards are fairly complicated documents in which the appropriate underlying relations are not immediately apparent. In such a case, it is a good idea to first list all the attributes in the report card and assign them appropriate names, as shown in Figure A-11 on the next page. After identifying the attributes, you should list the functional dependencies that exist between these attributes. The information necessary to determine functional dependencies must ultimately come from the user, although you can often guess most of them accurately.

NOTE: Notice that there are duplicate names in the list. CreditsEarned, for example, appears three times: once for the course, once for the semester, and once for the cumulative number of credits earned by the student. You could assign these columns different names at this point. The names could be CreditsEarnedCourse, CreditsEarnedSemester, and CreditsEarnedCumulative. Alternatively, you could assign them the same name with an explanation of the purpose of each one in parentheses, as shown in Figure A-11. Of course, after you have determined all the tables and assigned columns to them, you must ensure that the column names within a single table are unique.

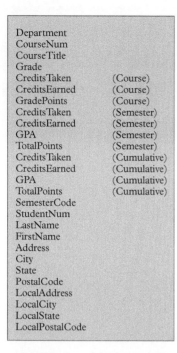

FIGURE A-11   Attributes on a report card from Douglas College

Assume the system's users have verified the attributes listed in Figure A-11 and your work is correct. Figure A-12 shows the functional dependencies among the attributes you identified on the report card. The student number alone determines many of the other attributes.

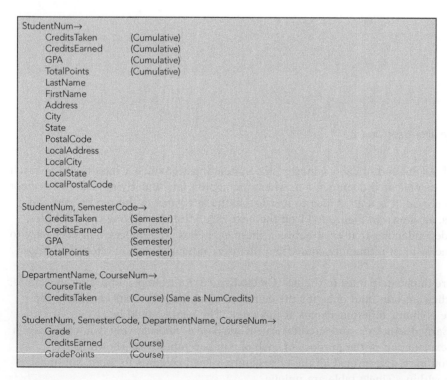

FIGURE A-12   Functional dependencies among the attributes on a report card

In addition to the student number, the semester must be identified to determine credits taken and earned, grade point average (GPA), and total points each semester. The combination of a department name (such as Computer Science) and a course number (such as 153) determines a course title and the number of credits.

Finally, the student number, the semester (semester and year), the department, and the course (department and course number) are required to determine an individual grade in a course, the credits earned from the course, and the grade points in a course. (The semester is required because the same course might be offered during more than one semester at Douglas College.)

NOTE: There is a parenthetical comment after CreditsTaken in the section determined by DepartmentName and CourseNum. It indicates that CreditsTaken is the same as NumCredits, which is a column already in the cumulative design. Documenting that the name you have chosen is a synonym for a name already in the cumulative design is a good practice.

The next step is to create a collection of tables that will support this user view. A variety of approaches will work. You could combine all the attributes into a single table, which you then would convert to third normal form. (In such a table, the combination of department, course number, course title, grade, and so on, would be a repeating group.) Alternatively, you could use the functional dependencies to determine the following collection of relations:

```
Student (StudentNum, LastName, FirstName, PermStreet, PermCity,
      PermState, PermPostalCode, LocalStreet, LocalCity, LocalState,
      LocalPostalCode, CreditsTaken, CreditsEarned, GPA, TotalPoints)
StudentSemester (StudentNum, SemesterCode, CreditsTaken,
      CreditsEarned, GPA, TotalPoints)
Course (DepartmentCode, CourseNum, CourseTitle, NumCredits)
StudentGrade (StudentNum, SemesterCode, DepartmentName,
      CourseNum, Grade, CreditsEarned, GradePoints)
```

All these relations are in third normal form. The only change you should make involves the DepartmentName attribute in the StudentGrade table. In general, if you encounter an attribute for which there exists a determinant that is not in the table, you should add the determinant. In this case, DepartmentCode is a determinant for DepartmentName, but it is not in the table, so you should add DepartmentCode. In the normalization process, DepartmentName will then be removed and placed in another table whose key is DepartmentCode. This other table will be merged with the Department table without the addition of any new attributes. The resulting StudentGrade table is as follows:

```
StudentGrade (StudentNum, SemesterCode, DepartmentCode,
      CourseNum, Grade, CreditsEarned, GradePoints)
```

Before representing this design in DBDL, examine the StudentSemester entity. Some of the attributes it contains (CreditsTaken, CreditsEarned, GPA, and TotalPoints) refer to the current semester, and all appear on a report card. Assume after further checking that you find that all these attributes are easily calculated from other fields on the report card. Rather than storing these attributes in the database, you can ensure that the program that produces the report cards performs the necessary calculations. For this reason, you will remove the StudentSemester table from the collection of tables to be documented and merged. (If these attributes are also required by some other user view in which the same computations are not as practical, they might find their way into the database when that user view is analyzed.)

Q & A A-1

Question: Determine the tables and keys required for User View 3. Merge the result into the cumulative design and draw the E-R diagram for the new cumulative design.

Answer: Figure A-13 shows the new cumulative design.

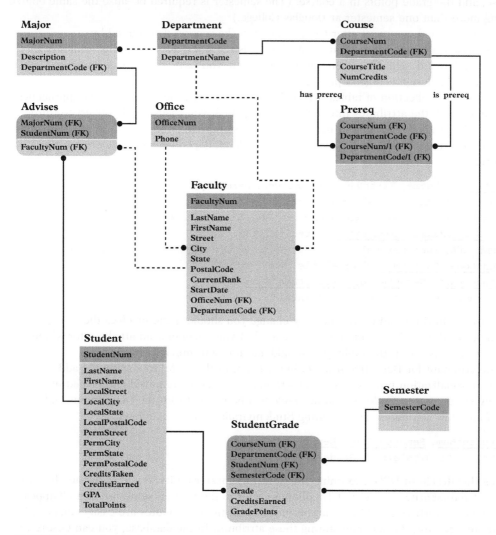

FIGURE A-13 Cumulative design after User View 3

User View 4—Class list: The system must produce a class list for each section of each course. Space is provided for the grades. At the end of the semester, the instructor enters each student's grade and sends a copy of the class list to the records office. Assume that, after examining the sample class list report (see Figure A-2), you decide to create a single table (actually an unnormalized table) that contains all the attributes on the class list, with the student information (number, name, class standing, and grade) as a repeating group. (Applying the tips for determining the relations to support a given user view would lead more directly to the result, but for the sake of developing the example, assume you have not done that yet.) The unnormalized table created by this method would be as follows:

```
ClassList (DepartmentCode, DepartmentName, SemesterCode,
    CourseNum, CourseTitle, NumCredits, SectionLetter,
    ScheduleCode, Time, Room, FacultyNum, FacultyLastName,
    FacultyFirstName, (StudentNum, StudentLastName,
    StudentFirstName, ClassStanding, Grade) )
```

NOTE: Because attribute names within a single table must be unique, it is not permissible to assign the attribute name LastName to both the faculty and student last names. Thus, the attributes that store the last and first names of a faculty member are named FacultyLastName and FacultyFirstName, respectively. Similarly, the attributes that store the last and first names of a student are named StudentLastName and StudentFirstName, respectively.

Note that you have not yet indicated the primary key. To identify a given class within a particular semester requires the combination of a department code, course number, and section letter or, more simply, the schedule code. Using the schedule code as the primary key, however, is not adequate. Because the information from more than one semester will be on file at the same time and because the same schedule code could be used in two different semesters to represent different courses, the primary key must also contain the semester code. When you remove the repeating group, this primary key expands to contain the key for the repeating group, which, in this case, is the student number. Thus, converting to first normal form yields the following design:

```
ClassList (DepartmentCode, DepartmentName, SemesterCode,
    CourseNum, CourseTitle, NumCredits, SectionLetter,
    ScheduleCode, Time, Room, FacultyNum, FacultyLastName,
    FacultyFirstName, StudentNum, StudentLastName,
    StudentFirstName, ClassStanding, Grade)
```

Converting to third normal form yields the following collection of tables:

```
Department (DepartmentCode, DepartmentName)
Section (SemesterCode, ScheduleCode, DepartmentCode, CourseNum,
    SectionLetter, Time, Room, FacultyNum)
Faculty (FacultyNum, LastName, FirstName)
StudentClass (SemesterCode, ScheduleCode, StudentNum, Grade)
Student (StudentNum, LastName, FirstName, ClassStanding)
Course (DepartmentCode, CourseNum, CourseTitle, NumCredits)
```

NOTE: Because the last name of a faculty member is now in a separate table from that of the last name of a student, it is no longer necessary to have different names. Thus, FacultyLastName and StudentLastName have been shortened to LastName. Similarly, FacultyFirstName and StudentFirstName have been shortened to FirstName.

Q & A A-2

Question: Why was the grade included in the StudentClass table?
Answer: Although the grade is not actually printed on the class list, it will be entered on the form by the instructor and sent to the records office for posting. The grade verification report differs from the class list only in that the grade is printed. Thus, the grade ultimately will be required, and it is appropriate to deal with it here.

Q & A A-3

Question: Determine the tables and keys required for User View 4. Merge the result into the cumulative design and draw the E-R diagram for the new cumulative design.

Answer: Figure A-14 shows the new cumulative design.

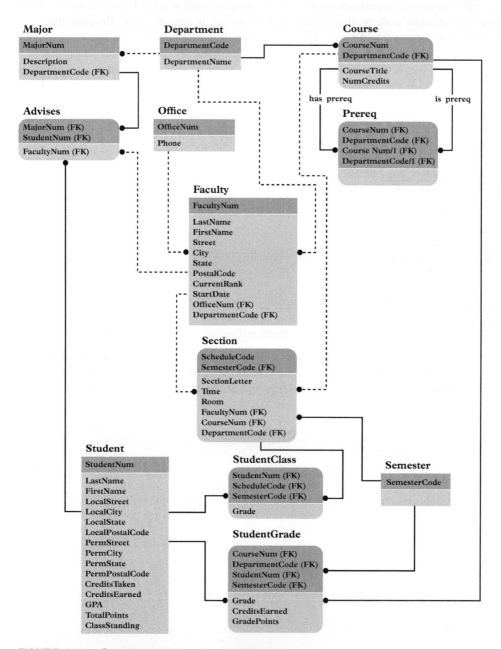

FIGURE A-14 Cumulative design after User View 4

User View 5—Grade verification report: After the records office processes the class list, it returns the class list to the instructor with the grades entered in the report. The instructor uses the report to verify that the records office entered the students' grades correctly. Because the only difference between the class list and the grade verification report is that the grades are printed on the grade verification report, the user views will be quite similar. In fact, because you made a provision for the grade when treating the class list, the views are identical and no further treatment of this user view is required.

User View 6—Time schedule: List all sections of all courses offered during a given semester. Each section has a unique four-digit schedule code. The time schedule lists the schedule code; the department offering the course; the course's number, section letter, and title; the instructor teaching the course; the time the course meets; the room in which the course meets; the number of credits generated by the course; and the prerequisites for the course. In addition to the information shown in the figure, the time schedule includes the date the semester begins and ends, the date final exams begin and end, and the last withdrawal date. The attributes on the time schedule are as follows: term (which is a synonym for semester), department code, department name, location, course number, course title, number of credits, schedule code, section letter, meeting time, meeting place, and instructor name.

You could create a single relation containing all these attributes and then normalize that relation, or you could apply the tips presented in Chapter 8 for determining the collection of relations. In either case, you ultimately create the following collection of relations:

```
Department (DepartmentCode, DepartmentName, Location)
Course (DepartmentCode, CourseNum, CourseTitle, NumCredits)
Section (SemesterCode, ScheduleCode, DepartmentCode, CourseNum,
    SectionLetter, Time, Room, FacultyNum)
Faculty (FacultyNum, LastName, FirstName)
Semester (SemesterCode, StartDate, EndDate, ExamStartDate,
    ExamEndDate, WithdrawalDate)
```

NOTE: Actually, given the attributes in this user view, the Section relation would contain the instructor's name (LastName and FirstName). There was no mention of instructor number. In general, as you saw earlier, it is a good idea to include determinants for attributes whenever possible. In this example, because FacultyNum determines LastName and FirstName, you add FacultyNum to the Section relation, at which point the Section relation is not in third normal form. Converting to third normal form produces the collection of relations previously shown.

Q & A A-4

Question: Determine the tables and keys required for User View 6. Merge the result into the cumulative design and draw the E-R diagram for the new cumulative design.
Answer: Figure A-15 on the next page shows the new cumulative design.

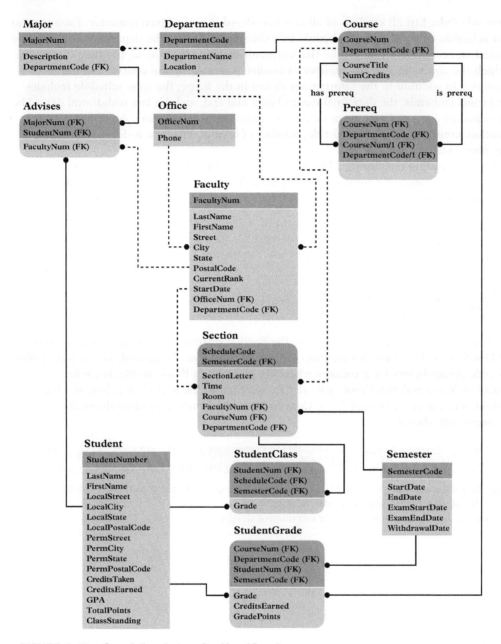

FIGURE A-15 Cumulative design after User View 6

User View 7—Registration request form: A student uses this form to request classes for the upcoming semester. Students indicate the sections for which they want to register by entering the sections' schedule codes; for each section, students may also enter a code for an alternate section in case the requested primary section is full. The collection of tables to support this user view includes a Student table that consists of the primary key, StudentNum, and all the attributes that depend only on StudentNum. These attributes include LastName, FirstName, and LocalStreet. Because all attributes in this table are already in the Student table in the cumulative design, this user view will not add anything new and there is no need for further discussion of it here.

The portion of this user view that is not already present in the cumulative design concerns the primary and alternate schedule codes that students request. A table to support this portion of the user view must contain both a primary and an alternate schedule code. The table must also contain the number of the student making the request. Finally, to allow the flexibility of retaining this information for more than a single semester (to allow registration for more than a semester at a time), the table must also include the semester in which the request is made. This leads to the following relation:

RegistrationRequest (<u>StudentNum</u>, <u>PrimaryCode</u>, AlternateCode, SemesterCode)

For example, if student 381124188 were to request the section with schedule code 2345 and then request the section with schedule code 2396 as an alternate for the FA18 semester, the row (381124188, 2345, 2396, "FA18") would be stored. The student number, the primary schedule code, the alternate schedule code, and the semester code are required to uniquely identify a particular row.

Q & A A-5

Question: Determine the tables and keys required for User View 7. Merge the result into the cumulative design and draw the E-R diagram for the new cumulative design.

Answer: Figure A-16 on the next page shows the new cumulative design. Notice that two relationships join the Section table to the RegistrationRequest table, so you must name each of them. In this case, you use "primary" and "alternate," indicating that one relationship relates a request to the primary section chosen and that the other relationship relates the request to the alternative section when there is one.

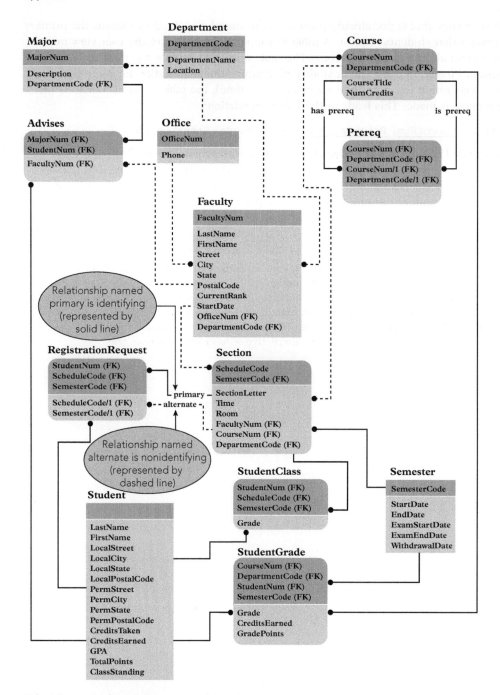

FIGURE A-16   Cumulative design after User View 7

NOTE: The foreign keys are the combination of PrimaryCode and SemesterCode as well as the combination of AlternateCode and SemesterCode. Because PrimaryCode and AlternateCode are portions of the foreign keys that must match the ScheduleCode in the Section table, they have been renamed ScheduleCode and ScheduleCode/1, respectively. Likewise, the second SemesterCode has been renamed SemesterCode/1.

User View 8—Student schedule: After all students are assigned to sections, the system produces a student schedule form, which is mailed to students to inform them of the classes in which they have been enrolled. Suppose you had created a single unnormalized relation to support the student schedule. This unnormalized relation would contain a repeating group representing the lines in the body of the schedule as follows:

```
StudentSchedule (StudentNum, SemesterCode, LastName, FirstName,
    LocalStreet, LocalCity, LocalState, LocalPostalCode, PermStreet,
    PermCity, PermState, PermPostalCode, (ScheduleCode,
    DepartmentName, CourseNum, CourseTitle, SectionLetter,
    NumCredits, Time, Room) )
```

At this point, you remove the repeating group to convert to first normal form, yielding the following:

```
StudentSchedule (StudentNum, SemesterCode, LastName, FirstName,
    LocalStreet, LocalCity, LocalState, LocalPostalCode, PermStreet,
    PermCity, PermState, PermPostalCode, ScheduleCode,
    DepartmentCode, CourseNum, CourseTitle, SectionLetter,
    NumCredits, Time, Room)
```

Note that the primary key expands to include ScheduleCode, which is the key to the repeating group. Converting this table to second normal form produces the following:

```
Student (StudentNum, LastName, FirstName, LocalStreet, LocalCity,
    LocalState, LocalPostalCode, PermStreet, PermCity,
    PermState, PermPostalCode)
StudentSchedule (StudentNum, SemesterCode, ScheduleCode)
Section (SemesterCode, ScheduleCode, DepartmentCode, CourseNum,
    CourseTitle, SectionLetter, NumCredits, Time, Room)
Course (DepartmentCode, CourseNum, CourseTitle, NumCredits)
```

Removing the attributes that depend on the determinant of DepartmentCode and CourseNum from the Section table and converting this collection of tables to third normal form produces the following tables:

```
Student (StudentNum, LastName, FirstName, LocalStreet,
    LocalCity, LocalState, LocalPostalCode, PermStreet,
    PermCity, PermState, PermPostalCode)
StudentSchedule (StudentNum, SemesterCode, ScheduleCode)
Section (SemesterCode, ScheduleCode, DepartmentCode, CourseNum,
    SectionLetter, Time, Room)
Course (DepartmentCode, CourseNum, CourseTitle, NumCredits)
```

Merging this collection into the cumulative design does not add anything new. In the process, you can merge the StudentSchedule table with the StudentClass table.

User View 9—Full student information report: List complete information about a student, including his or her majors and all grades received to date. Suppose you attempted to place all the attributes on the full student information report into a single unnormalized relation. The table has two separate repeating groups: one for the different majors a student might have and the other for all the courses the student has taken.

NOTE: Several attributes, such as name and address, would not be in the repeating groups. All these attributes are already in the cumulative design, however, and are not addressed here.

The table with repeating groups is as follows:

```
Student (StudentNum, (MajorNum, DepartmentCode, LastName,
    FirstName), (SemesterCode, DepartmentCode, CourseNum,
    CourseTitle, NumCredits, Grade, GradePoints) )
```

Recall from Chapter 5 that you should separate repeating groups when a relation has more than one. If you do not, you will typically have problems with fourth normal form. Separating the repeating groups in this example produces the following:

```
StudentMajor (StudentNum, (MajorNum, DepartmentCode, LastName, FirstName))
StudentCourse (StudentNum, (SemesterCode, DepartmentCode,
    CourseNum, CourseTitle, NumCredits, Grade, GradePoints))
```

Converting these tables to first normal form and including FacultyNum, which is a determinant for LastName and FirstName, produces the following:

```
StudentMajor (StudentNum, MajorNum, DepartmentCode, FacultyNum,
    LastName, FirstName)
StudentCourse (StudentNum, SemesterCode, DepartmentCode,
    CourseNum, CourseTitle, NumCredits, Grade, Grade Points)
```

The StudentCourse table is not in second normal form because CourseTitle and NumCredits depend only on the DepartmentCode, CourseNum combination. The StudentMajor table is not in second normal form either because DepartmentCode depends on MajorNum. Removing these dependencies produces the following tables:

```
StudentMajor (StudentNum, MajorNum, FacultyNum, LastName, FirstName)
Major (MajorNum, DepartmentCode)
StudentCourse (StudentNum, SemesterCode, DepartmentCode,
    CourseNum, Grade, GradePoints)
Course (DepartmentCode, CourseNum, CourseTitle, NumCredits)
```

Other than the StudentMajor table, all these relations are in third normal form. Converting the StudentMajor table to third normal form produces the following tables:

```
StudentMajor (StudentNum, MajorNum, FacultyNum)
Faculty (FacultyNum, LastName, FirstName)
```

Merging this collection into the cumulative design does not add anything new. (You can merge the StudentMajor table with the Advises table without adding any new attributes.)

User View 10—Work version of the time schedule: This report is similar to the original time schedule (see Figure A-3), but it is designed for the college's internal use. It shows the current enrollments in each section of each course, as well as each section's maximum enrollment. The only difference between the work version of the time schedule and the time schedule itself (see User View 6) is the addition of two attributes for each section: current enrollment and maximum enrollment. Because these two attributes depend only on the combination of the semester code and the schedule code, you would place them in the Section table of User View 6, and after the merge, they would be in the Section table in the cumulative design. The cumulative design thus far is shown in Figure A-17.

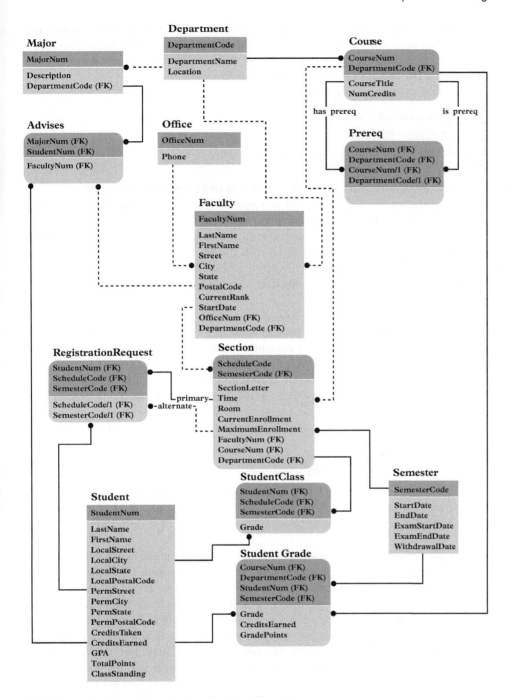

FIGURE A-17 Cumulative design after User View 10

Because the process of determining whether a student has had the prerequisites for a given course involves examining the grades (if any) received in these prior courses, it makes sense to analyze the user view that involves grades before treating the user view that involves enrollment.

User View 11—Post grades: For each section of each course, the system must post the grades that are indicated on the class list submitted by the instructor and produce a grade verification report. There is a slight problem with posting grades—grades must be posted by section to produce the grade report (in other words, you must record the fact that student 381124188 received an A in the section of CS 162 whose schedule code was 2366 during the fall 2018 semester). On the other hand, for the full student information report, there is no need to have any of the grades related to an actual section of a course. Further, because section information, including these grades, is kept for only two semesters, grades would be lost after two semesters if they were kept only by section because section information would be purged at that time.

A viable alternative is to post two copies of the grade: one copy will be associated with the student, the term, and the section, and the other copy will be associated with only the student and the term. The first copy would be used for the grade verification report; the second, for the full student information report. Report cards would probably utilize the second copy, although not necessarily.

Thus, you would have the following two grade tables:

```
GradeSection (StudentNum, DepartmentCode, CourseNum,
    ScheduleCode, SemesterCode, Grade)
GradeStudent (StudentNum, DepartmentCode, CourseNum,
    SemesterCode, Grade)
```

Because the DepartmentCode and CourseNum in the GradeSection table depend only on the concatenation of ScheduleCode and SemesterCode, they will be removed from the GradeSection table during the normalization process and placed in a table whose primary key is the concatenation of ScheduleCode and SemesterCode. This table will be combined with the Section table in the cumulative design without adding new fields. The GradeSection table that remains will be merged with the StudentClass table without adding new fields. Finally, the GradeStudent table will be combined with the StudentGrade table in the cumulative design without adding any new fields. Thus, treatment of this user view does not change the cumulative design.

User View 12—Enrollment: When a student attempts to register for a section of a course, you must determine whether the student has received credit for all prerequisites to the course. If the student is eligible to enroll in the course and the number of students currently enrolled in the section is less than the maximum enrollment, enroll the student. With the data already in place in the cumulative design, you can determine what courses a student has taken. You can also determine the prerequisites for a given course. The only remaining issue is the ability to enroll a student in a course. Because the system must retain information for more than one semester, you must include the semester code in the table. (You must have the information that student 381124188 enrolled in section 2345 in SP19 rather than in FA18, for example.) The additional table is as follows:

```
Enroll (StudentNum, SemesterCode, ScheduleCode)
```

The primary key of this table matches the primary key of the StudentClass table in the cumulative design. The fields occur in a different order here, but that makes no difference. Thus, this table will be merged with the StudentClass table. No new fields are to be added, so the cumulative design remains unchanged.

User View 13—Purge: Douglas College retains section information, including grades earned by the students in each section, for two semesters following the end of the semester, at which time this information is removed from the system. Periodically, certain information that is more than two terms old is removed from the database. This includes all information concerning sections of courses, such as the time, room, and instructor, as well as information about the students in the sections and their grades. The grade each student received will remain in the database by course but not by section. For example, you will always retain the fact that student 381124188 received an A in CS 162 during the fall semester of 2018, but once the data for that term is purged, you will no longer know the precise section of CS 162 that awarded this grade.

If you examine the current collection of tables, you will see that all the data to be purged is already included in the cumulative design and that you do not need to add anything new at this point.

FINAL INFORMATION-LEVEL DESIGN

Now that you are finished examining the user views, Douglas College can review the cumulative design to ensure that all user views have been met. You should conduct this review on your own to make certain that you understand how the requirements of each user can be satisfied. You will assume that this review has taken place and that no changes have been made. Therefore, Figure A-17 represents the final information-level design.

At this point, Douglas College is ready to move on to the physical-level design process. In this process, the appropriate team members will use the information-level design you produced to create the design for the specific DBMS that Douglas College selects. After it has done so, it will be able to create the database, load the data, and create the forms, reports, queries, and programs necessary to satisfy its requirements.

EXERCISES

1. Discuss the effect of the following changes on the design for the Douglas College requirements:
   a. More than one instructor might teach a given section of a course, and each instructor must be listed on the time schedule.
   b. Each department offers only a single major.
   c. Each department offers only a single major, and each faculty member can advise students only in the major that is offered by the department to which the faculty member is assigned.
   d. Each department offers only a single major, and each faculty member can advise students only in the major that is offered by the department to which the faculty member is assigned. In addition, a student can have only one major.
   e. There is an additional transaction requirement: given a student's name, find the student's number.
   f. More than one faculty member can be assigned to one office.
   g. The number of credits earned in a particular course cannot vary from student to student or from semester to semester.
   h. Instead of a course number, course codes are used to uniquely identify courses. (In other words, department numbers are no longer required for this purpose.) However, it is still important to know which courses are offered by which departments.
   i. On the registration request form, a student may designate a number of alternates along with his or her primary choice. These alternates are listed in priority order, with the first one being the most desired and the last one being the least desired.

2. Complete an information-level design for Holt Distributors.

   General description. Holt Distributors buys products from its vendors and sells those products to its customers. The Holt Distributors operation is divided into territories. Each customer is represented by a single sales rep, who must be assigned to the territory in which the customer is located. Although each sales rep is assigned to a single territory, more than one sales rep can be assigned to the same territory.

   When a customer places an order, the computer assigns the order the next available order number. The data entry clerk enters the customer number, the customer purchase order (PO) number, and the date. (Customers can place orders by submitting a PO, in which case, a PO number is recorded.) For each part that is ordered, the clerk enters the part number, quantity, and quoted price. (When it is time for the clerk to enter the quoted price, the computer displays the price from the master price list. If the quoted price is the same as the actual price, the clerk takes no special action. If not, the clerk enters the quoted price.)

   When the clerk completes the order, the system prints the order acknowledgment/picking list form shown in Figure A-18 on the next page and sends it to the customer for confirmation and payment. When Holt Distributors is ready to ship the customer's order, this same form is used to "pick" the merchandise in the warehouse and prepare it for delivery.

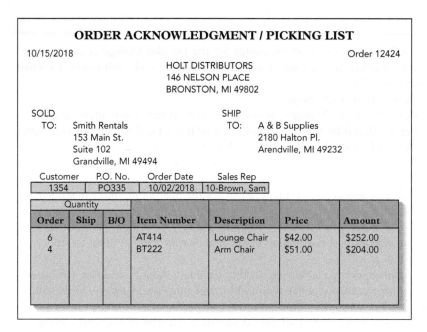

ORDER ACKNOWLEDGMENT / PICKING LIST

10/15/2018   Order 12424

HOLT DISTRIBUTORS
146 NELSON PLACE
BRONSTON, MI 49802

SOLD   SHIP
TO: Smith Rentals   TO: A & B Supplies
       153 Main St.   2180 Halton Pl.
       Suite 102   Arendville, MI 49232
       Grandville, MI 49494

Customer	P.O. No.	Order Date	Sales Rep
1354	PO335	10/02/2018	10-Brown, Sam

Quantity						
Order	Ship	B/O	Item Number	Description	Price	Amount
6			AT414	Lounge Chair	$42.00	$252.00
4			BT222	Arm Chair	$51.00	$204.00

FIGURE A-18   Order acknowledgement/picking list for Holt Distributors

An order that has not been shipped (filled) is called an open order; an order that has been shipped is called a released order. When orders are released, the system prints an invoice, sends it to the customer, and then increases the customer's balance by the invoice amount. Some orders are completely filled; others are only partially filled, meaning that only part of the customer's order was shipped. In either case, when an entire order or a partial order has been shipped, the order is considered to have been filled and is no longer considered an open order. (Another possibility is to allow back orders when the order cannot be completely filled. In this case, the order remains open, but only for the back-ordered portion.) When the system generates an invoice, it removes the order from the open orders file. The system stores summary information about the invoice (number, date, customer, invoice total, and freight) until the end of the month. A sample invoice is shown in Figure A-19.

10/15/2018   Invoice 11025

HOLT DISTRIBUTORS
146 NELSON PLACE
BRONSTON, MI 49802

SOLD   SHIP
TO: Smith Rentals   TO: A & B Supplies
       153 Main St.   2180 Halton Pl.
       Suite 102   Arendville, MI 49232
       Grandville, MI 49494

Customer	P.O. No.	Our Order No.	Order Date	Ship Date	Sales Rep
1354	PO335	12424	10/02/2018	10/15/2018	10-Brown, Sam

Quantity						
Order	Ship	B/O	Item Number	Description	Price	Amount
6	5	1	AT414	Lounge Chair	$42.00	$210.00
4	4	0	BT222	Arm Chair	$51.00	$204.00
				Freight		$42.50

	Pay This Amount
	$456.50

FIGURE A-19   Invoice for Holt Distributors

Most companies use one of two methods to accept payments from customers: open items and balance forward. In the open-item method, customers make payments on specific invoices. An invoice remains on file until the customer pays it in full. In the balance-forward method, customers have balances. When the system generates an invoice, the customer's balance is increased by the amount of the invoice. When a customer makes a payment, the system decreases the customer's balance by the payment amount. Holt Distributors uses the balance-forward method.

At the end of each month, the system updates and ages customers' accounts. (You will learn about month-end processing requirements and the update and aging processes in the following sections.) The system prints customer statements, an aged trial balance (described in the report requirements section), a monthly cash receipts journal, a monthly invoice register, and a sales rep commission report. The system then removes cash receipts and invoice summary records from the database and sets month-to-date (MTD) fields to zero. When the system processes the monthly data for December, it also sets the year-to-date (YTD) fields to zero.

Transaction requirements. The following transaction requirements are required by Holt Distributors:

a. Enter and edit territories (territory number and name).

b. Enter and edit sales reps (sales rep number, name, address, city, state, postal code, MTD sales, YTD sales, MTD commission, YTD commission, and commission rate). Each sales rep represents a single territory.

c. Enter and edit customers (customer number, name, first line of address, second line of address, city, state, postal code, MTD sales, YTD sales, current balance, and credit limit). A customer can have a different name and address to which goods are shipped (called the "ship-to" address). Each customer has a single sales rep who is located in a single territory. The sales rep must represent the territory in which the customer is located.

d. Enter and edit parts (part number, description, price, MTD and YTD sales, units on hand, units allocated, and reorder point). The Units allocated field is the number of units that are currently present on some open orders. The reorder point is the lowest value acceptable for units on hand without the product being reordered. On the stock status report, which will be described later, an asterisk indicates any part for which the number of units on hand is less than the reorder point.

e. Enter and edit vendors (vendor number, name, address, city, state, and postal code). In addition, for each part supplied by the vendor, enter and edit the part number, the price the vendor charges for the part, the minimum order quantity that the vendor will accept for this part, and the expected lead time for delivery of this part from this vendor.

f. Order entry (order number, date, customer, customer PO number, and order detail lines). An order detail line consists of a part number, a description, the number ordered, and the quoted price. Each order detail line includes a sequence number that is entered by the user. Detail lines on an order must print in the order of this sequence number. The system should calculate and display the order total. After all orders for the day have been entered, the system prints order acknowledgment/picking list reports (see Figure A-18). In addition, for each part ordered, the system must increase the units allocated for the part by the number of units that the customer ordered.

g. The invoicing system has the following requirements:

1. Enter the numbers of the orders to be released. For each order, enter the ship date for invoicing and the freight amount. Indicate whether the order is to be shipped in full or in part. If an order is to be partially shipped, enter the number shipped for each order detail line. The system will generate a unique invoice number for this invoice.

2. Print invoices for each of the released orders. (A sample invoice is shown in Figure A-19.)

3. Update files with information from the printed invoices. For each invoice, the system adds the invoice total to the current invoice total. It also adds the current balance and the MTD and YTD sales for the customer that placed the order. The system also adds the total to the MTD and YTD sales for the sales rep who represents the customer. In addition, the system multiplies the total by the sales rep's commission rate and adds this amount to the MTD commission earned and the YTD commission

earned. For each part shipped, the system decreases units on hand and units allocated by the number of units of the part or parts that were shipped. The system also increases the MTD and YTD sales of the part by the amount of the number of units shipped multiplied by the quoted price.

4. Create an invoice summary record for each invoice printed. These records contain the invoice number, date, customer, sales rep, invoice total, and freight.

5. Delete the released orders.

h. Receive payments on account (customer number, date, and amount). The system assigns each payment a number, adds the payment amount to the total of current payments for the customer, and subtracts the payment amount from the current balance of the customer.

Report requirements. The following is a list of the reports required by Holt Distributors:

a. **Territory List:** For each territory, list the number and name of the territory; the number, name, and address of each sales rep in the territory; and the number, name, and address of each customer represented by these sales reps.

b. **Customer Master List:** For each customer, list the customer number, the bill-to address, and the ship-to address. Also list the number, name, address, city, state, and postal code of the sales rep who represents the customer and the number and name of the territory in which the customer is located.

c. **Customer Open Order Report:** This report lists open orders organized by customer. It is shown in Figure A-20.

10/16/2018	**HOLT DISTRIBUTORS**				PAGE 1
	CUSTOMER OPEN ORDER REPORT				
Order Number	Item Number	Item Description	Order Date	Order Qty	Quoted Price
Customer 1354 - Smith Rentals					
12424	AT414	Lounge Chair	10/12/2018	1	$42.00
Customer 1358 - · · · · · · · ·					
·	·	·	·	·	·
·	·	·	·	·	·
·	·	·	·	·	·
·	·	·	·	·	·

FIGURE A-20 Open order report (by customer)

d. **Item Open Order Report:** This report lists open orders organized by item and is shown in Figure A-21.

10/16/2018	**HOLT DISTRIBUTORS**						PAGE 1
	ITEM OPEN ORDER REPORT						
Item Number	Item Description	Customer Number	Customer Name	Order Number	Order Date	Order Qty	Quoted Price
AT414	Lounge Chair	1354	Smith Rentals	12424	10/02/2018	1	$42.00
		1358	Kayland Enterprises	12489	10/03/2018	8	$42.00
				Total on order -		9	
BT222	Arm Chair	1358	Kayland Enterprises	12424	10/03/2018	3	$51.00
		·	·	·	·	·	·
		·	·	·	·	·	·
		·	·	·	·	·	·

FIGURE A-21 Open order report (by item)

e. **Daily Invoice Register:** For each invoice produced on a given day, list the invoice number, invoice date, customer number, customer name, sales amount, freight, and invoice total. A sample of this report is shown in Figure A-22.

10/16/2018		**HOLT DISTRIBUTORS** **DAILY INVOICE REGISTER FOR 10/15/2018**				PAGE 1
Invoice Number	Invoice Date	Customer Number	Customer Name	Sales Amount	Freight	Invoice Amount
11025	10/15/2018	1354	Smith Rentals	$414.00	$42.50	$456.50
.	.	.	.	.	.	.
.	.	.	.	.	.	.
.	.	.	.	.	.	.
.	.	.	.	$2,840.50	$238.20	$3,078.70

FIGURE A-22   Daily invoice register

f. **Monthly Invoice Register:** The monthly invoice register has the same format as the daily invoice register, but it includes data for all invoices that occurred during the selected month.

g. **Stock Status Report:** For each part, list the part number, description, price, MTD and YTD sales, units on hand, units allocated, and reorder point. For each part for which the number of units on hand is less than the reorder point, an asterisk should appear at the far right of the report.

h. **Reorder Point List:** This report has the same format as the stock status report. Other than the title, the only difference is that parts for which the number of units on hand is greater than or equal to the reorder point will not appear on this report.

i. **Vendor Report:** For each vendor, list the vendor number, name, address, city, state, and postal code. In addition, for each part supplied by the vendor, list the part number, the description, the price the vendor charges for the part, the minimum order quantity that the vendor will accept for this part, and the expected lead time for delivery of this part from the vendor.

j. **Daily Cash Receipts Journal:** For each payment received on a given day, list the number and name of the customer that made the payment and the payment amount. A sample report is shown in Figure A-23.

10/05/2018	**HOLT DISTRIBUTORS** **DAILY CASH RECEIPTS JOURNAL**		PAGE 1
Payment Number	Customer Number	Customer Name	Payment Amount
.	.	.	.
.	.	.	.
5807	1354	Smith Rentals	$1,000.00
.	.	.	.
.	.	.	$12,235.50

FIGURE A-23   Daily cash receipts journal

k. **Monthly Cash Receipts Journal:** The monthly cash receipts journal has the same format as the daily cash receipts journal, but it includes all cash receipts for the month.

l. **Customer Mailing Labels:** A sample of the three-across mailing labels printed by the system is shown in Figure A-24 on the next page.

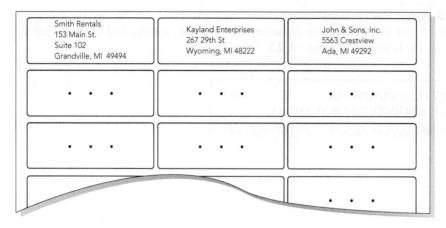

FIGURE A-24 Customer mailing labels

m. **Statements:** The system must produce a monthly statement for each active customer. A sample statement is shown in Figure A-25.

11/03/2018   **HOLT DISTRIBUTORS**
146 NELSON PLACE
BRONSTON, MI 49802

Smith Rentals   Customer Number: 1354
   153 Main St.   Sales Rep: 10 - Brown, Sam
   Suite 102
   Grandville, MI 49494   Limit: $5,000.00

Invoice Number	Date	Description	Total Amount
10945	10/02/2018	Invoice	$1,230.00
	10/05/2018	Payment	$1,000.00CR
11025	10/15/2018	Invoice	$456.50
	10/22/2018	Payment	$500.00CR

Over 90	Over 60		
$0.00	$198.50		
Over 30	Current	Total Due >>>>>>	$2,325.20
$490.20	$1,686.50		
Previous Balance	Current Invoices	Current Payments	
$2,138.70	$1,686.50	$1,500.00	

FIGURE A-25 Statement for Holt Distributors

n. **Monthly Sales Rep Commission Report:** For each sales rep, list his or her number, name, address, MTD sales, YTD sales, MTD commission earned, YTD commission earned, and commission rate.

o. **Aged Trial Balance:** The aged trial balance report contains the same information that is printed on each customer's statement.

Month-end processing. Month-end processing consists of the following actions that occur at the end of each month:

a. Update customer account information. In addition to the customer's actual balance, the system must maintain the following records: current debt, debt incurred within the last 30 days, debt that is more than 30 days past due but less than 60 days past due, debt that is 60 or more days past due but less than 90 days past due, and debt that is 90 or more days past due. The system updates the actual balance, the current invoice total, and the current payment total when it produces a new invoice or receives a payment; however, the system updates these aging figures only at the end of the month. The actual update process is as follows:

1. The system processes payments received within the last month and credits these payments to the past due amount for 90 or more days. The system then credits any additional payment to the 60 or more days past due amount, then to the more than 30 days past due amount, and then to the current debt amount (less than 30 days).

2. The system "rolls" the amounts by adding the 60 or more days past due amount to the 90 or more days past due amount and by adding the more than 30 days past due amount to the 60 or more days past due amount. The current amount becomes the new more than 30 days past due amount. Finally, the current month's invoice total becomes the new current amount.

3. The system prints the statements and the aged trial balances.

4. The system sets the current invoice total to zero, sets the current payment total to zero, and sets the previous balance to the current balance in preparation for the next month. To illustrate, assume before the update begins that the amounts for customer 1354 are as follows:

```
Current Balance:  $2,375.20    Previous Balance: $2,138.70
Current Invoices: $1,686.50           Current:    $490.20
Current Payments: $1,500.00           Over 30:    $298.50
                                      Over 60:    $710.00
                                      Over 90:    $690.00
```

The system subtracts the current payments ($1,500.00) from the over 90 amount ($690.00), reduces the over 90 amount to zero, and calculates an excess payment of $810.00. The system subtracts this excess payment from the over 60 amount ($710.00), reduces the over 60 amount to zero, and calculates an excess payment of $100.00. The system then subtracts the excess payment from the over 30 amount ($298.50) and reduces this amount to $198.50. At this point, the system rolls the amounts and sets the current amount to the current invoice total, producing the following:

```
Current Balance:  $2,375.20    Previous Balance: $2,138.70
Current Invoices: $1,686.50           Current: $1,686.50
Current Payments: $1,500.00           Over 30:    $490.20
                                      Over 60:    $198.50
                                      Over 90:      $0.00
```

The system then produces statements and the aged trial balance and updates the Previous Balance, Current Invoices, and Current Payments amounts, yielding the following:

```
Current Balance:  $2,375.20    Previous Balance: $2,375.20
Current Invoices: $0.00               Current:    $1,686.50
Current Payments: $0.00               Over 30:      $490.20
                                      Over 60:      $198.50
                                      Over 90:        $0.00
```

a. Print the monthly invoice register and the monthly cash receipts journal.

b. Print a monthly sales rep commission report.

c. Set all MTD fields to zero. If necessary, set all YTD fields to zero.

d. Remove all cash receipts and invoice summary records. (In practice, such records would be moved to a historical type of database for future reference. For the purposes of this assignment, you will omit this step.)

SQL REFERENCE

You can use this appendix to obtain details concerning important components and syntax for SQL. Items are arranged alphabetically. Each item contains a description and, where appropriate, both an example and a description of the query results. Some SQL commands also include a description of the clauses associated with them. For each clause, there is a brief description and an indication of whether the clause is required or optional.

ALTER TABLE

Use the ALTER TABLE command to change a table's structure. As shown in Figure B-1, you type the ALTER TABLE command, followed by the table name, and then the alteration to perform. (*Note*: In Access, you usually make these changes to a table in Design view rather than using ALTER TABLE.)

Clause	Description	Required?
ALTER TABLE *table name*	Indicates the name of the table to be altered.	Yes
alteration	Indicates the type of alteration to be performed.	Yes

FIGURE B-1   ALTER TABLE command

The following command alters the Customer table by adding a new column named CustType:

```
ALTER TABLE Customer
ADD CustType CHAR(1)
;
```

The following command alters the Customer table by changing the length of the CustomerName column:

```
ALTER TABLE Customer
CHANGE COLUMN CustomerName TO CHAR(50)
;
```

The following command alters the Item table by deleting the Storehouse column:

```
ALTER TABLE Item
DELETE Storehouse
;
```

COLUMN OR EXPRESSION LIST (SELECT CLAUSE)

To select columns, use a SELECT clause with the list of columns separated by commas. The following SELECT clause selects the CustomerNum, CustomerName, and Balance columns:

```
SELECT CustomerNum, CustomerName, Balance
```

Use an asterisk in a SELECT clause to select all columns in the table. The following SELECT command selects all columns in the Item table:

```
SELECT *
FROM Item
;
```

Computed Fields

You can use a computation in place of a field by typing the computation. For readability, you can type the computation in parentheses, although it is not necessary to do so.

The following SELECT clause selects the CustomerNum and CustomerName columns as well as the results of subtracting the Balance column from the CreditLimit column:

```
SELECT CustomerNum, CustomerName, CreditLimit-Balance
```

Functions

You can use aggregate functions in a SELECT clause. The most commonly used functions are AVG (to calculate an average), COUNT (to count the number of rows), MAX (to determine the maximum value), MIN (to determine the minimum value), and SUM (to calculate a total).

The following SELECT clause calculates the average balance:

```
SELECT AVG(Balance)
```

CONDITIONS

A condition is an expression that can be evaluated as either true or false. When you use a condition in a WHERE clause, the results of the query contain those rows for which the condition is true. You can create simple conditions and compound conditions using the BETWEEN, LIKE, and IN operators, as described in the following sections.

Simple Conditions

A simple condition includes the field name, a comparison operator, and another field name or a value. The available comparison operators are = (equal to), < (less than), > (greater than), <= (less than or equal to), >= (greater than or equal to), and < > (not equal to).

The following WHERE clause uses a condition to select rows on which the balance is greater than the credit limit:

```
WHERE Balance>CreditLimit
```

Compound Conditions

Compound conditions are formed by connecting two or more simple conditions using one or both of the following operators: AND and OR. You can also precede a single condition with the NOT operator to negate a condition. When you connect simple conditions using the AND operator, all the simple conditions must be true for the compound condition to be true. When you connect simple conditions using the OR operator, the compound condition will be true whenever any of the simple conditions are true. Preceding a condition with the NOT operator reverses the result of the original condition. That is, if the original condition is true, the new condition will be false; if the original condition is false, the new one will be true.

The following WHERE clause is true if those items for which the Storehouse number is equal to 3 *or* the number of units on hand is greater than 20:

```
WHERE Storehouse='3'
OR OnHand>20
```

The following WHERE clause is true if those items for which *both* the Storehouse number is equal to 3 *and* the number of units on hand is greater than 20:

```
WHERE Storehouse='3'
AND OnHand>20
```

The following WHERE clause is true if the Storehouse number is not equal to 3:

```
WHERE NOT (Storehouse='3')
```

BETWEEN Conditions

You can use the BETWEEN operator to determine whether a value is within a range of values. The following WHERE clause is true if the balance is between 1,000 and 5,000:

```
WHERE Balance BETWEEN 1000 AND 5000
```

LIKE Conditions

LIKE conditions use wildcards to select rows. Use the percent sign (%) to represent any collection of characters. The condition LIKE '%Oxford%' will be true for data consisting of any character or characters followed by the letters "Oxford" followed by any other character or characters. Another wildcard is the underscore character (_), which represents any individual character. For example, 'T_m' represents the letter T followed by any single character followed by the letter m and would be true for a collection of characters such as *Tim, Tom,* or *T3m*.

NOTE: In Access SQL, the asterisk (*) is used as a wildcard to represent any collection of characters. Another wildcard in Access SQL is the question mark (?), which represents any individual character. Many versions of SQL use the underscore (_) instead of the question mark to represent any individual character.

The following WHERE clause is true if the value in the Street column is Oxford Rd., Oxford, or any other value that contains "Oxford":

```
WHERE Street LIKE '%Oxford%'
```

Access version:

```
WHERE Street LIKE '*Oxford*'
```

IN Conditions

You can use the IN operator to determine whether a value is in some specific collection of values. The following WHERE clause is true if the credit limit is 7,500, 10,000, or 15,000:

```
WHERE CreditLimit IN (7500, 10000, 15000)
```

The following WHERE clause is true if the item number is in the collection of item numbers located in Storehouse 3:

```
WHERE ItemNum IN
(SELECT ItemNum
FROM Item
WHERE Storehouse='3')
```

CREATE INDEX

Use the CREATE INDEX command to create an index for a table. Figure B-2 describes the CREATE INDEX command.

Clause	Description	Required?
CREATE INDEX *index name*	Indicates the name of the index.	Yes
ON *table name*	Indicates the table for which the index is to be created.	Yes
column list	Indicates the column or columns on which the index is to be tested.	Yes

FIGURE B-2   CREATE INDEX command

The following CREATE INDEX command creates an index named RepBal for the Customer table on the combination of the RepNum and Balance columns:

```
CREATE INDEX RepBal
ON Customer (RepNum, Balance)
;
```

CREATE TABLE

Use the CREATE TABLE command to create a table by describing its layout. Figure B-3 describes the CREATE TABLE command.

Clause	Description	Required?
CREATE TABLE *table name*	Indicates the name of the table to be created.	Yes
(column and data type list)	Indicates the columns that make up the table along with their corresponding data types (see the "Data Types" section).	Yes

FIGURE B-3   CREATE TABLE command

The following CREATE TABLE command creates the Rep table and its associated columns and data types:

```
CREATE TABLE Rep
(RepNum CHAR(2),
LastName CHAR(15),
FirstName CHAR(15),
Street CHAR(15),
City CHAR(15),
State CHAR(2),
PostalCode CHAR(5),
Commission DECIMAL(7,2),
Rate DECIMAL(3,2) )
;
```

Access version:

```
CREATE TABLE Rep
(RepNum CHAR(2),
LastName CHAR(15),
FirstName CHAR(15),
Street CHAR(15),
City CHAR(15),
State CHAR(2),
PostalCode CHAR(5),
Commission CURRENCY,
Rate NUMBER )
;
```

NOTE: Unlike other SQL implementations, Access doesn't have a DECIMAL data type. To create numbers with decimals, you must use either the CURRENCY or NUMBER data type. Use the CURRENCY data type for fields that will contain currency values; use the NUMBER data type for all other numeric fields.

CREATE VIEW

Use the CREATE VIEW command to create a view. Figure B-4 describes the CREATE VIEW command.

Clause	Description	Required?
CREATE VIEW *view name* AS	Indicates the name of the view to be created.	Yes
query	Indicates the defining query for the view.	Yes

FIGURE B-4   CREATE VIEW command

The following CREATE VIEW command creates a view named Games, which consists of the item number, description, units on hand, and unit price for all rows in the Item table on which the category is GME:

```
CREATE VIEW Games AS
SELECT ItemNum, Description, OnHand, Price
FROM Item
WHERE Category='GME'
;
```

DATA TYPES

Figure B-5 describes the data types that you can use in a CREATE TABLE command.

Data Type	Description
INTEGER	Stores integers, which are numbers without a decimal part. The valid data range is –2147483648 to 2147483647. You can use the contents of INTEGER fields for calculations.
SMALLINT	Stores integers but uses less space than the INTEGER data type. The valid data range is –32768 to 32767. SMALLINT is a better choice than INTEGER when you are certain that the field will store numbers within the indicated range. You can use the contents of SMALLINT fields for calculations.
DECIMAL(p,q)	Stores a decimal number p digits long with q of these digits being decimal places. For example, DECIMAL(5,2) represents a number with three places to the left and two places to the right of the decimal. You can use the contents of DECIMAL fields for calculations.
CHAR(n)	Stores a character string n characters long. You use the CHAR type for fields that contain letters and other special characters and for fields that contain numbers that will not be used in calculations. Because neither sales rep numbers nor customer numbers will be used in any calculations, for example, both of them are assigned CHAR as the data type. (Some DBMSs, such as Access, use SHORT TEXT rather than CHAR, but the two data types mean the same thing.)
DATE	Stores dates in the form DD-MON-YYYY or MM/DD/YYYY. For example, May 12, 2015, could be stored as 12-MAY-2015 or 5/12/2015.

FIGURE B-5   Data types

DELETE ROWS

Use the DELETE command to delete one or more rows from a table. Figure B-6 describes the DELETE command.

Clause	Description	Required?
DELETE FROM *table name*	Indicates the name of the table from which the row or rows are to be deleted.	Yes
WHERE *condition*	Indicates a condition. Those rows for which the condition is true will be retrieved and deleted.	No (If you omit the WHERE clause, all rows will be deleted.)

FIGURE B-6   DELETE command

The following DELETE command deletes any row from the OrderLine table on which the item number is DL51:

```
DELETE
FROM OrderLine
WHERE ItemNum='DL51'
;
```

DROP INDEX

Use the DROP INDEX command to delete an index, as shown in Figure B-7.

Clause	Description	Required?
DROP INDEX *index name*	Indicates the name of the index to be dropped.	Yes

FIGURE B-7　DROP INDEX command

The following DROP INDEX command deletes the index named RepBal:

```
DROP INDEX RepBal
;
```

DROP TABLE

Use the DROP TABLE command to delete a table, as shown in Figure B-8.

Clause	Description	Required?
DROP TABLE *table name*	Indicates the name of the table to be dropped.	Yes

FIGURE B-8　DROP TABLE command

The following DROP TABLE command deletes the table named SmallCust:

```
DROP TABLE SmallCust
;
```

GRANT

Use the GRANT statement to grant privileges to a user. Figure B-9 describes the GRANT statement.

Clause	Description	Required?
GRANT *privilege*	Indicates the type of privilege(s) to be granted.	Yes
ON *database object*	Indicates the database object(s) to which the privilege(s) pertain.	Yes
TO *user name*	Indicates the user(s) to whom the privilege(s) are to be granted.	Yes

FIGURE B-9　GRANT statement

The following GRANT statement grants the user named Jones the privilege of selecting rows from the Customer table:

```
GRANT SELECT ON Customer TO Jones
;
```

INSERT

Use the INSERT command and the VALUES clause to insert a row into a table by specifying the values for each of the columns. As shown in Figure B-10, you must indicate the table into which to insert the values and then list the values to insert in parentheses.

Clause	Description	Required?
INSERT INTO *table name*	Indicates the name of the table into which the row will be inserted.	Yes
VALUES *(values list)*	Indicates the values for each of the columns on the new row.	Yes

FIGURE B-10 INSERT command

The following INSERT command inserts the values shown in parentheses as a new row in the Rep table:

```
INSERT INTO Rep VALUES
('75','Argy','Dorothy','424 Bournemouth','Grove',
'CA','90092',0.00,0.06)
;
```

INTEGRITY

You can use the ALTER TABLE command with an appropriate CHECK, PRIMARY KEY, or FOREIGN KEY clause to specify integrity. Figure B-11 describes the ALTER TABLE command for specifying integrity.

Clause	Description	Required?
ALTER TABLE *table name*	Indicates the name of the table for which integrity is being specified.	Yes
integrity clause	CHECK, PRIMARY KEY, or FOREIGN KEY	Yes

FIGURE B-11 Integrity options

The following ALTER TABLE command changes the Customer table so that the only legal values for credit limits are 5,000, 7,500, 10,000, and 15,000:

```
ALTER TABLE Customer
CHECK (CreditLimit IN (5000, 7500, 10000, 15000))
;
```

The following ALTER TABLE command changes the Rep table so that the RepNum column is the table's primary key:

```
ALTER TABLE Rep
ADD PRIMARY KEY(RepNum)
;
```

The following ALTER TABLE command changes the Customer table so that the RepNum column in the Customer table is a foreign key referencing the primary key of the Rep table:

```
ALTER TABLE Customer
ADD FOREIGN KEY (RepNum) REFERENCES Rep
;
```

JOIN

To join tables, use a SELECT command in which both tables appear in the FROM clause and the WHERE clause contains a condition to relate the rows in the two tables. The following SELECT statement lists the customer number, customer name, rep number, first name, and last name by joining the Rep and Customer tables using the RepNum fields in both tables:

```
SELECT CustomerNum, CustomerName, Customer.RepNum, FirstName, LastName
FROM Rep, Customer
WHERE Rep.RepNum=Customer.RepNum
;
```

NOTE: Many implementations of SQL also allow a special JOIN operator to join tables. The following command uses the JOIN operator to produce the same result as the previous query:

```
SELECT CustomerNum, CustomerName, Customer.RepNum, FirstName, LastName
FROM Rep
INNER JOIN Customer
ON Rep.RepNum=Customer.RepNum
;
```

REVOKE

Use the REVOKE statement to revoke privileges from a user. Figure B-12 describes the REVOKE statement.

Clause	Description	Required?
REVOKE *privilege*	Indicates the type of privilege(s) to be revoked.	Yes
ON *database object*	Indicates the database object(s) to which the privilege pertains.	Yes
FROM *user name*	Indicates the user name(s) from whom the privilege(s) are to be revoked.	Yes

FIGURE B-12 REVOKE statement

The following REVOKE statement revokes the SELECT privilege for the Customer table from the user named Jones:

```
REVOKE SELECT ON Customer FROM Jones
;
```

SELECT

Use the SELECT command to retrieve data from a table or from multiple tables. Figure B-13 describes the SELECT command.

Clause	Description	Required?
SELECT *column or expression list*	Indicates the column(s) and/or expression(s) to be retrieved.	Yes
FROM *table list*	Indicates the table(s) required for the query.	Yes
WHERE *condition*	Indicates one or more conditions. Only the rows for which the condition(s) are true will be retrieved.	No (If you omit the WHERE clause, all rows will be retrieved.)
GROUP BY *column list*	Indicates the column(s) on which rows are to be grouped.	No (If you omit the GROUP BY clause, no grouping will occur.)
HAVING *condition involving groups*	Indicates a condition for groups. Only groups for which the condition is true will be included in query results. Use the HAVING clause only if the query output is grouped.	No (If you omit the HAVING clause, all groups will be included.)
ORDER BY *column or expression list*	Indicates the column(s) on which the query output is to be sorted.	No (If you omit the ORDER BY clause, no sorting will occur.)

FIGURE B-13 SELECT command

The following SELECT command groups and orders rows by rep number. It displays the rep number, the count of the number of customers having this rep, and the average balance of these customers. It renames the count as NumCustomers and the average balance as AverageBalance. The HAVING clause restricts the reps to be displayed to only those whose customers' average balance is less than $2,000.

```
SELECT RepNum, COUNT(*) AS NumCustomers, AVG(Balance) AS AverageBalance
FROM Customer
GROUP BY RepNum
HAVING AVG(Balance)<2000
ORDER BY RepNum
;
```

SELECT INTO

Use the SELECT command with an INTO clause to insert the rows retrieved by a query into a table. As shown in Figure B-14, you must indicate the name of the table into which the row(s) will be inserted and the query whose results will be inserted into the named table.

Clause	Description	Required?
SELECT field list	Indicates the list of fields to be selected.	Yes
INTO table name	Indicates the name of the table into which the row(s) will be inserted.	Yes
remainder of query	Indicates the remainder of the query (for example, FROM clause and WHERE clause) whose results will be inserted into the table.	Yes

FIGURE B-14 SELECT command with INTO clause

The following SELECT command with an INTO clause inserts rows selected by a query into the SmallCust table:

```
SELECT *
INTO SmallCust
FROM Customer
WHERE CreditLimit<=7500
;
```

SUBQUERIES

In some cases, it is useful to obtain the results you want in two stages. You can do so by placing one query inside another. The inner query is called a subquery and is evaluated first. After the subquery has been evaluated, the outer query can be evaluated.

The following command contains a subquery that produces a list of item numbers located in storehouse 3. The outer query then produces those order numbers in the OrderLine table that are on any rows containing an item number in the list.

```
SELECT OrderNum
FROM OrderLine
WHERE ItemNum IN
(SELECT ItemNum
FROM Item
WHERE Storehouse='3')
;
```

UNION

Connecting two SELECT commands with the UNION operator produces all the rows that would be in the results of the first command, the second command, or both.

The following query displays the customer number and customer name of all customers that are represented by sales rep 15 *or* that have orders *or* both:

```
SELECT Customer.CustomerNum, CustomerName
FROM Customer
WHERE RepNum='15'
UNION
SELECT Customer.CustomerNum, CustomerName
FROM Customer, Orders
WHERE Customer.CustomerNum=Orders.CustomerNum
;
```

UPDATE

Use the UPDATE command to change the contents of one or more rows in a table. Figure B-15 describes the UPDATE command.

Clause	Description	Required?
UPDATE *table name*	Indicates the name of the table whose contents will be changed.	Yes
SET *column = expression*	Indicates the column to be changed, along with an expression that provides the new value.	Yes
WHERE *condition*	Indicates a condition. The change will occur only on those rows for which the condition is true.	No (If you omit the WHERE clause, all rows will be updated.)

FIGURE B-15 UPDATE command

The following UPDATE command changes the street address on the row in the Customer table on which the customer number is 502 to 1445 Rivard:

```
UPDATE Customer
SET Street='1445 Rivard'
WHERE CustomerNum='502'
;
```

"HOW DO I" REFERENCE

This appendix answers frequently asked questions about how to accomplish a variety of tasks using SQL. Use the second column to locate the correct section in Appendix B that answers your question.

How do I?	Review the Named Section(s) in Appendix B
Add columns to an existing table?	ALTER TABLE
Add rows?	INSERT
Calculate a statistic (sum, average, maximum, minimum, or count)?	1. SELECT 2. Column or Expression List (SELECT clause) (Use the appropriate function in the query.)
Change rows?	UPDATE
Create a data type for a column?	1. Data Types 2. CREATE TABLE
Create a table?	CREATE TABLE
Create a view?	CREATE VIEW
Create an index?	CREATE INDEX
Delete a table?	DROP TABLE
Delete an index?	DROP INDEX
Delete rows?	DELETE Rows
Drop a table?	DROP TABLE
Drop an index?	DROP INDEX
Grant a privilege?	GRANT
Group data in a query?	SELECT (Use a GROUP BY clause.)
Insert rows using a query?	SELECT INTO
Insert rows?	INSERT
Join tables?	Conditions (Include a WHERE clause to relate the tables.)
Order query results?	SELECT (Use an ORDER BY clause.)
Remove a privilege?	REVOKE
Remove rows?	DELETE Rows
Retrieve all columns?	1. SELECT 2. Column or Expression List (SELECT clause) (Type * in the SELECT clause.)
Retrieve all rows?	SELECT (Omit the WHERE clause.)

FIGURE C-1 How do I? reference *(continued)*

How do I?	Review the Named Section(s) in Appendix B
Retrieve only certain columns?	1. SELECT 2. Column or Expression List (SELECT clause) (Type the list of columns in the SELECT clause.)
Revoke a privilege?	REVOKE
Select all columns?	1. SELECT 2. Column or Expression List (SELECT clause) (Type * in the SELECT clause.)
Select all rows?	SELECT (Omit the WHERE clause.)
Select only certain columns?	1. SELECT 2. Column or Expression List (SELECT clause) (Type the list of columns in the SELECT clause.)
Select only certain rows?	1. SELECT 2. Conditions (Use a WHERE clause.)
Sort query results?	SELECT (Use an ORDER BY clause.)
Specify a foreign key?	Integrity (Use a FOREIGN KEY clause in an ALTER TABLE command.)
Specify a primary key?	Integrity (Use a PRIMARY KEY clause in an ALTER TABLE command.)
Specify a privilege?	GRANT
Specify integrity?	Integrity (Use a CHECK clause in an ALTER TABLE command.)
Specify legal values?	Integrity (Use a CHECK clause in an ALTER TABLE command.)
Update rows?	UPDATE
Use a computed field?	1. SELECT 2. Column or Expression List (SELECT clause) (Enter a calculation in the query.)
Use a compound condition in a query?	Conditions
Use a compound condition?	1. SELECT 2. Conditions (Use simple conditions connected by AND, OR, or NOT in a WHERE clause.)
Use a condition in a query?	1. SELECT 2. Conditions (Use a WHERE clause.)
Use a subquery?	Subqueries
Use a wildcard?	1. SELECT 2. Conditions (Use LIKE and a wildcard in a WHERE clause.)
Use UNION operation?	UNION (Connect two SELECT commands with UNION.)

FIGURE C-1   How do I? reference

INTRODUCTION TO MYSQL

INTRODUCTION

MySQL is a free, open source Relational Database Management System (RDBMS) from Oracle. **Open source** means that the software and its original code may be modified and redistributed freely. MySQL is one of the most popular RDMBS's, especially with database administrators, programmers, and web developers who use MySQL to create web, cloud, mobile, and embedded applications. MySQL is available under the GPL license and is well supported online. **GPL** stands for General Public License, which allows you the freedom to run, study, share, and modify the software.

There are several advantages to using MySQL:

- It is widely available and can be installed on many different platforms.
- It comes standard with most web hosting setups.
- It is fast, reliable, and flexible.
- Setting up and working with MySQL databases is relatively straightforward.
- It works well with web programming languages.

Whereas Microsoft Access creates a database file with the extension .accdb, MySQL creates a file with the extension .sql. An SQL file contains code that creates structures, such as tables, views, and queries, as well as allowing you to insert, delete, update, or extract data from a relational database via SQL statements.

This Appendix will introduce you to the MySQL server and a MySQL client interface called MySQL Workbench. Both will be illustrated using the Windows operating system. You will learn how to complete a basic installation of MySQL, open an SQL database file, and create a simple query. A copy of the SQL file for the BITS Corporation database is available in the data files associated with this text. The SQL code in previous chapters also can be used with MySQL.

DOWNLOADING AND INSTALLING MYSQL

In this section, you will download and install the MySQL server and the client interface, MySQL Workbench. Recall that a server is a computer or computer program that manages access to a resource or service. The **MySQL server** manages your database; it is also referenced by the name, **mysqld**. You must connect with the server via the Internet. The connection program runs in the background, behind the scenes, while you are using a MySQL client interface. One of the most popular interfaces for MySQL when working in a Windows environment is called **MySQL Workbench**, an integrated visual tool to run MySQL on Windows-based machines.

There are several places on the web to obtain the MySQL software; however, the easiest way is to open a browser and navigate to https://dev.mysql.com/downloads/installer/ (Figure D-1). The download works on both 32-bit and 64-bit machines.

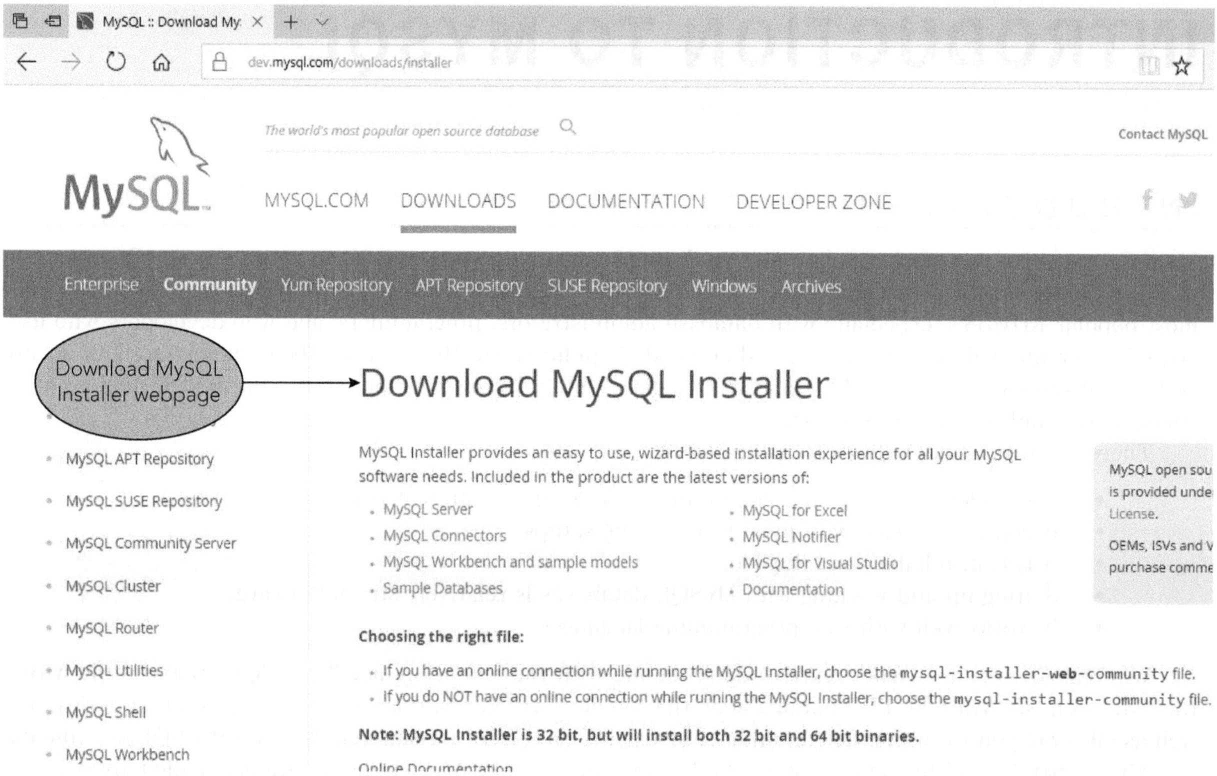

FIGURE D-1   Download MySQL Installer webpage

Scroll down to display the MSI installer Download button (mysql-installer-web-community-5.7.20.0.msi). The download is free, you do not have to create or login to an Oracle account. There is a link to start the download. Take note of the version number for future reference. The screens shown in this Appendix are version 5.7. Your version may differ.

When you click the download, you will be instructed to download an .msi file. An **MSI file** is a Microsoft installer package file format used by Windows for installation, storage, and removal of programs. Download the file and double-click it to proceed with the installation of the MySQL server. After a few moments, the opening screen of the MySQL Installer appears (Figure D-2).

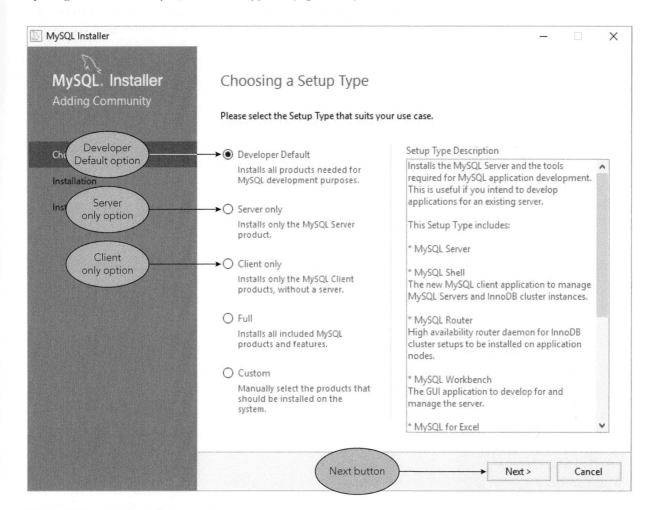

FIGURE D-2 MySQL Installer opening screen

The easiest solution is to choose the Developer Default option (shown in Figure D-2 on the previous page); however, at a minimum you should install the MySQL Server and the MySQL Workbench client. (That process would necessitate running the .msi file twice, one time for each.) Click the Next button and proceed through the next few screens accepting the default settings. The Developer Default option may want to install some helper programs for running other add-ons. You will not need them for this Appendix. See your instructor if you need help. After a few screens, the installer will ask you to create a password for your system (Figure D-3).

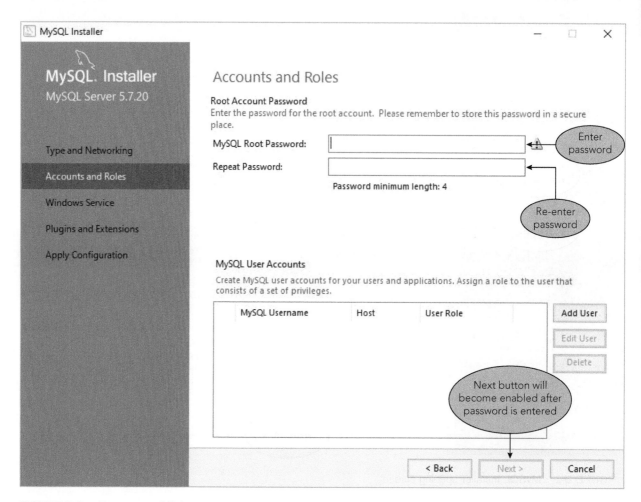

FIGURE D-3 Accounts and Roles screen

After entering the password, click the Next button several times, accepting the default values. When the installer asks, click the Execute button. After a few moments, the installer will complete (Figure D-4). You can click the Finish button.

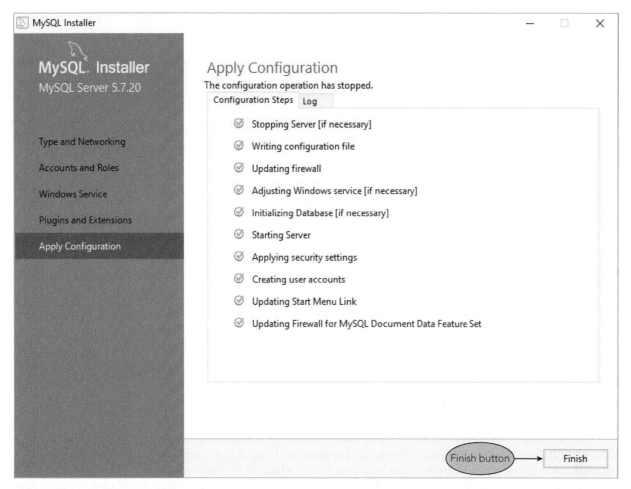

FIGURE D-4   Apply Configuration screen

Another common source to obtain MySQL is the downloads page at mysql.com/downloads shown in Figure D-5.

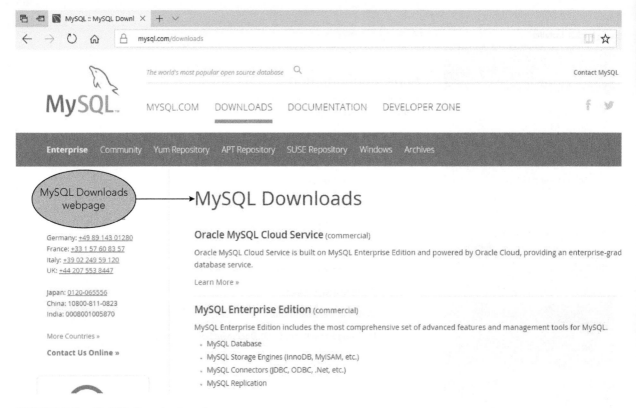

FIGURE D-5 MySQL Downloads webpage

On this page, you would scroll down and click the MySQL Community Edition (GPL). On the Community Edition webpage, you will need to download and install the server, then download and install MySQL Workbench. Your instructor can help you decide which platform is appropriate. The server download is an archival or compressed file which will have to be unzipped. Use the standard installation settings. See your instructor for specific questions pertaining to your system.

RUNNING MYSQL

The first time you run MySQL, you will need to name your server and connect it. Subsequent runs should connect automatically. MySQL usually downloads to the Programs folder on the Start menu. Scroll to MySQL in the list and then open the folder. Your version number may differ from the one shown in Figure D-6.

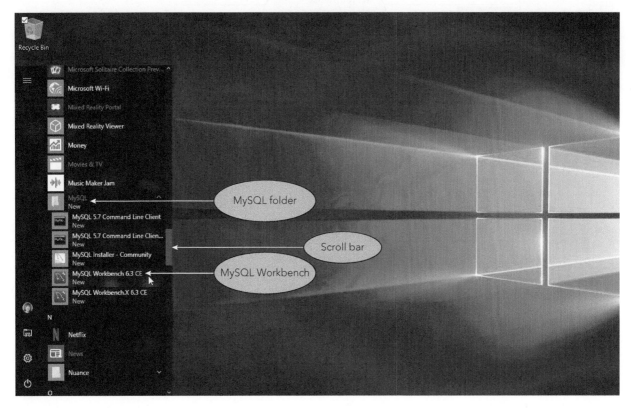

FIGURE D-6 Start Menu

Click MySQL Workbench to run the client program. The opening screen is displayed in Figure D-7.

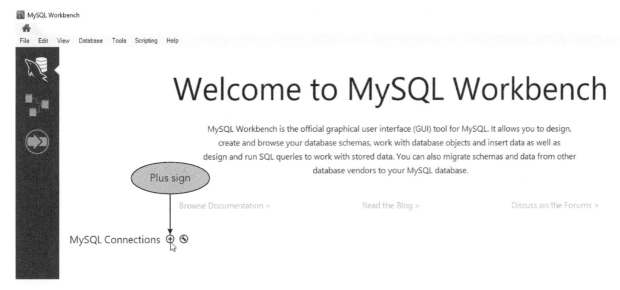

FIGURE D-7 MySQL Workbench opening screen

Click the plus button (Figure D-7 on the previous page) and enter a name for your instance of MySQL, such as MySampleServer (Figure D-8).

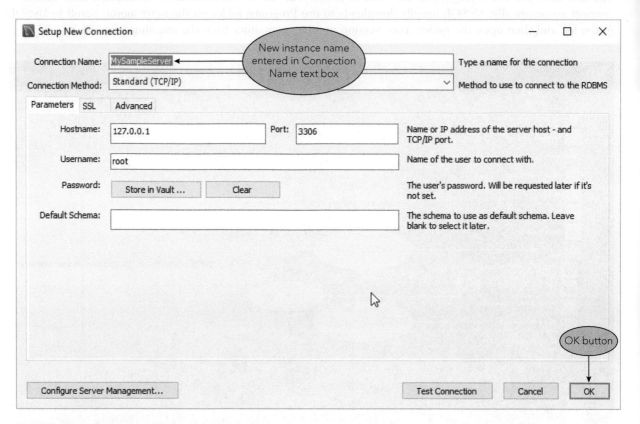

FIGURE D-8 Setup New Connection dialog box

Click the OK button. MySQL may ask you for your password. When the connection appears, right-click the connection and then click Open Connection on the shortcut menu. The MySQL Workbench client interface will begin.

Opening an SQL File in MySQL

To begin using MySQL Workbench, you must create a database or open a previously created database. Using the File menu, you can open a database SQL file which also is called a **script** (Figure D-9).

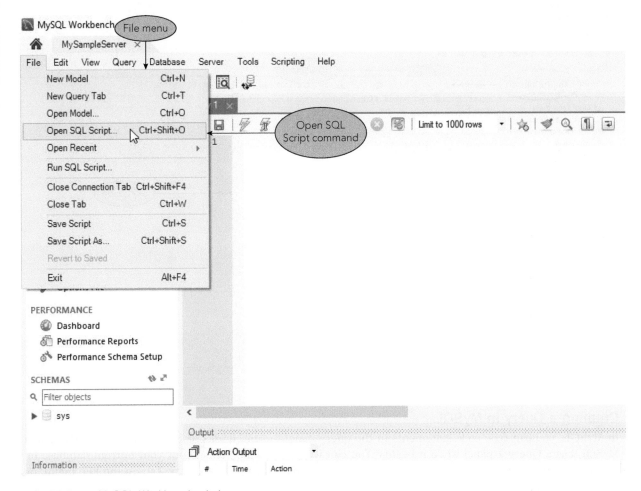

FIGURE D-9   MySQL Workbench window

YOUR TURN D-1

Open the BITS SQL script.

The command opens an Open SQL Script dialog box. Navigate to the location of your data files and double-click the BITS.sql file. It will display in a new panel (Figure D-10). Use the **Execute button** to run the script and place the database in RAM (local memory).

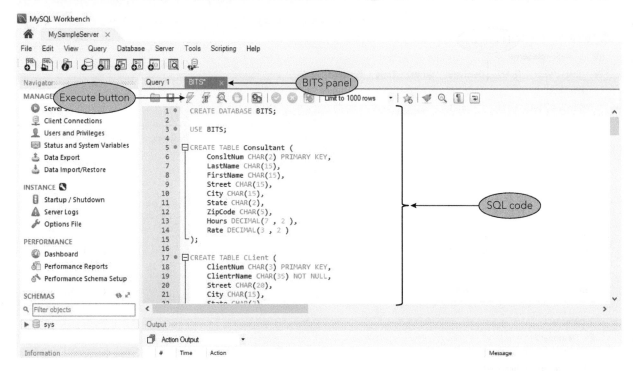

FIGURE D-10 SQL loaded into panel

Creating a Query in MySQL

In MySQL, you can type code statements in the query panel to run queries or create new tables. By default, MySQL has a Query 1 panel when it begins. You can write SQL statements about your current database in the panel and execute them. If you have closed it inadvertently, click New Query Tab on the File menu, or press CTRL+T.

YOUR TURN D-2

Create a query to display the Consultant table and execute it.

After the SQL command is entered and executed, the results of the query display in Figure D-11. Notice that a Result Grid displays the data in tabular form. The Action Output panel displays the action details.

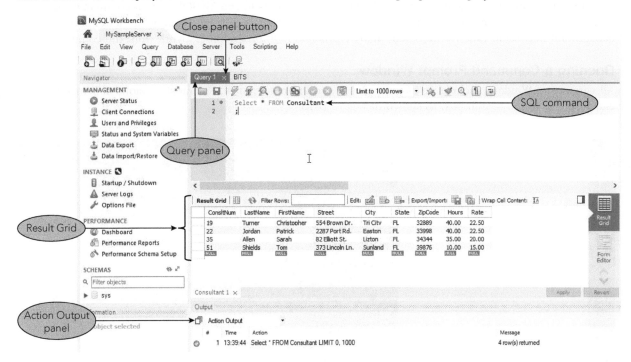

FIGURE D-11   Query results

Managing the MySQL Window

If you want to close a query panel, click the x button on the panel tab. To exit MySQL, click the Close button in the title bar. When you re-open MySQL Workbench in subsequent sessions, the BITS database should be loaded as a schema in the lower left panel. In MySQL, a **schema** is the same as a database. From that panel, you can view information about the schema by pointing to it and then clicking the Information (I) icon. Details about the database are displayed in the main panel, with tabs to examine specific parts of the database (Figure D-12). *Note:* The easiest way to open the SQL file, however, is still to use the File menu.

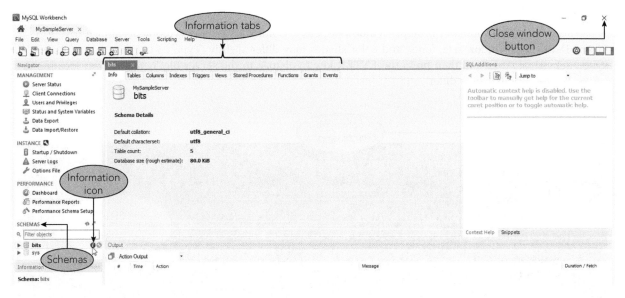

FIGURE D-12   Schema information tabs

RUNNING MYSQL FROM THE COMMAND LINE

An option to running the client interface, MySQL Workbench, is to run MySQL from a command line. A **command line** or **command prompt** is a text-based user interface screen. While white letters on a black background may seem rather antiquated, many DBAs and SQL programmers work from the command line.

Opening a Command Prompt Window

All versions of Windows include access to a Command Prompt window. For most versions of Windows, you can type cmd in the search box, as shown in Figure D-13.

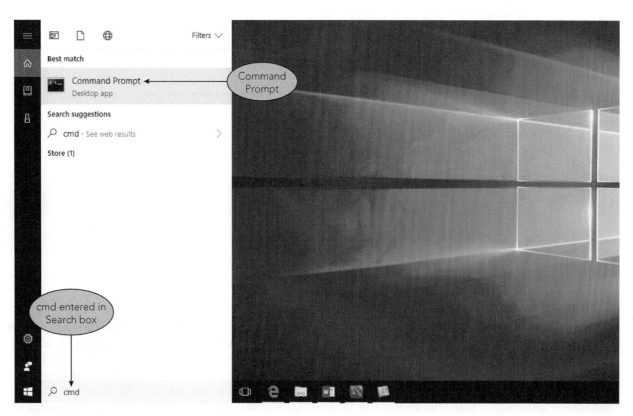

FIGURE D-13   Search box results

When you click Command Prompt, Windows opens a Command Prompt window as shown in Figure D-14. Your window size, fonts, and color shades may differ slightly. Type cd C:\Program Files\MySQL\ MySQL Server 5.7\bin and then press the ENTER key to change to the server file location. Your location or server version number may differ.

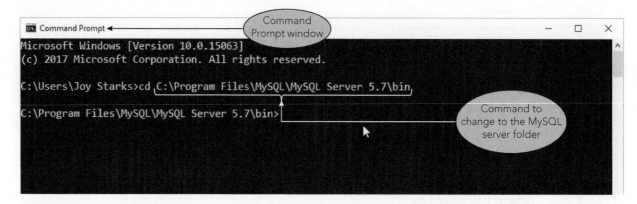

FIGURE D-14   Command Prompt window with change directory command

Starting the MySQL Command Line

To start MySQL, type `mysql -u root -p` and then press the ENTER key. You will be asked for the password you created earlier in this Appendix. A welcome message is then displayed (Figure D-15). Notice the command prompt changes to mysql>.

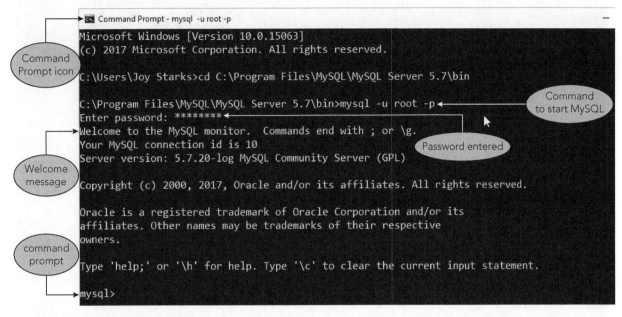

FIGURE D-15   Command to start MySQL

Q & A D-1

Question: I received an error message saying I could not connect. What should I do?
Answer: The steps assume that your server is still running from earlier in the Appendix. You may have inadvertently shut that down. In the Command Prompt window, type `mysqld` to start the server. If you still receive an error message, contact your instructor.

Q & A D-2

Question: Can I change the color or size of the font in the Command Prompt window?
Answer: Yes. Click the Command Prompt icon in the title bar and then click Properties in the resulting menu. Windows will display several tabs to customize your display.

To load a database into memory, MySQL requires the USE command. Type USE BITS and then press the ENTER key as shown in Figure D-16.

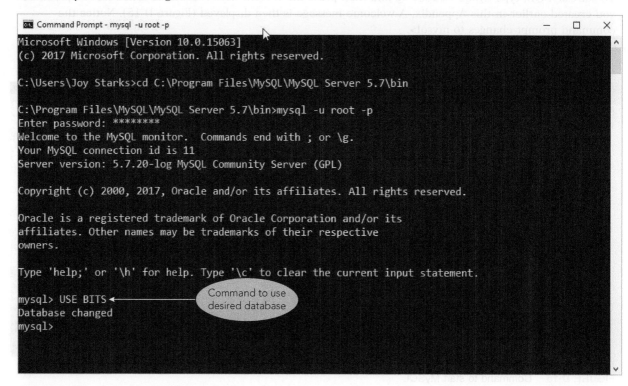

FIGURE D-16   Command to access database

Q & A D-3

Question: I received an error message saying no database was connected. What should I do?
Answer: MySQL is looking for the BITS database in its default storage location, C:\Program Files\MySQL\ MySQL Server 5.7\data\. If you saved your SQL data file in another location you will need to indicate that location before entering the name of the database. For example, you may need to enter a command similar to the following: USE C:\Users\Your Name\Documents\BITS.

YOUR TURN D-3

Using the Command Prompt window, enter the SQL command to display the entire Consultant table.

Once the database is loaded, you then can enter your SQL commands such as SELECT * FROM Consultant as shown in Figure D-17.

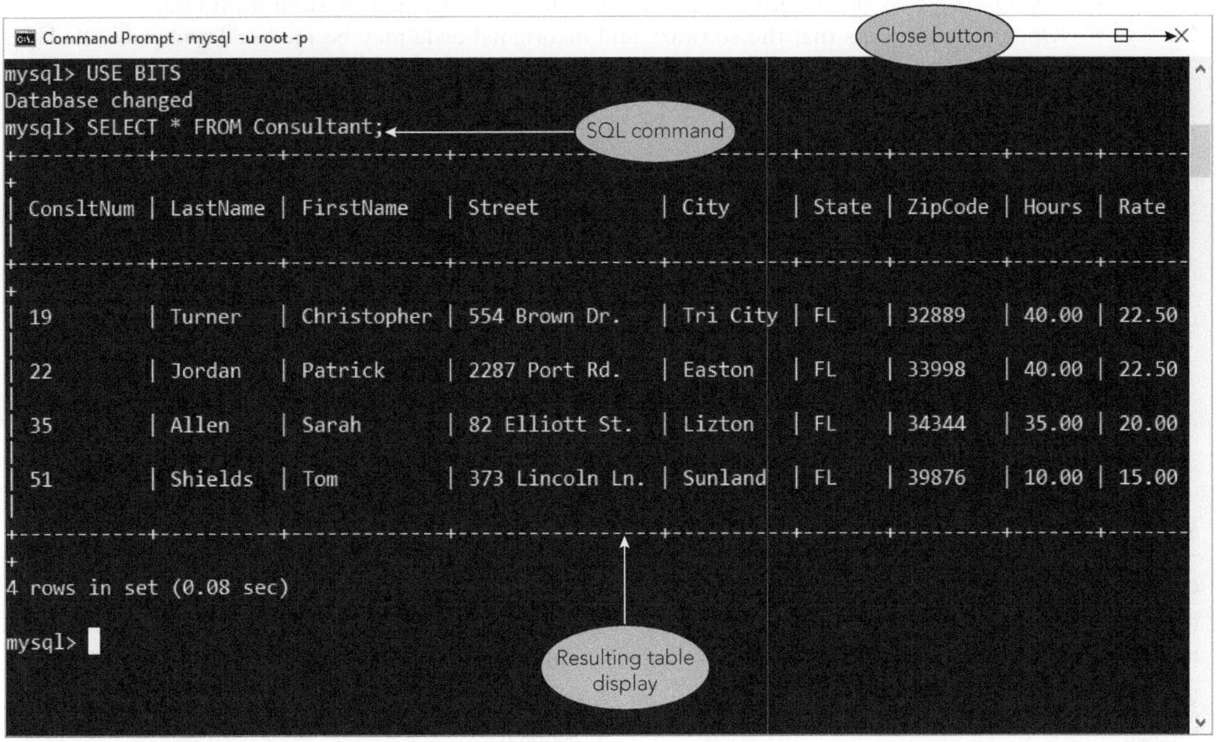

```
Command Prompt - mysql  -u root -p                              Close button        □ →X
mysql> USE BITS                                                                            ^
Database changed
mysql> SELECT * FROM Consultant;                        SQL command
+-----------+-----------+-------------+-----------------+-----------+-------+---------+-------+-------+
| ConsltNum | LastName  | FirstName   | Street          | City      | State | ZipCode | Hours | Rate  |
+-----------+-----------+-------------+-----------------+-----------+-------+---------+-------+-------+
| 19        | Turner    | Christopher | 554 Brown Dr.   | Tri City  | FL    | 32889   | 40.00 | 22.50 |
| 22        | Jordan    | Patrick     | 2287 Port Rd.   | Easton    | FL    | 33998   | 40.00 | 22.50 |
| 35        | Allen     | Sarah       | 82 Elliott St.  | Lizton    | FL    | 34344   | 35.00 | 20.00 |
| 51        | Shields   | Tom         | 373 Lincoln Ln. | Sunland   | FL    | 39876   | 10.00 | 15.00 |
+-----------+-----------+-------------+-----------------+-----------+-------+---------+-------+-------+
4 rows in set (0.08 sec)

mysql>                                            Resulting table
                                                     display
```

FIGURE D-17   Result of entering SQL code statement

To finish your session, simple close the Command Prompt window.

Summary

- MySQL is a free, open source Relational Database Management System from Oracle.
- Open source means that the software and its original code may be modified and redistributed freely.
- MySQL is one of the most popular RDMBS's, especially with database administrators, programmers, and web developers who use MySQL to create web, cloud, mobile, and embedded applications.
- Advantages of MySQL include multi-platform availability, standard with web-hosting setups, reliability, flexibility, and the ease of use with web programming languages.
- GPL stands for General Public License, which allows you the freedom to run, study, share, and modify the software.
- Mysqld is the name of the MySQL server. It must be installed and be running.
- MySQL Workbench is the name of a graphic user interface used to manage database files and write MySQL scripts.
- DBAs and programmers also run MySQL from the Command Prompt window.

Key Terms

command line	MySQL Workbench
command prompt	mysqld
Execute button	MSI file
GPL	open source
MySQL	schema
MySQL server	script

APPENDIX **E**

A SYSTEMS ANALYSIS APPROACH TO INFORMATION-LEVEL REQUIREMENTS

INTRODUCTION

In Chapter 6, you learned a method for creating information-level database designs, in which the starting point for the design process is a set of user views. Each user view is the set of requirements that is necessary to support the operations of a particular database user. In this appendix, you will learn how to determine the specific user views, or information-level requirements, required for a particular database.

INFORMATION SYSTEMS

A database is one of the components of an information system. As illustrated in Figure E-1, an **information system** is the collection of data, people, procedures, stored data, software, hardware, and information required to support a specific set of related functions. Examples of information systems are cell phone billing, payroll, airline reservation, point of sale, pharmacy management, property tax assessment, online bridal registry, and insurance premium processing. The BITS Corporation, Colonial Adventure Tours, and the Sports Physical Therapy cases are also examples of information systems, although this book has primarily focused on the database components of these information systems.

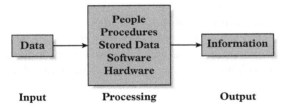

FIGURE E-1   Information system components

As described in Chapter 1, the primary goal of an information system is to turn data (recorded facts) into information (the knowledge gained by processing those facts). *Data* is input to an information system, and the information system outputs *information*. Data can be input to an information system manually using, for example, keyboards, telephones, or mobile devices, or by automated means using, for example, ATMs, point-of-sale scanners, credit or debit card readers, and external files and databases. Information can be output from an information system as printed reports, screen displays, external files, and databases, or it can be output to specialized devices or media such as wireless, audio, and fax.

Information systems exist within organizations that have some type of predefined structure. These organizations can range from multinational businesses to government agencies to local animal shelters. Information systems have goals that should be consistent with the goals and objectives of the organization. If a goal of BITS Corporation, for example, is to minimize the amount of time needed to process an order, then the order processing information system should be designed to meet that goal.

Each organization also has its own organizational structure and culture. **Organizational structure** refers to the hierarchical arrangement of lines of authority (who reports to whom), communication, rights, and duties. **Culture** includes the organization's values, beliefs, norms, and habits. Organizational culture influences the way people and groups interact with each other.

A thorough understanding of the organization's business (what does the organization do; how does it do it, and why does it do it), structure, and culture are necessary before designing any information system.

An information system is a success only when the *people* interacting with it and obtaining information from it view it to be successful. The people component of an information system include the end users (those directly interacting with the information system), management, auditing and other support staff groups, and often people in outside entities such as government agencies, suppliers, and financial institutions. The people component also includes technical staff, who develop and maintain the information system and who support the operating environment for the information system.

A **procedure** is a series of steps followed in a regular, specified order to accomplish one end result. Examples of procedures in information systems are signing up a new cell phone customer, auditing a payroll's direct deposits, and filling a prescription at a pharmacy. Procedures are often in written form in manuals or other information system documentation.

The data input to an information system must be retained for future processing and legal reasons. This data is retained as *stored data* in a database and, especially in older information systems, in files on hard drives and other storage media. The stored data is a critical information system component because all information either is produced directly from stored data or is derived from stored data in the form of calculated fields.

The *software* component consists of system software and application software. **System software** are the programs that control the hardware and software environment. These programs include the operating system, network managers, device drivers, and utility programs such as sorting and data backup. **Application software** consists of the programs that directly support the information system in processing the data to produce the required information.

The *hardware* component consists of all the physical equipment used within the information system. This equipment includes computer hardware, such as computers, telecommunications equipment, scanners, and printers, and noncomputer equipment such as copy machines.

Why is it important to focus on the components of an information system? This focus is important because you cannot analyze, design, develop, and implement a successful information system unless you consider all its components and their requirements and connect the components and requirements properly.

SYSTEM REQUIREMENT CATEGORIES

To create the user views for an information system, you must determine all of its system requirements. A **system requirement** is a feature that must be included in an information system to fulfill business, legal, or user needs. Using the definition of an information system, system requirements can be classified into output, input, and processing categories. You must also determine the technical and constraining requirements of an information system.

Output Requirements

To determine an information system's output requirements, you need to find answers to the following types of questions about each output:

- What is the content of the output? Specifically, you need to determine the fields to include in the output and their order and format.
- Does the output require a specified sort sequence?
- Are subtotals and totals needed in the output?
- Is the output intended to be printed, to appear on screen, to be transmitted to a special device, to be output to a file, or to be sent to another information system or company?
- Who are the recipients of the output?
- How often must the output be produced, and what triggers its output?
- What is the size of the output? For example, what is the estimated number of pages for a printed report, and how many records and what is the size of each record for an output file?
- Does the output have any security restrictions that limit who has access to it?

Input Requirements

To determine an information system's input requirements, you need to find answers to the following types of questions about each input:

- Who or what originates the input and what types of devices are used for that input?
- Does a source document, such as an application form or a work order, contain the data for the input? If so, obtain blank and filled-in copies of the source document.
- What is the content of the input? Specifically, what are the fields and in which order do they occur in the input? What is the best method for entering the content of the input into the information system?
- What are the attributes of each field in the input? What formatting and validation requirements are necessary for each field in the input?
- Are there unique fields in the input, so that each record can be distinguished from all other records?
- When is the data input, how often, and in what volume?

Processing Requirements

To determine an information system's processing requirements, you need to find answers to the following types of questions:

- Which input data must be retained as stored data to provide the required outputs?
- What calculations must be performed?
- Are there special cycle processing requirements that occur daily, weekly, monthly, quarterly, annually, or on some other frequency? For example, are there requirements for weekly or biweekly payroll processing, quarterly and annual tax processing, and quarterly shareholder processing?
- Are there auditing requirements for the data in the information system?
- Which stored data has special security requirements that permit only authorized users access or update privileges?
- Are there procedures that depend on other procedures?
- Are there procedures that occur in a specified sequence?
- Which procedures and other processing requirements are available to all end users, and which ones are limited to only authorized personnel?

Technical and Constraining Requirements

To determine an information system's technical and constraining requirements, you need to find answers to the following types of questions:

- Must the information system operate with a specific operating system or with multiple operating systems?
- Which DBMS will be used to store retained data?
- Does the hardware—entry, storage, output, and other devices—impose any restrictions or provide special capabilities?
- Which programming languages will be used for creating the application programs for the information system?
- How many end users must the information system support concurrently, and what response time is expected for online processing?
- Which portions of the information system must be available to end users 24/7?
- Does the company plan to utilize big data?

In addition to constraining requirements, you also need to determine the business rules for the organization. A **business rule** is a statement that defines or constrains some aspect of the business. A business rule for BITS Corporation could be: "BITS Corporation will not process an order if the order total will result in the customer exceeding its credit limit." Business rules must be captured and documented to ensure that the information system works correctly and that users understand the purpose and reasons for these constraints.

DETERMINING SYSTEM REQUIREMENTS

Many tools and methods have been developed to help you analyze and document the system requirements after you have determined what they are, but no similar aids exist to help you determine them in the first place. To determine the system requirements, you need to become a detective and collect the facts about the information system using basic fact-finding techniques. The most commonly used techniques for determining the facts about an information system are interviews, document collection, observation, and research.

Interviews

An **interview** is a planned meeting during which you obtain system requirements from other people. You conduct these interviews with the individuals who represent the people component of the information system, each of whom has a personal perspective about what the information system should do. You conduct individual and group interviews, during which you determine how the information system operates now, how it should operate in the future, and what requirements need to be in the new information system.

You should plan your interview questions in advance and revise the questions as necessary. Include both open-ended and closed questions. An **open-ended question** is one that requires a general response, such as "How do you fill orders for customers?" A **closed question** is typically a question that can be answered with a simple "yes" or "no" response.

Questionnaires

In large organizations with hundreds of end users and other people who have system requirements, especially when they work in a large number of locations, you cannot conduct interviews with everybody. In these situations, you can use questionnaires to allow everybody to participate and to obtain their system requirements. Questionnaires can include both open-ended and closed questions. You should test your questionnaire on a small group and use the feedback to refine the questionnaire before disseminating it to a larger audience. Questionnaires can be distributed electronically or in paper form.

Document Collection

Every information system has existing paper forms, online forms, reports, manuals, written procedures, and other documents that contain valuable system requirements. You should review all these documents and then confirm their validity with end users. Documents are a rich source for the data content of an information system, and are a quicker, more accurate way of determining the data, database, and information requirements than asking end users, although you need to verify the documents' accuracy with end users.

Observation

Observing current operating processing provides insight into how users interact with the system and how the interaction can be improved. Observation verifies what you learn during interviews and what is documented in procedure manuals. Observation can also identify undocumented processing and uncover processing that differs from standard practice.

Research

Few information systems are unique in their total system requirements. You can research journals, periodicals, books, and the Internet to obtain information, examples, and requirements related to a specific information system. You can also attend professional seminars and visit other companies to gain insight from other experts. Research can help you learn proper interviewing techniques, how to create questionnaires that are free of bias, and how to analyze the results of interviews and questionnaires.

TRANSITIONING FROM SYSTEMS ANALYSIS TO SYSTEMS DESIGN

After you have determined all the system requirements for an information system, you need to analyze and document the requirements. The Unified Modeling Language, briefly discussed in Chapter 9 is one approach you can use to model (analyze and document) system requirements; this approach uses class, use case, state, and other diagrams and modeling tools to model an information system. Another popular approach uses data flow diagrams to model the transformations of data into information, a data dictionary for data and table documentation, and various process description tools and techniques. System developers have additional approaches available to model system requirements. When you have completed the model, you have completed the systems analysis work, which consists of both the requirements determination step and the analysis and documentation step.

The approach you choose to transition from systems analysis to systems design will result in a large, complicated model of the information system. You use this model to perform the system design of the information system next. To simplify the design process, you can attack the design in smaller pieces by considering individual user views, as described in Chapter 6.

Key Terms

application software	open-ended question
business rule	organizational structure
closed question	procedure
culture	system requirement
information system	system software
interview	

Exercises

1. Use books, the Internet, and/or other sources to investigate how best to conduct interviews to determine system requirements and to understand and minimize the problems that can occur during interviews. Prepare a report that explains the results of your investigation. Be sure to cite your references.

2. Use books, the Internet, and/or other sources to investigate the proper way to create and manage questionnaires. Prepare a report that explains the results of your investigation. Be sure to cite your references.

3. Use books, the Internet, and/or other sources to investigate a modeling tool such as use cases, data flow diagrams, or any other tool approved by your instructor. Prepare a report that explains the results of your investigation. Be sure to cite your references.

& operator Combines the values of two fields into a single computed field.

Access delay A fixed amount of time required for every message sent over a network.

After image A record that the DBMS places in the journal or log that shows what the data in a row looked liked in the database after a transaction update.

Aggregate function A function used to calculate the number of entries, the sum or average of all the entries in a given column, or the largest or smallest of the entries in a given column; also called *function*.

ALTER TABLE The SQL command that is used to change the structure of a table.

Alternate key A candidate key that was not chosen to be the primary key.

Anomaly, update A data inconsistency that results from data redundancy, the use of inappropriate nulls, or from a partial update.

Anomaly, deletion The unintended loss of data due to deletion of other data.

Anomaly, insertion The anomaly resulting when you cannot add data to the database due to absence of other data.

AND criterion Combination of criteria in which both criteria must be true.

Application server In a three-tier client/server architecture, a computer that performs the business functions and serves as an interface between clients and the database server.

Application software The programs that directly support an information system in processing data to produce the required information.

Archive See *data archive*.

Argument Additional information required by an action in a data macro to complete the action.

Artificial key A column created for an entity to serve solely as the primary key and that is visible to users.

Association A relationship in UML.

Attribute A characteristic or property of an entity; also called a *field* or *column*.

Authentication A technique for identifying the person who is attempting to access a DBMS.

Authorization rule A rule that specifies which user has what type of access to which data in a database.

B2B See *business to business*.

Back-end machine See *server*.

Back-end processor See *server*.

Backup A copy of a database made periodically; the backup is used to recover the database when it has been damaged or destroyed. Also called a *save*.

Backward recovery See *rollback*.

Batch processing The processing of a transaction file that contains a group, or "batch," of records to update a database or another file.

Before image A record that the DBMS places in the journal or log that shows what the data in a row looked like in the database before a transaction update.

BETWEEN operator A compound condition that tests for a range of values, inclusive of the lower number, the higher number, and all numbers in-between.

Big data The large volume of data produced by every digital process, system, sensor, mobile device, and even social media exchange.

Binary large object (BLOB) A generic term for a special data type used by relational DBMSs to store complex objects.

Binding The association of operations to actual program code.

Biometrics A technique to identify users of a database or other resource by physical characteristics such as fingerprints, voiceprints, handwritten signatures, and facial characteristics.

BLOB See *binary large object*.

Bottom-up design method A design method in which specific user requirements are synthesized into a design.

Boyce-Codd normal form (BCNF) A relation is in Boyce-Codd normal form if it is in second normal form and the only determinants it contains are candidate keys; also called *third normal form* in this text.

Business rule A statement that defines or constrains some aspect of a business.

Business to business (B2B) E-commerce between businesses.

Calculated field See *computed field*.

Candidate key A minimal collection of columns (attributes) in a table on which all columns are functionally dependent but that has not necessarily been chosen as the primary key.

Cardinality The number of items that must be included in a relationship.

Cardinality, maximum The maximum number of entities that can participate in a relationship: one-to-one [1:1], one-to-many [1:N], or many-to-many [N:M].

Cardinality, minimum The minimum number of entities that must participate in a relationship: zero [0] optional or one [1] mandatory.

Cartesian product The table obtained by concatenating every row in the first table with every row in the second table.

Cascade delete A delete option in which related records are automatically deleted.

Cascade update An update option in which related records are automatically updated.

Catalog A source of data, usually stored in hidden database tables, about the types of entities, attributes, and relationships in a database.

Category The IDEF1X name for an entity subtype.

CHAR(*n*) The SQL data type for character data.

CHECK The SQL clause that is used to enforce legal-values integrity.

Class The general structure and actions of an object in an object-oriented system.

Class diagram A UML diagram that for each class, shows the name, attributes, and methods of the class, as well as the relationships between the classes in a database.

Client A computer that is connected to a network and that people use to access data stored on a server in a client/server system; also called a *front-end machine* or a *front-end processor*.

Client/server (system) A networked system in which a special site on the network, called the *server*, provides services to the other sites, called the *clients*. Clients send requests for the specific services they need. Software, often including a DBMS, running on the

server then processes the requests and sends only the appropriate data and other results back to the clients.

Client-side extension Instructions executed by a web client to provide dynamic webpage capability. These extensions can be embedded in HTML documents or be contained in separate files that are referenced within an HTML document.

Client-side script See *client-side extension*.

Closed question A question that can be answered with a simple "yes" or "no" response.

Cloud backup An easy, secure, and scalable strategy for backing up data that sends data to an off-site server. Fees are based on capacity, bandwidth, or the number of users.

Column A characteristic or property of an entity; also called an *attribute* or a *field*.

Command line or command prompt A way to interact with a database via a text-based user interface screen.

Commit A special record in a database journal or log that indicates the successful completion of a transaction.

Communications network Several computers configured in such a way that data can be sent from any one computer on the network to any other. Also called a *network*.

Comparison operator See *relational operator*.

Composite primary key A situation at occurs when more than one database column is necessary to make a row unique.

Complete category In IDEF1X, a collection of subtypes with the property that every element of the supertype is an element of at least one subtype.

Complex join A join of more than two tables.

Composite entity An entity in the entity-relationship model used to implement a many-to-many relationship.

Compound condition See *compound criteria*.

Compound criteria Two simple criteria (conditions) in a query that are combined with the AND or OR operators.

Computed field A field whose value is computed from other fields in the database; also called a *calculated field*.

Concatenation The combination of two or more rows in an operation, such as a join, or the combination of two or more columns for a primary key field to uniquely identify a given row in the table.

Concurrent update A situation in which multiple users make updates to the same database at the same time.

Constraint, data integrity A rule making sure the DBMS updates data accurately and consistently.

Constraint, interrelation A condition that involves two or more relations.

Constraint, key integrity An update rule consisting of primary key constraints and foreign key constraints.

Constraint, primary key A rule governed by entity integrity, which enforces the uniqueness of the primary key.

Context-sensitive help The assistance a DBMS provides for the particular feature being used at the time a user asks for help.

Cookies Small files written on a web client's hard drive by a web server.

Coordinator In a distributed network, the site that directs the update to the database for a transaction. Often, it is the site that initiates the transaction.

CREATE INDEX The SQL command that creates an index in a table.

CREATE TABLE The SQL command used to describe the layout of a table. The word *TABLE* is followed by the name of the table to be created and then by the names and data types of the columns (fields) that comprise the table.

Criteria The plural version of the word *criterion*.

Criterion A statement that can be either true or false. In queries, only records for which the statement is true will be included; also called a *condition*.

Culture An organization's values, beliefs, norms, and habits.

Cumulative design A design that supports all the user views encountered thus far in a design process.

Database operations manager (DM) Performs ongoing maintenance of established databases, manages data operations or DataOps, and makes sure the data gets from one place to another with integrity and security. He or she is responsible for ensuring the performance and availability of critical services and applications related to the database.

Data administrator A specialized data professional who handles most of the jobs involving data, such as setting data-handling policies, assigning data entry, organizing metadata, and acting as a liaison between the database administrator and the rest of the database staff.

Data architect A person who designs, builds, and deploys databases; in many cases, he or she manages or supervises the construction of large and comprehensive databases, working closely with software designers, design analysts, users, and others on the database team.

Data archive A place where a record of certain corporate data is kept. Data that is no longer needed in a corporate database but must be retained for future reference is removed from the database and placed in the archive. Also called an *archive*.

Data cube The perceived shape by a user of a multidimensional database in a data warehouse.

Data dictionary A catalog, usually found in large, expensive DBMSs, that stores data about the entities, attributes, relationships, programs, and other objects in a database.

Data file A file used to store data about a single entity. It's the computer counterpart to an ordinary paper file you might keep in a file cabinet, an accounting ledger, and so on. Such a file can be thought of as a table.

Data fragmentation The process of dividing a logical object, such as the records in a table, among the various locations in a distributed database.

Data independence The property that lets you change the structure of a database without requiring you to change the programs that access the database; examples of these programs are the forms you use to interact with the database and the reports that provide information from the database.

Data macro In Access, a collection of actions that are performed in response to an associated database operation, such as inserting, updating, or deleting records. Equivalent to an SQL trigger.

Data mining The uncovering of new knowledge, patterns, trends, and rules from the data stored in a data warehouse.

Data warehouse A subject-oriented, integrated, time-variant, nonvolatile collection of data used in support of management's decision-making process.

Database A structure that can store information about multiple types of entities, the attributes of these entities, and the relationships among the entities.

Database administration (DBA) The individual or group that is responsible for a database.

Database administrator (DBA) The individual who is responsible for a database, or the head of database administration.

Database design The process of determining the content and structure of data in a database in order to support some activity on behalf of a user or group of users.

Database Design Language (DBDL) A relational-like language that is used to represent the result of the database design process.

Database management system (DBMS) A program, or a collection of programs, through which users interact with a database. DBMSs let you create forms and reports quickly and easily, as well as obtain answers to questions about the data stored in a database.

Database password A string of characters assigned by the DBA to a database that users must enter before they can access a database.

Database server In a three-tier client/server architecture and in other architectures, a computer that performs the database functions such as storing and retrieving data in a database.

DATE The SQL data type for date data.

DBA See *database administration*. (Sometimes the acronym stands for *database administrator*.)

DBDL See *Database Design Language*.

DBMS See *database management system*.

DDBMS See *distributed database management system*.

Deadlock A situation in which two or more database users are each waiting to use resources that are held by the other(s); also called *deadly embrace*.

Deadly embrace See *deadlock*.

DECIMAL(*p,q*) The SQL data type for decimal data.

Decrypting A process that reverses the encryption of a database. Also called *decryption*.

Defining query The query that is used to define the structure of a view.

DELETE The SQL command used to delete a table. The word *DELETE* is followed by a FROM clause identifying the table. Use a WHERE clause to specify a condition. Any records satisfying the condition will be deleted.

Delete query A query that deletes all records that satisfy some criterion.

Denormalizing The conversion of a table that is in third normal form to a table that is no longer in third normal form. Denormalizing introduces anomaly problems but can decrease the number of disk accesses required by certain types of transactions, thus improving performance.

Dependency diagram A diagram that indicates the dependencies among the columns in a table.

Dependent entity An entity that requires a relationship to another entity for identification.

Design grid The portion of the Query Design window in Access where you enter fields, criteria, sort orders, and so on.

Determinant A column in a table that determines at least one other column.

Difference When comparing tables, the set of all rows that are in the first table but that are not in the second table.

Dimension table A table in a data warehouse that contains a single-part primary key, serving as an index into the central fact table, and other fields associated with the primary key value.

Disaster recovery plan A plan that specifies the ongoing and emergency actions and procedures required to ensure data availability, even if a disaster occurs.

Distributed database A single logical database that is physically divided among computers at several sites on a computer network.

Distributed database management system (DDBMS) A DBMS capable of supporting and manipulating distributed databases.

Division The relational algebra command that combines tables and searches for rows in the first table that match all rows in the second table.

Document Type Definition (DTD) A set of statements that specifies the elements (tags), the attributes (characteristics associated with each tag), and the element relationships for an XML document. The DTD can be a separate file with a .dtd extension, or can be included at the beginning of an XML document.

Documenter An Access tool that provides documentation about the objects in a database.

Domain The set of values that are permitted for an attribute.

Drill down The process of viewing and analyzing lower levels of aggregation, or a more detailed view of the data.

DROP INDEX The SQL command that drops (deletes) an index from a table.

DROP TABLE The SQL command that drops (deletes) a table from a database.

Dynamic webpage A webpage whose content changes in response to the different inputs and choices made by web clients.

Electronic commerce (e-commerce) Business conducted on the Internet and web.

Encapsulated In an object-oriented system, defining an object to contain both data and its associated actions.

Encryption A security measure that converts the data in a database to a format that's indecipherable to normal programs. The DBMS decrypts, or decodes, the data to its original form for any legitimate user who accesses the database.

Entity A person, place, object, event, or idea for which you want to store and process data.

Entity integrity The rule that no column (attribute) that is part of the primary key may accept null values.

Entity-relationship (E-R) diagram A graphic model for database design in which entities are represented as rectangles and relationships are represented as either arrows or diamonds connected to the entities they relate.

Entity-relationship (E-R) model An approach to representing data in a database that uses E-R diagrams exclusively as the tool for representing entities, attributes, and relationships.

Entity subtype Entity A is a subtype of entity B if every occurrence of entity A is also an occurrence of entity B.

Exclusive lock A lock that prevents other users from accessing the locked data in any way.

Existence dependency A relationship in which the existence of one entity depends on the existence of another related entity.

Extensible The capability of defining new data types in an OODBMS.

Extensible Hypertext Markup Language *See* *XHTML*.

Extensible Markup Language See *XML*.

Extensible Stylesheet Language See *XSL*.

Fact table The central table in a data warehouse that consists of rows that contain consolidated and summarized data.

Fat client In a two-tier client/server architecture, a client that performs presentation functions and business functions.

Field A characteristic or property of an entity; also called an *attribute* or a *column*.

File server A networked system in which a special site on the network stores files for users at other sites. When a user needs a file, the file server sends the entire file to the user.

First normal form (1NF) A table is in first normal form if it does not contain a repeating group.

Foreign key A column (attribute) or collection of columns in a table whose value is required either to match the value of a primary key in a table or to be null.

FOREIGN KEY clause The clause in an SQL CREATE TABLE or ALTER TABLE command that specifies referential integrity.

Form A screen object you use to maintain, view, and print data from a database.

Forward recovery A process used to recover a database by reading the log and applying the after images of committed transactions to bring the database up to date.

Fourth normal form (4NF) A table is in fourth normal form if it is in third normal form and there are no multivalued dependencies.

Fragmentation transparency The characteristic that users do not need to be aware of any data fragmentation (splitting of data) that has taken place in a distributed database.

FROM clause The part of an SQL SELECT command that indicates the tables in the query.

Front-end processor See *client*.

Function See *aggregate function*.

Functionally dependent Column B is functionally dependent on column A (or on a collection of columns) if a value for A determines a single value for B at any one time.

Functionally determines Column A functionally determines column B if B is functionally dependent on A.

Generalization In UML, the relationship between a superclass and a subclass.

Global deadlock In a distributed database, deadlock that cannot be detected solely at any individual site.

GPL (General Public License) A license which allows you the freedom to run, study, share, and modify the software.

GRANT The SQL statement that is used to grant different types of privileges to users of a database.

GROUP BY clause The part of an SQL SELECT command that indicates grouping.

Grouping The process of creating collections of records that share some common characteristic.

Growing phase A phase during a database update in which the DBMS locks all the data needed for a transaction and releases none of the locks.

HAVING clause The part of an SQL SELECT command that restricts the groups to be displayed.

Heterogeneous DDBMS A distributed DBMS in which at least two of the local DBMSs are different from each other.

Homogeneous DDBMS A distributed DBMS in which all the local DBMSs are the same.

Hot site A backup site that an organization can switch to in minutes or hours because the site is completely equipped with duplicate hardware, software, and data that the organization uses.

HTML (Hypertext Markup Language) A language used to create webpages.

HTTP (Hypertext Transfer Protocol) The data communication method used by web clients and web servers to exchange data on the Internet.

Hyperlink A tag in a webpage that links one webpage to another, or links to another location in the same webpage.

Hypertext Markup Language See *HTML*.

Hypertext Transfer Protocol See *HTTP*.

IDEF1X A type of E-R diagram; or, technically, a language in the IDEF (Integrated Definition) family of languages that is used for data modeling.

Identifying relationship A relationship that is necessary for identification of an entity.

Incomplete category In IDEF1X, a collection of subtypes with the property that there are elements of the supertype that are not elements of any subtype.

Independent entity An entity that does not require a relationship to another entity for identification.

Index A file that relates key values to records that contain those key values.

Index key The field or fields on which an index is built.

Information system The collection of data, people, procedures, stored data, software, hardware, and information required to support a specific set of related functions.

Information-level design The step during database design in which the goal is to create a clean, DBMS-independent design that will support all user requirements.

Inheritance The property that a subclass inherits the structure of the class as well as its methods.

INSERT The SQL command to add new data to a table. After the words *INSERT INTO*, you list the name of the table, followed by the word *VALUES*. Then you list the values for each of the columns in parentheses.

INTEGER The SQL data type for integer data.

Integrity A database has integrity if the data in it satisfies all established integrity constraints.

Integrity constraint A rule that must be followed by data in a database.

Integrity rules See *entity integrity*, *legal-values integrity*, and *referential integrity*.

Intelligent key A primary key that consists of a column or collection of columns that is an inherent characteristic of the entity.

Internet A worldwide collection of millions of interconnected computers and computer networks that share resources.

Internet Information Services (IIS) See *IIS*.

Interrelation constraint A constraint that involves more than one relation.

INTERSECT The relational algebra command for performing the intersection of two tables.

Intersection When comparing tables, an intersection is a new table containing all rows that are in both original tables.

Interview When determining system requirements, a planned meeting during which you obtain system requirements from other people.

INTO clause The SQL clause that inserts values into a table. An INTO clause consists of the word

INTO followed by the name of the table to insert the values into.

Intranet An internal company network that uses software tools typically used on the Internet and the World Wide Web.

Join In relational algebra, the operation in which two tables are connected on the basis of common data.

Join column The column on which two tables are joined. Also see *join*.

Join line In an Access query, the line drawn between tables to indicate how they are related.

Journal A file that contains a record of all the updates made to a database. The DBMS uses the journal to recover a database that has been damaged or destroyed. Also called a *log*.

Journaling Maintaining a journal or log of all updates to a database.

LAN See *local area network*.

Legal-values integrity The property that no record can exist in the database with a value in a field other than a legal value.

Live system See *production system*.

Local area network (LAN) A configuration of several computers connected together that allows users to share a variety of hardware and software resources.

Local deadlock In a distributed database, deadlock that occurs at a single site.

Local site From a user's perspective, the site in a distributed system at which the user is working.

Location transparency The property that users do not need to be aware of the location of data in a distributed database.

Locking A DBMS's denial of access by other users to data while the DBMS processes one user's updates to the database.

Log A file that contains a record of all the updates made to a database. The DBMS uses the log to recover a database that has been damaged or destroyed. Also called a *journal*.

Logical key A primary key that consists of a column or collection of columns that is an inherent characteristic of the entity.

Major sort key See *primary sort key*.

Make-table query An Access query that creates a table using the results of a query.

Mandatory role The role in a relationship played by an entity with a minimum cardinality of 1 (that is, there must be at least one occurrence of the entity).

Many-to-many relationship A relationship between two entities in which each occurrence of each entity can be related to many occurrences of the other entity.

Many-to-many-to-many relationship A relationship between three entities in which each occurrence of each entity can be related to many occurrences of each of the other entities.

Markup language A document language that contains tags that describe a document's content and appearance.

Message A request to execute a method. Also, data, requests, or responses sent from one computer to another computer on a network.

Metadata Data about the data in a database.

Metalanguage A language used to define another language.

Method An action defined for an object class.

Microsoft SharePoint Server A tool used to store, organize, and share information.

Minor sort key See *secondary sort key*.

MSI file A Microsoft installer package file format used by Windows for installation, storage, and removal of programs.

Multidependent In a table with columns A, B, and C, B is multidependent on A if each value for A is associated with a specific collection of values for B and, further, this collection is independent of any values for C.

Multidetermine In a table with columns A, B, and C, A multidetermines B if each value for A is associated with a specific collection of values for B and, further, this collection is independent of any values for C.

Multidimensional database The perceived structure by users of the data in a data warehouse.

Multiple-column index See *multiple-field index*.

Multiple-field index An index built on more than one field (column).

Multiplicity In UML, the number of objects that can be related to an individual object on the other side of a relationship; also called *cardinality*.

Multivalued dependence In a table with columns A, B, and C, there is a multivalued dependence of column B on column A (also read as "B is multide-pendent on A" or "A multidetermines B"), if each value for A is associated with a specific collection of values for B and, furthermore, this collection is independent of any values for C.

MySQL a free, open source RDBMS from Oracle.

MySQL Workbench One of the most popular interfaces for MySQL when working in a Windows environment.

Mysqld The name of the MySQL server which manages the database.

Natural join The most common form of a join.

Natural key A primary key that consists of a column or collection of columns that is an inherent charac-teristic of the entity.

Network See *communications network*.

Nonidentifying relationship A relationship that is not necessary for identification.

Nonkey attribute See *nonkey column*.

Nonkey column An attribute (column) that is not part of the primary key.

Nonprocedural language A language in which a user describes the task that is to be accomplished by the computer rather than the steps that are required to accomplish it.

Nonunique index An index used to improve query performance in frequently used columns by main-taining a sorted order; it does not enforce constraints.

Normal form See *first normal form, second normal form, third normal form,* and *fourth normal form*.

Normalization process The process of removing repeating groups to produce a first normal form table. Sometimes refers to the process of creating a third normal form table.

n-tier architecture See *three-tier architecture*.

Null A data value meaning "unknown" or "not applicable."

Object A unit of data (set of related attributes) along with the actions that are associated with that data.

Object-oriented database management system (OODBMS) A DBMS in which data and the methods that operate on that data are encapsulated into objects.

Office Open XML A Microsoft file format that is a compressed version of XML and first used in the Office 2016 suite.

OLAP See *online analytical processing*.

OLTP See *online transaction processing*.

One-to-many relationship A relationship between two entities in which each occurrence of the first entity is related to many occurrences of the second entity, and each occurrence of the second entity is related to at most one occurrence of the first entity.

One-to-one relationship A relationship between two entities in which each occurrence of the first entity is related to one occurrence of the second entity, and each occurrence of the second entity is related to at most one occurrence of the first entity.

Online analytical processing (OLAP) Software that is optimized to work efficiently with multidimen-sional databases in a data warehouse environment.

Online transaction processing (OLTP) A system that processes a transaction by dealing with a small number of rows in a relational database in a highly structured, repetitive, and predetermined way.

OODBMS See *object-oriented database management system*.

Open source A term describing software and its original code that may be modified and redistributed freely.

Optional role The role in a relationship played by an entity with a minimum cardinality of zero (that is, there need not be any occurrences of the entity).

OR criterion A combination of criteria in which at least one of the criteria must be true.

ORDER BY clause The part of an SQL SELECT command that indicates a sort order.

Organizational structure In an organization, the hierarchical arrangement of lines of authority (who reports to whom), communication, rights, and duties.

Outer join The form of a join in which all records appear, even if they don't match.

Parallel database system A system in which multiple computers to share access to data, software, or peripheral devices to improve performance through parallelization of operations, such as storing data, indexing, and querying. A parallel database provides for concurrent access to data while protecting data integrity.

Parameter query A query that allows you to enter criterion when you run the query, as opposed to placing it in the Access design grid.

Partial dependency A dependency of a column on only a portion of the primary key.

Password A string of characters assigned by a DBA to a user that the user must enter to access a database.

Permission The specification of the kind of access a user has to the objects in a database.

Persistence The ability to have a program remember its data from one execution to the next.

Physical-level design The step during database design in which a design for a given DBMS is produced from the final information-level design.

Polymorphism The use of the same name for different operations in an object-oriented system.

Primary copy In a distributed database with replicated data, the copy of the database that must be updated in order for the update to be deemed complete.

Primary key A minimal collection of columns (attributes) in a table on which all columns are functionally dependent and that is chosen as the main direct-access vehicle to individual rows. Also see *candidate key*.

PRIMARY KEY clause The SQL clause that is used in a CREATE TABLE or ALTER TABLE command to set a table's primary key field(s).

Primary sort key When sorting on two fields, the more important field; also called a *major sort key*.

Privacy The right of individuals to have certain information about them kept confidential.

Private visibility In UML, an indication that only the class itself can view or update the attribute value.

Procedural language A language in which a user specifies the steps that are required for accomplishing a task instead of merely describing the task itself.

Procedure A series of steps followed in a regular, specified order to accomplish one end result.

Product The table obtained by concatenating every row in the first table with every row in the second table.

Production system The hardware, software, and database for the users. Also called a *live system*.

PROJECT The relational algebra command used to select columns from a table.

Protected visibility In UML, an indication that only the class itself or public or protected

subclasses of the class can view or update the attribute value.

Public visibility In UML, an indication that any class can view or update the attribute value.

QBE See *Query-By-Example*.

Qualify To indicate the table (relation) of which a given column (attribute) is a part by preceding the column name with the table name. For example, *Customer.Address* indicates the column named Address in the table named Customer.

Query A question, the answer to which is found in the database; also used to refer to a command in a nonprocedural language such as SQL that is used to obtain the answer to such a question.

Query-By-Example (QBE) A data manipulation language for relational databases in which users indicate the action to be taken by completing on-screen forms.

Query optimizer A DBMS component that analyzes queries and attempts to determine the most efficient way to execute a given query.

RAID (redundant array of inexpensive/independent drives) A device used to protect against hard drive failures in which database updates are replicated to multiple hard drives so that an organization can continue to process database updates after losing one of its hard drives.

Record A collection of related fields; can be thought of as a row in a table.

Recovery The process of returning a database to a state that is known to be correct from a state known to be incorrect.

Recursive A condition in which the foreign key and the matching primary key are in the same table, sometimes called a self-referencing or recursive foreign key.

Redundancy Duplication of data, or the storing of the same data in more than one place.

Referential integrity The rule that if a table A contains a foreign key that matches the primary key of table B, then the value of this foreign key must either match the value of the primary key for some row in table B or be null.

Relation A two-dimensional table-style collection of data in which all entries are single-valued, each column has a distinct name, all the values in a column are values of the attribute that is identified by the column name, the order of columns is immaterial, each row is distinct, and the order of rows is immaterial. Also called a *table*.

Relational algebra A relational data manipulation language in which new tables are created from existing tables through the use of a set of operations.

Relational database A collection of relations (tables).

Relational operator An operator used to compare values. Valid operators are =, <, >, <=, >=, < >, and !=. Also called a *comparison operator*.

Relationship An association between entities.

Remote site From a user's perspective, any site other than the one at which the user is working.

Repeating group More than one entry at a single location in a table.

Replica A copy of the data in a database that a user can access at a remote site.

Replicate A duplicate of the data in a database that a user can access at a remote site.

Replication transparency The property that users do not need to be aware of any replication that has taken place in a distributed database.

Reserved word A word that is part of the SQL language.

REVOKE The SQL statement that is used to revoke privileges from users of a database.

Roll up View and analyze higher levels of aggregation.

Rollback A process to recover a database to a valid state by reading the log for problem transactions and applying the before images to undo their updates; also called *backward recovery*.

Row-and-column subset view A view that consists of a subset of the rows and columns in a table.

Run-book A log of all database maintenance, with dates, license keys, issues or updates, involved personnel, and resolutions.

Sandbox See *test system*.

Save See *backup*.

Scalability The ability of a computer system to continue to function well as utilization of the system increases.

Schema A term referring to a database in MySQL.

Script Another name for a database SQL file used in MySQL.

Second normal form (2NF) A relation is in second normal form if it is in first normal form and no non-key attribute is dependent on only a portion of the primary key.

Secondary key A column (attribute) or collection of columns that is of interest for retrieval purposes (and that is not already designated as some other type of key).

Secondary sort key When sorting on two fields, the less important field; also called *minor sort key*.

Security The prevention of unauthorized access to a database.

SELECT The relational algebra command to select rows from a table. Also, the retrieval command in SQL.

SELECT clause The part of an SQL SELECT command that indicates the columns to be included in the query results.

Server A computer that provides services to the clients in a client/server system; also called a *back-end processor* or a *back-end machine*.

Server-side extension Instructions executed by a web server to provide dynamic webpage capability. These extensions are usually contained in separate files that are referenced within the HTML documents.

Session The duration of a web client's connection to a web server.

SET command An SQL command to make changes to a database by indicating the field to be changed, followed by an equals sign and the new value.

Shared lock A lock that lets other users read locked data.

SharePoint Server See *Microsoft SharePoint Server*.

Shrinking phase A phase during a database update in which the DBMS releases all the locks previously acquired for a transaction and acquires no new locks.

Simple condition A condition that involves only a single field and a single value.

Single-field index An index built on a single field (column).

Slice and dice In a data warehouse, selecting portions of the available data, or reducing the data cube.

SMALLINT The SQL data type for integer data for small integers.

Smart card Small plastic cards about the size of a driver's license that have built-in circuits containing processing logic to identify the cardholder.

Sort The process of arranging rows in a table or results of a query in a particular order.

Sort key The field on which data are sorted; also called a *key*.

SQL See *Structured Query Language*.

Star schema A multidimensional database whose conceptual shape resembles a star.

Stateless A condition for a communication protocol, such as HTTP, in which the connection between the sender and the receiver, such as a web server and a web client, is closed once the sender responds to the sender's request and the sender retains no information about the request or the sender.

Static webpage A webpage that displays the exact same content for all web clients.

Stored procedure A file containing a collection of compiled and optimized SQL statements that are available for future use.

Structured data Data that is traditional in its retrieval and storage in database management systems.

Structured Query Language (SQL) A very popular relational data definition and manipulation language that is used in many relational DBMSs.

Stylesheet A document that specifies how to process the data contained in another document and present the data in a web browser, in a printed report, on a mobile device, in a sound device, or in other presentation media.

Subclass A class that inherits the structure and methods of another class and for which you can define additional attributes and methods.

Subquery In SQL, a query that appears within another query.

SUBTRACT The relational algebra command for performing the difference of two tables.

Superclass In UML, a class that has subclasses.

Surrogate key A system-generated primary key that is usually hidden from users.

Synchronization The periodic exchange by a DBMS of all updated data between two databases in a replica set.

Synthetic key A system-generated primary key that is usually hidden from users.

Syscolumns The portion of the system catalog that contains column information.

Sysindexes The portion of the system catalog that contains index information.

Systables The portion of the system catalog that contains table information.

System catalog A structure that contains information about the objects (tables, columns, indexes, views, and so on) in a database.

System requirement A feature that must be included in an information system to fulfill business, legal, or user needs.

System software The programs that control the hardware and software environment. These programs include the operating system, network managers, device drivers, and utility programs such as sorting and data backup.

Sysviews The portion of the system catalog that contains view information.

Table See *relation*.

Tag A command in a webpage that a web browser processes to position and format the text on the screen or to link to other files.

TCP/IP (Transmission Control Protocol and Internet Protocol) The standard protocol for all communication on the Internet.

Test system The hardware, software, and database that programmers use to develop new programs and modify existing programs. Also called a *sandbox*.

Thin client In a client/server architecture, a client that performs only presentation functions.

Third normal form (3NF) A table is in third normal form if it is in second normal form and the only determinants it contains are candidate keys.

Three-tier architecture A client/server architecture in which the clients perform the presentation functions, a database server performs the database functions, and the application servers perform the business functions and serve as an interface between clients and the database server. Also called an *n-tier architecture*.

Timestamp The unique time when the DBMS starts a transaction update to a database.

Timestamping The process of using timestamps to avoid the need to lock rows in a database and to eliminate the processing time needed to apply and release locks and to detect and resolve deadlocks.

Top-down design method A design method that begins with a general database design that models the overall enterprise and then repeatedly refines the model to achieve a design that supports all necessary applications.

Transaction A set of steps completed by a DBMS to accomplish a single-user task.

Transmission Control Protocol and Internet Protocol See *TCP/IP*.

Trigger An action that automatically occurs in response to an associated database operation such as INSERT, UPDATE, or DELETE.

Tuning The process of changing the database design to improve performance.

Tuple The formal name for a row in a table.

Two-phase commit An approach to the commit process in distributed systems in which there are two phases. In the first phase, each site is instructed to prepare to commit and must indicate whether the commit will be possible. After each site has responded, the second phase begins. If every site has replied in the affirmative, all sites must commit. If any site has replied in the negative, all sites must abort the transaction.

Two-phase locking An approach to locking that is used to manage concurrent update in which there are two phases: a growing phase, in which the DBMS locks more rows and releases none of the locks, and a shrinking phase, in which the DBMS releases all the locks and acquires no new locks.

Two-tier architecture A client/server architecture in which the clients perform the presentation functions, and a database server performs the database functions. In a fat client configuration, the clients perform the business functions, whereas in a thin client configuration, the database server performs the business functions.

UML See *Unified Modeling Language*.

Unified Modeling Language (UML) An approach used to model all the aspects of software development for object-oriented systems.

Uniform Resource Locator See *URL*.

UNION A combination of two tables consisting of all records that are in either table.

Union compatible Two tables are union compatible if they have the same number of fields and if their corresponding fields have identical data types.

Unnormalized relation A structure that satisfies the properties required to be a relation (table) with the

exception of allowing repeating groups (the entries in the table do not have to be single-valued).

Unstructured data Data not organized or easily interpreted by traditional databases or data models, which may involve a lot of text and metadata.

UPDATE The SQL command used to make changes to existing table data. After the word *UPDATE,* you indicate the table to be updated. After the word *SET,* you indicate the field to be changed, followed by an equals sign and the new value. Finally, you can include a condition in the WHERE clause, in which case, only the records that satisfy the condition will be changed.

Update anomaly An update problem that can occur in a database as a result of a faulty design.

Update query In Access, a query that updates the contents of a table.

UPS (uninterruptable power supply) A power source such as a battery or fuel cell, for short interruptions and a power generator for longer outages.

URL (Uniform Resource Locator) An Internet address that identifies where a webpage is stored—both the location of the web server and the name and location of the webpage on that server.

User view The view of data that is necessary to support the operations of a particular user.

Utility services DBMS-supplied services that assist in the general maintenance of a database.

Validation rule In Access, a rule that data entered in a field must satisfy.

Validation text In Access, a message that is displayed when a validation rule is violated.

Victim In a deadlock situation, the deadlocked user's transaction that the DBMS chooses to abort to break the deadlock.

View An application program's or an individual user's picture of a database.

Visibility symbol In UML, a symbol preceding an attribute in a class diagram to indicate whether other classes can view or change the value in the attribute. The possible visibility symbols are public visibility (+), protected visibility (#), and private visibility (−). With public visibility, any other class can view or change the value. With protected visibility, only the class itself or public or protected subclasses of the class can view or change the value. With private visibility, only the class itself can view or change the value.

W3C (World Wide Web Consortium) An international organization that develops web standards, specifications, guidelines, and recommendations.

Warm site A backup site that is equipped with an organization's duplicate hardware and software but not data.

Weak entity An entity that depends on another entity for its own existence.

Web (World Wide Web) A vast collection of digital documents available on the Internet.

Web app A database you use in a browser. Also called *Access app*.

Web browser A computer program that retrieves a webpage from a web server and displays it on a web client.

Web client A computer requesting a webpage from a web server.

Web server A computer on which an individual or organization stores webpages for access on the Internet.

Webpage A digital document on the web.

WHERE clause The part of an SQL SELECT command that indicates the condition rows must satisfy to be displayed in the query results.

Wildcard In Access SQL, the asterisk (*) is used as a wildcard to represent any collection of characters.

Workgroup In Access, a group of users who are assigned the same permissions to various objects in a database.

World Wide Web Consortium See *W3C*.

XHTML (Extensible Hypertext Markup Language) A markup language that is stricter version of HTML and that is based on XML.

XML (Extensible Markup Language) A metalanguage designed for the exchange of data on the web. You can customize XML tags to describe the data an XML document contains and how that data should be structured.

XML declaration An XML statement clause that specifies to an XML processor which version of XML to use.

XML schema A set of statements that specifies the elements (tags), the attributes (characteristics associated with each tag), and the element relationships for an XML document. The XML schema can be a separate file with a .xsd extension, or you can include it at the beginning of an XML document. It's a newer form of DTD that more closely matches database features and terminology.

XQuery A language for querying XML, XSL, XHTML, other XML-based documents, and similarly structured data repositories.

XSL (Extensible Stylesheet Language) A standard W3C language for creating stylesheets for XML documents.

XSL Transformations See *XSLT*.

XSLT (XSL Transformations) A language that defines the rules to process an XML document and change it into another document; this other document could be another XML document, an XSL document, an HTML or XHTML document, or most any other type of document.

Note: Page numbers in **boldface** indicate key terms.

E

F